Business Ethics

Business Ethics

Revised Edition

edited by
Milton Snoeyenbos
Robert Almeder
James Humber

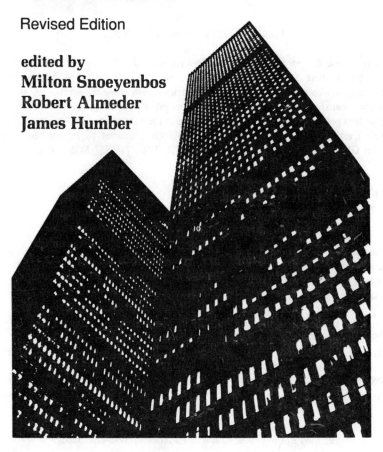

PROMETHEUS BOOKS ■ **BUFFALO, NEW YORK**

Published 1992 by Prometheus Books

96 95 94   5 4 3 2

Library of Congress Cataloging-in-Publication Data

Business ethics : corporate values and society / edited by Milton Snoeyenbos, Robert Almeder, James Humber.—Rev. ed.
    Easier said than done : moral decisions in medical
uncertainty / by Milton D. Heifetz.
        p.   cm.
    Includes bibliographical references (p.   ).
    ISBN 0-87975-725-6 (paper : acid-free)
    1. Business ethics—Case studies. I. Snoeyenbos, Milton. II. Almeder, Robert F.
III. Humber, James M.
HF5387.B87   1992
174′.4—dc20   92-8931
                                                                    CIP

Printed in the United States of America on acid-free paper.

CONTENTS

PREFACE

Many of the job-related decisions corporate employees must make are moral in nature. Recognizing this fact, most institutions of higher learning now offer business ethics courses in an attempt to provide students with the tools necessary to make such decisions. As business ethics courses have proliferated, the number of texts designed for teaching such courses has increased as well. Unfortunately, however, many of these texts are flawed in one of two ways: (1) those that address issues of interest to business students are generally not philosophically sophisticated, and (2) philosophically sophisticated texts are often *too* sophisticated, concentrating on issues that appeal to philosophers rather than business students.

In designing this book a conscious attempt has been made to avoid both of these extremes. We began with the intuition that business ethics courses should be designed primarily for business students, and should therefore address the issues faced by business men and women in their professional lives. Furthermore, we felt that only "essential" elements of ethical theory need be considered; lengthy discourses on distributive justice, Kant's categorical imperative, metaethics, and similar topics would only bore students and leave them with the impression that moral philosophy is unintelligible to all but a few "eggheads," and totally irrelevant to "real life."

To achieve our goals we worked closely with the College of Business at Georgia State University in an effort to identify moral issues relevant to business men and women. We have taught a number of business ethics courses to students enrolled in the school of business, and, in the process, a wide variety of teaching materials have been evaluated. Sometimes the extant literature did not fill our needs; and where we found this to be the case we wrote essays ourselves or commissioned others to write them. All the essays included in this text have been chosen for their intelligibility and their potential to encourage classroom discussion. The essays are not intended to *solve* moral problems. Rather, they raise moral issues and propose "bold hypotheses" that invite further discussion.

Business students who work through this text will learn some of the essentials

11

of ethical theory, and will acquire the basic tools needed to deal with the types of moral problems they will face during their professional lives. On the other hand, philosophy students will learn a great deal about the business world and the problems confronting corporate employees. Both philosophy and business have much to gain by a closer alliance; and if that alliance is strengthened in any way by our text, we will count it a success.

We wish to thank the faculty of the College of Business at Georgia State University for their advice and assistance in this project. Special thanks must also go to our wives, Peg Snoeyenbos, Virginia Almeder, and Helene Humber, whose patience and understanding make our work considerably easier than it might otherwise be.

It was our pleasure and good fortune to work with a highly skilled editor, Steven L. Mitchell of Prometheus Books. He brought not only diligence and editorial ability to his task, but philosophical acumen as well.

Milton Snoeyenbos
Robert Almeder
James Humber

Georgia State University

1

INTRODUCTION

This collection of essays is about ethical issues that arise within the context of business practices. As such, it does not describe actual business practices; its primary concern is not with detailing how businesspersons actually finance an enterprise, market products, or handle labor negotiations. Instead, its focus is on such issues as whether businesspersons should give preferential treatment to disadvantaged individuals, whether managers have moral and social obligations other than maximizing profits for their firms' shareholders, and whether some advertising is deceptive and therefore should be restricted or banned. All of us have opinions on these issues, and the readings in this volume contain contrasting points of view; but in order to understand fully such controversies and to resolve them rationally some acquaintance with ethical theory is required. This introduction presents some of the fundamentals of ethical theory; it provides a framework for informed discussion of the specific ethical issues taken up in the rest of the book.

Ethics is a discipline involving inquiry into the moral judgments people make and the rules and principles upon which such judgments are based. All of us are able to recognize moral judgments; we know, for example, that the following sentences express moral judgments:

1. The insider trading practices of Ivan Boesky were morally wrong.
2. The Lockheed payoffs to Japanese government officials to obtain sales of the TriStar were reprehensible and should not have been made.
3. Price fixing is wrong.

The following sentences, however, do not typically express moral judgments:

4. Ivan Boesky engaged in insider trading.
5. Lockheed officials made payments to Japanese government officials to obtain sales of the TriStar.

6. Price fixing occurred in the U.S. electrical equipment industry in the 1950s.

In examining these lists we can note that the sentences expressing moral judgments contain such *evaluative* terms as "good," "bad," "right," "wrong," "ought," and "should." The presence of these words frequently indicates that a moral judgment has been made. The presence of an evaluative word is not, however, sufficient for a judgment to be considered moral, for there are nonmoral judgments that also contain evaluative terms. For example,

7. The Mona Lisa is a good painting

makes an aesthetic, not a moral, judgment about the painting, and

8. If you want to get to Chicago in two hours, then you ought to take United flight 247

makes a nonmoral, prudential claim; it tells you the best means to employ to achieve a practical goal. There is no connection with morality here whatsoever. Furthermore,

9. Most Americans believe price fixing is wrong

does not express a moral judgment; it merely states a statistical fact about American opinion. It follows that we cannot simply say that a judgment containing an evaluative word is a moral judgment; nor is it the case that all moral judgments contain evaluative words, for there are contexts in which

10. Hooker Chemical polluted the Love Canal

could be used to judge that Hooker's action was wrong. Although there do not seem to be hard and fast linguistic rules for marking off moral from nonmoral judgments, it is the case that the former typically contain an evaluative term. Furthermore, most of us have a firm enough intuitive grasp of the moral/ nonmoral distinction so that we can recognize moral judgments when they are made, and this is enough for our present purposes.

Having said that ethics involves the systematic study of moral judgments and the rules and principles upon which such judgments are based, we should note that there are two major types of systematic inquiry regarding moral judgments: *descriptive ethics* and *normative ethics*. The former is concerned with facts about the moral judgments or moral beliefs of a person or a group of persons; for example:

11. John Jones believes Ford Motor ought to have installed a safer gas tank on the early models of the Pinto.

12. Most Americans believe it was wrong of Ivan Boesky to trade stocks on the basis of insider information.

These are factual claims, the truth or falsity of which is determinable by empirical investigation. Research regarding such issues is conducted by social scientists with the aim of finding out what moral beliefs people actually hold or what judgments they make. Thus, we can ask Jones whether he believes Ford should have installed a safer gas tank on the early Pinto and receive a yes or no answer, and if we poll a large, representative sample of the American people and find that most of the sample believe Ivan Boesky was morally wrong in trading on insider information, then 12 can legitimately be inferred to be true.

Now as we have noted, there are differences between the factual claim made in 12, the truth of which is determinable by a poll, and the following moral judgment:

13. Ivan Boesky acted immorally in trading on insider information.

Some people allow that 12 is true, while claiming that what Boesky did was morally permissible. Descriptive ethics, however, is not primarily concerned with the correctness or adequacy of moral judgments such as 13; the scientist focuses on establishing what moral beliefs are actually held by an individual or group of persons.

Normative ethics is a second important branch of ethical inquiry. It is concerned primarily with two questions: (A) What kinds of things are good? (B) What kinds of acts are right and should be performed? The latter question is of primary interest in business ethics, and we shall return to it after a brief discussion of (A).

Since the time of the ancient Greeks normative ethical theorists have attempted to develop a defensible account of what kinds of things are good or valuable. In the course of their investigations they have sorted out three distinct senses of "value." In one sense, the *preference* sense, a person values something if he prefers, likes, or takes an interest in it; some people, for example, value their work while others value leisure time. In this sense, those who take an interest in smoking, or who like to smoke, can be said to value smoking. In another sense, something can be valuable to a person even though he does not take an interest in it. We say that a person's health is valuable to him even though he may neglect it, and, in this sense, smoking is not of value to a person even though he likes to smoke. In the first sense, then, what is valuable is what is liked or preferred, and in the second sense what is valuable is what serves as a means to some end independent of whether it is preferred. For example, milk is valuable as a means to a healthy body, irrespective of whether an individual likes milk. A thing valued because it serves as a means to some end independent of whether it is preferred is said to be *instrumentally valuable*. There are many things—such as money, food, and security—that would normally be considered of instrumental value for humans, but are there things that are good in and for themselves and not merely of instrumental value; that is, are there things that are good for their own sakes, or *intrinsically valuable,* without reference to a further end? Many normative theorists have argued that there are such intrinsically good things, but there is considerable disagreement as to what things possess this sort of value. Pleasure, happiness, goodwill, freedom, honesty, knowledge, benevolence, and self-development have all been proposed as being intrinsically good, and one task of normative ethics is to assess these proposals. Can it be shown, for example, that one of the above-mentioned things is intrinsically valuable whereas the others are merely instrumentally valuable, or should we allow that several or all of them are intrinsically valuable?

Without resolving this issue, we can note the relevance of the instrumental/ intrinsic value distinction to issues in business ethics. In a general sense the defenses of the capitalistic economic system rest on emphasizing either its instrumental or intrinsic value. Given that people have basic intrinsic wants, and that a modern society requires capital to satisfy those wants, the instrumental defense of capitalism rests on showing that it can accumulate and allocate capital more effectively than alternative economic systems, and therefore better satisfy those wants. The defender of capitalism may also stress its intrinsic values. Freedom, for example, is often regarded as having intrinsic value, and economic freedom, the freedom to buy, sell, and compete for profits, can be regarded as one aspect of that intrinsic good. The distinction between instrumental and intrinsic value is also important in discussing issues within the framework of capitalism. For example, if freedom of speech has intrinsic value, and justified uses of advertising involve an exercise of free speech, then advertising can be said to have intrinsic value. On the other hand, if promotion of the public good is regarded as intrinsically valuable, then advertising may or may not have instrumental value, depending on whether it is regarded as a successful means toward realizing the public good. Furthermore, ethical problems may emerge within a firm if a manager and his employees stress different values. If a manager regards profit as the sole value whereas a subordinate emphasizes family life, the latter may be pressured to acquiesce in an illegal or immoral business practice due to his family obligations and the fear that failure to cooperate could cost him his job. And the amount of work required of a subordinate for profit maximization may lead to a form of "corporate bigamy" leaving little time for the family. Similarly, a manager may value corporate loyalty while an employee believes that the public has a right to know about a potentially unsafe product. In such cases an awareness that the disputants are emphasizing different values is an important first step in resolving the conflict.

Having noted three distinct uses of "good" or "value," and their relevance for business contexts, we should also note that when we morally assess a person's acts we generally speak of "right" and "wrong." The second major branch of normative ethics, the branch that is perhaps most relevant to business ethics, is concerned with establishing standards for assessing acts as right or wrong, that is, with the development of a theory of right conduct. For purposes of illustration, suppose that a struggling minority firm submits the second lowest bid to supply a large corporation with a machine part, and suppose the corporation's purchasing agent, P, rejects the minority firm's bid; then consider the following conversation P has with his corporation's affirmative action officer, A:

A_1: Rejecting that minority firm's bid was wrong; although there is no law governing this sort of purchase, the rule we should adopt is to help those who have been disadvantaged, whenever it does not put our own company in serious economic jeopardy. Since the bids are so close, we should award the contract to the minority firm.

P_2: I disagree. We have an obligation to our company, and my act was right because, as a rule, the best course of action in these cases, the right thing to do, is to accept the lowest bid.

A_3: Wait a minute. We should treat our suppliers fairly; that's just an instance of the Golden Rule: treat others as you wish them to treat you. But in order to be fair to minority firms we must take past discriminatory practices into account in order to give them a fair shake.

P_4: I still think I am right. I think it is the case that economic efficiency— and that means accepting the lowest bid—leads to the best consequences for everyone, black and white, in the long run.

For our present purposes we need not extend this argument to try to determine who is right. What is noteworthy about this exchange is how one usually goes about justifying moral judgments. Ordinarily, moral disagreements occur within a context of action, and what one judges are *acts* (in this case P's act of rejecting the minority firm's bid). Furthermore, when a person judges an act, he usually appeals to some *moral rule* to justify his judgment: A_1 and P_2 both involve appeals to moral rules. But appeals of this type do not invariably settle a moral dispute, because, as A_1 and P_2 illustrate, moral rules may differ; and if two people accept different moral rules, their moral judgments may differ. To fully justify his moral judgments, then, a person must show why *his* moral rules are correct while his adversary's are not. To accomplish this a person appeals to a more general rule, a *moral principle* or standard. A_3 contains an appeal to the Golden Rule, while P_4 appeals to the principle that an act is right if and only if it has the best consequences for everyone.

Let us say that a set of moral rules justified by an appeal to a moral principle constitutes a moral theory. If a person has a *moral theory,* he makes moral judgments based on moral rules and he justifies his moral rules by appeal to a moral principle. When A judges P's act to be wrong he does so by appealing to the moral rule in A_1, and he justifies that rule in terms of the moral principle expressed in A_3. On the other hand, P justifies his act by appealing to the moral rule in P_2, and he justifies that rule by having recourse to the moral principle in P_4. Our example indicates that moral theories differ; distinct moral judgments may be based on different rules and principles. To adjudicate this dispute, then, A and P will have to assess the adequacy of the moral principles expressed in A_3 and P_4. Normative ethics involves the attempt to discover, formulate, and defend fundamental moral principles.

If the field of ethics has descriptive and normative domains, and if our primary concern in business ethics is with the normative domain, it would seem that our next task is to discuss and assess the various moral principles that normative ethical theorists have set forth. Before we can justifiably do so, however, we must take up two challenges that seem at the outset to undercut the relevance of the normative enterprise to the actions of businesspersons. First, it is often maintained that morals are relative. As we shall see, this claim can be interpreted in a variety of ways, but it is often taken to mean that, since all moral judgments, rules, and principles are relative to a particular cultural context, there can be no adequate universal normative theory, i.e., no normative moral theory that is binding on all people in all circumstances. It is claimed that if relativism is correct, there is simply no point in examining the various normative theories proposed as universal and hence asserted to be relevant within business contexts. Second, it is often claimed that the relation between morality and the law is such that, while businesspersons should obey the law, morality is in some fashion irrelevant in the context of business. If this view is defensible, there is surely no point in trying to formulate a normative ethical theory applicable within the business community. Let us examine these challenges in turn.

Many people believe that some form of moral relativism is acceptable— you have your moral rules and principle(s), I have mine, and that's that. In fact, however, there are different versions of relativism, and it is worthwhile to distinguish some of them to see whether they are acceptable and to note their relevance to issues in business ethics. In line with our previous discussion, let us focus on factual and normative versions of moral relativism.

It is often claimed that moral beliefs are in fact relative, that different people do make different moral judgments and advocate different moral rules and principles. Let us call this position *factual moral relativism* (FMR). As a factual matter, the truth of FMR can be decided by empirical investigation; the study of FMR falls within the domain of descriptive ethics. We can distinguish several specific claims within the domain of FMR; being factual claims, each is either true or false:

(R₁) *Individual moral belief relativism*: the moral beliefs of one individual may differ from those of another.

(R₂) *Societal moral belief relativism*: the moral beliefs widely accepted in one society may differ from the moral beliefs widely accepted in another society.

(R₃) *Societal moral rule relativism*: the moral rules widely accepted in one society may differ from the moral rules widely accepted in another society.

(R$_4$) *Societal moral principle relativism*: the moral principle(s) widely accepted in one society may differ from the moral principle(s) widely accepted in another society.

R$_1$ is true because one person may believe that Lockheed was morally right in making payoffs to Japanese officials to secure sales of its Tristar aircraft, while another person believes Lockheed's actions were wrong. R$_2$ and R$_3$ also seem to be true. In many areas of the Middle East, the Far East, and Africa, where a private-sector market economy governed by competitive pricing does not exist, the exchange of goods is governed by a complex network of tribal, social, and familial relations and obligations. In this context bribery is often regarded as a morally acceptable practice. In some cases it is governmentally sanctioned; civil servants' salaries, for example, may be kept low with the expectation that they will supplement their wages with bribe money. In America, on the other hand, bribery is widely acknowledged to be morally wrong. Lockheed's officials, for example, allowed that the bribes paid to Japanese officials were morally wrong; they defended the payoffs only as necessary for commercial success. It seems clear, therefore, that the specific moral beliefs widely accepted in one society may differ from those in another society, and the rules used to justify such acts may differ as well; R$_2$ and R$_3$ are true.

The truth or falsity of R$_1$ is not as easily established as the other forms of FMR. Certainly the truth of R$_1$, R$_2$, and R$_3$ does not establish the truth of R$_4$. Suppose that in society S$_1$ the judgment that a specific act of bribery is morally right and the belief that bribery is morally right are both widely accepted, while in society S$_2$ it is widely held that the act is wrong and that in general bribery is reprehensible. R$_2$ and R$_3$ are then true. But suppose the members of S$_1$ justify their moral rule by claiming that the practice of bribery has the best consequences for everyone concerned, while the members of S$_2$ justify their moral rule by maintaining that bribery does not have the best consequences for everyone. Both societies would then have justified incompatible moral rules by appeal to the same moral principle. Therefore, the truth of R$_1$, R$_2$, and R$_3$ does not substantiate R$_4$. Of course, the truth or falsity of R$_4$ is, as previously noted, a factual matter determinable by scientific investigation. The problem is that at present the anthropological evidence is not conclusive; there is data both for and against the truth of R$_4$.

Let us assume, however, that all the versions of FMR are true, including R$_4$, and proceed to raise the question of whether relativism's truth has any relevance for normative ethics. We have already noted that R$_1$, R$_2$, and R$_3$ do not necessarily conflict with the acceptance of one normative principle. Furthermore, even if R$_4$ is true, and societies do actually accept different normative moral principles, we still cannot conclusively infer that there is no single normative principle binding on all humans. If people in society S$_1$ accept moral principle P$_1$ while people in S$_2$ accept P$_2$, and P$_1$ and P$_2$ are incompatible, then the most we can infer is that one of the principles must be mistaken. In fact, both may be mistaken. But it does not follow that there is no true normative principle. Even if it could be shown that all the normative principles accepted by all societies to this point in time are, for one reason or another, inadequate, it would still not follow that there is no true normative principle; it may simply be the case that no person has discovered that principle. In short, the truth of the varieties of FMR does not preclude our finding a universally binding normative theory. The best that can be said for relativism is that if R_4 is, as a matter of fact, true, and if there is considerable disagreement on fundamental moral principles (a claim that anthropologists have yet to establish), then there is some inductive evidence for the claim that there is no such universal normative principle to be found.

Relativism is sometimes presented as a normative principle; *normative ethical relativism* (NER) is the claim that an act A in society S is right if and only if most people in S believe A is right. This is a universal normative principle insofar as it applies to any person in any society; it is relativistic insofar as it allows that an act that is right in one society may be wrong in another society. NER may be attractive to businesspersons, especially those doing business in the international arena. There is a democratic ring to NER, and it seems to capture the truth in the maxim "When in Rome do as the Romans do." Actually, there seem to be rather conclusive reasons for rejecting NER, and, in addition, the arguments commonly advanced to support it are weak.

One argument against NER is that it may have morally objectionable consequences. If the majority of people in a society believe that owning slaves is an acceptable business practice, then it is morally right to own slaves in that society. Many people claim that the very possibility of allowing and sanctioning such practices is morally indefensible, and they reject NER on this basis alone. A second objection to NER is that it entails the infallibility of the majority, for what the majority believes to be right *is* right. Surely, we want to say, there are at least some cases in which the majority is wrong. A third criticism of NER is that it precludes the possibility of intersocietal comparisons. Suppose society S_1 regards slavery as right while S_2 regards it as wrong. Other things being equal, we would want to say the members of S_2 are more moral than the members of S_1. But if NER is true, we cannot justifiably say this. For the members of S_1 are right in following the majority's beliefs in S_1, and the same holds for S_2; both are performing right acts. We cannot fault the members of S_1 for not following the wishes of the members of S_2, because, according to NER, the members of S_1 are acting morally when they follow the majority opinion in S_1. Since NER is society-relative, there is no basis for condemning the members of S_1 for failing to adopt the majority opinion in S_2. Since we do want to make intersocietal moral comparisons, but NER precludes them, NER seems unacceptable.

In addition to these objections the arguments used to support NER are weak. First, it is sometimes claimed that the facts of factual moral relativism (FMR) provide evidence for NER. But even if it is true that individuals and societies have different moral beliefs, rules, and principles, as stated in R_1, R_2, R_3, and R_4, what people actually *believe* to be morally right cannot establish what *is* right, for, as we previously noted, some or even all of the individuals or groups may have mistaken beliefs. Hence, the facts of FMR seem irrelevant to the establishment of any normative principle, including NER. Second, it is argued that if we accept the principle of tolerance, namely, that we should not try to impose our moral beliefs on others, then we should accept NER because it is the only normative principle compatible with a commitment to tolerance. However, that conclusion does not follow. According to NER, if the majority believes in forcing a minority to accept some moral belief, then the act they are committing (an act of intolerance) is right. So NER need not foster tolerance. Furthermore, the denial of NER, and the acceptance of a nonrelativist normative principle, need not necessarily lead to intolerance, for the nonrelativist may accept the principle of tolerance as a moral rule. In general, then, the standard defenses of NER seem rather weak, and there do seem to be good arguments against its acceptability as a normative principle.

Let us now turn to the claim that although businesspersons should obey the law, if for none other than pragmatic reasons, ethical issues are in some sense irrelevant in the context of business, and hence, there is no point in attempting to formulate a normative theory that is applicable to business contexts.

One version of this position is that the jurisdictions of morality and the law are the same, so that the businessperson need not pay attention to moral rules or principles supposedly expressed independently of, or distinct from, the law—there are no such independent rules or principles. What is moral can be determined by simply examining the law. Furthermore, in following the law a businessperson is acting morally; to act morally is just to act in accordance with the law.

This view certainly simplifies moral matters; to check whether an act is morally wrong a businessperson need only check the legal statutes. But there are difficulties with this view of the relation between law and morality. First, if morality is synonymous with the law, then we cannot morally criticize the law. If act x is morally wrong only because it is considered illegal, then a person cannot legitimately claim that x is morally right even though it is illegal. So the view tends to entrench a form of societal conservatism; if slavery is legal in a society, and selling slaves an acceptable business practice, it cannot be legitimately claimed that the law should be changed because it is immoral. Furthermore, it should be noted that the law is coercive; enforcement is essential to the law, whereas, apart from societal pressures, our actions in the moral realm seem to be rooted in rational persuasion, conscience, and personal choice. These features of morality often serve as a basis for moral criticism of the law. The identification of law and morality, however, undercuts this voluntary or personal dimension and places considerable emphasis on enforcement. Individuals at odds with the public morality expressed in law are subjected to enforced penalties and at the same time are precluded from raising moral objections to the law, i.e., precluded from attempting to change the law by independent moral persuasion. In addition, on this view a change in law is a change in morality; so slavery is now illegal and immoral in America, yet in 1780 it was not only legal but also moral. Those who claim that slavery is always immoral must reject the identification of morality with the law.

A second version of the irrelevance of morality to business contexts rests on the claim that the law is totally independent of morality, and that although the law should be obeyed just because it is the law, moral considerations should not enter into the context of business.

This view seems partially correct insofar as it points out some differences between legality and morality. The law, as we noted, is coercive—it is connected with enforcement—whereas morality is not. Again, laws are made or enacted by humans, whereas it seems odd to say that moral rules or principles are *made* or *enacted*. But these differences do not entail a complete separation of law and morality. In fact, if we separate them completely, and claim that the law should be obeyed, then we once again seem to have no basis for failing to obey the law. If the law said slavery was legal, the question of its moral status would be irrelevant. On this view the law tends to be reduced to the domain of enforcement, and questions of the morality and justice of the law are simply set aside.

If moral rules are not synonymous with or reducible to positive law, and if legality is not totally independent of morality, it seems reasonable to say that legality often rests, in some sense, on morality. Legal obligation is not the basis of moral obligation, for the law is not as ultimate as fundamental moral principles. Laws are made and then repealed, but a genuine moral obligation is categorical and not repealable. For example, we should treat people with respect, not because of any legal considerations but because humans intrinsically ought to respect each other. And laws are often repealed on the basis of moral considerations. If a person argues that some laws are morally bad and ought to be changed, that the Constitution (morally) should be amended to preclude, say, abortion, or that a judge's decision ought to be reversed in the interest of justice, he is acknowledging the dependence of law on morality.

The upshot of our discussion is that normative ethics does seem relevant to the actions of businesspersons. We found that relativism does not undercut the attempt to find a universal normative theory, and we argued that the relation between law and morality is such that the former rests on the latter; and therefore it cannot be maintained that, although businesspersons should obey the law, morality is irrelevant in the business world. In light of our discussion, we can expand our notion of a moral theory to include legal rules or laws. Moral rules often serve as the justification for legal enactments, and moral rules, in turn, are justified on the basis of ultimate moral principles. This ordering of reasons reflects our claim that legality rests on morality.

If there were only one moral theory to which appeal could be made in making moral judgments, ethical disputes would be relatively easy to resolve. Unfortunately, things are not so simple in real life; and what we discover as we go about the process of living is that there are a number of competing moral theories from which we must choose. Although these theories can differ radically, some of them do have characteristics in common. The existence of these shared traits allows for the classification of moral theories into specific types. Traditionally, the broadest classification of moral theories is into one or the other of two classes: consequentialist and nonconsequentialist. Consequentialist theories hold that the rightness or wrongness of an act is ultimately determined by the act's *consequences*; i.e., an act is said to be morally right if it produces good consequences, and wrong if it produces bad results. Nonconsequentialists reject this view and claim that, ultimately, an act is right or wrong because of some aspect of its character, form, or nature. In addition, most nonconsequentialists insist that an action cannot be judged morally unless one knows why the person who performed the action did what he did. In other words, nonconsequentialists tell us that a person's motives for acting are important, and that an action cannot be morally right unless the person (the agent) who performed it did what he did for the right reasons.

Many businesspersons and economists accept a moral theory that attempts to combine elements of both consequentialism and nonconsequentialism into one all-encompassing system. For reasons that will become apparent later, we have chosen to call this moral theory "restricted egoism." In what follows we shall examine restricted egoism in some detail. In addition, four other moral theories will be analyzed. Two of these theories (ethical egoism and utilitarianism) are consequentialist, and two (Kantianism and theologism) are nonconsequentialist. Our purpose in introducing these theories is not simply to make the reader aware of certain "traditional" moral positions. Rather, our discussion is prompted by two considerations. First and foremost, we want the reader to have a clear understanding of what it is that restricted egoism asserts; and this is made most evident by considering the four theories listed above. Our second purpose is critical. Restricted egoism is not a "perfect" moral theory; and many of the problems one encounters in restricted egoism find their roots in ethical egoism and utilitarianism. Thus, analysis of these "traditional" theories will better enable us to evaluate the claims of restricted egoism.

CONSEQUENTIALISM: ETHICAL EGOISM, UTILITARIANISM AND RESTRICTED EGOISM

Ethical Egoism

Ethical egoists claim that an act is morally right if and only if it tends, more than any alternative act open to the agent at the time, to promote the interests of the agent. That is to say, what is right, or what one ought to do, is to act in accordance with one's own self-interest.

Ethical egoism should be distinguished from psychological egoism, which is the claim that people do, as a matter of fact, always act in their own self-interest. Ethical egoism is an ethical theory that purports to tell us what people should do; psychological egoism, on the other hand, is a factual or empirical theory that makes a claim about what people actually do or what motivates them to act. Psychological egoism is sometimes used to support ethical egoism; the claim is that if people do invariably act in their own self-interest, then the only moral theory compatible with this fact is ethical egoism. If psychological egoism is true, though, ethics becomes pointless. This is so because a moral theory must tell us either that there are times when we ought to sacrifice our own self-interests or that we always ought to do what is in our own interests. If psychological egoism is true, it would make no sense to say that we *ought* to sacrifice our own interests (because we cannot, or as a matter of fact do not, do this), and it is pointless to tell us to maximize our self-interest (because we will do this anyway).

In discussing ethical egoism it is important to note that the theory advocates the long-term self-interest of the agent, and hence it is not a fair objection against ethical egoism to say that it favors short-term or immediate self-interest. In business, for example, an employee who is an ethical egoist may be very loyal and hard-working in the belief that these traits will promote the firm's interests, and that promotion of the firm's interests, e.g., profit maximization, is the best means to serve his own long-term self-interest. Similarly, an ethical egoist shareholder may advocate that the firm defer dividend payments and reinvest them in order to maximize capital gains, which he takes to be in his long-term self-interest. Acting in a self-sacrificing way is compatible with being an ethical egoist as long as the act leads to the long-term best interest of the agent. One advantage of ethical egoism in a business context, then, is that the egoist is obligated to act in the firm's interest so long as that interest is the best means to achieve his own long-term self-interest; in a large percentage of cases egoism is compatible with the firm's interests.

A second advantage of ethical egoism is that it provides a basis for the flexibility that seems to be needed in business decision-making. Normally a businessperson should keep his contracts, and the ethical egoist can explain why this is so; in most cases it is in his interest that contracts be kept. But the egoist claims that moral rules, e.g., "Always keep your contracts," are not inviolate. In fact, the principle of ethical egoism makes no reference to moral rules, for the rightness of an act is solely determined by whether it maximizes self-interest, and in certain cases strict adherence to a moral rule will not maximize self-interest. The egoist claims that business decision-making is too complex to be bound by strict rules and that the principle of ethical egoism provides the moral basis for both breaking and adhering to such rules.

In spite of these advantages, egoism has several weaknesses as an ethical theory in business contexts. First, if a businessperson believes that profit maximization is in his self-interest, then any means that he can employ and "get away with" to maximize profit are regarded as morally right. Thus, if in certain cases a businessperson can maximize profit by dumping a harmful pollutant or marketing an unsafe product, and the chances of his getting caught are slim, then he ought to commit such acts. In such cases the flexibility afforded the businessperson by ethical egoism allows him to commit acts that intuitively seem wrong.

More generally, one can argue that the ethical egoists' definition of "right act" does not reflect society's ordinary ways of speaking, and that, as a result, ethical egoists must be wrong when they say that we ought to pursue our own interests. Let us say, for instance, that we know a person, *P,* who acts only to further his own interests. Whenever *P* helps others he does so only because this ultimately serves his own ends. At the same time, he never allows anyone to "get in his way." Furthermore, if it will ultimately benefit P to lie about someone, or hurt someone, he will do so. Now would we ordinarily say that P was a moral person, or that he was acting in morally right ways? It seems clear that we would not. Consequently, it seems that ethical egoists' understanding of what is right to do is mistaken and that their moral theory must be rejected.

Few ethical egoists would be convinced by the above criticism of their position. It might well be the case, they would say, that by "right act" most people do not mean "action which serves one's self-interest." Nevertheless, they would claim, this is what people should mean, and if they hold a contrary view they are mistaken. At this point, however, there is a second criticism that can be brought against the ethical egoists' position; namely, that the position is inconsistent. After all, ethical egoists claim that everyone should act to further his own interests. But how can business X enjoin a competing firm Y to seek only what is in Y's best interest when there certainly will be competitive situations in which those acts serving Y's interest will be detrimental to X's interests? And in such cases X seems to be telling Y that it is morally right for Y to work against X's interests, that is, to do what X considers to be morally wrong.

In conclusion, then, insofar as the calculation of interests and consequences enters into moral decision-making, it seems that impartiality is required of the agent; i.e., he should attempt to impartially consider the interests of all affected parties when calculating the consequences of an action. Ethical egoism's failure to meet the test of impartiality is a basic weakness of the theory.

Utilitarianism

A consequentialist ethical theory that does attempt to take everyone into account is utilitarianism. There are a number of versions of utilitarianism, two of which we shall consider: act utilitarianism and rule utilitarianism.

According to the act utilitarian, an act is morally right if and only if it maximizes utility, i.e., if and only if the ratio of benefit to harm calculated by taking everyone affected by the act into consideration is greater than the ratio of benefit to harm resulting from any alternative act. In deciding to act, then, the act utilitarian will first set out the alternatives open to him. Second, he calculates the ratio of benefit to harm for each individual, including himself, affected by the alternative acts. Third, he adds up the ratios for each alternative act. Finally, he chooses the act that results in the greatest total ratio of benefit to harm. Assume, for example, that there are three alternative acts (A_1, A_2, A_3) open to person P_1, and that there are three people (P_1, P_2, P_3) affected by each alternative act. Assume, furthermore, that the ratio of benefit to harm for each person affected by each act can be expressed quantitatively, with a plus value indicating a benefit and a negative value indicating a harmful effect. Finally, assume a calculation yields the following result:

	P_1	P_2	P_3	Totals
A_1	+4	–5	+8	+7
A_2	+6	+2	–3	+5
A_3	–2	–5	+4	–3

In this situation the act utilitarian will choose act A_1 because it produces the greatest ratio of benefit to harm (+7) when everyone affected by the act is taken into consideration. Thus, the act utilitarian often recommends a course of action different from that recommended by the ethical egoist. In the above situation the ethical egoist as agent P_1 would choose A_2, for that act maximizes P_1's self-interest.

In setting up our example we assumed that benefit/harm (or benefit/cost) ratios can be measured and compared, but these are assumptions that have been questioned. First, it is not altogether clear in some cases what is to count as a benefit or harm. In locating a plant, for example, what some people regard as a benefit others may see as a cost. Second, in some cases it may be difficult to assign quantitative values; for example, how does one measure the value of aesthetically pleasant surroundings or the value of a human life? Analogously, can something like aesthetic value ever be meaningfully compared with the value of a life? Third, the act utilitarian is concerned with the long-term consequences of acts, and in such contexts it may be very difficult to delimit the alternative acts available and to obtain reliable predictions as to the long-term consequences of performable acts.

If such difficulties could be overcome, however, act utilitarianism would have several advantages as an ethical theory in business contexts. First, unlike ethical egoism, act utilitarianism is impartial in that it takes each person's interests into account, and requires that act which maximizes utility irrespective of who benefits. Thus, the businessperson who accepts act utilitarianism has a basis for claiming that he is acting in a socially responsible manner in the sense that he takes everyone's interests, including employees, consumers, suppliers, etc., into account in decision-making. Second, the theory is able to account for why we typically hold certain business practices, e.g., contract-breaking, to be immoral; in most cases such practices do not maximize utility. But the act utilitarian denies that there are any unbreakable moral rules, e.g., "always keep your contracts," for in certain contexts breaking such a rule may maximize utility. A third advantage for the businessperson employing act utilitarianism is that it does not force him to accept binding rules; it allows for the flexibility that some people believe is necessary in today's complex business environment. In contrast with the egoist, however, such flexibility is based on overall utility considerations and not solely on self-interest.

Act utilitarianism, however, is not free of problems. For example, let us assume that executive X in company A has worked for months in order to bring about a contractual agreement between his company and another company, B. Whether or not the agreement actually does take place is dependent, in large part, upon what X does, for negotiations are at a crucial stage. If the agreement is secured, both companies A and B will profit and many new jobs will be created. During the final negotiations the president of company A by chance discovers that X has embezzled \$5,000 from the corporation. The company's books are scheduled to be audited in a day or two, and the president of A knows that the accountants will discover X's theft. The president of A confronts X and tells him what he has learned. X explains that he needed the money to pay for an operation for his wife, but that his wife has died and he never again will be pressed to steal money from the company. Also, X says that if his theft is made known the people he is negotiating with in company B will no longer trust him, and the agreement between companies A and B will fall through. Since X's theft will be detected by the impending audit, the president says there is very little he can do. As luck would have it, however, there is a low-level executive, Y, in company A who has had bad relations with all his supervisors and is about to be fired. X suggests that the president make it appear as though Y embezzled the \$5,000. When Y is fired, the company will not press charges, and X quietly will repay the money he stole. The question then is this: should the president of A frame Y for the embezzlement actually perpetrated by X? It appears as though an act utilitarian would have to say yes, but this violates our ordinary moral intuitions regarding justice and fair play. Furthermore, the following sort of utility calculation could be employed to justify an unjust act such as enslavement.

	P_1	P_2	P_3	Totals
A_1	+22	+22	–25	+19
A_2	+ 6	+ 6	+ 6	+18

It is conceivable that enslavement of P_3 via act A_1 would produce slightly greater total utility than act A_2, the other act open to the agent, even though A_2 results in a more equitable distribution. In that case the morally right act, according to the act utilitarian, is A_1. In such a case, however, act utilitarianism seems to clearly violate our ordinary perceptions of what is right.

Many utilitarians believe it is possible to avoid criticisms of the sort we have brought against act utilitarianism by reformulating the theory so that it has a place for moral rules. So reformulated, the position is known as *rule* utilitarianism. According to rule utilitarians, an act A in circumstance C is morally right if and only if the consequences of everyone acting on the rule "Do A in C" are better than the consequences of everyone acting on any alternative rule. The notion of "best consequences" here is specified in terms of utility maximization. Thus, an act is right if and only if it is in conformity with a particular moral rule, and that rule is chosen because, of all alternative rules, it maximizes utility. For example, a rule utilitarian might claim that "We must not hold a person accountable for a crime he has not committed" is a proper rule of conduct because if this rule were followed by everyone, it would maximize utility. Using this rule, the rule utilitarian could conclude that in our first counterexample to act utilitarianism it would be wrong for the president of company A to frame Y for the crime committed by X. Since this result seems to accord with our moral intuitions, the rule utilitarian contends that his theory represents an advance over act utilitarianism.

Critics of rule utilitarianism, however, point out that if rule utilitarians are committed to the moral rule that maximizes utility, then they will have to allow that the acceptable rule in any case is one that allows exceptions that maximize utility. Thus, instead of the rule "We must not hold a person accountable for a crime he has not committed," the rule utilitarian must adopt the rule "We must not hold a person accountable for a crime he has not committed, unless doing so maximizes utility." In that case, rule utilitarianism collapses into the equivalent of act utilitarianism, and the objections we raised against act utilitarianism resurface. Analogously, in the enslavement counterexample to act utilitarianism, the rule utilitarian might argue that the rule "never enslave" maximizes utility. But he would have to allow that there are at least conceivable exceptions that maximize utility, and hence the rule he advocates is "Never enslave, except when utility is maximized by doing so." The result is that under certain circumstances rule utilitarianism, like act utilitarianism, does appear to sanction intuitively immoral practices such as slavery.

Restricted Egoism

Ethical egoists advise us to act in our own self-interest whereas utilitarians advise us to maximize utility, and hence it might seem that these theories are incompatible. Interestingly, however, their incompatibility has been challenged by a number of economists and businesspersons (see, for example, the selections from Milton Friedman in this volume). Following Adam Smith, these people claim that the universal pursuit of self-interest is a process guided by an "invisible hand"—an invisible hand ultimately assuring that the public interest or total utility will be served. One qualification is needed here. Those who accept the invisible hand theory do not believe that it is morally right, in the pursuit of one's own self-interest, to break either the laws of the land or the established rules of competition. Thus, their moral theory is one that might be labeled "restricted egoism"; the theory is egoistic because it tells us that it is right to promote our own interests, yet this egoism is restricted by the demand that we obey certain laws and rules. On this view a corporation acts in a morally right manner if and only if it: (a) obeys the laws of the land as well as the accepted rules of competition, and (b) pursues its own self-interest, thereby automatically furthering the interests of society as a whole.

There are two major advantages with this theory. First, it commits businesspersons to conformity with the law, which can be looked up in the legal statutes. Second, it sanctions corporate self-interest, which typically means profit maximization, on the basis that pursuit of such self-interest in a competitive context will maximize utility, or further the overall interests of society. Whereas ethical egoism asserts that the pursuit of self-interest is moral, restricted egoism justifies the pursuit of self-interest in terms of utility.

In turning to criticisms of the theory, the first thing one notices about restricted egoism is that it is not clear why its proponents assert (a). Two possibilities present themselves: (1) restricted egoists might claim that it is right to obey society's laws and the rules of competition because such action serves self-interests (of course, since the invisible hand is at work, such action also will further society's interests), (2) restricted egoists could say that laws and rules must be obeyed because without a context of rule-governed behavior the competitive game itself is impossible. That is to say, if one corporation or business were to claim the right to be exempted from having to follow laws and rules, all businesses legitimately could claim that right. And in this situation—a situation in which any corporation could disregard any rule or law that it did not want to obey—business would be impossible.

Problems arise no matter which interpretation of restricted egoism one chooses to accept. If restricted egoists are interpreted as asserting (1), then why must corporations obey laws and rules in order to do what is morally right? For example, assume that the executives of a corporation know that they can break a law and not get caught. Furthermore, they know that breaking the law will benefit both the corporation and society. If the only justification for following laws and rules is that this ultimately conduces to the interests of business and society, why, in the absence of such a justification, should the corporation obey the law? Indeed, if any corporation refused to break the law when it was obvious that to do so would be in its own best long-term interests, as well as society's, would not that corporation be failing in its moral duty? Surely it would seem so. And if this is the case, restricted egoists should not tell us that businesses ought to obey certain rules and laws in order to do what is morally right, but rather that corporations have every right to break these laws and rules when it is clearly in their interests and the interests of society to do so.

If we interpret restricted egoists as using (2) rather than (1) to justify the inclusion of laws and rules within their moral theory, it now becomes impossible for any corporation to break the laws of society or the established rules of business practice without suffering moral condemnation. Still, on this view it is not necessarily true that a corporation acts morally when it obeys society's laws and the rules of good business practice. To be moral a corporation must follow rules *and* promote its own interests together with the interests of society. Both conditions are needed; and neither condition by itself is sufficient. That is to say, if a corporation is promoting its own interests and the interests of society, but breaks a law or rule in the process, then it is acting immorally. On the other hand, if it obeys society's laws and the accepted rules of competition but at the same time does not contribute to anyone's interest, then the corporation does not do what is morally right. It does not do anything wrong; but it does not do anything right either, according to restricted egoism.

If restricted egoism is represented in the above manner, the theory suffers from at least two difficulties. First, justification could be given for virtually *any* set of rules and laws. (Rules prohibiting competition or corporate activity could not be justified, but almost any other set of rules could be accepted as unbreakable guidelines for corporate conduct.) This being the case, restricted egoists could argue for the morality of many acts that we would ordinarily call immoral. For example, if some corporation was doing business in a country where bribes and kickbacks were accepted as part of the "competitive game," restricted egoists should argue that the company is morally bound to follow this established rule. But surely such a position is questionable. Or again, assume that a racist government is in power in a foreign country. It passes a law requiring all businesses to charge blacks more for goods and services than other citizens pay. Presumably, restricted egoists would now have to claim that it would be wrong for any corporation to break this law. But this runs counter to our ordinary moral intuitions. How, after all, can a corporation have a moral duty to further the ends of racism?

If, as we now are assuming, restricted egoism holds that laws and rules are unbreakable, there is a second, even more severe problem with the theory. That is, what happens if there is a conflict between one or more of society's laws and the established rules of the "competitive game"? Should businesspersons obey the law or follow informal rules of competition? In other words, in cases of conflict, which set of rules has priority? And whatever the choice, how would businesspersons justify their decision? Both questions must be answered before restricted egoism can be considered a "complete" moral theory.

We have seen that restricted egoism can be interpreted in at least two different ways, and that each form has its problems. But things are really worse than we have made out, for there is another difficulty plaguing *any* form of restricted egoism. Regardless of how they justify the inclusion of laws and rules within their moral theory, all restricted egoists agree that a morally right act furthers both self-interest and the interests of society. Restricted egoists see no problem with this "dual consequence" theory, because they firmly believe in Adam Smith's invisible hand. That is to say, corporate executives need worry about nothing but maximizing the interests of their own corporations; for if they are successful in this enterprise, Smith's "invisible hand" will see to it that society's interests are also served. But is this true? Certainly in *some* cases societal and business interests are in accord; but it is not at all clear that this is true in every case. For example, prior to the advent of child labor laws it was in the interest of business to have children work 12 to 14 hours a day at low wages. Given the amount of human suffering involved, however, it is not apparent that this served the public interest. Indeed, the fact that laws were passed prohibiting such practices tends to indicate that our society did not see child labor as fostering its best interests. Thus the problem for the restricted egoist is this: what should a corporation do when some action it is contemplating would benefit society but not the corporation, or *vice-versa*? In circumstances such as these, restricted egoists are forced to choose between ethical egoism and utilitarianism. Neither choice is problem free.

Consider a case in which the corporation's interests and those of society do not mesh, and the corporation chooses to act egoistically. Now ordinarily ethical egoism makes no reference to moral rules, for the rightness of an act is solely determined by whether it maximizes self-interest. On the other hand, the restricted egoist who wants to accept ethical egoism will have to claim two things: (1) that a right act is one that maximizes self-interest, and (2) that a right act must conform to society's laws and the rules of competition. It seems clear, however, that there will be times when (1) and (2) will conflict, e.g., times when it will be in a corporation's own interest to break a law. In cases such as these, restricted egoists seem to want to say that the corporation should obey the law. But why should (2) take precedence over (1)? Restricted egoists give us no clear answer. This is not to say that no answer can be given, only that such an answer must be forthcoming if restricted egoists are to present us with a fully worked-out moral theory. If in such cases the restricted egoist claims that (1) takes precedence over (2), then his position essentially reduces to ethical egoism, and we have already enumerated several difficulties with that theory.

Now consider a case in which the corporation's interests and those of society do not mesh, and the corporation acts on the basis of utilitarianism. First consider act utilitarianism. Because act utilitarianism is a theory that typically makes no reference to moral rules, the restricted egoist who opts for act utilitarianism faces a problem similar to that discussed in the previous paragraph. That is, how ought one to act when utility mandates action contrary to some law or rule? As we have noted, the businessperson's moral theory seems to hold that laws and rules are unbreakable. But how is this ordering of priorities justified? Why, in other words, should society's laws and the rules of competition take precedence over the demands of utility? On the other hand, if utility takes precedence over the laws and rules, then this version of restricted egoism reduces to pure act utilitarianism, several difficulties of which we have previously noted. Now consider rule utilitarianism. It would not be easy to combine rule utilitarianism with the rules and laws accepted by restricted egoists, for it is not clear that all these rules and laws could be justified by an appeal to utility. Or to put it another way, what would happen if, through application of the principle of utility, rule utilitarians were led to formulate a set of rules that differed significantly from the laws of our society and the rules of competition? Which rules would the businessperson accept? If he were to accept the utilitarian rules he would have to admit openly that he was not morally bound to follow either the laws of society or the accepted rules of competition. And this seems to be a conclusion that businesspersons are loath to accept. On the other hand, acceptance of the rule utilitarian's rules opens one up to the previously noted difficulties with that theory.

We have seen that there might well be circumstances in which corporate policy makers would be forced to choose between ethical egoism and utilitarianism, and that, regardless of the decision made, problems would arise. But what if we assume that Adam Smith's invisible hand is at work so that whatever conduces to a corporation's interests also operates to secure the best interests of society as a whole? Even in these circumstances we could not say that restricted egoism was a problem-free moral theory. Consider this example.

A company manufactures aerosol spray containing chemicals that destroy ozone. This is the cheapest method of production, and if the company continues to use ozone-destroying elements in its manufacturing process, profits will be maximized and stockholders will be paid the highest possible dividends. As stockholders are rewarded this creates greater demand in other sections of the economy, etc. In sum, the *short-term* consequences of using ozone-destroying chemicals are beneficial both to the manufacturer and to society. If one looks to the *long-term* effects, however, things could be quite different. For instance, as the ozone layer is destroyed, incidents of skin cancer could increase. And once people realize what is causing the destruction of the ozone layer they could refuse to buy any aerosol spray. Indeed, even if the manufacturer were to stop using destructive chemicals in its product, public distrust could be so great that the company might never recover its original market. Now, in these circumstances, what should the aerosol manufacturer do? Specifically, should the manufacturer take the short-term or the long-term consequences of its actions as determining moral rightness? Restricted egoists give us no answer to this question. We can also conceive of a situation in which enslavement of a small part of a society is legal, that it is in a corporation's interest to employ slaves, and that such a practice actually maximizes utility for society. In such a case all the conditions are satisfied for right action according to restricted egoism, but the use of slaves in a business is clearly immoral.

The criticisms of restricted egoism, ethical egoism, and utilitarianism are all limited in scope in that they call attention to specific problems within particular moral theories. We must, however, consider a much broader challenge to these moral theories. Some moral philosophers reject all forms of egoism and utilitarianism because these theories are consequentialist in nature. Moral theorists who reject consideration of consequences in ethics are called nonconsequentialists. Usually nonconsequentialists claim that the rightness or wrongness of an action is to be determined by two things: (1) the action's form or character, and (2) the motives of the agent, i.e., the motives of the person who performs the act. In what follows we shall examine two nonconsequentialist moral theories, briefly enumerate some of the problems faced by those who advocate them, and then see how nonconsequentialism constitutes a challenge to restricted egoism.

NONCONSEQENTIALISM: THEOLOGISM AND KANTIANISM

Although there are many different versions of theological ethics, theologism, as we shall use the term, asserts that an act is right if, more than any alternative open to the agent at the time, it is the one most consistent with what God wills, either directly or indirectly. Usually, theologism provides us with a set of rules (e.g., the Ten Commandments) thought to express God's will. Whether or not an act is right or wrong, then, is determined *in part* by reference to these rules. We say that the rightness or wrongness of an action is *partially* determined by reference to moral rules because most theologians hold that an act may conform to the requirements specified by a legitimate rule of conduct and still not be morally proper. For example, let us say that a person accepts the Ten Commandments as specifying God's will, and refuses to steal when he has an opportunity to do so. In this case, then, he has followed one of God's commands. But if the individual refused to steal because he was afraid of being caught, or because he wanted to be rewarded in heaven for his good behavior, his action would not be truly right. The motives for action would be "impure," and this impurity would affect (perhaps "infect" is a better word) the moral character of his action. For his action to be truly right, God's command must be followed for the right reason, viz., stealing must be rejected, not out of concern for oneself, but rather out of love for God and fellow men. Given *this* motive, then, the action would be right. In short, most versions of theologism hold that God not only wants us to act in certain ways, but also to act in those ways for the right reasons.

Kantianism, named after the German philosopher Immanuel Kant (1724–1804), is similar to theologism in a number of ways. Like theologism, Kantianism holds that an action's rightness or wrongness is to be determined by: (1) the action's form or character (i.e., the action must be such that it conforms to certain rules of conduct), and (2) the motives or intentions of the agent. On the other hand, Kantianism differs from theologism in certain significant respects. For one thing, it might well be the case that Kant's moral rules and the rules of theologism differ. The reason this is so is that while theologism justifies its rules by an appeal to God as the moral lawgiver, Kant appeals to what he calls the *categorical imperative*. This principle is an imperative because it is a command. It is categorical because it is a command that holds without qualification. Unfortunately, Kant states the categorical imperative in a variety of different ways. In what follows we shall discuss the two best known formulations.

Sometimes Kant states the categorical imperative as follows: "One ought never to act except in such a way that one can also will that one's maxim should become a universal law." Using such a guideline, Kant claims that practices such as lying, killing, stealing, and cheating are all forbidden by the moral law. And the reason they are forbidden is that if these acts were universalized (i.e., if they were practiced by everyone) it no longer would make any sense to speak of such practices occurring. To put it another way, universalization of the practice would destroy the practice itself. For example, consider lying. Unless there is a general context of truth telling, the concept of lying makes no sense, for to lie is not to tell the truth. But if everyone always lied, there would be no truth, i.e., nothing with which lying could be contrasted, and hence no way meaningfully to say that one was lying. On the other hand, the same considerations do not apply to truth telling. If everyone always told the truth, it still would make sense to say that people were speaking truly. This is so because "truth" is not defined in terms of "lying," but rather in terms of other criteria, e.g., a statement is true if it corresponds with fact.

Using the universalization formulation of the categorical imperative, Kant believes he can derive a set of moral rules that must *always* be obeyed. In other words, to break one of these rules is always to do something wrong, regardless of the particular circumstances in which one acts. On the other hand, simply to act in the ways specified by these rules is not to insure that one's actions are morally right. Like the theologian, Kant insists that an action cannot be counted as morally right unless the agent performs the action for the right reason. For Kant, however, one should not act from the motives specified by the theologian. Rather, one must obey moral rules *simply because this is the right thing to do.* In short, one's motive for action must be respect for the moral law. And when one obeys a rule for this reason, one is doing what is morally right.

Kant's second formulation of the categorical imperative is as follows: "Act so that you treat humanity, whether in your own person or that of another, always as an end and never as a means only." Kant's point here seems to be that all persons deserve respect simply because they are persons. If this principle is accepted, everyone has a moral duty to treat others fairly and equitably, to refrain from "using" humans as means for the procurement of one's own or others' ends, etc. In effect, the second statement of the categorical imperative, like the first, leads one to formulate a set of moral rules that must be obeyed if one is to act in morally right ways.

Because Kantianism and theologism are similar, there are criticisms which apply equally to both moral theories. Perhaps the best-known criticism applicable to both theories is that they provide us with moral rules that cannot be violated without doing something wrong. Take, for instance, the Kantian injunction against lying. For Kant, lying is *always* wrong; there are no exceptions to this rule. But surely there are some circumstances in which we ordinarily would say it was right to lie. Consider this case. You are a security guard for a large company that you know does secret work for the CIA. One day while making your rounds you discover an old friend of yours planting a bomb on the premises. He pulls a gun, holds it to your head and says that he is bombing the building and its occupants because he suspects the company does work for the CIA. At the same time he says that he trusts you, and that if you swear on everything you hold holy that the company does not work for the CIA, he will take his bomb and leave. Surely we believe that in these circumstances it would be morally right to lie, for to tell the truth would have truly disastrous consequences. This being the case, we must conclude that there is something wrong with any moral theory that tells us to wholly disregard consequences and to concern ourselves only with obeying pre-established, unbreakable moral rules.

Although Kantianism and theologism are alike, they are also dissimilar in various ways. And because of these dissimilarities there are specific criticisms applicable to each theory. For example, we have seen that Kant states the categorical imperative in a variety of different ways. On the face of it, these various formulations do not appear to assert exactly the same things. This being so it is quite likely that different moral rules could be justified, depending upon which formulation of the categorical imperative one happened to accept. But then, which moral rules ought to be accepted? All of them?

At first glance this may sound fine; but what if some of the rules derived from one formulation of the categorical imperative should happen to conflict with rules derived from another formulation? Kantianism gives us no way to resolve a conflict of this sort.

Unlike Kantianism, theologism appeals only to one principle to justify its set of moral rules. Supposedly, the rules of theologism specify right action because these rules, and no others, express God's will. It is at this point, however, that a problem arises. Namely, do the theologians' moral rules express what is right because of God's command or not? If the theologian says that the rules express what is right because of God's command, two untoward consequences follow. First, it no longer makes any sense to say that God is good. (Since *anything* God wills is good, for God himself there is no difference between good and evil; and when we say God is good we assert nothing.) And second, theologians have to admit that if God commanded murder, theft, or cruelty, these actions would be right and morally obligatory. But few people—theologians included—want to admit that actions of this sort ever could be morally right. On the other hand, if the theologians were to claim that their set of moral rules specified right action independently of God's command, then they would have to find a new justification for their moral rules. This is so because the theologians' present position would then be that *regardless* of what God commands, their set of moral rules specifies right action. And in these circumstances it simply would be contradictory for the theologians to assert that it is because of God's command that their moral rules delineate right conduct.

Although theologism and Kantianism have their problems, these theories nevertheless call attention to the fact that moral judgments are rarely if ever made on the basis of consequences alone. Ordinarily, moral rules play a part in our moral considerations; and any moral theory seeking widespread acceptance must take notice of this fact. Apparently, restricted egoists would agree with this assessment, for they try to make a place for rules in their moral theory. However, nonconsequentialists would not be satisfied with the rules of restricted egoism, because neither the laws of society nor the rules of competition are *moral* rules. Indeed, Kantians and theologians would insist that restricted egoists have been far too hasty in their rule selection; for rather than taking the difficult road of attempting to justify rules of conduct by appealing to a moral principle, these individuals simply have accepted a "handy" set of rules. However, operating in this fashion ultimately leaves one open to the possibility that one will accept rules of conduct that mandate immoral action. And, nonconsequentialists would insist, this is exactly what has happened to restricted egoists. For instance, at one time southern states had laws requiring that blacks and whites be segregated. Rather than opposing these laws, companies located in the south (even large national and international corporations) obeyed them. Or again, some members of the business community argue that there are circumstances in which one businessperson may lie to another because lying is an accepted part of the "competitive game." Such a position is surely unacceptable to a Kantian. And theologians would be just as anxious to reject the businessperson's "game" theory. After all, the Mafia sees itself as being engaged in a competitive game, too. In this game, however, killing as well as lying is an accepted rule. Are we then forced to conclude that a hired killer does not act immorally when he kills a Mafia official?

Even if restricted egoists were to justify their rules of conduct by appealing to a moral principle, it is unlikely that nonconsequentialists would be happy with the end product. This is so because restricted egoists do not seem to fully recognize that an agent's motives for acting are important in assessing the moral quality of his or her act. This is not to say that restricted egoists never speak of motives. However, when motives are mentioned by restricted egoists one gets the feeling that they believe humans always should be motivated by self-interest. Given our discussion of Kantianism and theologism, we know that nonconsequentialists disagree concerning the proper motives for human conduct. Despite this disagreement, however, nonconsequentialists are unanimous in their rejection of self-interest as a morally proper motive for action. And here, the nonconsequentialists' position would seem to be in accord with our ordinary ways of thinking and speaking (see above, pp. 24–25). Furthermore, restricted egoists also seem to realize that there is some problem with claiming that humans ought always to be motivated by self-interest, for they invoke the "invisible hand" theory and thus imply (albeit tacitly) that self-interest is acceptable as a universal motive for human action because actions prompted by self-interest ultimately contribute to the interests of society. But the invisible hand theory is questionable at best; in fact, it is probably false. However, even if it were clear that self-interested actions always secured society's best interests, it is not likely that nonconsequentialists would be satisfied with restricted egoism. Nonconsequentialists would insist that in addition to a desire to further society's interests there also are other motives that contribute to right actions. This claim is certainly disputable, but it is undeniable that restricted egoists have not paid careful attention to the important role motives play in moral judgment.

In addition to the above, all nonconsequentialists would reject restricted egoism because it fails to take note of the fact that human beings are deserving of respect. Kant insists that we should be treated as "ends" and not as "means." Theologism claims that we are all equally "children of God." However the doctrine is stated, the point is that we have certain rights as human beings, and abrogation of these rights cannot be justified either by an appeal to self-interest or by an appeal to the interests of society as a whole. That businesses often treat persons as mere "means" seems undeniable; there are cases in which workers are considered simply as pieces of equipment in the production process. Whether such action is justifiable by appeal to profit or utility is not an easy question to answer. What is true about the nonconsequentialists' charge is that restricted egoists must pay some attention to the issue. If businesspersons believe they sometimes are justified in treating people as "means" rather than as "ends," then they must be able to support this position. And at this point in time, no acceptable justification has been given.

Finally, nonconsequentialists would object to the restricted egoists' moral position by claiming that its concept of moral duty is too narrow. At first glance, at least, restricted egoism seems to impose only two moral duties upon us: (1) a duty to maximize self-interest, and (2) a duty to follow certain rules and laws. But nonconsequentialists claim that because human beings are "ends" rather than "means," they have certain rights. And where there are rights there are correlative duties. For example, if *P* promises his dog that he will feed him chicken livers tomorrow, *P* has no moral duty to keep that promise, for dogs are not intrinsically valuable ends-in-themselves. However, if *P* promises to pay *Q* for services the latter has performed, then *Q* has a right to expect payment and *P* has a moral duty to pay *Q*.

To be fair, restricted egoists do try to make a place for duties of the sort just mentioned, for they claim that employees must be regarded as having certain duties to their employer, e.g., employees have a duty to be loyal, a duty to follow orders, etc. Still, nonconsequentialists would argue that there are duties not recognized by restricted egoists, and that these duties are at least as important as those accepted by restricted egoists. For example, in addition to the duties employees have to their employers, they also have special duties to their families and friends, etc. Furthermore, there are duties that each person has to all other persons, e.g., we all have a duty to treat others fairly and justly. Now there are times when these duties conflict with the duties recognized by restricted egoism. Such cases arise most often in so-called whistle-blowing incidents. Generally, restricted egoists condemn whistle-blowing because they feel such action harms the company and violates the employee's duty to be loyal to his employer. But once a person admits that employees have duties to people outside the corporation, the morality of whistle-blowing is debatable. For instance, let us say that employee *P* knows that his company's head of personnel *Q* is a racist, and that *Q* always hires as few blacks as he can. In effect, *P* knows that *Q* does not treat blacks fairly. What is *P* to do? He has a duty to help others when they are in need of aid; and the blacks who are being mistreated are in need of aid. But *P* also has a duty to be loyal to his employer and not to do harm to his company's reputation. In these circumstances would it be right for *P* to blow the whistle on *Q*? Luckily, we need not decide the issue; for even if a person thinks that *P* should not blow the whistle, it seems unlikely that this is because he or she believes *P* has no duty to help other people. That is to say, if our example shows anything it is that we ordinarily do acknowledge employees as having duties that are not recognized by restricted egoists. And until restricted egoism makes some place for these duties in its moral theory, that theory cannot be considered fully adequate.

We have examined restricted egoism in some detail and have found the theory lacking. Whether or not the theory can be modified so as to overcome some or all of its shortcomings is another question entirely, one that each reader will have to decide for himself after examining the essays in this volume. If nothing else, an analysis of these readings will convince the reader of the enormity of the task facing the businessperson.

SELECT BIBLIOGRAPHY

Beauchamp, T. *Philosophical Ethics*. New York: McGraw-Hill, 1982.

Beauchamp, T., and N. Bowie, eds. *Ethical Theory and Business*. 3d ed. Englewood Cliffs, N.J.: Prentice-Hall, 1988.

Braybrooke, D. *Ethics in the World of Business*. Towota, N.J.: Rowman and Allanheld, 1983.

DeGeorge, R. *Business Ethics*. 2d ed. New York: Macmillan, 1986.

DesJardins, J., and J. McCall, eds. *Contemporary Issues in Business Ethics*. Belmont, Calif.: Wadsworth, 1985.

Donaldson, T. *Corporations and Morality*. Englewood Cliffs, N.J.: Prentice Hall, 1982.

Donaldson, T., and P. Werhane, eds. *Ethical Issues in Business*. 3d ed. Englewood Cliffs, N.J.: Prentice-Hall, 1988.

Frankena, W. *Ethics*. 2d ed. Englewood Cliffs, N.J.: Prentice-Hall, 1973.

Hoffman, W., and J. Moore, eds. *Business Ethics*. New York: McGraw-Hill, 1984.

Iannone, A., ed. *Contemporary Moral Controversies in Business*. New York: Oxford, 1989.

Newton, L., and M. Ford, eds. *Taking Sides*. Guilford, Conn.: Dushkin, 1990.

Rachels, J. *The Elements of Moral Philosophy*. New York: Random House, 1986.

Regan, T., ed. *Just Business,* New York: Random House, 1984.

Shaw, W., and V. Barry. *Moral Issues in Business*. 4th ed. Belmont, Calif.: Wadsworth, 1989.

Solomon, R., and K. Hanson. *Above the Bottom Line*. New York: Harcourt Brace Jovanovich, 1983.

Velasquez, M. *Business Ethics*. 2d ed. Englewood Cliffs, N.J.: Prentice-Hall, 1988.

2

ETHICS AND ORGANIZATIONS

INTRODUCTION

The concept of responsibility introduces two issues that recur throughout this book. First, if we assume we are reasonably clear about what is involved in saying that people have moral and legal responsibilities, in what sense can corporations or organizations be said to be responsible? Second, if we assume that either corporations or the individuals in them can be said to have responsibilities, what sorts of responsibilities do they have, and, in particular, do they have responsibilities to society, i.e., social responsibilities extending beyond that of making as much money as is legally possible?

In "Morality and the Ideal of Rationality in Formal Organizations," John Ladd argues that corporations have goals such as profit maximization, that the rational act for the firm's agents is to employ the best means to achieve the corporation's goals, and that because of the firm's structure moral considerations cannot factor into rational decision-making in corporations. In their reply, C. Richard Long and Milton Snoeyenbos criticize several premises of Ladd's argument, which leaves open the possibility that corporations, as well as the individuals in such organizations, can be said to have moral and/or social responsibilities. The case study discusses the basis of organizational decision-making in Aero Products.

In his two articles, Milton Friedman argues that corporations have only one social obligation, namely, to maximize profits within the constraint of the law and ethical custom. Friedman offers two primary arguments, one based on property rights, the other on utility. The rights argument is that shareholders who own the firm typically want profits maximized; managers, as the agents of the owners, should maximize profit. He also argues that if a manager acts other than to maximize profit, his act will probably have social disutility. Friedman sees institutions as having distinct functions; e.g., business should maximize profit and government should fulfill a separate set of social obligations.

If businesses play a socially responsible role beyond that of profit maximization, they not only undercut shareholder rights and social utility, they actually encourage a blurring of institutional functions, which may lead to socialism. In response, Robert Almeder argues that Friedman's arguments are unsound. Furthermore, he claims that from a moral point of view there are certain acts a corporation should not perform even though those acts have utility and are not legally prohibited. Almeder goes on to argue that it is strict adherence to the Friedman position that will most likely lead to socialism; the only kind of capitalism that can survive in the long run is one that repudiates certain central tenets of Friedman's position. The case study in this section considers Ford Motor Company's rationale for placing the gas tank in its early Pinto model, and provides a specific context for discussing the Friedman-Almeder debate.

A discussion of ethics and organizations should take into account the ethical issues that managers themselves regard as central in corporate life. This is the focus of the article by Milton Snoeyenbos. He pays particular attention to industry-wide ethical issues and controversies that arise inside organizations due to their hierarchical structure. The ethical issues discussed generally in this paper are precisely those to be covered in more detail in the later chapters. The author also suggests general strategies for improving ethical behavior in organizations.

ETHICS WITHIN ORGANIZATIONS

Case Study

Organizational Decision Making at Aero Products

Aero Products is the aerospace division of XYZ Corporation, a U.S. capital goods conglomerate. Aero is a major producer of subassemblies for the aerospace industry, and in 1967 it placed the low bid for an order of brake assemblies for an Air Force aircraft under contract to PQR Corporation. Aero's president, Jack Dale, assigned responsibilities as follows:

John Sunday: Chief Engineer, Aircraft Wheel Section:

Tim Hart:
Manager, Design Engineering

Carl Sinclair: Production Manager

Earl Ward: Design Engineer

Jim Lauris: Production Engineer

Ed Link:
Manager, Technical Services

Stan Gove: Test Lab Supervisor

Ward designed the brake, called B-9. Ward was regarded as a brilliant design engineer; he had an excellent track record of product innovation. He also had a nasty temper, which flared when his work was questioned. No one questioned his preliminary design for B-9 when it was submitted. Ward selected Lauris for the task of producing the final production design. Lauris,

41

24, and one year out of Caltech, had shown great promise. This was his first major assignment; his task was to determine the best brake lining materials and make minor design adjustments in the brake. Lauris would work out the kinks prior to production and submit a brake assembly to the dynamometer qualification tests required by the government. These tests, which simulate the aircraft's weight and speed, must be passed prior to production. Lauris was told by Tim Hart, Design Manager, that PQR wanted to begin flight testing in mid-1968, hence Lauris had to work fast. Since Aero's suppliers had not delivered the housing and other parts, Lauris made a prototype using the disc brake Ward had designed and the suggested lining material.

In September 1967, Lauris tested the prototype for thermal build-up and wear. Normal aircraft brake lining temperatures run to 1000 degrees but the test showed the B-9 prototype reached 1500 degrees, and the linings disintegrated. After three more similar failures Lauris began to suspect the brake's design. He reworked the design computations, and it seemed to him that the brake was too small; five discs, he figured, should be used instead of four. Lauris's calculations indicated that the four disc brake's total surface area was just too small to stop the plane without generating heat sufficient to disintegrate the linings.

Lauris then took his test results and computations to Ward, who said that it was a borderline case between the two computations. He indicated that Lauris could improve results by testing more materials. The four-disc brake, he noted, would be very cost effective, very light—which pleased the Air Force—and could help Aero land new contracts. Ward stressed that the four-disc design was a revolutionary advance of particular importance to the Air Force: the lighter the part, the greater the plane's payload. He informed Lauris that brake subassemblies designed for the four disc assembly had begun arriving, that to redesign and reorder new subassemblies would be costly, and that flight testing was still scheduled for mid-1968. Ward was also aware, but did not inform Lauris, that his superior, Sinclair, had reported to PQR that initial tests of the B-9 were very successful. Sinclair had checked with Ward just prior to the second test, and asked how things were going. Ward said: "The kid has some problems, but he'll work them out. It will be okay. We have to give these smart kids a chance to show their stuff; we can't solve all their problems for them." On that basis Sinclair sent his optimistic report to PQR.

Lauris ran two more tests in mid-November. Both failed government specifications, but he did reduce the temperature to 1300 degrees. Still unsatisfied, he decided to talk it over with Sinclair. As an MBA in industrial management, Sinclair was not an engineer. He said that he trusted Ward's experience and judgment, and noted that it would be a coup if the B-9 could be made to work. His advice was to retest. He pointed out that this was a big contract and that everyone was relying on Lauris to work out the bugs. Finally, Sinclair pointed out that PQR was the number one brake contractor and that some ten years earlier Aero had designed and built a brake for PQR that was not a success. For ten years PQR had eliminated Aero as a source of brakes. Aero needed a contract with PQR. This time around, Sinclair said, Aero had submitted a very low bid based on its new design—an offer that PQR had to accept. So a lot was riding on this contract.

By this time the main housing had arrived, so Lauris built a production model. It was this model that had to pass formal qualifications tests for the military. Using a new lining, Lauris got the temperature down to 1150 degrees, but this was still 150 degrees too high and there was still some disintegration beyond normal wear. Lauris ran a dozen tests between January and March 1968, with similar results. He reported to Ward that he didn't think the B-9 could qualify. He was convinced a five-disc brake was necessary.

Ward then met with Sinclair, who called in his boss, Tim Hart. Hart was aware of the problems, but said that John Sunday told him to "Get that brake qualified." Hart inquired as to the best strategy. Sinclair said they were close but needed more time. He suggested that Ward show Lauris how to run a controlled test and how to work up the data. Ward agreed.

When Lauris met with Ward he again stated that his theoretical calculations showed that the four-disc brake would not work. Ward said: "Jim, you're part of a big operation here—a small part. You're not in school now; it's no longer just theory. We have deadlines we have to hit, and to hit them you do what you are told. The big boys up above know more about the big picture than someone who isn't dry behind the ears. You take Sinclair; he's no engineer, but he knows how the game is played. Just do your job."

Ward and Lauris retested. The brake had to stand up under fifty simulated stops. Fans were employed as a cooling device. Instead of maintaining pressure on the brake until the wheel stopped, the pressure was reduced when the wheel decelerated to 15 mph. This meant the wheel had to "coast to a stop." In some cases it rolled over 16,000 feet, whereas normal stopping distance was 3,000 feet. This data was deleted. After each stop the brake was disassembled and parts were machined to reduce friction. In this way the disintegration was reduced to a satisfactory level, but the temperature was still too high. Some of the data recording instruments were then recalibrated to read lower temperatures than were actually recorded. Ward assured Lauris that there was no problem, that standards were always set too high, and the brake would perform well in flight tests. He said: "Sinclair and the big boys know what's going on. They'll back us up." Lauris then turned the data over to Stan Gove, Test Lab Supervisor, who would prepare the qualification report for the military.

In checking the data, Gove caught several errors and discrepancies, and consulted with Lauris. The latter readily allowed that there were calibration errors, but said he thought they were minor. Gove said he thought there were some serious problems, for example, a thermometer had been recalibrated so that while the actual test temperature was 1100 degrees the instrument recorded 1000 degrees. Lauris said that this was the first qualification test he had ever conducted and that he wasn't exactly aware of the proper procedures, but he assured Gove that he followed the test procedures set out by Ward. And he said that Ward assured him that Sinclair wanted the tests done as they were performed. Gove then checked with Ed Link, Technical Services Manager. He told Link he could not sign a report that had errors. Link said he had talked with Sinclair and Hart; the two had indicated that testing was rushed because of the time factor, but that the data was basically all right and could be cleaned up. Link said that he would try to take Gove off the hook; if Gove would prepare the data, he would get someone upstairs to actually write the report. "After all," he said, "we're just filling in blanks and drawing curves, we're not responsible for it after it leaves here." Gove suggested that Link could discuss the issue with Sunday, but Link said: "Look, this is no big deal. Sunday probably already knows about it, but if he doesn't I'm not going to be the one to tell him." Gove asked Link if his conscience would bother him if the plane crashed on test-flight landing. Link said: "I only worry about things I have control over. I have no control over this; neither do you, so why worry? Look, you've got five kids—worry about them and the wife. We'll take care of you; we'll get somebody to sign it."

Gove prepared the data and graphs. He was told by Ward to review the data and then deliver it to Sunday, who would assign someone in the engineering section to write the report and sign it. After his review, however, he was visited by Hart, Link, and Lauris. Hart said that no one was available to write it, and that the job fell to Lauris and Gove. Lauris protested that it would violate his professional code as an engineer. Hart said: "Look, there is always some latitude in experimental design and data interpretation; professionals have to use judgment." Gove said that he knew there had been data manipulation and falsification—he could see it in the contradictory data he had been given. Link said: "You always have to rationalize the data when it comes in from a number of sources, that's part of engineering know-how. Besides, the military has a fudge factor built in—nobody will ever know the difference. Sure you changed the data, but only to make it consistent with the big picture." Gove said he thought he should discuss the matter with Sunday. "Sunday won't touch this thing," said Hart. "Somebody's got to write and sign it, and you two are it. If the government checks us, well, Lauris did the tests and Gove drew the curves. You can defend it better than anyone. So you guys write it up and sign it, that's it. You'll get a big bonus for this, and we'll work out the kinks after the flight tests. We'll take care of you; write it up and sign it."

For Discussion

Do Lauris and/or Gove face a moral problem? Why or why not? If so, describe the problem. What alternative courses of action are available to solve the problem? What course of action should Lauris and/or Gove pursue? Why? Do Gove and/or Lauris have obligations to: (1) their superiors, (2) XYZ Corporation, (3) society? If so, what obligations do they have, and how should they be fulfilled? Discuss the organizational context in which this problem arose. If you were brought in as chief engineer to replace John Sunday and this issue became known to you, what steps would you take in the present case? Why? Would you change future decision-making procedures in your section of the organization? Why? How?

SOURCE

This case is based on Kermit Vandiver's "Why Should My Conscience Bother Me?" in *In the Name of Profit*, Robert L. Heilbroner, et al., eds. (New York: Doubleday, 1972), pp. 3-31.

John Ladd

Morality and the Ideal of Rationality in Formal Organizations

INTRODUCTORY

The purpose of this paper is to explore some of the moral problems that arise out of the interrelationships between individuals and formal organizations (or bureaucracies) in our society. In particular, I shall be concerned with the moral implications of the so-called ideal of rationality of formal organizations with regard to, on the one hand, the obligations of individuals both inside and outside an organization to that organization and, on the other hand, the moral responsibilities of organizations to individuals and to the public at large. I shall argue that certain facets of the organizational ideal are incompatible with the ordinary principles of morality and that the dilemma created by this incompatibility is one source of alienation in our contemporary, industrial society. The very conception of a formal organization or bureaucracy presents us with an ideological challenge that desperately needs to be met in some way or other.

The term "formal organization" will be used in a more or less technical sense to cover all sorts of bureaucracies, private and public. A distinctive mark of such organizations is that they make a clear-cut distinction between the acts and relationships of individuals in their official capacity within the organization and in their private capacity. Decisions of individual decision-makers in an organization are attributed to the organization and not to the individual. In

From *The Monist* 54, no. 4 (October, 1970). Reprinted by permission of the author and *The Monist*.

that sense, they are impersonal. Individual officeholders are in principle replaceable by other individuals without affecting the continuity or identity of the organization. In this sense, it has sometimes been said that an organization is "immortal."

This kind of impersonality, in particular, the substitutability of individuals, is one way in which formal organizations differ from other kinds of social systems, e.g., the family, the community or the nation, which are collectivities that are dependent for their existence on specific individuals or groups of specific individuals and that change when they change.

Under formal organizations I shall include not only all sorts of industrial, military, and governmental bureaucracies but also formal organizations like large universities (multiversities), hospitals, labor unions, and political machines. For our purposes, we may even include illegal and undercover organizations like the Mafia, the Communist Party, the FBI, and the CIA. The general characteristics of all these organizations are that they are "planned units, deliberately structured for the purpose of attaining specific goals,"[1] and such that each formal organization is a "continuous organization of official functions bound by rules."[2] One of the distinctive features of formal organizations of the type we are interested in is that they are ordinarily hierarchical in structure; they not only have a "horizontal" division of labor but a "vertical" one as well—a "pyramid of authority."[3]

*   *   *

Social critics, e.g., W. H. Whyte, use phrases like the "smothering of the individual" to describe the contemporary situation created by organizations. It is not my purpose here to decry once more the unhappy condition of man occasioned by his submergence as an individual in the vast social, economic, and political processes created by formal organizations. Instead, I shall try to show that the kind of alienation that we all feel and complain about is, at least in part, a logical necessity flowing from the concept of formal organizations itself, that is, it is a logical consequence of the particular language-game one is playing in organizational decision-making. My analysis is intended to be a logical analysis, but one that also has important ethical implications.

*   *   *

Here we may find the concept of a language-game, as advanced by Wittgenstein and others, a useful tool of analysis. The point about a language-game is that it emphasizes the way language and action are interwoven. . . . A particular language-game determines how the activities within it are to be conceptualized, prescribed, justified, and evaluated. Take as an example what is meant by a "good" move in chess: we have to refer to the rules of chess to determine what a "move" is, how to make one, what its consequences will be, what its objective is, and whether or not it is a good move in the light of this objective.[4] Finally, this system of rules performs the logical function of defining the game itself.

One advantage of the language-game model is, therefore, that it enables us to describe a kind of activity by reference to a set of rules that determine not only what should or should not be done, but also how what is done is to be rationally evaluated and defended. And it allows us to describe the activity without reference to moral rules (or norms). In other words, it provides us with a method of analyzing a rational activity without committing ourselves to whether or not it is also moral.

If we pursue the game-analogy one step further, we find that there may be even more striking similarities between the language-game of formal organizations and the language-game of other types of games. For instance, the rules and rationale obtaining in most typical games like chess and baseball tend to make the activity logically autonomous, i.e., the moves, defenses, and evaluations are made independently of external considerations. In this sense they are self-contained. Furthermore, while playing a game it is thought to be "unfair" to challenge the rules. Sometimes it is even maintained that any questioning of the rules is unintelligible. In any case, there is a kind of sanctity attached to the rules of a game that renders them immune to criticism on the part of those engaged in playing the game. The resemblance of the autonomy of the activity and the immunity of the rules governing the game to the operations of bureaucracies can hardly be coincidental![5]

THE CONCEPTS OF SOCIAL DECISION AND SOCIAL ACTION

Let us take as our point of departure Herbert Simon's definition of a formal organization as a "decision-making structure."[6] The central concept with which we must deal is that of a decision (or action) that is attributable to the organization rather than to the individuals who are actually involved in the decisional process. The decision is regarded as the organization's decision even though it is made by certain individuals acting as its representatives. The latter make the decision only for and on behalf of the organization. Their role is, i.e., is supposed to be, impersonal. Such nonindividual decisions will be called *social decisions,* choices, or actions. (I borrow the term "social choice" from Arrow, who uses it to refer to a choice made on behalf of a group as distinct from the aggregate of individual choices.)[7]

The officials of an organization are "envisaged as more or less ethically neutral . . . (and) the values to be taken as data are not those which would guide the individual if he were a private citizen. . . ."[8] When the official decides for the organization, his aim is (or should be) to implement the objectives of the organization *impersonally,* as it were. The decisions are made for the organization, with a view to its objectives and not on the basis of the personal interests or convictions of the individual official who makes the decision. This is the theory of organizational decision-making.

One might be tempted to call such organizational decisions "collective decisions," but that would be a misnomer if we take a collective decision to be a decision made by a collection of individuals. Social decisions are precisely decisions (or actions) that are to be *attributed* to the organizations themselves and not to collections of individuals. In practice, of course, the organizational decisions made by officials may actually be collective decisions. But in theory the two must be kept separate; for the "logic" of decisions attributed to organizations is critically different from the "logic" of collective decisions, i.e., those attributed to a collection of individuals.

Underlying the concept of social decisions (choices, actions) as outlined here is the notion that a person (or group of persons) can make decisions that are not his, i.e., are not attributable to him. He makes the decisions on behalf of someone else and with a view to the latter's interest, not his own. In such cases, we ordinarily consider the person (or group) that acts to be a representative or agent of the person or thing he is acting for.

*   *   *

The theory of social decision-making that we are considering becomes even clearer if we examine the theory of organizational authority with which it is conjoined. Formal organizations are hierarchical in structure, that is, they are organized along the principle that superiors issue commands to those below them. The superior exercises authority over the subordinates. . . .

In summary, then, the organizational order requires that its social decisions be attributed to the organization rather than to the individual decision-maker, the "decision is to be made nonpersonally from the point of view of its organization effect and its relation to the organizational purpose,"[9] and the officials, as its agents, are required to abdicate their choice in obedience to the impersonal organizational order.

We now turn to another essential facet of the organizational language-game, namely, that every formal organization must have a goal, or a set of goals. In fact, organizations are differentiated and defined by reference to their aims or goals, e.g., the aim of the Internal Revenue Service is to collect taxes. The goal of most business ventures is to maximize profits, etc. We may find it useful to distinguish between the real and stated goals of an organization. Thus, as Galbraith has pointed out, although the stated goal of large industrial organizations is the maximization of profits, that is a pure myth; their actual, operative goals are the securing of their own survival, autonomy, and economic growth."[10] There may, indeed, be a struggle over the goals of an organization, e.g., a power play between "officials."[11]

For our present purposes, we may consider the real goal of an organization to be that objective (or set of objectives) that is used as a basis for decision-making, i.e., for prescribing and justifying the actions and decisions of the organization itself as distinct from the actions and decisions of individual persons within the organization. As such, then, the goal is an essential element in the language-game of a formal organization's activities in somewhat the same way as the goal of checkmating the king is an essential element in the game of chess. Indeed, formal organizations are often differentiated from other kinds of social organizations in that they are deliberately constructed and reconstructed to seek specific goals."[12]

The logical function of the goal in the organizational language-game is to supply the value premises to be used in making decisions, justifying and evaluating them. "Decisions in private management, like decisions in public management, must take as their ethical premises the objectives that have been set for the organization."[13]

It follows that any considerations that are not related to the aims or goals of the organization are automatically excluded as irrelevant to the organizational decision-making process. This principle of the exclusion of the irrelevant is part of the language-game. It is a logical requirement of the process of prescribing, justifying, and evaluating social decisions. Consequently, apart from purely legal considerations, decisions and actions of individual officers that are unrelated to the organization's aims or goals are construed, instead, as actions of those individuals rather than of the organization. If an individual official makes a mistake or does something that fails to satisfy this criterion of social decision, he will be said to have "exceeded his authority," and will probably be sacked or made a vice-president. Again, the point is a logical one, namely, that only those actions that are related to the goal of the organization are to be attributed to the organization; those actions that are inconsistent with it are attributed to the individual officers as individuals. The individual, rather than the organization, is then forced to take the blame for whatever evil results.

Thus, for example, a naval officer who runs his ship aground is court-martialed because what he did was inconsistent with the aims of the naval organization; the action is attributed to him rather than to the Navy. On the other hand, an officer who successfully bombards a village, killing all of its inhabitants, in accordance with the objectives of his organization, is performing a social action, an action that is attributable to the organization and not to him as an individual. Whether or not the organization should take responsibility in a particular case for the mistakes of its officials is a policy decision to be made in the light of the objectives of the organization.

In other words, the concept of a social decision or action is bound up logically with the notion of an organizational aim. The consequence of this co-implication of action and aim is that the notion of an action or decision taken by an organization that is not related to one of its aims makes no sense. It is an unintelligible notion within the language-game of formal organizations. Within that language-game such an action would be as difficult to understand as it would be to understand how a man's knocking over the pieces in a chess game can be part of playing chess.

We finally come to the concept of "rationality," the so-called "ideal of pure rationality."[14] From the preceding observations concerning the organizational language-game, it should be clear that the sole standard for the evaluation of an organization, its activities and its decisions, is its effectiveness in achieving its objectives—within the framework of existing conditions and available means. This kind of effectiveness is called "rationality." Thus, rationality is defined in terms of the category of means and ends. "Behavior . . . is rational insofar as it selects alternatives which are conducive to the achievement of previously selected goals."[15] And "the rationality of decisions . . . is their appropriateness for the accomplishment of specified goals."[16]

"Rationality," so construed, is relative, that is, to be rational means to be efficient in pursuing a desired goal, whatever that might be. In the case of organizations, "a decision is 'organizationally' rational if it is oriented to the organization's goals."[17] Rationality is consequently neutral as to "what goals are to be attained."[18] Or to be more accurate, "rationality" is an incomplete term that requires reference to a goal before it is completely intelligible.

* * *

Let us return to the organizational language-game. It was observed that within the game the sole standard of evaluation of, e.g., a decision, is the "rational" one, namely, that it be effective in achieving the organization's goal. Hence, any considerations that are taken into account in deliberation about these social decisions and in the evaluation of them are relevant only if they are related to the attainment of the organization's objectives. Let us suppose that there are certain factual conditions that must be considered in arriving at a decision, e.g., the available means, costs, and conditions of feasibility. The determination of such conditions is presumably a matter of empirical knowledge and a subject for empirical investigation. Among these empirical conditions there is a special class that I shall call *limiting operating conditions*. These are conditions that set the upper limits to an organization's operations, e.g., the scarcity of resources, of equipment, of trained personnel, legal restrictions, factors involving employee morale. Such conditions must be taken into account as *data,* so to speak, in organizational decision-making and planning. In this respect information about them is on a par logically with other information utilized in decision-making, e.g., cost-benefit computations.

Now the only way that moral considerations could be relevant to the operations of a formal organization in the language-game that I have been describing is by becoming limiting operating conditions. Strictly speaking, they could not even be introduced as such, because morality is itself not a matter of empirical knowledge. Insofar as morality in the strict sense enters into practical reasoning it must do so as an "ethical" premise, not as an empirical one. Hence morality as such must be excluded as irrelevant in organizational decision-making—by the rules of the language-game. The situation is somewhat parallel to the language-game used in playing chess: moral considerations are not relevant to the decisions about what move to make there either.

Morality enters in only indirectly, namely, as moral opinion, what John Austin calls "positive morality."[19] Obviously the positive morality, laws and customs of the society in which the organization operates must be taken into account in decision-making and planning. The same thing goes for the religious beliefs and practices of the community. A decision-maker cannot ignore them, and it makes no difference whether he shares them or accepts them himself personally. But the determination of whether or not there are such limiting conditions set by positive morality, customs, laws, and religion is an empirical matter. Whether there are such limitations is simply a matter of fact and their relevance to the decision-making is entirely dependent upon how they affect the efficiency of the organization's operations.

Social decisions, then, are not and cannot be governed by the principles of morality, or, if one wishes, they are governed by a different set of moral principles from those governing the conduct of individuals as individuals. For, as Simon says: "Decisions in private management, like decisions in public management, must take as their ethical premises the objectives that have been set for the organization."[20] By implication, they cannot take their ethical premises from the principles of morality.

Thus, for logical reasons it is improper to expect organizational conduct to conform to the ordinary principles of morality. We cannot and must not expect formal organizations, or their representatives acting in their official capacities, to be honest, courageous, considerate, sympathetic, or to have any kind of moral integrity. Such concepts are not in the vocabulary, so to speak, of the organizational language-game. (We do not find them in the vocabulary of chess either!) Actions that are wrong by ordinary moral standards are not so for organizations; indeed, they may often be required. Secrecy, espionage, and deception do not make organizational action wrong; rather they are right, proper, and, indeed, *rational,* if they serve the objectives of the organization. They are no more or no less wrong than, say, bluffing is in poker. From the point of view of organizational decision-making they are "ethically neutral."

Of course, I do not want to deny that it may be in the best interests of a formal organization to pay lip service to popular morality (and religion). That is a matter of public relations. But public relations operations themselves are evaluated and justified on the same basis as the other operations of the organization. The official function of the public relations officer is to facilitate the operations of the organization, not to promote morality.

*   *   *

The upshot of our discussion so far is that actions are subject to two entirely different and, at times, incompatible standards: social decisions are subject to the standard of rational efficiency (utility) whereas the actions of individuals as such are subject to the ordinary standards of morality. An action that is right from the point of view of one of these standards may be wrong from the point of view of the other. Indeed, it is safe to say that our own experience attests to the fact that our actual expectations and social approvals are to a large extent based on a tacit acceptance of a double standard—one for the individual when he is in his office working for the company and another for him when he is at home among friends and neighbors. Take as an example the matter of lying: nobody would think of condemning Joe X, a movie star, for lying on a TV commercial about what brand of cigarettes he smokes, for it is part of his job. On the other hand, if he were to do the same thing in private among friends, we should consider his action to be improper and immoral. Or again, an individual who, acting in his official capacity, refuses help to a needy suppliant, would be roundly condemned if he were to adopt the same course of action in his private life.

The pervasiveness of organizational activity throughout modern society makes the impact of this double-standard on the individual particularly unsettling. It produces a kind of moral schizophrenia which has affected us all. Furthermore, the dilemma in which we find ourselves cannot so easily be conjured away; for it has its logical ground as well as basis in the dynamics of social structure.

* * *

THE MORAL RELATIONSHIP OF INDIVIDUALS TO ORGANIZATIONS

It follows from what has already been said that the standard governing an individual's relationship to an organization is likely to be different from the one governing the converse relationship, i.e., of an organization to individuals. The individual, for his part, is supposed to conduct himself in his relationship to an organization according to the same standards that he would employ in his personal relationships, i.e., the standards of ordinary morality. Thus, he is expected to be honest, open, respectful, conscientious, and loyal toward the organization of which he is a member or with which he has dealings. The organization, represented by its officials, can, however, be none of these in return. "Officials are expected to assume an impersonal orientation. . . . Clients are to be treated as cases . . . and subordinates are to be treated in a similar fashion."[21]

THE MORAL RELATIONSHIP OF ORGANIZATIONS TO INDIVIDUALS

For logical reasons that have already been mentioned, formal organizations cannot assume a genuine moral posture toward individuals. Although the language-game of social decision permits actions to be attributed to organizations as such, rather than to the officials that actually make them, it does not contain concepts like "moral obligation," "moral responsibility," or "moral integrity." For the only relevant principles in rational decision-making are those relating to the objectives of the organization. Hence individual officers who make the decisions for and in the name of the organization, as its representatives, must decide solely by reference to the objectives of the organization.

According to the theory, then, the individuals who are officers of an organization, i.e., those who run it, operate simply as vehicles or instruments of the organization. The organization language-game requires that they be treated as such. That is why, in principle at least, any individual is dispensable and replaceable by another. An individual is selected for a position, retained in it, or fired from it solely on the grounds of efficiency, i.e., of what will best serve the interests of the organization. The interests and needs of the individuals concerned, as individuals, must be considered only insofar as they establish limiting operating conditions. Organizational rationality dictates that these interests and needs must not be considered in their own right or on their own merits. If we think of an organization as a machine, it is easy to see why we cannot reasonably expect it to have any moral obligations to people or for them to have any to it.

For precisely the same reason, the rights and interests of persons outside the organization and of the general public are *eo ipso* ruled out as logically irrelevant to rational organizational decision, except insofar as these rights and interests set limiting conditions to the effectiveness of the organization's operations or insofar as the promoting of such rights and interests constitutes part of the goal of the organization. Hence it is fatuous to expect an industrial organization to go out of its way to avoid polluting the atmosphere or to refrain from making napalm bombs or to desist from wire-tapping on purely moral grounds. Such actions would be irrational.

It follows that the only way to make the rights and interests of individuals or of the people logically relevant to organizational decision-making is to convert them into pressures of one sort or another, e.g., to bring the pressure of the law or of public opinion to bear on the organizations. Such pressures would then be introduced into the rational decision-making as limiting operating conditions.

Since formal organizations cannot have moral obligations, they cannot have moral responsibilities in the sense of having obligations toward those affected by their actions or subject to their actions because of the power they possess. Organizations have tremendous power, but no responsibilities. . . .

Hence, as I have pointed out, the only way to influence such a rational organization is through coercion, legislative or otherwise. And the more rational it is, the more necessary it is that such external pressures be maintained.

Since, as I have argued in some detail, formal organizations are not moral persons, and have no moral responsibilities, they have no moral rights. In particular, they have no *moral* right to freedom or autonomy. There can be nothing morally wrong in exercising coercion against a formal organization as there would be in exercising it against an individual. Hence, the other side of the coin is that it would be irrational for us, as moral persons, to feel any moral scruples about what we do to organizations. (We should constantly bear in mind that the officials themselves, as individuals, must still be treated as moral persons with rights and responsibilities attached to them as individuals.)

*   *   *

UTILITARIANISM AND ALIENATION

It is abundantly evident that the use of a double standard for the evaluation of actions is not confined to the operations of formal organizations, as I have described them. The double standard for social morality is pervasive in our society. For almost all our social decisions, administrative, political, and economic, are made and justified by reference to the "rational" standard, which amounts to the principle that the end justifies the means; and yet as individuals, in our personal relations with one another, we are bound by the ordinary principles of morality, i.e., the principles of obligation, responsibility and integrity.

*   *   *

A great deal more needs to be said about the effects of working from a double standard of morality. In our highly organized (and utilitarian) society, most of us, as individuals, are forced to live double lives, and in order to accommodate ourselves to two different and incompatible standards, we tend to compartmentalize our lives, as I have already pointed out. For the most part, however, the organizational (or utilitarian) standard tends to take over.

Accordingly, our actions as individuals are increasingly submerged into social actions, that is, we tend more and more to use the social standard as a basis for our decisions and to evaluate our actions. As a result, the individual's own decisions and actions become separated from himself as a person and become the decisions and actions of another, e.g., of an organization. They become social decisions, not decisions of the individual. And in becoming social decisions, they are, in Hobbes's terms, no longer "his," they are "owned" by another, e.g., an organization or society.

This is one way of rendering the Marxian concept of alienation. As his actions are turned into social decisions, the individual is alienated from them and is *eo ipso* alienated from other men and from morality. In adopting the administrator's point of view (or that of a utilitarian) and so losing his actions, the individual becomes dehumanized and demoralized. For morality is essentially a relation between men, as individuals, and in losing this relation, one loses morality itself.

CLOSING REMARKS ON THE SOURCE OF THE PARADOX

It is unnecessary to dwell on the intolerable character of the moral schizophrenia in which we find ourselves as the result of the double standard of conduct that has been pointed out. The question is: what can be done about it? The simplest and most obvious solution is to jettison one of the conflicting standards. But which one? The choice is difficult, if not impossible. If we give up the standard of "rationality," e.g., of organizational operations, then we surrender one of the chief conditions of civilized life and progress as well as the hope of ever solving mankind's perennial practical problems, e.g., the problems of hunger, disease, ignorance, and overpopulation. On the other hand, if we give up the standard of ordinary moral conduct, then in effect we destroy ourselves as moral beings and reduce our relationships to each other to purely mechanical and materialistic ones. To find a third way out of the dilemma is not only a practical, political, and sociological necessity, but a moral one as well.

*   *   *

NOTES

[The notes for this essay have been renumbered.—Eds.]

1. Amitai Etzioni, *Modern Organizations* (Englewood Cliffs, N.J.: Prentice-Hall, 1964), p. 4. Hereinafter cited as MO.

2. Max Weber, quoted in Etzioni, MO, p. 53.

3. Herbert A. Simon, *Administrative Behavior*, 2d ed. (New York: Free Press, 1965), p. 9. Hereinafter cited as Simon, AB. For a useful survey of the subject of formal organizations, see Peter M. Blau and W. Richard Scott, *Formal Organizations* (San Francisco: Chandler Publishing Company, 1962). Hereinafter cited as Blau and Scott, FO. I am indebted to my friend Richard Taub for many helpful suggestions in writing this paper.

4. These rules are called "constitutive rules" by John Searle. See his *Speech Acts* (Cambridge: The University Press, 1969), Ch. 2, Sec. 5.

5. For further discussion of the game-model and this aspect of rules, see my "Moral and Legal Obligation," in J. Roland Pennock and John W. Chapman, eds., *Political and Legal Obligation, Nomos,* 12 (New York: Atherton Press, 1970).

6. See Simon, AB, *passim*. Also, Blau and Scott, PO, p. 36.

7. See Kenneth Arrow, *Social Choice and Individual Values* (New York: John Wiley, 1951), *passim*.

8. Quoted from A. Bergson by Kenneth Arrow in "Public and Private Values," in *Human Values and Economic Policy,* S. Hook, ed. (New York: New York University Press, 1967), p. 14.

9. Quoted from Chester I. Barnard in Simon, AB, p. 203.

10. See John Kenneth Galbraith, *The New Industrial State* (Boston: Houghton Mifflin, 1967), pp. 171-78. Hereinafter cited as NIS.

11. See Etzioni, MO, pp. 7-9.

12. Etzioni, MO, p. 3. See also Blau and Scott, PO, p. 5. In a forthcoming article on "Community," I try to show that communities, as distinct from formal organizations, do not have specific goals. Indeed, the having of a specific goal may be what differentiates a *Gesellschaft* from a *Gemeinschaft* in Tönnies' sense. See Ferdinand Tönnies, *Community and Society,* trans. Charles P. Loomis (New York: Harper and Row, 1957), *passim*.

13. Simon, AB, p. 52.

14. "The ideal of pure rationality is basic to operations research and the modern management sciences." Yehezkel Dror, *Public Policymaking Reexamined* (San Francisco: Chandler Publishing Company, 1968), p. 336. Dror gives a useful bibliography of this subject on pp. 336-40.

15. Simon, AB, p. 5.

16. Simon, AB, p. 240.

17. Simon, AB, p. 77.

18. Simon, AB, p. 14.

19. "The name *morality,* when standing unqualified or alone, may signify the human laws which I style positive morality, without regard to their goodness or badness. For

example, such laws of the class as are peculiar to a given age, or such laws of the class as are peculiar to a given nation, we style the morality of that given age or nation, whether we think them good or bad, etc." John Austin, *Province of Jurisprudence Determined,* H. L. A. Hart, ed. (New York: Noonday Press, 1954), p. 125. The study of positive moralities belongs to what I call "descriptive ethics." See my *Structure of a Moral Code* (Cambridge, Mass: Harvard University Press, 1957).

20. Simon, AB, p. 52.
21. Blau and Scott, FO, p. 34.

C. Richard Long
Milton Snoeyenbos

Ladd on Morality and Formal Organizations

In "Morality and the Ideal of Rationality in Formal Organizations," John Ladd argues as follows:

1. Corporate, military, and governmental organizations are formal organizations.
2. A formal organization is a decision-making structure characterized by:
   a. a goal or set of goals,
   b. the concept of an organizational (or "social") act or decision whereby an individual, as an agent for the organization, makes decisions for and on behalf of the organization.
   c. a hierarchical structure of authority for establishing and implementing organizational decisions, and,
   d. a standard of rationality according to which the rational organizational act is the one that best achieves the organization's goal(s).
3. The only way moral principles could enter into organizational decision-making is by either being organizational goals or limiting operating conditions.
4. All limiting operating conditions are factual conditions.
5. Moral principles are not factual conditions.
6. Moral principles are not organizational goals.
7. Therefore, organizational decisions cannot be based on moral principles.

If Ladd's argument is sound it has unsettling implications both for corporate behavior and for how ordinary citizens regard corporations. On the one hand, in fulfilling his organizational role the individual cannot legitimately appeal to moral principles. But, since people do have a moral dimension, which at times conflicts with decisions demanded by one's organizational role, individuals in organizations experience a moral schizophrenia or alienation that Ladd contends can be eliminated only by abandoning either the standard of organizational rationality or the standards of moral conduct. Since the former underpins the efficiency of organizational operations necessary for our complex society and the latter are the glue of social civility, this indeed is a dilemma. On the other hand, if, as Ladd suggests, corporations have no moral responsibilities or rights, it is not morally wrong to coerce them. But, since this can be only realistically accomplished by governmental action, it pits one type of formal organization against another (neither of which has moral responsibilities), and, given the power of government, this threatens the private/public distinction.

If we accept (2), (3), and (5), this still leaves us with (1), (4), and (6) as controversial premises. Let us first consider (4). If limiting operating conditions (i.e., those factors that set limits to or place constraints on achievement of a firm's goals) *could* include moral principles, then there could be moral constraints on corporate decision-making. And if there were cases in which moral principles actually served as limiting operating conditions, then (4) would be false.

According to Ladd, moral principles cannot be introduced as limiting operating conditions, because the latter are factual whereas the former are evaluative and not factual. But Ladd simply *asserts* that limiting operating conditions are factual; no argument is offered for the assertion. He does distinguish moral principles from moral beliefs or opinions. And there is a difference between the moral claim "act x is morally right," and moral beliefs of the form "person P (or the members of society S) believe act x is morally right"; the former is evaluative, the latter is factual. Accordingly, Ladd allows that moral beliefs, "the positive morality, laws, and customs of the society . . . must be taken into account in decision-making." The moral beliefs of a society, being factual, can, on Ladd's view, serve as limiting operating conditions. Again, however, this distinction does not entail that moral principles could not *also* be limiting operating conditions. Once one adopts a moral principle it is a fact that the principle has been adopted, but it does not cease to be a moral principle because one adopts, believes, or accepts it. So, Ladd simply asserts, but does not support, his claim that limiting operating conditions must be factual.

If we now consider *actual* corporate behavior, we must acknowledge that while we have numerous theoretical models of organizational decision-making, we have few concrete, empirical studies that would enable us to decide whether moral principles in fact do sometimes serve as limiting operating conditions. Perhaps the best we can do, then, is to examine corporate policy statements under the assumption that corporate behavior is sometimes in accord with such statements. Now, certainly, in some cases it appears that moral customs or beliefs are regarded as limiting operating conditions. General Mills, while acknowledging that its economic goals are primary, also recognizes an "obligation to conduct ourselves in a way that is consistent with social goals . . . compliance with these social goals is an important way of retaining an environment in which we can conduct our economic activity."[1] Exxon says that in addition to its economic functions it is "acutely aware that it must conduct its activities in a responsible and ethical manner . . . it is in the best interest of business to continue to meet public expectations." Exxon's Chairman, C. C. Garvin, recently elaborated on this, saying that ". . . business managers must begin by understanding the laws of the countries in which they operate—and, beyond this, develop a sensitivity to the spirit of the law. . . . Second, they must stay sensitive to shifts in public policy. . . . At Exxon we make frequent use of opinion research surveys to identify social concerns and to gauge their importance in the public mind."[2] While somewhat ambiguous, such statements have a prudential ring to them; consistent with Ladd's position, both could be interpreted as meaning that, although economic goals are primary, moral beliefs or customs, when adequately factored into organizational decision-making as constraints or limiting operating conditions, can better enable the firm to achieve its economic goals. But other corporations, while also acknowledging the primacy of economic goals, seem to allow that moral principles themselves can serve as limiting operating conditions. Alcoa lists traditional economic goals as "fundamental" corporate objectives, but states that in "achieving its fundamental objectives, Alcoa . . . pledges to conduct its business in a legal and ethical manner." Similarly, in achieving its economic "objectives," Bankers Life is "dedicated to conducting all its operations with high ethical and moral standards." On the face of it, these statements directly place evaluative constraints on the achievement of basic, economic corporate goals. In such cases, (4) seems false.

Our point, then, is that an argument rather than an assertion is required if Ladd is to establish that limiting operating conditions are factual and hence (assuming the truth of [5]) that moral principles are not (or cannot be) limiting operating conditions. For even if no firm has ever acted by using a moral principle as a limiting operating condition, this would not preclude the possibility or desirability of their so acting. And, as we noted, some corporate policy statements commit firms to regard moral principles as limiting operating conditions. If such firms act in accordance with their policy statements, then (4) is certainly false.

Premise (6) may also be questioned, because it is not obviously true that moral principles are not (in some cases) corporate goals. On the face of it, there seem to be no reasons why moral principles *could not* be corporate goals. While it may be true that many corporations do not include moral principles as explicitly stated goals, Ladd himself allows that corporations may have a multiplicity of goals, that formal organizations are "deliberately constructed and reconstructed to seek specific goals," and that there may be a "struggle over the goals of an organization." Since corporations lacking moral principles and obligations as corporate goals could be "reconstructed" to include them, there appears to be nothing intrinsic to the notion of a formal organization that precludes incorporation of moral principles into a corporate goal structure.

If we consider actual corporate policy statements, we find that firms frequently specify a variety of objectives, and some include moral goals. In certain cases, e.g., Hewlett-Packard and IBM, a firm simply provides a non-ordered list of corporate aims that includes moral obligations to employees, customers, society, etc., in addition to profit and growth objectives. In other cases, firms order their goals, and, interestingly enough, some corporations list profit as a means to goals that could reasonably be said to be moral:

> *The Dow Chemical Co. Objectives:* To seek maximum long-term profit growth as the primary means to ensure the prosperity of our employees and stockholders, the well-being of our customers, and the improvement of people's lives everywhere. To attract and hire talented, competent people, and pay them well for their performance. To provide our employees with equal opportunity for career growth and personal fulfillment. To give our employees greater opportunity to participate in decision-making. To strengthen our commitment to individual freedom and self-renewal. To be scrupulously ethical in the means to our ends and in the ends themselves. To be responsible citizens of the different societies in which we operate. To grow through continuous innovation of our products and processes. To make price a measure of true market value for our products and services. To practice stewardship in the manufacture, marketing, use and disposal of our products. To share in the responsibility of all peoples for protection of the environment. To make wise and efficient use of the earth's energy and natural resources. To make this world a better place for our having been in business.

Dow is quite explicit in claiming that profit maximization is a means to moral and social ends:

> To seek maximum long-term profit growth. . . . This is our first and overriding concern, of course. It is totally consistent with our view of social responsibility and should come as no surprise. Some people might prefer to see us downplay our concern for profit in favor of doing great and good things for society. Somehow, they misunderstand the role of business. They have been lulled into thinking of profit as an end in itself. It is not. At Dow, we do not squirrel away our money in an old sock like some corporate Scrooge. We use profit as a tool as the *means* to an end. That end, we feel, is very simple and very clear: . . . To ensure the prosperity of our employees and stockholders, the wellbeing of our customers, and the improvement of people's lives everywhere. This is our reason for being. It is a legitimate one. Profit is not a reward, but a way to achieve our objective. Indeed, our reward for continuing to provide the goods and services people want and need is to *stay* in business, to keep doing what we are very good at doing. Profit makes that possible.

Profit enables the firm to survive, but neither profit nor survival are the end of the firm; they are means to ends that embed moral and social principles. American Can Company has a similar policy statement:

The American Can Creed: American Can Company is a business enterprise dedicated to supplying goods and services of the highest quality to all of our customers worldwide, at the same time satisfying the needs of our share-owners and employees. Our fundamental goal is to provide a reasonable return on the investment made by our shareowners. By achieving this basic objective, we retain the strength and vigor needed to promote healthy competition and fulfill our social and moral responsibilities. We are committed to the highest standards of personal integrity in our daily work, and are pledged to respect both the letter and the spirit of the laws under which we operate. Through constant dedication to these principles, we will exemplify responsible leadership in the business community and ensure the continued confidence of the publics we serve.

The company acknowledges a number of goals, and then specifies a fundamental, *instrumental* goal ("a reasonable return on investment") that is a means of fulfilling the firm's "social and moral responsibilities."

Although there seem to be no reasons why firms cannot incorporate moral and social goals in their corporate goal structures, and although some firms explicitly *state* such goals as basic or central aims of the organization, Ladd differentiates stated from *actual* organizational goals. For example, he claims, following John Kenneth Galbraith, that profit maximization is a "mythical" (although frequently stated) corporate goal, and that firms actually seek their own survival, autonomy, and growth. Is it the case, then, that stated moral goals such as those expressed in the policy statements of Dow Chemical and American Can are a form of window dressing that masks actual economic goals?

Only detailed empirical research that we do not now possess could adequately answer this question, but three points are worthy of note. First, Ladd's distinction between stated and actual goals cuts both ways; it may be that firms stating profit maximization, survival, etc., as goals also accept adherence to moral principles as an actual but unstated goal. If a firm implicitly expects moral behavior from its employees in relation to the organization, it may analogously expect such behavior in their organizational decisions. Second, not every stated and actual goal has to be set down in a written, formal company policy statement. A corporate president recently made this observation: "Over the years we have insisted that our employees have the highest possible ethical principles in doing business in all areas of our company. This philosophy is impressed upon the employees when they are hired and it is maintained through our various supervisors and department heads. The standard of ethics of this company is considered one of the highest in our industry and I believe that the word-of-mouth procedure has been effective over the years."[3] Presumably, these principles are actual goals, and they are orally stated, although they are not stated in the company's formal statement of objectives. Third, the increased incorporation of moral objectives in recent corporate policy statements is accompanied by an increased institutionalization of explicit ethical codes with attendant enforcement mechanisms. Since these codes typically cover employees' organizational decisions, they are *prima facie* evidence that moral principles are actually being incorporated as organizational goals.

The upshot is that premise (6) seems false. Ladd provides no evidence for the claim that moral principles cannot be part of a corporate goal structure. Even if there were no empirical evidence of the adoption of moral principles as corporate goals, nothing precludes the "reconstructing" of firms to incorporate such goals. In certain cases such principles are stated goals, and where they are not stated they may be actual goals. In fact, there is some evidence that such goals are actual, in which case (6) definitely is false.

Finally, given that (2) is a reasonable definition or characterization of a formal organization, is a corporation a formal organization, i.e., is (1) true? This can be determined by examining whether corporations satisfy (2a), (2b), (2c), and (2d). Although a comprehensive investigation is beyond the scope of this paper, we can offer some comments indicating that corporations are not fully formal.

As Ladd allows, corporations may have multiple goals; for example, Hewlett-Packard lists profit, customer and employee satisfaction, growth, and fulfillment of societal obligations as goals. Although such goals are not necessarily incompatible, they may at times conflict: profit maximization may, in certain circumstances, conflict with the fulfillment of social obligations and also with corporate growth. In such cases it will not do to say simply, as in (2a), that corporations pursue a *set* of goals; some weighting of goals will have to be made to preserve the rationality mentioned in (2d). The mathematical apparatus is available to preserve rationality in a context of multiple goals *if* stable weights can be assigned to goals; but, given the rather large number of goals corporations typically pursue and the complexity and unpredictability of environmental factors that would affect weighting in specific contexts, it is doubtful that corporations can or do follow the dictates of the formal model.

It should also be noted that Herbert Simon, to whom Ladd frequently refers in setting up his formal model, does not give a purely formal account of organizations.[4] Simon, and subsequent Carnegie theorists, provide a descriptive rather than a normative account, i.e., they attempt to tell us what organizations are like, not what they should be like. Their account is based on several observations about humans; they view humans as (1) intending to be rational but possessing limited and imperfect information processing capabilities; (2) exercising selective perception based on interests and preconceptions, which in organizations leads to coalitions or factions based on similar interests; and, consequently, (3) seeking "satisficing" solutions to problems, i.e., solutions that are "good enough" rather than the best or optimal, as in (2d). Rationality in organizations is, to use Simon's term, "bounded" or limited rationality. In addition, Amitai Etzioni, cited by Ladd as an organizational theorist who articulates the goal-oriented formal model, actually argues that the goal model is not the best way to examine and understand organizations. Instead, he advocates a systems approach that takes into account complicating factors beyond the simplified means-end formalist model.[5] If the end-oriented formalist model does not match what can reasonably be expected of humans (Simon), and it is not the best way to study and understand organizational behavior (Etzioni), then the two main sources of Ladd's conceptual analysis of organizations actually undercut his analysis if it is meant to apply to actual organizational behavior.

The work of James March and Herbert Simon casts doubt on the sharp distinction between organizational and personal decisions that underlies (2b) and (2d).[6] March and Simon claim that actions in organizations are affected by an individual's identification patterns, which typically are multiple and often are rooted in sources other than the organization and its goals. An employee may identify with his sub-group in an organization, and the sub-group's goals may vary from those of the organization or top management. The individual may have sources of identification outside the organization, e.g., one's family or profession, that affect his decision-making role in the organization. Even if one's primary identification is with the firm, it may be that overidentification with one's organizational role turns out to be dysfunctional for the firm. Robert K. Merton and Victor Thompson have documented how excessive organizational identification, particularly with respect to organizational means, can lead to inflexible behavior that may not benefit the firm.[7] In addition, the bureaucratic (or hierarchical) and rational dimensions of the formal model of organizations (2c and 2d) do not necessarily mesh. Stanley H. Udy, Jr.'s study found, for example, that these factors tend to be mutually inconsistent, and Richard H. Hall's study suggests that these dimensions have only weak or negative correlations.[8]

To summarize, then, we have suggested that, even if (2a-d) does adequately characterize a formal organization, there are some grounds to question whether (1) is true, i.e., whether corporations are formal organizations. Moreover, even if the truth of (1) is granted, we argued there is no reason to accept (4). Ladd asserts, but does not establish, that limiting operating conditions are factual. Even if we grant Ladd's distinction between moral beliefs and principles, we found no reason to suggest that the latter could not serve as limiting operating conditions; in fact, we cited corporate policy statements that do seem to place moral constraints on primary economic goals. Finally we argued that moral principles certainly can be factored into a corporate goal structure. Indeed, if corporate behavior sometimes matches with corporate policy statements, we found evidence that some corporations do include moral principles as corporate goals. Hence, (6) seems false. If most firms neither include moral objectives in their goal structures nor construe moral principles as limiting operating conditions, we suggest that they consider doing so as one strategy for overcoming the alienation that Ladd mentions.

NOTES

1. This and subsequent citations of corporate policy statements are from: *A Study of Corporate Ethical Policy Statements,* The Foundation of the Southwestern Graduate School of Banking (Dallas, Texas: Southern Methodist University, 1980).

2. Address to shareholders at the 1981 Exxon annual meeting.

3. Sorrel M. Mathes and C. Clark Thompson, "Ensuring Ethical Conduct in Business," *The Conference Board Record* 1, no. 12 (December 1964), pp. 17–18.

4. Herbert Simon, *Administrative Behavior,* 2d ed. (New York: Free Press, 1957), pp. 61–109.

5. Amitai Etzioni, *Modern Organizations* (Englewood Cliffs, N.J.: Prentice-Hall, 1964), pp. 16–19.

6. James March and Herbert Simon, *Organizations* (New York: Wiley, 1958), pp. 35-171.

7. Robert K. Merton, "Bureaucratic Structure and Personality," *Social Forces* 18, no. 4 (May 1940): 560–68; Victor Thompson, *Modern Organizations* (New York: Knopf, 1961), pp. 152–77.

8. Stanley H. Udy, Jr., " 'Bureaucracy' and 'Rationality' in Weber's Organization Theory," *American Sociological Review* 24, no. 6 (December 1959): 791–95; Richard H. Hall, "The Concept of Bureaucracy: An Empirical Assessment," *American Journal of Sociology* 69, no. 1 (July 1963): 32–40.

BUSINESS AND SOCIAL RESPONSIBILITY

Case Study

Cost-Benefit Analysis and the Ford Pinto

In the late 1960s, American automakers were faced with serious competition from German and Japanese firms in the subcompact market. Some Detroit executives felt that they should concentrate on medium-size and large models and let foreign competitors with their lower costs have the small car market. Others argued that the subcompact market was potentially lucrative and should be pursued. Ford, whose market position had eroded, opted for the latter strategy, and in 1968 it decided to produce the Pinto.

Lee Iacocca, Ford's President, conceived the idea of building a car that would cost less than $2,000 and weigh less than 2,000 pounds. Mr. Iacocca oversaw the project with Vice Presidents Robert Alexander and Harold Mac-Donald, all of whom were members of Ford's Product Planning Committee, which reviewed the Pinto project as it developed.

Although production planning for a new model normally takes about three and one-half years, Ford decided to try to move from conception to production in two years; it wanted the Pinto ready for the 1971 model year. In the normal time frame, design changes and quality assurance standards are in place largely before production line tooling. But tooling requires about a year and a half, and hence, in the case of the Pinto, tooling and product development overlapped considerably. In large part because of the overlap, design decisions controlled engineering decisions to a degree greater than in normal planning. The Pinto's design required that its gas tank be located behind the rear axle, placing it tightly between the axle and rear bumper. Upon rear impact, the gas tank could be driven against the Pinto's differential housing, which was designed with a series of exposed bolt heads and a flange that were sufficient to puncture the gas tank.

Prior to production of the Pinto, Ford crash-tested several autos modified to resemble the rear-end structure of the Pinto. These tests were conducted in part with an eye to Federal Motor Vehicle Safety Standard 301, which was proposed for adoption by the National Highway Traffic Safety Administration (NHTSA) in 1969. Standard 301 proposed that all autos be required to withstand an impact of 20 mph, with only a small fuel loss. Specifically, an auto struck by a 4,000 lb. object moving at 20 mph should leak less than one ounce of fuel per minute. Of four Pinto prototypes tested, one failed completely when the fuel tank ruptured at a poorly welded seam, and the other three leaked slightly more fuel than permitted under the proposed standard. Court testimony later described some of these tests: "Prototypes struck from the rear with a moving barrier at 21 mph caused the fuel tank to be driven forward and to be punctured, causing fuel leakage." Subsequent to these tests, Ford modified the fuel tank's design and then proceeded to production in August, 1970.

After the Pinto was in production, Ford continued its crash-test program. All crash tests on production Pintos resulted in leakage in excess of that permitted by NHTSA's proposed Standard 301. As subsequent court testimony indicated: "A production Pinto crash tested at 21 mph into a fixed barrier caused the fuel neck to be torn from the gas tank and the tank to be punctured by a bolt head on the differential housing. In at least one test, spilled fuel entered the driver's compartment."

Ford also studied options for improving the Pinto's rear-end design in order to meet NHTSA's proposed standard. For example, it examined locating the gas tank over the axle. However, Ford engineers presented evidence that this design actually increased the risk of fuel leakage into the passenger compartment. Such placement also raised the Pinto's center of gravity, and thereby led to increased auto control problems. Finally, placing the gas tank over the axle significantly reduced trunk space. In addition, Ford modified the Pinto's gas tank design, and ran several crash tests on cars so modified. In one successful test, a plastic baffle was placed between the front of the gas tank and the differential housing. In a second successful test, a piece of steel was placed between the tank and rear bumper. The third successful test was of a Pinto with a rubber-lined gas tank. The rubber-lined tank, which would have increased the cost of a Pinto by $6, was seriously considered. But the liners failed in both very hot and very cold weather. Harley Copp, Ford's executive in charge of crash testing, said that all crash test results were forwarded to Ford's Product Planning Committee.

Ford decided to go ahead with its gas tank design, and not alter the tank in light of its crash-tests. It did so for several reasons. First, cost-benefit analysis, as detailed in a Ford memorandum titled "Fatalities Associated with Crash-Induced Fuel Leakage and Fires," suggested that there were no advantages in upgrading the Pinto's fuel tank. In the early 1970s, NHTSA decided that cost-benefit analysis was an appropriate basis for safety design standards. To make such an analysis some specific value had to be placed on a human life, and NHTSA decided on a figure of $200,725 as the estimated cost to society every time a person is killed in an auto accident:

Future Productivity Losses	
Direct	$132,000
Indirect	41,300
Medical Costs	
Hospital	700
Other	425
Property Damage	1,500
Insurance Administration	4,700
Legal and Court	3,000
Employer Losses	1,000
Victim's Pain and Suffering	10,000
Funeral	900
Assets (Lost Consumption)	5,000
Miscellaneous Accident Cost	200
Total Per Fatality	$200,725

Using NHTSA's data, Ford calculated costs and benefits by considering the variables of lives saved by product redesign and the cost of the product. For example, a Ford internal memorandum gives the following calculation of an $11 gas tank improvement, which was estimated to save 180 lives:

BENEFITS

Savings: 180 burn deaths, 180 serious burn injuries, 2,100 burned vehicles.

Unit Cost: $200,000 per death, $67,000 per injury, $700 per vehicle.

Total Benefit: 180 × ($200,000) + 180 × ($67,000) + 2,100 × ($700) = $49.5 million.

COSTS

Sales: 11 million cars, 1.5 million light trucks

Unit Cost: $11 per car, $11 per truck

Total Cost: 12,500,000 × ($11) = $137 million.

(This calculation was based on all of Ford's vehicles over an extended period of time, not just the Pinto.) Early in 1971 a Ford management committee reviewed the data discussed in "Fatalities Associated with Crash-Induced Fuel Leakage and Fires." Mr. MacDonald chaired the meeting and Mr. Alexander attended. Since the costs of the $11 safety improvement outweighed its benefits, Ford maintained it was not justified in making the improvement.

A second factor in Ford's decision was that the Pinto did meet all auto safety standards at the time. NHTSA Standard 301 was only a *proposed* rule. The rule was proposed early in 1969, and its objectives were initially supported publicly by Ford management. In fact, Ford voluntarily adopted the 20 mph standard as an objective for all its vehicles. In August, 1970, NHTSA specified the precise test method to meet Standard 301: all vehicles would be required to satisfy a 20 mph fixed-barrier test, i.e., the vehicle is towed backward into a fixed barrier at 20 mph. Ford and all other automakers objected to this test method. Ford favored a moving-barrier test, one in which an object impacts a stationary vehicle. Ford believed the moving-barrier test to be more realistic than the fixed-barrier test.

James Neal, speaking for Ford, said: "The Pinto met every fuel-system integrity standard of any Federal, State or Local Government." Neal also stressed that Ford was the only auto manufacturer in the world at that time to have set a 20 mph internal standard for rear collision without fuel leakage. Herbert Misch, Ford's Vice President of Environmental and Safety Engineering, said that Ford set the 20 mph standard as a performance goal to be met by future autos. Misch conceded that the Pinto failed rear-impact tests at 20 mph, but defended Ford's testing procedures. He also said that the tests with rubber-lined tanks were conducted to determine how to satisfy the 20 mph standard sometime in the future. Misch added: "It is simply unreasonable and unfair to contend that a car is somehow unsafe if it does not meet standards proposed for future years or embody the technological improvements that are introduced in later model years."

Third, Ford contended that the Pinto was as safe as comparable sub-compacts. It compared the Vega, Gremlin, Colt, and Toyota with the Pinto and argued that: (1) fuel tank metal thickness was above average on the Pinto; (2) only the Pinto had metal plates in the trunk to deflect impact; (3) all the subcompacts had puncture sources; and (4) bumpers were comparable on all five autos.

However, critics argued that the Pinto was not as safe as comparable subcompacts with respect to gas tank placement. Dr. Leslie Ball, head of safety for NASA's manned space program, said that all comparable Japanese and European subcompacts had safer gas tank positioning. Ball said the "production of the Pinto was the most reprehensible decision in the history of American engineering." Byron Block, auto safety expert, said Ford made an "extremely irresponsible decision when they placed such a weak tank in such a ridiculous location in such a soft rear end. It's almost designed to blow up premeditated."

A fourth factor was undoubtedly Ford's tight production schedule. When crash tests revealed the gas tank problem, Ford had $200 million worth of tools on line and in place. Redesign and retooling would have been very expensive.

A fifth factor was that Ford had to cut costs to be competitive. Ford wanted the Pinto to weigh less than 2,000 lbs. and cost less than $2,000. It felt that control of both variables was necessary to compete against Volkswagen and the Japanese imports. Within the scope of the law, it had to control both weight and cost.

The sixth factor in Ford's decision was a belief that Americans were not primarily interested in safety. As Lee Iacocca was fond of saying, "Safety doesn't sell."

From 1968 until its adoption by NHTSA in 1977, Ford opposed Standard 301, claiming that its cost-benefit analysis indicated that it was not rational to make the change sooner. However, critics claimed that Ford's lobbying against 301 indicated that it was not really serious about rear-impact safety. They claimed that Ford lobbied against 301 to block higher, and therefore more costly, legal safety standards in order to continue to sell the Pinto for a lower price and thereby increase its market share and profits.

Considerable controversy has ensued as to whether the Pinto is a safe automobile. Mark Dowie, Pinto critic, claims that more than 400,000 autos burned every year during the early 1970s, that every year 3,000 people were burned to death in autos, and that 40 percent of auto burn deaths could have been prevented by adoption of Standard 301. Dowie states that although Ford made 24 percent of the autos on American roads, its autos were involved in 42 percent of the accidents that involved fuel leakage. Dowie claims that between 1971-77 Pinto crashes caused at least 500 burn deaths of people who would not have been seriously injured if the auto had not burned. Dowie says the figure could go as high as 900.

Speaking for Ford, Mr. Misch cited statistics from NHTSA's Fatality Analysis Reporting System (FARS) to show that in 1975 there were 848 fire-related auto deaths, but only 13 involved Pintos. He claimed that in 1976, Pintos were involved in only 22 of 943 fire-related deaths. These data indicate that Pintos were involved in 1.9 percent of fire-related auto deaths, and Mr. Misch pointed out that Pintos constitute 1.9 percent of the autos in America. In addition, fewer than half of the Pintos mentioned in the FARS study were struck from the rear. Mr. Misch concluded the Pinto is a safe auto, and is not involved in 70 to 130 burn deaths annually, as Mr. Dowie claimed.

Reactions to the Pinto case have been very divergent. An industry spokesman said: "We have to make cost-benefit analyses all the time. That's part of business. Everyone knows that some people will die in auto accidents, but people do accept risks and they do want us to hold down costs. We could build an absolutely safe car, but nobody could afford it." A Pinto critic said, "One wonders how long the Ford Motor Company would continue to market lethal cars were Henry Ford II and Lee Iacocca serving twenty-year terms in Leavenworth for consumer homicide."

For Discussion

Should Ford have produced the Pinto? Why or why not? Is cost-benefit analysis the appropriate basis for safety design standards? Why or why not? If not, what other factors should be considered? Discuss NHTSA's figures regarding the estimated cost of an auto fatality. Analyze each factor in Ford's decision not to implement the $11 gas tank improvement. Do the reasons (individually or together) provide an adequate justification for Ford's decision? Discuss the moral basis of Ford's opposition to NHTSA Standard 301.

SOURCES

Grimshaw v. *Ford Motor Co.,* App., 174 Cal. Rptr. 348, pp. 359–88; Ralph Drayton, "One Manufacturer's Approach to Automobile Safety Standards," *CLTA NEWS* 8, no. 2 (February 1968), pp. 11 ff; "Magazine Claims Ford Ignored Pinto Fire Peril," *Automotive News* (August 15, 1977), p. 3; "Ford Rebuts Pinto Criticisms and Says Article Is Distorted," *The National Underwriter* (Prop. Ed.) 81 (September 9, 1977), p. 36; Mark Dowie, "How Ford Put Two Million Firetraps on Wheels," *Business and Social Review* no. 23 (Fall, 1977): 44–55; "Ford Fights Pinto Case: Jury Gives $128 Million," *Automotive News* (February 13, 1978), pp. 3 ff; J. Gamlin, "Jury Slaps Massive Fine on Ford in 1972 Pinto Crash," *Business Insurance* 12 (February 20, 1978), pp. 1 ff; "Ford Motor Is Indicted in Indiana Pinto Death," *Automotive News* (September 18, 1978), p. 2; "After Pinto," *U.S. News and World Report* 88 (March 24, 1980), p. 11; "Ford's Pinto: Not Guilty," *Newsweek* 95 (March 24, 1980), p. 74; "The Ford Motor Car," in Manuel Velasquez, *Business Ethics,* 2d ed., Englewood Cliffs, N.J.: Prentice-Hall, 1988, pp. 119–23; *Taking Sides,* L. Newton and M. Ford, eds., Guilford Conn.: Dushkin, 1990, pp. 130–47.

Milton Friedman

The Social Responsibility of Business Is to Increase Its Profits

When I hear businessmen speak eloquently about the "social responsibilities of business in a free-enterprise system," I am reminded of the wonderful line about the Frenchman who discovered at the age of 70 that he had been speaking prose all his life. The businessmen believe that they are defending free enterprise when they declaim that business is not concerned "merely" with profit but also with promoting desirable "social" ends; that business has a "social conscience" and takes seriously its responsibilities for providing employment, eliminating discrimination, avoiding pollution and whatever else may be the catchwords of the contemporary crop of reformers. In fact they are—or would be if they or anyone else took them seriously—preaching pure and unadulterated socialism. Businessmen who talk this way are unwitting puppets of the intellectual forces that have been undermining the basis of a free society these past decades.

The discussions of the "social responsibilities of business" are notable for their analytical looseness and lack of rigor. What does it mean to say that "business" has responsibilities? Only people can have responsibilities. A corporation is an artificial person and in this sense may have artificial reponsibilities, but "business" as a whole cannot be said to have responsibilities, even in this vague sense. The first step toward clarity in examining the doctrine of the social responsibility of business is to ask precisely what it implies for whom. Presumably, the individuals who are to be responsible are businessmen,

The New York Times Magazine, September 13, 1970, pp. 33, 122–26. © 1970 by The New York Times Company. Reprinted by permission.

which means individual proprietors or corporate executives. Most of the discussion of social responsibility is directed at corporations, so in what follows I shall mostly neglect the individual proprietor and speak of corporate executives.

*   *   *

In a free enterprise, private-property system, a corporate executive is an employee of the owners of the business. He has direct responsibility to his employers. That responsibility is to conduct the business in accordance with their desires, which generally will be to make as much money as possible while conforming to the basic rules of the society, both those embodied in law and those embodied in ethical custom. Of course, in some cases his employers may have a different objective. A group of persons might establish a corporation for an eleemosynary purpose—for example, a hospital or a school. The manager of such a corporation will not have money profit as his objective but the rendering of certain services.

In either case, the key point is that, in his capacity as a corporate executive, the manager is the agent of the individuals who own the corporation or establish the eleemosynary institution, and his primary responsibility is to them.

Needless to say, this does not mean that it is easy to judge how well he is performing his task. But at least the criterion of performance is straightforward, and the persons among whom a voluntary contractual arrangement exists are clearly defined.

Of course, the corporate executive is also a person in his own right. As a person, he may have many other responsibilities that he recognizes or assumes voluntarily—to his family, his conscience, his feelings of charity, his church, his clubs, his city, his country. He may feel impelled by these responsibilities to devote part of his income to causes he regards as worthy, to refuse to work for particular corporations, even to leave his job, for example, to join his country's armed forces. If we wish, we may refer to some of these responsibilities as "social responsibilities." But in these respects he is acting as a principal, not an agent; he is spending his own money or time or energy, not the money of his employers or the time or energy he has contracted to devote to their purposes. If these are "social responsibilities," they are the social responsibilities of individuals, not of business.

What does it mean to say that the corporate executive has a "social responsibility" in his capacity as businessman? If this statement is not pure rhetoric, it must mean that he is to act in some way that is not in the interest of his employers. For example, that he is to refrain from increasing the price of the product in order to contribute to the social objective of preventing inflation, even though a price increase would be in the best interests of the corporation. Or that he is to make expenditures on reducing pollution beyond the amount that is in the best interests of the corporation or that is required by law in order to contribute to the social objective of improving the environment. Or that, at the expense of corporate profits, he is to hire "hard-core" unemployed instead of better-qualified available workmen to contribute to the social objective of reducing poverty.

In each of these cases, the corporate executive would be spending someone else's money for a general social interest. Insofar as his actions in accord with his "social responsibility" reduce returns to stockholders, he is spending their money. Insofar as his actions raise the price to customers, he is spending the customers' money. Insofar as his actions lower the wages of some employees, he is spending their money.

The stockholders or the customers or the employees could separately spend their own money on the particular action if they wished to do so. The executive is exercising a distinct "social responsibility," rather than serving as an agent of the stockholders or the customers or the employees, only if he spends the money in a different way than they would have spent it.

But if he does this, he is in effect imposing taxes, on the one hand, and deciding how the tax proceeds shall be spent, on the other.

This process raises political questions on two levels: principle and consequences. On the level of political principle, the imposition of taxes and the expenditure of tax proceeds are governmental functions. We have established elaborate constitutional, parliamentary, and judicial provisions to control these functions, to assure that taxes are imposed so far as possible in accordance with the preferences and desires of the public—after all, "taxation without representation" was one of the battle cries of the American Revolution. We have a system of checks and balances to separate the legislative function of imposing taxes and enacting expenditures from the executive function of collecting taxes and administering expenditure programs and from the judicial function of mediating disputes and interpreting the law.

Here the businessman—self-selected or appointed directly or indirectly by stockholders—is to be simultaneously legislator, executive, and jurist. He is to decide whom to tax by how much and for what purpose, and he is to spend the proceeds—all this guided only by general exhortations from on high to restrain inflation, improve the environment, fight poverty and so on and on.

The whole justification for permitting the corporate executive to be selected by the stockholders is that the executive is an agent serving the interests of his principal. This justification disappears when the corporate executive imposes taxes and spends the proceeds for "social" purposes. He becomes in effect a public employee, a civil servant, even though he remains in name an employee of a private enterprise. On grounds of political principle, it is intolerable that such civil servants—insofar as their actions in the name of social responsibility are real and not just window-dressing—should be selected as they are now. If they are to be civil servants, then they must be selected through a political process. If they are to impose taxes and make expenditures to foster "social objectives," then political machinery must be set up to guide the assessment of taxes and to determine through a political process the objectives to be served.

This is the basic reason why the doctrine of "social responsibility" involves the acceptance of the socialist view that political mechanisms, not market mechanisms, are the appropriate way to determine the allocation of scarce resources to alternative uses.

On the grounds of consequences, can the corporate executive in fact discharge his alleged "social responsibilities"? On the one hand, suppose he could get away with spending the stockholders' or customers' or employees' money. How is he to know how to spend it? He is told that he must contribute to fighting inflation. How is he to know what action of his will contribute to that end? He is presumably an expert in running his company—in producing a product or selling it or financing it. But nothing about his selection makes him an expert on inflation. Will his holding down the price of his product reduce inflationary pressure? Or, by leaving more spending power in the hands of his customers, simply divert it elsewhere? Or, by forcing him to produce less because of the low price, will it simply contribute to shortages? Even if he could answer these questions, how much cost is he justified in imposing on his stockholders, customers and employees for this social purpose? What is his appropriate share and what is the appropriate share of others?

And, whether he wants to or not, can he get away with spending his stockholders', customers', or employees' money? Will not the stockholders fire him? (Either the present ones or those who take over when his actions in the name of social responsibility have reduced the corporation's profits and the price of its stock.) His customers and his employees can desert him for other producers and employers less scrupulous in exercising their social responsibilities.

This facet of "social responsibility" doctrine is brought into sharp relief when the doctrine is used to justify wage restraint by trade unions. The conflict of interest is naked and clear when union officials are asked to subordinate the interest of their members to some more general social purpose. If the union officials try to enforce wage restraint, the consequence is likely to be wildcat strikes, rank-and-file revolts, and the emergence of strong competitors for their jobs. We thus have the ironic phenomenon that union leaders—at least in the U.S.—have objected to government interference with the market far more consistently and courageously than have business leaders.

The difficulty of exercising "social responsibility" illustrates, of course, the great virtue of private competitive enterprise—it forces people to be responsible for their own actions and makes it difficult for them to "exploit" other people for either selfish or unselfish purposes. They can do good—but only at their own expense.

Many a reader who has followed the argument this far may be tempted to remonstrate that it is all well and good to speak of government's having the responsibility to impose taxes and determine expenditures for such "social" purposes as controlling pollution or training the hard-core unemployed, but that the problems are too urgent to wait on the slow course of political processes, that the exercise of social responsibility by businessmen is a quicker and surer way to solve pressing current problems.

Aside from the question of fact—I share Adam Smith's skepticism about the benefits that can be expected from "those who affected to trade for the public good"—this argument must be rejected on grounds of principle. What it amounts to is an assertion that those who favor the taxes and expenditures in question have failed to persuade a majority of their fellow citizens to be of like mind and that they are seeking to attain by undemocratic procedures what they cannot attain by democratic procedures. In a free society, it is hard for "good" people to do "good," but that is a small price to pay for making it hard for "evil" people to do "evil," especially since one man's good is another's evil.

I have, for simplicity, concentrated on the special case of the corporate executive, except only for the brief digression on trade unions. But precisely the same argument applies to the newer phenomenon of calling upon stockholders to require corporations to exercise social responsibility (the recent GM crusade, for example). In most of these cases, what is in effect involved is some stockholders trying to get other stockholders (or customers or employees) to contribute against their will to "social" causes favored by the activists. Insofar as they succeed, they are again imposing taxes and spending the proceeds.

The situation of the individual proprietor is somewhat different. If he acts to reduce the returns of his enterprise in order to exercise his "social responsibility," he is spending his own money, not someone else's. If he wishes to spend his money on such purposes, that is his right, and I cannot see that there is any objection to his doing so. In the process, he, too, may impose costs on employees and customers. However, because he is far less likely than a large corporation or union to have monopolistic power, any such side effects will tend to be minor.

Of course, in practice the doctrine of social responsibility is frequently a cloak for actions that are justified on other grounds rather than a reason for those actions.

To illustrate, it may well be in the long-run interest of a corporation that is a major employer in a small community to devote resources to providing amenities to that community or to improving its government. That may make it easier to attract desirable employees, it may reduce the wage bill or lessen losses from pilferage and sabotage or have other worthwhile effects. Or it may be that, given the laws about the deductibility of corporate charitable contributions, the stockholders can contribute more to charities they favor since they can in that way contribute an amount that would otherwise have been paid as corporate taxes.

In each of these—and many similar—cases, there is a strong temptation to rationalize these actions as an exercise of "social responsibility." In the present climate of opinion, with its widespread aversion to "capitalism," "profits," the "soulless corporation," and so on, this is one way for a corporation to generate good will as a by-product of expenditures that are entirely justified in its own self-interest.

It would be inconsistent of me to call on corporate executives to refrain from this hypocritical window-dressing because it harms the foundations of a free society. That would be to call on them to exercise a "social responsibility"! If our institutions, and the attitudes of the public, make it in their self-interest to cloak their actions in this way, I cannot summon much indignation to denounce them. At the same time, I can express admiration for those individual proprietors or owners of closely held corporations or stockholders of more broadly held corporations who disdain such tactics as approaching fraud.

Whether blameworthy or not, the use of the cloak of social responsibility, and the nonsense spoken in its name by influential and prestigious businessmen, does clearly harm the foundations of a free society. I have been impressed time and again by the schizophrenic character of many businessmen. They are capable of being extremely far-sighted and clear-headed in matters that are internal to their businesses. They are incredibly short-sighted and muddle-headed in matters that are outside their businesses but affect the possible survival of business in general. This short-sightedness is strikingly exemplified in the calls from many businessmen for wage and price guidelines or controls or incomes policies. There is nothing that could do more in a brief period to destroy a market system and replace it by a centrally controlled system than effective governmental control of prices and wages.

The short-sightedness is also exemplified in speeches by businessmen on social responsibility. This may gain them kudos in the short run. But it helps to strengthen the already too prevalent view that the pursuit of profits is wicked and immoral and must be curbed and controlled by external forces. Once this view is adopted, the external forces that curb the market will not be the social consciences, however highly developed, of the pontificating executives; it will be the iron fist of Government bureaucrats. Here, as with price and wage controls, businessmen seem to me to reveal a suicidal impulse.

The political principle that underlies the market mechanism is unanimity. In an ideal free market resting on private property, no individual can coerce any other, all cooperation is voluntary, all parties to such cooperation benefit or they need not participate. There are no "social" values, no "social" responsibilities in any sense other than the shared values and responsibilities of individuals. Society is a collection of individuals and of the various groups they voluntarily form.

The political principle that underlies the political mechanism is conformity. The individual must serve a more general social interest—whether that be determined by a church or a dictator or a majority. The individual may have a vote and a say in what is to be done, but if he is overruled, he must conform. It is appropriate for some to require others to contribute to a general social purpose whether they wish to or not.

Unfortunately, unanimity is not always feasible. There are some respects in which conformity appears unavoidable, so I do not see how one can avoid the use of the political mechanism altogether.

But the doctrine of "social responsibility" taken seriously would extend the scope of the political mechanism to every human activity. It does not differ in philosophy from the most explicitly collectivist doctrine. It differs only by professing to believe that collectivist ends can be attained without collectivist means. That is why, in my book *Capitalism and Freedom,* I have called it a "fundamentally subversive doctrine" in a free society, and have said that in such a society, "there is one and only one social responsibility to business—to use its resources and engage in activities designed to increase its profits so long as it stays within the rules of the game, which is to say, engages in open and free competition without deception or fraud."

Milton Friedman

Milton Friedman Responds

* * *

MCLAUGHRY: The question of environmental pollution is very much on the public's mind. There are various ways to approach this question. One is the completely laissez-faire approach; another is to tax pollution; another is to give tax incentives or subsidies to companies to encourage them to stop polluting; a fourth is to use police power to make pollution illegal and impose penalties. What would you view as the best way to attack the pollution problem in a free enterprise society?

FRIEDMAN: Well, there is a great deal of misunderstanding about the pollution problem in our society. First, it is often in the private interest not to pollute. That being said, we mustn't suppose that there are no mechanisms within the free enterprise society which lead to the "right" amount of pollution.

Let me stop here for a minute. An ideal of zero pollution is one of the fallacies mouthed about the problem. That is absurd. As in all these cases, you must balance returns with costs. People's breathing is one source of pollution. We breathe in oxygen and breathe out carbon dioxide. If too much carbon dioxide is breathed out, there is a lot of pollution. Now we can simply stop breathing, but most of us would consider the cost of eliminating that pollution greater than the return. We must

Excerpts from *Business and Society Review*, No. 1 (Spring 1972). Copyright © 1972. Reprinted by permission of *Business and Society Review*.

decide upon the "right" amount of pollution, that amount at which the cost of reducing pollution to all the people concerned would be greater than the gain from reducing the level.

In many cases, the private market provides precisely that incentive. For example, consider a town that has been cited as a horror—Gary, Indiana, where the U.S. Steel Company is the major source of pollution. Let's assume for a moment that contrary to fact, none of the pollution spreads into Chicago. Instead, it's all concentrated in Gary. Now, if U.S. Steel pollutes heavily in Gary, the Gary environment becomes unattractive. People don't want to live and work there. U.S. Steel has to pay higher wages to lure employees. You'll say to me that not all the people in Gary work for U.S. Steel. Some people run stores and gas stations. But exactly the same thing is true. If Gary is an unpleasant environment, nobody will run a grocery store there unless he can earn sufficiently more there than he can elsewhere to compensate for enduring the pollution. Consequently, food costs will be high and that again will raise the wages U.S. Steel will have to pay to attract a labor force. Under those circumstances, all the costs of pollution are borne by U.S. Steel, meaning a collection of its stockholders and customers.

MCLAUGHRY: Doesn't your argument depend on an assumption of perfect labor mobility?

FRIEDMAN: No, no. It depends on some labor mobility, but after all, there is labor mobility. It isn't necessary that every person be mobile. Wages are determined at the margin.

For example, the fact that 2 percent of the people are good shoppers makes it unnecessary for the other 98 percent to be good shoppers. Why is it that the prices are roughly the same in different stores? Doesn't that assume that every shopper is a good shopper? Not at all. It's a fact that because some people do compare prices and select the better buys, the rest of us don't have to pay such careful attention. The same is true here. Some people in the labor force will move in and out. The people in Gary will not live in Gary unless it offers better opportunity than they can get elsewhere. Maybe other things aren't very good; maybe by your standards and my standards these people are not very well off. But among the alternatives they have, that's best.

MCLAUGHRY: Don't the traditions and habits of people with lower income and lower education levels combine to frustrate that easy mobility of labor?

FRIEDMAN: On the contrary. There is enormous mobility of labor at the very lowest levels—not only in this country, but all over. How were Indians ever led from India to Africa, to Malaysia, to Indonesia, except for the fact that they heard of better opportunities? How was the United States settled? From the end of the Civil War to World War I, if I remember correctly, a third of the people in the United States had immigrated from abroad. The people who came here were not those who earned high wages; they were not the "jet set." They were poor, ignorant people who arrived with nothing but their hands. What encouraged them to migrate? The fact that they had heard at distances of five or six thousand miles that there were better jobs and better conditions in the United States than where they were. So it's absurd to say that because people in Gary, Indiana, are in the low-income bracket, they can't migrate elsewhere. Look at the enormous migration to the West Coast. Look at the Okie migration. If you count the number of people in the low-income class who every year move back and forth, it is quite obvious that there is enormous mobility of labor.

MCLAUGHRY: How does your argument relate to another topic of current interest—safety?

FRIEDMAN: What's the "right" number of accidents for Consolidated Edison to have? Now that seems like a silly question. All accidents are bad. But let's suppose for a moment that Con Ed does have an accident. One of its trucks hits your car. You have a case against them and they will have to pay damages. Well, that's part of their operating expense, and it has to be recouped from their customers. Suppose it costs them less to avoid a certain number of accidents than it does to pay for damages in these accident suits. Well, that would reduce the price they have to charge their customers. Obviously it's in their interest—and their customers' as well— to avoid these accidents. On the other hand, suppose it costs Con Ed more to avoid additional accidents than it does to pay damages—and it well might. To avoid all accidents, they might have to do all their work at night, give instructions that their trucks should never go faster than 2 MPH, and so on. You can see by this that Consolidated Edison must have the "right" number of accidents, that number where the cost of avoiding an additional accident would be more than the damages paid the victim.

Well now, what is the difference between this situation and the pollution case? There's only one: In the pollution case, it is often impossible to identify the individual victims and to require person-by-person compensation. In Consolidated Edison's case you can identify the victims early. In the U.S. Steel case, you can identify the victims as a group, and *all* the costs fall back on U.S. Steel. Therefore, in a single-company town like Gary, U.S. Steel has a private interest in maintaining the right level of pollution, because an extra $100 spent to reduce pollution would add less than $100 to the welfare of all of the people in the city of Gary. Under the circumstances where you cannot identify the victim, however, it is highly desirable to take measures to see that costs are imposed on the consumer. There is only one person who can pay the costs, and that's the consumer. If the people whose shirts are dirtied by Consolidated Edison could bring suit, Con Ed would have to pay the cost of cleaning their shirts—which is to say, Con Ed's customers would. If it were cheaper to stop polluting than it was to pay those costs, Con Ed would do so.

In those cases where you can determine what costs are being imposed on people other than the customer, the least bad solution seems to me to be a tax. Let's consider an industrial enterprise which pollutes a river. If you can calculate roughly that by putting in the effluent, an industry is causing a certain amount of harm to people downstream, then the answer would seem to be to tax it, roughly equal to the amount of harm it has imposed. This provides the right incentive. If it's cheaper for the corporation to put the effluent in the water and pay the tax than it is not to pollute or to clean up the river, then that is what should be done.

*   *   *

Robert Almeder

Morality in the Marketplace

I. INTRODUCTION

In order to create a climate more favorable for corporate activity, International Telephone and Telegraph allegedly contributed large sums of money to "destabilize" the duly elected government of Chile. Even though advised by the scientific community that the practice is lethal, major chemical companies reportedly continue to dump large amounts of carcinogens into the water supply of various areas and, at the same time, lobby to prevent legislation against such practices. General Motors Corporation, other automobile manufacturers, and Firestone Tire and Rubber Corporation have frequently defended themselves against the charge that they knowingly and willingly marketed a product that, owing to defective design, had been reliably predicted to kill a certain percentage of its users and, moreover, refused to recall promptly the product even when government agencies documented the large incidence of death as a result of the defective product. Finally, people often say that numerous advertising companies happily accept, and earnestly solicit, accounts to advertise cigarettes knowing full well that as a direct result of their advertising activities a certain number of people will die considerably prematurely and painfully. We need not concern ourselves with whether these and other similar charges are true because our concern here is with what might count as a justification for such corporate conduct were it to occur. There can be no question that such behavior is frequently legal. The question is whether corporate behavior should be con-

---

This paper is a revised and expanded version of an earlier paper, "The Ethics of Profit: Reflections on Corporate Responsibility," *Business and Society* (Winter 1980): 7–15.

strained by nonlegal or moral considerations. As things presently stand, it seems to be a dogma of contemporary capitalism that the sole responsibility of business is to make as much money as is legally possible. But the question is whether this view is rationally defensible.

Sometimes, although not very frequently, corporate executives will admit to the sort of behavior depicted above and then proceed proximately to justify such behavior in the name of their responsibility to the shareholders or owners (if the shareholders are not the owners) to make as much profit as is legally possible. Thereafter, less proximately and more generally, they will proceed to urge the more general utilitarian point that the increase in profit engendered by such corporate behavior begets such an unquestionable overall good for society that the behavior in question is morally acceptable if not quite praiseworthy. More specifically, the justification in question can, and usually does, take two forms.

The first and most common form of justification consists in urging that, as long as one's corporate behavior is not illegal, the behavior will be morally acceptable because the sole purpose of being in business is to make a profit; and the rules of the marketplace are somewhat different from those in other places and must be followed if one is to make a profit. Moreover, proponents of this view hasten to add that, as Adam Smith has claimed, the greatest good for society is achieved not by corporations seeking to act morally, or with a sense of social responsibility in their pursuit of profit, but rather by each corporation seeking to maximize its own profit, unregulated in that endeavor except by the laws of supply and demand along with whatever other laws are inherent to the competition process. Smith's view, that there is an invisible hand, as it were, directing an economy governed solely by the profit motive to the greatest good for society,[1] is still the dominant motivation and justification for those who would want an economy unregulated by any moral concern that would, or could, tend to decrease profits for some *alleged* social or moral good.

Milton Friedman, for example, has frequently asserted that the sole moral responsibility of business is to make as much profit as is legally possible; and by that he means to suggest that attempts to regulate or restrain the pursuit of profit in accordance with what some people believe to be socially desirable ends are in fact *subversive* of the common good since the greatest good for the greatest number is achieved by an economy maximally competitive and unregulated by moral rules in its pursuit of profit.[2] So, on Friedman's view, the greatest good for society is achieved by corporations acting legally, but with no further regard for what may be morally desirable; and this view begets the paradox that, *in business,* the greatest good for society can be achieved only by acting without regard for morality. Moreover, adoption of this position constitutes a fairly conscious commitment to the view that while one's personal life may well need governance by moral considerations, when pursuing profit, it is necessary that one's corporate behavior be unregulated by any moral concern other than that of making as much money as is legally possible; curiously enough, it is only in this way that society achieves the greatest good. So viewed, it is not difficult to see how a corporate executive could consistently adopt rigorous standards of morality in his or her personal life and yet feel quite comfortable in abandoning those standards in the pursuit of profit. Albert Carr, for example, likens the conduct of business to that of playing poker.[3] As Carr would have it, moral busybodies who insist on corporations acting morally might do just as well to censure a good bluffer in poker for being deceitful. Society, of course, lacking a perspective such as Friedman's and Carr's, is only too willing to view such behavior as strongly hypocritical and fostered by an unwholesome avarice.

The second way of justifying, or defending, corporate practices that may appear morally questionable consists in urging that even if corporations were to take seriously the idea of limiting profits because of a desire to be moral or more responsible to social needs, then corporations would be involved in the unwholesome business of selecting and implementing moral values that may not be shared by a large number of people. Besides, there is the overwhelming question of whether there can be any nonquestionable moral values or non-controversial list of social priorities for corporations to adopt. After all, if ethical relativism is true, or if ethical nihilism is true (and philosophers can be counted upon to argue for both positions), then it would be fairly silly of corporations to limit profits for what may be a quite dubious reason, namely, for being moral, when there are no clear grounds for doing it, and when it is not too clear what would count for doing it. In short, business corporations could argue (as Friedman has done)[4] that corporate actions in behalf of society's interests would require of corporations an ability to clearly determine and rank in noncontroversial ways the major needs of society; and it would not appear that this could be done successfully.

Perhaps another, and somewhat easier, way of formulating this second argument consists in urging that because philosophers generally fail to agree on what are the proper moral rules (if any), as well as on whether we should be moral, it would be imprudent to sacrifice a clear profit for a dubious or controversial moral gain. To authorize such a sacrifice would be to abandon a clear responsibility for one that is unclear or questionable.

If there are any other basic ways of justifying the sort of corporate behavior noted at the outset, I cannot imagine what they might be. So, let us examine these two modes of justification. In doing this, I hope to show that neither argument is sound and, moreover, that corporate behavior of the sort in question is clearly immoral if anything is immoral—and if nothing is immoral, then such corporate behavior is clearly contrary to the long-term interest of a corporation. In the end, we will reflect on ways to prevent such behavior, and on what is philosophically implied by corporate willingness to act in clearly immoral ways.

II.

Essentially, the first argument is that the greatest good for the greatest number will be, and can only be, achieved by corporations acting legally but unregulated by any moral concern in the pursuit of profit. As we saw earlier, the evidence for this argument rests on a fairly classical and unquestioning acceptance of Adam Smith's view that society achieves a greater good when each person is allowed to pursue her or his own self-interested ends than when each person's pursuit of self-interested ends is regulated in some way or another by moral rules or concern. But I know of no evidence Smith ever offered for this latter claim, although it seems clear that those who adopt it generally do so out of respect for the perceived good that has emerged for various modern societies as a direct result of the free enterprise system and its ability to raise the overall standard of living of all those under it.

However, there is nothing inevitable about the greatest good occurring in an unregulated economy. Indeed, we have good inductive evidence from the age of the Robber Barons that unless the profit motive is regulated in various ways (by statute or otherwise) untold social evil can (and some say *will*) occur because of the natural tendency of the system to place ever-increasing sums of money in ever-decreasing numbers of hands. If all this is so, then so much the worse for all philosophical attempts to justify what would appear to be morally questionable corporate behavior on the grounds that corporate behavior, unregulated by moral concern, is necessarily or even probably productive of the greatest good for the greatest number. Moreover, a rule utilitarian would not be very hard pressed to show the many unsavory implications to society as a whole if society were to take seriously a rule to the effect that, provided only that one acts legally, it is morally permissible to do whatever one wants to do to achieve a profit. Some of those implications we shall discuss below before drawing a conclusion.

The second argument cited above asserts that even if we were to grant, for the sake of argument, that corporations have social responsibilities beyond that of making as much money as is legally possible for the shareholders, there would be no noncontroversial way for corporations to discover just what these responsibilities are in the order of their importance. Owing to the fact that even distinguished moral philosophers predictably disagree on what one's moral responsibilities are, if any, it would seem irresponsible to limit profits to satisfy dubious moral responsibilities.

For one thing, this argument unduly exaggerates our potential for moral disagreement. Admittedly, there might well be important disagreements among corporations (just as there could be among philosophers) as to a priority ranking of major social needs; but that does not mean that most of us could not, or would not, agree that certain things ought not be done in the name of profit even when there is no law prohibiting such acts. There will always be a few who would do anything for a profit; but that is hardly a good argument in favor of their having the moral right to do so rather than a good argumunt that they refuse to be moral. In sum, it is hard to see how this second argument favoring corporate moral nihilism is any better than the general argument for ethical nihilism based on the variability of ethical judgments or practices; and apart from the fact that it tacitly presupposes that morality is a matter of what we all in fact would, or should, accept, the argument is maximally counterintuitive (as I shall show) by way of suggesting that we cannot generally agree that corporations have certain clear social responsibilities to avoid certain practices. Accordingly, I would now like to argue that if anything is immoral, a certain kind of corporate behavior is quite immoral although it may not be illegal.

III.

Without caring to enter into the reasons for the belief, I assume we all believe that it is wrong to kill an innocent human being for no other reason than that doing so would be more financially rewarding for the killer than if he were to earn his livelihood in some other way. Nor, I assume, should our moral feelings on this matter change depending on the amount of money involved. Killing an innocent baby for fifteen million dollars would not seem to be any less objectionable than killing it for twenty cents. It is possible, however, that some self-professing utilitarian might be tempted to argue that the killing of an innocent baby for fifteen million dollars would not be objectionable if the money were to be given to the poor; under these circumstances, greater good would be achieved by the killing of the innocent baby. But, I submit, if anybody were to argue in this fashion, his argument would be quite deficient because he has not established what he needs to establish to make his argument sound. What he needs is a clear, convincing argument that raising the standard of living of an indefinite number of poor persons by the killing of an innocent person is a greater good for all those affected by the act than if the standard of living were not raised by the killing of an innocent person. This is needed because part of what we mean by having a basic right to life is that a person's life cannot be taken from him or her without a good reason. If our utilitarian cannot provide a convincing justification for his claim that a greater good is served by killing an innocent person in order to raise the standard of living for a large number of poor people, then it is hard to see how he can have the good reason he needs to deprive an innocent person of his or her life. Now, it seems clear that there will be anything but unanimity in the moral community on the question of whether there is a greater good achieved in raising the standard of living by killing an innocent baby than in leaving the standard of living alone and not killing an innocent baby. Moreover, even if everybody were to agree that the greater good is achieved by the killing of the innocent baby, how could that be shown to be true? How does one compare the moral value of a human life with the moral value of raising the standard of living by the taking of that life? Indeed, the more one thinks about it, the more difficult it is to see just what would count as objective evidence for the claim that the greater good is achieved by the killing of the innocent baby. Accordingly, I can see nothing that would justify the utilitarian who might be tempted to argue that if the sum is large enough, and if the sum were to be used for raising the standard of living for an indefinite number of poor people, then it would be morally acceptable to kill an innocent person for money.

These reflections should not be taken to imply, however, that no utilitarian argument could justify the killing of an innocent person for money. After all, if the sum were large enough to save the lives of a large number of people who would surely die if the innocent baby were not killed, then I think one would as a rule be justified in killing the innocent baby for the sum in question. But this situation is obviously quite different from the situation in which one would attempt to justify the killing of an innocent person in order to raise the standard of living for an indefinite number of poor people. It makes sense to kill one innocent person in order to save, say, twenty innocent persons; but it makes no sense at all to kill one innocent person to raise the standard of living of an indefinite number of people. In the latter case, but not in the former, a comparison is made between things that are incomparable.

Given these considerations, it is remarkable and somewhat perplexing that certain corporations should seek to defend practices that are in fact instances of killing innocent persons for profit. Take, for example, the corporate practice of dumping known carcinogens into rivers. On Milton Friedman's view, we should not regulate or prevent such companies from dumping their effluents into the environment. Rather we should, if we like, tax the company after the effluents are in the water and then have the tax money used to clean up the environment.[5] For Friedman, and others, the fact that so many people will die as a result of this practice seems to be just part of the cost of doing business and making a profit. If there is any moral difference between such corporate practices and murdering innocent human beings for money, it is hard to see what it is. It is even more difficult to see how anyone could justify the practice and see it as no more than a business practice not to be regulated by moral concern. And there are a host of other corporate activities that are morally equivalent to deliberate killing of innocent persons for money. Such practices number among them contributing funds to "destabilize" a foreign government, advertising cigarettes, knowingly to market children's clothing having a known cancer causing agent, and refusing to recall (for fear of financial loss) goods known to be sufficiently defective to directly maim or kill a certain percentage of their unsuspecting users because of the defect. On this latter item, we are all familiar, for example, with convincingly documented charges that certain prominent automobile and tire manufacturers will knowingly market equipment sufficiently defective to increase the likelihood of death as a direct result of the defect and yet refuse to recall the product because the cost of recalling and repairing would have a greater adverse impact on profit than if the product were not recalled and the company paid the projected number of predictably successful suits. Of course, if the projected cost of the predictably successful suits were to outweigh the cost of recall and repair, then the product would be recalled and repaired, but not otherwise. In cases of this sort, the companies involved may admit to having certain marketing problems or a design problem, and they may even admit to having made a mistake; but, interestingly enough, they do not view themselves as immoral or as murderers for keeping their product in the market place when they know people are dying from it, people who would not die if the defect were corrected.

The important point is not whether in fact these practices have occurred in the past, or occur even now; there can be no doubt that such practices have occurred and do occur. Rather the point is that when companies act in such ways as a matter of policy, they must either not know what they do is murder (i.e., unjustifiable killing of an innocent person), or knowing that it is murder, seek to justify it in terms of profit. And I have been arguing that it is difficult to see how any corporate manager could fail to see that these policies amount to murder for money, although there may be no civil statute against such corporate behavior. If so, then where such policies exist, we can only assume that they are designed and implemented by corporate managers who either see nothing wrong with murder for money (which is implausible) or recognize that what they do is wrong but simply refuse to act morally because it is more financially rewarding to act immorally.

Of course, it is possible that corporate executives would not recognize such acts as murder. They may, after all, view murder as a legal concept involving one noncorporate person or persons deliberately killing another noncorporate person or persons and prosecutable only under existing civil statute. If so, it is somewhat understandable how corporate executives might fail, at least psychologically, to see such corporate policies as murder rather than as, say, calculated risks, tradeoffs, or design errors. Still, for all that, the logic of the situation seems clear enough.

IV. CONCLUSION

In addition to the fact that the only two plausible arguments favoring the Friedman doctrine are unsatisfactory, a strong case can be made for the claim that corporations *do* have a clear and noncontroversial moral responsibility not to design or implement, for reasons of profit, policies that they know, or have good reason to believe, will kill or otherwise seriously injure innocent persons affected by those policies. Moreover, we have said nothing about wage discrimination, sexism, discrimination in hiring, price fixing, price gouging, questionable but not unlawful competition, or other similar practices that some will think businesses should avoid by virtue of responsibility to society. My main concern has been to show that since we all agree that murder for money is generally wrong, and since there is no discernible difference between that and certain corporate policies that are not in fact illegal, then these corporate practices are clearly immoral (that is, they ought not to be done) and incapable of being morally justified by appeal to the Friedman doctrine since that doctrine does not admit of adequate evidential support. In itself, it is sad that this argument needs to be made and, if it were not for what appears to be a fairly strong commitment within the business community to the Friedman doctrine in the name of the unquestionable success of the free enterprise system, the argument would not need to be stated.

The fact that such practices do exist—designed and implemented by corporate managers who, for all intents and purposes, appear to be upright members of the moral community—only heightens the need for effective social prevention. Presumably, of course, any company willing to put human lives into the profit and loss column is not likely to respond to moral censure. Accordingly, I submit that perhaps the most effective way to deal with the problem of preventing such corporate behavior would consist in structuring legislation such that senior corporate managers who knowingly concur in practices of the sort listed above can effectively be tried, at their own expense, for murder, rather than censured and fined a sum to be paid out of corporate profits. This may seem a somewhat extreme or unrealistic proposal. However, it seems more unrealistic to think that aggressively competitive corporations will respond to what is morally necessary if failure to do so could be very or even minimally profitable. In short, unless we take strong and appropriate steps to prevent such practices, society will be reinforcing a destructive mode of behavior that is maximally disrespectful of human life, just as society will be reinforcing a value system that so emphasizes monetary gain as a standard of human success that murder for profit could be a corporate policy if the penalty for being caught at it were not too dear.

In the long run, of course, corporate and individual willingness to do what is clearly immoral for the sake of monetary gain is a patent commitment to a certain view about the nature of human happiness and success, a view that needs to be placed in the balance with Aristotle's reasoned argument and reflections to the effect that money and all that it brings is a means to an end, and not the sort of end in itself that will justify acting immorally to attain it. What that beautiful end is and why being moral allows us to achieve it, may well be the most rewarding and profitable subject a human being can think about. Properly understood and placed in perspective, Aristotle's view on the nature and attainment of human happiness could go a long way toward alleviating the temptation to kill for money.

In the meantime, any ardent supporter of the capitalistic system will want to see the system thrive and flourish; and this it cannot do if it invites and demands government regulation in the name of the public interest. A *strong* ideological commitment to what I have described above as the Friedman doctrine is counterproductive and not in anyone's long-range interest because it is most likely to beget an ever-increasing regulatory climate. The only way to avoid such encroaching regulation is to find ways to move the business community into the long-term view of what is in its interest, and effect ways of both determining and responding to social needs before society moves to regulate business to that end. To so move the business community is to ask business to regulate its own modes of competition in ways that may seem very difficult to achieve. Indeed, if what I have been suggesting is correct, the only kind of enduring capitalism is humane capitalism, one that is at least as socially responsible as society needs. By the same token, contrary to what is sometimes felt in the business community, the Friedman doctrine, ardently adopted for the dubious reasons generally given, will most likely undermine capitalism and motivate an economic socialism by assuring an erosive regulatory climate in a society that expects the business community to be socially responsible in ways that go beyond just making legal profits.

In sum, being socially responsible in ways that go beyond legal profit-making is by no means a dubious luxury for the capitalist in today's world. It is a necessity if capitalism is to survive at all; and, presumably, we shall all profit with the survival of a vibrant capitalism. If anything, then, rigid adherence to the Friedman doctrine is not only philosophically unjustified, and unjustifiable, it is also unprofitable in the long run, and therefore, down-right subversive of the long-term common good. Unfortunately, taking the long-run view is difficult for everyone. After all, for each of us, tomorrow may not come. But living for today only does not seem to make much sense either, if that deprives us of any reasonable and happy tomorrow. Living for the future may not be the healthiest thing to do; but do it we must, if we have good reason to think that we will have a future. The trick is to provide for the future without living in it, and that just requires being moral.[6]

NOTES

1. Adam Smith, *The Wealth of Nations,* ed. Edwin Canaan (New York: Modern Library, 1937), p. 423.

2. See Milton Friedman, "The Social Responsibility of Business Is to Increase Its Profits," in *The New York Times Magazine* (September 13, 1970), pp. 33, 122–126 and "Milton Friedman Responds," in *Business and Society Review* no. 1 (Spring 1972), p. 5ff.

3. Albert Z. Carr, "Is Business Bluffing Ethical?" *Harvard Business Review* (January-February 1968).

4. Milton Friedman in "Milton Friedman Responds," in *Business and Society Review* no. 1 (Spring 1972), p. 10.

5. Ibid.

6. I would like to thank C. C. Luckhardt, J. Humber, R. L. Arrington, and M. Snoeyenbos for their comments and criticisms of an earlier draft.

Shortly after this paper was initially written, an Indiana superior court judge refused to dismiss a homicide indictment against the Ford Motor Company. The company was indicted on charges of reckless homicide stemming from a 1978 accident involving a 1973 Pinto in which three girls died when the car burst into flames after being slammed in the rear. This was the first case in which Ford, or any other automobile manufacturer, had been charged with a criminal offense.

The indictment went forward because the state of Indiana adopted in 1977 a criminal code provision permitting corporations to be charged with criminal acts. At the time, twenty-two other states allowed as much.

The judge, in refusing to set aside the indictment, agreed with the prosecutor's argument that the charge was based not on the Pinto design fault, but rather on the fact that Ford had permitted the car "to remain on Indiana highways knowing full well its defects."

The case went to trial, a jury trial, and Ford Motor Company was found innocent of the charges. Of course, the increasing number of states that allow corporations to fall under the criminal code is an example of social regulation that could have been avoided had corporations and corporate managers not followed so ardently the Friedman doctrine.

Corporate Policy Statements

Views on Corporate Responsibility: The state provides a corporation with the opportunity to earn a profit if it meets society's needs. It follows inevitably that reported profits are the primary scorecard that tells the world how well a corporation is meeting its basic responsibility to society. This is all pretty simple and pretty elementary and I am sure you all studied it years ago in school. However, in recent times critics of our business structure seem to be losing sight of the primary purposes of the corporation and some want to blame the corporation for all of society's ills—real and imaginary. I have no quarrel with the citizenry, the bureaucrats, the legislators, or the educators who say that corporations have a responsibility to society beyond the obligation to generate a fair return or profit for the investor. The corporation—as I have said earlier—is a paper citizen, and every citizen has a responsibility to his fellow citizen. Democratic society is based on that fact. The corporation cannot ignore the truth any more than an individual human being can. However, I take real issue with the critics when they propose that corporations must put their other citizenship responsibilities ahead of their responsibility to earn a fair return for the owners. The only way in which corporations can carry their huge and increasing burden of obligations to society is for them to earn satisfactory profits. If we cannot earn a return on equity investment, which is more attractive than other forms of investment, we die. I am not aware of any bankrupt corporations which are making important social contributions.

. . . There are times when it is hard to define and quantify our responsibility. How much of our shareholders' money should the managers of the business give away in the interest of higher education, and to the United Way campaigns of our base communities? To the fostering of culture and the arts? How much should we spend in money and time attempting to persuade the public to adequately finance public schools, or to help reorganize local government? There is no charity for charity's sake in our handing out the company's money or in our asking the company's people to give of their time. Procter & Gamble's support of civic campaigns is now and always will be limited to what we believe represents the enlightened self-interest of the business. Here in the term self-interest we are back to the word "profit" again. Let's take our own home city of Cincinnati as an example. The future earnings of this company rest first and foremost on our ability to attract and hold bright, capable, dedicated, and concerned people as our employees. If one-quarter of those people are expected to spend their careers in Cincinnati, then it serves the interests of the stockholders for us to support soundly conceived efforts to maintain and enhance this community as a good place to live and raise families.

Procter and Gamble Co.

Alcoa's Fundamental Objectives: Aluminum Company of America, as a broadly owned multinational company, is committed to four fundamental, interdependent objectives, all of which are essential to its long-term success. The ideas behind these words have been part of Alcoa's success for many years—as has the company's intention to excel in all these objectives: 1. provide for shareholders a return superior to that available from other investments of equal risk, based on reliable long-term growth in earnings per share; 2. provide employees a rewarding and challenging employment environment with opportunity for economic and personal growth; 3. provide worldwide customers with products and services of quality; 4. direct its skills and resources to help solve the major problems of the societies and communities of which it is a part, while providing these societies with the benefits of its other fundamental objectives. Supporting Principles—in achieving its fundamental objectives, Alcoa endorses these supporting principles and pledges to: conduct its business in a legal and ethical manner; provide leadership and support for the free market system through successfully achieving its corporate objectives, superiority in product development and production, integrity in its commercial dealings, active awareness of its role in society, and appropriate communication with all employees and with the public; maintain a working environment that will assure each employee the opportunity for growth, for achievement of his or her personal goals, and for contributing to the achievement of the corporate goals; without regard to race, color, national origin, handicap or sex, recruit, employ, and develop individuals of competence and skills commensurate with job requirements; make a positive contribution to the quality of life of the communities and societies in which it operates, always mindful of its economic obligations, as well as the environmental and economic impact of its activities in these communities; for the well-being of all employees at all locations, maintain safe and healthful working conditions, conducive to job satisfaction and high productivity.

Aluminum Co. of America

MORALS, MANAGEMENT, AND CODES

Milton Snoeyenbos

Management and Morals

A number of surveys on ethics in business have been conducted that not only provide us with data regarding the ethical issues businesspersons actually consider to be most troublesome, but also indicate that top and middle managers have different perspectives regarding the source and nature of business disputes containing an ethical component. This article discusses the data and offers some suggestions for resolving the ethical problems revealed.

In 1961, Raymond Baumhart surveyed a large sample of subscribers to the *Harvard Business Review,* and in 1977, Steven Brenner and Earl Molander reported the results of a survey that repeated some of Baumhart's questions.[1] These studies are not representative of businesspersons. Less than 30% of the readers queried actually replied, and it is known that subscribers are significantly above average in position, income, and education. In fact, 44% of the respondents were top managers, 35% were middle managers and 20% were either lower management or nonmanagement business personnel. Nevertheless, the large sample size (over 2,700 replies from 10,000 queried) gives us some indication of how businesspersons actually regard ethical issues and how their views have changed. In 1987, Vitell and Festervand extended the earlier surveys by analyzing the responses of 118 top managers from manufacturing firms located in the southeastern United States.[2] Many of the same questions from the earlier surveys were employed.

Of those who responded to the Brenner-Molander survey 80% believe there are ethical absolutes and that ethical matters are not relative. Furthermore, in the 1961 and 1977 surveys 98% agreed that "in the long run, sound ethics is good business." However, about half of the respondents in both surveys agree that "the American business executive tends not to apply the great ethical laws immediately to work. He is preoccupied chiefly with gain." Evidently, then, for the businessperson, as for most of us, there frequently is a gap between what the person knows or believes that he ought to do and what he actually does; behavior fails to match a professed standard.

One reason for this gap may be that the manager finds himself in a context in which there is pressure to follow generally accepted *industry* practices that he regards as unethical. In all three surveys respondents were asked: "In your industry, are there any generally accepted business practices which you regard as unethical?" The results in percentages are:

	1961	*1977*	*1987*
None	19	27	44
Yes, a few	59	49	47
Yes, many	9	6	3
Don't know	13	18	6

Although the differences could be largely due to the fact that the 1987 survey was regional in scope and the earlier surveys were national, businesspeople seem to believe that unethical practices are decreasing. But these results are difficult to interpret. The decrease may be due to a heightened sense of ethics by managers or increased law enforcement. On the other hand, it may reflect a greater ability to conceal unethical practices or an actual ethical decline, i.e., what was formerly viewed as unethical may presently be so commonplace that it is now regarded as ethically acceptable.

In all three surveys respondents were asked to indicate which industry practices they would most like to see eliminated. The results, in order of importance, are:

1961	*1977*	*1987*
1. Gifts, gratuities, bribes	1. Gifts, gratuities, bribes	1. Unfair pricing practices
2. Unfair pricing practices	2. Unfair competitive practices	2. Gifts, gratuities, bribes
3. Dishonest advertising	3. Cheating customers	3. Cheating of customers
4. Unfair competitive practices	4. Unfairness to employees	4. Competitors' pricing collusion
5. Cheating customers	5. Unfair pricing practices	5. Unfairness to employees
6. Competitors' pricing collusion	6. Dishonest advertising	6. Contract dishonesty
7. Contract dishonesty	7. Competitors' pricing collusion	7. Dishonest advertising
8. Unfairness to employees	8. Contract dishonesty	8. Unfair credit practices

Although it is difficult to discern trends here, it is clear that the respondents agree that they would most like to eliminate certain marketing practices they regard as unethical. Bribes often occur in selling or purchasing, and unfair pricing, cheating of customers, and dishonest advertising are all within the marketing orbit. Why managers would like to eliminate these particular practices is unclear. It may be that managers view these practices as the most serious ethical problems they face. Alternatively, as Vitell and Festervand suggest, these practices may be more conspicuous than others because of their proximity to the marketplace, and, therefore, managers may be more likely to receive public criticism when they occur.

Aside from the question of unethical industry practices, the 1961 and 1977 surveys asked managers whether they had ever *personally* experienced a role conflict between what was expected of them as efficient, profit-conscious managers and what was expected of them as ethical persons. In 1961, 75 percent reported such conflicts, compared with 59 percent in 1977. Again, while it may be that competitive pressures have lessened, so that there are fewer role conflicts today, it may also be the case that standards have fallen, so that practices formerly regarded as unethical are accepted today.

The types of role conflict most frequently experienced have changed:

1961	*1977*	*1987*
1. Firings and layoffs	1. Honesty in communications	1. Honesty in communication
2. Honesty in communication	2. Gifts, entertainment, kickbacks	2. Gifts and kickbacks
3. Price collusion	3. Fairness and discrimination	3. Fairness and discrimination
4. Gifts, entertainment, kickbacks	4. Contract honesty	4. Price collusion
	5. Firings and layoffs	5. Firings and layoffs

Honesty in communication is a more significant problem now than in 1961, with a major increase in number manipulation in reports submitted to top management, governmental agencies, and clients. The decreased experience of role conflicts connected with firings and layoffs may indicate that such practices are becoming accepted as routine or that there is more equity built into firing decisions.

As noted, the three surveys studied are weighted toward the opinion of top management. The 1965 Evans survey, focusing on middle managers, reveals that their most important moral conflicts are:

1. Complying with superior's requirements when they conflict with one's own ethical code,
2. Job demands infringing on home obligations,
3. Methods employed in competition for advancement,

4. Avoiding or hedging responsibility,
5. Maintaining integrity when it conflicts with being well-liked,
6. Impartial treatment of subordinates because of race, religion or personal prejudice,
7. Moral concern that your job does not fully utilize your capabilities.[3]

These data indicate that middle managers experience role conflicts primarily because of "pressure from the top," a conclusion reinforced by a recent survey by Archie Carroll.[4] In Carroll's survey, 64% of the managers surveyed agreed that "managers today feel under pressure to compromise personal standards to achieve company goals," but of those agreeing 50% of top managers, 65% of middle managers, and 84% of lower managers agreed with the statement. Apparently, then, the lower one is in the managerial hierarchy the more one feels pressure to act unethically. Of course, pressure *per se* is not unethical; in a competitive, profit-oriented environment, pressure to produce is necessary for the efficiency that benefits both consumer and producer. But unethical pressure arises when top management sets a return on equity, sales quota, market share, etc., that cannot reasonably be achieved without a subordinate's engagement in unethical behavior. Unethical pressure may be either intentional or inadvertent. In other words, the manager may or may not be aware that he is pressuring a subordinate to the point that the latter is likely to commit an unethical or illegal act. Some unethical pressure is undoubtedly intentional. A manager may adopt a "produce or else" attitude toward subordinates, knowing it will probably result in unethical behavior, but believing that it will yield greater production or sales and that the subordinate can be held responsible for the unethical acts. A manager may require a subordinate to manipulate figures in a report that requires the latter's signature, believing that responsibility for wrongdoing will fall on the subordinate. Many people in business believe that advancement is open only to those individuals who are unethical, and a manager may intentionally encourage unethical behavior in intrafirm competition.[5] More generally, a manager who deliberately fails to provide a context in which ethical concerns can be voiced, and wrongdoing reported and corrected, may encourage unethical behavior.

On the other hand, some top managers are undoubtedly unaware that they are placing unethical pressure on their subordinates. This hypothesis is consistent with the results of Carroll's survey and the data from our three surveys. First, many of the industry-wide practices that top managers do not themselves condone and would most like to see eliminated (e.g., gratuities and bribes, unfair competitive and pricing practices, cheating customers, and contract dishonesty) may arise in large part because of inadvertent pressure from above. Second, the role conflicts actually experienced by managers, and prominently mentioned in the surveys (e.g., honesty in communication, gifts and kickbacks, fairness and discrimination, and contract honesty), may arise in part because of pressure superiors inadvertently place on subordinates. The surveys indicate that the role conflicts and industry practices that managers most want to see eliminated are those they have personally experienced, and, although some managers may be familiar with unethical acts they believe they can pressure subordinates into committing, others may simply not be well enough acquainted with lower-level operational details to recognize the unreasonableness of particular demands they make of subordinates. This may be especially significant in large diversified firms in which a manager with training and experience in one department may be transferred to the upper levels of a department in which he has little or no lower-level experience. Third, this hypothesis could account for the fact that the top-level respondents to the 1961 and 1977 surveys profess to have absolute ethical standards but also claim both that their standards are higher than those of the average manager and that the average manager does not apply these standards. It seems reasonable to assume that the professed standards of top, middle, and lower managers are about the same. But inadvertent pressure from the top may force subordinates to act contrary to the standards both profess. In turn, the subordinate's actions may be interpreted by top managers as an indication that other managers actually have lower standards. The problem is compounded when general corporate policies or codes are not linked with a mechanism that permits ethical concerns to be relayed to top management, when top managers are unwilling to listen, or when no sanctions are fixed for transgressions and ethical behavior goes unrewarded.

What steps can be taken to improve ethical behavior in business? It seems clear from the surveys that there must be greater awareness on the part of top managers that their leadership is essential. In one sense, managers should already be aware of this, since it is a principle of management theory that top management sets the standards of behavior and subordinates imitate the behavior that is expected for success within the organization. The 1977 survey, however, indicates that 65 percent of managers believe that society, not business, has the primary responsibility for setting ethical standards. Certainly there is some basis for this opinion; individuals are members of society long before they enter business, and the manager should be able to assume that the persons he or she hires are already ethical. Yet the surveys also reveal the importance of an organizational influence. Respondents to the 1961 survey ranked the following as factors that influence a person to make ethical decisions.

> An individual's personal code of behavior,
> Behavior of a person's superiors in the firm,
> Formal company policy,
> Ethical climate of the industry,
> Behavior of a person's equals in the company.

The following were ranked as factors influencing a person to make unethical decisions:

> The behavior of a person's superiors in the company,
> Ethical climate of the industry,
> The behavior of a person's equals in the company,
> Lack of company policy,
> Personal financial needs.

In the 1977 survey, the following factors were ranked as most influencing a person to make unethical decisions:

> Behavior of superiors,
> Formal policy or lack thereof,
> Industry ethical climate,
> Behavior of one's equals in the company,
> Society's moral climate,
> One's personal financial needs.

We have already noted Evans's survey result that middle managers experience role conflicts primarily because of organizational pressure. Furthermore, that survey indicates that when middle managers are pressured to comply with a superior's directive that is contrary to their personal code of behavior, they most often comply rather than resign or object and leave themselves open to dismissal, demotion, or horizontal transfer. Similarly, the Carroll survey reveals that 61 percent of middle managers and 85 percent of lower managers would "go along with their bosses to show their loyalty" if asked to engage in behavior they personally believe to be unethical. Thus, the surveys unambiguously indicate that, although a person's socially acquired ethical beliefs may strongly influence his behavior, when faced with an ethical dilemma a person in a lower-level organizational position will typically seek guidance in his immediate organizational context and, in particular, will refer to his superiors' ethical behavior. Organizational factors are central both to a person's perception of an ethical dilemma and his subsequent behavior once a problem is recognized. And, since it is clear that pressure to commit unethical acts is in part traceable to the managerial hierarchy, it is unreasonable for a top manager to expect that a subordinate's decisions will be based solely or primarily on values acquired prior to and independent of his business experience. Unless top management sets the standards of behavior expected in the organization, the pressure to produce may well lead to unethical behavior of the sort revealed in the surveys. And top managers must not only exhibit leadership by professing high standards, they must clearly articulate them and see that they are enforced.

The importance of top management leadership is also stressed in two 1988 studies. A Touche Ross survey of top corporate executives, business school deans, and congressmen indicated that 73 percent believe the firm's chief executive officer plays the most significant role in setting ethical standards for employees, whereas 25 percent believe the employee's immediate supervisor plays the most significant role.[6] A Business Roundtable study of ten firms considered leaders in ethics concluded that: "In the experience of these companies with regard to corporate ethics, no point emerges more clearly than the crucial role of top management. To achieve results, the Chief Executive Officer and those around the CEO need to be openly and strongly committed to ethical conduct, and give constant leadership in tending and renewing the values of the organization.[7]

How can top management develop and enforce high ethical standards in business? We can begin to answer this question by addressing the trouble spots our surveys reveal. Since we have noted that a considerable amount of unethical behavior arises from questionable industry practices, one suggestion is that top managers take an active role in curbing such practices through the implementation of industry-wide ethical standards (or codes) that not only are clearly articulated but also have an adequate enforcement mechanism. Respondents to both the 1961 and 1977 surveys indicate that they favor industry-wide codes. In 1961, 71% favored codes, 19% were neutral, and 10% were opposed. In 1977, 55% were in favor, 20% neutral, and 25% opposed. In practice, however, industry-wide self-regulation has never been widely practiced in America. As Ian Maitland explains, self-regulation is potentially anti-competitive, i.e., the very power needed to prevent industry-wide ethical problems could well be used to restrain trade and result in industry protectionism.[8]

Top management can, however, improve the ethical climate of business by institutionalizing ethics within the corporation. Of course, in the small firm there may not be a need for an elaborate formal structure, but in the large corporation there is a need for articulated objectives, relatively formal procedures and rules, and communication and enforcement mechanisms. If people want their organizations to be ethical as well as productive, then in complex firms there is a need to articulate and communicate ethical standards that are both equitable and effectively enforced. To accomplish these ends, the standards of expected behavior should be institutionalized, i.e., they should become a relatively permanent aspect of the organization. To institutionalize ethics we suggest that the firm: (a) adopt a corporate ethical code, (b) designate an ethics committee at a relatively high level in the organization, and (c) make ethics training part of its management development program.

The first step in institutionalizing ethics is to articulate the firm's values or goals. Many corporations do have general objectives; 3M Corporation, for example, has goals relating to profits, customers, employees, and society. With respect to profit, it states, "3M management will endeavor to maintain optimum profit margins in all product lines in order to finance 3M's future growth and to provide an adequate return to stockholders." The corporation also states that in pursuing its goals the firm will adhere to "uncompromising honesty and integrity . . . manifested in the commitment to the highest standards of ethics throughout the organization and in all aspects of 3M's operations." So 3M's code, developed by top management, has committed the firm's employees to ethical behavior in the achievement of general corporate goals. However, since our surveys reveal that the pressure to achieve goals can and does override ethics, the emphasis should be on setting *reasonable* goals and subgoals, i.e., goals should be set so that unethical pressure is not placed on subordinates. In addition to a general statement of goals and the means to implement them, a top management committed to ethics should: (a) extensively consult with personnel at all levels of the firm regarding goals and subgoals; (b) see to it that reasonable, specific subgoals are set; and (c) articulate a fine-grained ethical code that addresses ethical issues likely to arise at the level of subgoals.

A code, then, should be relatively *specific*. In addition to general policy statements mentioning overall corporate objectives and means, it should spell out in some detail policy regarding ethical issues that are liable to arise in the conduct of a particular corporation's business. It should detail the individual's obligations to the organization in areas such as: confidential information, trade secrets, bribes, gratuities, gifts, conflicts of interest, expense accounts, honesty, etc. But it should also mention employer obligations in areas such as: hiring, affirmative action, promotion, layoffs, termination, privacy, dissent, grievances, communication, worker and product safety, contributions, employee development, and job quality. In addition, specificity can be enhanced by integrating a firm's ethical concerns with its legal requirements. In the areas of safety and health, for example, specific ethical policy could be integrated with the law in areas such as: equipment, apparel, handling and testing of materials, testing of employees, treatment, compensation, and employment of the handicapped.

If a code is to be more than window-dressing, it must be enforced, equitable, and effective; it must be a living document that organizational members are aware of, comprehend, and to which they are committed. If top managemmt is genuine in its ethical commitment, there are a variety of ways to institutionalize a code; the "best" way will largely depend on the individual organizational context. In some cases, a board of directors' subcommittee comprised of inside and outside directors will be effective. In other cases, a committee comprised of managers and employees from different organizational strata will be successful. However it is constituted, the committee should have the authority and responsibility to: (1) communicate the code, pertinent changes, and decisions based on it to all members of the firm; (2) clarify the code and issues relating to its interpretation; (3) facilitate the code's use; (4) investigate grievances and possible code violations; (5) enforce the code by disciplining violators and rewarding those who comply with and uphold it; and (6) review, update, and upgrade the code.

In addition to an explicit ethical code and ethics committee, institutionalization can be aided by devoting part of the employee training program to ethics. Ideally this would embrace all employees, and could focus on the code, the ethics committee, and the responsibilities of employer and employee. At Chemical Bank, for example, new employees have a general orientation in which they receive and read the Code of Ethics and sign an agreement to abide by it. Training personnel discuss the code and answer questions. The new employees then view a film in which Chemical's Chairman emphasizes the importance of ethical behavior. Employees also receive instruction in ethical standards as part of their functional training and when they are promoted. Chemical Bank also utilizes a Decision Making and Corporate Value seminar to train managers in ethics. Held twice a year, the seminar articulates Chemical's values and helps managers recognize the ethical implications of their business decisions.

Within the firm, then, top management can create an ethical environment by: (1) articulating goals for the firm, and, in particular, by developing a two-way communicative process that sets realistic subgoals, such as sales quotas, for employees; (2) encouraging the development of an ethical code applicable to all members of the firm; (3) instituting an ethics committee to oversee, enforce, and develop the code; and (4) incorporating ethics training in the employee development program. Establishment of such internal programs, in the context of developing industry-wide codes of ethics to deal with issues that transcend a particular firm, would be a significant step in establishing an ethical climate in business.

Are corporations institutionalizing ethics? A 1986 survey by Bentley College's Center for Business Ethics addresses this question.[9] The center queried the Fortune 500 industrial firms and the Fortune 500 service firms and received 279 responses (28%). The survey indicates that 223 (or 80%) of the firms responding have taken steps to incorporate ethical values in their organizations. Of the 223, 93% have written ethical codes and 44% have ethics training for employees, with a majority of those having training actually requiring it. In spite of these rather encouraging results, the survey indicates that full institutionalization is far from realized. Only 18% of the 223 firms incorporating ethics have an ethics committee, and of those having ethics committees only 40% handle code infractions and only 23% handle employee complaints. Furthermore, of those companies which stated that they have taken steps to incorporate ethics, 74% also state that they are not planning to expand their present efforts to further incorporate ethics into the corporate environment.

It is, however, important to note that many firms have comprehensive ethics programs. Boeing's strategy consists of five key elements. First, the company has an ethics code titled *Business Conduct Guidelines*. It covers: marketing practices; offering of business courtesies; conflicts of interest; acceptance of business courtesies; and use of company time, materials, and proprietary information. The code consists of brief statements of the company's basic principles, followed by interpretations of those principles. Second, each of Boeing's operating units has an Ethics Advisor to interpret the firm's ethics policies and provide clarification and advice before employees act. Third, Boeing's Corporate Headquarters has an Office of Business Practices, which can be contacted directly via telephone by any employee who believes the ethics code has been violated. Fourth, Boeing has an Ethics and Business Conduct Committee that reports to the company's Board of Directors, and is composed of board members and upper management. This committee oversees all of Boeing's ethics programs and handles any questions referred to it by Ethics Advisors or the Office of Business Practices. Fifth, Boeing has extensive ethics training programs throughout its operating divisions. Each division has developed its own three-hour ethics program centered on the ethics code. The programs utilize case studies and focus on techniques for ethical decision-making relating to the principles set forth in the code.

NOTES

1. Raymond C. Baumhart, "How Ethical Are Businessmen?" *Harvard Business Review* 39, no. 4 (July–August 1961), pp. 6 ff; *Ethics in Business* (New York: Holt, Rinehart and Winston, 1968); Steven N. Brenner and Earl A. Molander, "Is the Ethics

of Business Changing?" *Harvard Business Review* 55, no. 1 (January–February 1977): 57–71.

2. Scott J. Vitell and Troy A. Festervand, "Business Ethics: Conflicts, Practices, and Beliefs of Industrial Executives," *Journal of Business Ethics* 6, no. 2 (February 1987): 111–22.

3. Appendix B to Thomas F. McMahon's "Moral Problems of Middle Management," in *Proceedings of the Catholic Theological Society of America* 20 (1965): 23–49.

4. Archie B. Carroll, "Managerial Ethics: A Post-Watergate View," *Business Horizons* 18, no. 2 (April 1975): 75–80.

5. Harrison Johnson, "How to Get the Boss's Job," *Modern Office Procedure* 6, no. 5 (1961): 15–18.

6. *Ethics in American Business,* Touche Ross, 1988, p. 2.

7. *Corporate Ethics: A Prime Business Asset,* The Business Roundtable, 1988, p. 4.

8. Ian Maitland, "The Limits of Business Self-Regulation," in *Ethical Theory and Business,* Tom L. Beauchamp and Norman E. Bowie, eds. (Englewood Cliffs, N.J.: Prentice-Hall, 1988), 3d ed., pp. 145–46.

9. M. Hoffman et al., "Are Corporations Institutionalizing Ethics?" *Journal of Business Ethics* 5, no. 2 (April 1986): 85–91.

SELECT BIBLIOGRAPHY

Anshen, M., ed. *Managing the Socially Responsible Corporation.* New York: Macmillan, 1974.

Carroll, A., ed. *Managing Corporate Social Responsibility.* Boston: Little, Brown and Co., 1977.

———. *Business and Society.* Boston: Little, Brown and Co., 1981.

Chamberlain, N. *The Limits of Corporate Responsibility.* New York: Basic Books, 1973.

Donaldson, T. *Corporations and Morality.* Englewood Cliffs, N.J.: Prentice-Hall, 1982, Chs. 2-6.

Donaldson, T., and P. Werhane, eds. *Ethical Issues in Business.* 3d ed. Englewood Cliffs, N.J.: Prentice-Hall, 1988, pp. 84–163. Contains articles on the moral status and moral responsibility of corporations.

Flew, A. "The Profit Motive." *Ethics* 86 (July 1976): 312-21.

French, P. *Collective and Corporate Responsibility.* New York: Columbia University Press, 1984.

Friedman, M. *Capitalism and Freedom.* Chicago: University of Chicago Press, 1962.

———. *Free to Choose.* New York: Harcourt Brace Jovanovich, 1980.

Hesson, R. *In Defense of the Corporation.* Stanford: Hoover Institution Press, 1979.

Hoffman, M., ed. *Proceedings of the Second National Conference on Business Ethics.* Washington, D.C.: University Press of America, 1979. Contains articles by T. Donaldson and K. Goodpaster on Ladd, and a response by Ladd, pp. 81–115.

Hoffman, W., J. Moore, and D. Fedo, eds. *Corporate Governance and Institutionalizing Ethics.* Lexington, Mass.: Lexington Books, 1984.

Humber, J. "Milton Friedman and the Corporate Executive's Conscience." *Philosophy in Context* 10 (1980): 71–80.

Johnson, B., ed. *The Attack on Corporate America.* New York: McGraw-Hill, 1978.

Stone, C. *Where the Law Ends: The Social Control of Corporate Behavior.* New York: Harper and Row, 1975.

Werhane, P. *Persons, Rights, & Corporations.* Englewood Cliffs, N.J.: Prentice-Hall, 1985.

3

EMPLOYEE OBLIGATIONS

INTRODUCTION

The work contract establishes employee obligations to the employer; in return for his wage the employee is expected to utilize his knowledge and skills for the benefit of the organization. Employees have clear, specific, and extensive legal obligations to their employers, and these are spelled out in C. G. Luckhardt's article "Duties of Agent to Principal." The rest of this chapter discusses employee obligations in the areas of conflict of interest, gifts, payoffs, trade secrets, and honesty in organizational communication.

If employees have an obligation to adhere to their work contracts, the firm also has an obligation to be relatively specific about the details of the work contract. This point is clearly made in Robert E. Frederick's discussion of conflicts of interest. Although firms have a right to preclude conflicts of interest, Frederick's discussion of Inorganic Chemical's policy points up the fact that corporate policies are often excessively general and biased in favor of the organization. The need for specificity in corporate policy statements is echoed in Robert Almeder's discussion of bribes and gifts.

We commonly regard knowledge as a social good and value its dissemination, which raises the question of whether we should allow corporations to protect the information they generate. Robert E. Frederick and Milton Snoeyenbos argue that there is a moral basis for allowing patents and trade secrets, but they also argue that an individual has a right to use *his* skills and knowledge to better himself, and hence the firm has an obligation to make sure that its secrets are legitimate trade secrets. The case study in this section points up the conflict between corporate and individual rights within the context of trade secrets.

Surveys reveal that honesty in communication is a major problem in organizations, and the Von Products case study illustrates communication dilemmas that can arise. James M. Humber argues that employees have a *prima facie* responsibility to tell the truth, and he points out that it is very difficult to justify lying in corporate communications. Humber also discusses conditions under which the liar would legitimately be excused from responsibility for his act. H. B. Fuller's corporate policy statement details specific methods a firm can adopt to keep lines of communication open.

AGENTS' DUTIES

C. G. Luckhardt

Duties of Agent to Principal

Agency is defined as "the fiduciary relation which results from the manifestation of consent by one person to another that the other shall act on his behalf and subject to his control, and consent by the other so to act."[1] The person for whom action is taken is called the principal, and the person who takes the action is called the agent. In order to understand the extent of and rationale for the various duties agents have with regard to their principals, it is important to distinguish and understand four elements of this definition of agency. The first is the concept of acting on behalf of, or for, another. "Acting for another" implies that the agent is a kind of stand-in for the principal, for *were* the principal able to act, there would be no need for him to employ an agent. But since the principal is unable to act, perhaps because of constraints of time or ability, he deputizes another person to act in his place. This suggests that the agent is, in effect, a "mini"-principal, i.e., a person whose own identity is submerged, and who takes on the identity of the principal. Ideally, the agent would be identical with the principal, but obviously this is impossible in practice. As your agent, I cannot have *exactly* the same intentions, thoughts, desires, abilities you have; nor can I make the same decisions as you. But one of the guiding thoughts behind the law of agency is the idea that I should resemble you in as many ways as is relevantly possible. As we shall see, the ramifications of this idea for the duties of agents are vast, and the questions it raises legion. Must the agent, for example, have all of the interests of the principal at heart when he represents him? If not, then what kinds and how many? And if so, does that mean that he must have none of his own? And if he may have his own interests, may these conflict with those of the principal?

A second important element of the definition of agency given above is that of consent. The principal must consent to the agent's acting on his behalf, and the agent must consent to work for the principal. Intuitively, this requirement of an agency relationship is understandable: I can represent your interests only if you want me to, and you can't force me to represent your interests if I don't want to. But plausible though it may be, this requirement is fraught with many legal difficulties. What constitutes consent, for example? How may the principal and the agent manifest their respective consents? Can either consent tacitly, or implicitly? And how may either revoke his consent? The general rule is that failure of the agent to perform his duties will constitute adequate grounds for the principal to revoke his consent, and so the requirement of consent is closely linked with the duties that the agent is determined to have.

A third aspect of this definition of agency is the notion of control. This element gives the principal the right to direct and control the agent's activities. But this means that the agent must be subject to that control, i.e., that he must obey the instructions and directions of the principal. The duty of obedience is, as we shall see, one of the most strictly enforced of all the duties agents bear.

The fourth important aspect of the definition of agency given above is that of a fiduciary relationship. For purposes of understanding the duties agents bear to principals, this is perhaps the most important aspect of agency. In general, a fiduciary relationship is one based on trust, or faith (from the Latin *fidere*), and in the case of agency the legal requirements stemming from this concept extend beyond mere obedience to those of care and loyalty. Even though we may have mutually consented for me to be your agent, the idea here is that you must be able to trust me in order for the relationship to persist. Therefore, if I show through my lack of care or loyalty that I cannot be trusted, you may unilaterally terminate my employment as your agent. In addition you may have further causes of action against me for violating this requirement of trust.

Care, loyalty, and obedience are the three major elements constituting the agent's duties towards his principal. But in the minds of the courts, they have far-reaching connotations and sometimes surprising applications. In what follows we shall examine how these requirements are commonly interpreted and applied.

DUTIES OF CARE AND SKILL

The duties of care and skill arise from the courts' understanding that an agent who is paid for his services is required to act with "standard care and with the skill which is standard in the locality for the kind of work which he is employed to perform."[2] When the agent contracts with the principal, the former is ordinarily presumed to possess the skills standardly required for carrying out his agency. There are two exceptions to this, however. If the agent represents himself as possessing more than standard skills, he can be held liable if he does not possess them. And if the principal knows that the agent does not possess the standard skills, then he may not hold the agent liable for not possessing them. Suppose *P* employs *A* as his attorney to sue *T*. Ordinarily *A* can be held liable only if he does not possess the skills and exercise the care of other attorneys in the locality in which he is employed. But if *A* holds himself out as being a specialist in tax law, for example, then *P* may reasonably expect him to possess the skills and exercise the care of a tax specialist. (These do not, of course, amount to his being expected to win every case he represents.) Conversely, if *P* knows that *A* is not a tax specialist when the latter is hired, he may not expect that *A* should exercise the skills or care of a specialist. An interesting question arises when the agent possesses special skills not known to the principal, but fails to exercise them. Technically speaking, the principal cannot expect the agent to exercise them. Nevertheless, most holdings suggest that the agent may nevertheless be held liable for not exercising such special skills.

Furthermore, agents are under a general obligation to exercise a standard degree of care in their transactions and behavior. In other words, they should not act negligently. If an agent *A* is hired to buy milk-cows for *P* from *T*, and he discovers at the time of delivery that the cows are on the verge of death, normal discretion and care would dictate that he would not go through with the purchase. Failure to exercise such discretion would constitute a violation of his duties.

Nor would a person exercising a standard degree of care attempt to do the impossible or the impracticable. If the agent discovers that he cannot do what he has been told to do, or that it is impracticable to do so, it is his duty not to waste his time and effort (and possibly the prinicpal's money) attempting to do so. Thus if just before he sets out to buy *T*'s cows, *A* discovers that they are dead, he is not only not under a duty to purchase them, but he also has a duty not to continue in his efforts, such as going to *T*'s place of business. The standard that is commonly used in determining whether he should continue his efforts is whether the agent could reasonably expect that the principal wanted him to do so. That is, he is to put himself in what he reasonably views as the principal's shoes. Of course, if he has been able to determine the principal's desires directly, then the agent is under a duty to do just that, even if this means that he continues his best efforts to attain what he, the agent, might regard as impracticable goals.

DUTY TO GIVE INFORMATION

Closely related to the duty of care is the duty to give information. If the agent receives information bearing on the principal's interests, he has a duty to communicate this information to the principal. If *P* instructs *A*, his agent, to sell some real estate to *T*, and *A* meantime acquires the information that *F* would be willing to pay more for the property than *T*, he is obliged to tell this to *P*. Or if the agent is unable to carry out the directions of his principal, because events make it impossible, impracticable, or illegal for him to do so, he should make that known to his principal. In the milk-cow examples above, the agent is also under an obligation to tell the principal that he has not bought the nearly dead or dead cows. Or again, an agent unable to obtain fire insurance for a principal must tell the principal that he has not been able to do so. Otherwise, in addition to being lawfully fired, he may be held liable for the amount of the insurance settlement that the principal might have received for his uninsured goods. The exceptions to this duty occur in cases where the agent has a superior duty to a person other than the principal. Thus, an attorney who acquires confidential information from one client is under no obligation to disclose it to another client whose interests it might affect.

DUTY OF GOOD CONDUCT

The requirements of skill, care, and the giving of information on the part of the agent are all related to actions for which the agent is employed. But the agent may also be held liable for some actions that are clearly outside the ambit of his employment. Thus, the duty of good conduct is usually understood as part of the agent's duty to care for the principal's interests. Actions that bring disrepute upon the principal, although not within the scope of the agent's employment, may be grounds for dismissal. Thus in a famous McCarthy-era case, a Hollywood screenwriter was found to have been legitimately dismissed from his job when he was convicted of contempt of Congress for refusing to answer whether he was a communist.[3] Furthermore, the duty of good conduct requires that the agent not act towards the principal in such a way as to "make continued friendly relations" with him impossible.[4] Insubordination, either in speech or by other means which jeopardize the "friendly relations," may subject an agent to lawful dismissal.

DUTY TO OBEY

All agents have a duty to refrain from knowingly violating the reasonable directions of the principal. This is an essential element of agency, stemming from the requirement of control. If the agent does violate the reasonable instructions of the principal, either as to acts to be performed, or the manner of performing them, he may lose his job and incur liability for any loss his violation has caused the principal. If, however, the principal's directions were unreasonable, then the agent may disobey, and may even have a valid claim against the principal for breach of his employment contract. Unreasonable directions include: (a) those which are illegal, unethical, or (according to a few holdings) contrary to public policy; (b) those which threaten the physical condition of the agent; (c) those which violate the ordinary customs of business with regard to such agency; (d) those which are impossible or impracticable for the agent to carry out; and (e) those which conflict with interests the agent is otherwise privileged to protect, whether such interests be his own or those of a third party. It is not proper for an agent to refuse to carry out orders solely on the grounds that doing so will harm the principal's interests. However, the agent may refuse to obey instructions if he stands directly to lose by doing so. Thus, if A is on salary, he may not refuse to sell P's goods at the price P demands, even if the price is so low that A knows that P will lose money selling them at that rate. If, however, A is working on commission, and knows that such a price will adversely affect his own income, he may refuse to sell at that price. Or, alternatively, if he knows that following the principal's directions will damage his own business reputation, he may refuse to follow them.

In the absence of instructions to the contrary the agent is ordinarily free to carry out the principal's orders in a manner customary to such undertakings. Thus real estate agents are free to advertise their clients' property in newspapers, unless the clients instruct them otherwise. If the principal's instructions are ambiguous and the agent is unable to receive clarification from the principal before the time to act, then his obligation is to act reasonably, in light of the facts of which he is aware.

DUTY TO ACT ONLY AS AUTHORIZED

The duty to obey requires that the agent do what the principal tells him to do. The duty to act only as authorized is the other side of that coin, insofar as it requires the agent not to do what he has been told or should infer that he is not to do, except when he is privileged to protect his own or another's interests. The usual standard that is applied here is that the agent act in accordance with "reasonable customs or, if there are no customs, that he is to use good faith and discretion."[5] Ordinarily, if his actions are based on a misinterpretation of the principal's unambiguous instructions, the agent can be held liable for the costs of his actions. Thus, if A is instructed to buy T's milk-cows, and he buys a bull as well, he may then be held liable to P for its value. Furthermore, the agent may be liable to the principal where he makes a mistake concerning the facts upon which his instructions depend. If P directs A to deliver some goods to T, then A may be liable for the cost of recovery of goods, or for the cost of the goods themselves, if they are delivered to F and cannot be recovered. Factors determining whether an agent is liable for acting mistakenly include "the subject matter of the authorization, the language used in conferring it, the type of agent, and the kind of business done by him."[6]

DUTY OF LOYALTY

The duty to obey is predicated on the view that the agent should not do anything the principal directs him not to do. The duty of loyalty extends beyond the doing of intentionally forbidden acts. It states that the agent has a duty to act solely for the interests of the principal. In its narrowest sense, the duty of loyalty requires that an agent not "act or speak disloyally in matters which are connected with his employment."[7] Outside his employment, however, the agent is not prevented from acting in good faith in a way that might injure his principal's business. Thus the agent for a soft drink company may not use his title as employee of that company, nor the special information he has acquired as an employee of the company, to advocate legislation banning the use of saccharine in soft drinks, when such legislation could harm his company's interests. However, as a citizen he may advocate such legislation, so long as he does not use the information he has acquired as an employee of the company. One important upshot of this rule is that employees are under a duty not to advise the public to buy elsewhere than from their employers, nor are they to suggest that their employers' products are inferior to those of a competitor.

DUTY NOT TO ACQUIRE AN ADVERSE INTEREST

Closely related to the duty of loyalty (and often construed as one element of it) is the duty not to acquire an adverse interest. This requires that an agent not acquire any interest adverse to that of the principal unless the latter agrees that the agent may do so. Thus a buyer for a department store may not acquire an interest in a manufacturing business from which he purchases goods for the store, either directly or through a "straw." Neither may a seller purchase the principal's goods for himself, either directly or through a "straw." To act in either of these ways would put the agent in a position in which he would have an adverse interest: to buy for less insofar as he represents the principal, while at the same time buying for more in terms of self-interest, or selling for more in terms of the principal's interest, while selling for less in terms of his own interest. Such divided interest means that the agent is not being completely loyal to the principal, as the law requires, and it subjects the agent to liability, to discharge from his employment, breach of contract, loss of compensation, as well as tort liability for losses caused and for profits made. If the agent makes his potential adverse interests known to the principal, however, and takes no unfair advantage of him, then the agent is not liable if the principal agrees that he may act in this way.

DUTY NOT TO COMPETE

In addition to acquiring an adverse interest, agents are also required not to compete with their principals, unless the principals consent to it. A real estate agent who represents a seller may not also show his own property to prospective buyers, in competition with that of the seller whom he represents. Nor may he buy property for himself which had originally been sought by the principal. Both of these actions would constitute a breach of duty during the time of the agent's employment. But during this time the agent is free to make plans to compete with the principal at the end of such employment, so long as he does not use confidential information in order to do so. After his employment has ended he may even hire the principal's employees for himself, as well as solicit customers for his competing business.

DUTY TO ACCOUNT FOR PROFITS

The duty to account for profits requires that the agent account for the value of goods received from third parties. Thus, bribes, kickbacks, and gifts to the agent, regardless of whether they are received corruptly, must be forfeited to the principal, even if he incurs no loss by the agent's receiving them. In addition, the principal may hold the agent liable for any harm that may arise because of the bribe or kickback, as well as breach of contract and actions based in tort. The general rule with regard to such matters is that "an agent who, without the knowledge of the principal, receives something in connection with, or because of, a transaction conducted for the principal, has a duty to pay this to the principal."[8] The burden of proving that the value received was not "in connection with, or because of, a transaction conducted for the principal" lies strictly with the agent. This duty has been interpreted to extend even to opportunities for gain which an agent's employment has made possible, such as information acquired in the course of his employment which benefits the agent, even though it causes no harm to the principal.

DUTY OF CONFIDENTIALITY

The duty of confidentiality requires that an agent not use or communicate confidential information for anyone's benefit other than that of the principal. The use of such information, acquired as a result of a person's agency, is prohibited both for the agent's own benefit, as well as for the benefit of third parties, even though the information does not relate to the subject of his agency. Thus a dairy worker who overhears the owner discussing plans to buy adjacent land may not use this information for his own advantage, nor may he disclose it to others for their advantage. Included within this restriction are such matters as "unique business methods of the employer, trade secrets, lists of names, and all other matters which are peculiarly known in the employer's business."[9] After the termination of his employment the agent has a continuing duty not to reveal such information, with the exception of "the names and customers retained in his memory as the result of his work for the principal and also methods of doing business and processes which are but skillful variations of general processes known to the particular trade."[10]

NOTES

1. *Restatement, Second, Agency* § 1.
2. Ibid., § 379.
3. *Twentieth-Century Fox Film Corp.* v. *Lardner*, 216 F.2d 844.
4. *Restatement,* § 380.
5. Ibid., § 383, a.
6. Ibid., § 383, c.
7. Ibid., § 387.
8. Ibid., § 388, a.
9. Ibid., § 395, b.
10. Ibid., § 396, b.

CONFLICT OF INTEREST

Sorrel M. Mathes
G. Clark Thompson

Sorrel M. Mathes
G. Clark Thompson

Inorganic Chemicals Company's Conflict of Interest Policy

GENERAL STATEMENT OF POLICY

The company expects and requires directors, officers, and employees (herein "employees") to be and remain free of interests or relationships and to refrain from acting in ways which are actually or potentially inimical or detrimental to the company's best interests.

APPLICATION OF POLICY

1. *"Conflicts of Interests" Defined*

A conflict of interest exists where an employee

(a) has an outside interest which materially encroaches on time or attention which should be devoted to the company's affairs or so affects the employee's energies as to prevent his devoting his full abilities to the performance of his duties.

From Sorrel M. Mathes and G. Clark Thompson, "Ensuring Ethical Conduct in Business," in *The Conference Board Record* 1, no. 12 (December 1964), p. 22. Reprinted by permission of The Conference Board.

(b) has a direct or indirect interest in or relationship with an outsider such as a supplier (whether of goods or services), jobber, agent, customer, or competitor, or with a person in a position to influence the actions of such outsider, which is inherently unethical or which might be implied or construed to

i. make possible personal gain or favor to the employee involved, his family, or persons having special ties to him, due to the employee's actual or potential power to influence dealings between the company and the outsider,

ii. render the employee partial toward the outsider for personal reasons, or otherwise inhibit the impartiality of the employee's business judgment or his desire to serve only the company's best interests in the performance of his functions as an employee,

iii. place the employee or the company in an equivocal, embarrassing, or ethically questionable position in the eyes of the public, or

iv. reflect on the integrity of the employee or the company.

Practically, conflicts of interests of the types just mentioned are reprehensible to the degree that the authority of the employee's position makes it possible for him to influence the company's dealings with the outsider; thus, for example, the situation of those who buy or sell for the company, or who can influence buying or selling, is particularly sensitive,

(c) has any direct or indirect interest or relationship or acts in a way which is actually or potentially inimical or detrimental to the company's best interests.

2. Examples of Improper Conflicts

There follow a few obvious examples of relationships which probably would run afoul of the foregoing definition, but any relationship covered by the definition is subject to this policy:

(a) Holding an outside position which affects the performance of the employee's work for the company.

(b) Relatively substantial (whether with reference to the enterprise invested in or to the employee's net worth) equity or other investment by the employee or members of his immediate family in a supplier, jobber, agent, customer, or competitor. Under normal circumstances, however, ownership of securities of a publicly held corporation is not likely to create a conflict of interests unless the ownership is so substantial as to give the employee a motive to promote the welfare of that corporation and unless the employee, through his position with the company or otherwise, is able to promote such welfare.

(c) The acquisition of an interest in a farm with which, to the employee's knowledge, the company is carrying on or contemplating negotiations for merger or purchase. In some cases, such an interest may create a conflict even though the interest was acquired prior to the time the company evinced any interest in merger or purchase. Similar considerations are applicable to real estate in which the company contemplates acquiring an interest.

(d) The receipt of remuneration as an employee or consultant of, or the acceptance of loans from, a supplier, jobber, agent, customer, or competitor of the company.

(e) The acceptance by the employee or members of his family from persons or firms having or seeking to have dealings with the company of any cash gifts, or of gifts or entertainment which go beyond common courtesies extended in accordance with accepted business practice or which are of such value as to raise any implication whatsoever of an obligation on the part of the recipient.

(f) Speculative dealing in the company's stock on the basis of information gained in the performance of the employee's duties and not available to the public, or other misuse of information available to or gained by the employee by reason of his employment.

Robert E. Frederick

Conflict of Interest

The employee has legal obligations to the organization he works for via the law of agency. For example, an agent has a "duty to his principal to act solely for the benefit of the principal in all matters concerned with his agency" (*Restatement,* Sec. 385). Again, the agent is barred from acting for individuals whose "interests conflict with those of the principal in matters in which the agent is employed" (*Restatement,* Sec. 394). However, the agent's interests may conflict with those of his principal. Perhaps only the total "organization man" completely identifies his interests with those of his employer, but that individual is a caricature not found in reality. These differing interests can lead to conflicts unless the broad and nonspecific language of the law of agency is clarified by an explicit and detailed work contract between employer and employee.

A conflict of interests in the corporate setting arises when an agent has an interest that influences his judgment in his own behalf or in behalf of a third party, and which is contrary to the principal's interest. The moral and legal basis of conflicts of interest is relatively clear. Via the work contract the agent agrees to further the principal's interest. If the agent acts for himself or a third party in a manner contrary to the principal's interest, he breaks his contract with the principal. Contract breaking is unfair to the principal, and, if generally practiced, would undermine the institution of business, with attendant social disutility. Given the asymmetry in the law of agency, however, which places obligations of loyalty, obedience, and confidentiality on the agent, and given that the employer typically sets the majority of the provisions in the work contract, it seems morally, if not legally, incumbent on the employer to clearly specify in the contract what constitutes a conflict of interest.

In many cases there is little in the way of such specification. An example is (1a) of Inorganic Chemicals' policy, which says that a conflict of interest occurs when an employee "has an outside interest which materially encroaches on time or attention which should be devoted to the company's affairs or so affects the employee's energies as to prevent his devoting his full abilities to the performance of his duties." As it stands, this is rather vague, particularly for the at-will employee whose work contract may not contain an explicit job description and clauses proscribing certain sorts of management directives. Thus, a sales manager might find that his "duty" is to maximize sales—a rather open-ended task. But that manager may have "outside interests," such as family interests and obligations, which may "prevent his devoting his full abilities to the performance of his duties."

We can begin to devise more specific guidelines by dividing employees' outside interests into the broad categories of those that the employer believes do not conflict with his interests, and those the employer believes do conflict with his interests. The latter category is divided into those interests of the employee that the employer *mistakenly* believes are in conflict with his interests, and interests of the employee that the employer *correctly* believes conflict with his. This last category is in turn divided into those areas in which the employer has a *legitimate* claim that the employee modify his activities, and those in which he does *not* have a legitimate claim. Our schema, then, looks like this:

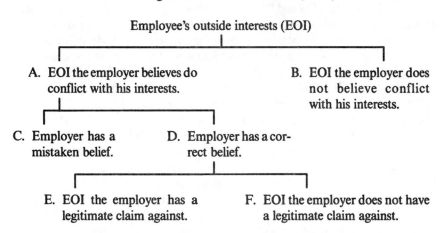

Let us say that Jones is Smith's employee. Then we can give the following examples of the various categories:

B. Jones collects stamps and Smith does not believe Jones's hobby conflicts with his interests. Nevertheless, Smith, in his capacity as Jones's employer, demands that Jones stop collecting stamps.

C. Jones collects stamps, and, for reasons we need not speculate on, Smith mistakenly believes this conflicts with his interests, and demands that Jones stop collecting stamps.

E. Jones is a government civil rights lawyer and in his spare time is an organizer for the local Ku Klux Klan. Smith demands that Jones cease this activity.

F. Jones works for XYZ Publishing Company and in his spare time writes successful novels. Company rules prohibit Jones from publishing at XYZ. Smith correctly believes that Jones's novels detract from XYZ's sales and demands that Jones stop writing novels.

Each of the above examples follows the same pattern: the employee engages in certain outside activities that the employer attempts to interfere with or prevent. Typically, clauses in the work contract, e.g., Inorganic's (1a), give the employer the right to interfere, in some cases, with the employees' outside activities. However, such clauses should not give the employer the right to interfere in all of the employee's outside activities since the employee has legitimate outside interests that are protected by his right to privacy and freedom of action. For instance, example B is a clear case where Jones's rights to privacy and free action are violated by Smith. In order to prevent this sort of abuse the work contract should unequivocally state that employees have legitimate outside interests and that the employer has no right to regulate those interests either by design or suggestion. Another example is employees' interests in and duties to their families. We all know of firms that place undue burdens on employees to the detriment of family life. However, employees are properly interested in their families and have a right to act so as to satisfy those interests. Hence the work contract should not be such that it can be construed as giving the employer the right to interfere in all of the employees' outside activities.

But there are many cases where the interests of the employer and the employee genuinely conflict. And since each has a right, within legal limits, to serve those interests, the work contract should provide some mechanism for determining whose rights prevail in particular instances. Example C is a situation in which Jones's rights to privacy and free action prevail since Smith has no interests that are at stake, although he incorrectly believes he has. Example E is more difficult. In a free society such as ours, individuals have great latitude when engaging in activities that satisfy their interests. Indeed, many people would say that individuals have a right, providing they do not violate the law, to engage in any activity they please as long as it does not result in significant harm to others. Now, Jones has a legal right to organize for the Klan, but even if his outside activity does not impair his job performance, it is highly likely that his activities will severely damage the credibility of the organization for which he works. Thus Smith can legitimately demand that Jones cease this sort of activity. Similar considerations apply to example F, but it seems that in the circumstances in question Jones's rights should prevail rather than Smith's.

The issue of outside interests, then, is relatively clear. In E and F both the employer and the employee have interests that are protected by rights. Each can justify his position by appeal to those rights, but there has to be some determination of whose rights are overriding. There are two ways that work contracts can apply in such cases. First, if the contract specifically prohibits a certain activity, e.g., organizing for the Klan, then by entering into the contract the employee forfeits his right to engage in that activity. If he does so anyway, he breaks the contract and is thereby subject to the appropriate penalty. Second, since the contract cannot possibly deal specifically with all potential conflicts, it should provide a means for settling disputes. I will discuss both of these points more fully in a moment, but first there are some other difficulties with Inorganic's policy that should be noted.

Thus far I have not considered conflicts of interest that occur in the actual work setting. Most of these conflicts should be specifically dealt with by the work contract. But note that 1(c) of Inorganic's policy defines a conflict as any act that is "actually or potentially inimical or detrimental to the company's best interests." If we suppose the company's "best interest" is profit maximization, then in every situation there is only one proper act, and an indefinite number of acts which are, perhaps unbeknown to the agent, "potentially inimical or detrimental" to maximizing profit. If an employee performs an act that does not maximize profit, then, even though he is interested in maximizing profit and believes his act to be in the company's best interest, according to 1(c) there is a conflict of interest. However, it seems more reasonable to describe his act as a performance shortcoming rather than a conflict of interest, since the employee acted in what he believed was the company's interest. If the employee's performance continually exhibits such shortcomings, management has the right to take appropriate measures to correct it, but they cannot justify such measures by an appeal to conflict of interest. Thus, since Inorganic's policy applies to performance shortcomings as well as genuine conflicts of interests, it is too broad to serve as a useful guideline for identifying cases of conflict of interest.

Furthermore, Inorganic's 1(c) states that a conflict arises when an agent has an interest that is "potentially inimical or detrimental to the company's best interests." If an actual conflict arises when an agent's self-interest influences his act contrary to a principal's interest, then a potential conflict arises when an agent has not acted but does have a self-interest or motive contrary to the principal's interest. Now the *Restatement* (Sec. 385) says that an agent has a "duty to his principal to *act* solely for the benefit of the principal," not that he must have no self-interests. Some individuals, after all, are able to place self-interests aside; they do not act on them. So, a potential conflict of interest is not inherently unethical. The issue rests on how the agent acts.

Since the Inorganic policy is typical of corporate policy statements, the foregoing suggests that such policies are often too general and tend to be biased in favor of the organization, particularly where factors such as performance shortcomings can be regarded as conflicts of interest. The remedy would seem to be a list of more specific guidelines covering particular areas where conflicts arise. The hazard with this approach is that the scope of such conflicts is difficult to circumscribe solely with specific guidelines. There will always be exceptions or borderline cases.

This suggests the following strategy: (1) the firm should have a brief, general, but accurate conflict of interest policy statement; (2) it should establish specific guidelines to cover clear-cut interests; (3) it should establish a committee, officer, or procedure to: (a) handle borderline cases, and (b) set policy in new areas by articulating and developing specific guidelines: (4) new policies should be disseminated to employees; (5) employees should be required to consult with the conflict of interest body prior to acting in borderline or new but questionable areas; and (6) the firm should make clear the penalties for violation of corporate policy in conflicts cases.

The following should suffice as a general policy statement covering all conflict of interest cases:

> The law states that employees have a legal obligation to use their best judgment to act solely for the benefit of the company in all job related matters. The law also prohibits employees from acting for individuals (including themselves) and parties whose interests conflict with the firm's interests in matters related to the employee's employment. The company has established guidelines to cover company policy regarding situations in which conflicts of interest frequently arise. Managers have the responsibility to see that their employees understand these guidelines. The company has a Conflict of Interest Board that handles situations not clearly covered by the guidelines. If an employee is in doubt as to whether an act constitutes a conflict, he should consult with the board before he engages in the act. If at any time the company determines that an employee has acted in a way such that he has an interest in his act that influences his judgment in his own behalf or in the behalf of a third party, and which is contrary to the company's interest as spelled out in the following guidelines, the employee will be disciplined as deemed appropriate to the act(s) involved.

Now the key is the list of specifics delineating this policy statement. Fortunately, such specifics can be articulated in the four major areas in which most conflict of interest cases arise: bribes, gifts, external affiliations, and insider information.

Bribes, kickbacks, payoffs, etc., in a competitive context, are immoral for two reasons: (1) Kantian universalization of maxims allowing bribery would undermine the institution of business, which rests on competitive bidding based on price, and (2) although bribes may be advantageous to the few persons involved, they generally have disutility for the vast majority of society's members, and hence rule utilitarian considerations weigh against bribery. Since such practices are also illegal, a firm's conflict of interest policy should be very straightforward:

> Bribes, kickbacks, payoffs, etc., are illegal and immoral; any employee who engages in or encourages others to engage in such acts will be summarily fired and his acts will be reported to the appropriate legal authorities.

Specific, clear-cut policy statements can also be developed regarding gifts and entertainment. In some firms individuals cannot give any gift to, or receive any gift from, another party. Where specific sanctions are listed for violations, one has a clear-cut policy. If gifts are allowed, morally relevant variables can be specified, e.g., data on the value of the gift, the context in which it was given or received, the intent behind giving the gift, and the position of the giver or receiver in the organization. Borderline cases will invariably arise, but these can be handled by (3), (4), (5), and (6) of our suggested strategy for dealing with conflicts. That is, all gifts should be reported to the conflict of interest body in the firm. Consultation with the body should be required before a borderline case or a new but questionable case is acted upon by the gift giver or recipient in the firm. Finally, new guidelines should be disseminated to employees.

A similar strategy applies to external affiliations. Conflicts of interest frequently arise when an employee has a financial interest in another organization with which the firm does business. Such conflicts can be precluded by explicitly forbidding employees to invest in suppliers, distributors, or customers associated with their employer. If investments are allowed they may be limited in a variety of ways (e.g., percentage of stock limits), and the firm may also require disclosure of outside interests. Borderline cases can be handled by the firm's conflict of interest body.

A corporate policy on insider information can also be spelled out more completely than Inorganic's policy. Saying, with 1(c), that a conflict occurs when an employee "has any direct or indirect interest or relationship or acts in a way which is actually or potentially inimical or detrimental to the company's best interests" is simply too general. Employees should know that the law states that insider information must be disclosed to the public before anyone possessing it can trade in or recommend the purchase or sale of the securities involved. Disclosure of insider information should be done in strict accordance with company policy. Insider information is material, nonpublic information; the test of materiality being that the information itself would affect investment decisions of investors and, if generally known, affect the price of the security. The following have been held by the courts to involve insider information based investment decisions: (a) dividend change, (b) indication of a new discovery or product, (c) corporate projections indicating a change in rate of earnings, (d) a sharp drop in earnings, (e) a sharply downward revised projection of earnings, and (f) significant unexpected losses. Finally, if there is any question about whether an item is insider information, the company's Conflict of Interest Board should be consulted prior to acting on the information.

It should be stressed that each firm will have to articulate its own specific guidelines. For example, a privately held firm may not need a policy on insider information, and a bank may want to have very specific guidelines regarding lending officers who might have a personal financial interest in a business that makes loans with the bank. All in all, however, the strategy I have developed promises to diminish the conflict of interest problem if a firm is serious about its implementation.

GIFTS AND ENTERTAINMENT

Corporate Gift-Giving

Priority Parts, Inc. is a mid-sized corporation engaged in the manufacture of rivets, bolts, clamps, screws, latches, and other metal-fastening mechanisms. Early in 1990, Priority Parts was taken over by a much larger corporation, Universal Motors and Electric, Inc. (UME). Immediately after the takeover, UME replaced many of Priority's top-level managers, but retained others. Ronald Frump, Head of Purchasing, and Tim Pakker, Sales Manager, were among those retained.

Until the takeover by UME, Priority Parts had no corporate policy on gift giving. However, UME had a policy, and in less than a week after UME's acquisition of Priority, both Pakker and Frump received a copy of a memo which read, in part:

> No employee of Priority Parts shall (1) *offer* gifts, favors, gratuities, meals, or entertainment to others at company expense, or (2) *accept* gifts, favors, gratuities, meals, or entertainment from persons with whom they are doing business, unless the following three conditions are met. First, the offer (or acceptance) must be public, consistent with generally accepted business prac- tices, and in accord with society's prevailing moral standards. Second, the value of the goods given (or received) must be small enough that the goods cannot reasonably be viewed as a bribe, kickback, or payoff. Third, all transfers of goods must be such that public knowledge of those transfers will not prove embarrassing to the company.

When Pakker received the company's memo on gift giving, he felt worried. For one thing, when UME took over Priority it created a new position— Assistant Sales Manager—and filled that position with a bright and extremely ambitious young man named Ed Rabbitt. Pakker felt that Rabbitt wanted his job, and with the new top-level management at Priority, Pakker did not feel secure in his position. Pakker knew that he had been retained at Priority after the UME acquisition because of his many sales contacts. However, in a year or two Rabbitt would be familiar with most of those contacts, and Pakker's advantage over Rabbitt would be nullified. Furthermore, if Pakker somehow embarrassed Priority by violating the directives spelled out in the company's memo on gift giving, this might give Rabbitt the edge he needed to oust Pakker and take over his job as Sales Manager.

Feeling that his position at Priority was precarious, Pakker resolved to adhere strictly to the company's guidelines on gift giving. However, the more Pakker studied the memo he had received, the more confused he became. What *exactly* was prohibited by the company's new policy, and what *exactly* was permitted? Pakker was not sure, for he found the company's memo to be extremely unclear. In the end, Pakker decided that he needed help in interpreting Priority's new policy. Pakker knew that his long-time friend, Ronald Frump, had received a copy of the gift-giving memo; thus, he called Frump and arranged with him to discuss the issue over lunch.

When Pakker and Frump got together for lunch, Pakker soon discovered that Frump was as confused by the memo as he was. Frump said that he rarely received gifts that were valuable; but as it happened, just two weeks earlier he had been given something which was worth a fairly substantial sum. After receiving the company's memo on the receipt of gifts, Frump now wondered whether he should keep what he had been given. He related several facts to Pakker, and then asked for his opinion on the subject. The facts were as follows.

For over ten years Priority Parts sold all of its scrap metal to Triple S Salvage, Inc. Throughout the ten-year period, Frump's contact at Triple S was Tom Toonces. Over the years Frump and Toonces became close friends— they had family picnics together, played tennis together, etc. Recently, Toonces had a falling out with his co-workers at Triple S; as a result, Toonces left the company to take a new job out of state. When Toonces left he gave Frump his season tickets for the local professional football team. Toonces said that Triple S had given many of its executives tickets earlier in the year, and that he had been one of those receiving tickets. Toonces chose to give Frump his tickets because the two were close friends, and Toonces knew that Frump was an avid football fan. Also, Toonces was still angry at the people at Triple S, and he refused to give the tickets to anyone who worked at that company.

Frump told Pakker that he wanted to keep the football tickets. To be sure, the tickets were worth hundreds of dollars. However, the tickets were given to Frump by Toonces personally, and not by Toonces acting as a representative of Triple S. Also, Toonces was going out of state and it was extremely unlikely that he and Frump would be doing business in the future. How, then, could the tickets be viewed as a bribe? Furthermore, Frump pointed out that the tickets had to be classified as a *public* gift, for as soon as Frump attended a football game he'd be sitting among Triple S executives who also had been given season tickets.

When Frump asked for Pakker's view on the subject of the football tickets, he was disappointed by Pakker's response. Pakker advised Frump to return the tickets to Toonces because keeping them could place Frump in a compromising position. Each year Frump examined bids from various salvage companies to determine which firm would purchase Priority's scrap. What would happen, Pakker said, if, in the upcoming year, some company other than Triple S were to submit the high bid for Priority's scrap? If Frump awarded the contract to that company, might not the personnel at Triple S conclude that Toonces had given Frump the football tickets as an incentive to *stop* doing business with Triple S? And what if someone at Triple S were to voice such an opinion to top management at Priority? Even if the charge were wholly untrue, Priority Parts would be put in an embarrassing position.

Frump thought about Pakker's advice, but in the end decided to reject it. So far as Frump was concerned, Pakker was overly cautious because he had Ed Rabbitt breathing down his neck, seeking to usurp his job. Further, Frump was honestly convinced that the football tickets were a *personal* gift, given to him by a close friend, and that the tickets had nothing whatsoever to do with business. Also, Frump was sure that the tickets would have no influence on him when he awarded contracts for the sale of Priority's scrap; thus, he resolved to keep the tickets.

Apart from his questions concerning the football tickets, Frump raised one other issue for discussion with Pakker. Virtually all of the gifts Frump received were given to him at his office by salespersons. However, each year Frump was given a Christmas turkey and four bottles of domestic champagne by the chief sales representative at Bestwest Steel. The gifts invariably were delivered to Frump's house rather than to his office. Because the gifts were sent to his home, it was unlikely that anyone at Priority knew that he received them. However, Frump never tried to keep the receipt of these gifts secret; everyone in his family knew that the gifts came from Bestwest Steel. Were the gifts publicly received? Frump was not sure, and neither was Pakker. After some discussion, Pakker and Frump decided that the best course of action would be for Frump to inform people in his office whenever he received a gift at home. This could be done informally. For example, when Frump received his traditional gifts from Bestwest, he could make a point of mentioning to several of his co-workers and secretaries that he was happy to receive the turkey and champagne from the sales personnel at Bestwest Steel, because these gifts came in handy at Christmas.

Like Frump, Pakker had two questions relating to the memo on gift giving. First, Pakker had directed his sales personnel at Priority to give small gifts—pocket protectors, plastic pens, key chains, etc.—to all customers at other firms. All these gifts were embossed with Priority's *logo,* and all were imprinted with the company's name, address, and telephone number. Pakker had always viewed these gifts as advertisements, and assumed that any gift that had the company's name, address, and phone number on it was properly classified as an advertisement. Now, however, Pakker was beginning to have doubts. In the previous year, for example, Pakker noticed that Priority Parts had been doing business with China-Cabinets, Inc. for ten years. To commemorate the occasion, Pakker gave the purchasing agent at China-Cabinets a gift of two gold-plated pens. The pens were inset with diamond chips and set in a marble base. The base had a brass plate on which Pakker had engraved the names of both companies, together with the phrase, "1980–1990: A Decade of Togetherness." When Pakker gave the pen set to the purchasing agent at China-Cabinet, he thought of it as an ingenious advertisement. However, the pens cost almost $500. Was that sum so large that the set could "reasonably be viewed" as a bribe, kickback, or payoff rather than as an advertisement? Pakker was not sure, and he asked Frump for his opinion.

Frump took no time in responding to Pakker. So far as Frump was concerned, *anything* that had a company's name, address, and phone number permanently attached to it was an advertisement, and this held true regardless of the value of the object being given or received. On the other hand, Frump told Pakker that he would not classify the pen set as an advertisement, because the pens had nothing engraved on them, and they were able to be separated from their base and used in non-business contexts. At the same time, Frump was not sure whether the pens were valuable enough to be "reasonably" viewed as a bribe, kickback, or payoff. Frump thought that the memo's guideline on this issue was hopelessly vague because different people could be influenced by different amounts—one person might be swayed to do something wrong for $500, while another might not do the same thing for $5,000.

After thinking the matter over, Pakker decided that he would adopt a "play it safe" attitude and no longer give any gifts on behalf of the company that were worth more than $50. Frump, on the other hand, refused to set any specific limit on the value of gifts he would accept. He said that he would evaluate each gift individually, and reject those which he felt were sufficiently large to have an influence upon the objectivity of his decision making.

Pakker's final difficulty with the gift-giving memo concerned those portions of the memo that dealt with "accepted business practices" and "prevailing moral standards." What, Pakker asked Frump, was an "accepted" business practice? And how was he to determine society's "prevailing" moral standards? To illustrate his point, Pakker used two examples. The first concerned his dealings with a former business associate, Brooks Brothers. For years Pakker and Brothers did business together, and over the years they had formed a close friendship. In 1988, Brothers retired. Still, Pakker and Brothers got together occasionally for lunch or golf, and whenever they did get together Pakker treated Brothers at company expense. The Pakker-Brothers gatherings were purely for fun and reliving old times; business was never discussed. Now, Pakker asked, was this an "accepted" business practice? In one sense it was, for every salesperson Pakker had ever known had, at one time or another, used his or her expense account to pay for non-business-related expenses. Top-level management knew this sort of thing went on, but, as long as expenses of this kind occurred infrequently and were kept to a minimum, management tended to wink at the practice. Still, the company's official position was that expense accounts were for business-related expenses only. In this sense, then, Pakker's actions could not be classified as an "accepted" business practice.

Pakker's second example concerned his biggest account, Bluejay Aircraft, Inc. Bluejay's corporate headquarters was in Cincinnati, and Pakker's contact at Bluejay was Dion Y. Sius. Whenever Pakker was in Cincinnati to do business with Bluejay, Sius insisted that Pakker not take him out to dinner at company expense, but rather use his expense account to finance a trip to some of Kentucky's best strip bars—establishments such as the Leopard's Lair and the Kitty Kat Lounge. Places such as these were outlawed in Cincinnati, though they were perfectly legal in Kentucky. When Pakker next did business with Sius, should he consider society's prevailing moral standards to be those established in Cincinnati, or those accepted in Kentucky? Indeed, should he look to the law at all? After all, though nude dancing was legal in Kentucky, this did not prove that it was commonly thought to be moral. In fact, the majority of Kentucky's citizens might well believe that the voyeurism and exhibitionism which occurred in nude dancing establishments was perverted and immoral.

When Pakker asked for Frump's opinion concerning his activities with Brothers and Sius, Frump said that he thought Priority's management was not so much interested in morality as in maximizing profits and strengthening Priority's position in the market. This being the case, he felt that Pakker would be treading on dangerous ground if he continued to use company funds to pay for Brothers' lunches and greens fees. On the other hand, if using company funds at Kentucky's strip joints was necessary to secure lucrative contacts with Bluejay Aircraft, Pakker should continue that practice. After all, Pakker was doing nothing illegal. How, then, could his actions embarrass Priority Parts?

After some thought, Pakker concluded that Frump's advice was sound. In the future, he would take "generally accepted business practices" to mean "practices which are officially sanctioned by the company," and not "commonly practiced business activities." Further, when considering the morality of his use of his corporate expense account, his only concern would be to obey the law in the jurisdiction where he was operating; he would not try to determine society's shared moral beliefs, or to adhere to those moral standards.

For Discussion

When Pakker and Frump reach different conclusions concerning gift giving, whose view do you think is closer to being correct? Explain why you believe as you do. When Pakker and Frump reach the same conclusion, do you agree with their position? Explain why you accept or reject their view. Many of the problems faced by Pakker and Frump arise because of vagueness and unclarity present in Priority Parts' gift-giving memo. Can you think of ways to reword the memo so as to eliminate, or at least reduce, that vagueness and unclarity?

Robert Almeder

Morality and Gift-Giving

A bribe is the offering of some good, service, or money to an appropriate person for the purpose of securing a privileged and favorable consideration (or purchase) of one's product or corporate project. Typically, but not necessarily, the person offering the bribe does so in secret and only when the person receiving the bribe antecedently agrees (either explicitly or implicitly) to accept the bribe under the conditions indicated by the briber. Understandably, the briber's business posture is enhanced by the successful bribe and it would not be otherwise enhanced, because, presumably, without the bribe the briber's product or project would not merit any special consideration as against the product or projects of the briber's competitors.[1]

For various reasons, few people in the business community are willing to defend the morality of the practice of bribery. Most people in the business community see the practice of bribery as one that, if adopted on a wide-scale basis, tends to undermine a free, competitive, and open economy by encouraging a lack of real competition for quality products. After all, where bribery is an acceptable practice, the briber (or the company with the biggest bribe) gains unfair advantage because the briber's product secures preferential treatment not based upon the merits or price of the product. Even at its best, the practice of bribery, *as a rule,* tends to undermine open competition along with the usual efficiencies and quality-of-goods characteristic of the open economy. Thus, what is basically wrong with bribery is that, *as a rule,* it strikes at the heart of capitalism by undermining a free and strenuously competitive economy.

I would like to thank James Humber for his comments on an earlier draft of this paper.

If capitalism is to survive as the best of economic systems, it can do so only where there is earnest and open competition.

The practice of bribery can also be faulted for the reason that the briber violates the golden rule because the briber, presumably, would not want his product discriminated against for reasons that had nothing to do with the quality of his product.

But what about the practice of giving gifts to persons with whom one is doing business? Is gift-giving of this sort a clear case of bribery? If it is, then for the reasons just mentioned it, like bribery, should be considered immoral. In other words, if one gives a gift in order to secure a business advantage that would not otherwise occur, and if in the typical case the person receiving the gift accepts it under the conditions indicated by the giver, then this act of gift-giving is in fact a bribe and should be considered a bribe. Many businessmen, however, do not see *all* gift-giving to one's clients as a clear case of bribery. They see nothing wrong with the practice of gift-giving if it is done under certain circumstances.

Those who favor some form of gift-giving in the marketplace do so because they think such a practice, unlike bribery, need not be an instance of deliberately intending to secure a decision that enhances one's business posture. A salesman, for example, may or may not intend his gift as a bribe. He may give a gift not for any special treatment, but only for fair treatment, or to insure equal treatment. He may even give the gift simply because in the years of doing business with someone he has become genuinely friendly with the person who just happens to be able to enhance the salesman's business posture and profit.

In response to this last line of reasoning, however, others are quick to note that what is wrong with bribery is not simply that those who offer bribes do so with the *intent* of securing special treatment, although certainly they do so. Rather, what is essentially wrong with bribery is that the practice has the effect of influencing the judgments of the bribed to provide special treatment not based on the merits or price of the product. This same effect can occur even when one merely offers a gift, that is, provides a service without intending or wishing that that service secure special treatment for the gift-giver. The person who receives the gift may, consciously or otherwise, be disposed predictably to favor the interests of the gift-giver. All that is needed to move a gift into the category of a bribe is that (a) the person receiving the gift be in a position to make a decision that enhances the assets of the giver and (b) the gift be of such a nontoken nature that it is reasonable to think that it may put the interests of the giver in a privileged status even when all else is equal.

As a result of these last considerations some corporations have in the past allowed gift-giving to their clients, or potential clients, only under the conditions that (a) the gift is not substantial enough to put the receiver into a conflict of interest position, and (b) the gift is given publicly and is not in any way a secret offering. Although these conditions seem sound in light of the reflections noted above, still we need to answer the question "Under what circumstances, if any, does an employee have a proportionate reason for running the risks involved in accepting gifts?" In answering this last question, Thomas Garrett urges that the basic question to be asked with regard to the practice of gift-giving is this: "Will this gift, entertainment or service cause any reasonable person to suspect my independence of judgment?"[2] Garrett goes on to urge that it should

> be clear that infrequent gifts of only a nominal cost, ten dollars or less, and small advertisement gifts will be acceptable by policy or law. On the other hand, practically any cash gift is liable to raise eyebrows and create a suspicion of bias.[3]

These same considerations would, presumably, apply with respect to entertainment. In other words, if the cost of entertainment is nominal, public, customary, and infrequent, there would be nothing morally wrong with the practice if it could not hamper the independence of the judgment of the person gifted or entertained. So, then, as Garrett would have it, if the gift is nominal, publicly given, and not intended to secure any special advantage, the practice of gift-giving would seem to be acceptable.

In spite of the sweet reasonableness of Garrett's conclusion, however, some people still think that even a nominal gift could, all else being equal, secure an advantage not merited in terms of quality or price of product. Even an annual gift of $10 (or its equivalent in goods or services) has the *potential* for securing an advantage for the giver, an advantage not merited by the quality or price of the product. Accordingly, even though Garrett's proposal seems quite sensible, any gift, depending on the nature of the receiver and the circumstances involved *could* have the effect of a bribe, even when the gift is nominal and public.

Given these last reasons, it would appear that the only safe moral position to adopt is the one that prohibits *all* gift-giving between corporate representatives and those with whom they would do business. In this latter regard, it is interesting to note that in a survey conducted by the Conference Board in 1964, most of the corporations surveyed were moving strongly in the direction of adopting policy statements prohibiting *all* gift-giving, even of the most nominal kind.[4] Only a few companies allowed, *officially,* small gifts provided the cost did not exceed $25 and did not occur more than three times annually. And, of course, some companies (perhaps too many) had perfectly ambiguous policy statements that provided no clear direction except to indicate that one should be "reasonable" and not do anything such that were it publicly disclosed it would embarrass the company.

In the end, the wisest policy to adopt would seem to be one of complete prohibition of any gift-giving between companies (and their representatives) and persons with whom companies do (or wish to do) business either directly or indirectly.

NOTES

1. Usually, but not necessarily, people are bribed not to do their job. We seldom talk about bribing someone to do his or her job rather than bribing them not to do their job. Still, it is possible to bribe somebody to do his or her job *faster* (thereby securing the briber a special advantage) than he might otherwise do it.

2. Thomas Garrett, *Business Ethics,* (New York: Appleton-Century Crofts, 1966), p. 78.

3. Ibid., p. 79.

4. *The Conference Board Record* 1, no. 12 (December 1964): 17–27.

Corporate Policy Statements

No company employee shall *ask for* or *accept* (directly or indirectly) payments, gifts, favors, or meals and entertainment (except as customary in the trade) from a . . . government official, government employee, or any other person in consideration for assistance or influence, or upon the representation that such assistance or influence has been or will be rendered, in connection with a purchase or any other transaction affecting the company. No company employee shall *offer* or *give* (directly or indirectly) payments, gifts, or favors (except as customary in the trade) to . . . a government official, government employee, or any other person in consideration for assistance or influence, or upon the representation that such assistance or influence has been or will be rendered, in connection with a sale or any other transaction affecting the company. Acceptance or giving of gifts must be limited to incidentals which are obviously a custom of the trade, are acceptable as items of insignificant value, or in no way would cause the company to be embarrassed or obligated. Gifts which do not fit in these categories must be returned. If return of a gift is not practicable because of its nature, it may be given to a charitable institution and the supplier informed of its disposition.

Honeywell

Gifts, favors, and entertainment may be given to others at company expense only if they meet *all* of the following criteria: (a) they are consistent with accepted business practices, (b) they are of sufficiently limited value, and in a form that will not be construed as a bribe or payoff, (c) they are not in contravention of applicable law and generally accepted ethical standards, and (d) public

133

disclosure of the facts will not embarrass the company. Secret commissions or other compensation to employees of customers (or their family members or associates) are contrary to company policy.

E. I. DuPont de Nemours & Co.

No IBM employee, or any member of his or her immediate family, can accept gratuities or gifts of money from a supplier, customer, or anyone in a business relationship. Nor can they accept a gift or consideration that could be perceived as having been offered because of the business relationship. "Perceived" simply means this: If you read about it in your local newspaper, would you wonder whether the gift just might have something to do with a business relationship? No IBM employee can give money or a gift of significant value to a supplier if it could reasonably be viewed as being done to gain a business advantage. If you are offered money or a gift of some value by a supplier or if one arrives at your home or office, let your manager know immediately. If the gift is perishable, your manager will arrange to donate it to a local charitable organization. Otherwise, it should be returned to the supplier. Whatever the circumstances, you or your manager should write the supplier a letter, explaining IBM's guidelines on the subject of gifts and gratuities. Of course, it is an accepted practice to talk business over a meal. So it is perfectly all right to occasionally allow a supplier or customer to pick up the check. Similarly, it frequently is necessary for a supplier, including IBM, to provide education and executive briefings for customers. It's all right to accept or provide some services in connection with this kind of activity—services such as transportation, food, or lodging. For instance, transportation in IBM or supplier planes to and from company locations, and lodging and food at company facilities are all right.

IBM

Gifts: Federal law restricts the extent of the deductibility of gifts to non-government clients, prospects, or suppliers to an amount not exceeding $25 per year to any individual. ARA strongly discourages gifts in excess of $25 per year to any individual, but in the event a gift is proposed to be made in excess of $25, approval must be secured in advance from both the General Counsel and the most senior Management Committee member to whom the operating component involved ultimately reports. Any gifts given must meet the following criteria: (a) gifts in the form of cash, stocks, bonds (or similar types of items) shall not be given regardless of amount; (b) gifts are in accord with normally accepted business practices, and comply with the policies of the organization employing the recipient; (c) such a practice would be considered legal and in accord with generally acceptable ethical practices in all governing jurisdictions; (d) subsequent public disclosure of all facts would not be embarrassing to ARA. *Entertainment:* Where entertainment of a nongovernment client, prospect, or supplier is involved, lavish expenditures are to be avoided. The cost and nature of the entertainment should be planned and carried out in a way which appropriately and reasonably furthers the conduct of the business of ARA. This, of course, does not mean that employees of prospective nongovernment clients may not be transported to, shown, and served at comparable service installations as part of the normal sales effort, at ARA expense.

ARA Services

TRADE SECRETS AND PATENTS

Case Study

Trade Secrets at Atlas Chemical Corp.

Rudy Kern joined Atlas Chemical just after obtaining his master's degree in chemical engineering from Purdue University in 1976. His thesis was on the catalysis of heavy metal-chlorine reactions, and he was hired by Atlas to work on a chloride process for the production of titanium dioxide, TiO_2, an important ingredient in paints and paper. Kern took the position for several reasons. First, the job was based squarely on his area of expertise. Second, Kern was a born tinkerer; he wanted to get out of the laboratory and into the solving of large-scale production problems. Finally, he saw a good promotion opportunity in that the TiO_2-chloride process was relatively new; as Atlas moved from the research stage to production some of the technical staff had a good chance to move into management slots.

Atlas encountered major problems in scaling up its TiO_2 process. It had begun experimental work in 1971, but did not get its first small plant into production until 1986, and it wasn't until 1991 that the firm's TiO_2 project broke even. From 1976 on, Kern was the major innovator in the project's development. He was responsible for most of the breakthroughs that enabled Atlas to move from the pilot-plant stage to full-scale production. Kern received excellent performance evaluations, above average salary increases, and by 1984 he applied for a management position, but was rejected on the grounds that he was too valuable as an engineer. Management explained that he was the only person aware of all the TiO_2 production technology and that he was needed on the plant floor. Kern did receive a significant raise that put him just a notch below the plant's manager on Atlas's pay scale, and he was titled Master Engineer, the top engineering title at Atlas. Nevertheless, by 1991, Kern was dissatisfied with his position at Atlas. He could see that from here on the project would be a moneymaker for Atlas. Most of the bugs had been worked out of the process, which didn't leave Kern with much to do that was not routine. It didn't look like Kern would make the management ranks. As Kern saw it, his career had plateaued at Atlas. He began to read engineering publications with an eye on the help-wanted ads.

Finding a position with another firm was more difficult than Kern initially envisaged. He was narrowly specialized in a particular field of chloride chemistry, and furthermore, Atlas was the only firm using a chloride process to produce TiO_2; other firms used a sulfate process. This made it very difficult for Kern to utilize his skills for another TiO_2 producer. The fact that his expertise was narrowly based and highly technical seemed to preclude him from finding a new position.

In early 1991, however, Kern noticed the following ad:

Major, innovative, chemical firm seeks experienced TiO_2 process engineer. Excellent opportunity for a person presently at the senior process engineering or plant production foreman level. Must have extensive TiO_2 production process experience. Salary open. Title: Plant Engineer, Technical Services. Equal Opportunity Employer.

Kern applied, and soon was contacted by Vulcan Chemical Corporation, which informed him that it was interested in interviewing him, since it was planning to use a chloride process to produce TiO_2. Prior to the interview, however, and prior to contact with any Vulcan representatives, Vulcan asked Kern to sign and mail an agreement pledging that he would "not disclose to Vulcan Chemical Corp., either during pre-employment contacts or in the course of any subsequent employment with Vulcan, any information that I know to be the proprietary information, data, or trade secrets of any third party." Once Kern complied with the request, he was interviewed by Vulcan and got the job. He received a 25 percent salary boost, and a promise that he would be considered for a management position as the project developed.

When Atlas learned of Kern's plan to join Vulcan, it already knew of Vulcan's strategy to develop a TiO_2-chloride process. It immediately went to the State Court in New Jersey and obtained a restraining order blocking Kern from working for Vulcan in the TiO_2 position.

In subsequent court proceedings, Atlas allowed that there was nothing mysterious or secret about TiO_2 itself; any physical chemist could accurately enumerate its characteristics. Basically it is a white powder that has a high capacity for scattering light, and is hence opaque. This accounts for its ability to impart whiteness (or opacity) to paint, paper, rubber, etc.

About 92 percent of world TiO_2 production of roughly 3 million tons is produced by the sulfate process, which begins by dissolving titanium ore in sulfuric acid. The process is relatively uncomplicated, but it does use a lot of sulfuric acid, and it contaminates the acid to the extent that much of it cannot be recycled readily. The sulfate process leaves its producer a significant disposal problem, a distinct disadvantage in a highly competitive context and an era of environmental concern. The chlorine process involves simple chemistry. Titanium ore is reacted with chlorine to produce titanium tetrachloride, which is then oxidized to produce TiO_2 and chlorine. The advantage of the chlorine process is that chlorine, one of the initial reactants, can be recovered in relatively pure form and reused. Although any high school science student would understand the basic chemical reaction of the chlorine process, the production process is technologically complex. The oxidation of titanium tetrachloride must be accomplished at 2200° F, at which temperature the tetrachloride is very corrosive. Furthermore, a complex catalyzing procedure must be employed to optimize reaction time. It had taken Atlas almost twenty years to work out the technical problems in its TiO_2 process.

Atlas is at present the only producer of TiO_2 via the chloride process. It produces 88 percent of TiO_2 worldwide. It started work on the process in 1971, along with three other firms, but Atlas was the only firm to move beyond the pilot plant to production. It began producing TiO_2 commercially via the process in 1986, encountered numerous problems, and only started to realize a profit on the process in 1991. Atlas calculates its research and development expenses for the process to be $42 million over twenty years. The process is reliably estimated to have a lower operating cost than the sulfate process.

In court proceedings, Atlas stated that its TiO_2 process was based on trade secrets. It maintained that none of its trade secrets were patentable; its success was based on innumerable tricks of the trade that would be readily understood by any process engineer but which were based on extensive trial and error research that would be very difficult to duplicate in total. Atlas stated that Kern had developed most of these secrets and that he knew more about them than anyone else in the firm. Atlas made available its Trade Secret Policy Statement, which all employees are required to read and sign in agreement. The policy requires that employees not disclose Atlas's trade secrets or use them for their own or others' advantage either while at Atlas or after they leave the company. Atlas also said that it requires each scientist to record his discoveries and sign a document stating that the discoveries so recorded were the sole property of Atlas. Furthermore, Atlas indicated that it has a policy to restrict access to research data. As its top engineer, Kern had to have access to all such data, but Atlas claimed that Kern was the only scientist with access to all its TiO_2 trade-secret research data irrespective of who developed the data. Atlas argued that it would be impossible for Kern, as Plant Engineer for Vulcan's TiO_2 project, to serve without making use of Atlas's extensive trade secrets. Atlas also pointed to its heavy research and development expense over many years, and the fact that it only recently had begun to cover these costs. Atlas admitted that sooner or later someone would solve the complex production problems and develop a similar chloride process to make TiO_2. But, having spent $42 million to develop its process, Atlas argued that it should be allowed to keep any competitor from solving the difficult engineering problems by illegitimately securing Atlas's trade secrets.

In its memorandum to the court, Vulcan declared that it had invented its own chloride process and now wanted to move to the pilot plant stage and then to production. Its new process, it asserted, was a trade secret. It added that it in no way was seeking, and would not seek, Atlas's trade secrets. Atlas responded by saying the basic chemistry has to be essentially the same, hence, Kern would almost of necessity encounter the same or very similar scale-up problems he had already encountered and solved at Atlas.

In Kern's memorandum to the court, he acknowledged that Atlas had legitimate trade secrets in the TiO_2 area and that he knew the secrets, but he claimed he would not disclose or use such information. Vulcan, he stated, had not asked him to reveal Atlas's secrets, and he fully intended to abide by the document Vulcan asked him to sign saying he would safeguard Atlas's secrets. He noted that he had never signed a covenant with Atlas not to work with a competitor if he left Atlas. He asked the court to remember that Atlas was not alleging that he used Atlas's secrets, or that he took or copied Atlas's documents, or in any way actually violated Atlas's confidentiality. He reminded the court of his narrow background in TiO_2 chemistry, noted that Atlas and Vulcan were the only two firms currently experimenting with the chloride process, and argued that he had a legitimate right to change jobs and attempt to better himself as long as he did not violate his confidentiality pledge to Atlas.

In response, Atlas claimed the issue was not whether Kern intended to disclose or use Atlas's trade secrets, but, rather, whether he could avoid doing so. Atlas claimed that even if Kern had the best of intentions, the processes would be so similar that it would strain credulity to believe that Kern would: (1) not indicate to his employees when they were going into a blind alley, (2) fail to in fact point his employees down the trail that Atlas had successfully pursued, and hence (3) reveal Atlas's trade secrets. As project engineer for Vulcan, Kern's task is to maximize production efficiency. Since Kern had already attained that end for Atlas via its trade secrets, Atlas asked how Kern could do the same for Vulcan without violating Atlas's trade secrets.

For Discussion

In your opinion is Atlas legally entitled to bar Kern from working as TiO_2 project enigineer for Vulcan? Why or why not? Is Kern morally justified in accepting the position at Vulcan? Why or why not? Is Vulcan morally justified in hiring Kern? Why or why not?

Robert E. Frederick
Milton Snoeyenbos

Trade Secrets, Patents, and Morality

Suppose that company M develops a super-computer that gives it a competitive advantage, but decides that, rather than marketing it, it will use the computer to provide services to users. In doing so, it keeps its technical information secret. If another company, N, were to steal the computer, N would be subject to moral blame as well as legal penalty. But suppose that, without M's consent, N obtained M's technical information, which thereby enabled N to copy M's computer. Should N then be subject to moral blame and legal penalty?

At first glance it seems that N should be held morally and legally accountable; but N has a line of defense which supports its position. Information, or knowledge, unlike a physical asset, can be possessed by more than one individual or firm at any one time. Thus, in obtaining M's information N did not diminish M's information; since M possesses exactly the same information it had before, N cannot be said to have stolen it. Furthermore, everyone regards the dissemination of knowledge as a good thing; it has obvious social utility. M's competitive advantage, moreover, was not a good thing, since it could have enabled M to drive other firms out of the computer service business; M might have established a monopoly. Thus, M has no right to keep the information to itself, and, in the interests of social utility, N had a right to obtain M's information. Hence, N should be praised rather than blamed for its act.

This defense of N raises the general question of whether a firm's use of trade secrets or patents to protect information is justifiable. If it is not, then N may at least be morally justified in using clandestine means to obtain M's information. If there is a justification for allowing trade secrets and patents, then, not only is N's act unjustifiable, but we also have a basis for saying that the release of certain information in certain contexts to N by an employee of M is unjustifiable. In this paper we argue that there are both consequentialist and nonconsequentialist reasons for allowing firms to protect *their* proprietary information via patents and trade secrets. On the other hand, an individual has a right to liberty and a right to use *his* knowledge and skills to better himself. These rights place certain constraints on what can qualify as a trade secret or patentable item of information. We begin with a discussion of present patent and trade secret law.

Patents differ significantly from trade secrets. A patent provides a legal safeguard of certain information itself, but the information must be novel. Some internal information generated by a firm may not meet the U.S. Patent Office's standards of inventiveness. Then, too, even if an item is patentable, there may be disadvantages to the firm in seeking and securing a patent on it and/or advantages to the firm in just trying to keep the information secret. There are legal costs in securing a patent, and patents have to be secured in every country in which one wishes to protect the information. In the U.S. a patent expires in 17 years, and, since it is not renewable, the information then becomes public domain. Furthermore, since a patent is a public document, it both reveals research directions and encourages competitors to invent related products that are just dissimilar enough to avoid a patent infringement suit. So there are ample reasons for a firm to keep information secret and not attempt to secure a patent. If a firm can keep the information secret, it may have a long-term advantage over competitors. The disadvantage is that, unlike a patented device or information, the law provides no protection for a trade secret itself. A competitor can analyze an unpatented product in any way, and, if it discovers the trade secret, it is free to use that information or product. For example, if a firm analyzes Coca-Cola and uncovers the secret formula, it can market a product chemically identical to it, although, of course, it cannot use the name "Coca-Cola," since that is protected by trademark law.

It is, however, unlawful to employ "improper means" to secure another's trade secret. Legal protection of trade secrets is based on the agent's duty of confidentiality. Section 395 of the *Restatement of Agency* imposes a duty on the agent "not to use or communicate information confidentially given to him by the principal or acquired by him during the course of or on account of his agency . . . to the injury of the principal, on his own account or on behalf of another . . . unless the information is a matter of general knowledge." This duty extends beyond the length of the work contract; if the employee moves to a new job with another firm, his obligation to not disclose his previous principal's trade secrets is still in effect.

Since patents are granted by the U.S. Patent Office in accordance with the U.S. Patent Code, patent law cases are federal cases, whereas trade secrets cases are handled by state courts in accordance with state laws. Although there is no definition of "trade secret" adopted by every state, most follow the definition in Section 757 of the *Restatement of Torts,* according to which a trade secret consists of a pattern, device, formula or compilation of information used in business and designed to give the employer an opportunity to obtain an advantage over his competitors who neither know nor use the information. On this definition virtually anything an employer prefers to keep confidential could count as a trade secret.

In practice, however, the *Restatement* specifies several factors it suggests that courts should consider in deciding whether information is legally protectable: (1) the extent to which the information is known outside the business, (2) the extent to which it is known to employees in the firm, (3) the extent to which the firm used measures to guard secrecy of the information, (4) the value of the information to the firm and to its competitors, (5) the amount of money the firm spent to develop the information, and (6) how easily the information may be developed or properly duplicated.

According to to (1), (2), (4), (5), and (6), not all internally generated information will count legally as a trade secret. And, via (3), the firm must take measures to guard its secrets: ". . . a person entitled to a trade secret . . . must not fail to take all proper and reasonable steps to keep it secret. He cannot lie back and do nothing to preserve its essential secret quality, particularly when the subject matter of the process becomes known to a number of individuals involved in its use or is observed in the course of manufacturing in the plain view of others" (*Gallowhur Chemical Corp.* v. *Schwerdle,* 37 N. J. Super. 385, 397, 117 A2d 416, 423; *J. T. Healy & Son, Inc.,* v. *James Murphy & Son, Inc.,* 1970 Mass. Adv. Sheets 1051, 260 NE2d 723 [Ill. App. 1959]). In addition to attempting to keep its information secret, the firm must inform its employees as to what data are regarded as secret: there "must be a strong showing that the knowledge was gained in confidence," (*Wheelabrator Corp.* v. *Fogle,* 317 F. Supp. 633 [D. C. La. 1970]), and employees must be warned that certain information is regarded as a trade secret (*Gallo* v. *Norris Dispensers, Inc.,* 315 F. Supp. 38 [D. C. Mo. 1970]). Most firms have their employees sign a document that (a) specifies what its trade secrets or types of trade secrets are, and (b) informs them that improper use of the trade secrets violates confidentiality and subjects them to litigation.

If a firm has information that really is a legitimate trade secret, if it informs its employees that this information is regarded as secret, and informs them that improper use violates confidentiality, then it may be able to establish its case in court, in which case it is entitled to injunctive relief and damages. But the courts also typically examine how the defendant in a trade secret case obtained the information. For example, if an employee transfers from company M to company N, taking M's documents with him to N, then there is clear evidence of a breach of confidentiality (or "bad faith") if the evidence can be produced by M. But trade secret law is equity law, a basic principle of which is that bad faith cannot be presumed. In equity law the maxim "Every dog has one free bite" obtains, i.e., a dog cannot be presumed to be vicious until he bites someone. Thus, if the employee took no producible hard evidence in the form of objects or documents, but instead took what was "in his head" or what he could memorize, then M may have to wait for its former employee to overtly act. By then it may be very difficult to produce convincing evidence that would establish a breach of confidentiality.

In considering possible justifications of patents and trade secrets, we have to take into consideration the public good or social utility, the firm's rights and interests, and the individual's rights and interests. Our aim should be to maximize utility while safeguarding legitimate rights.

As Michael Baram has noted, "A major concern of our society is progress through the promotion and utilization of new technology. To sustain and enhance this form of progress, it is necessary to optimize the flow of information and innovation all the way from conception to public use."[1] Given the assumption that technological progress is conducive to social utility, and that the dissemination of technological information is a major means to progress, the key issue is how to maximize information generation and dissemination.

One answer is to require public disclosure of all important generated information, and allow unrestricted use of that information. In some cases this is appropriate, e.g., government sponsored research conducted by a private firm is disclosed and can be used by other firms. Within a capitalistic context, however, it is doubtful that a general disclosure requirement would maximize social utility. The innovative firm would develop information leading to a new product only to see that product manufactured and marketed by another firm at a lower price because the latter firm did not incur research costs. The proposal probably would also result in less competition; only firms with strong financial and marketing structures would survive. Small, innovative firms would not have the protection of their technological advantages necessary to establish a competitive position against industry giants. If both research effort and competition were diminished by this proposal, then the "progress" Baram mentions would not be maximized—at least not in the area of marketable products.

In a market economy, then, there are reasons grounded in social utility for allowing firms to have some proprietary information. The laws based on such a justification should, in part, be structured with an eye to overall utility, and in fact they are so structured. Patents, for example, expire in 17 years. While the patent is in force it allows the firm to recoup research expenses and generate a profit by charging monopolistic prices. Patent protection also encourages the generation of new knowledge. The firm holding the patent, and realizing profits because of it, is encouraged to channel some of those profits to research, since its patent is of limited duration. Given that its patent will expire, the firm needs to generate new, patentable information to maximize profits. Competitors are encouraged to develop competing products that are based on new, patentable information.

Patent protection should not, however, extend indefinitely; it would not only extend indefinitely the higher costs that consumers admittedly bear while a patent is in force, but in certain cases, it could also stifle innovation. A firm holding a basic patent might either "sit on" it or strengthen its monopoly position. A company like Xerox, for example, with the basic xerography patent, might use its profits to fund research until it had built up an impenetrable patent network, but then cut reproductive graphics research drastically and rest relatively secure in the knowledge that its competitors were frozen out of the market. Patents allow monopoly profits for a limited period of time, but patent law should not be structured to forever legitimatize a monopoly.

Richard De George has recently offered another argument to the conclusion that the right to proprietary information is a limited right:

> Knowledge is not an object which one can keep locked up as long as one likes. . . . Whatever knowledge a company produces is always an increment to the knowledge developed by society or by previous people in society and passed from one generation to another. Any new invention is made by people who learned a great deal from the general store of knowledge before they could bring what they knew to bear on a particular problem. Though we can attribute them to particular efforts of individuals or teams, therefore, inventions and discoveries also are the result of those people who developed them and passed on their knowledge to others. In this way every advance in knowledge is social and belongs ultimately to society, even though for practical purposes we can assign it temporarily to a given individual or firm.[2]

Allowing the firm to use proprietary information has utility, but the right to such information is limited. In point of fact, although we have stressed the utility of allowing use of proprietary information, U.S. patent and copyright laws were enacted during the industrial revolution to reduce secrecy. Patent laws allow limited monopolies in return for public disclosure of the information on which the patent is based. Thus, patent laws provide information to competitors and encourage them to develop their own patentable information that not only generates new products, but also adds to the store of available knowledge.

If allowing limited use of proprietary information has utility, it is still an open question as to the proper limits of such use. Does the present 17 year patent limit maximize utility? This is an empirical question that we will not attempt to answer. Although most experts and industry representatives believe the present limit is about right, U.S. drug firms have recently argued that research and development time and Federal Drug Administration (FDA) testing and licensing requirements are so extensive that social disutility results, as well as disutility for innovative firms.

Although patents expire and the information protected can then be used by anyone, trade secrets can extend indefinitely according to present law. In 1623, the Zildjian family in Turkey developed a metallurgical process for making excellent cymbals. Now centered in Massachusetts, the family has maintained their secret to the present day, and they still produce excellent cymbals. Preservation of such secrets may well have utility for firms holding the secrets, but does it have social utility? Not necessarily, as the following case illustrates. Suppose that Jones, a shadetree mechanic, develops a number of small un-patentable improvements in the internal combustion engine's basic design. The result is an engine that is cheap, reliable, and gets 120 miles per gallon. With no resources to mass produce and market his engine, Jones decides to sell to the highest bidder. XYZ oil company, with immense oil reserves, buys the information. To protect its oil interests, it keeps the information secret. Now suppose it is in fact against XYZ's interests to divulge the information. Then, to calculate overall utility we have to weigh the social disutility of keeping the information secret against the social utility of keeping the existing oil industry intact. Although utility calculations are difficult, it seems clear that disutility would arise from allowing the information to be kept secret.

If the preservation of *some* secrets has social disutility, it also seems clear that requiring immediate disclosure of *all* trade secrets in a capitalistic context would have disutility as well. The arguments here parallel those we developed in discussing patents. Again, specification of the appropriate duration of a trade secret is a utility calculation. The calculation will, however, have to take into consideration the fact that the law provides no protection for the secret itself. The firm with a significant investment in a trade secret always runs the risk that a competitor may legitimately uncover and use the secret.

Allowing patents and trade secrets has obvious utility for the firm that possesses them, but the firm also has a *right* to at least the limited protection of its information. It has a *legal* right to expect that its employees will live up to their work contracts, and employees have a correlative duty to abide by their contracts. The work contract is entered into voluntarily by employer and employee; if a prospective employee does not like the terms of a (legitimate) trade secret provision of a contract, he does not have to take the job. The normal employment contract specifies that the firm owns all employer-generated information. Even if the employee transfers from firm M to firm N, M still owns the information produced when he was employed there, and the employee is obligated not to reveal that information.

The moral basis of contract enforceability, including contractual provisions for the protection of proprietary information, is twofold. First, as argued, allowing trade secrets has social utility in addition to utility for the firm. The institution of contract compliance is necessary for the systematic and orderly functioning of business, and a sound business environment is essential to general social utility. However, if only a few people broke their contracts, business would continue to survive. This leads to the second moral basis for adhering to the provisions of one's contract.

If an individual breaks his contract, then he must either regard himself as an exception to the rule banning contract-breaking, or he must believe, in Kant's terms, that a maxim concerning contract-breaking is universalizable. But if we agree that in moral matters everyone ought to adopt the moral point of view, and that point of view requires that one not make himself an exception to the rule, it follows that the person in question is not justified in breaking the rule. On the other hand, if he claims that breaking the contract is in accordance with a maxim, then we can properly demand to have the maxim specified. Clearly the maxim cannot be something like: "I will keep my promises, except on those occasions where it is not to my advantage to keep the promises." For if everyone followed this maxim, there would be no institution of promising or promise-keeping. Since the maxim is not universalizable, it cannot legitimately be appealed to as a sanction for action. Of course, other maxims are available, and the contract-breaker may claim that his act is in accordance with one of these maxims. But note that this reply at least tacitly commits the person to the moral point of view; he is agreeing that everyone ought to act only on universalizable maxims. The only dispute, then, is whether his maxim is in fact universalizable. If we can show him that it is not, he is bound to admit that he is not morally justified in breaking the contract. As a standard, then, contracts should be kept, and where an individual breaks, or contemplates breaking, a contract, the burden is on him to produce a universalizable maxim for his action.

Our analysis does not, however, imply that a person is morally obligated to abide by all contracts; some contracts, or provisions of certain contracts, may be morally and/or legally unacceptable. A person does have a right to liberty and a right to use his knowledge and skills to earn a living. Thus, firm M cannot legitimately specify that *all* knowledge an employee gains while at M is proprietary. This would prohibit the person from obtaining employment at another firm; in effect the work contract would amount to a master-slave relationship. As the *Restatement of Torts* appropriately specifies, only certain information qualifies as a legitimate trade secret. Furthermore, the employee brings to his job certain knowledge and skills that typically are matters of public domain, and, on the job, the good employee develops his capacities. As the court noted in *Donohue v. Permacil Tape Corporation:* an ex-employee's general knowledge and capabilities "belong to him as an individual for the transaction of any business in which he may engage, just the same as any part of the skill, knowledge, information or education which was received by him before entering the employment. . . . On terminating his employment, he has a right to take them with him."[3]

Given that an individual's rights to liberty and to use his knowledge and skills to better himself are primary rights, and hence cannot be overriden by utility considerations, the burden clearly is on the firm to: (1) specify to employees what it regards as its trade secrets, and (2) make sure the secrets are legitimate trade secrets. In addition, a company can employ certain pragmatic tactics to protect its trade secrets. It can fragment research activities so that only a few employees know all the secrets. It can restrict access to research data and operational areas. It can develop pension and consulting policies for ex-employees that motivate them not to join competitors for a period of time. More importantly, it can develop a corporate atmosphere that motivates the individual to remain with the firm.

We began by sketching an argument that company N was justified in obtaining information about company M's computer without M's consent. Our conclusion is that N's argument is specious. Utility considerations justify allowing M to keep its information secret for a period of time, and any employee of M who divulges M's secret information to N is morally blameworthy because he violates his contractual obligations to M.

NOTES

1. Michael Baram, "Trade Secrets: What Price Loyalty," *Harvard Business Review* 46, no. 6 (November-December 1968): 64–74.

2. Richard T. DeGeorge, *Business Ethics* (New York: Macmillan, 1982), p. 207.

3. Cited in Baram, p. 71.

Corporate Policy Statement

TI's trade secrets, proprietary information, and much other internal information are valuable assets. Protection of this information plays a vital role in TI's continued growth and in our ability to compete. Under the law of most countries, a trade secret is treated as property, usually in the form of information, knowledge, or know how, the possession of which gives the owner some advantage over competitors who do not possess the 'secret.' A trade secret must be secret, that is, not generally or publicly known; but it need not be patentable subject matter to qualify as a trade secret. Our obligations with respect to proprietary and trade secret information of TI are: not to disclose this information to persons outside of TI, for example, by conversations with visitors, suppliers, family, etc.; not to use this information for our own benefit or for the profit or benefit of persons outside of TI, and; not to disclose this information to other TIers except on a "need to know" basis, and then only with a positive statement that the information is a TI trade secret. TIers who have the "need to know" are those who can do their jobs properly only with knowledge of the proprietary or trade secret information. TI's trade secret and proprietary information is not always of a technical nature. Typical of such important information are TI business, research, and new product plans; Objectives, Strategies, and Tactical Action Programs; divisional and department sales, profits, and any unpublished financial or pricing information; yields, designs, efficiencies, and capacities of TI's production facilities, methods, and systems; salary, wage, and benefit data; employment levels for sites or organizations; employee, customer, and vendor lists; and detailed information regarding customer requirements, preferences, business habits, and plans except where such information is publicly available. This list, while not complete, suggests the wide scope and variety of TI proprietary information that must be safeguarded. Special safeguards should be observed for TI information classified "TI Strictly Private" or "TI Internal Data." Each of these classifications imposes restrictions of a need to know within TI. But even without these classifications, most of what we know about our own jobs and the jobs of others should remain in the plant or office when we finish the day's work. If we leave TI, our legal obligation is to protect TI's trade secret and proprietary information until the information becomes publicly available or TI no longer considers it trade secret or proprietary. We should remember also that correspondence, printed matter, documents, or records of any kind, specific process knowledge, procedures, special TI ways of doing things—whether classified or not—are all the property of and must remain at TI.

Texas Instruments

HONESTY IN COMMUNICATION

Case Study

A Communication Decision at Von Products, Inc.

Gerald Fowler inherited some money in 1959 and he used it to found Von Products, a company that manufactured air driers for use in refrigeration and air conditioning equipment. In 1959, Fowler was convinced that air conditioning was the new wave of the future. Fowler was right, and Von Products prospered. In 1973 and 1982, Fowler expanded his operations, each time selling stock in the corporation. In 1991, Von Products employed 406 people, with Fowler retaining ownership of 51 percent of the corporation's stock. The organization of Von Products' top-level management was as follows:

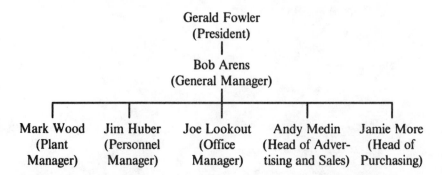

Fowler felt that Von Products was "his baby," and he strictly reviewed most management decisions in the corporation. One of the things Fowler insisted upon was that he personally make all management-level appointments and promotions. Below the level of management, the personnel manager was empowered to make all decisions regarding hiring, firing, and promotion. When management positions were to be filled, however, Bob Arens, the general manager, made recommendations to Fowler, who then made the ultimate decision.

On November 10, 1991, Jim Huber was called into Fowler's office. Fowler told him that Andy Medin was leaving the corporation, and that he, Fowler, was going to appoint a new head of advertising and sales. At present no one except Medin, Fowler, Arens, and Huber knew of Medin's upcoming resignation, and Fowler said that he wanted the information to be kept confidential. Fowler further told Huber that the list of candidates for promotion to Medin's position had been narrowed to two: Milt Snobiski, currently manager of the advertising department, and Bob Allen, sales manager. Fowler asked Huber to go over the files of both men and make a recommendation for promotion. The request was unusual; however, Fowler explained that Arens had strongly recommended one person for promotion, while he favored the other. Before he made his final decision, then, Fowler wanted a third opinion. And since Huber was personnel manager, he was selected for the task. Fowler refused to tell Huber whom Arens had recommended or whom he, Fowler, favored, because he did not want to prejudice Huber's judgment.

From the outset Huber felt uneasy about making the decision requested of him. He knew both Snobiski and Allen well, for all three men had grown up together and had gone to the same high school. Still, Huber was not familiar with the dossiers of either man. Huber had joined Von Products only two years ago; and both Allen and Snobiski had been hired over 12 years ago by Huber's predecessor, a man who recently had died of a heart attack.

Even before he looked at the résumés of the two men, Huber knew whom he favored for promotion. Huber felt that Snobiski was hard working, loyal, and competent. Furthermore, Huber and Snobiski were good friends. On the other hand, Huber knew that Allen had been made sales manager by Fowler on the recommendation of Arens, even though Andy Medin, a competent department head, had not favored the decision. In Huber's opinion, Allen had risen high in the corporation only because he constantly "buttered up" Arens. Furthermore, Huber knew that Allen had assumed Andy Medin's duties for two months in 1990 while Medin was sick, and that during that time advertising and sales suffered.

When Huber examined Allen's file he found that the subject had a slightly better than average record. At the same time, there was nothing outstanding about it. Snobiski's file, on the other hand, was, with one exception, truly impressive. Great leaps in sales were recorded in 1983, 1985, and 1989, and all were traceable to aggressive advertising campaigns masterminded by Snobiski. Furthermore, the file was replete with complimentary evaluations by Medin. Yet there was a problem with Snobiski's record. When Huber examined data concerning Snobiski's educational background, he found that Snobiski claimed to have a bachelor's degree in business from Ohio State and a master's in business administration from Indiana University. The dates of the degrees accorded with times when Huber felt sure Snobiski was serving in the Navy.

To check, Huber called both Ohio State and Indiana and found that his friend had no degree from either university.

Huber knew Fowler very well. If Fowler found out that Snobiski had falsified his employment application, not only would Snobiski be fired, Fowler would do his best to see that he was not hired anywhere else, Furthermore, Fowler certainly would make Allen head of advertising and sales, a move that Huber honestly felt would be disadvantageous for the corporation. With this in mind, Huber considered the various options that he felt were open to him:

(1) He could tell Fowler all that he had found, and argue for Snobiski's promotion. But Huber knew that Fowler felt that falsification of records was among the worst of all evils. Thus, choice of this course of action probably would do little more than cause Fowler to doubt Huber's trustworthiness. Furthermore, Huber's report would cause Snobiski to be fired, and a truly productive person would be lost to Von Products.

(2) He could tell Fowler that he favored Allen, justify the recommendation by some strained arguments, and omit any mention of Snobiski's educational record.

(3) He could argue for Snobiski's promotion, withholding all information concerning Snobiski's educational background.

(4) He could give all the information at his disposal to Fowler, and then argue against the promotion of either man. Once again, however, Snobiski would be fired. Further, Huber felt sure that if Snobiski was removed from consideration, Allen would be promoted regardless of what he had to say in opposition to the appointment.

As Huber considered the various alternatives available to him, he felt caught between a rock and a hard place. To tell all he knew would bring about dismissal of a valuable employee and a good friend, and almost certainly put Allen in a position Huber felt he did not deserve. However, the alternative was to withhold information, and this made Huber feel uncomfortable.

For Discussion

Are there other plausible courses of action that Huber could pursue? Of the available alternatives, which should Huber select? Why?

James M. Humber

Honesty in Organizational Communication

Top corporate executives consistently complain of problems involving communications within the organization.[1] In one study of 100 businesses and industries it was found that only 20 percent of the information downward from the level of the board of directors was understood at the worker level.[2] And if anything, problems with upward communications are even more severe than those encountered in downward transmissions of information.[3]

There are a variety of reasons to explain why communication problems arise within corporate structures. Upward communication is hampered by the very structure of the corporation itself. Top men insulate themselves from all but a few key employees to avoid undue interruptions and embarrassing encounters. Pressures of time and the routine demands of jobs also hinder the upward flow of information. The chain of command in most companies makes it impossible for employees to talk to decision makers in their organizations without first presenting their messages to each higher management echelon. Then too, some workers are not able to communicate clearly, either orally or in writing; and those who receive information sometimes misinterpret. In addition, subordinates are reluctant to pass on "bad" information to their superiors; and employees claim to feel pressures (sometimes real, sometimes imagined) to tell their bosses "only what they want to hear." With all of these impediments to upward communication, it is amazing that any undistorted information gets to the top.

There are at least as many factors operating to distort downward communication in corporations as there are factors working to hamper the upward flow of information. For example, some executives withhold bad news from their employees for fear of upsetting morale. In a large international or multi-national corporation, top management and local management rarely come into contact. Furthermore, it is sometimes difficult, in a very large company, to identify the person or persons to whom information should be sent. Then too, managers, like their subordinates, are often burdened by routine tasks. Sometimes persons in executive positions are incapable of communicating clearly; and oftentimes those below top-level management misunderstand the messages they receive. Overarching all of this, of course, is the problem of the "authoritarian" executive. A person of this sort does not feel that company information is any of the worker's business. And naturally, in these circumstances very little information is communicated downward.

There are a host of books and studies in management theory that attempt to provide employers with the means for improving internal corporate communications. My purpose in this essay is not to add to that body of literature, but rather to assess the moral quality of certain kinds of intentional distortions in the flow of information within business and industry. The following three cases will help to illustrate the kinds of communicative distortions I want to examine.

Case #1. Joe Doe and Jim Roe are coworkers competing for a promotion. Doe purposely passes on false information to Roe. As Doe expects, Roe acts on the false information and so "looks bad" in the eyes of his superiors.

Case #2. A department manager (DM) must write a report evaluating the work of four employees in his department. The first three employees are good friends of his, but he does not like the fourth employee. In writing his report the DM does not omit any pertinent information, but goes out of his way to stress his friends' strengths while emphasizing the weaknesses of the employee he does not like.

Case #3. A regional manager (RM) must report to top level executives concerning the operations of the various districts for which he has responsibility within the organization. The RM instructs an assistant, *A,* to collect data and prepare a report, telling *A* in the process that it is very important for his region to "look good" to the bosses. *A* prepares a report that makes no mention of the problems plaguing various districts in the RM's region.

In case #1 above, one employee straightforwardly tells another something that he knows to be false. In case #2, the truthfulness of communication is distorted by emphasis or "coloring." And in the final example, important information is withheld. What all three cases have in common, of course, is that in each instance an intentional deception or lie has been perpetrated.[4] Distortions of all three sorts occur in all organizations with varying degrees of frequency. But are such deceptions morally wrong? And if they are morally wrong, are the deceivers morally blameworthy? These are the questions that will serve as the focus of this essay. Before we can attempt to answer these questions, however, we first must decide whether employees in business and industry have any moral obligation to tell the truth in their corporate communications.

Ethicists and moral philosophers differ widely in their views concerning whether there is a moral duty to tell the truth. At one extreme we find people like Kant and St. Augustine claiming that there is an absolute, unconditional, or unbreakable moral obligation to tell the truth. Since an unbreakable moral duty is one that holds in all circumstances without exception, acceptance of this view would force the conclusion that *all* lies are morally wrong. But there are good reasons to believe that this theory, which we could call deontological extremism, is not correct.[5] For example, deontological [i.e., nonconsequentialist] extremists claim that there are other inviolable moral duties in addition to the absolute moral obligation to tell the truth. How is one to act if two or more of these unbreakable moral duties conflict? Kant took note of the problem; but in the end claimed that there was no real difficulty because "a conflict of duties and obligations is inconceivable"[6] This "solution," however, is far too facile. For instance, let us assume that we have only two absolute moral duties—one is to keep our promises, and the other is to tell the truth. Let us say further that S is a soldier who promises faithfully to do all in his power to confuse the enemy and protect his comrades. During one battle S is captured, imprisoned, and repeatedly interrogated regarding troop placements. Though S is tortured, he gives the enemy no information. One day, however, S learns that the enemy is planning to attack his army's headquarters. S knows that he is due to be questioned the next day, and that if he pretends to "break" under pressure, he may lie convincingly concerning the location of his army's headquarters and so cause the enemy's attack to be misdirected. What should S do? If he deceives his captors, he breaks his absolute moral duty to tell the truth. If he does not lie, he fails to keep his unbreakable promise to protect his comrades and confuse the enemy. In this case, at least, absolute moral duties do seem to conflict, and deontological extremism would appear to make it impossible for S to act in a morally right way.

Another problem with deontological extremism is that we ordinarily believe moral duties may be broken when the consequences of not violating those duties would be disastrous. For example, assume that the captain of a fishing boat is smuggling innocent political prisoners out of a country ruled by a corrupt dictator. Just before the captain is about to leave port with his surreptitious cargo, his vessel is boarded by the police. The police chief is a good friend of the captain, and will believe whatever the captain tells him. Thus, if the captain lies about the location of the prisoners he will save all of their lives. On the other hand, if the captain tells the truth or refuses to say anything, the boat will be searched and all the innocent prisoners killed. Now if the captain were to lie in these circumstances would he really do something wrong? Kant and St. Augustine would have to answer affirmatively; but a judgment of this sort violates our most basic moral intuitions.

Although the above two criticisms of deontological extremism proceed along different lines, they make essentially the same point, i.e., even if we believe there is a moral duty to tell the truth, we ordinarily do not think that this obligation must *always* be obeyed if we are to act in morally right ways. Indeed, this belief is held so strongly by the vast majority of mankind that, historically, deontological extremism proved unworkable. For example, discontent with St.

Augustine's absolute rejection of all lies gave birth to a theory known as the doctrine of mental reservations.[7] In its most extreme form this doctrine holds that it is not wrong for one person to say something misleading to another, just so long as the speaker is careful to add a qualifier to the statement in his or her mind so as to make the verbal statement true. For instance, let us say that I am at Dick's house and that I pocket a $5.00 bill which I find on the floor. Dick enters the room and asks me if I have seen $5.00. According to the doctrine of mental reservations I would not be lying if I said, "I did not see $5.00," and then silently completed the statement by saying something to myself like "yesterday" or "on the table."

Although those who accept the doctrine of mental reservations insist that we have an absolute moral duty to tell the truth, they allow us to "mentally qualify" any false statement so as to make it true. Hence the actual effect of the doctrine is to deny that we have any moral duty at all to communicate truthfully. The reason this is so is that there can be no such thing as a private language. That is to say, if I tell Dick (x) "I did not see $5.00," what I communicate to Dick is nothing more or less than the meaning of (x), for the "mental addition" to (x), which I make in my mind, is no communication at all. In reality, then, when I assert (x)—albeit a "mentally qualified" (x)—I lie to Dick; for what I have actually communicated [viz., the meaning of (x)], is something that I know to be false. And if the doctrine of mental reservations allows me to do this with any statement, at any time, without fear of doing something wrong, it effectively denies that there is any moral duty to tell the truth.

Those who accept the doctrine of mental reservations leap from dissatisfaction with St. Augustine's absolute injunction against lying to a position that denies there is any moral duty at all to tell the truth. Proponents of the mental reservations doctrine make no attempt to justify this "leap," because they do not understand the true nature of their own position. That is, they believe there is an absolute duty of veracity, but that they do not violate this duty when they assert mentally qualified statements because all such statements are true. We now know that this view of things is wrong. But this still leaves one question unanswered; specifically, is it possible to justify the mental reservationists' true position? Or to put it another way, can we construct an argument showing that there is no moral duty to tell the truth? Perhaps the best known attempt to provide such a justification has been made by a group of moral philosophers whom we may call teleological extremists.[8] Teleological [i.e., consequentialist] extremists believe that we have one and only one moral duty, and that is to maximize good consequences. Thus stealing, lying, killing, etc. cannot be said to be wrong because they violate moral injunctions against such actions. If actions of this sort are wrong, they are wrong only because they produce bad consequences. And of course, teleological extremists insist that there may be cases where it would be morally right to steal, lie, or kill. Specifically, it would be right whenever such action maximized good consequences. For example, teleological extremists might well claim that it would be right for the fishing boat captain to lie to the police chief in our earlier example because lying in this instance would save many innocent lives.

Insofar as teleological extremists claim that it sometimes may be morally permissible to lie, cheat, steal, etc., they no doubt are correct. On the other hand, there seems to be no reason to agree that we have no moral duties other than the duty to maximize good consequences. If this truly were the case, we would feel no moral qualms whatsoever about a person lying, stealing, cheating, etc., whenever it was clear that good consequences were produced by such action. But in fact, we often do feel morally troubled when such actions are performed and justified by an appeal to good consequences. For example, if I steal $50,000 from a millionaire who will never miss the money, and then give that money to charity, have I done something morally right? Or again, if I tell a dying friend on his deathbed that I will use his fortune to care for his pet cats, but after his death use his money to relieve human misery, is my lie justified? In cases such as these we do not feel that the moral issues are as clear-cut and simple as teleological extremists would have us believe. And we feel this way because we think there are many moral duties, and not just one as teleological extremists would have us believe.

We have rejected deontological extremism because it imposes *absolute* moral obligations upon us. On the other hand, teleological extremism goes too far in the opposite direction when it asserts that there are no moral obligations other than the duty to maximize good consequences. In the end, then, the truth would seem to lie somewhere between these extremes. And indeed, if the examples given throughout the text of this essay indicate anything, it is that we ordinarily acknowledge the existence of many moral duties (including the duty to tell the truth), but that we do not hold these duties to be absolute or unbreakable. Duties that are not absolute are called *prima facie* moral duties. *Prima facie* moral duties are so-called because violating them constitutes *prima facie* evidence of moral wrongdoing. That is to say, unless the person violating a *prima facie* duty can *justify* his or her violation, the person performing the action will be said to have done something morally wrong. Of course, what counts as an adequate justification for breaking a *prima facie* moral duty is the subject of much dispute; and more will be said of this later. For now, however, we need only note that our inquiries thus far would seem to require that we acknowledge the existence of a *prima facie* moral duty to tell the truth.

Having determined that there is a *prima facie* moral duty to tell the truth, it might appear that we now should try to specify those conditions under which violation of that duty would be justified. Before we can approach this task, however, there is another issue to be faced. There are some who allow that we ordinarily have a *prima facie* duty of veracity, but they go on to argue that the actions of employees in business and industry must be judged by a special moral theory. If this claim is true, and if this "special" moral theory imposes no duty on employees to tell the truth with respect to their internal corporate communications, we need not worry about seeking a justification for deceptive corporate communiques. Before we proceed further, then, we need to examine the major tenets of this "special" moral theory.

Milton Friedman is the propounder and chief advocate of a special moral theory that he feels must be used to judge the actions of employees in business and industry.[9] Admittedly, Friedman says, all persons have ordinary moral responsibilities. However, when individuals become employees of a company, they assume two duties that supersede their ordinary moral obligations. For Friedman, all employees must: (1) do their best to maximize profits for the corporation, and (2) obey the law and follow the rules of ethical custom.

Friedman's theory has been criticized from a number of quarters. Elsewhere, for example, I have argued that Friedman's theory is so beset by theoretical and conceptual difficulties that it must be rejected out of hand.[10] Also, Alan Goldman rejects the view that, as a general rule, professional obligations override or supersede ordinary moral obligations.[11] For the purposes of this paper, however, we may ignore these challenges to Friedman's position; even if we accept Friedman's theory we still must admit that employees in business and industry have a *prima facie* duty to communicate truthfully. There are two reasons for saying this. First, if our earlier reasonings are accepted, the *prima facie* moral duty to tell the truth is one of our society's "ordinary rules of ethical custom." Thus, insofar as Friedman imposes a moral duty upon employees to follow these rules, he also enjoins them to tell the truth. And second, virtually no one would dispute the claim that, generally, truthfulness in internal corporate communications is an aid to maximizing corporate profits. Indeed, recognition of this fact has spawned the many books, articles, and studies intended to provide employers with the means for improving the quality of information flow within their companies. If we accept Friedman's theory, then, we can say that corporate employees have a moral duty to be truthful in their communications because this helps to maximize company profits. On the other hand, this duty cannot be absolute, because we can imagine situations in which deception might be required for maximization of profits. For instance, one employee may have to lie in order to catch another who is stealing trade secrets.

No matter which way we turn it seems we must admit that company employees have a *prima facie* moral obligation not to distort the truth in their corporate communications. But if the duty to tell the truth is only *prima facie,* under what conditions would it be morally permissible for an employee to lie? Or, to put it another way, how could an employee morally justify lying in a corporate communication? In an essay of this length we cannot hope to take individual note of all the various cases in which lying might be justified. Nevertheless, we can say something in general about the process of justification, and so provide a means for testing the acceptability of moral justifications as they arise in actual practice. If nothing else, this examination should illustrate how very difficult it is to justify distorting the truth in corporate communications.

First, there seems to be agreement among many philosophers that a justification, if it is to be adequate, must be capable of being made public.[12] That is to say, appeals to personal conscience, secret moral knowledge, intuitions not shared by mankind in general, etc., will not do. Thus, if a moral view is to be adequately justified, the person doing the justifying must be able to present reasons and arguments capable of supporting the reasonableness of his or her position.

Second, because justifications must be capable of being made public, we would seem to have no alternative but to appeal to *consequences* in our justifications. For example, if an employee, *E,* were to lie in a corporate communication and then attempt to justify that lie by telling us that his lie was necessary to increase corporate profits, *E*'s "justification" could not be accepted; as it stands it tells us nothing more than that, in this particular instance, *E* feels that his duty to maximize profits supersedes his duty to tell the truth. But why should we accept this belief? It is hardly self-evident. To fully justify his position, *E* must appeal to some publicly accessible facts supporting his contention that the duty of veracity is outweighed by the duty to increase profits. And the only facts that would appear to be publicly accessible are the probable consequences of the two alternative courses of action. That is to say, if *E* is to justify his contention that he did not act wrongly when he lied, he must at the very least show that lying probably produced a greater balance of benefits over harms than not lying. If *E* cannot produce such factual support for his position, he cannot be said to have justified his belief that the duty to maximize profits outweighed his duty to tell the truth. And so long as this state of affairs remains, *E*'s action must be counted as morally wrong.

We have seen that we must appeal to the consequences of our actions whenever we attempt to justify lying in corporate communications. And this fact makes it so very difficult to justify deceptive communications in business and industry. The collective experience of mankind testifies to the fact that lying usually, if not always, produces harmful consequences. The individual who lies must worry about getting caught. If he is caught, his reputation suffers. If he is not caught, he oftentimes must continue to lie in order to conceal the original deception. Furthermore, trust is essential for the success of any cooperative venture; and lying, if it occurs frequently, undermines trust. In the corporate context an atmosphere of mistrust can have especially deleterious consequences: for if lying is continually expected, employees will tend to act on their own, oftentimes at cross purposes. In addition, when false information is passed on, decisions at various levels in the organization are made on the basis of incorrect data. And in these circumstances it is highly unlikely that decisions will be correct. Finally, if lying in internal corporate communications hurts business and industry, it also hurts society as a whole; for the more efficient and economically viable are our corporations, the stronger our economy.

Lying in corporate communications usually has harmful consequences for the liar, the corporation, and society. From past experience we *know* these effects customarily attend deceit; and it is from these negative consequences that this *prima facie* obligation not to lie in corporate communications derives its force. And this force is considerable. Of course, it is conceivable that an employee could show that some competing moral obligation superseded his duty not to lie; but this is quite unlikely. The reason this is so is that an employee who contemplates passing on false information is seldom in possession of the facts necessary to justify a deceptive communication. Even top-level executives do not have a complete and true picture of the organization's operations. As a result, they cannot predict the ultimate consequences of their actions with a high degree of certainty. On the other hand, they know perfectly well that lying will most likely produce the negative results noted previously. If it is difficult for persons at this level in the organization to justify deception, how much more so for individuals in middle-level management and below.[13]

We have seen that deceiving fellow employees in corporate communications is, in virtually all instances, morally wrong. But one question remains: are all those who lie in corporate communications morally blameworthy? Or, to put it another way, are there any conditions that would excuse a liar from responsibility for a wrongful act? In an essay of this length we cannot consider all possible excusing conditions. Nevertheless, we can consider the three most often appealed to, and see whether any succeeds in relieving the liar of responsibility.

First, we do not hold persons responsible for their actions when those actions are compulsory. For example, if we believe a murderer is mentally ill and unable to control his or her actions, we do not think the crime warrants punishment. Similarly, an employee could be a compulsive liar, and so not morally blameworthy if he or she were to lie. Cases such as this will be very rare, however; and if such an individual were discovered in an organization, he or she should be relieved of all responsibilities, at least until the illness has been corrected by proper medical attention.

Second, persons who act wrongfully out of ignorance are usually excused for their wrongdoing. I say "usually," because mere appeal to ignorance will not suffice to relieve one of responsibility. For instance, if an employee, E, purposely withholds information because of a mistaken belief that information is privileged, E is *not* excused if any reasonable person in the same position would have known that the information was not privileged. In every instance, the test is that of the "reasonable person," i.e., would a reasonable person have known what the person who passes on misinformation claims not to have known? If we believe a reasonable person would have known, we hold the employee who passes on distorted data responsible for his or her action. If we hold the contrary view, we do not blame. The difficulty, of course, is that the "reasonable person" test is very vague, and so difficult to apply in particular instances of wrongdoing. (How, after all, can we be sure what a reasonable person would have known in any given set of circumstances?) Thus, if an employee errs once or twice and then attempts to excuse his or her action by appealing to ignorance, it may be best to give the employee the benefit of the doubt. On the other hand, if an employee repeatedly passes on incorrect information, continued appeals to the excuse of ignorance cannot persist without placing the employee in a "no win" situation. Reasonable persons do not make the same mistake over and over again. Hence, if E continually misinforms coworkers, and then attempts to excuse these actions by appealing to ignorance, we must conclude: (a) that E is a reasonable person who is lying about being ignorant (in which case E is a liar), or (b) that E is a reasonable person who is purposely ignorant (in which case E is responsible for his or her false communication), or (c) that E is not a reasonable person (in which case E is incompetent).

Finally, Aristotle long ago realized that all persons have a breaking point, and that when this point is reached wrongdoers are not held responsible for their actions. For instance, a prisoner of war (POW) may "break" under torture and divulge information leading to the death of many of his comrades. In this case we would ordinarily say that the POW has done something wrong (after all, his action has caused the deaths of many fellow soldiers); at the same time, we would not blame the POW for breaking under torture. Similarly, employee E may be subjected to great pressures by his or her superior to "color" reports, cover up damaging information, etc. If E is caught in such a situation, if the pressures are severe (e.g., loss of job, permanently damaged reputation, etc.), and if there is no way for E to escape the situation by appealing to authorities in the organization above the level of his or her immediate superiors, then E may well have an excuse for forwarding deceptive information. Indeed, the person immediately responsible for E's wrongful action would appear to be E's superior. At the same time, one well might want to ask why responsibility for E's wrongful act should not extend further up in the organization. That is to say, one could claim that top-level executives have a duty to do their best to ensure truthful communications within their organizations, and that as a result, these individuals have an obligation to provide means for persons such as E to take action against superiors who pressure them to distort company communications. If these claims are true, and if an organization does not take steps to provide protection for employees who are pressured to deceive, does this mean that top-level management must assume some (or all) of the responsibility for lies prompted by pressure from above? The question is an interesting one; and it is one I will, quite happily, allow readers the freedom to answer for themselves.

NOTES

1. Throughout, I will be using "communications" to refer to all messages internal to the occupations of the organization. For example, all employees' oral, written, formal, and informal comments concerning business will be covered, while discussions among workers concerning football games or parties will not be counted as communications. Also excluded will be different communications of all sorts between and among corporations.

2. R. P. Cort, *Communicating with Employees* (Prentice-Hall, 1963), p. 10.

3. R. M. D'Aprix, *How's That Again?* (Dow Jones-Irwin, 1971), p. 10.

4. The term "lie" has a variety of different uses in our language. In one use, "lie" and "deception" are synonymous. On the other hand, there are some philosophers who believe it is important to distinguish between lying and deception [see, for example, J. Ellin, "The Solution to a Dilemma in Medical Ethics," *Westminster Institute Review* 1 (1980): pp. 3ff.] I do not wish to become embroiled in this conflict; and throughout, I will use "lie" to mean "intentionally deceptive statement." For all intents and purposes, this is the definition accepted by Sissela Bok in her classic work on lying. [See S. Bok, *Lying* (Vintage Books, 1979), p. 14.]

5. Proponents of this extreme view almost always accept some version of deontology; hence the name "deontological extremism." For a discussion of deontology in ethics see the introduction to this text.

6. I. Kant, *The Doctrine of Virtue,* trans. M. J. Gregor (Harper & Row, 1964), p. 23.

7. For an excellent discussion of this doctrine see Bok, *Lying* pp. 37ff.

8. For a detailed discussion of teleology (consequentialism) in ethics see the introduction to this text.

9. For a statement of Friedman's views see M. Friedman, "The Social Responsibility of Business Is to Increase Its Profits," *The New York Times Magazine* (September 13, 1970): pp. 33, 122–126, and "Milton Friedman Responds," *Business and Society Review* (Spring 1972): 5–16.

10. J. Humber, "Milton Friedman and the Corporate Executive's Conscience," *Philosophy in Context* 10 (1980): 71–80.

11. A. H. Goldman, *The Moral Foundations of Professional Ethics* (Littlefield, Adams and Co., 1980).

12. This view is accepted by philosophers who disagree about almost everything else. For example, Bok notes that Hume, Wittgenstein, and Rawls all agree that moral justification needs to have the capability of being made public (see Bok, *Lying,* p. 97).

13. There are numerous studies which show, as R. Cort says, that "the divergence between what the employee thinks and what the supervisor *thinks* he thinks is nothing less than astounding" (see Cort, *Communicating with Employees,* p. 11.) If misunderstanding in the corporation is this widespread, how can anyone predict, with any degree of certainty, the beneficial effects which a deceptive communication will have?

Corporate Policy Statement

Within H. B. Fuller the ability to communicate with each other takes on added dimensions as we continue to grow as a company and as society becomes more complex. We must communicate purposefully, clearly, openly, and with understanding. Our responsibilities are:

(1) The manager will inform you of the goals and objectives of your department and how this relates to the company's total business, and maximize the flow of information to all employees with regard to company plans and decisions. We must maintain an atmosphere where all employees can openly discuss their views and the views of management. This will be accomplished through the following methods: (a) individual and group meetings, (b) internal publications, (c) budget reports, (d) productivity and/or sales reports, (e) written or verbal explanation of management's views on a particular subject.

(2) Your ideas and suggestions will be listened to and evaluated by your supervisor and an answer provided. This will be accomplished through the following methods: (a) verbal suggestion acknowledged in the discussion, (b) written suggestion will be acknowledged in writing by the manager.

(3) The company will let you know what is expected of you in the performance of your job by the following methods: (a) instructions and directions from your supervisor, (b) job description, (c) formal performance appraisal on request.

(4) The company will communicate a description and explanation of all fringe benefits and facilitate the utilization of all benefit programs by providing easily accessible assistance and interpretations. This will be accomplished by

(a) Personnel Handbook, (b) Employee Benefit Statement, (c) your calling the Human Resources Department, 800-328-6816.

(5) The company will periodically determine the attitudes of employees on a variety of subjects as a basis for continued development of our employee relations function. The results will be reported to the employees.

(6) At our periodic meetings, managers and executives combined will work to develop continuing understanding of corporate philosophy and programs.

(7) The company will implement a system of periodic employee/management communications meetings at all organizational levels with appropriate feedback systems to assure communications to employees and from employees to management. At each location a committee will meet quarterly to discuss: (a) current operations, (b) corporate goals and performance, (c) local operational goals, (d) new or existing programs, (e) employee suggestions or requests. The committee will consist of the local manager and an employee representative, appointed by the local manager from each job category. A report of each meeting will be submitted to all employees at the local operation, plus copies of the report will be submitted to all line management not in attendance at the meeting, the company's president, and the Human Resources Department. Any member of the committee has the option of calling a special meeting if circumstances warrant.

H. B. Fuller Company

SELECT BIBLIOGRAPHY

Bacon, M. *The Moral Status of Loyalty*. Module Series in Applied Ethics. Dubuque, Iowa: Kendall/Hunt, 1984.

Blumberg, P. "Corporate Responsibility and the Employee's Duty of Loyalty and Obedience: A Preliminary Inquiry," in *The Corporate Dilemma*. Votaw, D., and Sethi, S., eds. Englewood Cliffs, N.J.: Prentice-Hall, 1973, pp. 82–113.

Bok, S. "Trade and Corporate Secrecy," in *Secrets*. New York: Random House, 1983, chapter 10.

Garrett, T. *Business Ethics*. Englewood Cliffs, N.J.: Prentice-Hall, 1966, ch. III.

Huseman, R., Logue, C., and Freshley, D., eds. *Readings in Interpersonal and Organizational Communication*. 2d ed. Boston: Holbrook, 1973.

Jacobs, L. "Business Ethics and the Law: Obligations of a Corporate Executive." *The Business Lawyer* 28 (July 1973): 1063–88.

Kintner, E., and Lahr, J., eds. *Intellectual Property Law Primer: A Survey of the Law of Patents, Trade Secrets, Trademarks, Franchises, Copyrights, Personality, and Entertainment Rights*. New York: Macmillan, 1974.

Lieberstein, S. *Who Owns What Is in Your Head?: Trade Secrets and the Mobile Employee*. New York: Hawthorne Books, 1979.

McGuire, J. "Conflict of Interest: Whose Interest? And What Conflict?" in *Ethics, Free Enterprise, and Public Policy*. R. DeGeorge and J. Pichler, eds. New York: Oxford University Press, 1978, pp. 214–31.

Michalos, A. "The Loyal Agent's Argument," in *Ethical Theory and Business*. T. Beauchamp and N. Bowie, eds. Englewood Cliffs, N.J.: Prentice-Hall, 1979, pp. 338–48.

Seavey, W. *Agency*. St. Paul, Minn.: West Publishing Co., 1964.

Shaw, W. *Business Ethics*. Belmont, Calif.: Wadsworth, 1991, pp. 227–69. Employee obligations to the firm and conflicts of interest.

Stevenson, R. *Corporations and Information: Secrecy, Access, and Disclosure*. Baltimore: Johns Hopkins University Press, 1980.

Thayer, L. *Communication and Communication Systems*. Homewood, Ill.: Richard D. Irwin, 1968.

Velasquez, M. *Business Ethics*. 2d ed. Englewood Cliffs, N.J.: Prentice-Hall, 1988, pp. 353–64. Employee obligations to the firm.

4

EMPLOYEE RIGHTS

INTRODUCTION

Corporations are goal oriented and often hierarchically organized, which places a premium on efficiency and the attendant employee obligations of loyalty, obedience, and confidentiality. In recent years it has been argued that employees have certain rights that cannot morally be overridden on grounds of efficiency. This chapter explores some of the moral rights that have been proposed in the areas of hiring, reverse discrimination, termination, privacy, worker safety, and whistleblowing.

In their article on hiring practices, Snoeyenbos and Almeder argue that the 1964 Civil Rights Act is consistent with and reinforces a private enterprise, free market conception of the economy. They go on to offer what they believe to be fair suggestions having utility across the scope of the hiring procedure: job analysis, job description, job specification, recruitment, testing, and interviewing. The ethical basis of recent court cases regarding hiring practices is also explored. The case study in this section provides a specific context for discussing hiring practices.

Although there is no doubt that women, blacks, and members of certain other minority groups have been discriminated against in business practices in our society, there is considerable disagreement as to whether they are entitled to preferential employment treatment. Ernest van den Haag argues that reverse discrimination is both unfair and has disutility. In response, Humber develops a specific proposal for preferential treatment of disadvantaged individuals, which he claims not only has overall utility but is fair to all. These articles are prefaced by contrasting judicial comments regarding the recent Weber case, in which white craft workers at Kaiser Aluminum charge that their firm's affirmative action program violates the Civil Rights Act of 1964 by discriminating against white employees in favor of blacks.

The trauma of being fired has been compared to that attending divorce or the death of a loved one. Snoeyenbos and Roberts examine the legal basis of termination policy and provide an ethical rationale for altering present law. Criteria for a just cause dismissal are offered, along with a policy for due process within the firm, and an argument that the harmful effects of termination should be mitigated even if the firing is based on just cause and the employee has received due process. The case study invites discussion regarding a specific discharge and the way it is handled.

In "Privacy in the Corporation," Humber points out difficulties corporations have in formulating and applying guidelines once a decision has been made to acknowledge privacy rights. He concludes by recommending a general strategy to resolve the central problems that arise in balancing the moral right to privacy with other corporate interests and rights. The case studies in this section explore two areas of concern with respect to privacy: a general moral issue concerning the kinds of employee data firms should be allowed to gather and retain, and the issue of specifying the morally permissible means used to gather such data.

In his article on worker safety, Manuel Velasquez lists three conditions necessary for a fair contract in the area of worker safety. Almeder and J. D. Millar argue that the worker has a *prima facie* moral right to know about any materially harmful working condition. The case in this section focuses on the issue of whether employees working under certain conditions have a right to know whether fellow employees have tested HIV positive.

If a firm is engaged in immoral or illegal activity, does an employee have a right or obligation to blow the whistle? Norman Bowie defines "whistleblower" and then sets out conditions under which whistleblowing is justifiable. Alan Westin lists certain complexities that should be considered in framing whistle-blowing policies.

HIRING

Hiring Procedures at World Imports, Inc.

World Imports, Inc. purchases a variety of unassembled chandeliers and lamps from foreign producers for assembly at its manufacturing facility in Philadelphia and for sale through ten local outlets. The company also manufactures a variety of electrical items: fixtures, wall receptacles, plugs, switches, etc., for use in its own products and for sale to other assemblers of more complex electrical equipment. The company, privately owned and an employer of 550 people, has the following organizational structure:

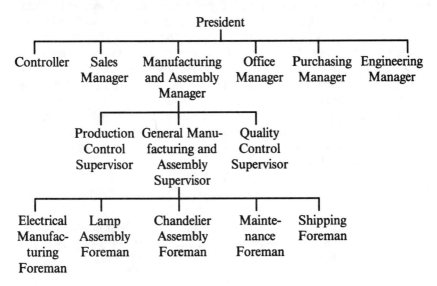

In 1992, World Imports's President Tom Naylor became concerned with quality-control problems. A disturbing percentage of electrical items the company manufactured were defective and rejected by quality-control testing. Most of these items had to be scrapped, which cut directly into profits. Rejection ratios were also increasing in the two assembly divisions. Discussions with his top managers indicated that the firm had a high personnel turnover ratio and significant personnel problems; absenteeism, for example, was on the rise, and more employee complaints were percolating upward. Naylor concluded that personnel problems were a big factor in World Imports's quality problems.

In the past, World Imports's personnel relations were handled by the office manager, but this manager had no formal training in personnel management and little experience with, or knowledge of, manufacturing or assembly work. These facts, coupled with strong growth in recent years, led Naylor to conclude that the time had arrived to create a personnel department at the manager level. Naylor knew just who he wanted to hire—Joan Miller, the daughter of his controller, a recent masters-level graduate in management, and a part-time office worker in the firm for several years. Naylor took Ms. Miller to lunch, offered her the position, and she accepted.

Joan immediately set out to analyze and resolve the firm's personnel problems. Since Naylor had clued her to the problems in manufacturing and assembly, she decided to start with those areas. Although Joan had not worked in these divisions, she was aware that work of this sort can be routine and boring, but also that exacting standards must be maintained in the production of consumer electrical products. Since she was a bit uneasy about the way in which she had been hired, and had focused on selection procedures in her graduate work, she decided to start by examining hiring procedures. She first checked for compliance with Equal Employment Opportunity Commission (EEOC) guidelines, and found that the company was well within the 80 percent selection ratio guidelines for blacks and women, although she did find that the vast majority of both groups were hired at the lowest level and remained there. She noted that no job analysis data were available for positions in the manufacturing and assembly division. When a foreman felt a new position needed to be filled, he made an oral request to his supervisor and the latter's manager, who then made the decision. If approved, the foreman and office manager discussed the issue, and the latter wrote up a brief job description and specification, which also served as an ad in the local newspaper. A recent ad ran as follows:

ELECTRICIAN-ASSEMBLER

Electrician for mfgr., assembly and testing of electrical products. Responsible for equipment maintenance. Supervises 5 helpers. Experience preferred. Good benefits. Day shift. 634-0297.

Candidates for the position were asked to submit three references, and the office manager selected one to be queried about facts of previous employment. To facilitate the process, an informal telephone reference check was conducted. After undesirable candidates were eliminated, the remaining candidates were given the Wonderlic Personnel Test. This is a general intelligence test that contains items relating to verbal, arithmetical, clerical, and judgmental abilities, and is used as a quick means of estimating the general mental ability of adults in industrial situations. Standard questions are:

1. The eleventh month of the year is _____.
2. SEVERE is the opposite of:
   (1) harsh (2) stern (3) tender (4) rigid (5) unyielding
3. Which word is different from the others?
   (1) certainty (2) dubiousness (3) assuredness (4) confidence (5) sureness
4. Answer yes or no. Does B.C. mean "before Christ?" _____.

In order to be considered for hiring, a candidate's scores must exceed the norm on this test. The remaining candidates are interviewed by the general supervisor and the foreman. The interview is unstructured, but the following items are to be considered and subsequently discussed: appearance and mannerisms, home and family background, education, motivation, work history, personality, and health.

After the interviews are complete, the foreman, his general supervisor, and the division manager review reference checks, test results, and interviews, and then make a joint selection.

For Discussion

Are World Imports's selection procedures acceptable? Why or why not? If you believe the firm's selection procedures can be improved, state specifically what improvements should be made and why.

Milton Snoeyenbos
Robert Almeder

Ethical Hiring Practices

Whether one owns a firm, manages it, invests in it, works for it, purchases its products, or relies on others who purchase its products, in some way we all have an important stake in a company's hiring practices. The firm seeks to hire those individuals who will contribute to its goals of efficiency and profitability. The individual seeks a position that is commensurate with his skills and will reward his efforts. Consumers want a quality product at the lowest possible cost, and this is, in part, a function of the quality of labor hired. In addition, our society also has an interest in hiring practices; since passage of the 1964 Civil Rights Act, we have attempted to ensure that candidates will be considered on the basis of merit rather than race, color, religion, sex, or national origin. An important question, then, is whether the stated interests of the firm, the prospective employee, and the larger society can all be met successfully and simultaneously within a private enterprise, free market economy.

In this article we argue for an affirmative answer to this question. In particular, we argue that the Civil Rights Act is consistent with and reinforces the private enterprise, free market economic framework. Thus, in addition to the interests of employer and prospective employee, the interests of society, as expressed in the Civil Rights Act, must be taken into consideration in developing an ethics of hiring. Keeping these interests in balanced perspective, we then discuss ethical dimensions of the employee selection procedure: job analysis, job description, job specification, recruitment, testing, and interviewing.

I. THE FREE MARKET AND THE MORALITY OF THE CIVIL RIGHTS ACT

Although a private enterprise, free market based economy may be characterized in a variety of ways, the following features are commonly regarded as central:

1. A system of property in which private individuals are the primary owners.
2. A method of enforcing contracts between individuals and also between the economic units individuals construct.
3. An open, competitive market structure in which:
   a. Individuals have free access to the market as producers and consumers.
   b. Resources and products can be moved freely among firms and geographic locations.
   c. Prices and wages are set voluntarily without governmental interference.
   d. Producers and consumers have reasonably complete information about market transactions, prices, and wages.
   e. Each producer has a small enough share of a particular product that it cannot significantly affect market price.

Like the frictionless wheel, this idealized conception is an abstraction only more or less approximated, while never fully realized. For example, in many cases consumers do not actually have relatively complete market information, and in a number of our industries today a small group of firms have oligopolistic power that clearly affects market prices. On the whole, however, with the exception of legislation sanctioning monopolistic utilities and labor legislation such as the Clayton and Wagner Acts granting anti-trust exemption to unions, American society has basically supported this type of economic structure. We see this, for example, in the Sherman Act, which encourages competition by precluding restraints of trade and monopoly; in the Pure Food and Drug Act, which requires accurate labeling of products and thereby helps consumers realize (3d); and, more to the point of this article, the 1964 Civil Rights Act.

Although the United States has long had a significant amount of legislation on the statute books banning discrimination (in particular, the Fifth, Thirteenth, and Fourteenth Amendments to the Constitution), specific legislation regarding discrimination in employment was not enacted until 1964. Title VII of the 1964 Civil Rights Act (as amended by the Equal Employment Opportunity Act of 1972) mandates that employers cannot discriminate on the basis of race, color, religion, sex, or national origin; specifically, it is illegal for an employer to:

A. Fail or refuse to hire or to discharge an individual or otherwise to discriminate against any individual with respect to his compensation, terms, conditions, or privileges of employment, because of such individual's race, color, religion, sex, or national origin.

B. Limit, segregate, or classify his employees or applicants for employment in any way that would deprive or tend to deprive any individual of employment opportunities or otherwise adversely affect his status as an employee, because of such individual's race, color, religion, sex, or national origin.[1]

There is no doubt that this legislation restricts an employer's right to freely establish contractual agreements with employees; if an employer hires only white males, and openly discriminates against other classes of people, his act is simply illegal. In a sense, then, it limits the contractual rights of individuals presupposed by (2) above, and represents a governmental intrusion in the market. On the other hand, the act enhances (3a), for, if discrimination occurs, individuals are denied access to the market. In this sense, the Civil Rights Act is like the Sherman Act. In limiting contractual agreements that restrain trade or lead to the formation of monopolies, the Sherman Act enhances competition by encouraging the existence of competing firms in an industry. Similarly, by banning discriminatory employment agreements, the Civil Rights Act enhances market competition by ensuring that all individuals have fair access to the market, and that hiring, compensation, and promotion decisions are based on merit or job performance, not on characteristics that are unrelated to job success.

The ethical justification for the Civil Rights Act rests on both consequentialist and nonconsequentialist grounds. From management's standpoint, hiring, compensation, and promotion decisions should be based on merit and job performance-related factors rather than race, sex, etc., because the efficient, productive employee maximizes profit. Since such a worker also enhances product quality and lowers product price, he also benefits the consumer. Thus, it is simply bad business to hire, compensate, and promote on the basis of factors unrelated to merit and job performance. Moreover, even if a firm could successfully compete with a product manufactured by persons hired under policies that violate the principle embedded in the Civil Rights Act, such policies tend, as a rule, to limit access to and participation in the market. Depending on the size of the discriminated group, such policies may have serious social consequences. If the group in question is large, the result may be massive social upheaval. In such cases, utility points in the direction of adoption of a nondiscriminatory employment principle. If the group is small, however, the consequences of discrimination may also be relatively small, and utility may be difficult to calculate. Nonetheless, many utilitarians argue that unjust policies generally produce bad social consequences over the long term. Nonconsequentialist factors must also be considered. Discrimination in hiring is wrong because the person discriminating would never want to be treated in the manner that he is treating the prospective employee. On the whole then, the Civil Rights Act is morally justified on both consequentialist and nonconsequentialist grounds. Furthermore, insofar as it enhances market access, it is consistent with and reinforces the private enterprise, free market economic model that most Americans advocate. Keeping the interests of the firm, prospective employee, and society in balanced perspective, let us now focus on the ethics of hiring practices.

II. HIRING PRACTICES

In the initial stages of the hiring process, a job opening is identified and the personnel manager performs a *job analysis*. Relevant information is collected and written up as a *job description* that details the job's main features and activities necessary for effective performance; it lists what the worker does and how he is to do it. In turn, the job description is used to develop a job specification which lists the necessary qualifications, i.e., knowledge, abilities, and experience needed to successfully perform the job. The organization then develops a pool of candidates by *recruiting*, and selects a person, primarily on the basis of *tests, interviews*, and reference checks. Although there can be other dimensions to the hiring process, the aspects denoted by the italicized terms above are the most important and the most commonly used, and on them our discussion will focus.

Job Analysis

From an ethical and practical standpoint, it is important for the personnel manager to conduct an accurate and thorough job analysis. The firm is interested in effective and efficient job performance that will enable it to maximize its goals. An accurate job description and job specification rest on having a detailed analysis of the position to be filled, and testing and interviewing should focus on those factors mentioned in the job description and specification, i.e., factors relevant to job performance. Utility for the firm thus requires a thorough analysis of the position to be filled. Fairness to the prospective employee also entails a thorough, accurate job analysis. The applicant should seek placement in a position where he can be rewarded commensurate with his ability, motivation, and output. If a job far exceeds or falls far short of a person's potential, these aims will not be realized. Since an individual typically seeks a position on the basis of a job description and job specification, and these rest on a job analysis, a person cannot seek a position commensurate with what he has to offer unless the employer conducts an accurate, thorough job analysis. Job analysis is also important in securing compliance with society's equal employment legislation. As we shall see, the law and federal guidelines require that personnel selection procedures must have validity, i.e., such procedures must represent actual, relevant aspects of job behavior. Since an accurate account of such behavior is typically developed in a job analysis, the law mandates that an employer conduct a thorough job analysis.

Let us now focus on the specifics of job analysis. If we assume we are dealing with an existing position to be filled, the personnel manager should not merely rely on the existing job description and job specification. A thorough job analysis requires a detailed understanding of the position as seen by its present jobholder and his supervisors. To acquire this understanding, the personnel manager can conduct interviews, observe the present employee on the job, or utilize questionnaires.

Questionnaires are frequently used to analyze a job. The employee is given a list of questions relating to various tasks and is asked to check whether he performs them and, if so, how long it takes. Other questions may be more open-ended, and simply ask the person to describe in writing the nature of some aspect of the job. But it is doubtful that a questionnaire can itself provide a thorough job analysis, since it places emphasis on the jobholder's ability to report accurately on his job functions. In practice this ability is often lacking, and hence information secured by a questionnaire is often incomplete or inconsistent. Questionnaires can, however, provide background information for a more thorough interview.

Observation of the incumbent jobholder can provide relevant information if the job involves routine or repetitive physical skills, but it is hardly sufficient for jobs requiring the exercise of judgment (e.g., paramedic) or those requiring a considerable amount of unquantifiable mental activity (e.g., draftsman). In these cases, observation must be coupled with an interview to obtain a thorough job analysis.

Interviews with the job incumbent and his supervisors are perhaps the most common way of conducting a job analysis. In many cases the utility of an interview is strengthened if it is used in conjunction with a questionnaire and direct observation of the incumbent jobholder. The interview can reveal information not obtainable by observation and can be used to confirm and clarify data gathered by both observation and the questionnaire. Since job incumbents frequently view the job analysis interview as an evaluation procedure, the most serious problem with such interviews is that the information received may be distorted. Edwin Flippo offers the following practical advice to avoid misunderstandings and to secure accurate information:

1. Prepare for the interview; rapport is facilitated if the worker feels he is not talking to a person totally ignorant of his job.
2. Introduce yourself so the worker and supervisor know who you are and why you are there.
3. Show a sincere interest in the worker and the job being analyzed.
4. Do not try to tell the employee how to do his job; your task is to obtain and organize information.
5. Verify the information obtained.[2]

Job Description

Assuming the personnel manager has a thorough, accurate job analysis, the next step is to write up a job description. This typically includes: (1) a job identification, which lists items such as the job title, department, division, plant location, and pay range; (2) a job summary detailing the position's procedures and responsibilities; it describes the duties performed, how they are to be performed, and the purpose of each duty, and (3) an account of working conditions.

A controversy has arisen recently concerning the degree of specificity necessary or desirable for job descriptions. Some management theorists argue for a detailed account of tasks, duties, and working conditions, whereas others favor a more unstructured or general job description. It is difficult to resolve this issue in a comprehensive manner because the nature of the job plays an important part in selecting the proper approach, e.g., managerial positions will typically require a more general description than a job on a factory line. In most cases, however, we favor a relatively specific job description. Arguments against a detailed job description are that it: (1) limits the jobholder's initiative and creativity, (2) is easily dated with job changes, and (3) can be used by the employee to avoid additional duties. But (3) is a motivational issue; the unmotivated employee could also seek to avoid additional duties by appeal to the vagueness of a nonspecific job description, in which case changes as mentioned in (2) would also have to be addressed and the job description made more specific. And, against (1), the employee with initiative might be able to develop responsibilities in addition to those already specified in some detail, which might lead to a job description revision that increases the productivity of other employees holding the same type of job. An additional factor related directly to hiring is that if the job description is used to help train new workers how to perform their jobs, it should contain specifics.

There are two major reasons favoring a specific, complete job description. The pragmatic reason is that the law now requires it. In the case of hiring, selection tests are based on the job description; one tests for the ability to perform tasks specified in the job description. In *Griggs* v. *Duke Power Co.* (1971), the Supreme Court held that selection tests must have validity, i.e., they must accurately represent actual on-the-job activities. In *Albemarle Paper* v. *Moody* (1975), the Supreme Court held that if tests are used to screen candidates for a job, then the duties and responsibilities of that job must be carefully analyzed and described prior to testing. More fundamentally, utility for the firm and fairness to the prospective employee are enhanced when the employee knows what is expected of him. Turnover costs relating to mismatched employees who resign, and the long range consequences of retaining mismatched employees, favor having the employer provide a relatively specific and complete job description.

Job Specification

A job specification lists qualifications needed to perform the job. In some cases this may seem straightforward, as in law or accounting, where specific training is required and professional standards are well articulated. Where the firm intends to hire an untrained person and train him for a job, careful consideration must be given to developing a set of qualifications. In either case, however, morality and legality require that the employer use only those qualifying criteria that relate directly to success on the job.

The legality of this principle was established in the case of *Griggs* v. *Duke Power Co.* (1971). From 1955 on Duke Power required a high school educa-tion for all positions in its Dan River power plant except the lowest level janitorial jobs. In 1966, Willie Griggs brought suit against Duke, claiming the educational requirement for the position of coal handler was discriminatory because it was not valid, i.e., not related to success on the job. Coal handlers unload, weigh, and transport coal via the use of heavy equipment. Duke argued that, as its business became more technologically oriented, it needed the education requirement, that, for example, a coal handler must have language facility in order to read manuals relating to the use of machines and equipment he operates. Duke also argued that the educational requirement provided some basis for believing that its employees would be able to advance to supervisory positions. But Duke allowed that no studies had been conducted to that time to establish that the educational requirement was related to job performance and success.

Although lower courts had decided the case basically in favor of Duke, the U.S. Supreme Court heard the case in part to resolve the question of whether an employer is prevented by the 1964 Civil Rights Act from requiring a high school education as a condition of employment when such education has not been shown to be significantly related to successful job performance and when it disqualifies a disproportionally high number of minority applicants. The Court found that "Congress has placed on the employer the burden of showing that any given requirement must have a manifest relationship to the employment in question."[3] In an 8–0 ruling, the Court decided against Duke because the educational requirement was not shown to be related to successful job performance. In fact, it was pointed out that white employees without a high school education (who had become coal handlers before the educational requirement was instituted) performed the job satisfactorily.

The morality of employing only qualifying criteria that relate to job success rests on both consequentialist and nonconsequentialist grounds. If job qualifications are set too high for the actual job, the individual hired may not be able to work to potential; and if they are set too low, the individual hired may not be able to perform successfully. In either case, job satisfaction is not liable to be achieved and the firm's efficiency and profitability are liable to be impaired, with consequent disutility to the firm and society. In addition, those individuals not hired have been denied fair access to the market.

Recruitment

In recruiting candidates a firm typically attempts to obtain a large selection ratio, i.e., a large number of applicants relative to the positions open. In this way the company has a better chance of selecting the best person for the job. However, fairness to the job seeker and utility for the firm both require that the personnel manager seek to attract only relevant candidates. Interviewing and testing are expensive activities for the firm, and a considerable amount of applicants' time and money can be wasted if an overzealous recruiter, intent on maximizing his selection ratio, fails to recruit only relevant candidates who can fill the job description and specification. Also, we should not overlook the psychological damage to an otherwise qualified applicant who is rejected in the early stages of the screening process (perhaps with no subsequent explanation) because of a recruiting mismatch.

A recruiting device, such as an advertisement, should therefore be relatively complete. It should contain items such as the job title, duties, qualifications and experience required, working conditions, salary, and fringe benefits. It should also be somewhat detailed, if that is possible; relevant portions of the job description and specification could in certain cases be included. Of course, the amount of information included must be balanced with the cost of the advertisement. In addition, fairness requires that the employer reveal his identity if he expects the job seeker to provide detailed biographical data. It also requires that the advertisement portray the firm in a realistic manner. Hiring is only one aspect of personnel management; retaining good employees is another important function. Job satisfaction is a key element in attaining a high retention ratio, and a considerable amount of job dissatisfaction is traceable to unrealistic recruitment efforts that attempt to make a firm "look good" to applicants. Thus, utility to the firm and fairness to the applicant necessitate realistic recruiting techniques.

Testing

The hiring process through the recruitment stage involves gathering applicants. Subsequent steps involve the rejection of candidates until available positions are filled. While the actual selection process may involve many stages, including application blanks and reference checks, we will discuss only the testing and interviewing steps.

Psychological testing became an important tool in the hiring process in the 1920s. It held the promise of bringing scientific objectivity to selection procedures, and this promise has certainly been partially realized. The psychologists' intelligence, physical, achievement, aptitude, and personality tests have enabled many people to make better career selections and have helped firms to better match employees and available job, both of which lead to increased employee job satisfaction, productivity, and profitability. During the 1960s, however, with increased concern over civil rights, scientists were led to restudy tests because of the fact that a high percentage of minorities were failing them. For example, one study showed that only 6 percent of blacks could pass a battery of standardized tests, compared with 58 percent of whites.[4] Critics of such tests pointed out that they were culture bound, and reflected the majority culture. Also, the predictive ability of such tests was questioned; one study found that most industrial occupations tests had little validity.[5] Other studies indicated that many workers who could not pass commonly used tests could, nevertheless, perform tasks the tests were designed to measure as well as individuals who did pass.[6]

The 1964 Civil Rights Act banned tests that were designed or used to discriminate, but it did not ban all tests:

... nor shall it be an unlawful employment practice for an employer to give and to act upon the results of any professionally developed ability test provided that such test, its administration or action upon the results is not designed, intended or used to discriminate because of race, color, religion, sex, or national origin.[7]

The Equal Employment Opportunity Commission, established to enforce employment antidiscrimination laws, interpreted "professionally developed ability test" to mean a test that,

fairly measures the knowledge or skills required by the particular job or class of jobs which the applicant seeks, or which fairly affords the employer a chance to measure the applicant's ability to perform a particular job or class of jobs. The fact that a test was prepared by an individual or organization claiming expertise in test preparation does not, without more, justify its use.[8]

Now, in addition to addressing the issue of educational requirements, the *Griggs* v. *Duke Power* case also addressed testing. Griggs argued that there were no scientific studies establishing Duke's tests as job related and that they did not "fairly measure the knowledge or skills required by the particular job" sought. The plaintiff also claimed that Duke's tests discriminated against blacks. Duke argued that, although there were no formal studies validating its tests for the particular jobs available in its power plants, nevertheless some *general* measure of intelligence and aptitude was required for hiring people to work in its complex plants and for ensuring their capability of advancement to supervisory levels. The company also argued that its tests should be acceptable because they were "professionally developed" as required by law, and served a legitimate business purpose.

In its 8–0 decision, the U.S. Supreme Court rejected Duke's claim that its general intelligence and ability tests were permitted by the 1964 Civil Rights Act. The Court held that employment tests must be *validated*, i.e., they must demonstrably measure what they propose to measure, which, in the case of a selection test, means the test must bear a predictive relationship to *actual* job performance regarding a particular job or type of work. Since Duke's general intelligence and ability tests were not validated, they could not be used:

Congress has placed on the employer the burden of showing that any given requirement must have a manifest relationship to the employment in question ... nothing in the (Civil Rights) Act precludes the use of testing or measuring procedures; obviously they are useful. What Congress has forbidden is giving these devices and mechanisms controlling force unless they are demonstrably a reasonable measure of job performance.[9]

There are both consequentialist and nonconsequentialist grounds for the Supreme Court's decision. The firm's aim is to staff positions with people who can best enable it to attain its goals, and the Court's decision forces the employer to show that his test is actually related to job performance. This should lead to greater efficiency and profitability for the company. The consequences for the jobholder, in terms of success and satisfaction, should be better for the person whose qualifications fit the position than for a person who is mismatched with a job via an invalid test. Also, society not only benefits from the avoidance of mismatches, but also from the lessening of social unrest resulting from awareness that selection tests must be based on merit rather than factors unrelated to job performance. On the nonconsequentialist side, a test that is not valid can hardly be fair to an otherwise qualified candidate who is rejected via the test. And not only does the decision help ensure fairness in selection, it also reinforces the private enterprise, free market conception of the economy by helping to provide equal employment opportunity and fair access to the market. Hence, the decision promotes both social justice and economic efficiency.

Special care must be taken to ensure the validity of certain sorts of tests that may be used in screening candidates. Some firms use polygraphs to screen, and carefully fashioned tests of this sort can have validity. But the nature of the device is such that the questioner typically follows up on a response, and this can easily lead into non-job-related areas of investigation that may represent a serious invasion of privacy. Similarly, personality tests, used to measure stability, motivation, and other aspects of character, are frequently problematic. They may invade privacy and are difficult to evaluate properly. In many cases the relationship between personality traits and job success is tenuous. Where such a relationship can be established, however, it can both help the employee to better himself and his placement in the organization, and also enable the employer to provide the applicant more adequate placement. The American Psychological Association has ethical standards that, together with the requirement of test validity, would protect significantly the rights of test takers:

1. The individual test taker has the right to the confidentiality of the test results and the right to informed consent regarding the use of those test results.
2. The individual has the right to expect that only people qualified to interpret the scores will have access to those scores, or that sufficient information will accompany the test scores to ensure their appropriate interpretation.
3. The individual has the right to expect that the test is equally fair to all test takers in the sense of being equally familiar or unfamiliar, so that the test results reflect the test taker's true abilities.[10]

Interviewing

Tests are infrequently used as the only selection technique; most often they are used in conjunction with interviews. In fact, after passage of the Civil Rights Act, when it was found that some of the standard tests were invalid, many personnel managers dropped testing altogether and based their selection decisions primarily on interviews. But there are two major problems with this approach to hiring. On the one hand, as Robert Dipboye, Richard Arvey, and David Terpstra have pointed out, there are problems with the interview itself. Interviewers frequently:

1. Issue judgments that are less reliable than objective tests; they frequeutly disagree in their assessments of a job candidate.
2. Miss or suppress information, and weigh negative data more than positive data.
3. Judge candidates via an ideal stereotype, e.g., white caucasian interviewers have the ideal of a young, white male.
4. Allow initial impressions to influence subsequent decisions.
5. Judge candidates on the basis of superficial traits such as physical attractiveness or manner of dress.[11]

Thus the interview method is often unreliable and invalid; it yields inconsistent results and fails to accurately predict job success. On the other hand, the courts have extended the validity requirement from tests to any selection procedure. In *Rowe* v. *General Motors* (1972), the Fifth Circuit Court of Appeals ruled against General Motors's practice of relying on its foremen to recommend employees for promotion; the Court stated, "The foremen base their recommendations on subjective and vague standards, there are no safeguards designed to avert discriminatory practices and a disproportionately small percentage of Negro hourly employees have been promoted or transferred to salaried positions."[12] A 1971 Equal Employment Opportunity Commission decision regarding interviewing held that "It is essential that the system be objective in nature and be such as to permit review."[13]

The ethical basis of the Court's decisions requiring interviewing validity is the same as we sketched in our discussion of testing. Fairness and utility regarding the person hired, the firm, and members of society require that interviews, and indeed any selection procedure, have validity. Gary Dessler offers some practical suggestions for structuring the interview process in a way that complies with the law and enables the firm to select the best candidate:

1. Select interviewers carefully and train them properly.
2. Know the requirements of the job via a fully developed job analysis, description, and specification.
3. Use a structured guide so that job related questions are asked.
4. Structure the process so that a decision is not premature.
5. Avoid a total reliance on interviews; balance them with tests, reference checks, etc.
6. Validate interviewer decisions as predictors of job success.[14]

Apart from its place in the hiring process, interviews also are used to give job candidates a preview of life in the firm. In many cases a preview is used to make the firm "look good" and "sell" it to the candidate. But there are reasons why a preview should be realistic, i.e., why it should balance the positive and negative aspects of the job and organization. If the candidate has unrealistic expectations, he may become dissatisfied and resign, with attendant turnover costs to the firm and himself; or he may stay on as a dissatisfied employee who affects the firm's productivity and other workers' morale. Dessler's study indicates that job longevity and satisfaction are increased if a job preview is realistic.

III. SUBSEQUENT DEVELOPMENTS

The underlying principle of the *Griggs* v. *Duke Power* case is this: employer practices that adversely impact on minorities *and* are not validated are illegal. Put another way, if a selection procedure is to be legal then it either has no adverse impact, or if it does have an adverse impact, then the procedure has to be validated. Congress confirmed this principle in the 1972 amendments to Title VII of the 1964 Civil Rights Act. By 1976, however, two different sets of compliance guidelines were being employed by the Equal Employment Opportunity Commission and other federal agencies (Justice, Labor and Civil Service). In 1978, a new, uniform set of compliance guidelines was issued stating, in part, that:

> A procedure having adverse impact constitutes discrimination unless justified . . . unless the procedure has been validated.[15]

Although this is equivalent to the Griggs principle, the guideline is interpreted to mean that:

> A selection procedure which has no adverse impact generally does not violate Title VII. . . . This means that an employer may usually avoid the application of the guidelines by use of procedures which have no adverse impact. If adverse impact exists, it must be justified on grounds of business necessity. Normally, this means by validation which demonstrates the relation between the selection procedure and performance on the job.[16]

In other words, on this interpretation if a selection procedure has no adverse impact, then it is legal; *but* if a selection procedure has an adverse impact and is not validated, then it is illegal. An "adverse impact" is vaguely defined as "a substantially different rate of selection in hiring, promotion, or other employment decisions which works to the disadvantage of members of a race, sex, or ethnic group."[17] In practice, however, the guidelines spell out "adverse impact" in terms of selection ratios, i.e., the number of applicants hired divided by the total number of applicants. A selection ratio for any minority group that is less than 80% of the ratio for the group with the highest ratio is generally regarded as evidence of adverse impact.[18]

Now, from both the *Griggs* principle and the above interpretation of the new guidelines we can infer that a legal selection procedure that has adverse impact must be validated. However, from the *Griggs* principle we cannot infer that if an invalidated selection procedure has no adverse impact, then it is legal; whereas we can infer this from the above interpretation of the new guidelines. Furthermore, the *Griggs* principle cannot be interpreted to imply that if a validated selection procedure has no adverse impact, then it is legal; but we can infer this from the new guidelines. Hence, although we cannot infer from the *Griggs* principle that if a selection procedure has no adverse impact (whether or not it is validated), then it is legal, we can infer this from the new guidelines. Accordingly, under the new guidelines a firm would only have to hire in accordance with the 80 percent selection ratio rule to be in compliance with the law. This raises the difficult question of the morality of hiring in terms of "quotas" or via affirmative action programs, a topic to which the next section is devoted.

NOTES

1. Civil Rights Act of 1964, Title VII, Section 703 (a).
2. Edwin B. Flippo, *Principles of Personnel Management* (New York: McGraw-Hill, 1966) 2d ed., pp. 117–119.
3. *Griggs* v. *Duke Power Co.,* 401 US 424, p. 432.
4. *Griggs* v. *Duke Power Co.,* 420 F.2d., p. 1239.
5. E. E. Ghisselli, *The Validity of Occupational Aptitude Tests* (New York: J. Wiley & Sons, 1966), p. 127.
6. T. A. Fermen, *The Negro and Equal Employment Opportunities* (New York: Frederick A. Praeger, 1968), p. 47.
7. Civil Rights Act of 1964, Title VII, Section 703 (h).
8. *Griggs,* 915 Ct., p. 855.
9. *Griggs,* 401 US 424, pp. 432, 436.
10. Based on Marilyn K. Quantance, "Test Security: Foundation of Public Merit Systems," *Personnel Psychology* 33, no. 1 (Spring 1980): 25–32.
11. Robert L. Dipboye, Richard D. Avrey, and David E. Terpstra, "Equal Employment and the Interview," *Personnel Journal* 55, no. 10 (October 1976): 520–24.
12. *Rowe* vs. *General Motors Corp.,* U.S. Court of Appeals, Fifth Circuit (New Orleans), no. 28959, March 2, 1972 (Summarized in the *Bureau of National Affairs Fair Employment Practices Cases,* vol. 4, pp. 445–54).
13. Equal Employment Opportunity Commission Decision no. 72-0703, December 27, 1971 (Summarized in the *Bureau of National Affairs Fair Employment Practices Cases,* vol. 4, pp. 435–37).
14. Gary Dessler, *Personnel Management* (Reston: Reston Publishing, 1981), 2d ed., pp. 134–42.
15. "Uniform Guidelines on Employee Selection Procedures," *Federal Register* 43, no. 166 (August 25, 1978), p. 38297.
16. Ibid., pp. 38290–1.
17. Ibid., p. 38307.
18. Ibid., pp. 38291, 38297–8.

REVERSE DISCRIMINATION

United Steelworkers v. *Weber*

[*What follows are portions of the majority opinion by Justice Brennan, together with selected passages from the dissenting opinion of Justice Rehnquist. Some footnotes have been dropped, with those remaining having been renumbered.*—Eds.]

Mr. Justice Brennan delivered the opinion of the Court.

In 1974 petitioner United Steelworkers of America (USWA) and petitioner Kaiser Aluminum & Chemical Corporation (Kaiser) entered into a master collective-bargaining agreement covering terms and conditions of employment at 15 Kaiser plants. The agreement contained, *inter alia,* an affirmative action plan designed to eliminate conspicuous racial imbalances in Kaiser's then almost exclusively white craft work forces. Black craft hiring goals were set for each Kaiser plant equal to the percentage of blacks in the respective local labor forces. To enable plants to meet these goals, on-the-job training programs were established to teach unskilled production workers—black and white—the skills necessary to become craft workers. The plan reserved for black employees 50% of the openings in these newly created in-plant training programs.

This case arose from the operation of the plan at Kaiser's plant in Gramercy, Louisiana. Until 1974 Kaiser hired as craft workers for that plant only persons who had had prior craft experience. Because blacks had long been excluded from craft unions, few were able to present such credentials. As a consequence, prior to 1974 only 1.88% (five out of 273) of the skilled craft workers at the Gramercy plant were black, even though the work force in the Gramercy area was approximately 39% black.

From *United Steelworkers, Etc.* v. *Weber* 443 U.S. 193, S.Ct. 2721 (1979).

Pursuant to the national agreement Kaiser altered its craft hiring practice in the Gramercy plant. Rather than hiring already trained outsiders, Kaiser established a training program to train its production workers to fill craft openings. Selection of craft trainees was made on the basis of seniority, with the proviso that at least 50% of the new trainees were to be black until the percentage of black skilled craft workers in the Gramercy plant approximated the percentage of blacks in the local labor force.

During 1974, the first year of the operation of the Kaiser-USWA affirmative action plan, 13 craft trainees were selected from Gramercy's production work force. Of these, 7 were black and 6 white. The most junior black selected into the program had less seniority than several white production workers whose bids for admission were rejected. Thereafter one of those white production workers, respondent Brian Weber, instituted this class action in the United States District Court for the Eastern District of Louisiana.

The complaint alleged that the filling of craft trainee positions at the Gramercy plant pursuant to the affirmative action program had resulted in junior black employees receiving training in preference to more senior white employees, thus discriminating against respondent and other similarly situated white employees in violation of §§703 (a)[1] and (d)[2] of Title VII (of the Civil Rights Act of 1964). The District Court held that the plan violated Title VII, entered a judgment in favor of the plaintiff class, and granted a permanent injunction prohibiting Kaiser and the USWA "from denying plaintiffs, Brian F. Weber and all other members of the class, access to on-the-job training programs on the basis of race." . . . A divided panel of the Court of Appeals for the Fifth Circuit affirmed. . . . We reverse.

We emphasize at the outset the narrowness of our inquiry. Since the Kaiser-USWA plan does not involve state action, this case does not present an alleged violation of the Equal Protection Clause of the Constitution. Further, since the Kaiser-USWA plan was adopted voluntarily, we are not concerned with what Title VII requires or with what a court might order to remedy a past proven violation of the Act. The only question before us is the narrow statutory issue of whether Title VII *forbids* private employers and unions from voluntarily agreeing upon bona fide affirmative action plans that accord racial preferences in the manner and for the purpose provided in the Kaiser-USWA plan. That question was expressly left open in *McDonald* v. *Santa Fe Trail Trans. Co.*, 427 U.S. 273 (1976) . . . which held, in a case not involving affirmative action, that Title VII protects whites as well as blacks from certain forms of racial discrimination.

Respondent argues that Congress intended in Title VII to prohibit all race-conscious affirmative action plans. Respondent's argument rests upon a literal interpretation of §§703 (a) and (d) of the Act. Those sections make it unlawful to "discriminate . . . because of . . . race" in hiring and in the selection of apprentices for training programs. Since, the argument runs, *McDonald* v. *Santa Fe Trail Trans. Co.*, settled that Title VII forbids discrimination against whites as well as blacks, and since the Kaiser-USWA affirmative action plan operates to discriminate against white employees solely because they are white, it follows that the Kaiser-USWA plan violates Title VII.

Respondent's argument is not without force. But it overlooks the significance of the fact that the Kaiser-USWA plan is an affirmative action plan voluntarily adopted by private parties to eliminate traditional patterns of racial segregation. In this context respondent's reliance upon a literal construction of §§703 (a) and (d) and upon *McDonald* is misplaced. . . . It is a "familiar rule that a thing may be within the letter of the statute and yet not within the statute, because not within its spirit nor within the intention of its makers." *Holy Trinity Church v. United States,* 143 U.S. 457. . . . The prohibition against racial discrimination in §§703 (a) and (d) of Title VII must therefore be read against the background of the legislative history of Title VII and the historical context from which the Act arose. . . . Examination of those sources makes clear that an interpretation of the sections that forbade all race-conscious affirmative action would "bring about an end completely at variance with the purpose of the statute" and must be rejected. . . .

Congress' primary concern in enacting the prohibition against racial discrimination in Title VII of the Civil Rights Act of 1964 was with "the plight of the Negro in our economy." 110 Cong. Rec. 6548 (remarks of Sen. Humphrey). Before 1964, blacks were largely relegated to "unskilled and semi-skilled jobs." *Id.,* at 6548. . . . Because of automation the number of such jobs was rapidly decreasing. . . . As a consequence "the relative position of the Negro worker (was) steadily worsening. In 1947 the non-white unemployment rate was only 64% higher than the white rate; in 1962 it was 124% higher." *Id.,* at 6547. . . . Congress considered this a serious social problem. As Senator Clark told the Senate:

> The rate of Negro unemployment has gone up consistently as compared with white unemployment for the past 15 years. This is a social malaise and a social situation which we should not tolerate. This is one of the principal reasons why this bill should pass. *Id.,* at 7220.

Congress feared that the goals of the Civil Rights Act—the integration of blacks into the mainstream of American society—could not be achieved unless this trend were reversed. And Congress recognized that that would not be possible unless blacks were able to secure jobs "which have a future." . . . As Senator Humphrey explained to the Senate:

> What good does it do a Negro to be able to eat in a fine restaurant if he cannot afford to pay the bill? What good does it do him to be accepted in a hotel that is too expensive for his modest income? How can a Negro child be motivated to take full advantage of integrated educational facilities if he has no hope of getting a job where he can use that education? *Id.,* at 6547.

Accordingly, it was clear to Congress that "the crux of the problem (was) to open employment opportunities for Negroes in occupations which have been traditionally closed to them," *Id.,* at 6548 . . . , and it was to this problem that Title VII's prohibition against racial discrimination in employment was primarily addressed.

It plainly appears from the House Report accompanying the Civil Rights Act that Congress did not intend wholly to prohibit private and voluntary affirmative action efforts as one method of solving this problem. The Report provides:

> No bill can or should lay claim to eliminating all of the causes and consequences of racial and other types of discrimination against minorities. There is reason to believe, however, that national leadership provided by the enactment of Federal legislation dealing with the most troublesome problems *will create an atmosphere conducive to voluntary or local resolution of other forms of discrimination.* H.R. Rep. No. 914, 88th Cong., 1st Sess. (1963), at 18. (Emphasis supplied.)

Given this legislative history, we cannot agree with respondent that Congress intended to prohibit the private sector from taking effective steps to accomplish the goal that Congress designated Title VII to achieve. The very statutory words intended as a spur or catalyst to cause "employers and unions to self-examine and to self-evaluate their employment practices and to endeavor to eliminate, so far as possible, the last vestiges of an unfortunate and ignominious page in this country's history," *Albemarle* v. *Moody,* 422 U.S. 405 . . . , cannot be interpreted as an absolute prohibition against all private, voluntary, race-conscious affirmative action efforts to hasten the elimination of such vestiges.[3] It would be ironic indeed if a law triggered by a Nation's concern over centuries of racial injustice and intended to improve the lot of those who had "been excluded from the American dream for so long," 110 Cong. Rec., at 6552, constituted the first legislative prohibition of all voluntary, private, race-conscious efforts to abolish traditional patterns of racial segregation and hierarchy.

Our conclusion is further reinforced by examination of the language and legislative history of §703 (j) of Title VII.[4] Opponents of Title VII raised two related arguments against the bill. First, they argued that the Act would be interpreted to require employers with racially imbalanced work forces to grant preferential treatment to racial minorities in order to integrate. Second, they argued that employers with racially imbalanced work forces would grant preferential treatment to racial minorities, even if not required to do so by the Act. Had Congress meant to prohibit all race-conscious affirmative action, as respondent urges, it easily could have answered both objections by providing that Title VII would not require or *permit* racially preferential integration efforts. But Congress did not choose such a course. Rather Congress added § 703 (j) which addresses only the first objection. . . . The section does *not* state that' 'nothing in Title VII shall be interpreted to *permit*" voluntary affirmative efforts to correct racial imbalances. The natural inference is that Congress chose not to forbid all voluntary race-conscious affirmative action.

The reasons for this choice are evident from the legislative record. Title

VII could not have been enacted into law without substantial support from legislators in both Houses who traditionally resisted federal regulation of private business. Those legislators demanded as a price for their support that "management prerogatives and union freedoms . . . be left undisturbed to the greatest extent possible." . . . Section 703 (j) was proposed . . . to prevent § 703 of Title VII from being interpreted in such a way as to lead to undue "Federal Government interference with private businesses because of some Federal employees ideas about racial balance or imbalance." 110 Cong. Rec., at 14314. Clearly, a prohibition against all voluntary, race-conscious, affirmative action efforts would disserve these ends. Such a prohibition would augment the powers of the Federal Government and diminish traditional management prerogatives while at the same time impeding attainment of the ultimate statutory goals. . . .

We need not today define in detail the line of demarcation between permissible and impermissible affirmative action plans. It suffices to hold that the challenged Kaiser-USWA affirmative action plan falls on the permissible side of the line.

(T)he plan does not unnecessarily trammel the interests of the white employees. The plan does not require the discharge of white workers and their replacement with new black hires. . . . Nor does the plan create an absolute bar to the advancement of white employees; half of those trained in the program will be white. Moreover, the plan is a temporary measure; it is not intended to maintain racial balance, but simply to eliminate a manifest racial imbalance. Preferential selection of craft trainees at the Gramercy plant will end as soon as the percentage of black skilled craft workers in the Gramercy plant approximates the percentage of blacks in the local labor force.

We conclude, therefore, that the adoption of the Kaiser-USWA plan for the Gramercy plant falls within the area of discretion left by Title VII to the private sector voluntarily to adopt affirmative action plans designed to eliminate conspicuous racial imbalance in traditionally segregated job categories. Accordingly, the judgment of the Court of Appeals for the Fifth Circuit is *Reversed.*

Mr. Justice Rehnquist, with whom the Chief Justice joins, dissenting.

In a very real sense, the Court's opinion is ahead of its time: it could more appropriately have been handed down five years from now in 1984, a year coinciding with the title of a book from which the Court's opinion borrows, perhaps subconsciously, at least one idea. Orwell describes in his book a governmental official of Oceania, one of the three great world powers, denouncing the current enemy, Eurasia, to an assembled crowd:

> It was almost impossible to listen to him without being first convinced and then maddened. . . . The speech had been proceeding for perhaps twenty minutes when a messenger hurried onto the platform and a scrap of paper was slipped into the speaker's hand. He unrolled and read it without pausing in his speech. Nothing altered in his voice or manner, or in the content of what he was saying, but suddenly the names were different. Without words said, a wave of understanding rippled through the crowd. Oceania was at

war with Eastasia! . . . The banners and posters with which the square was decorated were all wrong!

[T]he speaker had switched from one line to the other actually in mid-sentence, not only without pause, but without even breaking the syntax. G. Orwell, *Nineteen Eighty-Four,* 182–3 (1949).

Today's decision represents an equally dramatic and equally unremarked switch in the Court's interpretation of Title VII.

The operative sections of Title VII prohibit racial discrimination in employment *simpliciter.* Taken in its normal meaning and as understood by all Members of Congress who spoke to the issue during the legislative debates, this language prohibits a covered employer from considering race when making an employment decision, whether the race be black or white. Several years ago, however, a United States District Court held that "the dismissal of white employees charged with misappropriating company property while not dismissing a similarly charged Negro employee does not raise a claim upon which Title VII relief may be granted." *McDonald* v. *Santa Fe Trail Trans. Co.,* 427 U.S. 273, 278. This Court unanimously reversed, concluding from the "uncontradicted legislative history" that Title VII prohibits racial discrimination against the white petitioners in this case upon the same standards as would be applicable were they Negroes. . . ." 427 U.S., at 280.

We have never wavered in our understanding that Title VII "prohibits *all* racial discrimination in employment, without exception for any particular employees." *Id.,* at 283. . . . In our most recent discussion of the issue, we uttered words seemingly dispositive of this case: "It is clear beyond cavil that the obligation imposed by Title VII is to provide an equal opportunity for each applicant regardless of race, without regard to whether members of the applicant's race are already proportionately represented in the work force." *Furnco Construction Corp.* v. *Waters,* 438 U.S. 567,569 (1978).[5]

Today, however, the Court behaves much like the Orwellian speaker earlier described, as if it had been handed a note indicating that Title VII would lead to a result unacceptable to the Court if interpreted here as it was in our prior decisions. Accordingly, without even a break in syntax, the Court rejects "a literal construction of §703 (a)" in favor of newly discovered "legislative history," which leads it to a conclusion directly contrary to that compelled by the "uncontradicted legislative history" unearthed in *McDonald* and our other prior decisions. Now we are told that the legislative history of Title VII shows that employers are free to discriminate on the basis of race. . . . Our earlier interpretations of Title VII, like the banners and posters decorating the square in Oceania, were all wrong.

As if this were not enough to make a reasonable observer question the Court's adherence to the oft-stated principle that our duty is to construe rather than rewrite legislation, . . . the Court also seizes upon §703 (j) of Title VII as an independent, or at least partially independent, basis for its holding. Totally ignoring the wording of that section, which is obviously addressed to those charged with the responsibility of interpreting the law rather than those who are subject to its prescriptions, and totally ignoring the months of legislative debates preceding the sections introduction and passage, which demonstrate clearly that it was enacted to prevent precisely what occurred in this case, the Court infers from §703 (j) that "Congress chose not to forbid all voluntary race-conscious affirmative action."

Thus, by a *tour de force* reminiscent not of jurists such as Hale, Holmes, and Hughes, but of escape artists such as Houdini, the Court eludes clear statutory language, "uncontradicted" legislative history and uniform precedent in concluding that employers are, after all, permitted to consider race in making employment decisions. . . .

Were Congress to act today specifically to prohibit the type of racial discrimination suffered by Weber, it would be hard pressed to draft language better tailored to the task than that found in § 703 (d) of Title VII. . . . Equally suited to the task would be §703 (a) (2), which makes it unlawful for an employer to classify his employees "in any way which would deprive or tend to deprive any individual of employment opportunities or otherwise adversely affect his status as an employee, because of such individual's race, color, religion, sex, or national origin."

Entirely consistent with these two express prohibitions is the language of §703 (j) of Title VII, which provides that the Act is not to be interpreted "to require any employer . . . to grant preferential treatment to any individual or to any group because of race. . . ." Seizing on the word "require," the Court infers that Congress must have intended to "permit" this type of racial discrimination. Not only is this reading of §703 (j) outlandish in the light of flat prohibitions of §§ 703(a) and (d), but it is totally belied by the Act's legislative history.

Quite simply, Kaiser's racially discriminatory admission quota is flatly prohibited by the plain language of Title VII. This normally dispositive fact,[6] however, gives the Court only momentary pause. An "interpretation" of the statute upholding Weber's claim would, according to the Court, "bring about an end completely at variance with the purpose of the statute." To support this conclusion, the Court calls upon the "spirit" of the Act, which it divines from passages in Title VII's legislative history indicating that enactment of the statute was prompted by Congress's desire "to open employment opportunities for Negroes in occupations which (had) been traditionally closed to them." But the legislative history invoked by the Court to avoid the plain language of §§703 (a) and (d) simply misses the point. To be sure, the reality of employment discrimination against Negroes provided the primary impetus for passage of Title VII. But this fact by no means supports the proposition that Congress intended to leave employers free to discriminate against white persons. In most cases, legislative history . . . is more vague than the statute we are called upon to interpret. Here, however, the legislative history of Title VII is as clear as the language of §§703 (a) and (d), and it irrefutably demonstrates that Congress meant precisely what it said in §§703 (a) and (d)—that *no* racial discrimination in employment is permissible under Title VII, not even preferential treatment of minorities to correct racial imbalance.

Introduced on the floor of the House of Representatives on June 20, 1963, the bill—H.R. 7152—that ultimately became the Civil Rights Act of 1964 contained no compulsory provisions directed at private discrimination in employment. The bill was promptly referred to the Committee on the Judiciary, where it was amended to include Title VII.

After noting that "[t]he purpose of (Title VII) is to eliminate . . . discrimination in employment based on race, color, religion, or national origin," the Judiciary Committee's report simply paraphrased the provisions of Title VII without elaboration. In a separate Minority Report, however, opponents of the measure on the Committee advanced a line of attack which was reiterated throughout the debates in both the House and Senate and which ultimately led to passage of §703 (j). Noting that the word "discrimination" was nowhere defined in H.R. 7152, the Minority Report posited a number of hypothetical employment situations, concluding in each example that the employer "*may be forced to hire according to race,* to 'racially balance' those who work for him *in every job classification* or be in violation of Federal law."

When H.R. 7152 reached the House floor, the opening speech in support of its passage was delivered by Representative Celler, Chairman of the House Judiciary Committee. . . . A portion of that speech responded to criticism "seriously misrepresent(ing) what the bill would do and grossly distort(ing) its effects":

> [T]he charge has been made that the Equal Employment Opportunity Commission to be established by Title VII of the bill would have the power to prevent a business from employing and promoting the people it wished, and that a "Federal Inspector" could then order the hiring and promotion only of employees of certain races or religious groups. This description of the bill is entirely wrong. . . .
>
> Even (a) court could not order that any preference be given to any particular race, religion or other group, but would be limited to ordering an end of discrimination. The statement that a Federal Inspector could order the employment and promotion only of members of a specific racial or religious group is therefore patently erroneous.
>
> . . . [T]he bill would do no more than prevent . . . employers from discriminating against or *in favor of* workers because of their race, religion, or national origin. 110 Cong. Rec. 1518 (1964) (emphasis added).

Representative Celler's construction of Title VII was repeated by several other supporters during the House debate.

The Senate debate was broken into three phases: the debate on sending the bill to Committee, the general debate on the bill prior to invocation of cloture, and the debate following cloture. (1). When debate on the motion to refer the bill to Committee opened, . . . Senator Humphrey . . . was the first to state the proponents' understanding of Title VII. Responding to a political advertisement charging that federal agencies were at liberty to interpret the word "discrimination" in Title VII to require racial balance, Senator Humphrey stated: "[T]he meaning of racial or religious discrimination is perfectly clear. . . . [I]t means a distinction and treatment given to different individuals because of their different race, religion, or national origin." Stressing that Title VII "does not limit the employer's freedom to hire, fire, promote, or demote for any reasons—or no reasons—so long as his action is not based on race," Senator Humphrey further stated that "nothing in the bill would permit any official or court to require any employer or any labor union to give preferential treatment to any minority group." (2). In the opening speech of the formal Senate debate on the bill, Senator Humphrey addressed the main concern of Title VII's opponents, advising that not only does Title VII not require use of racial quotas, *it does not permit* their use. "The truth," stated the floor leader of the bill, "is that this title forbids discriminating against anyone on account of race. This is the simple and complete truth about Title VII." 110 Cong. Rec. 6549 (1964).

At the close of his speech, Senator Humphrey returned briefly to the subject of employment quotas: "It is claimed that the bill would require racial quotas for all hiring, when in fact it provides that race shall not be a basis for making personnel decisions." *Id.,* at 6553.

Senator Kuchel delivered the second major speech in support of H.R. 7152. Senator Kuchel emphasized that seniority rights would in no way be affected by Title VII: "Employers and labor organizations could not discriminate *in favor of or against* a person because of his race, his religion, or his national origin. . . ." *Id.,* at 6564 (emphasis added).

A few days later the Senate's attention focused exclusively on Title VII, as Senators Clark and Case rose to discuss the title of H.R. 7152 on which they shared floor "captain" responsibilities. . . . Of particular relevance to the instant case were their observations regarding seniority rights. As if directing their comments at Brian Weber, the Senators said:

> Title VII would have no effect on established seniority rights. Its effect is prospective and not retrospective. Thus, for example, if a business has been discriminating in the past and as a result has an all-white working force, when the title comes into effect the employer's obligation would be simply to fill future vacancies on a nondiscriminatory basis. He would not be obliged— *or indeed permitted*—to fire whites in order to hire Negroes, *or to prefer Negroes for future vacancies, or, once Negroes are hired, to give them special seniority rights at the expense of the white workers hired earlier. Ibid.* (emphasis added)

Thus with virtual clairvoyance the Senate's leading supporters of Title VII anticipated precisely the circumstances of this case and advised their colleagues that the type of minority preference employed by Kaiser would violate Title VII's ban on racial discrimination. . . .

While the debate in the Senate raged, a bipartisan coalition . . . was working with House leaders . . . on a number of amendments to H.R. 7152 designed to enhance its prospects of passage. . . . One of those clarifying amendments (was) §703 (j). . . .

The Court draws from the language of §703 (j) primary support for its conclusion that Title VII's blanket prohibition on racial discrimination in employment does not prohibit preferential treatment of blacks to correct racial imbalance. . . .

Contrary to the Court's analysis, the language of §703 (j) is precisely tailored to the objection voiced time and again by Title VII's opponents. Not once during the 83 days of debate in the Senate did a speaker, proponent or opponent, suggest that the bill would allow employers *voluntarily* to prefer racial minorities over white persons. In light of Title VII's flat prohibition on discrimination "against any individual . . . because of such individual's race," such a contention would have been, in any event, too preposterous to warrant response. Indeed, speakers on both sides of the issue, as the legislative history makes clear, recognized that Title VII would tolerate no *voluntary* racial preference, whether in favor of blacks or whites. The complaint consistently voiced by the opponents was that Title VII, particularly the word "discrimination," would be *interpreted* by Federal agencies such as the Equal Employment Opportunity Commission to *require* the correction of racial imbalance through the granting of preferential treatment to minorities. Verbal assurances that Title VII would not require—indeed, would not permit—preferential treatment of blacks having failed, supporters of H.R. 7152 responded by proposing an amendment carefully worded to meet, and put to rest, the opposition's charge. Indeed, unlike §§703 (a) and (d), which are by their terms directed at entities—e.g., employers, labor unions—whose actions are restricted by Title VII's prohibitions, the language of §703 (j) is specifically directed at entities—federal agencies and courts—charged with the responsibility of interpreting Title VII's provisions.

In light of the background and purpose of §703 (j), the irony of invoking the section to justify the result in this case is obvious. The Court's frequent references to the "voluntary" nature of Kaiser's racially discriminatory admission quota bear no relationship to the facts of this case. Kaiser and the Steelworkers acted under pressure from an agency of the Federal Government, the Office of Federal Contract Compliance, which found that minorities were being "underutilized" at Kaiser's plants. That is, Kaiser's work force was racially imbalanced. Bowing to that pressure, Kaiser instituted an admissions quota preferring blacks over whites, thus confirming that the fears of Title VII's opponents were well founded. Today §703 (j), adopted to allay those fears, is invoked by the Court to uphold imposition of a racial quota under the very circumstances that the section was intended to prevent. . . .

(After introduction of §703 (j)), the Senate turned its attention to an amendment proposed by Senator Cotton to limit application of Title VII to employers of at least 100 employees. During the course of the Senate's deliberations on the amendment, Senator Cotton had a revealing discussion with Senator Curtis. . . . Both men expressed dismay that Title VII would prohibit preferential hiring of "members of a minority race in order to enhance their opportunity. . . ." 110 Cong. Rec. 13086 (1964). Thus in the only exchange on the Senate floor raising the possibility that an employer might wish to reserve jobs for minorities in order to assist them in overcoming their employment disadvantage, both speakers concluded that Title VII prohibits such, in the words of the Court, "voluntary, private, race-conscious efforts to abolish traditional patterns of racial segregation and hierarchy. . . ." (3). (In) the limited debate that followed (cloture), Senator Moss . . . had this to say about quotas:

> The bill does not accord to any citizen advantage or preference—it does not fix quotas of employment or school population—it does not force personal association. What it does is to prohibit public officials and those who invite the public generally to patronize their businesses or to apply for employment, to utilize the offensive, humiliating, and cruel practice of discrimination on the basis of race. In short, the bill does not accord special consideration. It establishes *equality*. *Id.,* at 14484 (emphasis added).

Reading the language of Title VII, as the Court purports to do, "against the background of (its) legislative history . . . and the historical context from which the Act arose, ". . . one is led inescapably to the conclusion that Congress fully understood what it was saying and meant precisely what it said. Opponents of the civil rights bill did not argue that employers would be permitted under Title VII voluntarily to grant preferential treatment to minorities to correct racial imbalance. The plain language of the statute too clearly prohibited such racial discrimination to admit of any doubt. . . .

Our task in this case, like any other case involving the construction of a statute, is to give effect to the intent of Congress. To divine that intent, we traditionally look first to the words of the statute and, if they are unclear, then to the statute's legislative history. Finding the desired result hopelessly foreclosed by these conventional sources, the Court turns to a third source— the "spirit" of the Act. But close examination of what the Court proffers as the spirit of the Act reveals it as the spirit animating the present majority, not the Eighty-eighth Congress. For if the spirit of the Act eludes the cold words of the statute itself, it rings out with unmistakable clarity in the words of the elected representatives who made the law. It is *equality*. . . .

In passing Title VII Congress outlawed *all* racial discrimination, recognizing that no discrimination based on race is benign, that no action disadvantaging a person because of his color is affirmative. With today's holding, the Court introduces into Title VII a tolerance for the very evil that the law was intended to eradicate, without offering even a clue as to what the limits on that tolerance may be. We are told simply that Kaiser's racially discriminatory admission quota "falls on the permissible side of the line." By going not merely *beyond* but directly *against* Title VII's language and legislative history, the Court has sown the wind. Later courts will face the impossible task of reaping the whirlwind.

NOTES

1. Section 703(a), 42 U.S.C.'2000e-2(a), provides: (a) It shall be an unlawful employment practice for an employer—

(1) to fail or refuse to hire or to discharge any individual, or otherwise to discriminate against any individual with respect to his compensation, terms, conditions, or privileges of employment, because of such individual's race, color, religion, sex, or national origin; or

(2) to limit, segregate, or classify his employees or applicants for employment in any way which would deprive or tend to deprive any individual of employment opportunities or otherwise adversely affect his status as an employee, because of such individual's race, color, religion, sex, or national origin.

2. Section 703 (d), 42 U.S.C. §2000e-2(d), provides: It shall be an unlawful employment practice for any employer, labor organization, or joint labor-management committee controlling apprenticeship or other training or retraining, including on-the-job training programs, to discriminate against any individual because of his race, color, religion, sex, or national origin in admission to, or employment in, any program established to provide apprenticeship or other training.

3. The problem that Congress addressed in 1964 remains with us. In 1962 the nonwhite unemployment rate was 124 percent higher than the white rate. . . . In 1978 the black unemployment rate was 129 percent higher. See Monthly Labor Review, U.S. Department of Labor Bureau of Labor Statistics 78 (Mar. 1979).

4. Section 703 (j) of Title VII, 42 U.S.C. §2000e-2(j), provides: Nothing contained in this subchapter shall be interpreted to require any employer, employment agency, labor organization, or joint labor-management committee subject to this subchapter to grant preferential treatment to any individual or to any group because of the race, color, religion, sex, or national origin of such individual or group on account of an imbalance which may exist with respect to the total number or percentage of persons of any race, color, religion, sex, or national origin employed by any employer, referred or classified for employment by any employment agency or labor organization, admitted to membership or classified by any labor organization, or admitted to, or employed in, any apprenticeship or other training program, in comparison with the total number or percentage or persons of such race, color, religion, sex, or national origin in any community, state, section, or other area, or in the available work force in any community, state, section, or other area. . . .

5. Our statement in . . . *Furnco Construction* (which is) patently inconsistent with today's holding, (is) not even mentioned, much less distinguished, by the Court.

6. "If the words are plain, they give meaning to the act, and it is neither the duty nor the privilege of the courts to enter speculative fields in search of a different meaning."

". . . (W)hen words are free from doubt they must be taken as the final expression of the legislative intent, and are not to be added to or subtracted from by considerations drawn . . . from any extraneous source." *Caminetti* v. *United States,* 242 U.S. 470, 490, 37 S.Ct. 192, 196 (1917).

Ernest van den Haag

Reverse Discrimination: A Brief Against It

"How am I, as Secretary of HEW ever going to find first-class black doctors, first-class black lawyers, first-class black scientists, first-class women scientists, if these people don't have the chance to get into the best [schools] in the country?"—Joseph A. Califano Jr., *New York Times*, March 18, 1977.

I

On April Fool's Day Mr. Califano wisely fudged these words he had spoken two weeks earlier. However, he still does not understand that reversing discrimination is inconsistent with enforcing equality of opportunity. Preferential admissions to colleges and professional schools are now widely practiced. So is "affirmative action," which is basically analogous to preferential admissions: it applies to hiring, promotion, and employment in general. Persons belonging to selected minorities or under-represented groups (such as women, or blacks) are admitted or hired if they meet scholastic standards which are specially lowered for them. Or, they are given preference over others who have performed as well or better in meeting requirements. This practice, which Secretary Califano endorses, discriminates, in effect, against those who are being displaced in favor of those who displace them. Its legality has been attacked with respect to state institutions. But the Supreme Court, although it heard the DeFunis case (*DeFunis* v. *Odegaard,* 1974), avoided deciding it because DeFunis, who had sued the university, had by that time been admitted and graduated.

From *National Review* 29, no. 16 (April 1977). Reprinted by permission of the author.

Both preferential admissions and affirmative action are meant to discriminate against discrimination, to reduce discrimination by favoring those discriminated against in the past, or elsewhere. Is this reversal morally justifiable? Can it be effective in achieving its purpose?

In the past Oxford and Cambridge gave preference to the sons of great English families even when their qualifications did not justify it. They were preferred because they would exercise power and influence whether admitted or not. It was thought that society would benefit more by educating these students than by educating others who, even if more meritorious, would be likely to exercise less influence on the course of social affairs. The advantage to the universities was expected to be greater as well—a matter that probably did not escape the attention of the admitting authorities. For similar reasons, American universities in the past gave preference to students likely to inherit great wealth. Is a reversal of this pattern required by justice, or is it socially useful, as the old pattern was thought to be? Let me consider the social usefulness before turning to the justice of reversal.

Could society benefit from the preferential admission of the disadvantaged as it might have benefited from the preferential admission of the privileged? Scarcely. There is no reason to believe that members of groups previously discriminated against will exercise disproportionate social power or influence, regardless of higher education denied or received. Hence their preferential admission cannot be justified by reasoning that their education deserves preference because it would be socially more useful than that of the more meritorious.

Preferential admissions might be useful in other respects. If one assumes that society consists of separate communities, each wanting indigenous leaders, preferential admissions (even quotas) might help provide higher education for the requisite number of members of each group. (This was the justification English universities advanced for giving some preference to potential Indian and African leaders.) But women, or even blacks, do not form segregated political or cultural communities. Where they do, our present policy is to integrate or at least to desegregate them. Although the "melting pot" image of America simplifies and exaggerates, the Swiss paradigm of full geographical and cultural separation is neither feasible nor desirable in the United States. (Anyway, those who desire it can avail themselves of the private colleges exclusively attended by the groups of their choice.) Preferential admission of the previously disadvantaged cannot rest, then, on the social benefit to be gained by educating the independently powerful, or on the need for indigenous leadership.

Another argument for preferential admissions conceives of institutions of higher learning and of other nonpolitical institutions as representative bodies, in which all classes, races, sexes, and religions—however well integrated—ought to be represented in proportion to their share of the population, even if admission standards have to differ for each group to secure its proportional representation. Yet educational or business, unlike political, institutions are not meant to be representative. In politics, representativeness, rightly or wrongly, plays a major role, although it is often hard to see who, and what, is represented: the occupational, class, age, and sex ratios of our representative bodies scarcely reflect those of the population. Still, it would be hard for a white man to be elected in Harlem; and political tickets wisely tend to represent important ethnic, religious, or geographical groupings of voters.

However, institutions of higher learning are not political bodies and cannot represent the voters without defeating their function, which is to teach and do research, not to make political decisions. So too with business enterprises: to require representativeness in faculties, or student bodies, is no more justified than to require representativeness in Chinese restaurants, prisons, hospitals, or opera houses. These institutions have nonrepresentative functions which require admission (or confinement) criteria relevant to those functions, regardless of representativeness. So too with graduate or professional schools. We want the most able and gifted to be prepared for the tasks at hand by the most able and gifted, regardless of sex or race. To demand representativeness would be contrary to the social interest which requires the best surgeon, or the best singer, to be educated for his task, not the racially or sexually most representative.

I can find no utilitarian justification, then, for preferential admission of previously under-represented national, racial, or sexual groups. On the contrary, it would be dysfunctional, favoring persons less able to learn and teach than those rejected, and thus causing society to be served by the less able in the professions education prepares for. *Mutatis mutandis,* this applies to non-educational institutions as well. Let me turn now to nonutilitarian justifications.

II

Should the preference given the powerful in the past be reversed for the sake of justice? Surely, to do so would shift rather than repair injustice. Injustice would not be reduced, but merely inflicted on a different group. If the preference given the powerful was wrong because it violated equality of individual opportunity and the rule of admission by relevant qualification only, then violation of that rule in favor of a different group, the powerless, would be no less wrong, however generous the reparative intent.

Individual reparations can be justified if the victim of discrimination and the victimizer are individually identifiable. Thus, qualified persons who were not hired because they were discriminated against may be compensated for their loss. There is a case even for collective compensation, if losses are tangible (e.g., racial firings, confiscations, or de-licensings as in Nazi Germany), and if victimizers and victims, though not individually identifiable, are roughly contemporary as groups. Matters become murky, however, if one considers granting compensation to persons not allowed to acquire the qualifications they might have acquired had they been admitted and which might have led to higher incomes than they actually did earn. Unjust losses certainly were suffered, but we cannot know their incidence and size.

Matters become even more murky if the discriminatory rules were imposed over a long period in the distant past. The incidence of the unjustly achieved advantages and of the unjustly imposed disadvantages becomes diffuse and uncertain, as does the liability for both. Moreover, current generations can bear no responsibility for discrimination imposed by generations past, other than to discontinue it. Can today's Italians be held liable for Caesar's invasion of Gaul, or today's Frenchmen for Napoleon's invasion of Germany? Can Polish or Italian workers be held liable for the fate inflicted on American Indians by the colonists? Or Jewish teachers and students for disabilities imposed on blacks in the past? Or contemporary males for past discrimination against women? We are told (Deuteronomy 24:16): "The fathers shall not be put to death for the children, neither shall the children be put to death for the fathers: every man shall be put to death for his own sin." It is a good rule. Those not responsible for it cannot be asked to compensate for the damage. They can only be restrained from causing further losses.

Justice, then, requires the cessation of discriminatory activities, including discrimination in admissions or hiring, but no reversal. Preferential admissions to repair past injustice might "discriminate for" persons who themselves suffered no "discrimination against" at the expense of persons not responsible for past "discrimination against."

The problem of compensation for the present consequences of past injustice cannot be met, then, by preferential admissions. Still, efforts to solve it are demanded by generosity, if not by justice. Some members of the formerly "discriminated against" groups have native abilities which would justify admission to the schools or hiring by the enterprises to which they have applied, had these abilities not remained undeveloped because of unfavorable circumstances co-produced by past discrimination. Colleges and universities may play a role in helping such applicants to overcome hardships, in order to prepare them for (nonpreferential) admission. Preadmission tutoring may be a reasonable effort to offset the present effects of past injustices in which colleges participated, and thus to make amends.

III

Occasionally it is argued that preferential admissions are needed to offset unfairness inherent in the tests which universities and professional schools use to decide on admissions. These tests are thought to discriminate against qualified persons who belong to disadvantaged groups. Actually, they are quite reliable in predicting the likely degree of success in the professional and graduate schools which use them. They measure relevant abilities, regardless of sex or race. Their value is limited: the tests do not measure nonacademic abilities or human characteristics, nor predict the degree of success in activities for which they are not designed. However, though less than perfect, the tests serve well the limited purpose for which they are used. Preferential admissions, far from offsetting unfairness, instead would introduce it by setting aside the objective measurement the tests permit, in favor of racial or sexual privileges.

IV

Sexes and races are not proportionally represented among students admitted to professional and graduate schools, nor among faculties, nor in the ranks of corporations. This has been regarded as evidence of discrimination against the under-represented. Radicals insist that disproportionate representation is unfair even when it does reflect actual differences in abilities, qualifications, or motivations. Others, philosophically more moderate, believe that equal treatment necessarily would lead to proportional representation of all groups. Thus, disproportionate representation *eo ipso* demonstrates "discrimination against" the under-represented, even if it cannot be verified independently, and preferential admission may become an appropriate remedy.

If one assumes that all relevant aptitudes, talents, and motivations are equally distributed among classes, sexes, nationalities, and races, then over- or under-representation of any one group in desirable activities necessarily indicates unequal treatment. Such an assumption has never been shown to be true. Widespread abilities, e.g., the ability to be a farmer, a janitor, or a clerk, seem to be distributed fairly equally among groups. But the ability to study mathematics or teach it, or to run a major enterprise, is not that widespread. Universities and corporations cannot draw on a number of talented people in each group proportional to the size of the group. And if the members of different groups are not necessarily equally qualified *ab initio,* objective tests need not lead to proportional representation. Over- or under-representation does not indicate bias any more than proportional representation of groups among admitted candidates indicates unbiased admissions standards. Racist theories notwithstanding, the over-representation of Jews in important professions in Germany, and the consequent under-representation of non-Jewish Germans, did not indicate a discriminatory policy to place the latter at a disadvantage in favor of the former.

V

Is preferential admission of students, or affirmative action in hiring faculty or executives, a suitable remedy for actual or suspected discrimination? Both policies set numerical goals which, when achieved, would make faculties and student bodies, or executive units, reflect the proportions in which women or various racial groups occur, either in the general population, or among candidates with appropriate prior degrees and specializations.

Outside academic institutions, the advantages of using affirmative action to establish equality of opportunity may at times outweigh the disadvantages, when a licensing or admissions board, or an employer, currently discriminates against a group. There is a *prima facie* indication of discrimination if all those admitted, employed, or licensed are white, or male, even though others wish to be, and if (1) no distinctive qualifications are needed for the job or license; or (2) the distinctive qualifications needed can be shown to be possessed by the rejected candidates in substantially the same degree as by the accepted ones; or (3) the relevant qualifications can be tested, yet no suitable tests are used (or the tests used discriminate irrelevantly). In such cases numerical goals help to attain equality of opportunity. Yet they should be abandoned as soon as improper discriminatory practices cease, for numerical goals necessarily reduce the appropriate discriminations in hiring, promotion, firing, or licensing in terms of actual skill, reliability, diligence, etc.

Numerical goals *ipso facto* disregard the distinctive individual qualifications of candidates, or reduce the decisive weight they should have in most cases. They certainly cannot be appropriate for educational institutions, where these distinctive qualifications must be paramount. Further, academic institutions can (and do) properly test individual qualifications for admission. Therefore, numerical goals, far from reducing irrelevant discrimination, perpetuate or introduce it into academic institutions by placing more qualified persons at a disadvantage relative to less qualified or equally qualified ones who belong to an under-represented race or sex. (Where individual qualifications, although of decisive importance, are not always objectively testable—e.g., in hiring or promotions—universities and professional schools usually are willing to submit disputes to arbitrators.)

VI

Consider now the effect on persons, rather than institutions. The effect of academic affirmative action, or of preferential admissions, on those discriminated for is likely to be unhelpful. There are three possibilities. First, there is the unqualified law student who was preferentially admitted. He will drop out because of low grades which were predictable from his entrance test. He may be worse off than before.

Second, some preferentially admitted students graduate by dint of preferential grading or undemanding curricula specially fashioned for them. They profit from the credentials obtained. But the group which was to be favored pays a high price: the black college graduate, Ph.D., or lawyer who graduated because lower standards were applied to him than to his white counterparts is not as competent as they are and will reinforce the prejudice which maintains that blacks are necessarily less competent than whites.

Third, there is the preferentially admitted black student who, despite low entrance scores, actually catches up and does well without preferential grading. Yet he may never know whether he graduated because he was black or because he deserved to. If he does know, others will not: he will suffer from the image perpetuated by his fellow student whose preferential admission was complemented by preferential grading. Similarly, female or black professors hired or promoted because of affirmative action will not know whether they were hired because they were qualified or because they were female or black; nor will others. Those hired because they belong to an under-represented group though they are not the most qualified persons also will perpetuate the image of low competence of the under-represented group—the image that contributed to discrimination against it in the first place.

The persons excluded because of preferential admissions or affirmative action naturally are no less bitter than those who in the past were excluded by discrimination. Since "discrimination for" merely reverses "discrimination against," it cannot but perpetuate the group hostilities of the past. This applies as well to all enterprises which practice reverse discrimination.

There is also an unattractive arbitrariness about the whole procedure. Unless inclusion into the groups discriminated for is determined by sex, it often must be capricious. Puerto Ricans, Spaniards, Argentinians, and Mexicans are all "Spanish surnamed." It is hard to see what else they have in common, or why they should receive different treatment than Portuguese, Brazilians, or Arabs. And it is not obvious that various white "ethnics" suffered less from discrimination than females did. Yet they are not preferentially admitted, or hired, by affirmative action. These remedies, then, are not only counterproductive and unjust most of the time, but also arbitrarily selective. Perhaps this is a minor defect compared to those already mentioned: if an idea is bad, arbitrary application does not make it much worse. Nonetheless the inherent capriciousness of the scheme and the unavoidable arbitrariness in execution are psychologically repulsive.

VII

Affirmative action and preferential admissions were aided and abetted by persons who felt guilty enough about past discrimination to make amends, even at the expense of innocent third persons. Groups which, rightly or wrongly, felt discriminated against in the past also have supported affirmative action and preferential admissions. But in the main these are creatures of the federal bureaucracy and judiciary. The bureaucracy actually gave birth to the illegitimate child; the judiciary adopted and legalized it.

Fears that a bureaucratic monstrosity would be foisted on the country were voiced in Congress during the debate on the Civil Rights Act of 1964. Such fears were laid to rest when the managers of the bill, Senators Joseph Clark and Clifford Case, submitted a memorandum stating:

> There is no requirement in Title VII that an employer maintain a racial balance in his work force. On the contrary, any deliberate attempt to maintain a racial balance, whatever such balance may be, would involve a violation of Title VII because maintaining such a balance would require an employer to hire or refuse to hire on the basis of race. It must be emphasized that discrimination is prohibited as to any individual . . . the question in each case would be whether that individual was discriminated against. [110 *Congressional Record* 7213, April 8, 1964.]

Further, at the behest of the bill's sponsors, the Department of Justice submitted a memorandum stating:

> Finally, it has been asserted that Title VII would impose a requirement for "racial balance." This is incorrect. There is no provision, either in Title VII or in any part of this bill, that requires or authorizes any federal agency or federal court to require preferential treatment for any individual group for the purpose of achieving racial balance.
>
> No employer is required to hire an individual because that individual is Negro. No employer is required to maintain any ratio of Negroes to whites, Jews to gentiles, Italians to English, or women to men. [110 *Congressional Record* 7207, April 8, 1964.]

Despite the clear language of these memoranda, the bureaucracy has perverted the intent of the legislation. Racial balance and the group preferences needed to attain it are prescribed and enforced. The courts have found constitutional arguments to help administrative agencies override the intent of Congress. Bureaucracy has replaced both democracy and common sense. They can be reinstated only when the citizens push Congress and the courts into disciplining and limiting the bureaucracy.

James M. Humber

Reversing the Arguments Against Reverse Discrimination

I

Generally, those who seek to defend reverse discrimination do so by appealing to some variation of either of the following arguments.[1]

(1) Women and members of certain minority groups have been consistently discriminated against. Justice demands that members of these groups be given compensation for their injuries; and compensation is best secured by practicing reverse discrimination.

(2) In our society equality of opportunity is recognized as a good. At present, women and minority group members do not have true equality of opportunity because they have been "conditioned" to think of themselves as inferior, or at least as unsuited for certain tasks. To remove these psychological constraints (and so to ensure genuine equality of opportunity), women and blacks need "role models," i.e., individuals from "disadvantaged" groups who are successful in positions of importance. And to guarantee that there are persons serving as role models, it is necessary to practice reverse discrimination.

The arguments in favor of reverse discrimination have been attacked in various ways.[2] In opposition to the second argument, critics respond as follows:

(i) If equality of opportunity is a good to be realized in our society, it cannot be achieved by means of reverse discrimination. This is so because reversing discrimination is inconsistent with equalizing opportunity. After all,

---

Comments by Milton Snoeyenbos were helpful to me in the formulation of my ideas.

to favor blacks and women in hiring and school admission is simply to discriminate against (and hence to deny equal opportunity to) white males.

(ii) Although equality of opportunity is recognized as a desirable end in our society, it is not the only desirable end. And to give preference to some simply because of their race or sex could well hamper achievement of another recognized "good" in our society, namely, that of putting the most qualified people in responsible positions. The reason this is so is that race and sex as properties are irrelevant qualifications for either hiring or school admission. Business serves society by making a profit while turning out a quality product. Institutions of higher learning, on the other hand, exist to foster research and to disseminate knowledge. This being the case, race and sex do not qualify one either to be a scholar or a businessperson. Thus, if an employer gives preference to one job candidate over another simply because of a candidate's race or sex, the person hired might well have fewer properties relevant to success than the person who was not hired. And if this were to happen, society as a whole would suffer because it would be served by the less able.

(iii) Finally, even if preference in hiring and school admission did not cause society to be served by the less able it could: (a) have deleterious effects for those hired under affirmative action programs, and (b) have an undesirable effect upon other minority group members. Both effects would follow because everyone (including the persons hired or admitted to school) would know that they were given preferential treatment. And in these circumstances the persons given such "special" treatment would never know whether they were truly competent or merely "kept on" by their employers to demonstrate that their companies hired without regard to race, sex, or creed. Furthermore, other blacks and women might soon become aware of the advantages of being disadvantaged. After all, their "role models" had been hired because they were members of disadvantaged groups. Why, then, should they struggle to succeed? Would it not be far easier simply to complain of their disadvantaged status? Rather than inspiring, then, women and blacks who were preferentially hired as role models could influence behavior in nonbeneficial ways.

As against the claim that reverse discrimination is required by the demands of justice, critics offer the following three counter-arguments.

(A) First, it is said, practicing reverse discrimination may not serve the interests of justice, because there is no way to identify either those discriminated against or those responsible for discrimination. For example, let us say that person P carelessly drives his car into person Q. In this case we can identify the injury, find the individual responsible for that harm, and determine what is needed as just compensation for Q's injuries. And given this knowledge we can serve the ends of justice. (In the case at hand, for instance, we can take just compensation for Q's injuries from P and give that compensation to Q.) However, when we use reverse discrimination in an attempt to rectify the wrongs done by discrimination we do not have the sort of knowledge illustrated in our P/Q example. To be sure, we know that blacks and women have been discriminated against, principally at the hands of white males. To know this, though, is just to know that one *group* has wronged other groups.

We do not know which *individuals* within these groups have suffered or practiced discrimination; and because we lack this information, reversing discrimination could well produce more injustice than justice. For example, imagine that a white male (*WM*) and a black woman (*BW*) are competing for a job. *WM* is slightly better qualified for the position than *BW* but the employer (*E*) practices reverse discrimination and hires *BW*. Has *E* done something to compensate blacks and women for the debilitating effects of discrimination? Not necessarily, for *BW* may never have been a victim of discrimination, and *WM* may never have discriminated against anyone. And if this were the case *E* would have done nothing more than discriminate against *WM*, thus perpetrating rather than rectifying an injustice. Furthermore, if reverse discrimination were practiced widely in the United States there is no telling how often this scenario would be repeated. In the end, then, reverse discrimination should be rejected because it might produce more instances of injustice than justice.

(B) Unlike argument (A), which only tries to show that reversing discrimination *could* produce more injustice than justice, argument (B) attempts to show that reverse discrimination *is likely to* produce more injustice than it rectifies. Who, it is asked, would be the most likely beneficiaries of reverse discrimination? Would it not be the best educated, most sophisticated blacks and women? Surely it would seem so; for if employers were required to practice reverse discrimination they would give preference to these individuals, hiring them first, before their "lower ranking" counterparts. But the best educated, most highly sophisticated members of any disadvantaged group are the very ones who, in all likelihood, have suffered the least discrimination within that group. Thus, the objection goes, reversing discrimination *probably* would produce more injustice than justice; it would deny employment to those who, in all probability had suffered the most from discrimination, while at the same time "compensating" those within disadvantaged groups who least deserved compensation.

(C) If argument (C) were sound it would be the strongest of all the arguments for the injustice of reverse discrimination, for this argument, unlike, either (A) or (B), attempts to show that reversing discrimination *would* produce a greater amount of injustice than justice. As usually presented the argument proceeds as follows: First, it is said, discrimination against women and blacks was most severe in the past, for it was then that blacks were enslaved and women denied suffrage. The effects of such discriminatory actions may linger in the present but it would be wrong to attempt to rectify this unfortunate situation by practicing reverse discrimination. This is so because today's white males are not responsible for the actions of their forefathers. Consequently, to hold today's white males accountable (by taking jobs from them and giving them to blacks and women), is to treat these white males in ways that are manifestly unjust. Of course, this is not to deny that women, blacks, and members of other minority groups need to be recompensed for past wrongs. It is just to say that reverse discrimination is not the proper means for achieving that end.

Given the debate as presented above, I believe the arguments against reverse discrimination are far more persuasive than those offered in support of the practice. Still, I think there is more that can be said on the matter; and in what follows I intend to show that the arguments in favor of reverse discrimination can be modified so as to undercut all of the above-noted objections. Indeed, I want to go further and argue that reverse discrimination is justified, not only by the principle of justice, but also by the principle of utility. I will begin by reconsidering argument (C) for the injustice of reverse discrimination.

II. THE DEMANDS OF JUSTICE

Critics charge that reverse discrimination must be unjust because it denies jobs to today's white males, thus holding these individuals responsible for the sins of their forefathers. For this objection to have force, however, one must be willing to assume that discrimination is not being practiced in our society today; and there are two reasons why this assumption is false. The first reason may be made evident by means of an analogy.

Let us say we have two fighters, X and Y. Two months prior to their meeting in the ring X is given the best exercise, training, advice, food, etc., by the Fighting Commission. On the other hand, the Fighting Commission does not allow Y to sleep, forces him to live on a subsistence diet, and does not permit him to train. Now, if on the day of the fight the rules of the game were enforced "impartially" by the Fighting Commission, would we say that the fight was fair? I think not. Indeed, I believe we would say, not merely that Y *had been* discriminated against, but that he *was* being discriminated against because he was being forced to fight under rules favoring X. To make the fight fair, and so not to discriminate against Y, X needs to be handicapped in some way (e.g., he could be made to wear oversized gloves and a heavy weight belt). Today, women and blacks are in a situation similar to that of our starved fighter, for these individuals often are forced to compete in the marketplace under rules which, if enforced "impartially," favor white males. And to end this sort of discrimination, white males need to be handicapped.

Actually, our fighter example only tells one-half of the story, for in today's society it simply is not true that the rules of the game are being enforced "impartially." What Irving Thalberg calls "visceral racism" still exists.[3] Many of the important "extras" that spell success in business (e.g., exclusive club memberships, housing in upper class neighborhoods, etc.) are denied to blacks. And for the most part, women with intelligence and ambition are looked upon with suspicion. Furthermore, even though feminist and liberation movements have made great strides, the vast majority of women are "conditioned" from birth to seek only marriage and motherhood. To be sure, we have come a long way from the days of slavery and the denial of women's voting rights. But anyone who claims that women and minority group members today have no special obstacles to overcome in order to successfully compete is simply living in a dream world.

If our reasoning thus far is correct, we can say that discrimination is being practiced in our society today, not only because the "rules of the game" are unfair when enforced "impartially," but also because these rules are not truly being enforced impartially. Thus, if we were to engage in reverse discrimination we would not necessarily be punishing the sons for the sins of their fathers. Having shown this, however, we have not demonstrated that reverse discrimination is a just procedure. To do this we must show that reversing discrimination will compensate those who have suffered injury without harming those who have failed to practice discrimination.

The problem seems simple enough: We know that members of some groups are being discriminated against by members of another group. But reverse discrimination operates on an individual level; and if the critics of reverse discrimination are to be believed it is quite likely that reversing discrimination would produce more instances of injustice than justice. Are the opponents of reverse discrimination correct? I think not. Indeed, if a program of reverse discrimination were properly administered, I believe the facts would be quite otherwise than the critics assert. In order to see why this is the case it will be helpful to consider another example.

Let us say that two people are being considered for a job—a black woman, *BW,* who has been discriminated against, and a white male, *WM,* who knows *BW* has been the victim of discrimination. *WM* has a more impressive dossier than *BW* and so insists that he be hired. What should be our reaction? Remember our earlier example of the fighters. What would we think if fighter *X* were to balk at having to wear a weight belt and extra-large gloves, even though he knew how *Y* had been treated before the fight? Would we not say that he was seeking an unfair advantage? Similarly, if *WM* knew *BW* had been the subject of discrimination but insisted nevertheless that he be hired because his qualifications were superior to hers would he not be endorsing the past discrimination against *BW* by seeking to perpetuate it? It does not matter that *WM* had not himself discriminated against *BW* in the past. Fighter *X* did not starve fighter *Y* or refuse to allow him to sleep either; but if *X* refuses to handicap himself in his fight with *Y,* he is approving of those past practices and attempting to take unfair advantage of *Y.* In the same way, if *WM* knows that *BW* has been the victim of discrimination, and yet insists that he rather than *BW* deserves the job they both seek, *WM* is condoning the earlier discrimination against *BW* and trying his best to treat her unfairly. And in this case it would be in the interest of justice to employ *BW* rather than *WM,* for this action would compensate a victim of discrimination and penalize one whom we knew condoned discriminatory practices.

At this point our argument may seem subject to a criticism. Throughout our *WM/BW* example we assumed that *WM* knew *BW* had been the victim of past discrimination. The assumption is important; for if *WM* had no reason to believe that *BW* had been discriminated against, it would be proper for him to demand that he rather than *BW* be given the sought-after job. And, our critics will insist, this is precisely the point: it is impossible for white males to know that *individual* minority group members with whom they are competing for jobs have been the victims of past discrimination. But is this true? Surely it is so if by "to know" we mean "to be absolutely certain," for we cannot be absolutely certain about any matter of fact. But do we not have evidence that most blacks and women have been subject to discrimination? Surely we do. I suggest then, that whenever a woman or minority group member applies for employment or school admission, the initial assumption ought to be that this individual has been discriminated against. Furthermore, I do not think it would take much effort for an employer or school admissions officer to find evidence tending to support or disconfirm this initial assumption. Indeed, such an employer or admissions officer would only need information of the following two sorts: (1) relevant autobiographical information concerning the job candidate or school applicant (e.g., where the applicant lived between the ages of one and eighteen, what the candidate's family income had been during his formative years, what level of education the applicant's parents had attained, etc.), and (2) brief psychological profiles of all applicants for employment or school admission. If information of these sorts were appended to all applications for jobs and school admission, employers and admissions officers could determine, with a high degree of probability, whether or not a particular applicant had been the subject of discrimination. For example, consider the following two cases:[4]

Case #1. Three persons are applying for a job—a white male (WM), and two white women (WW1 and WW2). All three candidates meet the minimum requirements for employment, but according to all "objective" criteria, WM is best qualified for the job, WW1 next best qualified, and WW2 least qualified. The fact that WW2 seems least qualified to compete in a "man's domain" gives some evidence of her having been subject to the psychological "conditioning forces" so often brought to bear upon women in our society. It is hardly overwhelming evidence; but what if we assume that it is supplemented by psychological data indicating that WW2, unlike WW1 and WM, lacks aggressiveness and assertiveness, and is somewhat unsure of herself in her role as a businessperson? Further, WW2 (again unlike WW1 and WM) scores much higher on her verbal tests than on her mathematical examinations. All else being equal, I believe the employer then could say that it was highly probable that WW2 had been subjected to stronger "conditioning" forces than either WM or WW1. At this point it would not be improper for the employer to tell WM and WW1 that although WW2 did not score as high as they did on "objective" tests, she was being hired because she was qualified and most likely the subject of discriminatory pressures far more severe than those experienced by either of them. If either WM or WW1 protested, they would be advocating continued discrimination against WW2 and so justly denied employment. If neither protested, both would recognize what was in fact the case, namely, that they had competed fairly with WW2 for a position of employment and had lost.

Case #2. A white male (WM) and a black male (BM) are applying for admission to a school with one remaining opening. Although BM scores lower than WM on all examinations he nevertheless meets all the minimum requirements for admission. Furthermore, while the autobiographical history of WM shows that he comes from a solid middle class background, *BM*'s history indicates that he grew up in a ghetto, did not know his father, etc. Given these facts, it would be proper for the admissions officer to reason that in all probability, one of the principal reasons *BM* suffered as he did in his early life was that he and his family, being black, were victims of discrimination. And at this juncture *BM* could be admitted to school, and *WM* told why he was being rejected. Specifically, *WM* would be told that although his examination scores were better than *BM*'s, he was judged not to be as qualified an admissions candidate as *BM* in a fair competition, i.e., in a competition in which *BM* was given an advantage so as to offset the debilitating effects of probable past discrimination. And at this stage *WM* could react in either of two ways. He could accept the admissions officer's judgment, admit that he had lost in fair competition with *BM,* and so acknowledge that no injustice had been done. Or, he could claim that he should not be handicapped in his competition with *BM* even though *BM* probably had been the victim of discrimination. In the latter case, however, *WM* would be demanding that the past discrimination of *BM* be perpetuated. And in this circumstance it would be proper to tell *WM* that it was in the interest of justice to admit *BM* because this action compensated a victim of discrimination by taking away from one who condoned discriminatory practices.

At this point one might wish to object to both of our examples. What we have failed to notice, the critic could say, is that there is a third option open to those who believe they have been victimized by reverse discrimination. Namely (to use case #2 as an example) *WM* could object to the admissions officer's decision by claiming that he had been handicapped too severely in his competition with *BM.* And if this were the basis for *WM*'s protest he would not be condoning the past discrimination against *BM.* Indeed, *WM*'s point simply would be that his competition with *BM* had not been fair because of the degree of handicap. But what gives *WM* the authority to make such a judgment? Consider, once again, our earlier example of the fighters. Fighter *X* is handicapped in his bout with *Y;* the fight goes the distance and *Y* is declared the winner. What would we think if *X* objected to the decision, claiming that he had been overly penalized, e.g., his weight belt should have been ten pounds instead of twenty? Would we say, "Yes, *X* is right, the fighter who is being handicapped should be the one to determine the type and degree of handicap"? Surely this would be absurd. Rather, we would tell *X* that he was a sore loser, and that the best means we have been able to devise for guaranteeing fair fights is to let an impartial panel of judges determine handicaps and make judgments concerning victory. And the same rules should apply in the market-place. *WM* cannot be allowed to determine the degree to which he should be handicapped in his competition with *BM*—indeed, to let him do so would virtually assure an *unfair* competition.

We have considered the major arguments for the injustice of reverse discrimination and concluded that none carries the day. Many of today's white males *are* responsible for discrimination. Thus, if we were to practice reverse discrimination we would not necessarily be "punishing the sons for the sins of their fathers." Furthermore, if the right information were made available to employers and admissions officers, victims of discrimination could be identified with a high degree of probability. And in these circumstances, reverse discrimination could be used to rectify many of the injustices of discrimination without harming anyone.

Before discussing the utilitarian claim that it would be harmful to society to practice reverse discrimination, I would like to say a few words about how programs of preferential treatment might actually function in practice. If we assume that all applicants for employment and school admission were required to file autobiographies and take psychological tests, there are five general rules or guidelines which, if followed, might go a long way toward assuring justice in hiring and admissions.

First, whenever two or more *equally qualified* individuals[5] apply for a job or school admission, and only one of these candidates (say candidate *C*) is a member of a disadvantaged class, preference ought to be given to *C*. And this holds true regardless of whether or not *C* has been the victim of discrimination. If *C* has suffered discrimination, he or she deserves to be preferentially treated as compensation for past injuries. If, on the other hand, *C* has not been a discrimination victim, he or she should be preferred because (as we shall see in the next section) such action would benefit society.

Second, an employer who practices reverse discrimination ought to consider only those candidates judged to be minimally qualified when evaluated according to "ordinary" standards (e.g., examinations, school grades, on-the-job experience, etc.). This is because nonqualified candidates probably would fail in their endeavors and, as critics of reverse discrimination quite rightly point out, such failures would be detrimental both to society as a whole and to the persons who failed.

Third, employers and school admissions officers (like impartial fight judges) should determine the degree of handicap in any competition for jobs and school admission. Furthermore, the handicap should increase as does the evidence of discrimination. Under this rule, of course, white males need not always "lose out" in competitions with individuals who have been victimized by discrimination. It is quite possible, for instance, that a white male's qualifications could be so outstanding that he would be selected over all candidates who had been given a preferential advantage due to past discrimination.

Fourth, in order to ensure that employers and school admissions officers do their best to practice reverse discrimination fairly, their applications for admission and employment should be reviewed periodically by officials of the government. And where differences of opinion arise, employers and admissions officers should be required to *justify* their decisions. If they could not justify their decisions, they should be required to make amends to the wronged parties.

Finally, critics of reverse discrimination often point out that reversing discrimination would be unfair to disadvantaged group members themselves because the most likely beneficiaries of such a practice would be the best qualified (and hence least discriminated against) minority group members. The assumption upon which this argument depends, namely, that the least qualified individuals will, in general, be those who have suffered the most from discrimination, seems plausible if not probable. Thus we are led to formulate a fifth "guideline": whenever an employer or admissions officer is deciding between two or more disadvantaged group members, he should select the least qualified person unless the autobiographies and/or psychological test *clearly indicate* that a better qualified individual has suffered more from discrimination.

I do not want to claim that the above five guidelines for practicing reverse discrimination are exhaustive. Nor am I so idealistic as to believe that it would be easy for employers and admissions officers to make judgments of merit using these guidelines. Injustices would be done, and honest mistakes would be made. However, if reverse discrimination were practiced in the manner broadly specified above it seems highly probable that more instances of injustice would be corrected than would be produced. And this is all the supporter of reverse discrimination need show in order to make the case that reverse discrimination is a just procedure. Indeed, it would be illegitimate to demand that the advocate of reverse discrimination show more than this, for there can be no such thing as certainty in the practical affairs of human life.

III. THE DEMANDS OF UTILITY

In order to fully defend reverse discrimination it is necessary to show not only that this practice serves the interests of justice, but also that it benefits the entire society. As a first step toward achieving this goal I will show why we must reject the major arguments in support of the view that reverse discrimination produces more harm than good.

(i) The first utilitarian objection to reverse discrimination recognizes that equality of opportunity is a good to be achieved in our society, but then claims that reversing discrimination is inconsistent with that goal. Given our earlier example of the fighters we can now see that this argument is plainly wrong. A boxer who has been starved and kept awake can have an equal opportunity to win a fight against one who has been well-fed and trained, only if the healthy fighter is handicapped in some way. Similarly, in order to give individuals who have been discriminated against a truly equal opportunity, those who have not been discriminated against must be handicapped.[6] Far from inhibiting equality of opportunity, then, reverse discrimination actually fosters that goal.

(ii) The second argument against reverse discrimination is that this procedure may well harm society by causing it to be served by the less able. Because I advocate hiring the least qualified individuals in some circumstances, it may seem that my defense of reverse discrimination is particularly susceptible to this criticism. But this is not so. On my view, every individual hired (or accepted in school) would be qualified. And to ensure that the persons who are given employment or accepted in school do a good job, we need only insist that it be made easy to dismiss those who fail to perform their tasks properly. Cases of incompetence could be documented, I think, with relative ease. And if incompetents could be dismissed without undue encumbrance, society would not suffer in the least.

(iii) The third objection to practicing reverse discrimination is that this procedure: (a) could have deleterious effects for those hired, and (b) could affect other minority group members in undesirable ways. But these arguments also miss the mark. Under the system as I have outlined it, those hired or accepted in school would know that they were qualified. And if they were not dismissed they would know that they were performing their tasks well. Thus, they could take pride in their achievements. And similar considerations also apply to minority group members seeking employment or school admission. These individuals would know that in order to be considered for a job or an opening in school, they would have to achieve at a certain level. But, the critic will assert, might not members of disadvantaged groups see the advantages of being disadvantaged and so do their utmost to appear "disadvantaged" and "minimally qualified" in order to obtain employment? I think not. After all, how does one prepare to be "disadvantaged" and "minimally qualified"? And even if this were possible, what difference would it make? Those hired or admitted to school would be qualified. And to keep their positions, these qualified individuals would have to perform adequately. In the end, absolutely no one would suffer.

Given our brief examination of the utilitarian arguments against reverse discrimination certain conclusions seem mandated. First, rather than being at odds with equality of opportunity reverse discrimination is really a means for achieving that goal. Second, so long as it is relatively easy to dismiss incompetents hired under reverse discrimination programs, society will not suffer. And third, practicing reverse discrimination will give those who perform well a sense of pride, while at the same time providing other minority group members with truly inspiring "role models." To this we can add two further benefits. First, we have seen that practicing reverse discrimination will further the interests of justice. And although the demands of justice and the demands of utility may not always be in accord, in this instance, at least, they appear to be. Finally, once minority group members understand that they really are being given an equal opportunity to succeed in our society a giant step will have been taken toward achieving true harmony in our relations with one another. I am aware that there are those who would disagree with this assessment, and insist that reversing discrimination will do nothing but incite a white-male "backlash," thus ultimately making things worse. Of course, these pessimists may be right. For my own part, however, I much prefer the counsel of Hume, who tells us that men are motivated not only by self-interest, but also by humanity, fellow-feeling, and a desire for justice.

NOTES

1. For arguments in support of reverse discrimination see: J. J. Thomson, "Preferential Hiring," *Philosophy and Public Affairs* (Winter 1975): Bernard Boxhill,

"The Morality of Reparations," *Social Theory and Practice* (vol. 2, no. 1); Paul Taylor, "Reverse Discrimination and Compensatory Justice," *Analysis* (June 1973); M. G. Fried, "In Defense of Preferential Hiring," *Philosophical Forum* (vol. 5, 1973-1974).

2. For arguments in opposition to reverse discrimination see: Alan Goldman, "Limits to the Justification of Reverse Discrimination," *Social Theory and Practice* (vol. 3, no. 3) and "Reparations to Individuals or Groups?" *Analysis* (vol. 33, no. 5); E. van den Haag, "Reverse Discrimination: A Brief Against It," *National Review* (April 1977); and W. Blackstone, "Reverse Discrimination and Compensatory Justice," *Social Theory and Practice* (Spring 1975).

3. Irving Thalberg, "Visceral Racism," *The Monist* 56 (1972): 43–65.

4. Case #1 illustrates how psychological tests could be used to determine a person's "discrimination status"; case #2 makes the same point with regard to autobiographical data.

5. When I say "equally qualified" here I mean equally qualified before the imposition of any handicap to offset the debilitating effects of past discrimination.

6. Sometimes critics of reverse discrimination attack the practice by claiming that it "changes the rules" in the middle of the game. Put most simply, the claim is that employers practicing reverse discrimination will hire members of disadvantaged groups, and in many cases these individuals will not be as highly qualified as the white males who were denied employment. But this changes the rules of the game, because we have all been led to believe that the person who is best qualified for a job should be the one hired. Given what I have said above, it should be clear that I do not think this criticism is sound. I agree that today in our society we believe that highly qualified persons deserve to be employed before those who are not as well qualified. But we accept this "informal rule" only because we tacitly assume that all individuals competing for a job or admission to school have been given an equal opportunity to develop their talents. More accurately, then, the "informal rule" accepted in our society today is; *"where equality of opportunity obtains,* the best qualified individual ought to be selected for employment or school admission." This being so, employers or school admissions officers who practice reverse discrimination do not change the rules in the middle of the game. In fact, they abide by them; for what they do is handicap white males in their competition with disadvantaged group members so as to assure equality of opportunity, and then, given this adjustment, hire or admit the individual whom they consider to be best qualified.

Corporate Policy Statements

Why an Affirmative Action Program? Because minorities and women have been discriminated against. In addition to the necessity of complying with the law, our Affirmative Action Program predicates on three basic beliefs: First: We believe equality of opportunity to be a fundamental principle and a moral imperative. Second: We believe that the preservation and continuity of our company within this free society requires equal opportunity for all members of society. Third: We believe that equal opportunity will enlarge our talent pool and enable us, with imaginative and effective management, to have a more competent and productive work force.

Beyond legalistic concerns, we have become increasingly aware that we must respect and protect the individual rights of every human being to exercise the full range of options with regard to what purpose each particular life is to serve. Each of us must have the opportunity to be all we can be— to maximize our human potential and to become a fulfilled person, possessing a sense of identity, self-esteem and individual worth. Equal opportunity does not exist when just an exceptional "star" is promoted to the better, higher-level jobs. Equal opportunity comes when the woman or minority person of average ability is just as likely to be promoted as the average nonminority man, and just as likely, in the long run, to advance as far. . . . It has been traditional to think of Affirmative Action as being confined to a concern for equal employment opportunity. We now believe that this definition should be enlarged to encompass four components: I. *Equal Employment*—This is Affirmative Action that seeks to provide opportunity for equal access to jobs at all levels based upon qualifications (regardless of sex, race, color, ethnic

216

origin, age, or handicap) for all. II. *Entrepreneurial Development*—This is Affirmative Action aimed at increasing business ownership by women, minorities, and the physically handicapped. III. *Social-Priority Investment*—This is Affirmative Action aimed at deployment of capital where needed to meet societal goals and requirements essential to continuity of a whole and wholesome society. IV. *Corporate Support*—This is an opportunity to advance the achievement of societal goals through financial backing of selected nonprofit institutions and organizations whose work makes substantial contribution to the quality of life for all.

This four-part concept of Affirmative Action seems particularly fitting as we intensify efforts for "coming right with people" to assure a socioeconomic environment that is conducive to our corporate growth, progress and survival. . . . Our Affirmative Action policy for the Handicapped seeks to assure equality of opportunity through a barrier-free employment and advancement process. This policy applies to the handicapped no less than to minorities and women. Each Operations Area is responsible for implementing the policy with the counsel of the Employee Health Services Department. Specifically, Area personnel with hiring responsibilities are charged with seeking out and being responsive to those agencies which refer the employable handicapped. The Equal Opportunity Division has the responsibility for coordinating and monitoring the program in close cooperation with the Employee Health Services Department and will help area personnel in identifying potential sources of handicapped referrals. . . . It is Equitable's policy to avoid any appearance of sex discrimination or invasion of privacy. Therefore in written materials and oral references: Avoid *unnecessary* reference to the marital status of the individual in records and documents. Avoid the titles Miss or Mrs. (with recognizable exceptions, a woman's marital status is not of business interest). Ms. is an acceptable business form, as the counterpart to Mr. Avoid the erroneous inference that all Agents, Managers, Directors, Officers, physicians, clients, etc., are male; that all beneficiaries, spouses, and secretaries are female. In other words, check inadvertent inference of sex—male or female. As a way of avoiding such male-oriented usages as, the employer . . . he, use both male and female pronouns after a singular subject (he/she, his/hers, him/her). Or, as an alternative to tediously repeating these pairs of pronouns, don't use any pronoun with a singular subject or use the all-inclusive plural construction (employers . . . they or their). Common sense must govern. Avoid use of the word girls, ladies, gals, etc., relying on the more acceptable generic term: women.

Equitable Life Assurance Society

We will not discriminate against any minority groups nor will we discriminate against majority groups to facilitate minorities.

Fox & Jacobs

DISCHARGE

Discharge Policy at Pacemakers Inc.

When he took the job as manager of the circuit department in the technology division of Pacemakers Inc. four years ago, Jack Rice knew he was on a hot seat. Pacemakers, in business just twelve years, had achieved second place in sales in the industry in the short span of seven years. Then, a two-year series of product recalls based on circuit failures severely damaged the company's reputation and earnings. Sales slipped to fourth place in the industry and there were rumors that Pacemakers was a stockmarket takeover candidate. Top management, convinced there would be only two or three ultimate survivors in this business, and determined to be among them while also remaining independent, decided to clean house in the circuit department. To head the department they brought in Jack, largely because Stan Drew wanted him. Stan, manager of the technology division, had been Jack's old boss when they worked at Circuit Technology Inc., the leading U.S. firm in integrated circuits. Although he had never had management responsibilities, Jack had a reputation as an excellent new product man and he was hired to lead the development of a new series of pacemakers based on the latest work in integrated circuits.

Jack looked on the position as a real challenge. He was responsible for one of the three basic technological ingredients in a pacemaker: circuitry, battery, and pacing leads to the heart. And technology is the key to this business; doctors want the best pacemaker for their patients, and quality, not cost, is the primary factor. This was the challenge Jack desired; he'd had enough of designing circuits for products like electronic games, where cost factors dominated. Jack also got along well with his boss; he believed that Stan Drew knew what applied science was all about—hire creative people, increase the research and development budget, and quality products will emerge.

218

At first it was rough; Jack had to upgrade his staff—hire several new scientists, reorient others, and discharge a few. He also had to acquaint himself with battery technology, the basic aspects of biophysics, and his competitors' products. It took him two years to see clearly what sort of a product he wanted. And then he had to motivate his staff to pull with him, often by spending long hours with them working on design and materials problems.

About that time, Jack's boss, Stan Drew, was fired. Stan said little about his dismissal except that he had taken the long-range view and both sales and earnings were still unimpressive and erratic. Stan was replaced by Mark Burns, who had a finance background. There was some grumbling about this among members of the circuit department, but top management explained that the firm's condition was still precarious and attention had to be focused on the present bottom line as well as the long range.

Mark Burns met with Jack to discuss the problems at Pacemakers. Mark said he was uncomfortable with the way Stan Drew was terminated and was aware there was some discontent among the research personnel. Jack replied: "People are nervous. We are on track with the product. Our team knows that. But medical technology takes time. We have to cross the FDA's hurdles and their standards are tough. The main point from our end is that we are gaining even though our research budget is lower than our competitors'. So we are optimistic. Then we see our boss, the guy responsible overall for our progress, get clipped. You know, there are no golden parachutes at our level; most of our team isn't even vested in the pension plan. It's scary. You work hard, you produce, but you've got the mortgage to pay and college bills, and if you get cut you have little or nothing to fall back on. You're right. The troops are anxious." Mark said that a little fear was a good motivator, and added that the volatility in technological businesses meant there could be no job guarantees. He added: "We do need to provide more security, particularly for our managers. I'm going to see that you get a salary increase. I'm also going to do my best to get you a productivity incentive bonus. I also think managers at your level should be in on our profit-sharing plan. I'll discuss this with top management. Finally, I know that at age fifty-eight vesting in our pension plan is important to you, and I'll work on that. Do your job and don't worry. I'm behind you."

Over the next year, Jack's relations with Mark became strained. Jack had always talked with Stan Drew as one inventor to another. Management, to them, meant a deep involvement with and interest in the actual process of invention, a process that involved creativity and one not reducible to strict control, prediction, or rationalization. In contrast, Mark talked of management by objective and cost-benefit analysis; his vocabulary, to Jack, seemed textbook and unrelated to the unpredictability of inventive work. Jack also did not like the extended business lunches and group meetings that Mark favored; they seemed to be personnel relations ploys and unrelated to the job. Mark felt he was in charge of a bunch of wild horses which needed to be shaped into a team. He held meetings to develop lines of communication and a clearer sense of direction. Mark brought in several organizational consultants to talk to Jack's department but felt undercut when word got back to him that in response to an employee who brought up a circuit problem to Jack, the latter said: "Let's do it like Mark wants—sit down, hold hands, and meditate." Jack was also upset that, although his salary was increased, Mark said no more about bonuses, profit-sharing, or vesting in the pension plan. Finally, Jack felt that although Mark talked long term he really had his eye on the quarterly earnings report. Technology, Jack thought, takes time. But Jack also knew the company was now tracked on his product and he was confident that in time it, or a successor based upon it, would be a big winner.

Three and a half years into his job, a pacemaker with Jack's circuits hit the market. It had a good reception in tests, but market acceptance was mixed. Jack believed that this was largely due to the company's tarnished reputation, but he allowed that competitors had not stood still and that their recent products were still a bit ahead of Pacemaker's. As he entered the office of Bill Smith, executive vice president for manufacturing, to attend his quarterly meeting, Jack felt secure in the knowledge that Pacemakers was at least competitive and that they could gain the edge with the next generation of pacemakers he had on the drawing board.

Bill Smith informed Jack that recent sales figures were disappointing and that it did not seem to him that a turnaround was near. He added that top management had been disappointed with Jack's performance for some time and that he was being terminated effective at the end of the day. Jack was stunned. He protested that he clearly had turned his department around and asked Bill to bring in Jack's immediate boss, Mark Burns, to discuss the issue. Bill said the decision was his, not Mark's, and that it was final. Jack asked for some reasons. Bill said they were in the sales figures. He added that a new circuit department manager had already been hired from outside the firm, and he would be reporting in two days. Allowing that the termination was abrupt, Bill offered Jack two months severance pay and told him he would provide him with a good recommendation.

A few days later, in discussing Jack with the firm's personnel manager, Bill Smith said:

> Jack Rice and Mark Burns just didn't see eye to eye. There was some personality conflict that I could not put my finger on. Maybe I should have canned Mark; he couldn't explain the problem to Jack, and Jack wasn't really aware of it—he was too concerned with his tinkering in the lab. But I couldn't fire Mark; he's ticketed for a top-level managerial slot. And I couldn't transfer Jack—there's no other slot in the organization where he would fit. Instead of demoting him in his own department, I thought it was best to just let him go. He'll catch on as a new product man somewhere, but I won't recommend him for a managerial position.

Mark Burns said, in commenting privately on Jack's dismissal:

Jack was not on top of things; he was too unorganized. He was a brilliant Lone Ranger from Silicon Valley with a narrow, inventor's mentality, who was always jumping ahead of his staff to the next, vaguely thought out project. He had to do everything himself on the technical side of things, but he could not delegate or understand other aspects of the business. His product is okay, it'll help us survive. But as we grow we need more coordination and long-term planning, and Jack was uncomfortable with that approach. He thought it inhibited him. And he never understood that top management wanted at least a show of social responsibility. I found out that he did not even pass out the United Fund cards, and, as for affirmative action, Jack refused to hire on the basis of anything but merit; he'd just laugh and say, "Put 'em in your steno pool." He just did not have a feel for the human side of things. I talked with him about these matters, but it did not seem to have an impact. When I told Bill Smith that I thought we should dump Jack, I offered to do it and give reasons, but Bill said that he would take care of it. Sales, he said, were not that good, which was sufficient.

One of the supervisors formerly under Jack made these observations, three months after Jack's termination:

Things have changed some around here; we are not quite as free-wheeling as we used to be under Jack. The R and D budget has been cut a bit, and some of us are wondering who is next to go. In many ways I think Jack was a fall-guy for Burns and Smith. They are not innovators and this is a risk business. They got a good product out of him and solid ideas for future products. Sales are slow now, but they'll pick up and Burns and Smith will look good. The new boss has some good ideas. But that will mean he has to make changes to leave his mark. That might set us back a year or so. I'm just not sure what games are being played here.

Jack went to see Lem Hargett, a labor law attorney. Lem informed Jack that he got fired in the wrong state, that Georgia was the strongest "at-will" state, meaning that an employer can fire an employee at any time for a good reason, a bad reason, or no reason at all. The only exceptions in Georgia are that you cannot be fired because you receive a subpoena for a court appearance or because your wages are garnisheed one time. Hargett mentioned several federal statutes that restrict terminations, and, after hearing Jack's case, said he might have a basis for a lawsuit. Given his age, he might be able to bring an age discrimination action because a much younger man replaced Jack. Hargett also explained it is illegal to fire someone to deprive him of employee benefits. But he also noted that Jack had a relatively brief period of employment at Pacemakers. Hargett also thought that a fraud action might be brought because of the compensation promises made by Mark Burns. He cited a former IBM executive who was lured to another firm in 1979 with compensation promises that were not honored, and who won a $10 million case for breach of contract and fraud. However, he noted that Jack had nothing in writing. Hargett also said that lawsuits are painful, expensive, and often take five years to resolve. He said his fee for a case this questionable was fifty percent of a judgment and the client pays all expenses off the top. These include Xerox copies, $4 per-page court reporter's records, and fees charged by professional "expert witnesses."

Jack had this comment after reflecting on his dismissal and his three months of trying unsuccessfully to secure a similar position:

> I'm still bitter and baffled about this whole thing. I'm baffled because I put up the product that will eventually save this company. I'm bitter because I got the shaft. Mark and Bill Smith know that, and there's nothing I can do about it. Oh, I sent a zinger letter to the company's top dog, but I didn't even get a reply. I lie awake at night thinking about how those two toads above me will benefit from my work. Smith even had the gall to warn me not to take Pacemaker's trade secrets with me. *Their* secrets? Hah! In this business the next new product is in somebody's head—mine! I'll take that with me to a competitor and bury these clowns. So far though, I'll admit I haven't had any takers.

For Discussion

Was Pacemakers justified in firing Jack Rice? Why or why not? Discuss and evaluate the context of Jack's termination and the way it was handled. Could steps be taken to improve termination procedures at Pacemakers Inc.? If so, what steps would you take?

Milton Snoeyenbos
John Wesley Roberts

Ethics and the Termination of Employees

In signing a work contract an employee agrees to provide his abilities, time, and effort in return for a wage. Some work contracts extend additional benefits to employees; for example, most union collective bargaining agreements require the employer to provide "just cause" for dismissal of an employee, i.e., dismissal must be based on factors related to job performance or business necessities. However, less than one-fourth of American workers are presently covered by collective bargaining agreements. Although a few employees have just cause provisions specified in their individually negotiated work contracts, the vast majority of employees, perhaps 70 percent are not so covered. These employees not only have no contractual dismissal rights, they also have very little in the way of legal rights.

The traditional legal context regarding the at-will employee, i.e., one not having explicit work contract provisions regarding dismissal, is spelled out in the following legal cases:

> . . . employers "may dismiss their employees at will . . . for good cause, for no cause, or even for cause morally wrong, without being thereby guilty of legal wrong." *Payne* v. *Western & A. R.R.,* 81 Tenn. 507, 519–20 (1884).

> . . . the "arbitrary right of the employer to employ or discharge labor, with or without regard to actuating motives," is a proposition "settled beyond peradventure." *Union Labor Hospital Assn.* v. *Vance Redwood Lumber Co.,* 158 Cal. 551, 555, 112 p. 886, 888 (1910).

Over the years, several federal laws have diminished the scope of at-will terminations: (1) the National Labor Relations Act prohibits the termination of employees solely on the basis of labor organizing activities; (2) the Civil Rights Act protects individuals from dismissal solely on the basis of race, color, religion, sex, and national origin; (3) the Age Discrimination in Employment Act prohibits firings solely on the basis of age; (4) the Vocational Rehabilitation Act bans dismissals based solely on handicap; (5) the Occupational Safety and Health Act prohibits firing on the basis of an employee's refusal to perform a task the employee reasonably believes to be life-threatening; (6) terminations based on a reason that violates a significant public policy (e.g., refusal to commit perjury) may provide grounds for a court suit; and (7) refusal to engage in an ethically or legally prohibited act may provide the basis for court protection from unjust dismissal.[1]

Although such federal laws have undoubtedly prevented many firings, Congress and the courts have actually been fairly conservative in restricting employers' discharge rights. The cornerstone of this conservatism is the doctrine of contractual mutuality:

> An employee is never presumed to engage his services permanently, thereby cutting himself off from all chances of improving his condition; indeed, in this land of opportunity it would be against public policy and the spirit of our institutions that any man should thus handicap himself; and the law will presume . . . that he did not so intend. And if the contract of employment be not binding on thc employee for the whole term of such employment, then it cannot be binding upon the employer; there would be lack of "mutuality."
> *Pitcher* v. *United Oil and Gas Syndicate Inc.* 174 La. 66, 69, 139 So. 760, 761 (1932).

Just as the employee is free to resign, the employer is free to discharge the at-will employee at any time; there is a symmetry to the relationship. There is no doubt that this is an improvement over the complete asymmetry found in the master-slave relationship. In actuality, however, there is frequently an asymmetry in the employer-employee relationship that is slanted in favor of the employer. In times of high unemployment, or in fields of specialization or industries where there is a labor surplus, it will probably be more difficult for the discharged employee to find a new position than for the firm to hire a new employee. Consequently, the harm to the employee, in terms of economic hardship and psychological disruption, is often greater than the harm to the firm. In spite of this asymmetry, however, it is unlikely that sweeping federal limitations on the employer's right to discharge will be enacted in the near future, for, as Lawrence Blades has pointed out, "One need not be an extreme cynic to say that employers would not favor such legislation. Nor could organized labor be expected to favor laws which would give individual employees a means of protecting themselves without a union."[2]

It should be pointed out that, although the at-will doctrine was not restricted much at the federal level during the 1980s, about forty states have recently taken various actions to modify it. Some states, notably California, Montana, Alaska, and Wyoming, have specified that employees cannot be fired without just cause. Some state courts have held that employees who received assurances of benefits they did not obtain and who were subsequently fired should be reinstated, often with backpay and punitive damages. Other states have privacy laws, which courts have held were violated in termination proceedings. For example, a fast-food manager was fired after being orally questioned about drug use. He sued, arguing that his privacy had been invaded by the firm because he was polygraphed about drug use prior to taking the job. A jury awarded him $450,000 in compensatory and punitive damages. Defamation is the basis for many suits. A terminated manager who found it very difficult to find a new job hired a private detective to find out what his former associates were saying about him. When his former boss described him as a "sociopath . . . a total zero," he sued and won a $500,000 compensation award, with $600,000 in punitive damages tacked on.

In a survey of wrongful discharge cases, the *Wall Street Journal* reports that about one-half of managerial terminations today result in some form of legal action.[3] More than 25,000 such cases are pending in state and federal courts. The *Journal* cites a 1988 Rand Corporation survey of jury verdicts in 120 California wrongful discharge cases. The average salary of fired employees was $36,254. Plaintiffs won 68 percent of the cases, with an average award of $646,855. Clearly, the at-will doctrine has been severely curtailed in some states.

It is difficult to generalize about state law regarding the at-will doctrine; ten states, for example, have done little to modify it. Nonetheless, we can still inquire into the ethics of the matter and consider the question of whether there is a moral basis for restrictions or limitations on the discharge rights of employers. Let us discuss the ethics of dismissal under the rubrics of just cause, due process, and mitigation of harmful effects.[4]

JUST CAUSE

Although "just cause" is an admittedly vague phrase, let us see if we can sharpen it a bit by picking out some relatively clear-cut cases where discharge is justifiable and then some cases where it clearly is unjustifiable. Doing so will enable us to better discuss borderline cases.

What we might call "business necessity" may provide a sufficient basis for discharge. Automation necessary for competitiveness or survival of the firm, severe market shrinkage, product obsolescence, lack of capital—any number of such factors may require work force reduction. If managers calculate that benefits to the firm, remaining employees, and society at large outweigh the negative consequences to the discharged employees, and if the dismissal procedure is conducted fairly and the harmful effects of dismissal are mitigated, then there are both consequentialist and nonconsequentialist reasons for such dismissals. The key here is that the business necessity must be real; the firm must make a genuine attempt to calculate long-term consequences, the dismissal procedure must be fair, and the firm should make a real attempt to minimize harm to those dismissed. In many such cases there are alternatives to discharge that should be explored. For example, overall utility and fairness may be achieved by reducing everyone's work week by 20 percent for a period of time rather than discharging 20 percent of the work force.

In addition, many factors specifically related to job performance provide a just basis for discharge. If an employee is nonproductive, negligent, frequently absent without cause, and engages in disruptive conduct in violation of explicit guidelines, then the employer surely has just cause for dismissal. If internal due process procedures are available to employees, and the employer attempts to mitigate the harmful effects of discharge, then the employer is ethically justified in firing such an employee. From a utilitarian or consequentialist standpoint, the results of such a dismissal and the subsequent replacement with a more responsible employee would benefit fellow workers, the firm, and society at large. The dismissed worker demoralizes his fellows, reduces corporate efficiency, and the cost is passed to the consumer. In addition, the consequences of dismissal may be beneficial to such a discharged employee. Tacit consent to ineffectiveness, negligence, excessive absenteeism, laziness, etc., may only encourage such habits. If such an employee ignores company programs designed to help him, and explicit warnings prove ineffective, dismissal may help the person fully realize that his bad habits require reform.

Putting aside factors related to business necessity, if discharge should be related to job performance, then factors unrelated to job performance should not provide a basis for just discharge. Humans are adept at assuming a variety of roles, and *normally* there are many facets of a person's life, or roles he fulfills, that have little or no relevance to his role as employee. Where such roles do impinge on job performance, it is the criteria of the latter that form the basis for just dismissal.

Although the general principle is clear, namely, that factors unrelated to job performance do not provide a basis for just discharge, it is difficult to catalog all factors not related to job performance. At best we can set out some relatively clear-cut areas of immunity. Discharge is normally not just if it is based on the exercise of a constitutionally protected right. Thus, the employee has the right of free choice in the political arena and the right to free speech on most matters. Of course, if the employee spends so much time exercising his right to promote a political candidate or party that he impairs job performance, then discharge may be justified. Also, the employee should not be discharged for engaging in civic and cultural activities of his choice. On the other hand, where the employer can demonstrate *clearly* that job performance is closely tied to participation in certain sorts of civic and cultural activities, then a request to join may be reasonable. Typically, however, the connection is difficult to establish, and in fairness the employee should be given a wide range of options. Then, too, it should be noted that this principle can be carried to absurdity. The employee cannot be expected to join every organization that is related to job performance; good performance demands time *away* from the job, where a mix of roles can be fulfilled.

Finally, although employees are generally expected to abide by company regulations and procedures, and lawful management directives, no employee should be discharged for refusing to engage in behavior that is illegal or commonly acknowledged to be ethically unacceptable.[5] The manager who refuses to fix prices or lie should not be dismissed on such a basis. And firms need to be aware that courts take a dim view of managerial requests to engage in illegal behavior. For example, a state court reversed the dismissal of an employee who was fired because, on an off-duty rafting trip with her manager and other employees, she refused her manager's request to join in singing "Moon River" while mooning people on the shore. There are other areas where employees should have immunity from discharge, but, depending on the type of firm, these should be spelled out generally in an employee rights document and articulated via the firm's due process procedure.

It is important that the firm attempt to spell out as clearly as possible the various job related grounds for dismissal. It should also make these grounds known to its employees, for just cause should include only that conduct the employee knows is subject to discipline. Of course, some just cause grounds are obvious and need not be stated; an employee need not be told that physical assault on his supervisor will not be tolerated. But the employee should be informed of prohibited conduct that he would not reasonably understand to be prohibited. It is also important for employees to understand the enforcement status of a rule. If a firm has a no smoking rule, but the rule is not enforced and numerous employees do smoke on the job, then dismissal based solely on that rule is hardly just.

Although morality seems to require that a firm make explicit its job-related grounds for dismissal, it must be acknowledged that doing so makes it legally more difficult to fire employees; courts are increasingly holding that a firm must abide by its own ethical codes. For example, a female IBM manager filed suit after being fired for dating a former IBM employee who left to join a competitor. Her boss fired her one week after she received a merit raise, claiming that her relationship constituted a conflict of interest. She sued, claiming that even though she was nonunion she was protected by the firm's ethics code, which spelled out impermissible behavior but did not expressly forbid her relationship. She won a $300,000 judgment, with the court holding that a company must follow its own ethics code.

If we have marked off some clear cases where dismissal is justified and other cases where it is unjustified, it must, nevertheless, be admitted that there are numerous borderline cases, especially in the discharge of managers, where considerable judgment is required. The problem of managerial discharge is serious. James Gallagher claims that an "estimated 6 percent of the 250,000 executives and managers in major U.S. corporations—about 15,000 people are fired annually."[6] Donald Sweet argues that a total of 100,000 U.S. managers are fired each year.[7] Thomas Jaffe states that when high-level executives leave a firm the "reasons range from ill health and early retirement to irreconcilable policy differences. Sometimes the leaving is voluntary. Mostly the phrases in the press releases are euphemisms for firing."[8] Sweet points out a survey of personnel managers indicating that they are fired for a variety of reasons: " 'too emotional,' 'immature,' 'couldn't delegate,' 'not tough enough,' etc. Not one could say that these people were fired for lack of technical competence or deficiency of education, both of which are key considerations when a person is hired."[9] Gallagher, chairman of Career Management Associates, an outplacement firm, claims that "Contrary to conventional belief, job terminations are more often prompted by incompatibility than by incompetence. In seven out of ten outplacement cases we have managed, the fired executive has had a new boss within the previous eighteen months. Different styles, new goals, and conflicting personalities account for more terminations than plant closings, layoffs, and corporate mergers combined."[10]

Apparently, then, "incompatibility" is a major source of managerial dismissals. Now, in certain cases there may be organizational flaws that generate conflicts and incompatibility. Richard Huseman lists three causes of such conflict: (1) organizational incongruence, i.e., built-in opposition between task responsibilities; (2) inadequate performance measures, e.g., a purchasing department evaluated on the basis of the negative measure of excess inventory may fail to purchase adequately and this in turn may lead to conflict with the sales department; and (3) ambiguity, i.e., organizational complexity results in ambiguous communication, allowing employees to read what they want into communications.[11] In such cases, utility for the firm and fairness to its employees dictates that the flaws be remedied, and dismissals based on conflicts originating in such flaws do not have a just cause foundation.

We should note, however, that the comments of Donald Sweet and James Gallagher suggest that frequently it is simply *personality* conflicts or incompatibilities that are responsible for dismissals. Here we should keep in mind a hypothesis of recent management theory: "Organizations ought to thrive on most personal and professional differences, because in the long run they account for the dynamics of organizational growth."[12] If this is true, and if the person being considered for dismissal has a good job performance record, then utility for the firm and fairness to the employee indicate that such personality conflicts are not in themselves a just cause for discharge. At worst, the employee should be transferred to a position where such a conflict or difference either will not occur or can be used to advantage. Of course, some deep-seated, intractable personality differences may not lead to corporate growth. This is especially true at the top management level, where fundamental personality differences related to conflicting organizational objectives and strategies may harm the firm and its employees. Furthermore, in some top management slots transfer without demotion may be impossible, and the demotion may be unacceptable to the employee. In such circumstances one suspects that job performance frequently suffers and forms the basis for a just dismissal. But even if not, an overall assessment of utility may permit just discharge.

To summarize, we have suggested that business necessity and factors directly related to job performance provide a justifiable basis for dismissal. We also marked off several aspects of an employee's life that have little or no relevance to the employment relationship, and, hence, dismissals based on such factors do not have a just cause basis. Incompatibilities based on organizational flaws call for elimination of the flaw and do not provide just foundation for dismissal. Moreover, personality conflicts are not themselves a just cause for dismissal; in some cases transfer, not termination, is the answer. But in other cases personality conflicts may lead to disutility and thus provide a basis for just dismissal.

Finally, an employer should not only have just cause for terminating an employee, he should state in writing the reasons for discharge. No person should have to experience the following:

> Do you have any idea why you were fired?—I think ultimately because they didn't like me. I think it's probably that simple. There are still people in the company who are quasi-alcoholics or who don't do any work. They're still there. And people who don't make waves. I had a lot of people working for me, and I was under a lot of pressure. I'm probably the kind of person who under those circumstances is not invisible. Probably what it came down to was simply that I was not liked. But I don't really know.[13]

There is no moral basis for the anxiety, self-doubt, and resentment often caused by such terminations. Dismissal may be justified in some cases, but the discharged employee cannot learn from the action if he does not understand its rationale. In addition, a written explanation of reasons for dismissal would encourage the manager to give the same reasons to his superiors, the discharged employee, and those responsible for the firm's due process procedure, the second element in an ethical discharge system.

DUE PROCESS

The right to due process in discharge cases is based squarely on fairness to the employee affected and on utility for the company. As we have noted, fairness and utility require a just cause discharge; adequate due process helps assure both. In fairness to the employee, due process may unmask an unjust discharge; furthermore, the unjust firing of a person with a good job performance record will probably have disutility for the firm. And, insofar as it assures other workers that dismissal decisions are not arbitrary, due process increases employee morale, which has overall utility. Finally, the checks and balances of a good due process procedure encourage a more objective decision.

Objectivity is clearly needed in discharge cases. As we have noted, personality differences often play a central role in such cases, and emotion may cloud balanced judgment. Then, too, management texts and management training mention very little about the practice of discharge and almost nothing about the ethics of discharge. As a result, most managers are not prepared to adopt the synoptic viewpoint necessary for an objective decision. This is especially true of lower-level managers, who may have a limited perspective of the whole organization and the breadth of its responsibilities.

David Ewing has provided a succinct list of the characteristics of an ethical due process system:

1. It must be a procedure; it must follow rules. It must not be arbitrary.

2. It must be visible, well-known enough so that potential violators of rights and victims of abuse know it.

3. It must be predictably effective. Employees must have confidence that previous decisions in favor of rights will be repeated.

4. It must be "institutionalized." That is, it must be a relatively permanent fixture in the organization, not a device that is here today, gone tomorrow.

5. It must be perceived as equitable. The standards used in judging a case must be respected and accepted by a majority of employees, bosses as well as subordinates.

6. It must be easy to use. Employees must be able to understand it without fear that procedural complexities will get the best of them.

7. It must apply to all employees.[14]

Although there are a variety of ways that an ethical due process system can be institutionalized, and the best method will be somewhat dependent on the size and type of the firm, the following is offered as a procedure that promises objectivity and fairness for a relatively large firm. The firm's Ethics and Social Responsibility Committee of the Board of Directors (constituted by an equal number of inside and outside directors) selects a termination hearing panel of two company members and one member from the firm's legal counsel. Employees who have received a termination notice receive a written explanation for the termination five days before its effective date. Within this period the employee may elect to contest the dismissal by submitting a request for a termination hearing to the panel. The panel sets a hearing date ten to fourteen days after the effective termination date. The employee has the right to select a member of the firm's legal staff, a member of management, or an outside counsel to represent his case, and can make his selection any time after he has informed the panel that he requests a hearing. The manager who fired the employee is also entitled to representation. The member from the firm's outside legal counsel presides over the hearing. Both sides are entitled to call witnesses or additional resource people, and these may be cross-examined. A stenographer is present to record the hearing. The hearing panel renders its decision within ten days. If the decision favors the employee, it is binding on management; if it favors management, it does not abrogate the employee's right to seek relief or legal remedy from state or federal courts. If the decision favors the employee, no record of the termination or proceedings are retained in the employee's personnel file.

MITIGATION OF HARMFUL EFFECTS

Even though a dismissal is based on just cause and the employee has received due process, the employer still has an obligation to mitigate the harmful effects of dismissal. The obligation is in part based on the asymmetry in the employment relationship that we previously mentioned. It is generally more difficult for the dismissed employee to find a new position than for the firm to hire a new employee. And this asymmetry may still obtain even though the employer does mitigate the situation through his contribution to unemployment compensation, for, in addition to his economic loss, the psychological effect of discharge on an employee is often devastating. Sweet says, "there are three very traumatic separations in our life: divorce, the death of a loved one, and the separation that experts estimate faces 100,000 executives every year—separation from their jobs."[15] Fairness often dictates that the firm should help alleviate this harm. Utility also points in the direction of mitigating the harmful effects of discharge; Angelo Troisi nicely captures the shock of termination and the overall utility to be gained from mitigation:

> Although the emotional impact of being fired varies with the individual, studies show that the trauma associated with termination is so great that it can be compared in intensity to divorce or the death of a loved one. Shock, depression, anger, self-pity, confusion, and loss of identity are some common feelings and reactions. The person is filled with anxiety and self-doubt about the prospects of finding a new job, the reactions of family and peers, and finances. The individual may be extremely bitter and negative about the future to the point of seeking revenge. He or she may go to work for a customer or competitor, file a lawsuit against the company, or spread malicious rumors. Since such negative actions can substantially damage a company's reputation and can have serious effect on its recruiting efforts, community image, and employee morale and loyalty, it is in a company's best interests to handle terminations as positively as possible.[16]

The precise type of help the firm should provide a dismissed employee will depend on the circumstances: financial aid, employment references, logistical support in finding a new job, and job search training all may play a constructive role.

In concluding, we would point out that, although we have stressed termination costs to the employee, there are also costs to the employer. In the case of unjust dismissals, where an employee has a good job performance record, discharge may reduce efficiency. And many dismissals are harmful to morale and company image. Even just dismissals entail a waste of training and often a disruption of continuity. So, management should take a close look at what is causing terminations and resignations. It should start with a close look at its selection and performance appraisal systems: "a major factor in separations may be underhiring and overhiring . . . a great deal of the agony of separation could be eliminated by working harder at the front end—the selection process. Making sure not only that candidates can do the job, which is the easy part of the procedure, but that they *will* do the job."[17] Troisi asks three questions related to performance that if sufficiently answered, would prevent many terminations and resignations:

1. Was the employee's job description regularly reviewed to determine if the employee was performing the duties prescribed?

2. Was the correlation between the employee's salary and his job description reviewed?

3. Were the employee's performance reviews carefully studied?[18]

In addition, it seems reasonable to say that improvements in the quality of work-life would often reduce dismissals and resignations. Our main point here, then, is that even if the firm has an ethical discharge system, with just cause, due process, and mitigation mechanisms, the best solution to the problem is to structure the firm so that the dismissal issue seldom arises.

NOTES

1. Richard G. Vernon and Peter S. Gray, "Termination at Will—The Employer's Right to Fire," *Employee Relations Law Journal* 6, no. 1 (Summer 1980): pp. 25–40.

2. Lawrence E. Blades, "Employment at Will vs. Individual Freedom: On Limiting the Abusive Exercise of Employer Power," *Columbia Law Review* 67, no. 8 (December 1967), p. 1434.

3. "Fired Managers Winning More Lawsuits," *The Wall Street Journal*, Thursday, September 7, 1989, B1.

4. Thomas Garrett, *Business Ethics* (New York: Appleton-Century-Crofts, 1966), pp. 46–50.

5. In 1981 a law titled the Whistle-Blowers Protection Act was implemented in Michigan. The law makes it illegal for an employer to discharge or threaten a worker or to discriminate in salary, benefits, privileges, or location of employment because an employee has reported a violation of law to any public body. Courts are empowered to order reinstatement, along with seniority, back pay, and damages.

6. James J. Gallagher, "What Do You Owe the Executive You Fire?" *Dun's Review* 113, no. 6 (June 1969), p. 109.

7. Donald H. Sweet, "What's Wrong with Being Fired?" *Personnel Journal* 58, no. 10 (October 1979), p. 672.

8. Thomas Jaffe, "Is There Life After Downfall?" *Forbes* 124, no. 10 (November 12, 1979), p. 241.

9. Sweet, "What's Wrong with Being Fired?" p. 672.

10. Gallagher, "What Do You Owe the Executive You Fire?" p. 109.

11. Richard C. Huseman, "Interpersonal Conflict in the Modern Organization," in *Readings in Interpersonal and Organizational Communication,* 2d ed. Richard C. Huseman, Cal M. Logue, and Dwight L. Freshley, eds. (Boston: Holbrook Press, 1973), pp. 192–93.

12. Stephen S. Kaagen, "Terminating People from Key Positions," *Personnel Journal,* vol. 57, no. 2 (February 1978), p. 96.

13. Harry Maurer, *Not Working* (New York: Holt, Rinehart and Winston, 1979), p. 20.

14. David W. Ewing, *Freedom Inside the Organization* (New York: E. P. Dutton, 1977), p. 156.

15. Sweet, "What's Wrong with Being Fired?" p. 672.

16. Angelo M. Troisi, "Softening the Blow of 'You're Fired,' " *Supervisory Management* 25, no. 6 (June 1980), p. 16.

17. Sweet, "What's Wrong with Being Fired?" p. 672.

18. Troisi, "Softening the Blow of 'You're Fired,' " p. 14.

PRIVACY

Case Study

Employee Records at
Fantenetti Valve Corporation

Fantenetti Valve Corporation, headquartered in Patterson, New Jersey, is a specialty valve manufacturer with 1992 sales of $426 million. Unlike many of its competitors, Fantenetti does not mass produce standard valves, but instead focuses primarily on research and design work; it employs a relatively high percentage of scientific and technical personnel and spends about 6 percent of its annual sales on research. Most of its manufacturing is subcontracted with other firms. Fantenetti is not unionized. We interviewed Ross Mills, personnel manager at Fantenetti Valve Corporation, concerning that company's policy on employee records.

QUESTION: We hear a lot about files on employees these days Ross; what's the need for them in a firm such as Fantenetti?

MILLS: We are a large, technologically based firm, with about 6,000 employees in five states. Our technical data are our lifeblood, and we simply have to minimize risk with respect to trade secrets, formulas, marketing plans, and our growth strategies. Since most of the risk relates to the background and experiences of our employees, we must have data about them. We're in a tough position. We try to be sensitive to people's rights, but managers cannot make rational decisions without data, and this includes data on people—we certainly would be open to criticism if we acted without benefit of information on the people we hire and employ.

QUESTION: How do you get the data you want, and what's included?

MILLS: Well, each person's an individual. What's relevant in one case may

234

not be relevant in another. So, at the time of application we ask the applicant to sign the following authorization:

I understand that my employment at Fantenetti Valve Corporation is subject to verification of previous employment, data provided in my application, and any related documents, and will be contingent on my submitting to and passing both a physical examination administered by a company appointed physician and whatever psychological tests are authorized by Fantenetti Valve Corporation. I authorize educational institutions, law enforcement authorities, employers, and all organizations and individuals having information relevant to my employment at Fantenetti Valve Corporation, to provide such information. I release all organizations and individuals, including Fantenetti Valve Corporation, from any liability in connection with the release of information about me. I understand that an investigative report may be made by, or authorized by and submitted to, Fantenetti Valve Corporation, and that this report might include information concerning my character, reputation, and mode of living.

This gives us some flexibility on the data we collect about each applicant; what's important in the case of one person may not be with another.

QUESTION: But isn's this just too broad? Doesn't it authorize you to gather any data in whatever way without incurring any liability at all?

MILLS: Our experience is that you never know where an investigation will lead. So you need a blanket authorization. Of course we don't do anything outside the law. You know that the law today is very strict about what you can and cannot do. We stay strictly within the law. But if we want information that the law permits us to gather, we go after it. And once we hire someone, he's free to inspect his dossier anytime and to insert comments. I suppose we are unfair to some applicants. We do hire professionals to run our tests and background checks. And where we have only a few applicants we may invite in an otherwise promising candidate who has a few bad spots on his record. We sit down, talk about, and maybe clarify the problem. But, you know, in most cases we are swamped with candidates, so we can quickly narrow the list to the cream of the crop, most of whom have no problems with previous employers, school records, credit bureaus, health, and so on. But let me add that we also base our decisions on objective tests that we administer regarding aptitude, intelligence, and personality.

QUESTION: Aren't some of these sorts of tests of doubtful validity, especially personality tests?

MILLS: Let me say that we are an equal opportunity employer. We do some federal work, and we've always met Equal Employment Opportunity Commission (EEOC) and Office of Federal Contract Compliance (OFCC) guidelines. Beyond that, we are a scientific company. We believe in science. We believe that personality traits are measurable. You may have a person with the aptitude and brains for a job, but he has a personality flaw. In our sensitive business it's important that we measure a person's maturity, stability, and compatibility. Personality tests aren't infallible, but they're better than just a hunch about a person. They give us some idea about areas of a person's adequacy and inadequacy. They also help place people, to fit them into the right corporate slot.

QUESTION: Don't some of these tests touch on variables like masculinity/ femininity? Are you interested in this sort of adequacy?

MILLS: It might be relevant. You don't know what is relevant until you look at each particular case. By "adequacy" we are looking at two things: (1) Is this person going to fit into the job? We don't want an introvert as a salesman. The tests tell us whether an applicant is an introvert. And (2), is the applicant going to fit into Fantenetti? If an applicant isn't going to mesh with our corporate culture, we don't want him.

QUESTION: Is homosexuality a thing of interest here?

MILLS: It may be; you can't generalize. You have to look at each case as it comes up. If he is gay and going to be disruptive, we don't want him. But, then, we don't want anyone who is disruptive. We have our values, our traditions. We have this all worked out in our mission statement. And we want employees who are totally dedicated to those values. It's very simple: if you have certain measurable personality traits, it's probable that you will be happy at Fantenetti. And if you are happy here, you will probably be productive. So, we use personality tests. But let me stress that we are interested in the person as well as Fantenetti. The person whose values do not mesh with ours will often become frustrated or alienated. He should be someplace else. If we can measure these traits, we are doing some applicants a favor by not hiring them.

QUESTION: But in these cases aren't you faced with an invasion of privacy?

MILLS: Of course, people have a right to privacy. We don't invade a person's home. We don't force people to apply for a job here or force them to take our tests. People sometimes think only employees have rights, but Fantenetti also has rights. We have a right to hire only employees who will avoid doing what we tell them not to do. We have a right to expect loyalty. We have a right to hire people who will act exclusively for Fantenetti's benefit. And we have a right to know what type of person we are hiring.

QUESTION: Does all this data become part of one's permanent file?

MILLS: Yes, but he always has access to it, and can insert comments. We don't try to stereotype people with tests. Files are constantly updated. Everyone is evaluated annually, and the employee sees and signs his evaluation. He may add comments. Other data is constantly added: letters of commendation or warning, relevant memoranda, newspaper clippings, employee suggestions, health insurance information, and so on.

QUESTION: Do you separate job performance data from personal information?

MILLS: No. It's all related to job performance.

QUESTION: Can the employee see anything in his file at any time?

MILLS: There are only two things he cannot see. We have a form that compares workers for merit raises, promotions, and layoffs. Since this data is comparative, and includes personal information on several employees, it is not available. We also have a corporate development plan that contains management's general opinion of an individual's potential, any long-range plans the company might have regarding the employee, and a list of possible replacements. This isn't available either. But let me add that we're practically required to keep such files. We have to promote minorities, and so we have to get the data. To compare people and groups we have to have data on everyone.

QUESTION: Who has access to these files?

MILLS: A superior has access to the file of any subordinate responsible to him on the organizational chart. Those people designated "senior manager" have access to the file of anyone below that level. You must have this sort of access to facilitate the information flow. We're a "people" company, and we have to get the right people in the right jobs.

QUESTION: Do you allow outsiders access to your employee files?

MILLS: You have to. The Occupational Safety and Health Administration (OSHA) requires health information. The IRS wants payroll data. The Defense Department examines our security checks. I could go on. The police and the courts can get certain data. We also generally agree to provide data on job title, salary, and length of service to the credit bureaus and investigating agencies that screen our applicants. We don't release any other information unless the employee agrees to it.

For Discussion

Has Ross Mills presented an acceptable defense of Fantenetti's policies regarding employees' records? In what areas is his defense strong? In what areas is it weak? If it were your responsibility to redesign Fantenetti's employee record procedures, what changes would you make? Why?

Integrity Testing at Marvex Distributors

Marvex Distributors operates 157 convenience food stores and operates concessions at 26 airports in the United States. We interviewed Mary Bell, Marvex's vice-president responsible for security.

QUESTION: Ms. Bell, Marvex is known as a security conscious firm; explain some of your precautions and the reasons for them.

BELL: Let me say that every corporation in America today is security conscious. Studies show that worker theft of money and property amounts to about $60 billion annually. Intangible theft or time theft in the form of false sick days, making personal phone calls, punching an absent worker's time card, etc., costs the United States about $250 billion per year.

Now Marvex is in two low-profit-margin businesses. In our type of business about 2 percent of annual sales is lost to employee theft. We cannot afford that loss and make a profit. We used to have an extensive polygraph program, a program that was very effective in both detecting theft and deterring employees from stealing. Then, in 1988, polygraphs were essentially banned from the private-sector workplace as an invasion of privacy. This ruling has made it very difficult to detect a thief after the person's initial employment begins. So our present strategy is to screen applicants very carefully. We use a two-pronged strategy. First, we employ an investigative agency to run a check on each applicant who passes our initial screen tests. We want to know whether the person is stable and honest: What's the person's work record like? Has this person lied on our application? Is he or she extravagant? Does this person pay his or her debts? Is the person's home life stable?—things like that. In addition to examining past behavior, we also give each applicant a pencil and paper integrity test. What we are looking at here is the applicant's attitude toward theft; we try to determine whether the prospect is inclined to deviant behavior.

QUESTION: What's this test like?

BELL: Marvex didn't make up the test. It was constructed and is graded by Psytest Systems. We selected this test because a 1991 study by the American Psychological Association indicated that the test's results are validated by academic research. I don't doubt that many such tests are unscientific, but Psytest seems to have passed muster. The test basically is true/false. You mark down "true" or "false" to statements such as:

1. Most work-related accidents can be avoided.
2. There are some people I definitely hate.
3. I always try to do my best at work.
4. I find it difficult to make friends with people.
5. In most cases I insist on doing things my own way.
6. I have never told a lie.
7. Making personal phone calls while at work is not the same as stealing.
8. The typical supervisor generally puts in a full day of hard work.
9. In some cases I try to get even with someone who has hurt me.
10. I would trick someone out of their money if I could definitely get away with it.
11. I have never done anything I felt guilty about.
12. It would be nice to have enough money to not have to work again.

QUESTION: Doesn't this sort of smack of Big Brother? On the basis of what a pencil and paper test claims that you "might" do, you can be denied a job. Furthermore, you cannot say you won't take the test. Isn't this coercion?

BELL: Not really. We don't force anyone to apply for a job at Marvex. You have a choice. To be processed, each applicant must accept and sign the following:

As part of my application I agree to voluntarily submit to a job-related questionnaire, and I release and indemnify Marvex Distributors, and any persons
in any way connected therewith, of any and all liability with respect thereto.

So it's all voluntary. We aren't coercing these people.

QUESTION: But is this truly voluntary? You either take the test or you are not hired. Doesn't the Fifth Amendment say you have a right to remain silent and not incriminate yourself? Doesn't the test amount to an unreasonable search that the Fourth Amendment bars? And isn't it a form of coerced expression that essentially violates the First Amendment?

BELL: Look, I'm no Constitutional scholar, but these tests are used and there's no law explicitly banning them. The rights you mention are important, but they're not inalienable; they have to be balanced with Marvex's right to its property.

QUESTION: Are these tests valid?

BELL: Of course, these tests are not perfect; no test is. Some honest people get excluded from consideration, and some thieves slip through. Psytest does, however, have impressive data that show a reduction in what we call "shrinkage" in businesses that use its tests. We found at Marvex that our shrinkage has been cut by 30 percent. The American Psychological Association's 1991 study said the preponderance of evidence indicates that such tests work, i.e., they help predict which prospective employees may prove undependable or steal. The group concluded: "Despite all our reservations about honesty tests, we do not believe there is any sound basis for prohibiting their development and use. Indeed, to do so would only invite alternative forms of pre-employment screening that would be less open, scientific, and controllable."

QUESTION: This seems like letting the fox guard the henhouse. Can you really expect that the APA, which is after all deeply committed to the position that personality traits can be objectively measured, would say that such tests seem bogus?

BELL: Look, Marvex sells food. We are not test assessors. We rely on what the experts say.

QUESTION: But one of our strengths in the United States is that we take individual rights seriously. And this procedure reminds me of the frontier judge who, desirous of seeing that the guilty did not escape punishment, sentenced everyone before him to hang.

BELL: Well, an integrity test will, in some cases, deny a person a job. Yet any selection process culls people. A hundred people apply for a job. A personnel manager can discard 90 for any reason—or no real reason. Maybe one of them would have been the best for the job. Who knows? But the objective tests give one some basis that applies to every applicant and serves as a reasonable basis for rejection. Of course, applicants have privacy rights. Marvex realizes this. Yet we also have responsibilities to our shareholders, our customers, and our honest employees. A thief raises the price of an item, costing the consumer and reducing wages we can pay, while also robbing our stockholders. Is that fair? Does a thief have that right? If such testing is legally allowed, if it results in theft reduction, and if it benefits customers and honest employees, as well as Marvex, then don't we have an obligation to use such tests?

QUESTION: You say these tests are objective, but are they? It looks like the questions are loaded with ambiguity. Won't the really honest person simply fail the test? He thinks: "Sure, I lied—when I was a boy," or "I make a few calls on company time, say, to check up on a sick child, but I don't think that's theft," or "I don't always give 100 percent; I have bad days." So he fails. The clever liar, however, gives them what they want to hear and gets the job.

BELL: The tests aren't infallible. But Psytest includes certain questions, such as, "I have never told a lie, that tempt liars to answer "true," but which are clearly false. Everyone lies sometime. So the test-taker who answers "true" is assumed to be lying. Psytest sprinkles such questions throughout the test to unmask liars.

Psytest has some good evidence that their tests work. A four-year study of employees in a supermarket chain showed that testing reduced inventory loss along with employee terminations due to theft. We asked Psytest for references of firms that used their system, and everyone was satisfied. As I indicated, we are seeing some results.

QUESTION: You have given us some general results—theft is down 30 percent, etc., but how valid are the tests when applied to individuals?

BELL: The Psytest test has 100 questions. Each applicant scores a particular number. If Joe scores 60, this means 60 percent of the other applicants gave answers that were less honest. Marvex itself then sets the score below which we will not consider the applicant.

QUESTION: How accurate is the score, the 60 assigned to Joe?

BELL: Psytest tells us its test is 85 percent reliable. It is 85 percent sure Joe gave answers that were more honest than 60 percent of all applicants.

QUESTION: Many tests have been found to discriminate. How about integrity tests?

BELL: Psytest assures us their test is corrected for bias by assigning different weights to questions, depending on whether the test is given to blacks, whites or Hispanics. To make sure they are being fair, Psytest also scores test-takers against others in their own group in order to balance out differences in schooling, lifestyle, and family background. For the most part, the questions are readily understandable to a person with a sixth-grade level of reading comprehension. So we don't think the tests discriminate.

QUESTION: There are lots of studies that indicate employees today want to be trusted; they want autonomy, respect, responsibility, etc. And some research shows people produce better if they are trusted. But Marvex starts out by not trusting its applicants. Isn't this counterproductive?

BELL: We do want employees we can trust, but an applicant is not an employee. We believe integrity tests give us a higher percentage of employees we can trust than if we didn't use the tests. In business we have to keep our eye on the bottom line, and we think the bottom line looks better when we use these tests.

QUESTION: Mary, I know you came into Marvex as a vice president last year. Tell me, were you required to take an integrity test?

BELL: Well, the program is only two years old, and so far we have exempted top-manager applicants. The subject is still up for discussion. But the consensus at this point is that people at the upper levels are above testing. You look at their record.

QUESTION: Surely the potential harm of top management fraud dwarfs that of the convenience store employee who steals a carton of cigarettes, and fairness would seem to require that everyone take a test that Marvex believes to be effective in detecting theft.

BELL: As I said, the issue is not closed. You do have to realize that the convenience store business is tough. Competition is keen and margins are razor thin. This means that at the lower organizational levels salaries are low, benefits slim or nonexistent, and turnover is high. I wish it were different, yet this is the reality of this type of business, as is the fact that at the lower levels you have a theft problem unless you test. However, we do promote from within, so, over time, many of our top-level people will have been tested.

For Discussion

Does Mary Bell make a good case for Marvex's testing policies? What are the strengths of her position? What are the weaknesses? If you were managing Marvex, what testing practices would you retain? Why? What changes would you make? Why?

Drug Testing at Explo Inc.

Explo Inc. is a leading manufacturer and distributor of blasting powder, blasting caps, nitroglycerine-based explosives, ammonium nitrate, nitric acid, and sulfuric acid. Explo's main plant is located in the southeastern United States and employs approximately 400 nonunion employees, including 40 salaried and 320 hourly workers. In January of 1990 management at Explo decided that the company should investigate the possibility of implementing a drug-testing program for all of its employees. Management's decision was prompted by two noteworthy events. First, in November of 1989 an explosion occurred at a plant owned by one of Explo's main competitors, Acme Powder Company. The accident at Acme killed three employees and destroyed approximately one-third of Acme's manufacturing capacity. The cause of the accident was determined to be carelessness on the part of one of the Acme employees who was killed in the blast. When this employee's body was examined his pocket was found to contain marijuana, and an autopsy indicated that the employee was high on the drug at the time of his death.

Second, approximately two weeks after the Acme disaster, one of the foremen at Explo was arrested by local authorities for selling drugs from his home. This event convinced Explo's management that Explo employees were not immune to drug use, and that the company should take steps to protect its personnel and property from the sort of calamity that occurred at Acme. Having made this decision, management ordered Explo's director of human resources, Mr. T. T. Barnum, to investigate the feasibility of implementing a drug-testing program at Explo.

Barnum knew very little about drug-testing procedures or the legal problems that sometimes arise when companies institute employee drug-screening programs. However, Explo routinely bought raw materials from a local company, Chemico Chemicals, and Barnum knew that Chemico had established a drug-testing program for its employees two or three years earlier. Also, Chemico recently had appointed Ayn Oakley as its new director of personnel, and Barnum was well acquainted with Oakley. Barnum respected Oakley's abilities, and he resolved to call her and seek the benefit of her experience at Chemico before recommending anything to the management at Explo.

When Barnum contacted Oakley she told him that she had inherited Chemico's drug-testing program from her predecessor, and that it had been the source of nothing but problems since its inception. Because of these problems, she had suspended all drug testing at Chemico and was reviewing and re-evaluating every aspect of the program. When pressed by Barnum for details, Oakley described Chemico's testing program and enumerated the various problems spawned by the program's implementation.

According to Oakley, safety considerations prompted Chemico to establish its drug-testing program late in 1987. Development, implementation, and oversight of the program was the responsibility of Oakley's predecessor, Clive Beatty. Beatty anticipated few legal problems when he instituted the program at Chemico, for Chemico was a private employer acting on its own initiative, and Beatty knew that, in general, the constitutionality of drug testing was an issue only when the government served as employer, or testing in the private sector was mandated by the government. In addition, Beatty felt that labor relations issues would be of minor importance, for although substance testing of workers was a mandatory subject of bargaining for unions, Chemico, like Explo, was a nonunion employer.

After considering various alternative drug-testing programs, Beatty convinced Chemico's management that drug testing should be required as a condition of employment, and that testing should be conducted under the following circumstances:

1. All new job applicants would be tested as part of their pre-employment physical examination.
2. An employee would be tested whenever there was a sudden, unexplained and sustained decline in the job performance of that employee.
3. An employee would be tested whenever that employee was involved in an accident, violated a publicized safety precaution, or was reported by a supervisor to have acted in a careless and dangerous manner.
4. Random, company-wide testing would be conducted upon all employees. Names would be randomly selected by computer, and testing would take place during periodic, company-sponsored physical examinations.

During the initial job interview, all applicants for employment at Chemico were informed verbally that they would have to complete a pre-employment physical that included a drug screen. In addition, written notice of the drug test requirement was included on the company's job application form, and prospective employees were required to sign the form so as to indicate that they had been informed of the screening mandate.

Employees of Chemico were informed of the drug-testing requirement three months before implementation of the program. Fliers providing a detailed description of the screening program were included in the pay envelopes of all workers, and employees were required to sign a statement indicating that they had received a description of the testing program. Signed statements from all employees were returned to Chemico's personnel office.

Job applicants who tested positive for drugs during the pre-employment process were rejected from consideration for employment. Employees who tested positive were placed on a six-week leave of absence. At the end of this six-week period the employee would be retested. If the employee's test results were negative, he/she would return to work and be randomly retested over the next twelve months. Any employee who tested positive on more than one occasion would be discharged.

The mechanics of drug testing at Chemico were complex. Immediately prior to taking a test, subjects signed a drug-test consent form. At the same time, each test subject also provided a list of all prescription and nonprescription drugs which he or she had taken in the preceding month. To guard against employees tampering with their urine samples, the company physician witnessed the sample collection procedure for male workers, while the company nurse witnessed for female employees. After a sample had been obtained, the employee would initial the sample container and watch the container as it was labelled with his/her name. Next, the sample would be sealed in a tamper-proof pouch which the employee also initialed. A courier delivered all samples to a local laboratory. If any pouch showed signs of tampering when it was given to the lab technician, the sample in that pouch would not be tested, and a new sample would be secured.

Urine samples were tested by the Enzyme Immunoassay (EIA) process. This process screens for the presence of amphetamines, barbiturates, benzodiazepines, marijuana, cocaine, methadone, methaqualone, opiates, PCP, and propoxphene. Whenever a sample tested positive, that sample would be retested so as to ensure that the first test was free from error. If the second sample tested negative, the test results would be considered void, and a new sample would be secured from the employee for retest.

When Chemico instituted its drug-screening program, Beatty expected few difficulties. However, just the opposite was true; indeed, testing of new job applicants was about the only aspect of the program that did not cause problems. Random testing produced the greatest controversy. No sooner had the program been announced than workers began to express feelings of oppression, anxiety, and insecurity concerning the testing procedure. Many questioned the accuracy of the EIA process, and others insisted that the program's purpose was not to ensure safety, but rather to rid the corporation of workers whom management felt were malcontents. Over time, those who opposed random testing coalesced to form an organized group of resistance, and members of this group were now at the forefront of a movement to unionize workers at Chemico. Oakley told Barnum that she was convinced that the movement for unionization would never have gotten off the ground if Chemico had not implemented its drug-screening program.

In addition to the movement toward unionization, employee opposition to drug testing produced other problems for Chemico. For one thing, Chemico's drug-testing program gave rise to a plethora of lawsuits, most of which were still before the court. Not long after random testing was established, one female employee challenged the procedure by filing a common-law invasion-of-privacy tort. Company lawyers told Oakley that if this employee succeeded in showing that random testing intruded upon her privacy in such a manner that it would be considered "highly offensive" to a "reasonable person," then it was possible that she could be awarded a large sum as recompense for a wrongful intrusion upon her seclusion. The crux of the woman's argument was that drug testing at Chemico was "highly offensive" because, in the absence of any reasonable suspicion that she was a drug user, the procedure forced her to allow the company nurse to witness the collection of her urine sample. The issue was still before the court and Chemico's lawyers were not optimistic about the outcome. They noted that employees of other companies had successfully challenged random testing by bringing invasion-of-privacy torts, and that one such employee had been awarded $485,000 in damages. Further, they stated that whether or not a particular activity counts as a "highly offensive" intrusion upon seclusion is something to be decided by a jury, and that most jury members are employees rather than employers. Thus, juries are more likely to sympathize with plaintiffs than with defendants in invasion-of-privacy torts.

In addition to the female employee's invasion-of-privacy challenge to random testing, two male employees brought similar suits challenging other aspects of Chemico's drug-screening program. The first of these employees (E1) had been tested immediately after he was involved in a minor accident at the plant's loading dock. Chemico argued that involvement in an accident creates a reasonable assumption of drug use on the part of the worker(s) involved in the accident because approximately 50 percent of all industrial accidents are drug or alcohol related. In response, E1 argued that it was patently obvious that carelessness could not have been a contributing cause of the particular accident in which he was involved, and that forcing him to have a drug test in the absence of reasonable suspicion of individual impairment was a highly offensive intrusion upon his seclusion because it caused fellow workers and members of the community to suspect that he was a drug user. The second employee (E2) made a similar claim. E2 was tested after his job performance declined noticeably and his absenteeism rate increased. E2 claimed that his performance on the job had suffered because he was having problems with his teenage son who was addicted to cocaine and alcohol. Further, E2 argued that testing him for drugs in these circumstances was a highly offensive intrusion upon his privacy because it held him up to ridicule in the eyes of his son, and thus destroyed any ability he had to influence his son's actions.

Common-law invasion-of-privacy torts were not the only court cases spawned by Chemico's drug-screening activities. A class action suit had been brought by a number of minority status employees charging that Chemico was using its drug-testing program to harass minority workers. In addition, another employee (E3) claimed that drug testing in his particular case violated state common law because the testing was motivated by malevolent, non-job-related reasons. E3 had been tested for drugs when his supervisor (S) reported that he had repeatedly violated company safety precautions. E3 claimed that he had violated no safety precautions, and argued that S concocted the false report to punish him when he discovered that E3 was dating his estranged wife.

In addition to the court cases suing Chemico for damages under state common law, a number of employees who had been discharged because they tested positive for drug use sought reinstatement in their jobs. At least three employees went to court seeking such reinstatement. Two claimed that they should be rehired because the test results indicating that they were drug users were inaccurate. Basically, these employees argued that when their urine samples were tested by the EIA procedure, the method produced a false positive result which was replicated when the test was repeated. The employees noted that in addition to the EIA procedure for drug screening there are at least two other methods that can be used to test for drug use, namely, the thin layer chromatography (TLC) procedure, and the gas chromatography/mass spectrometry (GC/MS) test. The employees argued that Chemico should use all three procedures in its drug screening program, and only discharge employees when they test positive on all three tests.

The third employee who sought reinstatement after being dismissed for positive EIA test results openly admitted to drug use. However, this employee claimed that under state law, dependency on drugs was to be considered a handicap, and that as a result, Chemico had an affirmative duty to make reasonable accommodations on his behalf. Rather than being terminated, this employee argued that he should be allowed to enter a drug rehabilitation center, and then be permitted to return to work once he had completed the program of study at that center.

Finally, Oakley told Barnum that Chemico's drug-screening program had given rise to two disputes concerning eligibility for unemployment benefits. The first case involved a relatively new employee who was discharged when he tested positive on a random drug screen. Rather than seeking reinstatement, this individual filed for unemployment compensation. Chemico protested; however, the state division of employment security refused to disqualify the former employee for receipt of benefits. The division ruled that Chemico had not shown that the employee's discharge was for misconduct, because the company had failed to demonstrate either that the employee had used drugs in the workplace, or that the employee's work performance was below par. Chemico appealed this ruling, and the appeals referee's decision was pending.

Chemico's second case involving unemployment compensation was quite unlike its first. In this instance Chemico opposed the claim of a worker who sought unemployment compensation during the unpaid, six-week leave of absence that he was forced to take after he first tested positive on his drug test. This case had not yet been decided by the state division of employment security.

Oakley told Barnum that her decision to reevaluate the drug-screening program at Chemico was prompted by the many problems engendered by that program. She also said that she had come to the conclusion that the entire program needed to be reworked. Her present thinking on the subject was that the right course of action was to continue testing new job applicants, but to drop the testing of employees, and instead require that these individuals attend a series of drug education seminars. The seminars would be offered on company time and repeated annually. Oakley did not think that the drug education classes would be anywhere near as effective as drug testing in reducing drug use among company personnel. Still, substituting drug education for drug screening would go a long way toward mollifying employee discontent, and at the same time save the corporation a great deal of money.

After listening to Oakley, Barnum felt confused. He knew that at companies where drug testing had been implemented, 8 to 12 percent of the work force was found to have been using illegal drugs. If these figures applied to Explo's employees, Barnum felt that it was only a matter of time until Explo experienced a significant drug-related accident. Given the highly dangerous character of Explo's business, this was something that it was in *everyone's* interest—employer and employees alike—to avoid. On the other hand, Chemico's experience showed that implementing a drug-testing program at Explo could have quite deleterious consequences for the corporation. Further, Barnum was not sure whether he liked Oakley's solution to the problems faced by Chemico. By opting to drop all employee testing she was minimizing present costs for her corporation, for she was avoiding lawsuits, placating disgruntled employees, and reducing the cost of testing (testing cost Chemico $50.00 per employee). However, Oakley acknowledged that testing job applicants and instituting a drug education program would not be as effective as screening employees in reducing the possibility of a drug-related accident at Chemico. In essence, then, Oakley was taking a chance; for if a serious accident did occur at Chemico, losses in terms of lives and property easily could outweigh the benefits derived from the decision not to test employees for drug use.

It did not take Barnum long to see that his options were not limited simply to those of accepting or rejecting the course of action which Oakley had adopted. For one thing, Barnum noted that the drug-testing program established at Chemico lacked any mechanism for rehabilitating workers who were found to have a drug dependency. If Explo implemented a screening program, it could introduce such a mechanism. That is to say, rather than firing workers who were found to be using drugs, Explo could see that these workers were given counseling and medical help for their problems. Such action would benefit Explo's workers, contribute to the social good, and no doubt help to forestall employee discontent with any drug-testing program which Explo implemented. Still, if 10 percent of Explo's employees were to enter drug rehabilitation programs, health insurance costs at Explo could become prohibitively burdensome. Furthermore, Barnum was not sure that Explo had any duty to benefit society as a whole, or to cure its workers of drug abuse. Also, Barnum suspected that there might be less expensive ways to placate workers and undermine employee opposition to drug testing. In the end, then, Barnum was left uncertain as to what sort of report he should make to management concerning the feasibility of establishing a drug-testing program at Explo.

For Discussion

If you were T. T. Barnum, would you recommend that a drug-testing program be implemented at Explo Inc.? If not, why not? If so, what sort of program would you recommend be instituted, and why?

James M. Humber

Privacy in the Corporation

In our society we speak very loosely of "rights." Much of the discussion of the right to privacy in the literature reflects this looseness. Few commentaries on the right to privacy in corporations clearly distinguish between legal and moral rights, or attempt to explore the complex relationships between these different rights. Indeed, more often than not the two kinds of rights are confused.[1] Furthermore, the concept of a "moral right" is problematic. Are humans "endowed" with "inalienable" moral rights, or are moral rights ascribed to us by society? Philosophers have argued this issue for years; but those who discuss the right to privacy avoid the fray and rarely, if ever, tell us which theory of rights they accept.

In an essay of this length I cannot begin to resolve, or even take note of, all the problems involved in discussions of moral and legal rights. However, what I can and will attempt to do is the following: First, I will distinguish between moral and legal rights in general, and, in particular, the moral and legal right to privacy. Next, I will narrow my discussion to the *moral* right to privacy, and consider some of the problems involved in understanding and implementing such a right within the corporate structure. Finally, I will recommend a course of action aimed at resolving the more important problems corporations must face as they attempt to balance the moral right to privacy against opposing corporate interests.

I. RIGHTS: MORAL AND LEGAL

Ordinarily, statements about rights and statements about duties are taken to be reciprocal. For example, if I have a legal right to vote, one might say that society has a legal duty not to interfere with my voting. Similarly, if I have a moral right not to be killed, then it could be claimed that other persons have a moral duty not to kill me. In addition, rights and duties can be viewed as absolute or as *prima facie*. If my right not to be killed is absolute, then there are absolutely no circumstances under which one's duty not to kill me would not hold. (In essence, to kill me *must* be to do something wrong.) On the other hand, if my right not to be killed is merely *prima facie*, then if I am killed by another, there is nothing more than a presumption that my killer has done something wrong. That is to say, it is understood that there may be circumstances under which a person's duty not to kill me could be "overridden" or "negated," so that he or she could kill me and do nothing wrong (e.g., my killer might have to kill me in order to avoid his or her own death).

In our society few rights (legal or moral) are granted absolute status. However, a *prima facie* right is a right nonetheless. On the other hand, there are cases where we possess moral rights without corresponding legal rights, and *vice versa*. It is in these cases that the distinction between moral and legal rights is most clearly evidenced. For example, most people would agree that we have a moral duty to tell the truth, and that we have a (moral) right not to be lied to. However, we have no general legal obligation to tell the truth. For example, assume that you must catch a train in order to be present for a job interview, and that you ask me what time the train leaves. I dislike you and straightforwardly lie about the train schedule. Because of my lie you miss the train and do not make your interview. In this case you cannot take me to court and claim that I have violated one of your legal rights. Still and all, I have done something morally wrong; there is no justification for violating my moral duty to tell you the truth. Or to put it another way, you have a moral right to be told the truth (even though you have no legal right), and in the case at hand the circumstances are not such that I can morally justify violating that right.

If there are cases where we possess moral rights without corresponding legal rights, there also are cases where we have legal rights and no corresponding moral rights. Let us say, for instance, that I buy a used car only after the salesman gives me his "personal assurance" that he will make all necessary repairs within the first six months of my ownership. I secure a loan from the car dealership, and, after paying $500 down and making three monthly payments, my car's transmission falls out. When I return the car to the salesman and demand that he fix the transmission, he refuses. I withhold my fourth month's car payment and use that money to repair the car. The salesman responds by repossessing my car. In this case the salesman does not act illegally; indeed, he has a legal right either to be paid or to be given title to my car. From the moral point of view, however his right to repossess my car is questionable, for he has not kept his promise to repair my car when necessary.

II. PRIVACY RIGHTS: LEGAL AND MORAL

Companies doing business in the United States have no choice but to recognize a legal right to privacy, for that right has been held to be constitutionally guaranteed.[2] In addition, some states have passed legislation attempting to protect the employee's right to privacy.[3] Thus, unless a corporation is willing to break the law, it must do its utmost to ensure that its policies and practices accord with requirements set by law. Of course, this is not a simple procedure; there are times when the best lawyer can do no more than make an educated guess as to what is and is not required or prohibited by law. For example, a California law gives employees the right to inspect personnel files that are "used or have been used to determine that employee's qualifications for employment, promotion, and additional compensation, or termination. . . ."[4] Does this mean that *no* information in an employee's file can be kept "company confidential"? Or does it mean that no personal information can be kept from an employee? If the latter, what is meant by "personal information"? Are a company's salary forecasts for an employee personal information (after all, they may be used to determine the employee's additional compensation), or are they rather business planning information? Until the matter is tested in court, no one can be absolutely sure whether such forecasts are legally classifiable as personal information, or as business planning information. Furthermore, no lawyer can be expected to anticipate all the new directions the law will take. For instance, some legal scholars were quite surprised to discover that the right to privacy was used as a justification for allowing women the right to abort in the first and second trimesters of pregnancy.[5] Thus, a corporate law firm may have very good reasons to believe that certain corporate practices do not violate the legal right to privacy, and yet discover (to its dismay) that the court does not share its opinion.[6]

A corporation must grapple with difficult problems as it attempts to set its policies and practices foursquare with the law. As difficult as these problems are, however, they pale in comparison to the problems that arise once a corporation evidences a concern for the moral right to privacy; in many ways legal rights are less problematic than moral rights. The former are determined by statute and by case law; as such, they are fairly determinate, easily accessible, and uniformly applicable. In addition, they are subject to final arbitration; ultimately, the law is what the court says it is. Moral rights enjoy none of these advantages: moral views differ; the "moral law" is informal and indeterminate; and most troublesome of all, there is no group of moral "experts" empowered to serve as an ultimate court of appeal in resolving moral disputes. Because all moral rights share these characteristics, corporate attempts to formally recognize a moral right to privacy face numerous problems. It is to the most important of these problems that we must now direct our attention.

III. PROBLEMS INVOLVED IN UNDERSTANDING AND IMPLEMENTING THE MORAL RIGHT TO PRIVACY IN THE CORPORATION

Although any attempt to recognize a moral right to privacy within the corporate setting will generate problems, there seems to be a general feeling among corporate executives that such action is advisable. There are at least three reasons for this. First, as many managers realize, failure to acknowledge a moral right to privacy may well foster employee discontent.[7] Second, those companies exhibiting little or no concern for employee privacy beyond what is mandated by law risk projecting a bad public image. Finally, and most importantly, privacy concerns have prompted, and will continue to prompt, a swirl of legislative activities;[8] thus, if corporations do not act to provide some corporate mechanisms for avoiding and resolving privacy disputes, they may well find themselves hamstrung by severely restrictive privacy legislation.[9]

Once a company acknowledges that its own interests are served by concerning itself with the moral right to privacy, a host of problems must still be faced. Virtually all of these problems arise because, as we have seen, moral rights are quite different from legal rights. Moral rights are informal and indeterminate. They cannot be found "written down" in a moral constitution somewhere; and as a consequence, each corporation is left to its own devices as it attempts to understand the moral right to privacy. What exactly is that right, and how far does it extend? There appears to be general agreement that the right refers to the control an individual has over personal information; but once one proceeds beyond this point agreement breaks down. The major reason for disagreement is that different people accept different moral theories, and moral commitments affect one's views concerning moral rights. To illustrate this point, let us consider the importance that the right to privacy would have for advocates of two very different moral theories.[10]

Many persons argue for a moral right to privacy by appealing to consequences. According to Stanley I. Benn:

> The usual arguments against wiretapping, bugging, a National Data Center, and private investigators rest heavily on the contingent possibility that a tyrannical government or unscrupulous individuals might misuse them for blackmail or victimization. The more one knows about a person, the greater one's power to damage him.[11]

The argument here is that failure to recognize a right to privacy will, in all likelihood, produce more harm than good, and that as a consequence we ought to recognize such a right. As Benn realizes, however, this argument rests upon the "contingent possibility" that someone might misuse information secretly obtained. As such, we can imagine circumstances in which the argument would have little or no force. For example, let us say that I own a small business, that I interview all candidates for jobs in my company, and that only I have access to personnel files. I know that I would never misuse the employee information I have accumulated, and that the possibility of this information being misused by anyone else is virtually *nil*. Furthermore, my past experience has been that secretly obtaining personal information regarding sexual preferences, drinking habits, religious affiliations, etc., has been extremely helpful to me in hiring trustworthy employees. In these circumstances, I might well conclude that recognition of a right to privacy would do more harm than good, and so hold that there is no such right to be accorded those who seek employment in my business.

If we attempt to ground the moral right to privacy on considerations of consequences, there may be circumstances in which we would not want to recognize that right. But we are not forced to appeal to consequences in order to justify recognition of a moral right to privacy. For example, Benn argues that the moral right to privacy is founded on the principle of respect for persons. On this view:

> It is not just a matter of a fear to be allayed by reassurances (concerning the possible misuse of secretly obtained information), but a resentment that anyone—even a thoroughly trustworthy official—should be able to satisfy any curiosity, without the knowledge let alone the consent of the subject. For since what others know about him can radically affect a man's view of himself, to treat the collation of personal information about him as if it raised purely technical problems of safeguards against abuse is to disregard his claim to consideration and respect as a person.[12]

To ground the right to privacy on the principle of respect for persons is not to found that right on "contingent possibilities." Thus, if one accepts such an interpretation he or she must acknowledge that at least a *prima facie* right to privacy is *always* possessed by *all* persons. And even if one is convinced (as was the owner of the small business in our earlier example) that no harmful consequences would flow from secretly collecting information about another person's sex life or religious preferences, he or she must allow that action of this sort is morally questionable because it violates the right to privacy that all persons possess.[13]

Because the moral right to privacy is subject to various interpretations, any corporation wanting to recognize such a right must first decide how it wants, generally, to understand that right. That is to say, the corporation must determine whether it considers the right to privacy to be grounded on considerations of consequences, respect for persons, or some other foundation. Once a corporation has cleared this hurdle, however, it faces further difficulties. These problems arise because the moral right to privacy is commonly understood to be *prima facie* and not absolute. To say that privacy is a *prima facie* right is to acknowledge that there are circumstances in which it may be "overridden." Or to put it another way, it is to admit that there may be cases where it would be morally permissible to invade someone's privacy. The difficulty with all this, however, is that two or more people can: a) agree in their general understanding of the moral right to privacy, b) agree that the right is *prima facie*, and yet c) disagree completely as to what sorts of conditions justify overriding that right. To see how this can happen, it may be useful to examine an actual set of corporate privacy guidelines.

Probably no corporation has spent more time, money, and effort developing corporate guidelines regarding privacy than International Business Machines. IBM hired a consultant, Professor Paul Westin of Columbia University, an acknowledged expert on privacy, and did all that it could to achieve a comprehensive understanding of the moral right to privacy.[14] The end product of IBM's study—the corporation's guidelines to privacy—may well serve as a model for other businesses and industries. The following summarizes, in a very rough fashion, a number of IBM's most important views on employee privacy.

A. Only job-related facts about employees may be collected and kept in personnel files.

B. Employees have a right to see most of the information in their personnel files, and they are entitled to know how that information is being used.

C. Information over three years old is purged from personnel files.

D. No employee's conversation may be recorded or monitored without that employee's consent and knowledge.

E. Employers are restricted in the means they can use to "check up" on employees, e.g., they cannot hire an investigator to follow an employee on a trip

F. Personality and general intelligence tests may not be used by the personnel department.

G. Lie detectors can only be used if an employee gives his/her permission for their use. If the employee does not give his/her permission, this decision cannot be used against the employee.

H. Use of personal files within the corporation must be classified.

I. No information on an employee is given to an outsider unless the employee consents, or the requestor can furnish proper identification, prove his or her legal authority, and demonstrate that they need the information sought.

J. Information that is less than three years old and included in an employee's personnel file cannot be destroyed without the employee's consent.

IBM's attempt to formulate a comprehensive set of guidelines to privacy is laudable. Nevertheless, it is clear that different people can accept these guidelines and disagree as to what sorts of investigations they permit. For example, consider a problem that could arise under guideline A. The problem is one noted by Frank Cary, chairman and chief executive officer of IBM.

> Suppose one of our managers got an anonymous letter giving strong indica-
> tion that an employee was a child beater. The manager might judge this to
> be a private matter and not investigate. Of course he would be wrong.
> Humanitarian considerations aside, an accusation such as this, if true, might
> affect both the employee's performance and—if there were contact with
> customers—ability to represent IBM.[15]

For Cary it is clear that an anonymous charge of child beating warrants in-vestigation, because if the charge were true it could affect the employee's job performance. However, for a number of reasons one might want to disagree with Cary's judgment. First, the charge is anonymous; one could argue that charges from anonymous parties do not justify intrusions into areas of one's life that do not obviously and directly relate to one's job description. Second, one could claim that IBM's only interest is in its employees' *job perform-ances,* not in the *causes* for its employees' successes and failures. Or to put it another way, investigation into the child-beating charge is not called for, because means are readily available to determine whether or not the employee is accomplishing the tasks he or she has been assigned. Indeed, if Cary feels that he has a right to investigate anything that *might* affect job performance, this gives him license to intrude into virtually any area of his employees' lives. After all, if an employee is upset about his daughter being unwed and pregnant, or his wife overcharging a credit account, he might well perform poorly on the job. Should Cary be permitted to investigate these areas of his employees' lives too?

The point is not that Cary is wrong in judging that an anonymous child beating charge justifies collecting information about otherwise private areas of his employees' lives. The point is that it is a personal judgment whether such a charge justifies "overriding" an employee's right to privacy, and that as a consequence those empowered to apply IBM's guidelines may evidence hon-est and deepseated disagreement as to how this ought to be done. But if this is so, those corporations which formulate and employ a formal set of corporate privacy guidelines also must set some general policy for the application of those guidelines. Otherwise the corporation will not have one set of guidelines, but as many sets as there are people interpreting and applying them.

Finally, once a corporation has formulated its corporation privacy guide-lines and has set some policy for applying these standards, there is a third set of problems it must face. These problems arise because the moral right to privacy is affected by contingencies of time, place, and culture. One hundred years ago we did not worry about computers, tape recordings, and lie de-tectors, for these machines did not exist. In addition, we did not have the attitude (which seems to be evolving today), that elected officials' tax records are public property. In short, societal attitudes and circumstances change; what is not considered a violation of one's moral right to privacy at one time and place may be so considered in another, and *vice versa.* As a result, corporations must develop a procedure for modifying or extending their guidelines so as to cover new cases that arise because of changing circumstances and attitudes. Without such a procedure, the net effect would be that new cases would be decided in a totally *ad hoc* manner, without reference to any guidelines at all. And it is precisely this condition that a corporation seeks to avoid when it develops a formal set of guidelines reflecting the organization's understanding of the moral right to privacy.

IV. RECOMMENDATION FOR UNDERSTANDING AND IMPLEMENTING THE MORAL RIGHT TO PRIVACY IN THE CORPORATION

We have seen that there are at least three reasons motivating a corporation to go beyond what is required by law and to recognize that its employees have a moral right to privacy: (1) such action creates a good public image; (2) it significantly reduces the possibility of disputes with employees over privacy related issues; and (3) it provides a means for resolving privacy disputes within the corporation, thus obviating the need for restrictive privacy legislation. In addition, we have seen the problems that recognition of a moral right to privacy raises for a corporation: (a) the organization must develop a general understanding of the moral right to privacy; (b) it must develop a general policy for the application of its guidelines; and (c) it must formulate procedures for extending its guidelines to new cases. A truly successful program for recognizing the moral right to privacy within the corporation will accomplish goals (1) through (3) while at the same time resolving problems (a) through (c). It may be that no program can totally realize all of these ends.[16] I believe, however, that the following program holds out some hope of success.

First, I recommend that each organization look upon itself as a microsociety existing within, and at the pleasure of, the macro-society. Realization of this fact makes it clear that businesses and industries must obey existing statutory law. Thus, the first step any corporation must take is to get clear as to current privacy legislation, and do its utmost to ensure that its procedures concerning privacy are in accord with all legal requirements.

Second, corporations need to arrive at some general understanding of what they take the moral right to privacy to be. Because moral rights are informal and indeterminate, each corporation can—indeed must—determine this on its own. There is no indisputably "correct" interpretation of the moral right to privacy; corporations may adopt their own methods for arriving at their various interpretations of the privacy right. In the end, however, it is absolutely essential that a formal set of privacy guidelines be written, and that this be distributed to all employees and made available to all job applicants. Further-more, it should be clearly stated that the corporation's guidelines apply equally to *all* persons on the company payroll. For example, if the guidelines state that union workers who call in sick may be called at home or "checked up on" in other ways, such actions would also be permitted when the company president failed to show up for work.

A number of advantages would be secured if corporations were to proceed along the lines just noted. First, the requirement that the corporate guide-lines be distributed to all employees and be made available to all job appli-cants helps ensure employee consent for these guidelines. It is generally rec-ognized that there is no invasion of a person's privacy if that person freely consents to share information about himself. If we look upon a corporation as a micro-society, we can say that employees who are aware of their cor-poration's privacy guidelines and do not resign tacitly agree to accept them (much like the citizens of a state tacitly "sign" the social contract). Thus, if the guidelines were strictly adhered to, no employee could complain that his/her privacy was being invaded. After all, he/she has tacitly agreed that the corporation's guidelines determine his/her right to privacy in the corporation; and if those guidelines are not violated, his/her privacy has been respected.

Second, it seems clear that within any corporation, privacy guidelines would have to be approved and set in place by top-level management. Making the guidelines applicable to these managers assures that they will be honest and truthful in their understanding of the moral right to privacy. That is to say, it forestalls the possibility that top-level management will interpret the moral right to privacy in a very weak fashion for middle-level management and be-low, and then interpret that right in a much more strict fashion when they apply it to themselves.

Finally, if a corporation's privacy guidelines applied equally to everyone in the corporation, employees would not feel that they were being treated un-fairly or that there were two rights to privacy: one for themselves and one for top-level management. This would do much to avoid employee discontent.

Obviously, if a corporation's privacy guidelines are to apply equally to all employees, there must be some mechanism within the corporation to as-sure such equality of application. What seems to be called for is a privacy court, similar to the macro-society's judicial system. This court would have at least one representative from all major groups within the organization, e.g., union workers, management, research and development. In addition to ensur-ing that the guidelines are applied to everyone in the corporation, this court also would be responsible for interpreting and applying the corporation's guidelines, and extending them to new cases. As decisions of these sorts are made, they could be kept on file and used as precedents for later decisions.[17] This would solve the problems of developing a general policy for applying the guidelines, and formulating procedures for extending these guidelines to new cases (b and c).

Development of a privacy court within a corporation would not be an easy matter; there is no obviously "correct" method of operation for such a court. That is to say, one corporation might want all court decisions to be made in accordance with a majority rule doctrine, while another company might insist that a representative of top management serve as judge and final decision maker, with all other court members merely offering opinions and advice. Each corporation would have to work out its own method of operation. Even granting this, however, there do not seem to be any insuperable problems involved in setting up privacy courts within business organizations. Furthermore, if a privacy court were made operational in a corporation, and if knowledge of the judicial procedure for the application and extension of the guidelines were made available to all employees and job applicants, along with copies of the corporate privacy guidelines, employees who did not resign could be said to have tacitly consented to the corporation's judicial procedure as well as to its guidelines. In short, all problems involved in understanding and implementing the moral right to privacy in the corporation would be solved. And as these problems are solved, the goals the corporation had in mind when it decided to recognize the moral right to privacy would also be realized. Specifically: (1) the corporation would acquire a good public image; (2) it would minimize disputes over privacy concerns; and (3) it would provide a mechanism within the corporation for resolving disputes that do arise, thus making it less likely that society would pass laws imposing its views of privacy upon the corporation.

NOTES

1. To take just one example, International Business Machines has guidelines to employee privacy which clearly are intended to go beyond the law and specify moral standards for corporate behavior (see "IBM's Guidelines to Employee Privacy," *Harvard Business Review* 54, no. 5 [1976]: 82–90). When David Ewing discusses these guidelines, however, he contends their acceptance would not "hobble management in its security efforts" because (among other things) "where the checking of purses, briefcases, and bundles is legal today, it would still be legal" (David Ewing, *Freedom Inside the Organization* (E. P. Dutton, 1977), p. 137). But IBM is not making law when it formulates corporate guidelines to privacy; it is merely setting internal corporate policy relevant to its employees' *moral* right to privacy. Thus the question Ewing should ask is: "Do IBM's guidelines reflect what is morally right (so that security is morally justified in inspecting bundles, etc.), or does the moral right to privacy, when properly interpreted, prohibit such searches (in which case IBM's guidelines ought to proscribe such inspections)?"

2. *Griswold* v. *State of Connecticut* 381 U.S. 479, 85 S. Ct. 1678 (1965).

3. For example, seven states have laws giving private employees the right to see their personnel files. "Privacy at Work," *Wall Street Journal,* May 12, 1980, p. 26.

4. Virginia Schein, "Privacy and Personnel: A Time for Action," *Personnel Journal* 55, no. 12 (1976), p. 606.

5. John Ely, "The Wages of Crying Wolf" *The Yale Law Journal* 82 (1973): 923–37.

6. For further problems encountered by businesses and industries as they attempt to implement the legal right to privacy see Schein, *op. cit.*

7. For an example of such discontent see Vincent Barry's account of the strike at Adolph Coors brewery in 1977. V. Barry, *Moral Issues in Business* (Wadsworth, 1979), p. 149.

8. See Schein, *op. cit.,* p. 604.

9. This seems to be the principal motivation behind IBM's concern with privacy. In explaining his company's interest in privacy, Frank Cary, chairman and chief executive of IBM, says: "When I became chairman, it seemed to me that this subject (privacy) was going to become an issue for us, as auto safety has become a major issue for Ford and General Motors" ("IBM's Guidelines to Employee Privacy," *op. cit.,* p. 82). The major auto makers did not set strict enough auto safety standards for themselves, and this prompted legislation governing their actions. Apparently, Cary wants to avoid a repeat of this scenario.

10. Our purpose is served by considering only two moral theories. It should be noted, however, that there are numerous moral theories and hence numerous interpretations of the moral right to privacy. For a brief discussion of the right to privacy as it relates to a wide variety of moral theories see Barry, *op. cit.,* pp. 160-63.

11. Stanley I. Benn, "Privacy, Freedom, and Respect for Persons," in R. Wasserstrom, ed., *Today's Moral Problems* (Macmillan, 1975), p. 5.

12. Ibid., p. 9.

13. For a good example of how prior moral commitments can affect one's view of the strength and scope of the moral right to privacy see E. Pattullo, "The Limits of the 'Right' of Privacy," and R. Veatch, "Limits to the Right of Privacy: Reason, Not Rhetoric," *IRB* 4, no. 4 (1982): 3-7.

14. Although the evidence is not conclusive, it appears that IBM has decided that the moral right to privacy is grounded on respect for persons. For example, in discussing his corporation's privacy guidelines, Frank Cary, chairman of IBM, says: "There's absolutely no taping of a person's conversations on the telephone without express permission. . . . I consider this a simple matter of respect for the individual" ("IBM's Guidelines to Employee Privacy," *op. cit.,* p. 89).

15. *Ibid.,* p. 84.

16. IBM probably has devoted more time and energy to privacy related issues than any other corporation; and its program does not achieve all of the goals specified. IBM has resolved problem a; but as far as I can tell it has not solved problems b or c. Because IBM has solved problem a it has accomplished goal 1. However, so long as problems b and c remain unresolved, goals 2 and 3 remain unrealized.

17. For example, in the case cited earlier by Frank Cary, the privacy court would decide whether or not an anonymous charge of child beating would warrant investigation. And its holding in this case would have an influence on a later case in which an employee was charged with, say, wife beating or use of prostitutes.

Corporate Policy Statements

Employee Records. General Motors believes that its employees' private personal activities are not properly the concern of GM so long as they do not adversely affect attendance, job performance, working relationships with fellow employees, or the public image of the corporation.

General Motors does not consider such procedures as polygraph tests proper in the evaluation of job candidates, nor does the corporation include in personnel records non-business-related information, unless submitted or authorized in writing by the employee. Nonetheless, compliance with government regulations and administration of labor agreements and employee-benefit programs have greatly increased the amount of personal data GM is required to record.

GM policy dictates that such records be treated with the same strict confidentiality accorded to all GM's proprietary information. Any employee may examine his or her own personnel record.

Employees are advised, upon inquiry, of the kinds of files and data which the corporation must maintain concerning them. These may contain personally identifiable information only if it is relevant and necessary to the proper administration of the business or to compliance with the law or government regulation.

All written information about employees is to be recorded and maintained accurately, factually, and objectively. Employees have the opportunity to correct or amend any information concerning themselves, to ensure accuracy and fairness. Furthermore, GM personnel whose job responsibilities legitimately permit them access to such information are directed to protect employee records from unauthorized release, transfer, access, or use.

Personally identifiable information must not be disclosed outside the corporation unless the employee consents, with the following exceptions: the *fact* of employment may be verified for employee credit approval; *dates* of employment may be verified for employment reference checks; an employee's elected bargaining representative may be entitled by labor contract to certain information; and a law or a court order may require disclosure of certain information.

General Motors

IBM has four basic practices concerning the use of personal information about employees: To collect, use and retain only personal information that is required for business or legal reasons; To provide employees with a means of ensuring that their personal information in IBM personnel records is correct; To limit the internal availability of personal information about an individual only to those with a clear business need to know; and to release personal information outside IBM only with approval of the employee affected, except to verify employment or to satisfy legitimate investigatory or legal requirements. But even with these practices, not every case can be covered. What constitutes a legitimate business need for a particular piece of information? Should information about an employee ever be released without his or her knowledge, even if it might be to his or her benefit? Ultimately, you must balance the right of the organization to use information for valid business purposes with the individual's right to privacy. Your own conscience and judgment and the advice of your management and of IBM Personnel all should be considered in this delicate area.

IBM

The nature of the services offered by American Express Company necessitates collection and retention of a substantial amount of personal information about the individuals to whom services are provided. We must avoid any unjustifiable intrusion on an individual's right to privacy. We must strive for a reasonable balance between the operational needs of our businesses and the personal needs of individuals. In an effort to attain such balance we will be guided by the following principles with regard to the collection, custody, and distribution of personal information concerning the individuals to whom we provide services. (1) Obtain only that personal information which is necessary and relevant to the conduct of our business; (2) use only lawful means to collect information; obtain it directly from the individual to the extent practicable; and make reasonable efforts to assure the reliability of information acquired from others; (3) explain the general uses of personal information to all individuals who question the reasons that they provide such information, and refrain from using the information for other purposes without informing the individual; (4) establish appropriate administrative, technical, and physical safeguards to assure that access to records is limited to those who are authorized and that information is disseminated only by and to those with a legitimate business purpose or regulatory function, or where disclosure is required by subpoena or other legal process; (5) provide personal data records with secure storage and ensure that personnel who are involved with custody or maintenance of such records are aware of their responsibility to preserve their confidentiality; (6) promptly notify the individual in the case where records are subpoenaed, unless specifically prohibited from doing so by court order. Respond according to the law, but wait the full length of time allowed by the subpoena before providing the information in order to allow the individual the opportunity to exercise his or her rights; (7) advise the individual of the Company's policy with respect to mailing lists and provide the individual with the opportunity to have his or her name removed from such lists; (8) respond to all individuals who question the reasons that adverse determinations have been made about them, and advise them of the nature of information acted upon, except for information which relates to the investigation of an insurance claim or of a possible criminal offense. This will, of course, be subject to ethical considerations and applicable laws; (9) upon request, except with regard to insurance claims investigations, and within a reasonable period of time, advise an individual of factual data (maintained about that person) such as residence, address, place of employment, etc., and give the individual the opportunity to verify this factual data and to provide corrected or amended information where appropriate; (10) review periodically corporate policy regarding the collection, retention, use, and protection of individually identifiable data to ensure that this policy is in keeping with the shifting needs of both the business and the individual.

American Express Co.

WORKER SAFETY

AIDS on the General Motors Assembly Line

Bill Snelling is a twenty-eight-year-old married father of three who was rendered HIV positive from a blood transfusion two years ago when undergoing
surgery in the Glenview General Hospital for a ruptured appendix. For various reasons, Snelling suspected that the blood supply he had used might be
contaminated, and had himself tested at the HMO contracted under his health
plan with his employer, the General Motors Assembly Plant in Glenview. When
he was given the news, the HMO promised complete confidentiality.

Snelling, a robust athletic type who jogs and bikes every day after work
and does not drink or smoke, decided to continue working on the assembly
line at GM because, as he explained to his wife, "I still need to feed a family,
and I feel quite healthy." He promised his wife that if he ever got the disease,
he would quit when he felt too weak to do the job well. Snelling, incidentally,
is one of eight people who are testing HIV positive on the GM assembly line
according to the confidential records of the HMO. The director of the HMO
promised all of them strict confidentiality but has also recommended informally that they try to seek employment that would not expose them to any
risk of cutting themselves in the workplace. One of the problems with working
on the assembly line, they were each told, is that there is some minimal risk
that workers who become careless will cut themselves occasionally, even when
using gloves, while bolting and fitting parts to the chassis. When that occurs
the next person in the assembly line may become exposed to the blood and
become HIV positive. But, they were also told, the probability of contracting
HIV in this manner is extremely low and perhaps even lower than .0003, which
is the probability of contracting HIV from a deep needle puncture contaminated

with HIV virus. Snelling, like the others on the assembly line who were HIV positive, feels that the probability of anybody becoming HIV positive from contact with his blood, if he should ever cut himself, is so low that it could not be a problem for anybody but himself.

When asked, the director of the HMO reports to the the GM management, and the plant manager, Thomas Brown, that there are eight assembly line workers testing positive for HIV at the Glenview plant, that they have been guaranteed confidentiality, and that there is no significant threat to the health of anybody who may come in contact with the blood of any of them, should they cut themselves on the assembly line.

Shortly thereafter, Thomas Brown, the plant manager, is approached by the head of the local AFL-CIO auto workers union who reports that he has heard disturbing news that a number of people on the assembly line are HIV positive and that if that is true, the workers want to know their names. Brown tells him that there are some people on the line who are HIV positive but that he will not reveal their names, because they have been promised confidentiality and, besides, the risk to anybody else on the line is incredibly small—smaller, he says, "than the risk of being run over by a truck while sleeping in your bed." Even so, the union leader demands to know which people on the assembly line are HIV positive. He says, "We need to get them out of the plant, because no matter how small the probability of contracting the HIV virus, any probability at all, given the fatal effects, should be removed from the workplace." He then cites the Occupational Safety and Health Administration's (OSHA's) rule that workers have a right to know of any condition in the workplace that could possibly adversely affect their health. Brown responds that the right in question does not extend to knowing the names of the people who are HIV positive; to which the union leader responds that unless they know the the names of the people involved they cannot be sure "the problem" will be taken care of in a way that protects the safety and health of the workers. He threatens to go to OSHA and file suit to get the names, unless Brown voluntarily discloses the information in the morning.

For Discussion

Do the workers have a right to know the names of the persons on the line who are HIV positive? Does the union leader have a good reason for demanding the names of Snelling and others? If so, does Brown have a responsibility to reveal the names? Should the HMO have promised confidentiality? Can Brown turn over the list of names without violating Snelling's and the others' moral right to privacy? Do they in fact have a moral right to privacy in this case? Should the HMO agree to give the list of names to Brown to turn over to the union? What should Brown do if he wants to act in the morally correct way? Suppose the Union sues and the court decrees that this is a moral matter best decided among the parties involved because there is no legislation requiring the employer in these circumstances to reveal the names. Would such a decision alter your assessment?

Manuel G. Velasquez

Working Conditions: Health and Safety

Each year more than 5,900 workers are killed and over 5,700,000 are seriously injured as a result of job accidents.[1] Ten percent of the job force suffers a job-related injury or illness each year, for a loss of over 31 million work days annually. Delayed occupational diseases resulting from exposure to chemical and physical hazards kill off additional numbers. Annual costs of work-related deaths and injuries are estimated to be $8 billion.[2]

Workplace hazards include not only the more obvious categories of mechanical injury, electrocution, and burns, but also extreme heat and cold, noisy machinery, rock dust, textile fiber dust, chemical fumes, mercury, lead, beryllium, arsenic, corrosives, skin irritants, and radiation.[3] A government description of occupational injuries is dismaying:

> Three and a half million American workers exposed to asbestos face a dual threat: Not only are they subject to the lung-scarring pneumoconiosis of their trade, *asbestosis,* but they are endangered by *lung cancer* associated with inhalation of asbestos fibers. Recent studies of insulation workers in two states showed 1 in 5 deaths were from lung cancer, seven times the expected rate; half of those with twenty years or more in the trade had x-ray evidence of asbestosis; 1 in 10 deaths were caused by *mesothelioma,* a rare malignancy of the lung or pleura which strikes only 1 in 10,000 in the general working population. Of 6,000 men who have been uranium miners, an estimated 600 to 1,000 will die during the next twenty years as a result of *radiation exposure,*

From Manuel G. Velasquez, *Business Ethics: Concepts and Cases,* 3e © 1992, pp. 386–88. Reprinted by permission of Prentice-Hall, Englewood Cliffs, New Jersey.

principally from lung cancer. Fifty percent of the machines in industry generate *noise* levels potentially harmful to hearing. Hundreds of thousands of workers each year suffer skin diseases from contact with materials used in their work. The *dermatoses* are the most common of all occupational illnesses. Even the old, well-known industrial poisons, such as mercury, arsenic, and lead, still cause trouble.[4]

In 1970 Congress passed the Occupational Safety and Health Act and created the Occupational Safety and Health Administration (OSHA) "to assure as far as possible every working man and woman in the nation safe and healthful working conditions."[5] Unfortunately, from the beginning OSHA found itself embroiled in controversy. But in spite of the severe criticism it has received,[6] an inadequate number of field inspectors (800), and often inefficient forms of regulation, the existence of OSHA has led many firms to institute their own safety programs. A 1975 poll revealed that 36 percent of the firms surveyed had implemented safety programs as a result of OSHA, while 72 percent said that the existence of OSHA had influenced them in their safety efforts.[7]

Although more attention is now being paid to worker safety, occupational accident rates have not necessarily been declining. Between 1961 and 1970, the number of injuries per million working hours in manufacturing industries rose by almost 30 percent: from 11.8 injuries per million, to 15.2 per million.[8] By 1973, the rate had moved up to 15.3 per million, and by the late 1970s, the incidence of disabling injuries continued to be 20 percent higher than in 1958.[9]

Risk is, of course, an unavoidable part of many occupations. A race-car driver, a circus performer, a rodeo cowboy, all accept certain hazards as part of their jobs. And so long as they (a) are fully compensated for assuming these risks and (b) freely and knowingly choose to accept the risk in exchange for the added compensation, then we may assume that their employer has acted ethically.[10]

The basic problem, however, is that in many hazardous occupations, these conditions do not obtain:

1. Wages will fail to provide a level of compensation proportional to the risks of a job when labor markets in an industry are not competitive, or when markets do not register risks because the risks are not yet known. In some rural mining areas, for example, a single mining company may have a monopoly on jobs. And the health risks involved in mining a certain mineral (such as uranium) may not be known until many years afterwards. In such cases, wages will not fully compensate for risks.

2. Workers might accept risks unknowingly because they do not have adequate access to information concerning those risks. Collecting information on the risks of handling certain chemicals, for example, takes up a great deal of time, effort, and money. Workers acting individually may find it

too costly, therefore, to collect the information needed to assess the risks of the jobs they accept.

3. Workers might accept known risks out of desperation because they lack the mobility to enter other less risky industries or because they lack information on the alternatives available to them. Low-income coal miners, for example, may know the hazards inherent in coal mining, but since they lack the resources needed to travel elsewhere, they may be forced to either take a job in a coal mine or starve.

When any of the three conditions above obtain, then the contract between employer and employee is no longer fair; the employer has a duty, in such cases, to take steps to ensure that the worker is not being unfairly manipulated into accepting a risk unknowingly, unwillingly, or without due compensation. In particular:

1. Employers should offer wages that reflect the risk-premium prevalent in other similar but competitive labor markets.

2. To insure their workers against unknown hazards the employer should provide them with suitable health insurance programs.

3. Employers should (singly or together with other firms) collect information on the health hazards that accompany a given job and make all such information available to workers.

NOTES

1. Keith Davis and William C. Frederick, *Business and Society: Management, Public Policy, Ethics* (New York: McGraw-Hill Book Company, 1984), p. 266.

2. Rollin H. Simonds, "OSHA Compliance: Safety Is Good Business," *Personnel* (July–August 1973).

3. William W. Lowrance, *Of Acceptable Risk* (Los Altos, Calif.: William Kaufmann, Inc., 1976), p. 147.

4. U.S. Department of Health, Education and Welfare, "Occupational Disease . . . The Silent Enemy," quoted in ibid., p. 147.

5. *Occupational Safety and Health Act of 1970,* Public Law, 91–596.

6. See, for example, Robert D. Moran, "Our Job Safety Law Should Say What It Means," *Nation's Business* (April 1974), p. 23.

7. Peter J. Sheridan, "1970–1976: America in Transition—Which Way Will the Pendulum Swing?" *Occupational Hazards* (September 1975), p. 97.

8. Davis and Frederick, *Business and Society,* p. 266.

9. Barry, *Moral Issues in Business,* p. 178; see also "Workplace Injuries Increase," *San Francisco Chronicle,* November 14, 1985.

10. See Russell F. Settle and Burton A. Weisbrod, "Occupational Safety and Health and the Public Interest," in *Public Interest Law,* Burton Weisbrod, Joel F. Handler, and Neil K. Komesar, eds. (Berkeley: University of California Press, 1978), pp. 285–312.

Robert Almeder
J. D. Millar

The Moral Right to Know in the Workplace

INTRODUCTION

The complexities involved in explaining the notion of a basic moral right are certainly more than anyone can confront successfully in a short paper. Literally, hundreds of books and lengthy treatises have been written, and are still being written, on the nature of morality and moral rights. Collectively they reflect remarkably different and mutually exclusive basic views on the nature of moral rights and, although there are many thoughtful persons willing to defend what they regard as *the correct view* about the nature and scope of basic moral rights, the awful truth of the matter is that there is no consensus, either public or academic, on just what a moral right is. Accordingly, when it comes to stating the nature of moral rights, anyone taking a clear and dogmatic stand is much like the proverbial fool rushing in where angels fear to tread. Indeed, it almost seems that the most one can do is to adopt a particular view one finds congenial, and then "sallie forth to do battle with the heathen." Even so, a cautious and steadfast refusal to confront honestly and persistently the issue of human moral rights seems like a reprehensible abandonment of the responsibility to promote the public good. In short, woe to those who seek to understand human moral rights, and woe to those who don't.

This paper is a revised and expanded version of J. D. Millar's keynote address delivered to the New York Academy of Science and subsequently published in the *Annals of the New York Academy of Sciences* 572 (December 29, 1989).

In spite of these woes, we will outline, and then propose a way to over-come, the major obstacle to constructing an enlightened public policy on the moral right to know in the workplace. If we are correct in what we propose, there should be little doubt about the future general direction morally sensitive legislative enactment should take. But first let us examine the major obstacle just mentioned.

CONSEQUENTIALIST AND NONCONSEQUENTIALIST VIEWS ON MORAL RIGHTS

In examining the moral right to know in the workplace, we must keep in mind that there are two basic and mutually exclusive views about the nature of human rights. The first is the *consequentialist theory of rights,* and the second is the *nonconsequentialist theory of rights.* Under the first theory, a right is an obligation to be treated in a certain way and it exists if recognition of the right produces the best general outcome for all those affected by the exercise of the right. Accordingly, we must look to the consequences of exercising the right, and if the consequences (broadly conceived) prove to promote the best net outcome, given all the available alternatives, then the right exists; otherwise it does not exist. For example, on this view, the question of whether people have a right to life is simply a matter of determining the consequences of allowing people to kill others without a very good reason; and because the consequences of so acting do not produce the best general outcome for all those affected by the behavior, the consequentialist urges that everybody has the right to life—meaning thereby that nobody ought to take anybody else's life without having a very good reason for doing so.[1]

Under the second theory of rights, the nonconsequentialist theory of rights, rights do and can exist even if recognition of them does not produce the best general outcome. On the nonconsequentialist view, for example, even if killing an innocent person could guarantee the survival of a thousand innocent peo-ple who would otherwise most surely die, it would still be wrong to kill an innocent person. On the nonconsequentialist theory of rights, there are cer-tain things one ought never do no matter what the consequences. Immanuel Kant, for example, argued that no matter what the consequences, one should never lie, steal, or murder.[2]

Perhaps the best way to capture the difference between these two distinct theories on the nature of human rights is to examine an example moral phi-losophers sometimes probe when discussing the nature of morality. This is the famous "Commandant Example."[3] It goes like this: Suppose you are an occupant of a P.O.W. camp, and the commandant (who is reliable but wildly insane), approaches you and says, "Either kill one of the innocent babies in this camp, or I will kill 5,000 inmates, including women and children." Assum-ing that you cannot destroy the commandant, what would be the morally correct course of action? If one kills the innocent baby in order to save a larger number of innocent persons, then one has opted for the consequentialist theory of rights—the baby does not have the right to life, because recognition of the right does not produce the best general outcome. Conversely, if one refuses to kill the innocent baby, then one has opted for the nonconsequentialist theory of rights under which no matter what the consequences, it is never permissible to kill an innocent person. The important point here is that no matter what one's choice, there does not seem to be any effective decision procedure to resolve the dispute over what is the correct moral course of action. By implication, there is no known decision procedure to resolve the dispute over which view about human moral rights is correct.

Consequentialists typically criticize nonconsequentialists on the grounds that anybody who would *not* kill an innocent baby to save a larger number of innocent people is more like a moral fanatic than a committed moral agent acting on moral principle. After all, they say, anybody who is not willing to kill an innocent baby to save the world is surely morally blind. Nonconsequentialists, however, simply see morality as having nothing to do with the consequences of acts and stand in amazement over what they regard as the moral blindness of anybody who would kill an innocent baby to save a larger number of innocent people.[4] They would refuse to kill the innocent baby, and then ascribe responsibility for the death of the 5,000 innocent inmates to the evil commandant. Those who simply *see* morality as a matter promoting consequences productive of the greatest net good for the greatest number cannot help but regard the nonconsequentialist position as one of moral blindness; and those who simply *see* morality as a matter of doing certain things no matter what the consequences, are equally convinced of the moral blindness of the consequentialist position. The rest of us see no way of resolving the dispute by appeal to some agreeable principle or reason that would allow us to answer objectively the question of whether, or to what extent, the morality of an act is to be judged in terms of the overall effects of the act viewed as a rule. Consequently, the important point is that no matter which position one accepts on the nature of moral rights, there does not seem to be any viable decision procedure for effectively resolving the dispute over which view of moral rights is the correct one. Those who must make public policy in the presence of such a dilemma may well appreciate the feeling of existential despair.[5]

IN DEFENSE OF THE CONSEQUENTIALIST

When we turn to the debate about the moral right to know in the workplace, we recognize immediately these two distinct views on the nature of moral rights. On the one hand, there are those who will insist that no matter what the consequences of revealing information about possible harms in the workplace, workers have an absolute right to that information as an extension of their right to autonomy or even of their right to life.[6] On this latter view, the probable loss of life that results from recognizing a worker's right to know is totally irrelevant to the question of whether someone has the right to know about such harms in the workplace. On the other hand, the consequentialist view of the right to know inspires those who insist that a failure to look at the consequences of revealing information about possible harms seems too much like the moral fanaticism of those who insist that no matter what the consequences, certain things ought never be done. The problem, of course, is that those who fashion public policy must struggle with the question of whether the right to know in any particular case is a valid right only if revealing the information produces less human harm than withholding it. It is not difficult to refer to a number of instances in which more life was lost or harmed by revealing information about possibly harmful substances than would have been if that information had not been issued.[7] Some aspects of the present public reaction to providing information on AIDS suggest this. After all, the past surgeon general publicly said that "most of the people who are scared to death of contracting AIDS, couldn't catch it if they tried."[8] Typically, however, such cases are the exception; but what they establish is that we should be willing, when the situation demands it, to take a close look at the consequences of revealing information about possible harms in the workplace. Those who object to such a policy because they adopt a nonconsequentialist theory of rights must recognize that their position on human rights is no more privileged than the consequentialists, however strenuously voiced.

Furthermore, the nonconsequentialist often overlooks the crucial fact that this society has already spoken very strongly in favor of the consequentialist view on the moral right to life. Certainly, as a nation, we grant that human life is sacred and that everyone has a fundamental right to life. However, we do not hesitate to endorse an institution which knowingly conscripts and kills a number of innocent persons in the interest of preventing the predictable death of a larger number of innocent persons. We refer, of course, to the institution of war. If having a right to life meant that one's life could never be taken no matter what the consequences, then the institution of war would be inescapably and intrinsically evil. The bottom line here is that this society has not chosen, and is unwilling to live with, the principle that no matter what the consequences, one should never take a human life. Why should we act any differently when it comes to the moral right to know, especially when the latter is construed as an extension of the right to autonomy and life itself? Whether we talk about war, or even capital punishment, we stand as a society ready to endorse the view that the right to life means no more than that one must have a very good reason to take another person's life; and that reason may well be the greater harm in terms of loss of life that results from not taking that person's life. It is difficult to see why we should not adopt the same general attitude when it comes to the moral right to know in the workplace.

IN DEFENSE OF THE NONCONSEQUENTIALIST

Even though it makes sense to examine the consequences of revealing information in order to determine whether the right to know exists, the concern behind the nonconsequentialist posture should by no means be ignored. As we have already noted, the Kantian view that morality has nothing to do with the consequences has commanded the respect of a good number of serious and profound thinkers.

But what precisely is the concern motivating the nonconsequentialist on the right to know in the workplace? To begin with, there is a long-standing and deeply felt suspicion that some industries or corporations are only too willing to be indifferent to the safety and health of the worker if the cost of compassion is even marginally burdensome to the shareholder. Nobody will deny that abuses of this sort have occurred in the past. In the absence of a good watchdog, such abuses are likely to occur in the future. To a considerable extent this concern may be addressed by the remarkable effect of strict liability law and its capacity to engender real fear in the hearts of those who might otherwise have been tempted to play fast and loose with the health and safety of workers. There are those who feel that strict liability law may be quite unfair to employers; but nobody should deny that it places remarkable contraints, although no insuperable constraints, on the degree of indifference an employer can responsibly maintain with respect to the health and safety of employees. Of itself, however, liability law works only *after* certain harms (including loss of life) have occurred; and while it may allay some of the nonconsequentialist concern, liability law is certainly no substitute for a mechanism that would make an appeal to liability law less likely or necessary.

Second, what often bothers and motivates the nonconsequentialist is the ominous prospect of the life of the worker being measured purely in terms of economic units. Some people, of course, erroneously believe that this prospect is an integral part of any cost-benefit analysis associated with determining the costs incurred in protecting the health and safety of the workers. Certainly, however, the consequentialist theory of rights *does not imply* that the sanctity of human life is to be measured in terms of a certain dollar figure. Any conception of a suitable "cost-benefit analysis" that would ever imply as much is erroneous and doomed to moral extinction. The consequentialist theory of moral rights by no means implies that any worker can, without her enlightened consent, be exposed to certain material harms simply as part of the cost of doing business. If anything, such a policy would, if widely implemented, tend as a rule to produce the greatest amount of harm for all those affected.

And, finally, we can dispel the core concern of the nonconsequentialist simply by adopting the same policy toward the right to know that we, as a society, adopt with regard to the right to life. In other words, although saying that a person *has a moral right to life* is saying that nobody can take his life without a very good reason, those who would take it will need to assume a very heavy burden of proof and will be forced to demonstrate the presence of such a compelling reason if they are to avoid harsh punishment. Society reflects this moral right as primitive by making laws against killing, and in so doing specifies what it believes are suitably strong reasons for not considering particular acts of killing (such as capital punishment or war) legally reprehensible. *Prima facie* there is a law against such behavior and, if the law is willfully broken, then the stated penalty will be imposed in no uncertain terms. In other words, the law exists to protect a *prima facie* moral right, and that moral right we recognize because failure to do so would, as a rule, fail to promote the greatest amount of good for all affected.

Similarly, although saying that a person has a right to know does not *mean* that nobody can withhold relevant information without his permission, it does mean that nobody can withhold such information without having a very good reason which will need to be defended because withholding such information breaks the law. Those who would ostensibly withhold such information need to assume a heavy burden of proof and publicly defend such a procedure in a fully articulated legal context just because the law places such a special value on human life. Where the long-term good of society as a whole renders withholding relevant information demonstrably defensible, it will find its way into the law and public policy as a way of refining our understanding of the value of life. Otherwise, here again, the law prohibits very specifically any failure to disclose information on what is materially harmful to workers in the workplace.[9] Given that we may understand the right to know as a justifiable extension of the right to autonomy and, hence, by implication, the right to life, this sort of reasoning may alleviate somewhat the concerns at the root of the nonconsequentialist view on the nature of the right to know in the workplace. Importantly enough, this way of defending and alleviating the nonconsequentialist concern does not require of us that we abandon the consequentialist view of the right to know in the workplace.

Doubtless, there are nonconsequentialists who will insist that *their* concern will be respected only when, no matter what the consequences, nothing could ever possibly count as a reason for anybody's withholding information from the worker on what is possibly harmful in the workplace. As we have just argued, however, while there is no way to meet that concern stated in that way, this society has, as a whole, given special preeminence to the right to life by visiting with the harshest of penalties those who break well-defined laws respecting the *prima facie* right to life.

CONCLUSION

Naturally, there are many other problems or obstacles in fashioning and implementing a broadly agreeable public policy on the right to know in the workplace. There are fine questions involved in determining the nature of certain risks, just as there are important questions associated with determining how much risk of harm needs to be present before a worker's right to know is materially affected. And we have said little here about the legal right to know, or the status of that legal right. We have only sought to confront what we take to be the major obstacle to constructing a morally inspired policy on the right to know in the workplace. That obstacle is reflected in the nonconsequentialist view that, no matter what the consequences, no worker should ever be exposed, without his (or her) enlightened and informed consent, to significant risk to harm. While addressing the concerns that motivate this latter claim, we have, in sum, urged that the *moral* right to know in the workplace is best construed as the consequentialist construes it. This implies, among other things, that the worker has a *prima facie* moral right to know about any materially harmful condition or substance in his (or her) workplace; and this amounts to saying that nobody can morally withhold that information without having a demonstrably very good reason for doing so. Those who would withhold such information need to assume the burden of proof and demonstrate the presence of such a reason—which may be a compelling reason only because revealing the information is certifiably more likely to involve a greater loss of life. At any rate, whether they succeed in so demonstrating the presence of such a reason is incidental to the fact that such behavior is, as things presently stand, illegal.

In the end, makers of public policy cannot avoid profound public controversy over the nature and scope of basic moral rights. Invariably, there are passionate defenders on both sides of the issue. Forging public policy in the absence of a broad public consensus is nothing more than the arbitrary imposition by government of some preferred, but by no means necessarily privileged, moral view. It hardly seems the legitimate role of a democratic government, even in the name of moral leadership, to so impose views that are deeply controversial and incapable of broad-based support by the population at large. It is better by far, for reasons of stable public policy, that we seek the painful path of building a general public consensus among the well-informed and well-meaning citizenry. This involves pleading one's moral intuitions publicly in the interest of promoting as humane a society as we can imagine. If we can achieve no such consensus, then the law will, as a matter of necessity, settle the issue in the interest of an efficient discharge of social functions . . . and, from the viewpoint of evolution at least, that is not a particularly unfortunate outcome.

NOTES

1. For a general discussion of consequentialist and nonconsequentialist theories of ethics, see William Frankena, *Ethics* (New York: Prentice Hall, 1982), pp. 15–45. See also, David Lyons, "Human Rights and the General Welfare" in *Rights,* David Lyons, ed., (Belmont, Calif.: Wadsworth Publishing Company, 1979), pp. 187ff. and Bernard Williams and J. J. C. Smart, *Utilitarianism For and Against* (New York: Cambridge University Press, 1976).

2. For a general discussion of Kant's views see Frankena, *Ethics,* pp. 25–29, and Immanuel Kant, *The Foundation of the Metaphysics of Morals* (New York: Liberal Arts Press, 1959). See also, as an example of the nonconsequentialist position, G. E. M. Anscombe, "Modern Philosophy," *Philosophy* (1958), p. 7.

3. See Williams and Smart, *Utilitarianism For and Against.* The example was initially offered by Williams.

4. See, for example, G. E. M. Anscombe, "Modern Moral Philosophy," *Philosophy* (1958), p. 7. See also Alan Gewirth, *Moral Philosophy* (Chicago: University of Chicago Press, 1979).

5. The more practical dimensions of this problem occur, for example, when one is asked to devise public policy on matters affecting the permissibility and financing of abortion for various reasons. Another case in point, one more pertinent to the issue of the right to know in the workplace, was recently noted elsewhere by J. D. Millar, who, as Director of NIOSH (National Institute of Occupational Safety and Health), in 1981 consulted respectively (1) the Office of General Counsel of Public Health Service and (2) the Centers for Disease Control Ethics Committee on the question of whether NIOSH should inform some workers who, as a result of a retrospective cohort mortality study, were determined to be at some risk to death as a result of exposure to hazardous materials in the workplace. From the attorneys in the Office of General Counsel he was advised that NIOSH had no legal duty to advise the individuals involved and, moreover, if NIOSH were to so inform the workers, it would incur certain legal liabilites as a result. From the CDC Ethics Committee he was advised that he did have a moral duty to inform the workers as an instance of the general responsibility to ensure that workers have knowledge of their exposure to hazardous material. Because the CDC Ethics Committee was arguing that, regardless of the consequences (in this case the legal consequences as well as the effects on the conduct of business and all that that implies) all workers had a right to know, it was assuming a nonconsequentialist posture on the right to know and the responsibility to disclose.

6. See Ruth R. Faden and Thomas L. Beauchamp, "The Right to Know in the Workplace,"*The Canadian Journal of Philosophy,* Suppl. Vol. 8 (1982), p. 199ff. For another interesting discussion on the tension between consequentialist and nonconsequentialist theory as it affects occupational health, see Sherry I. and Paul W. Brant-Rauf, "Occupational Health Ethics: OSHA and the Courts," *Journal of Health Politics, Policy and Law* 5, no. 3 (Fall 1980).

7. On this point see Faden and Beauchamp, "The Right to Know in the Workplace," pp. 197–200. The point Faden and Beauchamp make is that one sometimes has a responsibility to beneficence, which may well conflict with the worker's right to autonomy. In which case, depending on the circumstances, we may have good reason to withhold information. There are, for example, cases in which female workers suffer a demonstrably low risk of sterility or fetal damage as a result of certain exposures. To reveal such information is likely to induce behaviors (such as certain types of x-raying) more life threatening than the original exposures.

8. Opening General Session, Annual Meeting of the Association of Military Surgeons of the United States. Las Vegas, Nevada, November 9, 1987.

9. Nobody should think, incidentally, that this paper condones or encourages the view that it is morally permissible to break the current laws pertaining to employer responsibilities to inform employees of what may materially and/or adversely affect them in the workplace. Those laws are, we submit, a product of the consequentialist posture we adopt as a society seeking the general common good. (For a clear statement of those laws, see J. D. Millar, "The Right to Know in the Workplace," *Annals of the New York Academy of Science* 572 [December 1989]). Our basic concern here is to determine how the law and public policy should be written to embody basic moral rights in the presence of what seems to be mutually exclusive views on the basic nature of those rights.

WHISTLEBLOWING

Whistleblowing at Northern Airlines

When Mack Thomas became foreman of Northern Airlines' Bay Six maintenance crew at Chicago's O'Hare Airport he knew he had his work cut out
for him. The crew ranked dead last in productivity over the previous year,
and Thomas's manager, Stan Gibbons, said he expected improvement pronto.

Northern ranked each of its mechanics from 1st (top) to 100th (lowest)
percentile on the basis of productivity, leadership, and attitude. Thomas noted
that, on average, his crew ranked in the 73rd percentile, with no individual
higher than 58th and the lowest ranked 97th. He would be working with mechanics, all of whom ranked below average. The lack of leadership ability among
the crew, its poor productivity record, and a generally sour attitude toward
Northern made for a difficult problem that would not be easily resolved.

Nevertheless, Thomas welcomed the challenge. He had moved his Bay
Three crew from fifth to second in productivity among Northern's eight crews
in two years. He knew the Bay Six crew was older and set in its ways, but
if he could improve its ranking, he thought he would be chosen for the foreman supervisor slot that would be coming open in about two years.

Thomas asked Stan Gibbons if he could bring in two top mechanics from
his old Bay Three crew to give him some role models. Gibbons said he didn't
want to break up a team that had momentum; he wanted Thomas to see
if he could turn the Bay Six crew around. On reflection, Thomas felt that
Gibbons had his eye on him for promotion. If he could succeed with the Bay
Six crew, he would prove his management abilities.

When he faced the Bay Six crew for the first time, Mack Thomas said:

The facts show that you guys are dead last. And in case you don't know it, you're the laughing-stock of Northern Airlines. We're going to change that. We're going to be number one in two years. That's our goal. Don't tell me to be patient. Patience is for those with no goals. My goal is to be number one; your goal is to be number one. To reach that goal we're going to do two things: work smarter and work harder.

We're not working hard enough here. In some cases we're not working. Northern's rule is that you get five unexplained sick days per year and you can be late for work six times per year. Now this policy hasn't been enforced with the Bay Six crew. One of you had 16 unexplained sick days last year. And one of you, Pacello, was tardy over 20 times last year—almost once every two weeks. I'm going to fire anyone who violates either rule. No exceptions. No excuses.

We're also going to work smarter. For example, we know we have to write up in the maintenance log every safety problem we encounter . The Federal Aviation Administration requires this, and it's Northern's policy. But I also have a rule here: you must consult with me before entering a problem in the maintenance log. I want to see that those problems are described correctly. When I first started as foreman over at Bay Three a lot of problems were logged that made for a lot of make-work. Guys would inflate a problem on paper, and then sit around in the hangar doing nothing. That won't happen here. We're going to move the metal.

Tony Pacello was a bit apprehensive about being singled out by Mack Thomas. Punctuality was not a real problem. Tony knew he had taken advantage of a lax foreman, but, as a former Air Force mechanic, he knew he could and would get to work on time. Talk about being "Number One" did bother Tony. The ranking system Northern used didn't take safety into account. Pacello had a low ranking of 77, but no person had ever been hospitalized because of a safety problem with a plane he helped maintain. For Pacello, safety was "Number One," and he hoped that legitimate safety concerns would not be labeled "make-work."

For three months Pacello reported on time, took no sick leave, and enjoyed his work. No major problems were encountered; only routine maintenance was required. Morale did seem to be improving in Bay Six. Pacello was a bit irritated with Thomas's temper tantrums and his hyperactive behavior, but he had to admit that the team was pulling together. Thomas took the team out for a few beers on occasion, and paid for a catered picnic for Bay Six family members.

The first reportable problem Pacello found was a chafed brake hose on a landing gear. He told Thomas it needed to be fixed immediately and logged it in the FAA file. Thomas said the replacement would cause a flight delay and inquired whether the problem was serious enough to require immediate attention or could be deferred until the plane's scheduled overhaul in a week. Pacello said it should be fixed. Thomas, a former mechanic, examined the brake, said it wasn't serious, ordered it taped, and told Pacello not to write it up in the FAA log. Instead, he told Pacello to be sure to fix the problem a week later. Pacello objected, saying that all such problems had been reported in the past and resolved immediately. Thomas repeated that the chafing wasn't serious enough to repair or report and said that the Bay Six team had not operated properly in the past. Pacello did not agree that there was no danger, and he knew that FAA rules required him to log a problem for which he had evidence. He mentioned this to Thomas, who boiled over: "I told you there's no problem, Pacello, no chance of a problem. I'm giving you a direct order to certify that plane. Get it? Now get out!" Pacello left and certified the plane for flight.

A month later, Pacello and his fellow mechanic Art Necassi reported to Thomas that a plane's engine housing latch had jammed after the engine's inspection and that they hadn't been able to release it. They believed the problem should be logged and resolved, which would mean a flight postponement. Thomas said: "Look, the engine was inspected. It's okay. The jamming you mention means the latch is locked; it just can't be unlocked. A locked latch will not come open. So, there's no problem, no real problem. Move the metal; we will clean it up later." Necassi said he thought the problem should be fixed and logged, but that he wanted to talk with Tyler Morgan, Stan Gibbons's boss, before he logged it. Thomas said he should talk with Gibbons if he talked with anyone, but he added that he wanted to look at the latch first. He did so and pronounced the flight ready to go. He told Necassi to think it over for 15 minutes before calling anyone. When Necassi called, Morgan told him he had talked with Thomas, who reported that he had seen this problem many times and that it was not reportable. Morgan also said that Thomas told him he had consulted with Gibbons. Morgan told Necassi to listen to Thomas and not let Pacello influence him: "Tony's a nice guy, but he's in the 77th percentile. We've repeatedly had to lay him off or transfer him. He's spent more time maintaining ground vehicles here than planes. He hasn't spent enough time on aircraft to really know what he's doing." Necassi certified the plane for flight after Pacello refused. When informed of Morgan's comments about him, Pacello said: "Something's gotta give here and it won't be me."

Three weeks later Necassi discovered a broken floor panel in a plane scheduled to fly in two hours. He conferred with Pacello, who said no panels were in inventory. Pacello immediately entered the item in the FAA logbook. A short time later, Thomas confronted Pacello, saying: "Of all the planes we're working, this is the only one with a chance of making the 7 A.M. takeoff, and you shoot it down." After ordering Necassi and Pacello to take a break, Thomas told another mechanic to patch the panel with sheet metal. When Pacello returned to the plane, he felt the panel sink beneath his feet, and had visions of it breaking and interfering with the steering control cables that run under the floor. Since he had filed the log notation, Pacello knew he could be held responsible by the FAA if he was party to a substandard repair. He went for a smoke, and, while there, watched the plane take off. Finally, he went to a phone and called the FAA. Northern was contacted immediately; the plane was located in Minneapolis, with the cables in normal working order; a new panel was shipped in, and after a day's delay, the plane was certified for flight.

When the plane returned to Chicago, Pacello noticed that his logbook entry had been changed; it now indicated the broken panel was in a different location. The log indicated that repairs had been completed. Since falsifying an aircraft logbook is a federal felony, Pacello again called the FAA, which investigated. Pacello said he had no doubt that Thomas did it. Speaking for Northern, Tyler Morgan said it was probable that another mechanic did it to discredit Thomas. The FAA could not decide who was at fault.

Nine days after the incident Thomas saw Pacello sitting in a first-class seat while Necassi was working on a loose seat behind the one Pacello was in. Thomas immediately suspended Pacello for loafing, though the latter insisted that he was helping by pushing the frame into place with his legs. Necassi supported Pacello's version. Thomas called in Gibbons and Morgan. What happened next is unclear. Thomas, Gibbons, and Morgan claim they told Pacello to return to the hangar the next day to meet and discuss his suspension. Necassi and Pacello say no such meeting was mentioned. After Pacello did not appear for the meeting, he was fired. Pacello was later reinstated through Northern's grievance procedure, although he was demoted to ground vehicle maintenance.

After his reinstatement, Pacello held a news conference in which he alleged that Northern had committed serious unethical and illegal acts. He laid out the specifics regarding the chafed hose, the engine housing latch, and the broken floor panel. He also mentioned the altered logbook, and the fact that Northern's grievance procedure had reinstated him after he had been fired. Pacello said he felt sure Northern would neither investigate the actions of Thomas, Gibbons, and Morgan nor discipline them, and he asked the media to conduct their own investigation.

For Discussion

How many times did Tony Pacello blow the whistle? Was he justified in blowing the whistle on Northern Airlines? Why or why not? Discuss Northern's responses to Pacello's acts. Were these responses justified? Why or why not? If you were placed in charge of Northern's response to safety issues, would you make any changes? If not, why not? If so, why would you make the specific changes you recommend?

Norman E. Bowie
Ronald F. Duska

Whistleblowing

Whether or not they are asked to participate in the act, employees are often in a position to know about the illegal or immoral actions of a supervisor or employer. Should an employee who is asked to participate in an illegal or immoral action, or who witnesses the illegal or immoral action of a supervisor or employer, inform the public? Whenever these questions are answered in the affirmative and the public is informed, we have cases of whistleblowing. On a first account, whistleblowing is the act by an employee of informing the public on the immoral or illegal behavior of an employer or supervisor.

One of the better-known cases in which whistleblowers have lost their jobs is the BART case. BART is the acronym for the Bay Area Rapid Transit system, a modern rail transit system in San Francisco. During construction of the line, three engineers became deeply concerned over the safety of certain features of the system. Holger Hjortsvang reported, to no avail, his concerns about the Automatic Train Control System that was being built by the Westinghouse Corporation. Just a few months later, another engineer, Robert Bruder, became concerned about Westinghouse's lack of tests on certain equipment. Still later, Max Blankenzee, a senior programmer, joined Mr. Hjortsvang in sharing his concerns. Having received no response from various memoranda they had filed, the three engineers met with a member of the BART board of directors. Following the meeting, confidential memos shared

From Norman E. Bowie and Ronald F. Duska, *Business Ethics*, 2e, © 1990, pp. 72–77. Reprinted by permission of Prentice Hall, Englewood Cliffs, New Jersey.

with board member Daniel Helex appeared in the *Contra Costa Times,* and the report of a private consultant in support of the three engineers was ridiculed after being presented to the full board. Three days later all three engineers were fired. The engineers sued and each won $25,000 in an out-of-court settlement. It took from eight to fifteen months for the three engineers to find satisfactory jobs elsewhere. In addition to the economic stress, the psychological stress was relatively severe on all of them.

Despite the apparent injustice that results when whistleblowers protect the public interest at great personal cost, many business people have little sympathy for them. According to these people, whistleblowers have violated one of the chief duties of an employee—the duty to be loyal to one's employer. This attitude is perhaps best captured in remarks by James M. Roche, former president of General Motors.

> Some critics are now busy eroding another support of free enterprise—the loyalty of a management team, with its unifying values of cooperative work. Some of the enemies of business now encourage an employee to be disloyal to the enterprise. They want to create suspicion and disharmony, and pry into the proprietary interests of the business. However this is labeled—industrial espionage, whistleblowing, or professional responsibility—it is another tactic for spreading disunity and creating conflict.[1]

However, the obligation of loyalty as an overriding obligation has recently come under attack.[2] The general consensus seems to be that one has a duty to be loyal only if the object of loyalty is one that is morally appropriate.

One cannot assume, however, that the claims of all whistleblowers are obviously true and that the demands of all employers are obviously false. Some whistleblowers may be trying to seize more power within the company. BART made just such a charge against engineer Hjortsvang. Others try to create a whistleblowing case for the purpose of covering up genuine personal inadequacies—inadequacies that represent the real reason for their being disciplined or dismissed. What is needed is a careful definition of whistleblowing along with guidelines outlining what considerations should be taken into account to justify acts of whistleblowing. To begin, let us define the whistleblower:

> A whistleblower is an employee or officer of any institution, profit or nonprofit, private or public, who believes either that he/she has been ordered to perform some act or he/she has obtained knowledge that the institution is engaged in activities which (a) are believed to cause unnecessary harm to third parties, (b) are in violation of human rights or (c) run counter to the defined purpose of the institution and who inform the public of this fact.[3]

With respect to corporations, the discerning reader will note that the whistleblower in business reports activities that violate either the basic moral presuppositions on which the business enterprise rests or that violate the purpose of the corporate enterprise.

What can be said on behalf of this definition? First, it limits the class of moral infractions that an employee should make public. A person who makes a point of informing on every discretion is a nuisance and is more appropriately an object of scorn rather than a subject of praise. Who wants to know every time someone utters an unkind word about one's supervisor or uses a piece of office stationery for a personal letter. Parents encourage their children not to tattle, and those in the business world should not be tattletales either. Whistleblowing is reserved conceptually only for those serious moral faults spelled out in the definition. Of course, people who commit these relatively minor moral faults ought not to do them. An injunction against tattling does not make the actions of the perpetrators blameless. Rather, the injunction against tattling is based on the view that it is inappropriate for everyone to have as his or her responsibility the task of informing others of the minor moral faults of everyone else. Given the rancor and ill will that are caused when people do tattle, there are good utilitarian arguments against tattling. In addition, the definition limits the scope of one's response to immoral behavior. A whistleblower's responsibility is limited to informing the public. The responsibility does not extend to taking any retaliatory action against the employer or firm. The concept of "whistleblower" must be kept distinct from the concept of "saboteur."

To define the whistleblower is not thereby to justify all acts of whistleblowing. The definition of something is one thing: its justification is another. The following list of conditions, when met, provides sufficient grounds for an act of whistleblowing:

1. The whistleblowing is done for the appropriate moral motive—namely, as provided in the definition of whistleblowing.

2. The whistleblower, except in special circumstances, has exhausted all internal channels for dissent before informing the public.

3. The whistleblower has made certain that his or her belief that inappropriate actions are ordered or have occurred is based on evidence that would persuade a reasonable person.

4. The whistleblower has acted after a careful analysis of the danger: (a) how serious is the moral violation? (b) how immediate is the moral violation? (c) is the moral violation one that can be specified?

5. The whistleblower's action is commensurate with one's responsibility for avoiding and/or exposing moral violations.

6. The whistleblowing has some chance of success.

This list of justifying conditions deserves some comment. The question of motive is extremely important. Since whistleblowing does violate a prima facie duty of loyalty to one's employer, whistleblowing must be based on moral grounds if it is to be justified. The moral aim of whistleblowing is deemed so central that it is made part of the definition—namely, whistleblowing aims at exposing unnecessary harm, violations of human rights, or conduct counter to the defined purpose of the corporation. However, the moral dimensions of whistleblowing are not exhausted by examining its aim. Many moral philosophers have insisted that consideration of motives is relevant in assessing the morality of a person's action. Suppose that a potential assassin attempts to push the president of the United States in front of a train. As the president stumbles, another assassin (whose existence is unknown to the first) fires a shot that misses the president. Surely the action of the first potential assassin is not morally justified even though the act had good results.

Now consider possible motives for whistleblowing. A desire to attract attention, to get ahead, to shift the focus away from one's genuine weakness, and a general propensity toward being a troublemaker all represent possible motives for whistleblowing, but obviously none of them passes the justificatory test. A whistleblower's motive should be to protect the public interest. Anything less than that undercuts the justification of whistleblowing.

Yet another justificatory constraint is that the whistleblower exhaust all internal channels for dissent. Because the whistleblower does have some obligations to the employer, he or she should—at least in normal circumstances—use the institutional mechanisms that have been created for the purpose of registering dissent with the policies or actions of the corporation. One can be cynical about such institutional mechanisms, but, as we will see in the next chapter, such self-regulating mechanisms are desirable. In fact, two contemporary theorists have argued that,

> The task of ethical management is to have anticipated the pressures which would give rise to the concealed and harmful practice, and to have helped create patterns of communication within the organization so that whistleblowing would not be necessary. The focus on attempting to assure protection for the whistleblower is, from the point of view of managerial ethics, basically misconceived—the managerial task is to prevent the necessity of whistleblowing.[4]

As such effective mechanisms develop, the whistleblower is under an obligation to use them.

Yet another element in justified whistleblowing refers to the evidential base on which the whistleblowing is done. Charges of immorality should be based on strong evidence. Definitions of what counts as strong evidence go far beyond the subject matter of this book. We rest content with the semilegal notion that the evidence should be strong enough so that any person in a similar situation would be convinced that the practice being protested is indeed immoral. We have already seen how the concept of the reasonable consumer functions in judgments of deceptive advertising. The reasonable consumer standard is also used in liability and negligence lawsuits; hence, we will let the concept suffice here.

Still another requirement for justified whistleblowing focuses on the nature of the moral violation itself. First, the seriousness of the violation should be considered. Just as parents should only call the doctor when their child is seriously ill and not when the illnesses are minor, whistleblowers should only inform on their employers for grave moral matters. Fastidiousness about moral matters is not a requirement for business ethics. Another element to be considered is how immediate the moral violation is. The greater the time before the violation is to occur, the greater the chances that internal mechanisms will prevent the anticipated violation. In general, whistleblowing is more justified the more immediate the violation is. Finally, the violation should be something specific. General claims about a rapacious company, obscene profits, and actions contrary to the public interest simply will not do. Such claims must be backed up with identifiable examples—examples that will stand up under the other justificatory tests.

Still another justificatory requirement enables us to return to the discussion of role morality. Some positions within the corporate structure have as part of the job description a concern with the morality of corporate actions. Some jobs such as ombudsman or vice-president for corporate responsibility are defined as being concerned with corporate moral behavior. In other cases, certain kinds of moral activities are the responsibilities of corporate personnel. Corporate auditors check the legitimacy of expense account statements. Quality control personnel have special responsibilities concerning consumer safety. When some moral matter is the specific assignment of an employee, that person has special responsibilities associated with that role. When the corporate role gives an employee explicit responsibility for some matter with ethical dimensions, the corporation is normally committed to following the advice of the person given the responsibility. After all, failure to do so would create a serious ethical dilemma for the employee with the moral responsibility. If the corporation overruled the advice, the employee would either have to acquiesce in an activity that he or she has already determined to be illegal or immoral or he or she would have to blow the whistle.

However, responsibilities for moral matters are not limited to job descriptions created by the business institutions themselves. Where corporations make use of *professional* employees, there are certain moral obligations associated with the role of that profession. Often those obligations are spelled out in a professional code of ethics. The best-known examples are in engineering and accounting. One provision of the code of the American Society of Civil Engineers is that an engineer "will use his knowledge and skill for the advancement of human welfare and refuse any assignment contrary to this good." The National Society of Professional Engineers has a rather extensive code of ethics consisting of 15 major sections. The National Association of Accountants also has a professional code of ethics, which among its admonitions requires that accountants "refrain from engaging in any activity that would prejudice their ability to carry out their duties ethically." Being a professional engineer or accountant binds those engineers and accountants to the code of conduct of the society and by implication binds the companies that employ these individuals as well. After all, in hiring a professional it is presumed that one wishes to employ someone who meets certain professional standards, and, unless specified otherwise, an employer accepts all the standards of professional behavior associated with that profession.

The final justificatory condition is more controversial. It requires that the whistleblowing have some chance of success. If there is no hope in arousing societal or governmental pressure, then one is needlessly exposing oneself and one's loved ones to hardship for no conceivable moral gain. It is not simply a matter of saying that an employee is not obligated to blow the whistle if there is no chance of success, but that whistleblowing that does not have a chance of success is less justified, all things being equal, than is whistleblowing that does have a chance of success. The reader should note that we are not saying that such whistleblowing is never justified and hence should never be done. Sometimes such whistleblowing should be done if, for example, the violation is especially grave and the whistleblower's other personal obligations are few. On balance, however, given the dangers that personal whistleblowers run, the more likely the chances of success, the more justified the act of whistleblowing is. So much for the obligation to blow the whistle.

NOTES

1. James M. Roche, "The Competitive System, to Work, to Preserve, and to Protect," *Vital Speeches of the Day* (May 1971), p. 445.

2. For example, see Ronald Duska, "Whistleblowing and Employee Loyalty" in *Ethical Theory and Business,* 3d ed., Tom L. Beauchamp and Norman E. Bowie, eds. (Englewood Cliffs, N.J.: Prentice Hall, 1988), pp. 299–303.

3. Norman E. Bowie, *Business Ethics,* 1st ed. (Englewood Cliffs, N.J.: Prentice Hall, 1982), p. 142.

4. This quotation is from a discussion draft prepared for the Hastings Center Project on "The Teaching of Ethics," by Charles W. Powers and David Vogel, p. 40. This comment was omitted from the published version.

Alan F. Westin

Whistleblowing: Loyalty and Dissent in the Corporation

. . . [O]ur society needs to rethink the current definitions of loyalty and dissent in corproate life. We must come up with a strategy that will apply a combination of new remedies to increase the protection of legitimate whistleblowing. And, we have to start discussing this issue with some urgency now. . . .

Having stated this conclusion, it may seem that this presents a relatively straightforward problem for American law and social policy: just create some new procedure to protect whistleblowers. But the problem is not at all simple. Consider the following factors that have to be taken into account in framing new public policies.

1. *Not all whistleblowers are correct in what they allege to be the facts of management's conduct, and determining the accuracy of whistleblowing charges is not always easy.* If it were possible to collect all the instances of corporate-employee whistleblowing charges in the United States in a given year and then determine how often managements were justified in their actions and the employees mistaken, my guess is that employers would deserve to win many of these disputes. This has been the experience under independent labor arbitration, when unionized workers challenge dismissals as not being for "just cause." It is also the experience when government employees have ap-

pealed to the courts to vindicate free-expression rights in government whistleblowing cases. Putting the whistle to one's lips does not guarantee that one's facts are correct.

2. *There is always the danger that incompetent or inadequately performing employees will take up the whistle to avoid facing justified personnel sanctions.* Forbidding an employer to dismiss or discipline an employee who protests against illegal or improper conduct by management invites employees to take out "antidismissal insurance" by lodging a whistleblowing complaint. Any new system to protect whistleblowers must find ways to deal with this possibility.

3. *Employees can choose some ways of blowing the whistle that would be unacceptably disruptive, regardless of their protest.* Suppose an employee at a chemical plant takes out an ad in the local newspaper that says, "My company is violating the law by polluting the town reservoir." Or suppose a black employee of the XYZ Corporation comes to work on the assembly line one day wearing a large button that says "XYZ is a Honkie Firm that Practices Racism against its Black Workers." Finally, suppose an automobile design engineer, without raising the issue with his supervisor or upper management, reports to the National Transportation Safety Board that he believes the gas tank of a new model just entering production will pose grave safety problems. These illustrations demonstrate that any system to protect rights of employee expression must consider the time, place, and manner in which an employee voices that dissent.

4. *Some whistleblowers are not protesting unlawful or unsafe behavior but social policies by management that the employee considers unwise.* When this is the case, should an employee be entitled to remain on the job? In considering this, it helps to recall that whistleblowing can come in a wide variety of ideological stripes. Most government and corporate whistleblowers have recently been people who are asserting liberal values when they call for changes in corporate policies. But in the late 1940s and early fifties, the most celebrated whistleblowers were persons leaking information to anti-Communist legislators or the press about allegedly "soft-on-communism" policies by members of the Truman administration or their private employers. It was Senator Richard M. Nixon who proposed legislation in 1951 to protect the jobs of such federal-employee whistleblowers if they revealed classified information about corruption or pro-Communists to congressional committees. At that moment, liberals and civil libertarians defended the need for autonomy and confidentiality in the executive branch, and deplored the totalitarian "informer" mentality being championed by the McCarthyites. This suggests that any policy protecting whistleblowers must reckon with the likelihood of shifting ideological directions among protesting employees, and consider how often society wants social policies to be determined in the private sector through whistleblowing disputes.

5. *The legal definitions of what constitutes a safe product, danger to health, or improper treatment of employees are often far from clear or certain.* It usually takes years and many test cases before the courts and regulatory agencies define just what is required in a given situation. This leaves open a wide range of judgments and choices as to what is proper compliance activity. Until the law becomes clear, shouldn't management have the authority to select compliance strategies, since management bears the legal responsibility for meeting standards? This is especially true since the harsh realities of foreign business competition and rising production expenses create legitimate concerns for management about containing costs, including the cost of complying with government regulations. In addition, the jobs of millions of corporate employees, the well-being of local communities in which companies operate, and the strength of the national economy are all involved in the determination of reasonable risk-to-cost calculations.

6. *The efficiency and flexibility of personnel administration could be threatened by the creation of legal rights to dissent and legalized review systems.* If it becomes legally protected to challenge management policies and procedures and to appeal directives to outside authorities, this could lead to a flood of unjustified and harassing employee complaints. It could require personnel managers to document every action as a defense to possible litigation, and embroil managements in consistent employee litigation. It could also create an "informer ethos" at work that would threaten the spirit of cooperation and trust on which sound working relationships depend.

7. *There can be risks to the desirable autonomy of the private sector in expanding government authority too deeply into internal business policies.* Although democratic societies have a major interest in allowing private organizations to run their own affairs and to make their own personnel decisions, they insist that these private organizations are also subject to obeying the law. Having courts or government tribunals pass on the validity of a wide range of personnel decisions could give the government more authority to define loyalty and disloyalty for 80 million private-sector employees than would be desirable, and could also give government too much authority to control what products are produced and how they are manufactured.

This catalogue of institutional and social problems does *not* mean that we should abandon the effort to install new whistleblower protections in the private sector. It does suggest that we need to be sensitive to the multifaceted aspects of the task, and to recognize that care now could save much regret later over the "unanticipated consequences" of a new policy.

SELECT BIBLIOGRAPHY

Arvey, R. *Fairness in Selecting Employees.* Reading, Mass.: Addison-Wesley, 1979.

Ashford, N., and J. Katz. "Unsafe Working Conditions: Employee Rights Under the Labor Management Relations Act and the Occupational Safety and Health Act." *Notre Dame Lawyer* 52 (1977): 802–37.

Cohen, M., T. Nagel, and T. Scanlon, eds. *Equality and Preferential Treatment.* Princeton: Princeton University Press, 1977.

Dessler, G. *Personnel Management.* 2d ed. Reston, Va.: Reston Publishing, 1981.

Elliston, F. et al. *Whistleblowing and Whistleblowing Research.* 2 vols. New York: Praeger, 1985.

Ewing, D. *Freedom Inside the Organization.* New York: McGraw-Hill, 1977.

Ezorsky, G., ed. *Moral Rights in the Workplace.* Albany: SUNY Press, 1987.

Faden, R., and T. Beauchamp. "The Right to Know in the Workplace." *Canadian Journal of Philosophy,* 8 (1982), 177–210.

Fullinwider, R. K. *The Reverse Discrimination Controversy.* Totowa, N.J.: Rowman and Littlefield, 1980.

Gibson, M. *Workers' Rights.* Totowa, N.J.: Rowman and Allanheld, 1983.

Goldman, A. *Justice and Reverse Discrimination.* Princeton: Princeton University Press, 1979.

Peterson, J., and D. Farrell. *Whistleblowing.* Module Series in Applied Ethics. Dubuque: Kendall/Hunt, 1985.

Preston, S. "A Right Under OSHA to Refuse Unsafe Work or a Hobson's Choice of Safety or Job?" *University of Baltimore Law Review* 8 (1979): 519–50.

"Protecting At-Will Employees Against Wrongful Discharge: The Duty to Terminate Only in Good Faith." *Harvard Law Review* 93 (June 1980): 1816–44.

Smith, R. *Privacy: How to Protect What's Left of It.* Garden City: Anchor Press, 1978.

Werhane, P. *Persons, Rights, and Corporations.* Englewood Cliffs, N.J.: Prentice-Hall, 1985.

Westin, A. *Privacy and Freedom.* New York: Atheneum Press, 1967.

Westin, A., ed. *Whistle Blowing: Loyalty and Dissent in the Corporation.* New York: McGraw-Hill, 1981.

Westin, A., and S. Salisbury, eds. *Individual Rights in the Corporation.* New York: Random House, 1980.

5

ETHICS AND FINANCE

INTRODUCTION

Finance was at the forefront of ethical concern in the 1980s. The collapse and subsequent federal bailout of a big part of the savings and loan business, the insider trading scandals that shook Wall Street's most prestigious investment banking houses, the wave of hostile corporate takeovers that threatened to gobble up and dismember even America's largest corporations, and the number of firms that went bankrupt shortly after receiving an auditor's "clean opinion"— all convinced many observers that Wall Street was consumed by greed. We discuss three finance-related issues: insider trading, corporate takeovers, and accounting ethics.

Henry Manne argues that insider trading has utility and also is the best way to reward those who originate corporate information, hence insider trading should be permitted. Milton Snoeyenbos counters that both consequentialist and nonconsequentialist reasons point to the immorality of insider trading. One actual case and ten hypothetical scenarios are presented for discussion.

Robert Reich argues that leveraged buyouts harm productivity in four interrelated ways. Robert Almeder and Robert Carey respond that it has not been established that even hostile liquidating takeovers, i.e., those in which corporate raiders buy a firm and then sell off the parts for profit, are unethical. The case here is the RJR Nabisco leveraged buyout, by far the largest corporate buyout in U.S. history, and one of the most controversial.

Snoeyenbos and Ray Dillon discuss in some detail the nature of the accounting profession, with particular reference to those parts of the American Institute of Certified Public Accountants' Code of Professional Conduct that address the issues of auditor independence, objectivity, and integrity. They then examine how the accounting profession attempted to handle eight important ethical problems that came to the forefront in the 1980s.

INSIDER TRADING

Scenarios

Discuss the morality of the various acts in each of the following scenarios. Provide reasons for your position. Although there are legal holdings related to some of these scenarios, focus primarily on the morality of the situation.

(1) As CEO of Mover Corp., you are aware of confidential good news that should soon propel Mover's stock above its present value of $6 per share. You sell stock short through a stockbroker who you know will tell his clients you are selling short and that the stock will decline. Mover's stock slips to $4. You cover your short, making $2 per share. You then buy more stock at $4, release the news, and when Mover stock hits $15, you unload.

(2) You work for Mine Inc. as an inventor and have just discovered an additive that seems to increase gas mileage three miles per gallon. Although you are sure of the discovery, your boss wants to wait two months to announce it to be sure the results are triple-checked. You are sixty-five in a month, the mandatory retirement age. Mine Inc. has no retirement benefits and pays its inventors no bonuses. You take out a home-equity loan, add it to your entire life savings, and buy $250,000 of Mine stock, tripling your investment when the news is announced.

(3) You and your golfing partner, both executives at Engulf Inc., are discussing Engulf's secret plan to acquire Flaccid Inc. Your caddy overhears your discussion and purchases Flaccid stock. Next week Engulf announces its bid and Flaccid stock doubles, whereupon the caddy sells.

(4) You are an upper-level manager with Torpor Inc. and you know Torpor will announce a disappointing earnings report in a week. You know the present law prohibits you from selling before the news, but you tell your best friend, who calls his stockbroker with the news. Your friend sells Torpor stock short

on his broker's advice, and the broker calls all his clients who hold Torpor and advises them to dump Torpor stock.

(5) You are having a beer with Ken Moore, attorney for Art Grab, a corporate raider, when Moore leans over and confides: "Grab is going to initiate purchases of Zilch Inc. next week. You immediately purchase 10,000 shares of Zilch and cash out in two weeks when the price doubles on public news of the takeover attempt.

(6) Upper Inc. is about to report fantastic earnings. You go to Fax Inc. to fax Upper's earnings to its printer, who will print the quarterly report. The fax operator sees the results and immediately places an order for Upper stock. The fax receiver at the printer also notices the results and buys Upper stock.

(7) You write the column "Wall Street Beat" for *Barrens,* the top-ranked financial daily. You know your influence is such that a positive or negative discussion of a stock will cause it to rise or fall 6 percent on average. All of your information comes from your analyses; none comes from insiders of the firms you discuss. When you have particularly strong comments on a stock, you trade in the stock before your column appears. You pass your information on to your friends, who also trade on it.

(8) You are working in the mergers and acquisitions department of Kidunot & Co. on a takeover concerning two companies, the details of which are confidential. You sell the information to Evan Booski, a well-known arbitrager, who buys stock in the takeover target, makes $3 million from the transaction, and gives you $400,000 for the information.

(9) You work for Golddigger & Co., which has a mergers and acquisitions (M & A) department that advises clients on financing, mergers, and takeovers, and an arbitrage department that trades in the stock of likely takeover targets. You are aware that the law requires there be no leakage of information between the two departments within a firm. You arrange through a counterpart at Kidunot & Co. to trade information between Kidunot's arbitrage and Golddigger's M & A departments, and between Kidunot's M & A and Golddigger's arbitrage departments. By trading on such information Kidunot and Golddigger each gain $30 million per year. You also trade in your own private account on the information passed to Golddigger from Kidunot.

(10) As an investment analyst knowledgeable about the banking industry, you have been approached by two bank officials who want you to expose serious wrongdoing at their bank, which will soon bring about a total collapse of the bank's stock. They do not wish to go public themselves, for fear of never working in the industry again. You investigate further and write a critical research report but do not release it until you have called all your clients who own the bank's stock and tell them to sell.

Waste Management Case Reflects Murkiness of Insider-Trading Laws

A group of top corporate executives buys thousands of shares of stock in a potential takeover candidate, then cashes in for big profits after the bid is made.

Insider trading or canny investing?

It's the kind of question most companies would prefer not to discuss. But last week Waste Management Inc. outlined details of just such a situation. A special committee of three outside Waste Management directors, faced with a stockholder lawsuit in Delaware chancery court alleging insider trading, investigated 19 purchases of ChemLawn Corp. stock by Dean L. Buntrock, Waste Management's chairman and chief executive, his family, and three other company executives. In all, the Waste Management executives bought 45,000 ChemLawn shares over two years, while intermittently discussing acquiring ChemLawn.

Ultimately, in February 1987, Waste Management bid for—and lost— the Columbus, Ohio, lawn-care concern. But the executives came out winners; they sold their ChemLawn holdings during the next two months for a combined profit of close to $1 million.

The special committee's verdict: The executives were simply sharp investors. In its report, filed in the Delaware chancery court, the committee says it based its decision on a legal reading of one of the murkiest areas of securi-

Bill Richards and Jeff Bailey, *Wall Street Journal,* Tuesday, February 9, 1988, p. 41. Reprinted by permission of *The Wall Street Journal,* © 1988 Dow Jones & Company, Inc. All Rights Reserved Worldwide.

ties law: When do companies' internal deliberations on a prospective tender reach a point where they can influence the market?

(*The Wall Street Journal* last year filed a motion in an unrelated case seeking some of the documents referred to in the special committee's report.)

Federal securities law says an insider-trading violation occurs once "any person has taken a substantial step or steps to commence, or has commenced, a tender offer," according to rule 14e-3 of the U.S. Securities Exchange Act. But the law doesn't spell out clearly what those "steps" could be, allowing for sharply different opinions on the matter.

"You look for the bright line beyond which you should not trade," says Wallace Timmeny, a former deputy director of the Securities and Exchange Commission's enforcement division who was hired by Waste Management's special committee to lead the investigation of the insider trading allegations. Mr. Timmeny, now in private practice in Washington, is frequently hired by corporate boards in such situations. That "bright line," he says, is a company's formal consensus to go after an acquisition. Mr. Timmeny says that individual traders within a company may reach that line before the company itself. But Waste Management's executives, he says, never crossed it.

Others say the line isn't quite so clear. David A. Sirignano, who heads the Securities and Exchange Commission's office of tender offers, says there are two camps: Those who sanction inside corporate stock deals right up to the board's decision to bid, and those who say the line could come much earlier than a formal determination to proceed with the offer.

"Our position is the latter," Mr. Sirignano says.

"This is a fuzzy area," adds Donald C. Langevoort, a securities-law expert and visiting professor at Harvard Law School. "But if I were a juror there are a lot of things I would consider significant before the price and structure of a deal were firmed up."

Some of the issues may be clarified when the Supreme Court rules in a pending stockholder case against Basic Inc., a unit of Stamford, Conn.-based Combustion Engineering Inc. Shareholders accused Basic in 1979 of falsely denying that merger talks were under way between the two companies—nearly a year after they began. The case touches on the question of when preliminary negotiations become material, a point that the SEC's Mr. Sirignano calls "an important issue" in clarifying insider-trading rules.

The SEC won't say whether it is investigating Waste Management's bid for ChemLawn. But the following chronology shows the difficulty of defining just what constitutes insider trading. Taken from the special committee's report, it gives a behind-the-scenes look at executives alternately tending to their employer's finances—and their own:

1985

March 13: Jerry E. Dempsey, Waste Management's vice chairman, completes a broad study on potential acquisition candidates, including ChemLawn, as part of a possible diversification plan. Mr. Buntrock says he reviewed it. A presentation is made to the board.

May 8: Mr. Buntrock buys 100 shares of ChemLawn for his personal account "to receive shareholder reports." On this day, he also buys 100 shares of 28 different companies for the same purpose, and larger stakes in 15 other companies.

1986

January 29: Mr. Buntrock sends to James E. Koenig, assistant to Waste Management's chief financial officer, Value Line and Standard & Poor's reports on ChemLawn and asks for his comment. Mr. Koenig responds that ChemLawn looks like "a good short-term play." Mr. Buntrock later replies that Waste Management, "as a matter of policy did not purchase securities to speculate." Mr. Buntrock makes a note to himself to tell his wife, Rosemarie Buntrock, to buy some ChemLawn stock.

January 31: Mr. Buntrock purchases 900 ChemLawn shares. Mrs. Buntrock, who—both she and her husband acknowledge—buys stocks on her husband's orders, acquires 2,000 ChemLawn shares. Mr. Koenig buys 400 ChemLawn shares.

July 8: Mrs. Buntrock buys 2,000 ChemLawn shares.

July 9-11: Waste Management holds its annual strategic planning meeting at the Buntrocks' summer home in Wisconsin, beginning with cocktails and dinner the evening of July 9. "Acquistions outside the solid-waste industry are not (repeat NOT) discussed at the . . . meeting," according to the committee's report. And none of those present "could recall any discussions—formal or informal—regarding ChemLawn."

On July 9 Mrs. Buntrock buys 2,000 ChemLawn shares. Peter Huizenga, a Waste Management vice president, also buys 2,000 ChemLawn shares. He says he made the purchase after Mrs. Buntrock, who "maintains an office at the company's headquarters adjacent to Mr. Huizenga's," came into his office and mentioned that she was considering buying ChemLawn stock. (Mrs. Buntrock denies this.)

On July 10, Mrs. Buntrock buys 2,000 ChemLawn shares.

July 15-16: Mrs. Buntrock buys 1,000 ChemLawn shares. Two Buntrock family trusts buy a combined 4,000 shares of ChemLawn. Mr. Huizenga buys 2,000 ChemLawn shares.

September 11: Mrs. Buntrock buys 10,000 ChemLawn shares.

September 12: Two Buntrock family trusts buy a combined 6,000 shares. Mr. Buntrock says he can't recall why shares were bought in this month, except that the trusts had an excess of cash around that time. Sometime during September, Mr. Buntrock and Gerald E. Seegers, president of the company's Waste Management Partners Inc. subsidiary, discuss another acquisition effort and the potential acquisition of ChemLawn comes up in their discussion.

October 6: Perry Lewis, an investment banker with Morgan, Lewis, Githens

& Ahn in New York, sends Mr. Buntrock a Smith Barney research bulletin on ChemLawn. The report also goes to Mr. Dempsey, Waste Management's vice chairman. Mr. Buntrock doesn't recall any prior talks with Mr. Lewis that "would have prompted" the letter, though he says "it is possible" the two might have previously discussed ChemLawn. Mr. Lewis says he had discussed ChemLawn with Mr. Buntrock before—"as one of the 25 or 30 companies (Waste Management) was interested in monitoring." Mr. Lewis says he had previously offered to introduce Mr. Buntrock to ChemLawn mangement but says ChemLawn was "back-burnered" because its price was "astronomical."

October 15: Mr. Buntrock buys 3,000 ChemLawn shares, raising his family's stake to 33,000 shares. He doesn't recall why he made the purchase, though he says it "could have been prompted by Mr. Lewis's letter." However, Mrs. Buntrock says the purchase could have been made by her on a weeks-old instruction from her husband. She often doesn't immediately buy stock, she says, "because the stock market is one of her lowest priorities."

October 16: Mr. Dempsey buys 1,000 ChemLawn shares. He and Mr. Buntrock say they didn't discuss Mr. Lewis's letter with each other or anyone else.

October 20: Phillip B. Rooney, Waste Management's president, sends Mr. Buntrock a memo saying: "Should we introduce the ChemLawn idea at the October 31 board meeting? We shouldn't wait too long before moving forward if we want to buy the company." Mr. Rooney says "the ChemLawn idea" and buying "the company" were intended to be "generic references to the lawn-care industry"—much like saying Coke for soft drinks, Kleenex for tissue, and Xerox for copying.

(The Waste Management special committee, in its conclusions, says the memo, "taken alone, and read literally, is problematic. It is clear, moreover, that ChemLawn and its trading discount had come to the attention of individuals within senior management by October 1986, and that such individuals considered ChemLawn specifically to be a possible acquisition candidate if (Waste Management) ever decided to expand into the lawn-care industry." The report also states that: "Other interviewees told the committee that they personally considered ChemLawn to be a specific acquisition candidate if for no other reason than that it was a leader in the lawn-care industry.")

October 27: Mr. Dempsey buys 1,000 ChemLawn shares. Agendas for the October 31 board meeting are distributed. ChemLawn appears on the agenda under the heading "pending acquisitions," along with five other companies.

October 31: Waste Management's board meets. ChemLawn is discussed only briefly, and is ruled out as a takeover target by Mr. Buntrock. Officials at the company say ChemLawn didn't belong on the agenda under "pending acquisitions" in the first place.

(Mr. Huizenga prepared the agenda and says it was his idea to add Chem-Lawn. He says Mr. Buntrock asked him before the meeting why ChemLawn was listed under "pending acquisitions." Mr. Huizenga replied that the company's efforts to get into residential services could lead it toward lawn care. "While clearly not endorsing the idea, Mr. Buntrock did not tell Mr. Huizenga to delete ChemLawn from the agenda," according to the committee's report. Mr. Buntrock recalls he "was upset with Mr. Huizenga for adding ChemLawn to the agenda" because it might confuse discussion of another company Waste Management wanted to buy. Minutes from the October 31 board meeting weren't prepared until late December.)

November 14: Mr. Buntrock buys 2,000 ChemLawn shares, his last purchase, bringing his family's stake to 35,000.

November 17: Waste Management's outside law firm sends recent Chem-Lawn financial disclosure filings to Mr. Seegers, president of Waste Management Partners Inc. He says he asked for these documents "looking ahead, hoping to anticipate a request from Mr. Buntrock to get information on ChemLawn and then being able to 'impress the boss' by having 'a leg up.' "

December: Sometime before Christmas, Mr. Lewis, the Morgan Lewis investment banker, talks with Mr. Buntrock about "making a preliminary approach to ChemLawn." Mr. Buntrock instructs Mr. Lewis to make "contact on an anonymous basis." Mr. Buntrock wanted a meeting on a "get-to-know" basis, and didn't want to generate speculation about a takeover, according to the special committee's report. (The report offers no explanation for Mr. Buntrock's abrupt change of attitude toward ChemLawn as a potential acquisition target.)

On December 19, Mr. Huizenga buys 2,000 ChemLawn shares.

In late December, minutes from the October 31 board meeting are prepared by Mr. Huizenga. ChemLawn was "not of interest and was not discussed," the minutes say.

1987

January: ChemLawn's investment banker, replying to Mr. Lewis's approach, says ChemLawn isn't "interested in talking to any anonymous parties." Mr. Buntrock authorizes Mr. Lewis to make another approach, this time identifying Waste Management.

At the January 12 board meeting, ChemLawn isn't mentioned.

January 22: Merrill Lynch investment bankers meet with company officials in New York to pitch a leveraged buyout of ChemLawn.

February 5: Mr. Dempsey buys 2,000 ChemLawn shares.

February 9: Mr. Buntrock is annoyed that Merrill Lynch is pressuring him to make an acquisition. He thinks Merrill Lynch plans to put Chem-Lawn "into play" regardless of what he does. "Mr. Buntrock left (Waste Management chief financial officer Daniel F.) Flynn's office without ever sitting down," the report says.

February 12: Messrs. Buntrock, Flynn, and Rooney meet, and Mr. Flynn now strongly endorses a Waste Management takeover of ChemLawn. Mr. Koenig is ordered to begin preparing data on a ChemLawn acquisition.

February 19: At a meeting with Merrill Lynch and outside lawyers, Waste Management decides to launch a tender offer for ChemLawn.

February 20: Mr. Lewis of Morgan Lewis tells Mr. Buntrock that ChemLawn officials won't meet with Waste Management. "These people will never be friendly," Mr. Buntrock says, adding he might as well make a hostile offer.

February 25: Waste Management's board authorizes a $27-a-share tender offer for ChemLawn at a special meeting. ChemLawn rejects the bid and ultimately is acquired by EcoLab Inc. of St. Paul, Minn., for $36.50 a share.

March 26 & 27; April 24 & 27: Mr. and Mrs. Buntrock, the Buntrock family trusts, Peter Huizenga and Mr. Dempsey sell their ChemLawn stock at $36.25-to-$36.50 a share, realizing a combined profit of about $1 million.

Henry G. Manne

In Defense of Insider Trading

In April 1965, when the Securities and Exchange Commission announced its action against executives of the Texas Gulf Sulphur Company for alleged violations of rules against insider trading, there was an outcry of public indignation against the defendants. It was as though men who were highly respected members of the community had suddenly been found out in heinous crime.

But this is only one more manifestation of a long and persistent trend. Leading academic figures, lawyers, businessmen, and spokesmen for the SEC, with almost boring uniformity, have castigated insider trading as being costly to shareholders and giving unfair and undeserved gains to insiders. The tone of most discussions on this subject suggests that there is no doubt whatever: insider trading is a sin, and the war against it is a holy one.

But, as in most holy wars, self-righteousness and hypocrisy may be the true order of the day. In the entire literature on insider trading there does not exist one careful analysis of the subject. Lawyers have been having a field day arguing about the meaning of words or the reach of the last case or any of a thousand technical and legal issues. Unfortunately, however, most lawyers do not have the skills to develop a careful economic analysis of the subject, and economists have remained essentially moralistic and question-begging. Logic has been totally lost to emotion.

It is very likely, however, that unless businessmen, commentators, and the courts wake up, far more than logic will be lost. For the current attack on

An excerpt from "In Defense of Insider Trading" by Henry G. Manne, 44, no. 6 (November-December 1966): 113-22. Copyright © 1966 by the President and Fellows of Harvard College. All rights reserved. Reprinted by permission of *Harvard Business Review*.

insider trading may prove to be a fundamental attack on free capital markets and entrepreneurial capitalism. It would be a shame to lose the battle by default.

This article constitutes at least a starting point for logical analysis of the subject. In particular, I shall argue that insider trading is the best, if not the only, method of adequately compensating corporate innovators, and I shall attempt to define and to answer objections to the practice of insider trading.

GAIN AND LOSS

What, if any, advantages would flow to participants in the stock market if insider trading were effectively stopped? Here we come to one of the most astounding facts in this whole astounding business: the only stock market participants who are likely to benefit from a rule preventing insider trading are the short-term speculators and traders, not the long-term investors who are regularly stated to be the objects of the SEC's solicitude.

The initial error of most commentators is the assumption that the persons who sold to insiders before disclosure of important news would not have sold at all if the insiders were not in the market. Obviously this is absurd; the average seller has no way in the world of knowing the identity of his buyer. One of the great virtues of an organized securities market is its automaticity, which results in anonymity of traders. Publicly traded companies are quite different in this respect from small, closely held corporations, and the rules governing them should also be different.

If insiders are in the market, however, they represent additional buying power over what would prevail without them. So there must be some sellers in the market who can be said to sell only because of the insider's buying. But this is only the beginning of analysis. We need to know the identity of these additional sellers, and also we want to see if there is any benefit from the insider's trading activities that may counteract any harmful effects of this additional purchasing power.

INVESTORS VERSUS TRADERS

To discover the identity of sellers who would not trade but for the insider's activities, we must first distinguish two types of shareholders—investors and traders. This distinction has certainly been overworked for many purposes, but it is of considerable value in the present analysis:

- Investors, the long-term shareholders, tend to select stocks based on so-called "fundamental" factors, such as earning potential, dividend history, growth prospects, or the reputation of management, to mention just a few. And they select stocks suitable for their own particular investment needs. They tend to sell either because their estimate of the fundamental factors proved wrong or because of some change in their personal circumstances or needs. They almost never buy or sell because of short-swing fluctuations in the price of a security.

Short-swing traders, whether we call them "speculators" or not, may also trade on so-called "fundamental" factors. But many of them, unlike any of the true investors, also buy or sell simply because of recent changes in the price of a security. That is, they assume their ability to predict future price changes from previous changes in price and volume—so-called "technical" factors. And very many of these traders simply are gambling.

This is not the place to enter the debate on whether technical strategies can ever be used successfully, though a growing academic literature is casting grave doubts on the validity of technical factors as determinants of stock price movements. The importance of this trading for our purposes is that any price change is taken as a signal by the "technicians" in the market, or by the gamblers, to buy or sell. Consequently, as insiders cause a price rise by adding their buying power to the market, the selling necessary to complete the additional transactions will ordinarily be supplied by short-term traders. It cannot and should not be denied that the stock market provides the greatest competition for Las Vegas and the racetracks we have. This is not intended as criticism. But it is seriously disturbing to find the SEC pressing hard for a rule designed either to aid this group or to encourage their gambling proclivities.

In aggregate, the gamblers in a perfectly free stock market, with no inflation, are bound to lose money. Just as the house's cut in the gambling casino guarantees the long-term gambler a loss, so stockbrokerage commissions on each transaction must injure the steady stock trader who has no valid information. Furthermore, as we noticed previously, he often supplies the stock on which insiders profit. Thus he is matching wits with an expert in a game which does not pay off for amateurs. Perhaps the analogy to gambling against someone with loaded dice or marked cards is most apt.

HOW MUCH HARM?

Though statistically this is probably not significant, the long-term investor may turn out to be the individual who in fact sells to the insider. But since he is normally selling for reasons unrelated to the insider's trading, and would be selling in any event, he should be indifferent to the identity of his buyer. Actually, he may benefit from the insider's buying on good news, as the average price received may be higher with than without insider trading. For example:

Let us assume that a stock is selling at $50, with undisclosed good news which will *ultimately* cause the stock to sell for $60, and that no factors other than the good news will affect the price.

Suppose, further, that with insider trading the price of the shares rises *gradually* to $60. The average price at which shares sell during this period is somewhere in the neighborhood of $55 (more or less depending on the shape of the time-price curve). At $60, anyone who has held his shares will have received the full benefit of the new information whether it is disclosed to him or not. This advantage to the ultimate holder remains even if we effectively prevent insider trading.

Without insider trading, however, the position of those who sell during the time required for the price to rise from $50 to $60 is radically altered. No longer do they receive an average price of $55. Assuming that the ultimate disclosure is made at the same time under either rule, they receive only $50 for their shares without insider trading. In short, they get less than they would with insider trading.

It may be argued that this overstates the direct advantages from insider trading. For, in fact, during the same relevant time period investors will be buying as well as selling, and—to take the same example—with insider trading they might buy at an average price of $55, while without it they would buy at an average price of $50. If the number of buyers among investors is the same as the number of sellers, then we are simply back where we started; the gains and losses cancel out (though not necessarily for the same individuals). It may be true, however, that a gradual price increase will cause fewer investment decisions to buy relative to decisions to sell than would be the case with an abrupt price change. (The difference, of course, is accounted for by other traders.) On balance, therefore, insider trading may still benefit investors.

Even if there is no appreciable net direct advantage or disadvantage to investors as a group from insider trading, it is likely that price fluctuations will not be so sharp, part of the excitement which attracts the gambler may be lost, and the occasionally valid "hot tip" will not pay off as much. Are not these all advantages, rather than disadvantages?

WARY INSIDERS

When it is further realized how rare significant insider trading must be, one wonders even more what all the shouting has been about. If insider trading does occur, insiders as a group trade in the stock market with greater certainty and success than do those not using fresh, reliable information. Accordingly, successful inside traders may tend to gamble in the stock market much less than all other traders, since they will more often have "sure things." This conservatism suggests that they have several likely attitudes toward their trading:

- The insider tends not to trade on information unless it will be very significant quantitatively. It must be of sufficient importance that the conservative trader, recognizing the natural uncertainties of the marketplace, will still trade.

- He must have some assurance that the information is not already or shortly to be in the hands of many other individuals; for if it is, he cannot expect to realize the full potential of his data.

- He will probably move very quickly to take his proift and get out of the market, since the longer he stays in, the more subject he will be to vagaries of the market which he can neither control nor know about in advance. Of course, the tax benefits for gains on assets held for six months influence him in the other direction, but an insider still has considerable incentive to buy and sell quickly.

Each of these phenomena reflects a recognition that the market is always full of uncertainties. A huge copper ore find may be followed closely by a collapse of world copper prices, and an important earnings increase may coincide with announcement of a tax hike. Thus even the most conservative insider can only deal in probabilities; and if he knows that he will regularly be privy to information, he will probably tend to trade only on that with the highest probability of allowing a gain.

Similarly, the longer stock is held, the greater becomes the risk that other factors will develop and counteract his existing paper profits. Again conservatism will dictate speed, not greed. Only rarely will all the necessary conditions for effective, regular insider trading be met. Great developments, measured in stock price impact, do not happen very often in any company. And news of these occurrences is not always the exclusive property of a few insiders. Therefore really significant trading by insiders is probably not a very common occurrence.

STIMULUS TO INNOVATION

If this is all that could be said for or against insider trading, the matter would not be a very interesting one. But there is another and far more crucial facet to the issue, one which has not been noted in the existing literature. Basically, the argument is that profits from insider trading constitute the only effective compensation scheme for entrepreneurial services in large corporations.

Critical Distinction

I should begin this discussion with some explanation of what is meant by the "entrepreneurial function." The term is used here in a technical, economic sense, and the function differs in critical aspects from that performed by managers:

Entrepreneur—An Innovator. Fundamentally the entrepreneur is a man who finds a new product or a new way to make or sell an old one. He may reorganize corporate administration, or he may be responsible for the merger of two companies. He may be a corporate promoter, or he may perform the job of selecting and guiding the managers. In short, he is the individual responsible for having or taking a new idea and causing it to be put into effect. A critical part of this definition is the "new idea," but there is no pay-off unless the idea is put into effect successfully.

Since the value of an entrepreneur's contribution cannot be known until it has been made, there is rarely any way of appraising his services in advance. This is undoubtedly why early economists, including Adam Smith, did not see the entrepreneurial function as being distinct from the capitalist's function, for in the eighteenth century one was generally required to risk his own money to prove the value of his innovation. The return for successful innovation looks, superficially at least, like the return to the owner of capital.

Today, however, a sizable portion of economic literature, introduced principally by the late Joseph A. Schumpeter of Harvard University, has been built on the distinction between the entrepreneur and the capitalist, though it has not yet had a great impact on popular thinking.

Manager—A Technician. The management function is, in the pure sense, simply to administer a business along lines already determined. Though it may be extraordinarily complex and highly paid, the manager's job is basically that of a technician. As soon as he begins to reorganize the existing arrangement, then and only then is the executive performing an innovational or entrepreneurial activity, rather than a management function. Again the distinction between functions remains even though the same individual performs both. As Schumpeter commented, it is "just as rare for anyone always to remain an entrepreneur through the decades of his active life as it is for a businessman never to have a moment in which he is an entrepreneur, to however modest a degree."[1]

Reward for Performance

In return for performing its function, management receives its compensation, generally termed by economists the "wage." This wage is simply the market price for managerial skills. No one knowingly pays more or takes less. Similarly, the capitalist receives "interest," which, whatever the legal form might be called, is the economic return to him. It may be relatively certain, as in the case of bonds, or it may be very indefinite, as with speculative securities; but its economic nature remains the same. Although the degrees of risk may vary greatly, interest is the price that has to be paid for the use of money over time.

But in the sense that wages and interest are the market return for capital and management, there is no such thing as a market price for entrepreneurial skills. In fact, almost by definition, it is impossible to value entrepreneurial activities *before they have paid off in some other form.* Economic theorists do, however, have a word for the entrepreneurial return; it is termed "profit," although that particular usage of the word has not received popular acceptance. But, aside from having a word for it, we have little knowledge about the particular form that this "profit" may take, or even whether it can redound to the benefit of entrepreneurs in large corporations.

Here it is important to turn once more to Schumpeter. Perhaps his greatest contribution to modern economic theory was the concept of dynamic competition. Schumpeter pointed out that where enterprise is allowed a free rein, no one can afford to stand still. His famous "perennial gale of creative destruction" is the process by which the most significant competition occurs. This is the competition created by the true entrepreneur, and it is a fierce thing.

Schumpeter thought that price competition, so loved by antitrusters, was effete indeed compared to the competitive effects of new products, new markets, and new ways of doing things. On this point he may well have been right. Price competition could probably be administered by pure managers, corporate bureaucrats, or today even by carefully programmed computers. But that kind of activity could never withstand the onslaught of the real entrepreneur.

Survival of Capitalism

For all his brilliance in developing the theory of entrepreneurship and dynamic competition, Schumpeter made a serious and well-known error concerning the American corporate system. This error occurred in his famous *Capitalism, Socialism and Democracy,* published in 1942.[2] Briefly, it was that the system of corporate capitalism simply could not survive. He believed that large corporations would become completely bureaucratized and management-oriented. He felt that innovation had been routinized, and the "romance of earlier commercial adventure" no longer characterized business leaders' activities. This routinization of innovations would first destroy the capitalist entrepreneurs as a class, and eventually capitalism would disappear for lack of an effective champion. "The true pacemakers of socialism," he said, "were not intellectuals or agitators who preached it but the Vanderbilts, Carnegies, and Rockefellers."

It requires no argument to realize how wrong Schumpeter was in this prediction. For all their organization and bureaucratization, American corporations seem as dynamic, innovative, and entrepreneurial today as they have ever been. What, then, could explain such a gross misconception by one of the leading economic scholars of the century? The answer to this question seems to have eluded theoreticians up to now.

Closer examination of Schumpeter's argument may explain his error. Schumpeter stated that any form of compensation for corporate executives other than salaries and bonuses was either "illegal or semi-illegal." Yet he realized that salary and bonuses were appropriate forms of compensation only for the pure management function. Entrepreneurs would require something much grander, though less certain. And since Schumpeter felt this could not be made available to them in the large corporation, he assumed that they would disappear from the large corporate scene.

But he did not see the possibility of using insider information as an appropriate form of compensation for entrepreneurs in large corporations.

One cannot argue with Schumpeter's theory of what would happen to large corporations if in fact no entrepreneurs within them could receive an appropriate return. Government agencies and heavily regulated or protected industries are probably sufficient proof of the validity of this idea. On this basis the prediction for which Schumpeter has been frequently criticized could be closer to the mark than his critics have realized—that is, if misguided proposals to abolish our most effective system for rewarding entrepreneurs in large corporations (insider trading in one form or another) are adopted.

Compensation Not Enough

To provide an effective incentive, entrepreneurial compensation has to be available when the benefits are realized by the corporation, and it must vary with the value of the contribution. Since neither of these eventualities can ordinarily be predicted in advance, most existing compensation plans are inadequate for the task. Obviously, salary is inappropriate. The amount of salary has to be decided on in advance, it does not allow for distinguishing the manager who only manages from one who also innovates, and it is not flexible enough to reward particular contributions.

At first glance the bonus does seem to answer most of these objections. However, most bonuses today are formulated in advance and depend on total profits rather than individual contributions. Bonus plans are incentive devices, but they probably tend to generate managerial improvements, such as small cost-cutting, rather than radical innovations. The bonus plan, as opposed to the special bonus, will not serve the entrepreneur's purpose.

The special bonus can, of course, be used to reward great innovations, though there are legal restrictions if authorization is not established in advance. But the main drawback is that the true value of a particular contribution, in the form of higher profits, may not be known for many years. So there frequently are gross disparities in judgment between the bonus committee and the executive as to the latter's true worth. This misjudgment may become even more serious if the innovation has caused the price of the stock to rise but has not yet affected profits, though the stock price rise is precisely what the entrepreneur should be rewarded for.

In addition, the entrepreneurial type who is motivated by the possibility of "getting rich quick" probably does not like the idea of negotiating his reward after his contribution has been made. This distinction is like that between a patent system and a system of bonuses or government awards for inventions. Few will be found to argue that the latter system encourages as much invention as the former.

Stock options also add some incentive to efficiency for managers, but it is doubtful that they can serve the needs of the entrepreneur for massive reward for great innovations. The difficulty should be obvious. The number of shares to be optioned to various executives normally has to be determined in advance of any entrepreneurial innovation. If the options are granted after the innovation, they are the same as the special bonus, except that payment is made in the form of a free call on corporate stock rather than in the form of cash. Stock options undoubtedly add greatly to incentive, but they may still promise too little to entrepreneurial types with ambition, enthusiasm, and a large measure of self-confidence.

Incentives from Trading

On the other hand, free trading by insiders in a company's securities meets the objections mentioned for other compensation schemes and has special advantages of its own. Perhaps this can best be seen by comparing systems of compensation for patentable and nonpatentable innovations.

Basically the patent system is designed to allow inventors to receive an appropriate reward for successful innovations by preventing others from copying and participating in profits which we might say were not earned by them. The granting of a temporary monopoly to the patentee assures two goals: (1) it excludes the would-be interloper; (2) it provides the patentee with a substantial reward for his idea, although that reward will vary with the economic importance of the invention.

The patent system seems to work reasonably well, but only for patentable ideas. How can we guarantee a similar reward to inventors of nonpatentable ideas? In this area our legal system has been rather weak and ineffective; it has developed few really successful techniques for the protection of such ideas. Most businessmen recognize that secrecy and speed of marketing are the two principal devices for realizing substantial profits for their companies from nonpatentable innovations—secrecy to keep competitors away and speed because they cannot be kept away for long. But nothing in this scheme provides any protection or reward for the individual who has an important, nonpatentable idea which he personally is in no position to exploit.

For the man who has not founded his own business to exploit his idea —historically the traditional course for an entrepreneur—trading in the stock market on inside information provides a reward system, and is the only effective device available for the entrepreneur who is employed by a large corporation.

Insider trading allows any individual who works for a publicly traded corporation to play the entrepreneurial role, a very important advantage. Individuals can, in effect, sell their own ideas without the necessity of having large amounts of capital available. The increase in stock price, though not perfect, will provide as accurate a gauge of the value of the innovation as can be found, and it will leave little room for argument about an individual's worth.

Large corporations will be able to compete more effectively for entrepreneurial talent with closely owned companies, since they can now hold out the promise of very great rewards for the successful innovator. The image of corporate executives as gray bureaucrats can and should be erased. Large corporations can furnish as much romance, excitement, and opportunity for rapid economic and social advancement as any other avenues pursued today. But if corporations get hung up on foolish moralizing, such as characterizes most discussions of insider trading, they cannot hope to compete successfully or to survive the subtle attacks of government agencies.

If there really is an economic service or function that can be termed entrepreneurship, then we must have some way of compensating it. The cases are legion of new corporate managers bringing in fresh, imaginative, but often untested ideas. If these individuals were to be limited to the same compensation as their dull, unimaginative, and overly conservative predecessors, what incentive would they have to innovate? Their salaries, bonuses, and pensions are usually secure, and few large companies face imminent bankruptcy. Their stock options and bonus plans will give some motivation to improve things, but not to take very great personal risks. For the true entrepreneur, the possibility of great riches will elicit more risk-taking activities and enterprise than will the possibility of smaller though more certain gain.

It might also be added that this promise attracts a different type of personality as well, one with which successful American businessmen have traditionally been proud to identify—the self-made, rags-to-riches, "Horatio Alger" hero. There is still room for such characters in the large modern corporation.

NOTES

1. Joseph Alois Schumpeter, *The Theory of Economic Development,* translated by Redvers Opic (Cambridge, Harvard University Press, 1934), p. 78.
2. New York, Harper & Brothers.

Milton Snoeyenbos

Insider Trading: Immoral

In 1959 a Texas Gulf Sulfur geologist in a helicopter equipped with magnetic detection gear discovered a possibly significant ore body near Timmins, Ontario. By 1963, TGS geologists had mapped out a geological anomaly that suggested an extensive area of mineralization. The company's first drill core was remarkably rich in zinc and copper, which were located near the earth's surface, indicating that the ore was mineable by the relatively inexpensive open-pit method.

When drilling began in late 1963, TGS stock sold for $17 a share. After the discovery, directors, officers, and employees began buying TGS stock and call options. Many of these purchases were by individuals who had never before bought TGS stock or calls. Some top managers were given stock options by TGS. At this time TGS also increased its drilling program and its efforts to secure mineral rights to property near the Timmins strike.

From the first drilling date in November 1963 to April 1964, TGS stock moved from $17 to $29. Rumors surfaced about the TGS strike. On April 12, 1964, TGS issued a press release which said that the company wanted to protect would-be buyers of its shares from what it regarded as exaggerated rumors, and it claimed that the Timmins drilling afforded only preliminary indications, and that more drilling was necessary for proper evaluation of the prospect. The announcement said: "The drilling to date has not been conclusive, but the statements made by many outside quarters are unreliable." The rumors were labeled "premature and possibly misleading" and were said to have originated with speculators unconnected with TGS. Several stock analysts were critical of TGS's press release. On April 16, 1964, TGS announced "a major ore discovery" of zinc, copper, and silver. TGS subsequently explained

310

that as of April 12 it only had one drill core available, but by April 16 it had seven cores that indicated the ore body's extent.

Shortly after the April 16, 1964 announcement, TGS stock moved to $37. It subsequently reached a high of $71 during early 1965. Along the way TGS insiders took profits on their earlier purchases. Timmins proved to be one of the Western Hemisphere's great copper and zinc finds.

Consider another actual case. J. Cheever Cowdin, a registered representative with Cady-Roberts, was also a Curtis-Wright director. Curtis was developing a new engine, which led to an increase in its stock price. During the increase, Robert Gintel, a friend of Cowdin and a partner at Cady-Roberts, bought Curtis stock for thirty of his customers, one of whom was his wife. The Board of Directors of Curtis-Wright then decided to cut its dividend. In the two days prior to the announcement of the dividend cut, Gintel sold half of the Curtis-Wright holdings in his accounts. During a break in the meeting in which the board cut Curtis' dividend, Cowdin telephoned Gintel with the news. Gintel then sold out his accounts, and in several accounts he sold short substantial blocks of Curtis's shares. When news of the dividend cut was subsequently made public, Curtis's stock plunged and Gintel covered his short positions, benefiting his customers.

Now something seems wrong in these cases. Remarkably, however, some economists and financiers believe the actions in both cases are moral.[1] They argue that such trading makes markets more efficient by helping to move stock prices in the "correct" direction, i.e., to the level the stock would be at if the information were known. They also argue that nobody is harmed by insider trading. Finally, they argue that insider trading is the best way to reward employees for benefiting the firm. So, although insider trading today is illegal, and although the insiders' actions in the Texas Gulf Sulfur and Cady-Roberts cases were held illegal,[2] these writers urge that we drop the prohibition of insider trading. In this essay I offer three reasons why insider trading is unethical. How such arguments connect with the issue of whether we should continue the legal ban on insider trading I leave to legal scholars.

FAIRNESS

Section 10b-5 of the 1934 Securities Exchange Act makes it illegal to defraud or deceive a person in connection with the purchase or sale of a security. Although 10b-5 is nonspecific, courts interpret it as barring corporate insiders possessing material, nonpublic, confidential information from trading in securities of their firms. Although the notion of an "insider" is not clearly specified, it certainly includes those who have a confidential relationship in the conduct of the business. The rule is called the "disclose or abstain" rule, for the insider generally has a choice between trading after disclosing the confidential information or refraining from trading until the information becomes public.

One legal basis of the "disclose or abstain" rule is found in the case involving

Texas Gulf Sulfur. Commenting on the SEC Act and Rule 10b-5, the Supreme Court said:

> By that Act Congress proposed to prevent inequitable and unfair practices and to insure fairness in securities transactions. . . . The Rule is based in policy on the justifiable expectation of the securities marketplace that all investors trading on impersonal exchanges have relatively equal access to material information.

Now there is something correct about the equal access idea, but we must interpret it carefully. Those who favor the permissibility of insider trading have uncharitably interpreted "fairness" as "equal access," and then dismissed the fairness grounding for insider trading restrictions by reducing the equal access notion to absurdity. Heatherington, for example, says fairness advocates believe that "the odds must be the same for everyone who plays the game," i.e., it is unfair for one person to trade with another unless the two are equally knowledgeable about transaction facts.[3] This is, of course, absurd. If equal knowledge is required for fairness, there will be no incentive to gain new market-related information. Why would a mining company search for ore on another's land if it had to reveal all its test results prior to acquisition of the land? The world of equal information would generate little new information.[4]

However, we need not interpret "equal access" in such an uncharitable manner. Victor Brudney says that unfairness arises because of the "inability of a public investor with whom an insider transacts on inside information ever lawfully to erode the insider's informational advantage."[5] Insider trading precludes equal access because the corporation has certain information to which the insider has access, but, because the corporation wishes to protect its information, the outside trader cannot acquire the information lawfully from the corporation. Furthermore, the insider knows the corporation has not released and, in all probability, will not release the information. So the insider has an unerodable informational advantage; the outsider cannot legally acquire access to what the insider knows.

Brudney's account of how insider trading precludes equal access and is unfair also enables us to see that some forms of access that are unequal are permissible. The outsider who generates information is entitled to benefit from it. So the person who devises a profitable stock-picking method by analyzing data found in Value Line's stock report data would be entitled to use the method. He would not have to make sure the person he was trading with had "equal information" about the method in order for the trade to be fair. If you are wealthy and can afford to buy investment information from a brokerage firm, that is ethical, even though I might not be able to afford such information, and hence have no access to it. The point is that I am not legally precluded from the information; if I had the money, I could purchase the same information you enjoy.

CONSEQUENCES FOR OUTSIDERS

The "unfairness" objections to insider trading would be swept aside if it could be demonstrated that nobody is actually harmed by the practice, which is Henry Manne's thesis. Let us assume insiders have information that would result in a share price increase if the information were commonly known. According to Manne, insider trading will tend to move the stock's price in the "correct" direction, i.e., the price it will reach when the news is out.[6] For example, if a stock sells at $10 when insider trading commences, it will help move the stock toward the $18 value it will reach when the information is made public. Since insider trading generally occurs during a relatively brief time span, shareholders who do not trade during that time will benefit, since their stock will be higher when the information is made public. Furthermore, anyone who sells as the stock moves from $10 to $18 benefits in the sense that he gets a higher price than he would if insider trading had not occurred. Manne says that the only shareholders who are harmed are those curious few who sell prior to information disclosure because of the price rise caused by insider trading and who would not have sold if the price had not risen due to insider trading.[7] For example, if Sam buys at $10 and wouldn't sell at $10, but he does sell at $12 when insiders trade it up quickly to that level, then Sam lost $6 under the assumption that he would have held the stock until it reached $18 when the news is out. So the only people harmed are those who sell only *because* of the insider's purchases *and* who would have held their shares longer if the insiders had not driven the price higher. There will not be many such people. Hence, only a few people can be harmed by insider trading.

Manne's argument, however, is not defect free. There are buyers in markets as well as sellers. If Joe intends to offer $10 for a stock fluctuating around that price but insider trading causes it to rise above $10 and then pushes it to $18, then Joe is out the $8 he would have realized if insiders had not pushed the price above his bid. If Joe jumps in at $15 on the way up, he benefits as the price moves to $18, yet he is harmed by the loss of the $5 he would have realized had not insiders driven the price above $10. Manne attempts to undercut these cases by assuming the long-term investor is not influenced by a stock's present price. This seems implausible. It is more reasonable to assume that price is a factor, and sometimes an important factor, in many long-term investors' purchase decisions.

Stocks go down as well as up. If unfettered insider trading is permitted and bad news is forthcoming, inside traders will sell stock short hoping to profit by buying it back cheaper upon disclosure. They may short the stock at $10, hoping to buy it back at $6, its price at disclosure. Outside investors buy all the way down at prices higher than they would have paid if disclosure occurred at $10. So, all those investors who buy between $10 and $6 are definitely harmed. Furthermore, if the outsiders sell at $6, they sell to an insider who shorted at $10 and knew the stock was headed lower. It is a curious theory that rewards managers for failure as well as success.

So it seems that many investors would be harmed by insider trading. Of course, we haven't shown that such trading would cause more harm than benefit. Apparently there are no empirical studies of this matter; Manne's work is entirely theoretical. Nonetheless, many investors would be harmed. It is interesting to note that in summarizing his argument on the consequences of insider trading Manne himself makes a very limited claim as to what he has established:

> This somewhat laborious discussion of what happens in the stock market does not constitute a strong argument *against* a proposal to bar all insider trading. Indeed it is not intended for that purpose at all, but merely to point out that no strong arguments along these lines are available in *defense* of such a proposal.[8]

So Manne regards his argument as a burden-of-proof argument, claiming that the burden is on those who would ban insider trading to show that insider trading is harmful overall. If opponents of insider trading cannot show it has overall bad consequences, Manne suggests unfettered insider trading should be permitted. However, the burden of proof is on those who would change a practice, and we do have a network of laws in place that prohibit or restrict certain forms of insider trading. So the burden of proof is on Manne to definitely show that insider trading is beneficial overall. By his own words he has not made the case.

Furthermore, Manne tends to cast his argument in black-or-white terms: either ban all insider trading or permit it totally unfettered. He seems to overlook the sensible middle position that some insider trading is unethical and ought to be banned. If we accept Manne's position, then Ivan Boesky, Dennis Levine, Martin Siegel, Boyd Jeffries, Michael David, R. Foster Winans, Paul Thayer, Adrian Antoniu, and Thomas Reed all become candidates for the Wall Street Hall of Fame.

One objection to Manne has been the contention that unfettered insider trading would reduce the public's confidence in markets. However, if Manne's argument is acceptable, then the public's "perceptions" do not match reality; if insider trading actually causes no harm, the public's perception should be changed. We have seen, however, that insider trading would harm many investors, which in turn would reduce public confidence in markets. In particular, many small investors would feel that the deck is stacked against them and decide not to play. Since all participants in the debate agree we should preserve public confidence, we should not permit unfettered insider trading.

OWNERSHIP

When a person goes to work for a company he receives a wage and benefits, and in return is expected to use his skills and knowledge for the firm's benefit. During employment an employee may create or acquire information, but that information belongs to the firm, not the employee. The employee has a duty of loyalty to the firm, i.e., he or she is obligated to act solely for the firm's interests. Furthermore, the employee has a duty of confidentiality, i.e., information should not be used for anyone's benefit other than the firm's. So, the company is entitled to *exclusive* use of information generated or acquired by its employees. However, inside traders take this information and use it for their own personal interest. In a sense, then, inside traders are taking corporate property, stealing it if you will, and using it for their own benefit.

As numerous commentators have noted, however, since the corporation owns its information, it should be entitled to do what it wants with it. So, if it decides to permit insider trading, it should be allowed to do so.[9] Manne's argument is that no outside traders are harmed by insider trading and that insider trading actually benefits the firm. We have examined and found fault with the first part of Manne's thesis; let us now examine the second part.

Manne argues that firms should be entitled to permit trading on insider information because they own such information, and they should allow such trading because adequate recognition of entrepreneurship within the firm is very important and insider trading is the best way to compensate employees for entrepreneurship.[10] Manne reasons that entrepreneurs within the firm, the inventors of information, may not be compensated adequately via salary for their contributions to the firm, in which case their incentive to produce is decreased. Hence, insider trading should be allowed to link the entrepreneurial inventiveness to its reward when the company's stock price rises because of this creativity.

This theory is problematic. First of all, an unproductive insider may well benefit more than the creator of information. If the creator of information lacks capital but a peripheral member of the research team happens to be wealthy, the latter will profit much more than the former. Second, insiders totally unconnected to the actual information-generating entrepreneurs may benefit because of rumor, luck, or other irrelevant factors. Hence, in many cases there will be no reasonable relationship between what the insider receives and what he or she contributes. Furthermore, there do seem to be compensation systems that provide incentive while maintaining the relationship between contribution and reward, e.g., stock options, bonuses, fringe benefits, and so forth. The bonus, for example, seems a good way to compensate corporate entrepreneurs. It is paid as an addition to the employee's salary, and once the invention's value is established the bonus can be set commensurate with that value. In this way, the bonus, unlike unfettered insider trading, will benefit nonwealthy corporate entrepreneurs as much as those who just happen to be wealthy. Furthermore, the bonus, unlike insider trading, is directed precisely at those who originate corporate information.

Still, the above problems for Manne's theory do not derail it, because they do not show that insider trading harms the firm. However, Robert Haft has argued that insider trading of the scope permitted by Manne will probably have "adverse effects of a pervasive and systemic nature upon internal decision-making and efficiency" in the large corporation.[11] Haft argues that the upward and downward information flow, necessary for accurate decision making, will be impeded as individuals seek to maximize their own opportunities for financial gain. Individuals and groups will also tend to distort information, to the firm's disadvantage. Such activities will tend to erode the trust between employees, a trust that is necessary for organizational efficiency. Organizational discord will increase as lower-level employees who originate information ultimately benefit less than upper managers, who have more extensive access to information and greater financial resources to invest.

In addition, if insider trading is allowed, insiders will have an incentive to manipulate the accuracy and timing of advice that is disclosed ultimately to the public. In certain cases, this will work to the firm's disadvantage. Then, too, insider trading will be an incentive to select high-risk projects that produce wide stock fluctuations.[12] The high-risk projects may harm the firm, but the inside trader can profit from any news, good or bad. The fact that the insider can profit from bad news by short selling means that the "entrepreneur" can profit from poor performance, a result that is hardly consonant with Manne's entrepreneurial theory. So there are many reasons why firms should ban insider trading.

The upshot is that insider trading is immoral for three primary reasons. First, the insider has an unerodable informational advantage; since the outsider cannot legally acquire access to what the insider knows, insider trading is unfair to the outsider. Second, contrary to Manne, many outside investors would be harmed by insider trading, and, because this is so, general public confidence in the market would decrease. Finally, although the firm owns its information, and, hence, other factors being equal, should be entitled to permit its insiders to trade on confidential information, insider trading will likely harm the firm, hence firms have a good reason not to permit insider trading. Furthermore, other things are not equal here. Given that insider trading is unfair to outside investors and harms many of them, firms have additional reasons to prevent insider trading irrespective of such trading's effects on the firm.

NOTES

1. Henry G. Manne, *Insider Trading and the Stock Market* (New York: The Free Press, 1966); Henry G. Manne, "In Defense of Insider Trading," *Harvard Business Review* 44, no. 6 (November–December 1966): 113–22; J. A. C. Heatherington, "Insider Trading and the Logic of the Law," *Wisconsin Law Review* 1967, no. 3 (Summer 1967): 720–37.

2. *SEC* v. *Texas Gulf Sulfur Co.*, 401 F. 2d 833 (2d Cir. 1968); *In re Cady, Roberts & Co.* 40 S.E.C. 907 (1961).

3. Heatherington, p. 720.

4. Frank H. Easterbrook, "Insider Trading, Secret Agents, Evidentiary Privileges, and the Production of Information," *The Supreme Court Review* (1981), p. 329.

5. Victor Brudney, "Insiders, Outsiders, and Informational Advantages under the Federal Securities Laws," *Harvard Law Review* 93, no. 2 (December 1979), p. 346.

6. Manne, pp. 93, 96–103; Heatherington, p. 722.

7. Heatherington, pp. 723–25.

8. Manne, *Insider Trading and the Stock Market*, p. 110.

9. Easterbrook, p. 331; Dennis W. Carlton and Daniel R. Fischel, "The Regulation of Insider Trading," *Stanford Law Review* 35, no. 5 (May 1983): 861–66.

10. Manne, *Insider Trading and the Stock Market,* pp. 131–41. In places, Manne makes a stronger claim as regards the merits of entrepreneurial insider trading, claiming that "profits from insider trading constitute the only effective compensation scheme for entrepreneurial services in large organizations." Manne, "In Defense of Insider Trading," p. 116.

11. Robert J. Haft, "The Effect of Insider Trading Rules on the Internal Efficiency of the Large Corporation," *Michigan Law Review* 80, no. 5 (April, 1982): 1051–71.

12. Easterbrook, p. 332.

CORPORATE TAKEOVERS

Case Study

RJR Nabisco

In a typical leveraged buyout (LBO) an investor group makes a bid for the shares of a publicly held company. Typically, the group puts up about 10 percent of the bid price in cash, and then, borrowing against the company's assets, it raises about 60 percent of its bid price from secured bank loans and the other 30 percent from junk bonds sold to pension funds, insurance companies, and other investors. The investor group then buys all the outstanding stock of the company, taking it private. Management may then sell off parts of the firm, close divisions, cut employees, and reduce capital spending in order to increase profitability and reduce debt. In some cases the firm is "liquidated," i.e., all the parts are sold. In other cases the group works to strengthen the firm in order to again take it public or sell it to another private firm.

Ross Johnson, RJR Nabisco's president, knew about the art of the deal. Johnson worked his way up to the president's slot at Standard Brands, the producer of Planters nuts and Butterfinger candy bars, and then in 1981 sold the company to Nabisco, the big cookie, cracker, and biscuit maker. In 1984, Johnson became Nabisco's president. He thought Nabisco was undervalued, so he shopped it around to cash-rich consumer companies; in 1985, R. J. Reynolds purchased Nabisco for $5 billion. The firm was renamed RJR Nabisco (RJR). By the end of a year Johnson became RJR's president. In 1987 he became chief executive officer of RJR.

From 1985 to 1987, RJR Nabisco's profits moved up nicely, but its stock lagged behind most diversified consumer stocks. In mid-1987, Johnson was playing golf with Donald Kelly, who had worked with Kohlberg Kravis Roberts & Co. (KKR) on the Beatrice LBO. Kelly thought RJR was undervalued and

318

suggested that Johnson consider taking it private. Johnson and Kelly subsequently had dinner with Henry Kravis of KKR and the three discussed an LBO. However, by this time the market had moved higher, carrying RJR stock to $70, a price that Johnson thought more realistic. In October 1987, however, the market crashed, taking RJR's stock to around $50. The LBO idea resurfaced in Johnson's mind.

Johnson considered several ways to enhance RJR's stock price. He sold Heublein to get out of a low-margin business. He considered buying another food company to go with Nabisco and Del Monte. But food companies were richly valued; a purchase would have diluted equity holdings in RJR. He considered the repurchase of RJR shares, but concluded that it wouldn't benefit RJR in the long run. He raised the dividend 15 percent, but the stock price went nowhere. Johnson then approached Shearson Lehman, which informed him that RJR was an ideal LBO candidate. Shearson told Johnson that RJR would bring $75 to $80 a share.

RJR certainly looked like a good LBO candidate. With the stock at $56 per share, the total market value of RJR was $12.6 billion. Smith Barney estimated the break-up sale value to range from $24.6 to $26.1 billion (from $109 per share to $116 per share). Taking the low estimate, Smith Barney estimated the sale value of RJR's businesses to be: tobacco, $12.5 billion; U.S. food businesses, $9.6 billion; international food businesses, $2.5 billion. Furthermore, RJR's businesses were discrete and could be sold off either as a package or in pieces. For example, the U.S. food business consisted of: Nabisco cookies and crackers, Del Monte canned fruit and vegetables, Shredded Wheat cereals, Planters Peanuts, Life Savers, Butterfinger candy bars, Carefree bubble gum, Fleischmann's margarine, Del Monte fresh fruit, Ortega Mexican food, A-1 Steak Sauce, and, Milkbone dog biscuits.

Johnson had every reason to believe that RJR's board, of which he was a member, would look favorably on a management offer. He had hand-picked most of the board's members. Furthermore, Johnson treated RJR's directors well. When he took office he doubled their salaries to $50,000, on the high side for salaries of directors of major corporations. Several directors also had lucrative consulting contracts with RJR. A former Shearson Lehman managing director had an annual consulting contract of $780,000. Charles Hugel, board chairman, had a $150,000 consulting agreement with RJR. Finally, three of the seven-member management team that would be making the LBO offer were RJR directors; in fact, over half of RJR's twenty board members would have links of one sort or the other to the buyout team.

In July 1988, RJR's board of directors granted "golden parachutes" to 117 of RJR's top managers, awarding them $52 million if a takeover occurred and Johnson either quit or was fired as a result of the takeover. Under such conditions, Johnson himself would receive $5.4 million.

In early October of 1988, Johnson took Hugel to dinner and informed him that he was considering a LBO of RJR. Hugel said he did not think it was a good idea. Two weeks later, on October 19, Johnson brought RJR's directors together for dinner the evening before the next day's regular board meeting. Johnson told the directors that he had tried everything to get the stock's price up, but to no avail. His solution was that he and a small management group would take control of RJR via an LBO. They would then sell some of the food brands and run the remaining divisions as a private firm. Hugel and the other directors decided Johnson should go ahead and make his best offer. Hugel said that Johnson could not make a frivolous offer; it would have to be above the highest price at which the stock had ever traded, namely, $71 per share. Johnson said this could be done, even though the stock traded currently at $56. Johnson consulted with Shearson Lehman and on October 20 Johnson announced publicly that his group was considering a $75 per share (or $17 billion) LBO of RJR, whereupon RJR stock moved from $56 to $77. Four days later, on October 24, KKR announced it would bid $90 per share ($21 billion) for RJR.

KKR was founded in 1976 by Jerome Kohlberg, Jr., Henry Kravis, and George Roberts. By 1988 it was by far the most powerful LBO firm. Between 1985 and 1988, KKR was centrally involved in four of the ten largest corporate buyouts. By 1988 it controlled twenty-three large companies with annual sales of $38 billion. These included: Stop & Shop (supermarkets), Beatrice (food), Duracell (batteries), Motel 6 (lodging), Jim Walter (construction), and Safeway (supermarkets). If KKR could add RJR, with its sales of $16 billion, KKR, with $54 billion in sales, would be just slightly smaller than IBM and would be the fifth largest U.S. firm.

When it takes over a company, KKR moves decisively to sell off assets and reduce costs. When it bought out Safeway, KKR sold off unprofitable pieces of the business to pay down debt. Analysts applauded the sales because the remaining company was more efficient and profitable. About 200 people in Safeway's home office were terminated, some with over twenty years of service. Some Safeway employees found their pay cut in half. One analyst said: "When you get into one of these LBOs you start to see bodies fly; at Safeway it was brutal."

KKR is a very small firm. In 1988 it consisted of eighteen people: three accountants and fifteen transaction specialists. KKR does not offer day-to-day management advice. Its members offer financial advice and sit on the boards of directors. It also directs the acquired firms' cost-cutting strategies. Once it has turned a company around, KKR looks for ways to take profits, either by taking the company public or selling it to a private buyer. KKR makes money three ways: (1) it gets a percentage of the profits, usually 20 percent, when a firm is sold; (2) it collects management fees of 1.5 percent on its equity fund (in 1988, it received roughly $75 million); and, (3) it gets transaction fees for carrying out deals, typically 1 percent of the purchase price. Because of its solid record and dominant LBO position, KKR attracts tremendous amounts of money from investors, who have benefited considerably from KKR's investment savvy.

Johnson's group bid $75 per share for RJR on October 20, 1988. KKR bid $90 on October 24. Johnson's investment banker from Shearson Lehman then met with Kravis on October 25 to work out a deal according to which

KKR and Johnson's management group would go together to buy RJR. When these talks fell through, Johnson's group bid $92 on November 3. RJR's board then met and decided that subsequent bids would be sealed and that final bids had to be submitted by November 18. Again, KKR and Johnson's group talked about a plan to jointly control KKR, but these talks also failed. On November 16, a group led by Forstmann Little & Co. dropped out of the bidding. On November 18, Johnson's group bid $100 and KKR bid $94. On that date a group led by First Boston Corp. made a tentative offer that was valued at between $105 to $118. The RJR board wanted time to evaluate this new bid, and hence extended the deadline to November 29.

Johnson was upset with the extension, saying: "I believe that we, along with our financial partners, submitted the winning bid, which met all of the stated objectives of the board's special committee." Jack Nussbaum, one of Johnson's legal advisers, said: "We won the bidding contest by the rules, we won the company, and we're disappointed we have to wait another week." A spokesman for the board said: "There are enough holes in the two bids and enough promise in the First Boston bid where you have to seriously say 'Hold it.' "

According to the *Wall Street Journal* (November 29, 1988, p. 4), on November 28, RJR advisers informed the three bidders that RJR's board would unveil its own restructuring plan unless the bids exceeded $100 per share. First Boston's November 29 bid was in excess of $100, but the firm still had not arranged adequate financing, and the bid was based on the group's ability to close the deal by the end of December in order to take advantage of a tax loophole. Since RJR's board felt this was impractical, First Boston's bid was rejected. Johnson's group bid $101 and KKR bid $106. RJR's board tentatively decided to accept KKR's bid. Johnson got word that KKR had outbid him and asked whether he could appear before the board to make another bid. On the morning of November 30, Johnson met with the board and bid $108. Later in the day he submitted another bid—for $112. KKR got word of Johnson's bids, asked to make a final bid, and offered $109. The final bids were combinations of cash, preferred stock, and convertible stock. KKR offered $81 a share in cash, $18 a share in exchangeable preferred stock, and $10 a share in debentures convertible into a total of about 25 percent of the acquiring company's equity. Johnson's group offered $84 in cash, $24 in preferred stock, and $4 a share in stock convertible into a total of 15 percent of the new company's stock. KKR's total bid was $25.07 billion ($109 per share); Johnson bid $25.76 billion ($112 per share). Each bid was more than the gross national product of Ireland or Portugal. On November 31, 1988, RJR's board declared KKR the winner.

Johnson's investment team was perplexed by the board's decision. The team's attorney said: "We have very sophisticated clients who are stunned by the fact that in an auction process they put in the high bid not once but three times and still didn't get the company." According to the *Wall Street Journal* (December 2, 1988, p. A1), the key factors in the board's selection of KKR were:

- The breakup factor. RJR directors wanted to keep the company as intact as possible. KKR promised to sell only $5 billion to $6 billion in RJR assets, primarily food companies, in the near future, while the management group intended to sell the entire food company for an estimated $13 billion.

- The equity factor. Directors wanted to allow stockholders to share in any KKR profits as much as possible. KKR proposed to distribute 25 percent of the equity in the future company to shareholders, compared with the management group's 15 percent offer.

- Bid structure. When directors cut through all the arcane details of preferred stock and debentures in the two packages, it became clear that KKR was offering $500 million more of equity than the management group was. Directors believed that this strengthened the KKR bid and reduced the debt payments that the future company would have to meet.

- Job commitments. Directors believed that KKR was more firmly committed to saving jobs at RJR than the management group was. In an interview published a few days before the bidding deadline, Mr. Johnson had shrugged off his group's planned firings.

KKR agreed that wages would not be reduced and would, in fact, be increased by at least 4 percent per year. KKR also agreed that all benefits would be retained, and pledged that when businesses were sold they would assume responsibility for seeing that benefits continued.

In the only interview he gave during the bidding process, Johnson responded to a question as follows:

> Question: What about the employees? You say at least 800 will have to be laid off. Isn't an LBO very hard on employees?
>
> Johnson: While you are going through the transition period it is. If you take 120,000 RJR Nabisco people, yes, there will be some dislocation. But the people that I have, particularly the Atlanta people, have very portable types of professions: accountants, lawyers, secretaries. It isn't that I would be putting them on the breadline. We have excellent severance agreements (*Time,* December 5, 1988, p. 71).

In contrast, KKR agreed to pay severance pay and moving expenses for those RJR employees who worked for businesses that would be sold. One RJR director said: "Those kinds of thoughts were absent on the other side."

Some of RJR's directors also believed Johnson was greedy. In his *Time* interview Johnson said: "My job is to negotiate the best deal that I can for my people. So I negotiated a deal where we'd get 8.5% and then have incentives that went to 12% and then to 18.5% if we hit certain targets along the way." Critics said that by "my people" Johnson meant the seven individuals in the management buyout group. In exchange for $20 million they would receive an 8.5% stake in the new firm. Upon completion of the deal, the 8.5% stake would be worth $200 million. If RJR could be turned into a more profitable firm, critics pointed out that the eventual 18.5% stake could be worth $2.6 billion in five years, of which Johnson's share would be over $1 billion. In response Johnson said in his *Time* interview:

> I wasn't going to take 18% of this company for seven people. You could multiply and get these incredible figures, that I could make a billion dollars. What was in the newspapers was only the seven that I could identify because they were the only ones working on the deal. If I'd known it was going to be in the newspapers, I would have said, "Look, there's going to be 15,000 people." They will get at least 5%. I always saw myself in there at around 1%. In seven or eight years, I could make $100 million.

Despite this rebuttal, Johnson was widely portrayed as greedy; the *Time* headline on its front cover was: "The Game of Greed." Johnson was pictured on the cover.

Finally, RJR's board had reviewed carefully RJR's operations when it explored restructuring the company itself, and it found that management was spending extravagantly on a fleet of corporate jets (so large that one director dubbed it the "RJR Air Force"), corporate lodgings in Palm Springs, and security measures for Mr. Johnson. Although the directors had themselves benefited from Johnson's lavishness, they hadn't realized its extent and cost. Some directors thought KKR could better manage RJR.

KKR financed the RJR LBO by putting up $1.5 billion of its own cash. It also lent $500 million to a holding company it set up to complete the deal. The financing plan also included $14 billion in bank debt, $5 billion in junk bonds, and $5.9 billion in convertible bonds and preferred stock.

Who won and who lost in the RJR LBO? Of course, we will not know for some time how the LBO will pan out. But eight groups can be said to have benefited. First of all, RJR's 114,000 shareholders benefited; the total value of RJR increased from $13 billion to $25 billion, an increase of $12 billion. Second, Johnson's management group benefited; they were in a no-lose situation. Johnson himself held 235,535 shares, which became worth $25.7 million. Johnson's golden parachute provided another $5.4 million, and he became eligible for retirement benefits in 1992. Third, KKR and the former shareholders of RJR (who hold a 25 percent equity stake in the new firm) will benefit if the LBO works out. They could make upwards of $2 billion. Fourth, the LBO investors backing KKR typically realize a 30 percent annual return. Fifth, the commercial banks who put up $14 billion impose an up-front fee of 1.4 percent for arranging the risky loans in addition to hefty interest charges of about 2 percent over the prime rate, which was 10.5 percent on December 1, 1988. Sixth, the junk bond, preferred stock, and convertible bond holders typically receive a 15 percent annual return. Seventh, the investment bankers who helped KKR and the management team put together their bids are estimated to have earned $400 million. Finally, merger and acquisition lawyers are estimated to have received in the area of $150 million.

Who were the losers? First of all, RJR's bondholders. Before Johnson announced his bid, RJR had $5 billion outstanding of high-grade bonds. Since the LBO would saddle RJR with a riskier debt load, the old bonds were immediately marked down by 20 percent, for a loss of $1 billion. Several bondholders sued RJR. In its suit Metropolitan Life Insurance Co. said: "One key ingredient in this financial alchemy is the expropriation of value from the company's long-term debt holders." Bondholders were also upset with Shearson Lehman, which had underwritten $1.4 billion of conservative RJR debt in early 1988. Shearson Lehman subsequently served as the investment banker to Johnson's group in their LBO bid. Although Metropolitan Life did not sue Shearson Lehman, it said in its RJR suit that Shearson was "a leader in expropriating the value of the securities it underwrote." Critics of the LBO also charged that it reduced the value of all existing corporate high-grade bonds. Given that RJR was America's nineteenth largest industrial corporation, no firm seemed immune from a takeover attempt. Not knowing which firm might be next, bondholders marked down all bonds accordingly. Robert McLaughlin, investment officer of the Ohio Public Employees Retirement System, said: "Corporations really don't care about the bondholder anymore. . . . People who buy industrial bonds these days have their eyes closed." The total amount of increased interest that corporations had to pay as a result of the RJR LBO has not been quantified.

The U.S. government was probably also a loser in the long term. Depending on each shareholder's purchase price, the capital gains on RJR stock may have been about $7 billion. At the 28 percent tax rate, the government would collect $2 billion in tax. However, interest payments on corporate debt are tax deductible, and the RJR LBO created a mountain of debt. In 1988, RJR had $2.9 billion of operating income on which it paid tax. In 1989 the debt interest wiped out operating income. Critics charge that U.S. taxpayers will be out some $2 to $5 billion over the long term.

Critics also allege that consumers will be harmed by the RJR LBO. They claim that to pay down debt RJR will introduce fewer new products, and will raise prices; competitors, they believe, will simply ride RJR's pricing coattails. Reduced research and capital expenditures can also be expected. RJR had planned to invest $2.8 billion in high-tech bakeries, investments that were shelved when the LBO was announced. RJR also shelved the Premier smokeless cigarette, which had a projected development cost of $1 billion.

Finally, the workers who were terminated as KKR cut costs would also be harmed. Again, this factor has not been quantified.

For Discussion

Did Ross Johnson and his RJR management team act in a morally responsible way in the RJR LBO? Why or why not? Did RJR's board of directors act in a morally responsible way in the RJR LBO? Why or why not? In general, do you believe corporate LBOs are morally justifiable? Why or why not? Because of the RJR LBO and other LBOs in the 1980s, many people thought Congress should act to regulate LBOs, and, in particular, the use of high-risk "junk" bonds to finance them. Should LBOs be controlled or restricted? Why or why not? If they should be regulated or curtailed, what general sort of regulation would you recommend?

SOURCES

Wall Street Journal: November 21, 1988, A3; November 22, 1988, A4; November 29, 1988, A4; December 1, 1988, A3; December 2, 1988, A1, A10, B1, C1; December 5, 1988, A3; December 7, 1988, A3; December 9, 1988, C1; December 14, 1988, C1; *Atlanta Constitution:* November 20, 1988, E1; November 27, 1988, E1; November 30, 1988, A1; December 1, 1988, A1, D1; December 2, 1988, D1, D6, D7; December 4, 1988. D7, E1; December 6, 1988, C1; December 9, 1988, D1; December 14, 1988, A11; January; 1, 1989, N7; *Time,* December 5, 1988, 66-74; *Fortune,* January 2, 1989, 66-76; F. M. Scherer and David Ravenscraft, *Mergers, Sell-offs, and Economic Efficiency* (Washington, D.C.: Brookings, 1987); Alan J. Auerbach, ed., *Corporate Takeovers: Causes and Consequences* (Chicago: University of Chicago, 1988); Bryan Burrough and John Helyar, *Barbarians at the Gate: The Fall of RJR Nabisco* (New York: Harper and Row, 1990). John F. Steiner, *Industry, Society, and Change* (New York: McGraw-Hill, 1991), pp. 241-70.

Robert B. Reich

Leveraged Buyouts: America Pays the Price

When the capital development of a country becomes a byproduct of the activities of a casino, the job is likely to be ill-done. The measure of success attained by Wall Street . . . cannot be claimed as one of the outstanding triumphs of laissez-faire capitalism.

John Maynard Keynes, *The General Theory*
of Employment, Interest and Money (1936)

First came the mammoth takeovers. Then the insider-trading scandals. Then the stock-market crash of October 1987. Then the giant leveraged buyouts, culminating in the $24.88 billion takeover of RJR Nabisco Inc. Then Drexel Burnham's guilty plea to criminal fraud.

America has had enough. Even by the cynical standards of the 1980s, Wall Street is giving greed a bad name.

In a typical takeover, the raider buys enough stock to gain control of a company; in a leveraged buyout, a company's own executives are often among the buyers. A popular way to finance these deals is through "junk" bonds— I.O.U.'s paying hefty interest, reflecting their higher-than normal risks.

Only a portion of the money involved in these activities is actually used up in the takeover and buyout process. Most of it circulates among investment bankers, arbitragers, portfolio managers, brokers, and other financial intermediaries, as they trade shares of stock in companies about to be taken over, or about to be disassembled, or they make bets on whether other fi-

---

nancial intermediaries will expect such companies to be taken over or disassembled, and so on, in an almost infinite regression of trades and takeover bets, and bets on takeover bets, and trades on bets on takeover bets.

Defenders of such antics argue that they are justified by "economic fundamentals." Corporate executives speak of wondrous gains from "synergy"— the dynamic effects of combining managerial talent, research laboratories, and production facilities, making the whole greater than the sum of the parts. They then wax with equal enthusiasm over the gains to be had from disassembling and selling off piecemeal such parts, thus making the sum of the parts (at least in dollar terms) greater than the whole.

Through it all, they exhibit faith—endless, indomitable faith—in the hidden, *potential* value of the companies being purchased, relative to the price they could currently fetch on the stock market. In other words, the prices listed on the stock exchange understate what the companies are potentially worth.

Most of this is nonsense, or worse. The record of the 1970s and '80s is dismally clear on this point. There is little evidence to suggest that mergers have on the average enhanced the profitability or productivity of merging enterprises. The subsequent rush to dismember suggests, in fact, the reverse.

In 1985, R. J. Reynolds, the giant tobacco corporation, merged with Nabisco, the giant food-processing company. At the time, the merger was hailed as a brilliant strategy, through which the tobacco company would diversify into foods. Just three years later, the newly merged company became the object of a mammoth contest between armies of investment bankers pledging billions of dollars for the privilege of breaking it up once again.

Although takeover defenders claim that mergers and acquisitions are not a speculative game but a means by which the financial market insures that money is available for new investment, close examination belies this view. Wall Street's dynamism has little to do with the financing of new commercial ventures. During the 1980s, new issues of common stock averaged only about 1 percent of the total stock outstanding; the action was in the 99 percent of shares already in circulation.

The American economy as a whole has not benefited demonstrably from all this activity. Since the mid-1970s, when most of this began, productivity gains have slowed. Adjusted for inflation, average wages have stagnated, corporate profits have been lackluster and the Dow Jones industrial average has yet to regain the peak it achieved in January 1973. And only the public-relations office of the United States Chamber of Commerce would contend that American companies have stayed competitive with those of Japan, West Germany, South Korea, and other places around the globe where, incidentally, hostile takeovers and leveraged buyouts rarely, if ever, occur.

If there is little economic justification, why does the wheeling and dealing continue?

Let us go back to 1974. That year, the International Nickel Company decided to buy up enough shares in the Electric Storage Battery Company to give International Nickel control over the board of directors of Electric

Storage, and thus allow International Nickel to run the company. International Nickel argued that its nickel powder used in rechargeable batteries made Electric Storage a perfect complement. But Electric Storage did not want to be taken over and thus regarded International Nickel's act as hostile. International Nickel won.

Before International Nickel made its takeover bid, Wall Street had viewed such aggression as unseemly, if not unethical. One didn't just take over a company. A company was its managers and employees, its trademark and reputation. These attributes could not be purchased against its will—or so it was assumed.

Then Wall Street's other shoe fell. In 1975, the Securities and Exchange Commission decreed that commissions paid on stock transactions were no longer to be based on fixed rates, but were to be negotiable. Henceforth, brokers' commissions were to be subject to the free market. Within two years, revenues on Wall Street plunged $600 million. This was no time for niceties. The Street had to forage for new sources of earnings, and hostile takeovers looked like just the place to start.

Of mergers and acquisitions each costing $1 million or more, there were just 10 in 1970; in 1980, there were 94; in 1986, there were 346. A third of such details in the 1980s were hostile. The 1980s also saw a wave of giant leveraged buyouts. Mergers, acquisitions, and L.B.O.'s, which had accounted for less than 5 percent of the profits of Wall Street brokerage houses in 1978, ballooned into an estimated 50 percent of profits by 1988. And profitable it has been. Last year, Wall Street firms earned about $2.2 billion before taxes, compared with $1.1 billion in 1987.

Deal-making has proved particularly lucrative because every time industrial assets are rearranged, the paper entrepreneurs earn money. The larger and more complex the escapade, the more money they earn. And here is the critical point: paper entrepreneurs not only do the deals, but also advise their clients (corporate directors, chief executives, pension-fund managers) about when and whether such deals should be made.

The RJR Nabisco deal generated almost $1 billion in fees, including an estimated $153 million in advisory fees; $294 million in financing fees for investment banks, and $325 million in commercial-bank fees. Lawyers' fees, which are usually not disclosed, are estimated to have run in the millions.

Should the economy collapse, paper entrepreneurs are prepared. Investment banks already have amassed funds for "deleveraged buyouts," which will do the reverse of what was done during boom times: buy back the I.O.U.'s of the bankrupt companies at a small fraction of their face value and issue new shares of stock to the remaining creditors. Then sell the newly reorganized companies—now free of debt—for a fat profit.

Through all this, the historical relationship between product and paper has been turned upside down. Investment bankers no longer think of themselves as working for the corporations with which they do business. These days, corporations seem to exist for the investment bankers.

Whole departments of investment banks now scan corporate America for businesses ripe for the plucking. It is as if doctors or auto mechanics went from house to house, instructing the occupants on what they must do to avoid death or breakdown, and then ripping them or their car apart to make the prescribed repairs.

In fact, investment banks are replacing the publicly held industrial corporations as the largest and most powerful economic institutions in America. Twenty-five years ago, most investment banks were small partnerships. Today, many are giants. In 1987, Drexel Burnham Lambert posted earnings estimated at $500 million, putting it right up there with Xerox, Monsanto, and Kraft.

A quarter-century ago, the titans of American industry were chief executive officers of major industrial corporations. Today, as in the late 19th century, they are investment bankers. Henry R. Kravis and George R. Roberts, two principal partners of Kohlberg, Kravis, Roberts & Company, each earn about $70 million a year. The firm is the majority owner of some 20 companies, including Owens-Illinois and Safeway and (as soon as the paperwork is completed) RJR Nabisco as well. Rarely have so few earned so much for doing so little. Never have so few exercised such power over how the slices of the American pie are rearranged.

I do not want to suggest that all efforts directed at rearranging corporate assets are necessarily wasteful. To the extent that they allocate capital more efficiently to where it can be most productive, they make our economy perform better. But given the recent record of rampant speculation and finagling, one must ask whether these beneifts are worth what we are paying for them, in terms of both direct cost and future productivity.

The current obsessions with asset-rearranging harms productivity in four related ways:

Myopia. Research aimed at developing fundamentally new technologies is apt to go slowly, yielding little or no profit for many years. Even many service businesses require years of steady investment in quality controls and personnel training. All this demands a willingness to invest now for returns in a distant future.

But fear of a takeover, or the necessity of paying off a large loan, forces managers to focus on the short term—and cut back on long-term investments. General Electric's costly acquisition of RCA, for example, resulted in less research for both. In 1987, G.E. cut its research spending by $300 million; under new management, RCA's famed David Sarnoff Research Center—for decades an incubator of television technology—slashed its staff by 25 percent. A survey last year by the National Science Foundation determined that takeovers and leveraged buyouts were to blame for a marked slowdown in corporate research-and-development spending.

The changing pattern of stock ownership has encouraged mergers and acquisitions, contributing to the emphasis on immediate gains. Not long ago, the majority of stocks were owned by individuals and many of them held onto their shares for years. It was not unusual for such an investor to take a mildly proprietary interest in how his or her company was doing, and what it was planning to do. Today, 70 percent of the volume of stock trading is done by institutions, mainly mutual funds, pension funds, and insurance companies—which are under pressure to produce the short-term earnings that clients demand.

On the management side, the motivation is similar. The frenetic movement of corporate assets engenders a similar shifting of managerial talent. Top executives are dismissed, or they are lured to another newly rearranged corporation. They feel no loyalty to their present company, which, after all, is regarded by its directors and stockholders as little more than a collection of financial assets. Thus, the average term of office for today's chief executive officers is only five to six years.

If you compare those industries in which our competitive position continues to decline—semiconductors, consumer electronics, machine tools—with those in Japan, South Korea, and West Germany, you will find the same myopic pattern. The American companies have lower research-and-development budgets and older plant and equipment.

Wasted Talent. Asset-rearranging also harms productivity by using up the energies of some of our most talented citizens. Paper entrepreneurs are responsible for the nation's most innovative economic strategies. The result is a "brain drain" from product to paper.

Today's corporate executives spend an increasing portion of their days fending off takeovers, finding companies to acquire or responding to depositions in lawsuits instead of worrying about the quality of their products and how they can be distributed more efficiently. More of our top corporate executives are trained in law and finance than in any other field—in contrast to the case three decades ago when most were trained in marketing, engineering, and sales.

Meanwhile, our best minds are increasingly drawn to the pie-dividing professions of law and finance, and away from pie-enlarging professions like engineering and science. (My most talented students continue to march to Wall Street where they are promised starting salaries and bonuses of $100,000 or more.) Although graduate programs in law and finance are booming, those in engineering and science are foundering—again in contrast to other industrialized nations.

In 1987, the majority of students graduating from American universities with doctorates in engineering were foreign nationals, most of whom, presumably, will return to their home countries. Out of every 10,000 citizens in Japan, only 1 is a lawyer and 3 are accountants; in the United States, 20 are lawyers and 40 are accountants. Out of the same group in Japan, 400 are engineers; in the United States, only 70 are engineers.

There is a basic distortion here. The bankers and lawyers who helped RJR Nabisco move out of equities and into debt late last year earned about $1 billion for their efforts. This sum exceeded the total amount devoted by the United States in all of 1988 to the search for a cure for AIDS.

Debt. Typically, the money required to rearrange industrial assets—to mount hostile takeovers, to defend against hostile takeovers, to return a company to private ownership by repurchasing the publicly owned shares of stock—is borrowed. High leverage creates extraordinary opportunities for profit, but it also creates substantial danger, should the economy sputter and interest payments be missed. This was the lesson we were supposed to have learned in the 1920s, when Americans last went on a speculative spree with borrowed money.

Corporate debt in the 1980s has reached alarming proportions. Twenty-five years ago, the average American corporation paid 16 cents of every dollar of pre-tax earnings in interest on its debt. In the 1970s, it was 33 cents. Since 1980, it has been more than 50 cents. Few highly leveraged corporations have yet succumbed to bankruptcy, but most of their debt has been accumulated since 1983, during an economic expansion.

Economic history suggests that recessions do occur periodically. The Brookings Institution, not known for its alarmist rhetoric, undertook to examine the effects on corporate America of a recession similar in severity to that which rocked the nation in 1974 and 1975. The Brookings computer simulation revealed that, with the levels of debt prevailing in the late 1980s, 1 in 10 American companies would succumb to bankruptcy.

Distrust. An economy based on asset-rearranging has a final disadvantage. It invites zero-sum games, in which one group's gain is another's loss. As those engaged in rearranging the slices of the pie become more numerous and far more wealthy than those dedicated to enlarging the pie, trust declines. Without trust, people won't dedicate themselves to common goals. They will turn their energies instead to defending their own interests. In a corporation this means declining productivity.

There are signs that a vicious spiral has begun, as each corporate player seeks to imporve its standard of living at the expense of another's.

Corporate raiders transfer to themselves, and other shareholders, part of the income of employees by forcing the latter to agree to lower wages. (TWA's stock price rose after Carl Icahn took over, largely because TWA employees were forced to accept reduced wages.)

Corporate borrowers utilizing high-yield "junk" bonds make off with the gains anticipated by regular bondholders and other creditors, who never bargained for the kind of risk to which the enterprise is now exposed. (After the mammoth deal was announced, regular RJR Nabisco bondholders suddenly discovered that their bonds were worth far less than before because of the new debt load.)

Executives deprive stockholders of their gains by paying greenmail—exorbitant payoffs—to would-be acquirers or by undertaking a leveraged buyout and then reselling the company at a higher price.

And then there are the investors who rob other investors of potential market gains by illegally trading on inside information.

The catch is that these groups seeking to grab assets from one another are often the very groups whose collaboration is necessary for real growth to occur. The surest path to greater productivity is through collaboration—blue collar and white collar, investors and managers, creditors and stockholders, investors and employees.

Robert Almeder
David Carey

In Defense of Sharks: Moral Issues in Hostile Liquidating Takeovers

I. INTROUCTION

In this essay we will examine the major arguments attacking the practice of hostile buyouts initiated solely for the purpose of liquidation. This practice occurs only when management is unable or unwilling to close a significant gap between the market value of the company's shares and the breakup value of the company. Accordingly, these buyouts are usually "hostile" to the intentions of the current management. The "corporate raider" (sometimes more affectionately described by management as "the shark"), after buying a significant percentage of the company's shares, then offers to buy the shares from the other shareholders at a price considerably higher than current market value, buys the company, and makes a profit by selling off the underlying assets of the company. The raider may, or may not, take on a great deal of expensive debt in order to succeed in buying the target company. Such debt-based takeovers are called "leveraged," and takeovers can be more or less "highly leveraged" or not leveraged at all—as would occur if the raider proposed to buy the company with cash. If the proposed hostile offer is leveraged (and especially if it is leveraged) the raider typically seeks to eliminate the debt with the sale of the underlying assets and then pocket the difference.

From the *Journal of Business Ethics* 10 (1991): 471–84. Copyright © 1991 Kluwer Academic Publishers. Reprinted by permission of Kluwer Academic Publishers.

The raider's practice is unlike the practice of a hostile takeover of one company by another where the primary purpose is not so much to liquidate the assets for a quick profit, but rather to increase market share or shareholder value for the buying company which may, or may not, involve liquidating assets of the purchased company.

Various corporate managers, employee groups, politicians and philosophers have argued strenuously against the raider's practice, and the first question is whether those arguments justify eliminating or constraining the practice legislatively or otherwise. After reviewing the proposed arguments against the practice, we shall argue negatively that such arguments are unsound, and positively that there are good rule-utilitarian grounds for allowing the practice. (Whether this is more of an indictment of rule-utilitarianism than a defense of hostile takeovers, of course, is beyond the scope of this essay.)

II. ARGUMENTS AGAINST THE SHARK

We find, distilled from the general rhetoric on the issue, three arguments against the practice of the hostile liquidating buyout. The first two apply even when the proposed buyout is not highly leveraged and all three apply when the buyout is highly leveraged.

The Argument from Human Cost

As Lisa Newton has argued, any business practice that causes massive employee firing, with all its attendant trauma and suffering, when the company is both profitable and the employees not demonstrably incompetent, requires a justification. Moreover, for Newton, the long-term human costs involved certainly cannot be justified in terms of the self-aggrandizement of a few. The pleasure and limited good of a few in making a large profit cannot be justified by the overwhelming human suffering typically involved when a large company is liquidated.[1] In describing the hostile corporate takeover as a form of assault with a deadly weapon, she says:

> A practice requires moral scrutiny if it regularly derrogates from human dignity, causes human pain, or with no apparent reason treats one class of human beings less well than another. Any practice that regularly throws people out of work has at least the first two of those . . . and unless we find the raider's urgent need for self-aggrandizement as a worthy reason for dismembering working units, it probably does the third also (p. 501).

She goes on to note that such takeovers are usually defended on a rule utilitarian basis with the claim that, however painful in the short run, such takeovers are in the public interest because they increase the long-term efficiency of the market and enhance shareholder return. However, Newton (and many others along with her) reject this reason by appealing to people, such as Andrew Sigler, who have argued that as reasons go, the rule-utilitarian defense of the practice is unacceptable even on its own terms because such practices in no way produce real wealth. Rather, as a rule, they cause great pain and destroy wealth by creating great debt. In testimony before the House Committee on Energy and Commerce, Sigler said:

> Hostile takeovers create no new wealth . . . they merely shift ownership, and replace equity with large amounts of debt. . . . More and more companies are being pushed . . . either in self-defense against the raiders or by the raiders once they achieve control—into unhealthy recapitalizations that run contrary to the concepts of sound management I have learned over thirty years. This type of leveraging exposes companies to inordinate risks in the event of recession, unanticipated reverses, or significant increases in interest rates. . . . Generation after generation of American managers have believed that there must be a solid equity base for an enterprise to be successful in the long term. This long-term equity base absorbs—in exchange for the expectation of higher returns—the perils of depression, product failure, strikes, and all the other dangers that characterize business in a free economy. That healthy conservatism is now being replaced by a new game in which the object is to see how far that equity base can be squeezed down by layers of debt. And too much of this debt is carrying interest rates far in excess of those a prudent manager can possibly be comfortable with.[2]

And a number of others have agreed with Sigler that the practice generally, as a rule, erodes equity necessary for long-term survival and promotes heavy debt by forcing corporations in the presence of the raider's threat to defend itself by taking on the sort of debt that undermines real productivity.[3] Appealing to these considerations, Newton rejects the utilitarian defense that the practice is in the general interest, and hence she finds no countervailing social benefit to compensate for the human suffering typically caused by the practice. There is a large number of people who will agree with her reasoning.

The Argument from the Destruction of Wealth

According to this second argument, the hostile liquidating buyout, whether leveraged or not, is unacceptable, quite independently of the human cost and trauma involved. The reasoning here is that even if there were no such suffering attending the practice, it would still be against the public interest because, as a general rule, even the threat of a hostile buyout destroys wealth by undermining competitiveness at home and abroad. If so, such a business practice should be stopped for being contrary to the general well-being of society. (Hence, this too may be construed as a rule-utilitarian argument.) In support of this particular argument, Harold Williams, after noting that fear of the raider forces management to seek ever high earnings at all costs, says:

> The pursuit of constantly higher earnings can compel managers to avoid needed writedowns, capital programs, research projects, and other bets on

the long term. The competitiveness of U.S. corporations has already been impaired by the failure to make long-term commitments. To compound the problem because of fears of takeovers is a gift to foreign competitors that we cannot afford.[4]

This point was made in Andrew Sigler's testimony cited above. So, whether leveraged or not, even the threat of a liquidating hostile takeover engenders corporate behavior that, as a rule, undermines long-term corporate productivity and hence, by implication, destroys wealth in the long run rather than creates it. Accordingly, even if in the short-term we could find mechanisms guaranteeing that all displaced employees could be rehired nearby with roughly the same salary and working conditions, the practice would still be against the long-term common good for these reasons. And all this is doubly true if the hostile buyout is heavily leveraged. On this argument it will be necessary for the long-term good of society that we sustain significant gaps between the market value of the shares of a profitable company and the breakup value of the company under a liquidating hostile buyout. This argument, and kindred variations of it, is probably the most persuasive and common argument against the practice of hostile liquidating buyouts. Certainly, it is in no small measure responsible for proposed legislation favoring the severe restriction and elimination of the practice.

Incidentally, proponents of this argument need not, and generally do not, deny that sharks and raiders spend their ill-gotten profits and hence redistribute these profits back into the economy. Their point is that as long as raiders make their money in this way, it is not at all conducive to the kind of capital formation necessary for the long term production of wealth and general prosperity. Financiers, investment bankers, attorneys, and stockbrokers are integral to a service economy, but service economies without a strong basis in productive manufacturing, or in companies that are generally capital intensive in the name of competitiveness, will wither on the vine.

The Argument from the Death of Ownership

Lisa Newton has offered a third argument to the effect that allowing the hostile liquidating buyout will as a rule tend to militate against the right to private property and the right to ownership. On her view, in addition to being a practice unconscionably inhumane and destructive of the common good (because destructive of long-term general wealth), the liquidating hostile buyout is, as a rule, an assault on the right of ownership. As we shall see, this argument too is rule-utilitarian in perspective.

Her argument begins with the premise that *ownership,* as a social institution essential for the survival of society, imposes a fundamental moral duty on the owner to take care of the thing owned. The duty arises from the fact that without such care the wealth necessary for survival is imperiled. Whether ownership is single or shared, the duty corresponds to personal interest. In explicating this premise, she says:

> If I own a sheep, it is very much in my interest and incumbent upon me
> to take care of the beast and see that it thrives. If you and I together own
> a sheep, the same interest applies to both of us, the same imperative fol-
> lows, and we shall divide up the responsibilities of caring for it. If you and
> I and 998 others own it, enormous practical difficulties attend that care. But
> however small my interest in that sheep, it is still in my interest that the
> animal should thrive. Similarly, partial ownership in a whole herd of sheep,
> or a farm or a factory, or a business that owns several factories, does not
> necessitate a change in the notion of ownership (p. 506).

The next premise in the argument is that *liquidation* of property turns property into money that can be spent on consumption, but with liquidation all
future good one might have gotten from the property disappears (p. 507). Hence,
so the argument concludes, the tendency to liquidation goes strongly against
the duty of owners to take care of property in the interest of producing long-
term wealth necessary for social good and survival. She adds that the moral
weight of the most successful cultures is not on liquidation, but rather on
the side of thrift and preservation. In spelling out this argument, she says:

> *Liquidation* consumes something that is owned, or turns it into money that
> can be spent on consumption. The easiest way to liquidate the sheep is to
> eat it. The way to liquidate most owned things is to sell them. Then you
> no longer own the thing, and your responsibilities terminate; but so, of course,
> does all future good you might have gotten of the thing. Part of the cultural
> evolution of ownership has been the elaboration of a tension between reten-
> tion and liquidation, saving and spending, with the moral weight of the most
> successful cultures on the side of thrift and preservation. The business sys-
> tem probably depends as much on Ben Franklin's "a penny saved is a penny
> earned" as it does on Adam Smith's "invisible hand." The foreseen result
> of the *hand,* we may remember, was to increase the wealth, the assets, of
> a nation. For the herdsman it is evident that if you slaughter or sell all your
> sheep, you will starve in the next year; for Smith it was equally self-evident
> that it is in a businessman's interest, whatever business he may be in, to save
> his money and invest in clearing more land, breeding more beasts or build-
> ing more plants, to make more money in the future. Hence the cleared land,
> the herds, and the factories—the assets of the nation—increase without limit,
> and all persons, no matter how they participate in th economy, in fact share
> in this increased wealth. Presupposed is the willingness of all players in the
> free enterprise game to acquire things that need care if they are to yield profit,
> hence to render that care, and to accept that responsibility, over the long
> run. Should that willingness disappear, and the population suddenly show
> a preference for liquidation, all bets are off for the wealth of the nation.
> And the problem is, of course, that the developments of ownership made
> possible in the last century create excess tendencies toward liquidation (p.
> 506).

As an example of such excess tendencies toward liquidation, she notes that
institutional investors own up to 70 percent of all publicly owned corporations

and their only contractual obligation is to profit-taking for the sake of having money available at some future date. They recognize no responsibilities to preserve companies for future growth (p. 507). Moreover, accounting procedures and tax laws shift the cost of hostile acquisitions and liquidations to taxpayers by allowing the raider to take tax deductions for interest payments and to re-evaluate assets so as to reduce his taxes. In summing up her position, she concludes:

> The evils of the takeover market, then, go to the philosophical base of our market system, striking at the root of moral habits evolved over 2500 years. The corporate raiders have yet to make their first widget, grow their first carrot, or deliver their first lunch. *All* they do is turn money into money, cantilevering the profit off the shell of responsible ownership. No doubt capital is more productively lodged in some places than in others, but it follows from no known economic theory that it is more beneficial to the world when lodged in T. Boone Picken's bank account than when lodged wherever it was before he got it. Possibly, it will end up in facilitating some industrial projects—he has no intention of keeping it in a mattress, after all— but only in those that promise quick profits. We need not look to him to revitalize our smokestack industries and make them competitive on the world markets. The whole productive capacity of the American economy seems at the mercy of money men on the rampage, with all productive companies under threat of being taken over, taken apart, and eradicated. Surely, this condition cannot be healthy or good (p. 507).

From this argument she concludes that regulation favoring the elimination of such takeover practices is certainly in order. We know of no other available arguments seeking to justify such regulation.

III. ARGUMENTS FAVORING THE SHARK

In response to the three arguments against the practice of hostile liquidation buyouts, the corporate raider will be able to offer the following replies in defense of the practice of hostile liquidating buyouts.

Responses to the Arguments from Human Cost and the Destruction of Wealth

The raider is by no means blind to the human costs and pain involved in liquidating a profitable company in order to sell off the underlying assets. But his position is that of a rule-utilitarian according to whom only those acts are wrong (and ought to be prohibited) which, *as a rule or as a practice,* tend to promote more harm than good in the long run for all those affected by the practice. Acts which have just the opposite effect, i.e., those which *as a rule* tend to promote more good than harm in the long run are morally obligatory; and those which cannot be shown to do either are permissible rather than obligatory or prohibited. Given this general moral position, the raider need only reply to the argument from human cost by asserting that he may pursue a practice until someone shows that, as a matter of fact, the practice as a rule tends *in the long run* to promote more suffering than benefit, all things considered. In situations of real uncertainty or invincible ignorance, raiders may bet that their activities have long-term net social benefits. That is, the raider can defend the practice as permissible on the grounds that nobody has *shown*, rather than simply asserted, that the practice will in all likelihood lead to more harm than good in the long run. If he is right in this last claim then the raider will have responded adequately to both the argument from human cost and also to the argument from the destruction of wealth. In so doing he will have established the *permissibility* of the practice rather than the stronger and more difficult thesis that the practice *should be encouraged* because it tends to promote more good than harm in the long run for all those affected. Later on we will see whether the raider might be successful in establishing the stronger thesis, but right now the question is whether his initial response to the first two arguments is persuasive.

In defense of the raider's first argument, it is important to note that nobody has conducted anything like a long-term or longitudinal study of the effects of the practice. Presumably, such a study would minimally involve examining how capital acquired from the practice was used over a suitably long period, and whether it was used to promote the kinds of efficiencies that utlimately create wealth. The claim that it will inevitably be used only to destroy the assets necessary for long-term prosperity is by no means obviously true, if true at all. As a matter of fact, it seems gratuitious because based on dubious assumptions about how the markets will perform in the long run. The truth of the matter seems to be that there is no sound reason to think the practice will inevitably destroy, rather than create long-term wealth. Let us explain and defend this last claim.

That the hostile liquidating buyout need not inevitably, or even be more likely to, destroy wealth can be established in the following way. Suppose, for the sake of argument, that we allowed "sharks" to buy and liquidate every publicly owned company whose breakup value was sufficiently higher than the market value of its shares to generate an above average return on capital for the breakup. The argument against such a practice, as we saw above, is that the practice will, as a rule, tend to be against the public interest because it will render impossible the kind of capital formation and asset base necessary for long-term productivity and competitive success in world markets. This latter argument *assumes* that, as a general rule, open market economies will need, in order to create and maintain the sort of wealth consistent with long-term social stability, publicly held companies whose asset base allows the kinds of efficiencies of scale that only truly successful competitive companies have. In other words, the creation and maintenance of social wealth will require an economy with at least a large number of publicly owned companies whose breakup value will sufficiently exceed the market share value to make them attractive as targets for hostile liquidating buyouts. But where is the evidence for such an assumption?

Does it not seem equally plausible to assume that if all such companies were liquidated, the wealth thereby acquired would then be concentrated in privately held companies (or companies 51 percent private) producing the efficiencies of scale that are necessary for maintaining and creating public wealth? Stated differently, why not assume, for the sake of argument, that if we eliminated all such publicly owned companies, it would just as likely lead not to a destruction of public wealth but rather to a change in the way such public wealth is held? Does this not seem equally plausible?

Take the steel industry, for example. Suppose we liquidate all major publicly owned steel producers in the interest of enhancing shareholder value by liquidating the underlying assets of the company. What would then happen? According to the main argument against such a practice, we would as a rule lose wealth and jobs to those large competitive companies with the sort of asset or capital base we have just destroyed. They would control ever larger shares of the market, and the real profit would leave the nation. As a matter of fact, however, it would seem as natural to expect that the price of steel, in the absence of domestic competition, would rise to that point where there was a suitable incentive to form privately held, or largely privately held, companies managed on a more efficient basis. This seems as natural to expect as any other scenario because of the plausibility behind the claim that large companies often become inefficient as long as they are not confronted with competition. Indeed, while the current breakup value of the steel operation at USX, for example, is worth considerably more than its corresponding value reflected in the share value, there has been an ever increasing number of smaller and largely private steel companies (such as Weirton Steel and Birmingham Steel) making a substantial profit and whose share value is very close to their breakup value. In short, we have good reason to think the main argument against the practice of "the shark" is unsound because, first and foremost, it is by no means obvious that if we allow the practice to liquidate all companies whose breakup value is considerably more than their share value, we will (either necessarily or in all likelihood) thereby decrease sooner or later public wealth rather than shift the way in which wealth is owned from largely public corporations. So, it is by no means clear that the practice will inevitably, or even likely, produce the economic Armageddon some managers have suggested. In itself, this conclusion seems sufficient to block any argument for outlawing the practice based upon the so-called long-term tendency of the practice to promote social harm by destroying public wealth.

There is a second argument, moreover, to the effect that the practice should be encouraged. While such an argument is not strictly necessary to defend the view that the practice should not be outlawed, it is nonetheless important to examine because if it is correct, then there is some positive reason to recommend the practice, rather than simply allow it. This second argument asserts, as we saw above, that in the long run the practice will not only not destroy public wealth, it will create more wealth. Typically, in the face of such a claim, those opposed to the practice tend to grant that the profits made by the liquidation of such companies flow to other parts of the economy, but, as Lisa Newton has said, only insofar as those parts produce a quick profit and never into those parts that require large underlying assets rendering the breakup value of a company considerably higher than its market share value. Here again, however, we can easily imagine T. Boone Pickens, for example, deciding to enter the oil drilling business if the price of crude got high enough as a result of a significant loss of competition resulting from hostile liquidating buyouts. The higher the price of crude, the quicker he could depreciate the cost of the underlying assets, thereby bringing the shares to their full value quickly. And if the company he establishes is private (or only 49 percent public) he would need to compete efficiently, or sooner or later lose his market share and profits to those who could raise capital and run a more efficient company. In short, as long as there is reason to think the market ultimately rewards an efficient use of capital, there is good reason to think that liquidating buyouts will promote more general market efficiency even though it may be in terms of private or largely private ownership. Thus, while various managers have often claimed that the creation of long-term wealth requires a kind of efficiency that necessitates a considerable gap between the breakup value of core industries and their share value, there is good reason to think that this claim is false. Rather, there is more reason to think that what is required in the interest of efficiency and the creation of long-term public wealth is that there be no interesting gap between breakup value and share value. This is the stronger argument favoring the promotion of the practice rather than the regulation of it.

To repeat, it seems evident that the argument for regulation would work only if one can *show* that, as matter of fact, hostile liquidating takeovers tend, as a rule and in the long run, to destroy public wealth by destroying publicly held companies whose breakup value is suitably higher than their market share value. But nobody has actually shown that *that* is more likely than that the process will simply sooner or later replace such large companies with more asset-efficient privately held ones or ones in which the public holds no more than 49 percent. This conclusion suffices to render the practice at least permissible as a way of enhancing shareholder return.

Of course, those opposed to the liquidating hostile buyout will be quick to urge, in response to the above arguments, that nobody has shown, rather than simply asserted, that the practice will in fact create more wealth in the long run.[5] As Lawrence Summers has noted:

> There is, in my view, almost no evidence, other than the dubious evidence
> of the stock market, that takeovers actually reflect improved economic efficiency as a result of acquisition.[6]

The shark's response to this is twofold.

In the first place, as we noted above, even if the point were well-taken, nobody needs to show as much in order to be justified in preventing regulation of the practice. Those who would outlaw the practice need to show that, as matter of fact, the practice *will* produce a net balance of general public harm over good *in the long run.* And that has not been shown. Newton's argument itself presupposes the social benefit of private ownership. Accordingly, the right to private ownership, and its free exercise, while *prima facie* and subordinate to the common good, should not be compromised except by rules constraining those practices which are shown on the whole to do long-term, and not merely short-term, net social harm. Society has other less objectionable options to alleviate the short-term pain incurred by the practice in question.

In the second place, Professor Summers notwithstanding, it seems fair to say that there is an argument from standard economic theory that the practice *will* indeed tend in the long run to produce the general public good. Craig Lehman, for example, has offered in his essay "Takeovers and Takeover Defenses: Some Utilities of the Free Market" a core argument favoring the practice as a mechanism that enhances capital allocation which is a necessary condition for an open market to run efficiently and, in the long run, produce the general good that justifies open-market economies as more conducive to real productivity and the creation of wealth than constrained market economies. In Lehman's view, rather than *destroy* large assets, the hostile liquidating buyout promotes efficient capital reallocation for a more efficient use of assets. On his argument, it is the primary responsibility of management to promote shareholder value and long-term public wealth by eliminating inefficiencies and waste; and when management fails in that responsibility the market can, and must, force reallocation of assets to eliminate those sorts of inefficiencies. Doing so *promotes,* rather than *undermines* the general welfare. He says:

> If the market is to respond efficiently to increasing demands for some producers and decreasing demand for others—and capitalism's defenders claim that this is one of the system's major virtues—then capital must be free to flow in and out of various sectors of the economy.
>
> This can happen in a variety of ways. Suppose, for instance, that widgets are the product of the future, but that right now there is only one widget manufacturer. The new megatrend has not yet arrived. So, right now the stock of Widget Corporation (which represents ownership of widget-producing assets and a flow of future earnings from widget sales) may well be selling for less than it is worth, according to various theories of securities valuation. As the boom in widgets becomes more visible and finally arrives, however, the price of Widget Corporation stock will be bid up, and eventually it will become high enough that some investors will prefer to put up capital for new widget-producing facilities (or alternative technologies), rather than paying for the stream of earnings from the current facilities. Thus the realization of asset values is the first step in a larger process that eventually leads to a greater supply of the products consumers desire, at a price constrained by competitive pressures. This is one of the basic and fundamental utilities of a capitalistic system.
>
> One way in which takeovers are part of this picture is that they can *speed* the process of asset value realization and capital flow. If individual investors who see the value of owning widget-producing assets start buying

up the stock of Widget Corporation, it may be several years before the stock is fully priced and there is an economic incentive to bankroll new widget facilities. (Common advice to asset-oriented investors is to be very patient.) But if Behemoth Corporation or Octopus Investors Group devour all the stock of Widget Corporation in one gulp, there is no pure play left in widgets; those who want to make a killing in this area will have to put their capital into new facilities. Takeovers can thus *accelerate* the process of asset-value realization and capital flow. In any case, however, capital flow is capital flow whether it comes from the treasury of a large, established corporation or the investment of individuals. . . .[7]

He goes on to note that in the light of the above, many oil company takeovers, in addition to many takeovers in other industries (where assets are more valuable unbundled than conglomerated) are to be seen simply as manifestations of the open market trying to reallocate capital efficiently. Lehman claims that while current managements may think bigger is better, capital markets have in effect been demanding that organizations with inefficient divisions grow smaller and devote resources only to operations in which they can achieve an acceptable return on investment (p. 514):

> Capitalism thus turns out to have a built-in mechanism that counteracts the drive toward bigness for its own sake, and the takeover appears in a new light, as a way in which the market can discipline managers who have failed to heed public demands for a reallocation of capital. "Villains," such as Pickens, Carl Icahn, or Sir James Goldsmith are recast as inevitable and impersonal outgrowths of market pressures (p. 514).

In short, the basic point behind this argument is that efficiency in market activities serves the long-term general public good; companies whose breakup asset value *suitably* exceeds the share value, are not acting efficiently, and the hostile liquidating takeover is a predictable and good mechanism for imposing efficiency and promoting the long-term general good. We submit that this general argument, without involving a long-term study of the effects of the practice, tips the scale in favor of the view that the practice tends to promote more long-term good than evil for society at large.

The only plausible reply to this argument would consist in asserting, as others have urged above, that, contrary to what has been suggested, good, profitable and efficient companies often have a breakup value considerably in excess of market share value and, as a rule, that is desirable as a cushion for economic bad times or for developing products and thereby running more efficiently in the future. Such companies may appear inefficient in the short-term for those interested in the quick buck, but good managers know that the ability to generate capital from such assets when necessary is essential to long-term efficiency and viability.

The problem with this counterreply, however, is that while it is certainly true that there must be some justifiable gap between breakup value and share value in some efficient industries, where that gap exists management can usually defend it. However, with few exceptions, good companies do not have for very long a breakup value considerably in excess of market share value.

Response to the Argument from the Destruction of Ownership

Finally, if everything we have just said is true, then far from destroying ownership, the hostile liquidating buyout not only does not destroy long-term wealth, it would tend to create it; and failure to support such buyouts as market mechanisms for long-term efficiency will likely promote the sort of inefficiency that will guarantee a loss of wealth and with it, ownership. This is not to say, of course, that the efficiency promoted by such a mechanism may not change the ways in which ownership is exercised. We may, as we saw above, see more corporations with less than 50 percent public ownership; but, barring monopolistic activities, if such companies become inefficient in having more breakup value than what is reflected in share value, we can expect the market to allocate capital in a way that provides real competition. But none of this implies the death of ownership in any interesting way.

Moreover, Newton's version of the argument from destruction of ownership too closely associates liquidation with consumption. To liquidate assets is often simply to convert them to a more socially useful form; it may merely allocate wealth rather than diminish it. To this extent, her argument fails.

So, it would appear that we have some fairly persuasive arguments in defense of the shark, and against the proposal to outlaw the liquidating hostile takeover.

NOTES

1. L. Newton, 1988, "The Hostile Takeover: An Opposition View," in T. Beauchamp and N. Bowie, eds., *Ethical Theory and Business,* 3d edition (Englewood Cliffs, N.J.: Prentice Hall), pp. 501-510.

2. Testimony of Andrew C. Sigler, Chairman and Chief Executive Officer of Champion International Corporation, representing the Business Roundtable, before hearings of the Subcommittee on Telecommunications, Consumer Protection and Finance of the House Committee on Energy and Commerce, Thursday, May 23, 1985.—as cited by Lisa Newton, p. 503.

3. For others who share the same view, see P. Drucker, 1983, *Wall Street Journal,* January 5; L. Wayne, 1985, "Buyouts Altering the Face of Corporate America," *New York Times,* November 23; H. Williams, 1985, "It's Time for a Takeover Moratorium," *Fortune,* July 22, pp. 133-136.

4. H. Williams, 1985, "It's Time for a Takeover Moratorium," *Fortune,* July 22, pp. 133-136, as cited by Newton, p. 504.

5. For example, Kohlberg Kravis Roberts and Company (KKR) conducted a study in which it argued that LBOs had five beneficial consequences, namely, increased employment, higher research-and-development spending, higher tax yield for the government, continued strong capital spending, and strengthening of companies against

recession. Criticizing the study, William Long and David Ravenscraft came to the conclusion that in fact LBOs, among other things, reduced employment, decreased research and development spending, and decreased capital spending. See T. Ricks, 1989, "Two Scholars Blast KKR Buy-Out Study that Reached Pro-Takeover Conclusions," *Wall Street Journal,* May 10, p. A2; and T. Ricks, 1989, "KKR Says Critics of Its Buy-Out Study Misconstrue—But They Don't Buy That," *Wall Street Journal,* May 22, p. A2.

The problem with this whole discussion is that it is hard to believe that the long-term benefits of the practice could be assessed in terms of a study conducted only three years after a company is bought out. KKR would have been well-advised to argue the case solely on the basis of the well-known fact that open-market economies sooner or later (but not necessarily in three years) reward the kinds of efficiencies typically promoted by the efficient flow of capital stimulated by liquidating LBOs and that, at any rate, until somebody could show that the long-term interests are not served by this process, the right of shareholders to sell at a price they think fit is a basic inalienable human right. The methodology of both parties to this argument is questionable because it seems unduly arbitrary to argue for the long-term economic effects of a practice on the basis of the effects preciptitated by the practice over a three-year period. Why not a twenty-year study?

6. See *Business Ethics Report,* op. cit., p. 23.

7. C. Lehman, "Takeovers and Takeover Defenses: Some Utilities of the Free Market," in *Ethical Theory and Business,* op. cit. pp. 512–13.

ETHICS AND ACCOUNTING

Case Study

Dilemma of an Accountant

In 1976 Senator Lee Metcalf (D-Mont.) released a report on the public accounting industry which rocked the profession. Despite a decade of revisions in rules and regulations (variously established by the Securities and Exchange Commission, Accounting Principles Board, and Financial Accounting Standards Board), public accounting firms were still perceived by many on Capitol Hill as biased in favor of their clients, incapable of or unwilling to police themselves, and at times participants in coverups of client affairs. Senator Metcalf even went so far as to suggest nationalizing the industry in light of these activities.

Just prior to the Metcalf report, Daniel Potter began working as a staff accountant for Baker Greenleaf, one of the Big Eight accounting firms. In preparation for his CPA examination, Dan had rigorously studied the code of ethics of the American Institute of Certified Public Accountants (AICPA), and had thoroughly familiarized himself with his profession's guidelines for morality. He was aware of ethical situations which might pose practical problems, such as maintaining independence from the client or bearing the responsibility for reporting a client's unlawful or unreasonably misleading activities, and he knew the channels through which a CPA was expected to resolve unethical business policies. Dan had taken the guidelines very seriously: they were not only an integral part of the auditing exam, they also expressed to him the fundamental dignity and calling of the profession—namely, to help sustain the system of checks and balances on which capitalism has been based.

Daniel Potter firmly believed that every independent auditor was obligated to maintain professional integrity, if what he believed to be the best economic system in the world was to survive.

Thus, when Senator Metcalf's report was released, Dan was very interested in discussing it with numerous partners in the firm. They responded thoughtfully to the study and were concerned with the possible ramifications of Senator Metcalf's assessment. Dan's discussions at this time and his subsequent experiences during his first year and a half at Baker Greenleaf confirmed his initial impressions that the firm deserved its reputation for excellence in the field.

Dan's own career had been positive. After graduating in Economics from an Ivy League school, he had been accepted into Acorn Business School's accountant training program, and was sponsored by Baker Greenleaf. His enthusiasm and abilities had been clear from the start, and he was rapidly promoted through the ranks and enlisted to help recruit undergraduates to work for the firm. In describing his own professional ethos, Dan endorsed the Protestant work ethic on which he had been raised, and combined this belief with a strong faith in his own worth and responsibility. A strong adherent to the assumptions behind the profession's standards and prepared to defend them as a part of his own self-interest, he backed up his reasoning with an unquestioning belief in loyalty to one's employer and to the clients who helped support his employer. He liked the clear-cut hierarchy of authority and promotion schedule on which Baker Greenleaf was organized, and once had likened his loyalty to his superior to the absolute loyalty which St. Paul advised the slave to have towards his earthly master "out of fear of God" (Colossans 3:22). Thus, when he encountered the first situation where both his boss and his client seemed to be departing from the rules of the profession, Dan's moral dilemma was deep-seated and difficult to solve.

The new assignment began as a welcome challenge. A long-standing and important account which Baker had always shared with another Big Eight accounting firm needed a special audit, and Baker had reason to expect that a satisfactory performance might secure it the account exclusively. Baker put its best people on the job, and Dan was elated to be included on the special assignment team; success could lead to an important one-year promotion.

Oliver Freeman, the project senior, assigned Dan to audit a wholly-owned real estate subsidiary (Sub) which had given Baker a lot of headaches in the past. "I want you to solve the problems we're having with this Sub, and come out with a clean opinion (i.e., a confirmation that the client's statements are presented fairly) in one month. I leave it to you to do what you think is necessary."

For the first time Dan was allotted a subordinate, Gene Doherty, to help him. Gene had worked with the project senior several times before on the same client's account, and he was not wholly enthusiastic about Oliver's supervision. "Oliver is completely inflexible about running things his own way —most of the staff accountants hate him. He contributes a 7:00 A.M. to 9:00 P.M. day every day, and expects everyone else to do the same. You've *really* got to put out, on his terms, to get an excellent evaluation from him." Oliver was indeed a strict authoritarian. Several times over the next month Dan and Oliver had petty disagreements over interpretive issues, but when Dan began to realize just how stubborn Oliver was, he regularly deferred to his superior's opinion.

Three days before the audit was due, Dan completed his files and submitted them to Oliver for review. He had uncovered quite a few problems but managed to solve all except one: one of the Sub's largest real estate properties was valued on the balance sheet at $2 million, and Dan's own estimate of its value was no more than $100,000. The property was a run-down structure in an undesirable neighborhood, and had been unoccupied for several years. Dan discussed his proposal to write down the property by $1,900,000 with the Sub's managers, but since they felt there was a good prospect of renting the property shortly, they refused to write down its value. Discussion with the client had broken off at this point, and Dan had to resolve the disagreement on his own. His courses of action were ambiguous, and depended on how he defined the income statement: according to AICPA regulations on materiality, any difference in opinion between the client and the public accountant which affected the income statement by more than 3% was considered material and had to be disclosed in the CPA's opinion. The $1,900,000 write-down would have a 7% impact on the Sub's net income, but less than 1% on the client's consolidated net income. Dan eventually decided that since the report on the Sub would be issued separately (although for the client's internal use only), the write-down did indeed represent a material difference in opinion.

The report which he submitted to Oliver Freeman contained a recommendation that it be filed with a subject-to-opinion proviso, which indicated that all the financial statements were reasonable subject to the $1.9 million adjustment disclosed in the accompanying opinion. After Freeman reviewed Dan's files, he fired back a list of "To Do's," which was the normal procedure at Baker Greenleaf. Included in the list was the following note:

1. Take out the pages in the files where you estimate the value of the real estate property at $100,000.
2. Express an opinion that the real estate properties are correctly evaluated by the Sub.
3. Remove your "subject-to-opinion" designation and substitute a "clean opinion."

Dan immediately wrote back on the list of "To Do's" that he would not alter his assessment since it clearly violated his own reading of accounting regulations. That afternoon Oliver and Dan met behind closed doors.

Oliver first pointed out his own views to Dan:

1. He (Oliver) wanted no problems on this audit. With six years of experience he knew better than Dan how to handle the situation.

2. Dan was responsible for a "clean opinion."
3. Any neglect of his duties would be viewed as an act of irresponsibility.
4. The problem was not material to the Client (consolidated) and the Sub's opinion would only be used "in house."
5. No one read or cared about these financial statements anyway.

The exchange became more heated as Dan reasserted his own interpretation of the write-down, which was that it was a material difference to the Sub and a matter of importance from the standpoint of both professional integrity and legality. He posited a situation where Baker issued a clean opinion which the client subsequently used to show prospective buyers of the property in question. Shortly thereafter the buyer might discover the real value of the property and sue for damages. Baker, Oliver, and Dan would be liable. Both men agreed that such a scenario was highly improbable, but Dan continued to question the ethics of issuing a clean opinion. He fully understood the importance of this particular audit and expressed his loyalty to Baker Greenleaf and to Oliver, but nevertheless, believed that, in asking him to issue knowingly a false evaluation, Freeman was transgressing the bounds of conventional loyalty. Ultimately a false audit might not benefit Baker Greenleaf or Dan.

Freeman told Dan he was making a mountain out of a molehill and he was jeopardizing the client's account and hence Baker Greenleaf's welfare. Freeman also reminded Dan that his own welfare patently depended on the personal evaluation which he would receive on this project. Dan hotly replied that he would not be threatened, and as he left the room, he asked, "What would Senator Metcalf think?"

A few days later Dan learned that Freeman had pulled Dan's analysis from the files and substituted a clean opinion. He also issued a negative evaluation of Daniel Potter's performance on this audit. Dan knew that he had the right to report the incident to his partner counselor or to the personnel department, but was not terribly satisfied with either approach. He would have preferred to take the issue to an independent review board within the company, but Baker Greenleaf had no such board. However, the negative evaluation would stand, Oliver's arrogance with his junior staff would remain unquestioned, and the files would remain with Dan's name on them unless he raised the incident with someone.

He was not at all sure what he should do. He knew that Oliver's six years with Baker Greenleaf counted for a lot, and he felt a tremendous obligation to trust his superior's judgment and perspective. He also was aware that Oliver was inclined to stick to his own opinions. As Dan weighed the alternative, the vision of Senator Metcalf calling for nationalization continued to haunt him.

Milton Snoeyenbos
Ray D. Dillon

Accounting Ethics

In 1986 the American Institute of Certified Public Accountants (AICPA) retained the Harris polling organization to conduct an opinion poll focusing on attitudes of the American public and special targeted groups toward the accounting profession.[1] Each group whose opinion was sampled was asked its views of the ethics of twelve key leadership and professional groups. Certified Public Accountants (CPAs) ranked at the top; the groups sampled believed that accountants rank higher in their ethical practices than, in order: professors, bankers, doctors, newspaper editors, television newscasters, corporate executives, financial planners, stockbrokers, members of Congress, lawyers, and insurance agents. Among those of the sampled groups with some detailed knowledge of accounting, the poll revealed a very high degree of confidence that CPAs are ethical. Top corporate executives have this opinion by 92% to 7%, corporate audit committee members by 93% to 5%, creditors by 95% to 2%, attorneys by 85% to 12%, state and federal officials by 96% to 3%, congressional aides by 81% to 14%, media members by 83% to 15%, academics by 93% to 5%, and security analysts by 79% to 18%.

Although these poll results must have cheered the profession, just prior to their release George Anderson, chair of an AICPA committee set up to examine the profession's ethical standards, said: "The accounting profession is facing a crisis of immense proportions. Public confidence in the profession is eroding, and this erosion can be directly attributed to the alarming amount of work that does not meet the profession's standards or the public's expectations."[2] How do we square Anderson's concerns with the poll results? One clue is that although Harris found that large majorities of the groups polled believe that CPAs are well qualified, competent, objective, honest, and independent, a 58% to 36% majority of the general public favor stricter governmental regulation of accountants. This poll finding matches Anderson's concern with the "public's expectations." Apparently, although the general public believes the vast majority of CPAs are ethical, it also believes that some are acting improperly. To curtail the practices of the few the general public favors more governmental regulation.

To address these and many other concerns, the AICPA restructured its ethics code in 1988. This essay discusses the new code and recent developments in accounting ethics. After a few general remarks about the nature and function of professional codes of ethics, we focus on the AICPA Code's structure. We close with a discussion of some of the ethical problems facing the profession.

A profession is a group of people characterized by:

1. possession of a technical body of knowledge;
2. a professional association establishing
   a. competence requirements for entry into the profession
   b. technical standards for use of the body of knowledge
   c. an ethical code
   d. a mechanism for code enforcement;
3. a commitment to socially responsible behavior.

That there is a need for accounting is obvious. Businesses and other organizations make claims concerning their activities by issuing financial statements; investors, government agencies, creditors, and other interested parties base a wide variety of decisions on these statements. Because financial information is complex and voluminous, and because those who use it seldom have direct access to the data, there is a need for an independent review of the provider's claims. So, yes, we need accountants; but do we need an accounting *profession*? In our society, yes, we do. Although there are a variety of possible review mechanisms, including governmental review bodies, our society has selected private accounting firms exclusively to perform the audit function. These accounting firms are also hired and paid by the organizations whose statements the accounting firms audit. Because accounting firms have been granted a collective monopoly and are paid by those whose statements they audit, society has every right to demand that the firms perform their tasks with competence, independence, integrity, and a sense of public responsibility. In short, we have every right to demand professional status of accounting.

Our society has consistently permitted the accounting profession to develop the two foundations that constitute accounting's technical body of knowledge: generally accepted accounting principles (GAAP) and generally accepted auditing standards (GAAS). Although the Securities and Exchange Commission (SEC) has legislative authority to promulgate GAAP, it has always relied primarily on the accounting profession to develop these principles. The Financial Accounting Standards Board (FASB), a body independent from the AICPA, but consisting of a majority of CPAs, formulates the GAAP that must be followed by accountants when preparing financial statements. The AICPA attempts to assure the *competence* of independent auditors by specifying entry-level requirements for admittance to the profession and by establishing GAAS for use by CPAs. Thus, a baccalaureate degree in accounting and passage of the CPA examination are required for admittance to the profession. In 1988 the AICPA stipulated that CPAs in public practice must complete 120 hours of continuing professional education over each three-year period in order to retain their AICPA membership. The GAAS were developed to assist the CPA in attesting to whether financial statements were prepared in accordance with GAAP and fairly reflect the organization's activities.

The GAAS provide a major basis for the profession's primary social responsibility—the client's and the user's need for reliable information—and there are three types of such standards.[3] The *general standards* require that auditors have adequate proficiency, maintain independence, and exercise professional care in job performance. *Field work standards* require that the auditor: (1) adequately plan and supervise work, (2) properly evaluate the audited firm's internal control mechanism, and (3) gather sufficient evidence to afford a reasonable basis for an opinion. *Reporting standards* specify guidelines for the auditor's report. Although the GAAS are general, the AICPA issues specific interpretations of the standards from time to time. The AICPA also issues industry audit guidelines for specific areas, e.g., Medicare audits. CPAs must attest that financial statements are prepared according to GAAP. In general, the profession's entry requirements and technical foundations as set forth in GAAP and GAAS establish a basis for professional competence and accountability to society, and also provide guidelines for job performance.

To this point we have sketched briefly (and very incompletely) three components of the accounting profession's code that we listed: 1, 2a and 2b. In GAAP the profession has a technical body of knowledge (1), in GAAS it has technical standards for the use of such knowledge (2b), and the AICPA sets various competency requirements for becoming a CPA (2a). The GAAS are a key part of (3), the profession's commitment to socially responsible behavior, since adhering to GAAS is necessary to providing reliable information to users. We now turn to the AICPA's ethics code and enforcement policies (2c and 2d), the remaining elements of a profession and the central focus of this essay. Along the way we will also comment on the profession's commitment to social responsibility.

Every viable professional code of ethics consists of three parts: concepts, rules, and interpretations. The concepts section defines and elucidates central terms. The rules section typically consists of negative injunctions of the form: "A member shall not do X." The interpretations section lists specific interpretations of the rules that a governing body makes over time; it delineates guidelines for the scope and applicability of the rules. Interpretations are also standardly stated as negative injunctions. Now there is some merit in listing rules and interpretations as negative injunctions, for these can be stated in relatively precise terms, whereas positive injunctions ("A member shall do X") must be worded generally to cover many possibilities of action. The problem with basing an ethical code exclusively on negative injunctions is that this allows the professional to search the rules and interpretations and, if an act is not explicitly prohibited, infer that it is ethically permissible. Such an approach regards ethics not as a set of ideals for which to strive, but rather a minimal set of standards to be obeyed.

The new 1988 AICPA code, called the Code of Professional Conduct (hereafter, the Code) represents a noticeable departure from and advance over other ethical codes. The concepts section, titled "Standards of Professional Conduct," sets forth positive, goal-oriented standards of behavior. For example, Article II on the public interest states:

> Members should accept the obligation to act in a way that will serve the public interest, honor the public trust, and demonstrate commitment to professionalism.[4]

Article III says the following about integrity:

> To maintain and broaden public confidence, members should perform all professional responsibilities with the highest sense of integrity.[5]

Throughout, the Standards state high ethical and performance standards that the CPA should strive to attain and maintain. These standards provide a positive framework for the eleven enforceable rules and numerous interpretations that follow, most of which are stated as negative injunctions. It should be stressed that the new code makes an unequivocal commitment to the public interest. Article II states that a "distinguishing mark of a profession is acceptance of its responsibility to the public,"[6] where this term is defined as all who use or rely on CPA services.

In addition to its public-interest commitment, the new code emphasizes the importance of integrity, objectivity, and independence. A casual reader of the code might object that these concepts are not tightly defined in the standards section, and hence the entire code suffers from vagueness. However, a close reading of the Standards, Rules, Interpretations, the AICPA's Supplementary Statements, and relevant sections of the GAAP and the GAAS reveals that these concepts are adequately specified.

In a general sense an *independent* person is not subject to others' control: "Independence precludes relationships that may appear to impair a member's objectivity in rendering attestation services."[7] In this sense the auditor should not be subordinate to the provider whose financial statements he audits. Legally he is not an agent of the firm he audits, hence he does not have the agent's duties of loyalty and obedience to that firm. From an ethical and social viewpoint the auditor is to review the provider's claims to assure users that these claims are both fair and meet professional standards. If the auditor subordinates his judgment to that of the provider, such assurance would be undercut. Insistence on independence from the provider is especially important given that the provider selects the auditor and pays his fees. The auditor, then, should assume responsibility for his own opinion, based upon professional standards.

It follows that the auditor must also be independent of vested interests, personal interest, and third-party interests or relationships that might impair his professional judgment. The auditor has the same obligation to the provider that he has to users: to establish that the provider's financial statements are fair and meet professional standards. If he subordinates his judgment to his own interests or the interests of third parties or users, he fails in his professional obligation to both the provider and the potential user. It is in this sense that the auditor is to remain *objective;* he is to focus just on the facts of the matter at hand. His task is to consider just the evidence in light of his profession's standards and not subordinate his judgment to anyone.

Independence and objectivity, however, are not sufficient to establish behavior as ethical; the auditor must also act with *integrity.* The auditor must base his opinions on the facts, not just a select set of facts, but the complete set of relevant facts in accordance with professional standards. Furthermore, he must be honest in presenting those facts. It is true that the new Standards do not say much about integrity other than saying the auditor must be honest and candid. However, Rules 201, 202 and 203 commit the auditor to compliance with the GAAP, the GAAS, and other technical standards, many of which are directly relevant to integrity. For example, the fieldwork standards of the GAAS read:

1. The work is to be adequately planned and assistants, if any, are to be properly supervised.
2. A sufficient understanding of the internal control structure is to be obtained to plan the nature, timing, and extent of tests to be performed.
3. Sufficient competent evidential matter is to be obtained through inspection, observation, inquiries, and confirmations to afford a reasonable basis for an opinion regarding the financial statements under audit.[8]

If the auditor intentionally or unintentionally fails to gather enough evidence to make an objective opinion, (3) is violated. Failure to disclose a material fact known to him but not indicated in the financial statements, the disclosure of which would be necessary to make the statements not misleading, also results in a violation of (3). If the auditor fails to report a material misstatement that he knows to be present in the financial statements, (3) is violated. Because of (2) the auditor cannot claim that a failure to satisfy (3) rests on an inadequate internal control system in the firm he audits. Standard (1) precludes dishonesty that might be masked by a claim of inadequate planning or supervision. In addition, the reporting standards of the GAAS require audit reports to be in accordance with GAAP, which precludes a failure to direct attention to any material departure from GAAP. Thus, the requirement of integrity is built solidly into the profession's technical and ethical standards. Accordingly, the new standards cannot be faulted for providing a loose definition of "integrity."

In our opinion, the AICPA through its new code of conduct has provided an adequate specification of professional obligations. It provides guidelines for appropriate behavior and criteria for enforcement action when behavior is inappropriate.

The accounting profession is not, however, without its critics. We discuss eight major problem areas, classifiable into four general types: (1) the issue of who should be responsible for setting the basic, technical precepts of the profession, namely, the GAAP and the GAAS; (2) three problems that arise because of obligations specified in the Code of Conduct, namely, whether the auditor can both satisfy the public interest and the client's right to confidentiality, whether auditor independence can be maintained when the client pays his fee and can dismiss him at will, and whether an auditor can maintain independence when his firm also provides business services to the same client; (3) three issues related to the audit, namely, what the audit report should say, what the auditor's responsibilities should be for fraud detection and reporting, and whether the audit function should include a projection into the future; and (4) the issue of whether the Code of Conduct is adequately enforced.

WHO SHOULD SET ACCOUNTING AND AUDITING PRECEPTS?

Critics of accounting claim that the GAAP and the GAAS are "the writings of persons who have impacted into them their own particular vested interests, and those of their clients," and the profession itself should not determine these basic precepts.[9] Now part of this criticism rests on an alleged threat to independence because of self-interest. The standard remedy proposed is governmental specification of standards. However, this position overlooks the fact that the government is the major user and provider of financial statements. Hence, the problem of independence would simply emerge in a new context. Although there are problems with the present system, it seems likely that the potential for abuse is greater if the government sets accounting and auditing standards.

The other basis of this criticism is that the standards exhibit a degree of flexibility that leads to auditor abuse in terms of self-interest. Two remedies have been proposed. One is that whoever sets the standards should set very specific standards that severely limit accounting and auditing alternatives. The problem here is that the factors that auditors attempt to record are dynamic; to strap the auditor with inflexible standards over time raises the possibility that he will record an illusion. The Interstate Commerce Commission required strict, uniform accounting standards for railroads in 1914, at which time the system was widely regarded as a model accounting system. Half a century later the system was still in use but very dated. In following the dated standards, many railroads' financial statements were no longer in accordance with the then current GAAP. Adherence to overly rigid standards in this case has not led to high levels of utility for the railroads or for users of their statements. The other remedy, suggested by Briloff, is to: (1) abandon the quest for tight rules and "leave it to the marketplace of ideas to judge the quality of the principles in practice," (2) shift responsibility for the financial statements from management to the auditor, and (3) assign the FASB responsibility to review accounting alternatives in practice.[10] The danger with (1), however, is that if standards are too loose, statements within an industry might not be comparable. With respect to (3), if there are a variety of principles and the FASB, with Briloff, is to ask "Did the auditor apply the best principles? . . . If not, why not?" the FASB is assigned an open-ended task. Indeed, there is this dilemma for auditors: if standards are too flexible, comparability is impaired; but if they are too rigid, they probably will not capture the dynamics of business. Hence, standards with some flexibility are required, whoever sets them. Our view is that the FASB, which currently sets the GAAP, does attempt to walk the proper line between rigidity and anarchy.

Furthermore, it is very difficult to make the charge of self-interest against the FASB stick.[11] The FASB is a board independent from the AICPA, consisting of seven members who come from a variety of business and accounting backgrounds. Members must have a knowledge of business disciplines and a concern for the public interest in matters related to financial accounting and reporting. The FASB members are appointed by the Financial Accounting Federation, an independent, nonprofit organization. The FAF's trustees periodically review the FASB's structure and procedures to assure they are functioning properly. Another independent advisory council provides technical advice to the FASB. All FASB meetings are open to the public. The SEC has legislative authority to establish the GAAP, but to this point it has trusted the private sector to set these principles. The FASB continues to be a good mechanism for responding to accelerating business change, which will continue to pose difficult problems for those who set GAAP.

PUBLIC INTEREST/CONFIDENTIALITY DILEMMA

As we have noted, a CPA has a duty of integrity, to be honest and candid, along with an obligation to act in the public interest. But a CPA also has a duty of confidentiality to his client. Rule 301, an enforceable rule, states: "A member in public practice shall not disclose any confidential client information without the specific consent of the client."[12] There are exceptions to the confidentiality requirement; for example, confidentiality does not relieve a member of his obligations to GAAP and GAAS. However, some courts have convicted accountants for breaches of confidentiality and others have convicted them for failure to disclose confidential information. So catch-22 situations will inevitably occur that are borderline as regards these two obligations. In such cases the ethical act may not be at all clear, and whatever decision he makes may open the auditor to legal liability.[13]

While we acknowledge that such dilemmas will occur, it is important to recognize that their mere existence is not a criticism of the profession. The criticism would have to be: a code that permits such dilemmas is poorly structured; it should be rewritten so they do not occur. But this involves a fundamental misconception of ethics codes. To write a code that avoids all problems is simply impossible. In this case two legitimate rights are involved: the client's right to confidentiality and the user's right to be protected from harm. Both are legitimate; neither is absolute. Although codes are written in absolute, categorical form ("A member shall not do X"), everyone acknowledges that these rules are prima facie, not absolute. The code's Interpretations section spells out qualifying conditions. Once an interpretation is made it guides behavior in certain limited types of cases. But in a profession as dynamic as accounting no code will cover the unforeseen borderline cases that will invariably crop up. Ethical decision-making in such instances is not mechanical; professional judgment is often required. It is interesting to note that the new 1988 AICPA code states in its Standards:

> A distinguishing mark of a profession is acceptance of its responsibility to the public. The accounting profession's public consists of clients, credit grantors, governments, employers, investors, the business and financial community, and others who rely on the objectivity and integrity of certified public accountants. . . . In discharging their professional responsibilities, members may encounter conflicting pressures from among each of these groups. In resolving those conflicts, members should act with integrity, guided by the precept that when members fulfill their responsibility to the public, clients' and employers' interests are best served.[14]

While this standard seems to tilt strongly in favor of the public interest, we must remember that the client is part of the "public" and that Rule 301 is enforceable whereas the standards are not. So how the public interest/confidentiality dilemma will play out is a matter for the profession and, of course, the courts. That option is far preferable to trying to achieve the impossible, namely, writing a problem-free code.

THE INDEPENDENCE/CLIENT PAYS-THE-FEE DILEMMA

Critics charge that clients exert a dominant influence over auditors because they contract with auditors and can dismiss them at will. The upshot is said to be an asymmetry of power that too often undermines the auditor's independence. The critics' remedy frequently is to suggest that the client/auditor contract be severed, and the auditor made truly independent by affording him public employee status. The idea is that the auditor's neutrality would be ensured in his relationship with providers and users of financial statements.

Again, however, this argument overlooks the fact that the government itself is the major user and provider of financial statements. So, the problem of independence would be shifted, not obviated. And the potential for abuse is probably greater under the critics' proposal. For example, at the height of the improper payments scandal that resulted from the Watergate investigations, the IRS required of 1,200 large corporations that they submit with their tax returns answers to questions about possible improper payments. The IRS also requested such responses from the companies' auditors, under threat of criminal charges for false responses. Furthermore, it threatened to refuse to finalize its examination of the firms' returns unless the auditors' statements were received. The threat to the private sector, the Orwellian implications of which are clear in the above case, would be magnified if auditors were governmental employees. It is doubtful that making him an employee of the major user and provider of financial statements would strengthen the auditor's independence.

If the critics' remedy is too extreme, this does not mean that their criticism of the profession entirely lacks force; there are troublesome cases where independence has been affected because of the asymmetry of power in the client/auditor relationship. For example, "opinion shopping" can threaten independence. This occurs when a company seeks an opinion from other CPA firms and, when it obtains a more favorable opinion, either threatens to replace or actually replaces the engaged audit firm to get the opinion it wants. The answer to such problems is for the AICPA to strengthen auditor independence, as it did on opinion shopping in 1986 with its Statement on Auditing Standards No. 50. It sets out requirements for providing opinions to firms that are not clients.

THE INDEPENDENCE/SCOPE-OF-SERVICES DILEMMA

As accounting firms have grown, they have developed the ability to serve their clients in certain capacities other than the audit function: for example, tax services and management advisory services. Critics allege that audit independence cannot be completely maintained when these other services are performed. The standard remedy proposed is that accounting firms should be banned from providing such services; the scope of their service should be narrowed to the audit function.[15]

The central question here is whether auditor independence is actually impaired. The answer is no. As Elliott and Jacobson point out: "There is no known case where performing management advisory services has been shown to impair independence. . . . The abundant evidence from litigated audits has provided no examples, and none have surfaced from the work of academic researchers and professional bodies."[16] If auditors' independence is in fact not compromised, then accounting firms clearly should be allowed to perform peripheral services, for doing so has numerous benefits. There is increasing demand for expertise, and accountants have skills that can directly benefit firms; we want the best advisor available to provide management with advice regarding, say, a cost accounting system, and that person will in all probability be a CPA. Furthermore, the ability to provide a wide range of services probably improves the audit's quality. Accordingly, utility for society and the client, as well as the CPA firm, favors allowing CPAs to provide auxiliary services.

The AICPA Code specifies that auditors must be independent in appearance as well as in fact. Critics contend that at least the appearance of independence is threatened when the auditor of a company also provides peripheral services. However, given that utility to society and the client are fostered by having experts, including CPAs, advise management, and given that in fact auditors are independent in such contexts, this is more an argument that favors strengthening the independence criteria for auditors rather than preventing the use of their services. And, of course, this is precisely what the profession has done; over the years the AICPA has issued numerous Statements concerning tax practice and management advisory services.[17]

THE AUDIT REPORT EXPECTATION GAP PROBLEM

The Harris poll revealed a distinct difference between what the general public believes auditors are responsible for and what auditors and those knowledgeable about the profession believe that auditors are responsible for. This difference is labeled the "expectation gap." Part of the expectation gap arose because, as the Harris poll revealed, the public systematically misunderstood the auditor's standard report in use since 1948: "almost all of the general public . . . simply do not understand the meaning of a clean opinion."[18] As Briloff and others have pointed out, however, the audit report contained ambiguous language that also contributed to the gap.[19] To close this part of the gap the AICPA auditing standards board issued a Statement on Auditing Standards (SAS No. 58), effective in 1989.[20] SAS 58, written in clearer language than the old audit report, differentiates management responsibilities for its financial statements from the auditor's responsibility to express an opinion on the statements. It also states clearly the work the auditor performs and the assurance he provides that the financial statements are free from material misstatement.

THE EXPECTATIONS GAP: FRAUD DETECTION AND REPORTING

Statistics indicate that theft is a major problem for corporations, and auditors (internal and independent) uncover only about 20 percent of those frauds that are detected.[21] Critics charge that auditors are not doing enough to detect and report fraud. However, the AICPA has a statement on fraud detection, namely, SAS No. 53: "The auditor should assess the risk that errors and irregularities may cause the financial statements to contain a material misstatement. Based on that assessment, the auditor should design the audit to provide reasonable assurance of detecting errors and irregularities that are material to the financial statements."[22] SAS No. 53 deals with "errors and irregularities," the former being unintentional, the latter involving intentional misconduct, including employee fraud or theft of assets. So the AICPA policy is quite clear. Furthermore, the CPA who fails to detect fraud that would have been uncovered if the GAAS had been followed is held responsible for damages the client incurs. But clearly the auditor cannot be held responsible for detecting immaterial fraud; the cost would be enormous if the auditor had to establish evidence sufficient to *guarantee* that no fraud existed at, say, IBM. Similarly, although the auditor has an obligation to examine and assess the audited firm's internal controls management can override internal controls, and engage in collusion or other improper actions. If total responsibility for detection of such activities were placed on the auditor, his detective work would be very expensive. Although utility calculations are difficult in this area, the above reasoning suggests that the present fraud detection responsibilities are appropriate.

Just as he cannot be expected to uncover all irregularities, the auditors cannot be expected to detect all illegal activities. For example, the auditor has no special expertise for determining whether a firm is in compliance with OSHA, FDA, and EPA rules and regulations. The auditor is neither a detective nor an attorney. So, the CPA cannot be expected to design the audit to detect all illegal acts. But SAS No. 54 states that when auditors believe there is a possible illegal act, they must obtain sufficient information to determine and assess its effect on the financial statements.[23]

When irregularities or illegal acts that are material to the financial statements are detected, SAS Nos. 53 and 54 require the auditor to report the information to the audited firm's senior management or audit committee. In certain cases the auditor is required to report to bodies outside the client firm. In recent years numerous proposals have been made to require or encourage auditors to blow the whistle to the government on management fraud. Perhaps the most interesting proposal, authored primarily by Representative Ron Wyden, would require auditors to report material management fraud to the government if the fraud is not corrected by management within a certain time period after the auditors give management notice. If this proposal could be crafted so that it didn't put the SEC in the business of setting audit standards and if it protected whistleblowing auditors from being sued, it would give auditors stronger powers to curb fraud. Whether the bill would have utility would depend on whether the amount of fraud deterred would outweigh the increased auditing costs.

THE EXPECTATION GAP: AUDIT PROJECTION

The audit report used from 1948 to 1988 provided an opinion on a firm's financial statements at a particular point in time; it presented no opinion on the firm's future status. The Harris poll found that most people believe that a clean opinion certifies the company as a good investment, which implies that it will at least be a going concern in the near future.[24] Given this belief, it is no wonder that many people question an audit's quality when a business fails soon after its statements receive a clean opinion.

To meet this part of the expectation gap the AICPA revised the auditor's standard report. Beginning in 1989, SAS No. 59 requires the auditor to: (1) evaluate every audit to determine whether a substantial doubt exists about whether the company will be able to continue as a going concern for a period of up to a year; (2) consider the adequacy of management's financial statement disclosure about the ability to continue as a going concern; and (3) include in the audit report an explanatory paragraph stating and describing the uncertainty when there is substantial doubt about the ability of a firm to continue as a going concern.[25]

CODE ENFORCEMENT

Many critics of accounting allege that the code is not adequately enforced. The charge is that the number of enforcement actions is not commensurate with the amount of accounting sin.[26] One problem with this criticism is that although we know the AICPA takes approximately twenty-five disciplinary actions per year, we don't know the number of serious code violations. The fact that only a few disciplinary actions are taken may simply mean there isn't much serious accounting sin going on. Then, too, the critics often erroneously assume that when financial statement sin occurs, it must be accounting sin; for example, they assume incorrectly that when management fraud occurs the auditors definitely have violated their code if they fail to detect it.

Although accounting critics often assume that code enforcement ought to be modeled on legal enforcement, the two are quite distinct in two important ways.[27] First, the state has vastly more punitive powers than a profession. Unlike the legal system, a profession cannot send someone to jail, assess fines, or even subpoena witnesses; maximally, a profession can only ban an individual from professional membership. In accounting, the ultimate responsibility for discipline lies with the state boards of accountancy, since they are the licensing bodies for accountants practicing within their jurisdictions. A state board can revoke a license to practice as its maximum punishment, which is tantamount to removal from the profession. Second, the law stresses punishment for transgressors, whereas a profession seeks to change behavior and avoid problems in the future. Even when sanctions are imposed in a profession, they are typically viewed as remedial. It follows that those who urge that professional self-regulation be modeled on legal enforcement are bound to be disappointed, but unjustifiably so.

In 1988, the AICPA adopted a quality review program for members in public practice; it requires periodic review by outsiders of a CPA firm as a condition of AICPA membership.[28] The profession required this review procedure because it recognized that complaint-based code enforcement procedures are often ineffective. Mandatory reviews will help spot substandard work and improve audit quality; consistent with the emphasis in self-regulatory enforcement programs, the focus is remedial and educational. Disciplinary actions are undertaken only when a firm refuses to cooperate or exhibits very substandard work. In addition to its quality review program, as of 1990 the AICPA requires that all firms auditing SEC clients must join the SEC practice section (SECPS) of the AICPA division for CPA firms. The SECPS's peer review program, in place since 1977, has proved highly successful in improving audit quality.[29] In addition to peer review, the results of which are open to the public, SECPS firms are subject to public oversight by a Public Oversight Board, which evaluates SECPS activities and recommends improvements. Finally, the SECPS has a quality control committee that reviews the audit practices of accounting firms that are defendants in SEC-related legal cases. In these ways the SECPS has implemented a remedial and educational enforcement program that benefits the accounting profession, clients, users, and society at large.

The GAAP, the GAAS, and the profession's Code of Conduct will most certainly require modifications in the future; but this is simply a corollary of the profession's dynamism. We live in a time of accelerating economic change, yet we have in place a system that provides the world's most believeable, fair, and accurate financial statements, and is also able to respond well to rapid change.

NOTES

1. "How the Public Sees CPAs," *Journal of Accountancy* 162, no. 6 (December 1986): 16–34.

2. George D. Anderson, "A Fresh Look at Standards of Professional Conduct," *Journal of Accountancy* 160, no. 3 (September 1985): p. 92.

3. *AICPA Professional Standards,* vol. 1 (Chicago: Commerce Clearing House, 1990), sections 200, 300, 400 and 500. Material from the Code, the GAAP, and the GAAS is paraphrased unless it is directly quoted. Both paraphrased and quoted sources are cited.

4. *AICPA Professional Standards,* vol. 2 (Chicago: Commerce Clearing House, 1990), ET Section 53, p. 4301.

5. Ibid., ET Section 54, p. 4311.

6. Ibid., ET Section 53, p. 4301.

7. Ibid., ET Section 55, p. 4321.

8. *AICPA Professional Standards.* vol. 1, AU Section 150, p. 81.

9. Abraham Briloff, "Codes of Conduct: Their Sound and Fury," in *Ethics, Free Enterprise, and Public Policy,* Richard T. de George and Joseph A. Pichler, eds. (New York: Oxford University Press, 1978), p. 267.

10. Abraham Briloff, "How Accountants Can Recover Their Balance," *Business and Society Review* No. 24 (Winter 1977–78): 64–68.

11. Dennis R. Beresford, "What's Right with the FASB," *Journal of Accountancy* 169, no. 1 (January 1990): 81–85.

12. *AICPA Professional Standards,* vol. 2, ET Section 301, p. 4671.

13. John E. Beach, "Code of Ethics: The Professional Catch-22," *Journal of Accounting and Public Policy* 3 (1984): 311–23.

14. *AICPA Professional Standards,* vol. 2, ET Section 53, p. 4301.

15. Briloff, "How Accountants Can Recover Their Balance," p. 67.

16. Robert K. Elliott and Peter D. Jacobson, "Reexamining Independence," *New Accountant* 7, no. 2 (October 1991), p. 23.

17. *AICPA Professional Standards,* vol. 2, pp. 15,001–15,054; pp. 18,003–18,192.

18. Harris Poll, "How the Public Sees CPAs," p. 34.

19. Abraham Briloff, "Old Myths and New Realities in Accounting," *The Accounting Review* (July 1966), p. 488.

20. *AICPA Professional Standards,* vol. 1, AU Section 508, pp. 651–75.

21. Joseph T. Wells, "Six Common Myths About Fraud," *Journal of Accountancy* 169, no. 2 (February 1990): 82–88.

22. *AICPA Professional Standards,* vol. 1, AU Section 316, p. 240.

23. Ibid., pp. 251–56.

24. "How the Public Sees CPAs," p. 34.

25. *AICPA Professional Standards,* vol. 1, AU Section 341, pp. 451–56.

26. Briloff, "Codes of Conduct: Their Sound and Fury," pp. 272–76.

27. Robert K. Mautz, "Self-Regulation—Perils and Problems," *Journal of Accountancy* 155, no. 5 (May 1983), pp. 76–84.

28. Bruce N. Huff and Thomas P. Kelley, "Quality Review and You," *Journal of Accountancy* 167, no. 2 (February 1989): 34–40.

29. "The Mandatory SECPC Membership Vote," *Journal of Accountancy* 168, no. 1 (July 1989): 40–44.

SELECT BIBLIOGRAPHY

AICPA Professional Standards, vols. 1 & 2. Chicago: Commerce Clearing House, 1990.

Auerbach, A., ed. *Corporate Takeovers: Causes and Consequences.* Chicago: University of Chicago Press, 1988.

Bagby, J. "The Evolving Controversy Over Insider Trading." *American Business Law Journal* 24, no. 4 (Winter 1987): 571–620.

Brudney, V. "Insiders, Outsiders, and Informational Advantages Under the Federal Securities Laws." *Harvard Law Review* 93, no. 2 (December 1979): 322–76.

Burrough, B., and J. Helyar, *Barbarians at the Gate: The Fall of RJR Nabisco.* New York: Harper & Row, 1990.

Carey, J., and W. Doherty, *Ethical Standards of the Accounting Profession.* New York: AICPA, Inc., 1966.

Causey, D. *Duties and Liabilities of Public Accountants.* Homewood, Ill.: Dow Jones-Irwin, 1982.

Commons, D. *Tender Offers: The Sneak Attack in Corporate Takeovers.* Berkeley: University of California Press, 1985.

Humbert, T. *Ten Myths About Leveraged Buyouts.* Washington, D.C.: Heritage Foundation, 1989.

Loeb, S., ed. *Ethics in the Accounting Profession.* Santa Barbara: Wiley, 1978.

Manne, H. *Insider Trading and the Stock Market.* New York: Free Press, 1966.

Scherer, F., D. and Ravenscraft, *Mergers, Sell-offs and Economic Efficiency.* Washington, D.C.: Brookings Institute, 1987.

Schotland, R. "Unsafe at any Price: A Reply to Manne." *Virginia Law Review* 53, no. 7 (November 1967): 1425–78.

Simon, J. et. al. *The Ethical Investor.* New Haven, Conn.: Yale University Press, 1972.

Stevens, M. *The Accounting Wars.* New York: Macmillan, 1985.

Weidenbaum, M., and K. Chilton, eds. *Public Policy toward Corporate Takeovers.* New Brunswick, N.J.: Transaction Books, 1988.

Windal, F., and R. Corley. *The Accounting Professional: Ethics, Responsibility and Liability.* Englewood Cliffs, N.J.: Prentice-Hall, 1980.

6

BUSINESS AND THE CONSUMER

INTRODUCTION

In producing and marketing goods and services, the firm incurs moral and legal obligations to the consumer. The consumer also has responsibilities with regard to the use of a product. This chapter discusses three key issues in the relationship between business and consumers: product safety, advertising, and selling.

Until 1916 a manufacturer was not legally liable for an injury to a consumer unless there was privity (private knowledge) of contract between manufacturer and consumer, i.e., purchasers could sue only those who sold an item directly to them. Since few manufacturers sold goods directly to the public, most were immune from suit. Recent times have seen a legal shift from *caveat emptor* (let the buyer beware) to *caveat venditor* (let the seller beware). Strict liability, the dominant product liability theory at present, only requires that a consumer prove the product was defective and caused the injury. Strict liability is grounded in part in utilitarian considerations; it encourages manufacturers to make safer products, which results in fewer accidents. George Brenkert argues that strict liability is also consistent with and, indeed, rests upon, the foundations of the free market. Robert Malott suggests a variety of problems with the strict liability doctrine and argues for a set of constraints on strict liability that he believes would make the law more reasonable and fair. In contrast, Beverly Moore argues that strict liability does not adequately protect consumers; he advocates the theory of absolute liability, i.e., the producer should be liable for any injury, regardless of fault. The two court cases presented were decided on the basis of strict liability laws.

Advertising has been subject to perhaps more criticism than any other business practice; the section on advertising discusses the central criticisms. John Z. Miller, following Galbraith, argues that advertisements create desires which the producer of the advertised product then satisfies. He claims that advertising actually undercuts the free market, which assumes the producer merely satisfies antecedently existing desires. Miller also argues that advertising is bad because it is so pervasive and promotes materialistic values exclusively. Finally, Miller argues that advertising is often deceptive, misleading, or simply provides no information to consumers. In response, Charles Collins argues that advertising is a form of speech, and hence producers have a right to advertise their products. He argues that all advertising provides consumers with some information, and that many advertisements labeled by critics as "deceptive" are not properly classified. Collins claims, against Galbraith and Miller, that advertising does not create desires; he also argues that advertising cannot be said to control consumer behavior. Two legal cases illustrate how the courts have treated "misleading" advertising; the third case asks you to assess the morality of producing and using a particular type of advertisement. Johnson Wax's policy statement points up one corporation's commitment to ethical advertising.

Although most business schools do not include a course on selling, more graduates probably start in sales than in any other area of business. David Holley accepts the basic framework of the free market and then describes three features that must be met in sales practices for the successful functioning of the free market. The case study presents five scenarios that we will all face as buyers or sellers. The corporate policy statement details Hewlett-Packard's extensive ethical commitments in sales.

PRODUCT SAFETY

Case Study

Biss v. *Tenneco Inc.*

Robert Biss was injured when a loader he was operating went off the road, collided with a telephone pole, and pinned him between the loader and the pole. Shortly before he died, Biss told witnesses that he lost control of the loader. Mrs. Biss brought suit against Tenneco, the loader's manufacturer, based on an alleged design defect in the loader since it was not equipped with a rollover protection structure, known as a ROPS.

The action involved a so-called "second collision" issue; that is, the claim was not that the loader itself had a design defect, thus causing the accident, but that there was a design defect that caused or enhanced the injuries arising from the accident. Tenneco, it was claimed, should have provided a ROPS as standard, rather than optional, equipment, and its failure to do so constituted a design defect that caused or enhanced Biss's injuries arising from the accident.

The New York Supreme Court considered the following to be the applicable rule of law:

> A manufacturer is obligated to exercise that degree of care in his plan or design so as to avoid any unreasonable risk of harm to anyone who is likely to be exposed to the danger when the product is used in the manner for which the product was intended, as well as unintended yet reasonably foreseeable use.

The court reasoned that manufacturers are not obligated to provide accident-proof merchandise but they are required to exercise reasonable care. There

---

409 N.Y.S. 2d 874 (A.D. 1978)

was no defect in the loader itself, and a ROPS was available to the purchaser, Vincent Centers, for whom Biss worked. Accordingly, the court ruled:

> That being so, defendants had fulfilled their duty to exercise reasonable skill and care in designing the product as a matter of law when they advised the purchaser that an appropriate safety structure for the loader was available.

The court pointed out that injury from a rollover accident is posed by the use of construction equipment, but noted that the danger varies according to the job and site for which the equipment is used:

> It is not a danger inherent in a properly constructed loader. Neither is it a danger which the manufacturer alone may discover or one which he is more favorably positioned to discover. If knowledge of the available safety options is brought home to the purchaser (Vincent Centers) the duty to exercise reasonable care in selecting those appropriate to the intended use rests upon him. He is the party in the best position to exercise an intelligent judgment to make the trade-off between cost and function, and it is he who should bear the responsibility if the decision on optional safety equipment presents an unreasonable risk to users. To hold otherwise casts the manufacturer and supplier in the role of insurers answerable to injured parties in any event, because the purchaser of the equipment for his own reasons, economic or otherwise, elects not to purchase available options to ensure safety.

Mrs. Biss's suit against Tenneco was dismissed, 3-0.

For Discussion

What theory of product liability has the court applied in this case? Do you agree with this theory? Why or why not? Do you agree with the court's decision in this particular case? Why or why not? If Mrs. Biss sued Vincent Centers, rather the Tenneco, do you believe she should (legally and morally) win? Why or why not?

Austin v. Ford Motor Co.

A variation of the second collision issue was presented in the case of Barbara Austin, who died in a one-car accident. A motorist testified that Ms. Austin passed him when he was travelling at a speed of 65 to 70 mph. The Austin auto, a Ford, was estimated to have been going 20 to 25 mph faster than the vehicle she passed—a speed of approximately 90 mph—when her car left the road, rolled over twice, and landed on its top. Ms. Austin was thrown from her car and killed. A state police officer found a portion of Austin's seatbelt on the ground and a portion still attached to the front seat.

The plaintiffs, Ms. Austin's children, produced two witnesses who provided evidence that she was wearing a seatbelt, and that a defective belt was a cause of death. According to the testimony of a state police technician, a microscopic examination of the belt showed that the webbing had been irregularly cut through. He said that a sharp instrument was needed to cut the belt, that the cut portion was not normally visible, and that nothing in the auto could have caused the cut. An engineer testified to the probable causal connection between the seatbelt's breaking and Austin's death. Ford countered that it was probable that the impact of the accident was of sufficient force to cause Austin's death.

The court's opinion focused on the issue of causation:

> The accident was a grievous one and the facts support a finding of negligent driving by the decedent. But the heart of the case is causation, not of the accident but of the death. In an action such as this, is it a permissible inference

273 N.W. 2d 233 (1979)

or conclusion that decedent's negligent driving was a cause of her death? . . .
The court is persuaded to the conclusion that it is not.

The court distinguished the cause of the accident from the cause of Austin's death. Ms. Austin's negligence caused the accident, but, since seat belts are designed to protect the wearer in the event of a collision, including a collision that is caused by the driver's own negligence, the court regarded Austin's negligent driving as an irrelevant factor in assessing the cause of her death. The court reasoned that Austin would have survived the accident had the seatbelt not been dangerously defective, and hence the defective seatbelt was a cause of death.

. . . Ford's negligence in furnishing an unsafe and defective seatbelt was found to be a cause of the death of Barbara Austin and there is no evidence to show that Barbara Austin's own negligence contributed to her death. . . .

Judge Coffey dissented from the majority's opinion:

The jury found that her (Austin's) excessive speed was the cause of her injuries. How can it be said that her negligence in driving 90 mph, which caused the accident, was not a cause of her death? The answer of the majority is that seat belts are designed to protect the wearer from injuries suffered in an accident which may be the wearer's fault. . . . As a policy matter, the majority has decided in this case that negligence as the cause of the accident (and therefore the injuries) of the deceased will not be compared with the product liability imposed on the manufacturer for the failure of the seat belt. I have reservations about the wisdom of this policy. When applied to the theory that an injury would have been prevented if the injured party had worn a seat belt, its corollary will result in re-introducing a form of assumption of risk into Wisconsin law.

For Discussion

What theory of product liability has the court applied in this case? Do you agree with this theory? Why or why not? Do you agree with the majority or the dissenting opinion in this case? Why do you agree with one opinion and disagree with the other?

George G. Brenkert

Strict Products Liability and Compensatory Justice

Strict products liability is the doctrine that the seller of a product has legal responsibilities to compensate the user of that product for injuries suffered because of a defective aspect of the product, even when the seller has not been negligent in permitting that defect to occur.[1] Thus, even though a manufacturer, for example, has reasonably applied the existing techniques of manufacture and has anticipated and cared for nonintended use of the product, he may still be held liable for injuries a product user suffers if it can be shown that the product was defective when it left the manufacturer's hands.

To say that there is a crisis today concerning this doctrine would be to utter a commonplace which few in the business community would deny. The development of the doctrine of strict products liability, according to most business people, threatens many businesses financially. Furthermore, strict products liability is said to be a morally questionable doctrine, since the manufacturer or seller has not been negligent in permitting the injury-causing defect to occur. On the other hand, victims of defective products complain that they deserve full compensation for injuries sustained in using a defective product whether or not the seller is at fault. Medical expenses and time lost from one's job are costs no individual should have to bear by himself. It is only fair that the seller share such burdens.

In general, discussions of this crisis focus on the limits to which a business ought to be held responsible. Much less frequently, discussions of strict products liability consider the underlying question of whether the doctrine of strict products liability is rationally justifiable. But unless this question is answered it would seem premature to seek to determine the limits to which businesses ought to be held liable in such cases. In the following paper I discuss this underlying philosophical question and argue that there is a rational justification for strict products liability which links it to the very nature of the free enterprise system.

To begin with, it is crucial to remember that what we have to consider is the relationship between an entity doing business and an individual. The strict liability attributed to business would not be attributed to an individual who happened to sell some product he had made to his neighbor or a stranger. If Peter sold an article he had made to Paul and Paul hurt himself because the article had a defect which occurred through no negligence of Peter's, we would not normally hold Peter morally responsible to pay for Paul's injuries.

It is different for businesses. They have been held to be legally and morally obliged to pay the victim for his injuries. Why? What is the difference? The difference is that when Paul is hurt by a defective product from corporation X, he is hurt by something produced in a socioeconomic system purportedly embodying free enterprise. In other words, among other things:

1. Each business and/or corporation produces articles or services it sells for profit.

2. Each member of this system competes with members of the system in trying to do as well as it can for itself not simply in each exchange, but through each exchange for its other values and desires.

3. Competition is to be "open and free, without deception or fraud."

4. Exchanges are voluntary and undertaken when each party believes it can benefit thereby. One party provides the means for another party's ends if the other party will provide the first party the means to its ends.[2]

5. The acquisition and disposition of ownership rights—that is, of private property—is permitted in such exchanges.

6. No market or series of markets constitutes the whole of a society.

7. Law, morality, and government play a role in setting acceptable limits to the nature and kinds of exchange in which people may engage.[3]

What is it about such a system which would justify claims of strict products liability against businesses? . . . In the free enterprise system, each person and/or business is obligated to follow the rules and understandings which define this socioeconomic system. Following the rules is expected to channel competition among individuals and businesses to socially positive results. In providing the means to fulfill the needs of others, one's own ends also get fulfilled.

Though this does not happen in every case, it is supposed to happen most of the time. Those who fail in their competition with others may be the object of charity, but not of other duties. Those who succeed, qua members of this socioeconomic system, do not have moral duties to aid those who fail. Analogously, the team which loses the game may receive our sympathy but the winning team is not obligated to help it to win the next game or even to play it better. Those who violate the rules, however, may be punished or penalized, whether or not the violation was intentional and whether or not it redounded to the benefit of the violator. Thus, a team may be assessed a penalty for something that a team member did unintentionally to a member of the other team but which injured the other team's chances of competition in the game by violating the rules.

This point may be emphasized by another instance involving a game that brings us closer to strict products liability. Imagine that you are playing table tennis with another person in his newly constructed table tennis room. You are both avid table tennis players and the game means a lot to both of you. Suppose that after play has begun, you are suddenly and quite obviously blinded by the light over the table—the light shade has a hole in it which, when it turned in your direction, sent a shaft of light unexpectedly into your eyes. You lose a crucial point as a result. Surely it would be unfair of your opponent to seek to maintain his point because he was faultless—after all, he had not intended to blind you when he installed that light shade. You would correctly object that he had gained the point unfairly, that you should not have to give up the point lost, and that the light shade should be modified so that the game can continue on a fair basis. It is only fair that the point be played over.

Businesses and their customers in a free enterprise system are also engaged in competition with each other. The competition here, however, is multifaceted as each tries to gain the best agreement he can from the other with regard to the buying and selling of raw materials, products, services, and labor. Such agreements must be voluntary. The competition which leads to them cannot involve coercion. In addition, such competition must be fair and ultimately result in the benefit of the entire society through the operation of the proverbial invisible hand.

Crucial to the notion of fairness of competition are not simply the demands that the competition be open, free, and honest, but also that each person in a society be given an equal opportunity to participate in the system in order to fulfill his or her own particular ends. Friedman formulates this notion in the following manner:

> . . . the priority given to equality of opportunity in the hierarchy of values . . . is manifested particularly in economic policy. The catchwords were free enterprise, competition, laissez-faire. Everyone was to be free to go into any business, follow any occupation, buy any property, subject only to the agreement of the other parties to the transaction. Each was to have the oppor-

tunity to reap the benefits if he succeeded, to suffer the costs if he failed. There were to be no arbitrary obstacles. Performance, not birth, religion, or nationality, was the touchstone.[4]

What is obvious in Friedman's comments is that he is thinking primarily of a person as a producer. Equality of opportunity requires that one not be prevented by arbitrary obstacles from participating (by engaging in a productive role of some kind or other) in the system of free enterprise, competition, and so on in order to fulfill one's own ends ("reap the benefits"). Accordingly, monopolies are restricted, discriminatory hiring policies have been condemned, and price collusion is forbidden.

However, each person participates in the system of free enterprise *both* as a worker/producer *and* as a consumer. The two roles interact; if the person could not consume he would not be able to work, and if there were no consumers there would be no work to be done. Even if a particular individual is only (what is ordinarily considered) a consumer, he or she plays a theoretically significant role in the competitive free enterprise system. The fairness of the system depends upon what access he or she has to information about goods and services on the market, the lack of coercion imposed on that person to buy goods, and the lack of arbitrary restrictions imposed by the market and/or government on his or her behavior.

In short, equality of opportunity is a doctrine with two sides which applies both to producers and to consumers. If, then, a person as a consumer or a producer is injured by a defective product—which is one way his activities might arbitrarily be restricted by the action of (one of the members of) the market system—surely his free and voluntary participation in the system of free enterprise will be seriously affected. Specifically, his equal opportunity to participate in the system in order to fulfill his own ends will be diminished.

Here is where strict products liability enters the picture. In cases of strict liability the manufacturer does not intend for a certain aspect of his product to injure someone. Nevertheless, the person is injured. As a result, he is at a disadvantage both as a consumer and as a producer. He cannot continue to play either role as he might wish. Therefore, he is denied that equality of opportunity which is basic to the economic system in question just as surely as he would be if he were excluded from employment by various unintended consequences of the economic system which nevertheless had racially or sexually prejudicial implications. Accordingly, it is fair for the manufacturer to compensate the person for his losses before proceeding with business as usual. That is, the user of a manufacturer's product may justifiably demand compensation from the manufacturer when its product can be shown to be defective and has injured him and harmed his chances of participation in the system of free enterprise.

Hence, strict liability finds a basis in the notion of equality of opportunity which plays a central role in the notion of a free enterprise system. That is why a business which does *not* have to pay for the injuries an individual suffers in the use of a defective article made by that business is felt to be unfair to its customers. Its situation is analogous to that of a player's unintentional violation of a game rule which is intended to foster equality of competitive opportunity.

A soccer player, for example, may unintentionally trip an opposing player. He did not mean to do it; perhaps he himself had stumbled. Still, he has to be penalized. If the referee looked the other way, the tripped player would rightfully object that he had been treated unfairly. Similarly, the manufacturer of a product may be held strictly liable for a product of his which injures a person who uses that product. Even if he is faultless, a consequence of his activities is to render the user of his product less capable of equal participation in the socioeconomic system. The manufacturer should be penalized by way of compensating the victim. Thus, the basis upon which manufacturers are held strictly liable is compensatory justice.

In a society which refuses to resort to paternalism or to central direction of the economy and which turns, instead, to competition in order to allocate scarce positions and resources, compensatory justice requires that the competition be fair and losers be protected.[5] Specifically, no one who loses should be left so destitute that he cannot reenter the competition. Furthermore, those who suffer injuries traceable to defective merchandise or services which restrict their participation in the competitive system should also be compensated.

Compensatory justice does not presuppose negligence or evil intentions on the part of those to whom the injuries might ultimately be traced. It is not perplexed or incapacitated by the relative innocence of all parties involved. Rather, it is concerned with correcting the disadvantaged situation an individual experiences due to accidents or failures which occur in the normal working of that competitive system. It is on this basis that other compensatory programs which alleviate the disabilities of various minority groups are founded. Strict products liability is also founded on compensatory justice.

An implication of the preceding argument is that business is not morally obliged to pay, as such, for the physical injury a person suffers. Rather, it must pay for the loss of equal competitive opportunity—even though it usually is the case that it is because of a (physical) injury that there is a loss of equal opportunity. Actual legal cases in which the injury which prevents a person from going about his or her daily activities is emotional or mental, as well as physical, support this thesis. If a person were neither mentally nor physically harmed, but still rendered less capable of participating competitively because of a defective aspect of a product, there would still be grounds for holding the company liable.

For example, suppose I purchased and used a cosmetic product guaranteed to last a month. When used by most people it is odorless. On me, however, it has a terrible smell. I can stand the smell, but my coworkers and most other people find it intolerable. My employer sends me home from work until it wears off. The product has not harmed me physically or mentally. Still, on the above argument, I would have reason to hold the manufacturer liable. Any cosmetic product with this result is defective. As a consequence my opportunity to participate in the socioeconomic system is curbed. I should be compensated.

There is another way of arriving at the same conclusion about the basis of strict products liability. To speak of business or the free enterprise system, it was noted above, is to speak of the voluntary exchanges between producer and customer which take place when each party believes he has an opportunity to benefit. Surely customers and producers may miscalculate their benefits; something they voluntarily agreed to buy or sell may turn out not to be to their benefit. The successful person does not have any moral responsibilities to the unsuccessful person—at least as a member of this economic system. If, however, fraud is the reason one person does not benefit, the system is, in principle, undermined. If such fraud were universalized, the system would collapse. Accordingly, the person committing the fraud does have a responsibility to make reparations to the one mistreated.

Consider once again the instance of a person who is harmed by a product he bought or used, a product that can reasonably be said to be defective. Has the nature of the free enterprise system also been undermined or corrupted in this instance? Producer and consumer have exchanged the product but it has not been to their mutual benefit; the manufacturer may have benefited, but the customer has suffered because of the defect. Furthermore, if such exchanges were universalized, the system would also be undone.

Suppose that whenever people bought products from manufacturers the products turned out to be defective and the customers were always injured, even though the manufacturers could not be held negligent. Though one party to such exchanges might benefit, the other party always suffered. If the rationale for this economic system—the reason it was adopted and is defended —were that in the end both parties share the equal opportunity to gain, surely it would collapse with the above consequences. Consequently, as with fraud, an economic system of free enterprise requires that injuries which result from defective products be compensated. The question is: Who is to pay for the compensation?

There are three possibilities. The injured party could pay for his own injuries. However, this is implausible since what is called for is compensation and not merely payment for injuries. If the injured party had simply injured himself, if he had been negligent or careless, then it is plausible that he should pay for his own injuries. No compensation is at stake here. But in the present case the injury stems from the actions of a particular manufacturer who, albeit unwittingly, placed the defective product on the market and stands to gain through its sale.

The rationale of the free enterprise system would be undermined, we have seen, if such actions were universalized, for then the product user's equal opportunity to benefit from the system would be denied. Accordingly, since the rationale and motivation for an individual to be part of this socioeconomic system is his opportunity to gain from participation in it, justice requires that the injured product user receive compensation for his injuries. Since the individual can hardly compensate himself, he must receive compensation from some other source.

Second, some third party—such as government—could compensate the injured person. This is not wholly implausible if one is prepared to modify the structure of the free enterprise system. And, indeed, in the long run this may be the most plausible course of action. However, if one accepts the structure of the free enterprise system, this alternative must be rejected because it permits the interference of government into individual affairs.

Third, we are left with the manufacturer. Suppose a manufacturer's product, even though the manufacturer wasn't negligent, always turned out to be defective and injured those using his products. We might sympathize with his plight, but he would either have to stop manufacturing altogether (no one would buy such products) or else compensate the victims for their losses. (Some people might buy and use his products under these conditions.) If he forced people to buy and use his products he would corrupt the free enterprise system. If he did not compensate the injured users, they would not buy and he would not be able to sell his products. Hence, he would partake of the free enterprise system—that is, sell his products—only if he compensated his user/victims. Accordingly, the sale of this hypothetical line of defective products would be voluntarily accepted as just or fair only if compensation were paid the user/victims of such products by the manufacturer.

The same conclusion follows even if we consider a single defective product. The manufacturer put the defective product on the market. Because of his actions others who seek the opportunity to participate on an equal basis in this system in order to benefit therefrom are unable to do so. Thus, a result of his actions, even though unintended, is to undermine the system's character and dignity. Accordingly, when a person is injured in his attempt to participate in this system, he is owed compensation by the manufacturer. The seller of the defective article must not jeopardize the equal opportunity of the product user to benefit from the system. The seller need not guarantee that the buyer/user will benefit from the purchase of the product; after all, the buyer may miscalculate or be careless in the use of a nondefective product. But if he is not careless or has not miscalculated, his opportunity to benefit from the system is illegitimately harmed if he is injured in its use because of the product's defectiveness. He deserves compensation.

It follows from the arguments in this and the preceding section that strict products liability is not only compatible with the system of free enterprise but that if it were not attributed to the manufacturer the system itself would be morally defective. And the justification for requiring manufacturers to pay compensation when people are injured by defective products is that the demands of compensatory justice are met.[6]

NOTES

1. This characterization of strict products liability is adapted from Alvin S. Weinstein et al., *Products Liability and the Reasonably Safe Product* (New York: John Wiley & Sons, 1978), ch. 1. I understand the seller to include the manufacturer, the

retailer, distributors, and wholesalers. For the sake of convenience, I will generally refer simply to the manufacturer.

2. F. A. Hayek emphasizes this point in "The Moral Element in Free Enterprise," in *Studies in Philosophy, Politics, and Economics* (New York: Simon and Schuster, 1967), p. 229.

3. Several of these characteristics have been drawn from Milton Friedman and Rose Friedman, *Free to Choose* (New York: Avon Books, 1980).

4. Milton Friedman and Rose Friedman, *Free to Choose*, pp. 123–24.

5. I have drawn heavily, in this paragraph, on the fine article by Bernard Boxhill, "The Morality of Reparation," reprinted in *Reverse Discrimination,* Barry R. Gross, ed. (Buffalo, N.Y.: Prometheus Books, 1977), pp. 270–78.

6. I would like to thank the following for providing helpful comments on earlier versions of this paper: Betsy Postow, Jerry Phillips, Bruce Fisher, John Hardwig, and Sheldon Cohen.

Robert H. Malott

Let's Restore Balance to Product Liability Law

When I began my business career 30 years ago, the liability of manufacturers and distributors for injuries suffered by a product user was limited and easily understood: businesses could be held responsible if their actions or conduct were negligent. During the past three decades, however, product liability law has changed dramatically, creating confusion among manufacturers and distributors as to what exactly constitutes liability. The focus has shifted from the conduct of product makers and sellers to the condition of the product itself. Liability can now result if a court or jury determines that a product's design, its construction, or its operating instructions and safety warnings make it unreasonably dangerous or hazardous to use.

These changes have produced a tremendous expansion in the scope of product-related injuries for which manufacturers and distributors are now held accountable. The most graphic evidence of this escalating exposure is the rapid growth in the number of product liability suits being filed and in the amounts of damages awarded. Between 1974 and 1981, for example, the number of product liability suits filed in federal district courts grew at an average annual rate of 28 percent, nearly three-and-a-half times faster than the average annual increase in civil suits filed in federal courts.[1]

For some, the changes of the past three decades represent merely a re-dressing of the balance of product liability law, which for too long was viewed as favoring product makers at the expense of product users. Other observers, however, are increasingly concerned that the pendulum has swung too far in favor of the injured product user, imposing on manufacturers and distributors enormous and inequitable costs that are ultimately passed on to society as a whole.

CHANGING FOCUS OF TORT LAW

Although the changes in product liability law of the 1960s and 1970s appeared to sweep onto the national scene with little forewarning, legal scholars note that the changes were, in fact, part of a continuous but quiet trend dating from the turn of the century.

Prior to about 1900, tort law, as a branch of the common law, had for several hundred years tended to limit liability to cases of "fault," or moral responsibility. In product liability cases, this meant that a buyer had no ground for recovering damages for injuries incurred while using a product, unless he or she could prove that the product's maker or seller had been negligent in its construction or sale.

The legal standards for determining liability on negligence grounds were clear: the court or jury had only to determine that the product maker or seller had failed to act reasonably and prudently. Despite the seeming vagueness of the terms *reasonable* and *prudent* as standards of conduct, the common law included a well-developed body of case law which enabled judges to instruct juries on the determination of *negligent conduct*.

For particular kinds of torts, such as damages caused by wild animals or illnesses caused by unwholesome food, the common law did, however, permit injured parties to recover damages without requiring that they prove the defendant guilty of negligent conduct. Because foodstuffs could become spoiled or impure through no fault of the producer or seller, and because wild animals pose unusual hazards or dangers, the law allowed courts and juries to assign liability even though there was no fault or lapse of conduct. This concept of liability without fault is known as *strict liability*.

Around the turn of the century, portions of the legal community began arguing that a concept of liability based solely on fault was inadequate to protect product users and consumers from the dangers of modern civilization. The advent of larger and more complicated machinery in the workplace and the introduction of labor-saving appliances into the home dramatically increased productivity and improved the standards of living. The new technologies, however, also exposed workers on the job and product users at home to greater hazards of injury than earlier generations faced.

As products and manufacturing processes became more and more complex, a negligence-based concept of liability posed an onerous burden on an injured victim seeking compensation: he or she was required to identify what part of a product failed or to prove that the failure or accident could be explained only by the manufacturer's or seller's negligence. Moreover, mass production techniques introduced the possibility that defective products could be produced and offered for sale, despite manufacturers' quality checks and testing.

Yet, a negligence-based liability doctrine precluded recovery by an injured consumer because the manufacturer had not acted negligently. Thus, there was a need—concerned lawyers, judges, and scholars agreed—for legal grounds other than negligence on which injured individuals could recover damages for injuries or loss.

In response, lawyers and judges expanded the concept of strict liability to products that have manufacturing defects. In so doing, they overturned the doctrine of "no liability without fault." Instead, as tort law expert William L. Prosser noted:

"In some cases the defendant may be liable, although he is not only charged with no moral wrongdoing, but has not even departed in any way from a reasonable standard of intent or care."[2]

By applying strict liability to product injury cases, the courts were, in one sense, simply expanding the common law, as they had been for hundreds of years. At a more fundamental level, however, the courts were engaged in judicial legislation, making sweeping changes in the relationship between producers and consumers. As Prosser also noted:

"The basis of this policy is a social philosophy which places the burden of the more or less inevitable losses due to a complex civilization upon those best able to bear them or to shift them to society at large."[3]

The liability was assigned to the manufacturer or distributor, according to Prosser, because business "is in a better position to administer the unusual risk by passing it on to the public than is the innocent victim."[4]

The application of the strict liability doctrine to product liability cases gained a stamp of legitimacy with its acceptance by the California Supreme Court in the 1963 decision in a case in which a man was injured while using a combination power tool in his home workshop.[5] The concept was further boosted a year later by its inclusion in the 1964 Restatement of Torts, a summary of tort law by the prestigious American Law Institute. By the early 1970s, strict liability had been accepted virtually nationwide.

QUESTIONABLE ISSUES

Now, the question is no longer "Whose fault is it?" Rather, "Is there a condition of the product that creates an unnecessary hazard or danger?"

Answering the product condition question, with respect to an alleged manufacturing defect, is easy: defective manufacturing is obvious because the product does not conform to the maker's design specifications. Had the extension of the strict liability doctrine been limited to injuries caused by manufacturing defects, liability exposure, although broader than it was under the negligence doctrine, would be clear and comprehensible.

Unfortunately, however, strict liability has been extended to product conditions other than manufacturing. In particular, some courts have determined that product designs may create hazardous conditions of use or that products may be sold without sufficient warning of hidden risks.

For an injured consumer, extending strict liability to design and warning "defects" was a logical next step in expanding the scope of damage recovery. To the manufacturers and sellers of those products, the step from manufacturing defects to design and warning defects was dramatic. Unlike the test for manufacturing defects, there are no standards to guide judicial decisions on the adequacy of a product's warnings or design.

Not surprisingly, each state has developed its own definition of strict liability for design and warnings. For instance, California deems a design defective if the product "fails to perform as safely as an ordinary consumer would expect it to when used in an intended or reasonably foreseeable manner." In Pennsylvania, on the other hand, a product's design is defective if it left the supplier's control "lacking any element to make it safe for its intended use or possessing any feature that renders it unsafe for the intended use."

Further complicating matters, phrases such as "intended use," "when used in a reasonably foreseeable manner," or "performs as safely as an ordinary consumer would expect" have no agreed-on meaning—and no common understanding based on case law built up over many years—to guide their application by the courts.

By making manufacturers liable for any aspect of a product's condition that causes it to be unreasonably dangerous, the strict liability doctrine has made design safety an issue to be decided by judges and juries. Because there are no judicial standards that define minimum safety requirements, the courts have enormous latitude in deciding cases. In practice, they have tended to come down on the side of the product user. Consider the following case.

In 1974 a Pennsauken, New Jersey police officer, responding to a burglar alarm, was severely injured when the Dodge Monaco police car he was driving spun off a rain-soaked highway. While moving backward, the car struck a steel pole 15 inches in diameter on the driver's side behind the front door. The police officer, Richard Dawson, sued the car's manufacturer, Chrysler Corporation, on the ground that the Monaco's design was unreasonably dangerous because it did not specify a rigid steel body, which would have prevented penetration of the passenger compartment.

In its defense Chrysler argued that the Monaco was designed with a flexible body to maximize passenger protection in front- or rear-end collisions, by far the most numerous types of accidents. A flexible frame absorbs the impact of these collisions by crumpling up. Moreover, Chrysler argued, a rigid side body construction would add about 250 pounds to the weight of the car, reducing its fuel efficiency and increasing its operating costs as well as price. Chrysler, faced with federal regulations both on fuel economy standards and front-end collision survivability, contended that the Monaco's design was optimal, given the infrequency of side collisions compared with front and rear accidents. The jury accepted the plaintiff's argument and awarded him damages of more than $2 million. On appeal, the federal appeals court upheld the trial court's verdict.[6]

This decision, and decisions in other cases like it, lead to the following conclusion: if a product's design will not prevent all accidents, then juries may choose to consider it inadequately safe. The result has been an almost unfathomable expansion of the scope of product liability, with exorbitant costs to society.

Manufacturers simply cannot design products that will prevent harm or injuries from all possible accidents. In creating a product, they must choose a design that affords the most practicable protection from injuries in the most frequent types of accidents. If a manufacturer can show, as Chrysler did, that its design was chosen to minimize the injuries from the types of accidents that are most likely to occur, is it reasonable to make the company liable simply because it did not use an alternative design that might have prevented injuries from a type of accident that occurs much less frequently?

Judges and juries have also been given the power to determine the adequacy of safety warnings and operating instructions under the strict liability doctrine. Again, the lack of any judicial standards has expanded the scope of liability. The lack of a warning specifically directed to any hazard that results in an accident or injury has been sufficient ground for courts and juries to judge the manufacturer liable. For an assessment of liability against the manufacturer, experience has taught that it does not matter whether the product is to be used only by skilled operators, not the general public, or how obvious the hazard is.

My own company, FMC Corporation, was sued in 1971 by a laborer injured when a crane operator maneuvered the boom of an FMC-built crane into high voltage electrical transmission lines. The plaintiff argued that FMC should be liable for his injuries because (1) the company had not posted warnings on the crane or in its cab of the dangers of operating the crane near high power lines, and (2) because it had not installed safety devices that, in the opinion of witnesses called by the plaintiff, could have alerted the operator to potential contact with electrical power lines.

In its defense, FMC argued that it had not put a warning in the crane's cab because the crane was intended to be used by trained heavy equipment operators thoroughly familiar with the hazards of working around electrical power lines. The company also noted that its engineers had concluded that proximity warning devices available at the time the crane was built (in 1957) did not operate with sufficient reliability to justify their use. An unreliable proximity warning device could pose a safety hazard of its own, in that workers who relied on it could be injured if they assumed that the device would protect them. Nonetheless, the court decided in the plaintiff's favor and awarded a judgment of $2.5 million.[7]

The doctrine of strict liability makes manufacturers liable for injuries if a product does not perform safely when used in "an intended" or "reasonably foreseeable manner." Again, it is up to the courts to determine what constitutes intended or reasonably foreseeable use. Recent cases have extended the boundaries of what may be construed as foreseeable use, with enormous implications for the liability exposure of manufacturers.

In one case, American Home Products, the makers of Pam, an aerosol which is sprayed on pots and pans to prevent food from sticking during cooking, was sued in 1979 by the mother of a 14-year-old boy who died after internally inhaling the freon propellant from a can of Pam. At the time of the youth's death, the can bore the following warning: "Avoid direct inhalation of concentrated vapor. Keep out of the reach of children." The boy's mother charged that the company should be held accountable because this warning was inadequate, particularly because the company had knowledge of 45 deaths, prior to her son's, involving teenagers concentrating the fumes and inhaling them in order to produce a tingling sensation in the lungs. The jury awarded her $585,000 in damages.[8]

The decision in this case disturbs me for two reasons. First, it is unreasonable to suppose that there is any kind of warning a manufacturer could use to prevent an individual from deliberately misusing a product. And second, the individual, not the manufacturer, should be responsible for the consequences of his or her own actions, particulary in cases of intentional misuse.

Should manufacturers be liable for hazards posed by their products that may result in injuries many years later, but which scientific knowledge cannot detect at the time a product is marketed? The answer courts give to this very difficult question will have extraordinary implications for the liability exposure of manufacturers of pharmaceuticals, toxic materials, and chemical products that may have harmful effects that take many years to develop.

The asbestos controversy has highlighted this issue in recent years. Prolonged exposure to significant amounts of asbestos in its fibrous form can cause asbestosis, a restrictive lung disease characterized by scarring of the tissues. It is also associated with the development of some cancers. Fibrous asbestos, however, has been widely used as a flame-retardant, fire-resistant insulating material. In particular, the U.S. Navy and the Maritime Commission required the use of asbestos in the construction of warships and cargo vessels during World War II to protect seamen against the spread of fire on board battle-damaged ships.

Today, asbestos makers face thousands of claims for damages from workers exposed to asbestos, half of which were filed by those exposed to asbestos in shipyards during and after World War II. In August 1982, Manville Corporation filed for bankruptcy, maintaining that although it was still solvent, the 16,500 pending asbestos claims, combined with a potential 30,000 additional claims, would exhaust its assets.

A recent New Jersey Supreme Court decision may extend the liability exposure of asbestos makers even further. In *Beshada, et al.* v. *Johns-Manville Products Corporation, et al.,* the court struck down the state-of-the-art defense used by asbestos makers. The companies argued that they should not be liable for failing to warn of the dangers of asbestos exposure because they were unaware of the danger at the time the product was marketed and because such dangers could not have been detected with the scientific techniques then available.

In its ruling the court differentiated between the defenses that are applicable in a suit based on negligence and one based on strict liability. A manu-facturer may use the state-of-the-art defense only when it is being sued for negligence: a company is not acting negligently by offering a product for sale that to its knowledge—given the state of scientific techniques—does not pose a hazard. In a strict liability suit, however, the state-of-the-art defense is not admissible because the product's condition—not the manufacturer's actions and what it knew or could not have known—is the focus of the action.

By holding manufacturers liable for injuries that may be incurred from products whose hazards cannot now be foreseen, this ruling may threaten the future viability of many companies or even of entire industries.

CONSEQUENCES OF IMBALANCE

The lack of clear and discernible standards means that the verdicts reached in product liability suits today are often inequitable and inconsistent.

This imbalance is not surprising, because courts and juries today are asked to make judgments that they are not well equipped to make. Strict liability has moved determinations of liability from the realm of the mainly objective to that of the substantially subjective. Judges and juries are required to deter-mine what constitutes a hazardous design or an inadequate warning—matters in which they are invariably not experts. They are required to render an eval-uation—through hindsight—of decisions made by manufacturer's engineers and experts after extensive study during the design process.

Another source of inconsistency in product liability verdicts today is the varying interpretations of liability from state to state. These cause different results in different jurisdictions, out of cases based on essentially the same facts. For instance, shortly after the Illinois court's judgment against FMC in the crane case, courts in New Mexico and Minnesota ruled in similar cases that the manufacturer was not liable because the hazard of driving a steel boom into high power lines was obvious.

Strict liability has dramatically increased the costs of product liability. The old negligence-based tort law, which assigned damages to the responsible party, has been converted into a business-financed "social insurance system" for product injury victims. Under this system the size and number of product liability awards have increased greatly, and they give every indication of con-tinuing to grow at astronomical rates.

It is therefore entirely appropriate to ask whether the costs imposed by current interpretations of product liability law are reasonable in relation-ship to the damages incurred, just as it is necessary to ask who will pay these costs.

Ultimately, of course, the costs are borne by consumers as the costs of liability insurance premiums and liability judgments are passed through to them. These costs can be quite high: one small machine tool manufacturer has re-ported that its cost of liability insurance went from $200 per machine in 1970 to $11,000 per machine in 1982.[9]

The defenders of the current state of product liability law often claim that manufacturers, aware of their potential liability, make better products than they would otherwise. Our experience suggests that exactly the opposite may also occur: companies may hesitate to introduce new products or expand into new markets because of the potential liability.

For example, FMC's former Power Transmission Group produced high-quality commercial bearings for use as components in machines and equipment built by other manufacturers. As a component manufacturer, FMC had no control over the design of the products into which bearings were placed. Yet, in the event of a failure, a claimant could sue the component manufacturer as well as the product manufacturer. In 1971 we concluded that the potential product liability exposure from the use of FMC bearings in helicopter rotors was too great, given the small share of our market that such use constituted. We therefore issued a directive stating that no orders for bearings would knowingly be accepted for use in manufacturing in-flight aircraft controls.

I should also point out that injured parties are poorly served by the adversary process of settling product liability suits. As much or more money is being paid to adjudicate a claim as is being paid to compensate victims. There is some indication that the contingency fee basis on which most plaintiffs' lawyers are engaged tends to escalate damage claims. James A. Henderson, Jr. of Boston University's School of Law has estimated that:

"Out of every dollar paid by consumers to cover the relevant liability costs, less than fifty cents—estimates vary downward from forty-five cents to thirty cents—are returned to the consumers in benefits. Most of the rest—between fifty-five and seventy cents out of every premium dollar—goes to pay the lawyers, adjusters, and the like. If I were a cynic, I would say that if this is a social insurance scheme, it is being run primarily to benefit the trial bar."[10]

REDRESSING THE BALANCE

If one accepts the conclusion that today's product liability system based on strict liability produces inequitable, inconsistent, and excessively costly judgments against manufacturers, then one ought to ask what can be done to reestablish reasonableness and fairness in liability decisions.

The answer—establishment of clear and precise standards of liability—seems simple enough. The challenge is to ensure standards that are understandable by manufacturers, equitable to product makers and users alike, and uniformly interpreted by courts and juries nationwide (thus ensuring consistency of results). Among the standards needed are:

1. A Negligence-based Standard for Judging the Adequacy of Product Design and the Appropriateness of Warnings.

The basic question in design and warning cases should be refocused on the manufacturer's conduct. Did the manufacturer use reasonable and prudent care in designing the product or providing warnings of hidden risks? Plaintiffs will almost always be able to show, as the plaintiff did in *Dawson* v. *Chrysler,* that an alternative design may, in the opinion of an expert chosen by the plaintiff, have prevented a particular accident.

Instead of making manufacturers liable because they cannot design a product in such a way as to prevent all accidents, would it not be more reasonable to focus on the degree of care taken by the manufacturer in designing the product?

2. A Standard Creating a Presumption that a Product Conforming to Government Safety Requirements is Reasonably Safe.

Currently, an injured product user may buttress his or her suit against a manufacturer by citing a product's failure to conform to government safety standards as evidence of inadequate design. The reverse, however, is not true. In many states, manufacturers are not permitted to cite the fact that a product meets or exceeds all applicable government standards as evidence of the adequacy of a product's design.

It would be more equitable (1) to allow compliance with government standards to create a presumption that a product is reasonably safe, and (2) to allow plaintiffs to rebut that presumption if they can show that the manufacturer knew that governmentally established standards were inadequate for a normal or intended use of the product.

3. A Standard Requiring Assignment of Liability and Damages on the Basis of Comparative Responsibility.

Frequently, injury from a product has several causes. For example, a person who misuses or alters a product may be responsible to some degree for his own or someone else's injury. In such cases, the courts should allocate liability among all responsible parties, and defendants should pay damages only in proportion to their share of the liability.

To require manufacturers to absorb the cost of someone else's carelessness creates an inequitable financial burden, a burden which the manufacturer must pass on to the consumer in the form of higher prices.

4. A Standard Limiting Liability for Manufacturing or Design Defects to a Specific Period of Time.

Products that have served their purpose without evidence of harm for a prolonged period should not be reexamined with regard to the manufacturer's liability for the adequacy of design and warning at a later date. No company should be forced to defend the adequacy of the design and safety warnings on a product that has operated safely for decades. In one egregious example, the Oliver Machinery Company was sued in the 1970s by a man who was injured while using a table saw manufactured by the company in 1942—more than 30 years before the accident!

At some point in time a manufacturer's responsibility should end. Appropriate allowances should be made, of course, when setting such limits, for chemical products or other toxic substances that may cause illness or damage only after prolonged exposure.

NOTES

1. Data compiled from the *Annual Report of the Director of the Administrative Office of the United States Courts, 1974–1981* (Washington, D.C.: U.S. Government Printing Office).

2. William L. Prosser, *Handbook of the Law Torts* (St. Paul, Minn.: West Publishing Company, 1955), p. 317.

3. Ibid., p. 315.

4. Ibid., p. 318.

5. *Greenman* v. *Yuba Power Products,* California Supreme Court, January 24, 1963.

6. *Dawson* v. *Chrysler Corporation,* U.S. Court of Appeals, Third Circuit, September 11, 1980.

7. *Burke* v. *Illinois Power Company, FMC Corporation, et al.,* Illinois Appellate Court, January 18, 1978.

8. *Harless* v. *Boyle-Midway Division, American Home Products Company,* U.S. District Court, Northern District of Florida, February 22, 1980.

9. Statement of Herbert W. Goetz, manager of product safety, Cincinnati Incorporated, on behalf of the National Product Liability Council, before the Subcommittee on Consumer, Committee on Commerce and Transportation, U.S. Senate (March 12, 1982).

10. Statement of James A. Henderson, Jr. before the Subcommittee on Consumer, Committee on Commerce and Transportation, U.S. Senate (March 9, 1982).

Beverly C. Moore, Jr.

Product Safety:
Who Should Absorb the Cost?

Product safety will be an important concern of the consumer movement until effective steps are taken to reduce the cost of accidents. Cost estimates for 1970 for three major categories of accidents are $5.5 billion for household product accidents (National Commission on Product Safety), $8 billion for work-related accidents (National Safety Council), and $16.2 billion for automobile accidents (Insurance Information Institute). The $30 billion total, encompassing 105,000 deaths and 390,000 permanent disabilities, is a substantial understatement.

In addition to significant underreporting, particularly of work-related accidents, such intangible damages as pain and suffering and the noneconomic value of lives lost are excluded. The comprehensive total cost of accidents in the United States may be in the vicinity of $50 billion, excluding the cost of administering a compensation system.

Presumably there will continue to be accident costs as long as there are accident prevention costs which are greater. These prevention costs are generally of two kinds:

One, *human carefulness,* in addition to having a relatively finite potential for further perfectibility, appears to be becoming more costly to exercise in a world which is increasingly complex, full of gadgets, warnings, directions, and distractions.

The other, *product* design, has quite the opposite potential. Its perfect-

Reprinted by permission from *Trial* magazine (January/February 1972). The Association of Trial Lawyers of America.

ibility—ultimately in preventing negligent, even intentionally caused accidents—and the cost of its perfectibility, is dependent solely on the progress of technology. Judging from the recent past, one can expect that technological progress, given the proper incentives, will be steady and dramatic.

It can be reliably forecast, therefore, that primarily through improvements in product design, accident prevention costs, and thus the net cost of accidents, will be reduced over time.

The pace at which that development unfolds depends upon what external pressures are brought to bear upon the corporations which design products (or employ workers or perform services).

Competition—the external force upon which we generally rely to spur product improvements and cost-saving technologies—is not always or even usually effective in forcing product safety improvements. Competition can work to the extent that the safety improvement is substantial enough to be noticed by a significant number of consumers who will pay the higher cost necessitated by the improvement in order to avoid a cognizable accident risk. Examples could be cited where this has occurred, but generally the consumer lacks the information to evaluate such particularized criteria.

While the problem could be ameliorated somewhat by mandatory disclosure of accident risk information at point of purchase, a further problem remains: Accident-prone products are often produced by oligopolistic firms which compete sluggishly, if at all, in safety improvements.

With a single adjustment, however, competition could be harnessed as the prime lever of cost-effective safety improvements—irrespective of consumer ignorance of accident risks, irrespective of the general absence of competition within oligopolistic industries.

The adjustment is to transfer the entire cost of a product's accidents from its victims to the producer, regardless of fault. By forcing corporations to internalize their social costs—i.e., treating them as ordinary business expenses—the price mechanism will force the adoption of cost-effective safety improvements.

Suppose, for example, that the auto industry was saddled with $20 billion annually for accident costs, not to mention an additional $10 billion liability for air pollution damage and other externalities. The average price of an automobile would increase by $2000. Sales would drop dramatically as consumers would resort to mass transit and other less costly means of transportation. This state of affairs would persist until the industry developed a car safe enough to reduce its damage liability to the point at which prices could be lowered sufficiently to generate a profitable sales volume.

One suspects that safer cars would soon be on the market. The continuing solvency of General Motors would depend upon that. And if, perchance, the industry is unable to reduce net accident costs sufficiently to stay in business, then it will have been demonstrated that automobiles have been economically feasible instrumentalities only by virtue of their costs being subsidized by their accident victims.

From the accident victim's viewpoint, this "enterprise liability" concept differs markedly from present and proposed compensation systems.

- It differs from the fault system in that not 42 percent, but 100 percent, of accident victims' economic losses are compensated.
- It differs from workmen's compensation formulas in that there is no schedule of maximum benefits preventing the victim from recovering his full economic and intangible losses.
- It differs from strict products liability doctrine in that no defect need be established.

Enterprise liability goes beyond no-fault in two important aspects:

First, except for very small or new firms, the producers of accident-prone products would be prohibited from resorting to liability insurance to spread their accident-damage risks. In light of the ultimate objective, these corporations cannot be permitted to avoid the safety competition touched off when an individual firm lowers its price after implementing a damage-reducing product-design change.

Second, enterprise liability would not tolerate any exceptions to no-fault principles, such as denial of compensation to drunk drivers.

There is no attempt here to be solicitous of accident victims generally or of drunk drivers in particular, or to impute "blame" to the auto industry. From society's perspective, any benefits to victims are purely incidental to the overriding purpose (which compensation serves)—preventing accidents so that there will ultimately be no victims to compensate.

This is accomplished by imposing the cost of any general category of accidents upon the party (i.e., producer or victim) who is best able to prevent that class of accidents. We have assumed that the producer will usually be that party.

In the case of automobile accidents, one is initially impressed with the argument that the fear of the accident itself is a sufficient deterrent to negligent driving even if the driver is assured of compensation for his own negligence. Likewise, there is no good reason for supposing that placing the loss upon the drunk driver will deter drunk driving to a greater extent then placing it upon the manufacturer according to the general rule. After all, the drunk driver persists, notwithstanding our having held him liable before.

It seems much more promising to encourage the industry to develop devices which will render intoxicated persons unable to operate a parked motor vehicle. Nor is this to say that additional measures, such as traffic fines and license suspensions, should not continue to act as a deterrent to individual carelessness.

Although the concept of internalizing social costs has been advocated by economists as a means of solving our pollution problems, it has not been seriously proposed, even by consumer advocates, as a means of reducing accident costs.

(There has been considerable academic discussion. *See* G. Calabresi, *The Costs of Accidents* (1970); Reviewed in 80 *Yale Law Journal* 647 (1971), 84 *Harvard Law Review* 1322 (1971); Coase, "The Problem of Social Cost," 3 *Journal of Law & Economics* 1 (1960).)

The traditional approach, advocated by the Product Safety Commission and already incorporated into federal auto safety legislation, has instead been to authorize a government agency to promulgate and enforce standards.

These may bring about a reduction in accident costs. But the cost-internalization alternative will generally bring about an even greater accident-cost reduction, and it will accomplish this result with a minimum of prevention costs.

The reasons for the superiority of cost internalization are not difficult to discern. At worst the government agency will become the captive of its regulatees. Congressional appropriations will be minimal, and sanctionless "voluntary compliance" will become the enforcement mode. At best, agency standard setting will be cumbersome and crude.

The basic dilemma is that regulators must operate in a milieu of static technology. Even if the standard that is promulgated—the air bag, for example—is or appears to be the most cost-effective means of reducing accidents at the time of its adoption, a more advanced technology may be developed shortly thereafter. Even if the agency is vigilant to replace the old standard with the new, there will always be some lag.

Also under cost internalization, the pressure to develop new technology is on the industry, where the greatest expertise presumably resides. Under the standards approach, however, this onus is placed upon the agency, which is likely to adopt a standard which either prevents too few accidents or is more costly than necessary with respect to the accidents it does prevent.

Under cost internalization, the industry has an incentive to do neither, but rather to follow the course which will reduce its damage liability at least cost to the consumer.

This is not to say that government standards can play no desirable role. Standards may complement cost internalization in cases where the accident damage cannot be measured with sufficient precision or where there is a small but real possibility of planetwide disaster—if the polar ice caps were to melt on account of increased atmospheric carbon dioxide levels attributable to fuel combustion, for example.

A relatively sure and simple legal apparatus can be fashioned to internalize accident costs without reliance upon government discretion.

A product safety commission would be established with a mandate to gather accident data to be used as evidence in private class-action lawsuits. These actions would seek recovery from the corporate defendants of a lump-sum damage fund (plus attorneys' fees and claims administration costs) in behalf of the class as an entity. Individual accident victims would then file claims against the fund, just as they would against a fire insurance company. In the likelihood that not all individual claims will be filed, the remainder of the damage fund will revert in trust "to the benefit of accident victims generally," to be disbursed under court supervision.

The data-collecting agency would be empowered to order corporations, doctors and hospitals to comply with accident reporting procedures. If the agency failed to gather the data necessary to establish class-action damages, any private citizen could file suit to compel the agency to act. If the citizen suit was successful, the agency would be ordered to pay the plaintiff's attorney's fees and expenses, plus a cash bonus to reward his initiative as a private attorney general.

No doubt it will be argued that the higher product costs resulting from cost internalization would be "regressive." This objection is really that *all* prices are regressive—for bread, postage stamps, whatever. To allocate resources most efficiently, prices should reflect costs. The costs of product accidents, pollution and other externalities are no less "costs" than are the costs of labor, land, and capital.

Nor must one resign himself to the inevitability of disproportionately burdening the poor with the cost of accidents. The reason why it is desirable to internalize those costs is that a net economic gain is thereby produced which can be directly transferred to the poor.

To illustrate, suppose that the total annual cost of accidents is $60 billion, including pain and suffering, other intangibles and administration of a compensation system. Suppose further that two-thirds, or $40 billion, of that cost could be eliminated at a prevention cost of $20 billion, leaving a net gain of $20 billion. Through a negative income tax device this sum could then be used to supplement the incomes of low-income persons to an extent which would far outweigh the regressive impact of higher product prices.

Corporate Policy Statement

We are committed to exercising responsible care for our products both in manufacturing and distribution and later in their handling by distributors and use by our customers. This means assessing the environmental impact of the products and then taking appropriate steps to protect employee and public health, and the environment as a whole. In addition to a safe production and distribution, as well as judicious customer use, it means we have a continuous concern for the ultimate disposal of our products in the environment. We expect Research and Development to: Direct Dow development activity to product applications which permit safe handling, use, and disposal. Determine that product testing is conducted at each stage of product development so that safety hazards and both short and long range environmental effects can be assessed before critical decision points. Give primary consideration to human safety and potential environmental hazards in selecting products for development and sale. In so doing, Dow employees, customers, plant communities and the public at large must be considered, as well as both short and long range environmental hazards in the distribution, use, and eventual disposal of our products. Provide information to production, distribution and marketing personnel so that employees, distributors of our products, and customers may be instructed in the safe handling, use and disposal of our products. We expect manufacturing to: adhere to Dow's Global Pollution Control Guidelines and company safety standards. Carefully review, before adoption, product specifications or process changes which may alter product properties, utility, or quality, including product impurities. . . . We expect marketing to: furnish customers and distributors of Dow products appropriate information to foster the safe handling, use and disposal of Dow products. . . . Alert Dow personnel immediately to problems of use involving human or environmental safety and assist in modifications of either products or use patterns, as required, to correct these problems. We expect distribution to: assess the safety and environmental impact to determine that appropriate steps will be taken while our products are being stored and transported in order to protect persons, property and the total environment. . . . Select carriers, warehouses and terminals to perform distribution functions consistent with Dow policies and guidelines.

Dow Chemical Co.

ADVERTISING

Case Study

FTC v. *Colgate-Palmolive Co.*

Colgate-Palmolive engaged the Ted Bates advertising agency to develop an advertising campaign based on the slogan "Rapid Shave outshaves them all." The result was a series of three one-minute commercials in which it was claimed that Rapid Shave could soften even the toughness of sandpaper. The test showed Rapid Shave being applied to what was claimed to be sandpaper. The ad used these words: "To prove Rapid Shave's super-moisturizing power, we put it right from the can onto this tough, dry sandpaper. It was apply, soak, and off in a stroke." Simultaneously, the viewer saw a razor shave the surface, leaving it completely smooth. But the actual surface was not sandpaper, rather, Plexiglas to which sand had been applied, because, it was claimed, sandpaper looks like ordinary colored paper when shown on television. Evidence brought to the attention of the Federal Trade Commission (FTC) also showed that, although Rapid Shave could actually shave the sand from real sandpaper, it could do so only after a soaking period of about 80 minutes, rather than the few moments shown on television.

In 1960 the FTC issued a complaint against Colgate and Bates claiming the commercials were false and deceptive. The hearing examiner dismissed the complaint, reasoning that neither misrepresentation—concerning moistening time or the identity of the shaved surface—would mislead the public. In 1961 the FTC reversed the hearing examiner, claiming that since Rapid Shave could not shave actual sandpaper in the time depicted in the ads, the product's moisturizing power had been misrepresented. The commission also held that undisclosed use of a Plexiglas substitute was deceptive.

U.S. Sp. Ct., 1965. 380 U.S. 374, 85 S. Ct. 1035, 13 L. Ed. 2d904.

In 1962 the First Circuit Court of Appeals twice upheld the FTC order against misrepresentation relating to the time factor, and Colgate conceded this issue. But the Appeals Court refused to allow enforcement of the FTC's claim of misrepresentation regarding the Plexiglas substitution. The issue facing the Supreme Court then was whether a commercial (portraying tests that supposedly confirm the claims made for a product) may use simulated props and devices that differ from materials the defendants originally claimed to be using in the tests.

A majority of the Supreme Court decided against Colgate. Television commercials that include a test were ruled deceptive if the test uses materials other than those which it purports to use. The majority argued mainly by analogy. Similar cases established that it is deceptive: (1) to state falsely that a product ordinarily sells for an inflated price but that it is being offered at a reduced price, even if the offered price represents the product's actual value; (2) to conceal that a product has been reprocessed even though it is as good as new; and (3) for a seller to misrepresent to the public that he is in a certain line of business, even though the misstatement in no way affects the quality of a product. Speaking for the majority, Chief Justice Warren went on to say:

> Respondents . . . insist that the present case is not like any of the above, but is more like a case in which a celebrity or independent testing agency has in fact submitted a written verification of an experiment actually observed, but, because of the inability of the camera to transmit accurately an impression of the paper on which the testimonial is written, the seller reproduces it on another substance so that it can be seen by the viewing audience. This analogy ignores the finding of the commission that in the present case the seller misrepresented to the public that it was being given objective proof of a product claim. In respondents' hypothetical the objective proof of the product claim that is offered, the word of the celebrity or agency that the experiment was actually conducted, does exist; while in the case before us the objective proof offered, the viewer's own perception of an actual experiment, does not exist. . . .
>
> The Court of Appeals has criticized the reference in the commission's order to "test, experiment or demonstration" as not being capable of practical interpretation. It could find no difference between the Rapid Shave commercial and a commercial which extolled the goodness of ice cream while giving viewers a picture of a scoop of mashed potatoes appearing to be ice cream. We do not understand this difficulty. In the ice cream case the mashed potato prop is not being used for additional proof of the product claim, while the purpose of the Rapid Shave commercial is to give the reviewer objective proof of the claim made. If in the ice cream hypothetical the focus of the commercial becomes the undisclosed potato prop and the viewer is invited, explicitly or by implication, to see for himself the truth of the claims about the ice cream's rich texture and full color, and perhaps compare it to a "rival product," then the commercial has become similar to the one now before us. Clearly, however, a commercial which depicts happy actors delightedly eating ice cream that is in fact mashed potatoes . . . is not covered by the present order.

Justice Harlan spoke for the minority, and in favor of Colgate, in the 7-2 decision:

> The only question here is what techniques the advertiser may use to convey essential truth to the television viewer. If the claim is true and valid, then the technique for projecting that claim, within broad boundaries, falls purely within the advertiser's art. The warrant to the Federal Trade Commission is to police the verity of the claim itself. . . .
>
> I do not see how such a commercial can be said to be "deceptive" in any legally acceptable use of that term. The Court attempts to distinguish the case where a "celebrity" has written a testimonial endorsing some product, but the original testimonial cannot be seen over television and a copy is shown over the air by the manufacturer. . . . But in both cases the viewer is told to "see for himself" in the one case that the celebrity has endorsed the product; in the other, that the product can shave sandpaper; in neither case is the viewer actually seeing the proof and in both cases the objective proof does exist, be it in the original testimonial or the sandpaper test actually conducted by the manufacturer. In neither case, however, is there a material misrepresentation, because what the viewer sees *is* an accurate image of the objective proof. . . .
>
> It is commonly known that television presents certain distortions in transmission for which the broadcasting industry must compensate. Thus, a white towel will look a dingy gray over television, but a blue towel will look a sparkling white. On the Court's analysis, an advertiser must achieve accuracy in the studio even though it results in an inaccurate image being projected on the home screen. . . . Would it be proper for respondent Colgate, in advertising a laundry detergent, to "demonstrate" the effectiveness of a major competitor's detergent in washing white sheets; and then "before the viewer's eyes," to wash a white (not a blue) sheet with the competitor's detergent? The studio test would accurately show the quality of the product, but the image on the screen would look as though the sheet had been washed with an ineffective detergent. All that had happened here is the converse: a demonstration has been altered in the studio to compensate for the distortions of the television medium, but in this instance in order to present an accurate picture to the television viewer.

For Discussion

Analyze carefully the reasoning of Justices Warren and Harlan. In your opinion which Justice presents the best argument? Why? Pay attention to their uses of "misrepresentation" and "deception." Do you yourself believe Colgate's advertisement was deceptive? If so, what aspects were deceptive, and why were they deceptive? If you believe the advertisement was not deceptive, what is the basis for your claim? What additional arguments can you provide for your view beyond the arguments presented by the justices?

FTC v. *Sterling Drug Inc.*

Sterling Drug, producer of Bayer Aspirin, had long chafed under rival analgesic makers' claims that their products were "twice as fast as aspirin," or "better than aspirin." So they must have been cheered by the December 29, 1962, issue of the *Journal of the American Medical Association,* which carried an article by two physicians and a statistician titled: "A Comparative Study of Five Proprietary Analgesic Compounds." The article assessed the efficacy and effects of Bayer Aspirin, St. Joseph's Aspirin, Bufferin, Anacin, and Excedrin. The latter two products are called "combination-of-ingredients" drugs. The study also employed a placebo consisting of lactose and cornstarch.

The study concluded: "The data failed to show any statistically significant difference among any of the drugs (that is, excluding the placebo) at any of the check points [fifteen minutes through four hours] . . . no important differences among the compounds studied in rapidity of onset, degree, or duration of analgesia." Fifteen minutes after ingestion "pain relief scores" were calculated, with Bayer scoring .94, while the next most effective drug after 15 minutes, namely Excedrin, scored .90; the others scored .76 or lower. The margin of statistical accuracy was .12. The researchers also studied the incidence of stomach upset after ingestion of the products, and concluded: "Excedrin and Anacin form a group for which the incidence of upset stomach is significantly greater than is the incidence after Bayer, St. Joseph's, Bufferin, or the placebo." Of those who took the placebo, .8 percent reported upset stomach, whereas 1.1 percent of those taking Bayer reported upset stomach.

Subsequent to the study, Sterling Drug prepared advertisements, one of which said:

---

317 Fed 669 (1963).

GOVERNMENT-SUPPORTED MEDICAL TEAM COMPARES BAYER ASPIRIN AND FOUR OTHER POPULAR PAIN RELIEVERS.

Findings reported in the highly authoritative *Journal of the American Medical Association* reveal that the higher priced combination-of-ingredients pain relievers upset the stomach with significantly greater frequency than any of the other products tested. While Bayer Aspirin brings relief that is as fast, as strong, and as gentle to the stomach as you can get.

This important new medical study, supported by a grant from the federal government, was undertaken to compare the stomach-upsetting effects, the speed of relief and the amount of relief offered by five leading pain relievers, including Bayer Aspirin, aspirin with buffering, and combination-of-ingredients products. Here is a summary of the findings.

UPSET STOMACH

According to this report, the higher priced combination-of-ingredients products upset the stomach with significantly greater frequency than any of the other products tested, while Bayer Aspirin, taken as directed, is as gentle to the stomach as a plain sugar pill.

SPEED AND STRENGTH

The study shows that there is no significant difference among the products tested in rapidity of onset, strength, or duration of relief. Nonetheless, it is interesting to note that within just fifteen minutes, Bayer Aspirin had a somewhat higher pain relief score than any of the other products.

PRICE

As unreasonable as it may seem, the products which are most likely to upset the stomach—that is, the combination-of-ingredients products—actually cost substantially more than Bayer Aspirin. The fact is that these products as well as the buffered product, cost up to 75 percent more than Bayer Aspirin.

The Federal Trade Commission (FTC) sought a temporary injunction against Sterling, claiming that the advertisements were false and misleading. The FTC charged that Sterling's advertisements falsely represented that: (a) the researchers' findings were endorsed and approved by the U.S. government; (b) the publication in *JAMA* was evidence of endorsements and approval by the American Medical Association and the medical profession; (c) the researchers found that Bayer Aspirin is not upsetting to the stomach and is as gentle as a sugar pill; (d) the researchers found that Bayer, after 15 minutes following ingestion, yields a higher degree of pain relief than any other product tested. The FTC said it sought the injunction because consumers would rely on the advertisements to their "irreparable injury," and because competitors would engage in similar tactics unless Sterling was stopped.

The Court's opinion was delivered by Judge Irving R. Kaufman, U.S. Court of Appeals Second Circuit. [What follows are portions of Judge Kaufman's opinion. Footnotes have been removed—Eds.]

The legal principles to be applied here are quite clear. The central purpose of the provisions of the Federal Trade Commission Act under discussion is in effect to abolish the rule of *caveat emptor* which traditionally defined rights and responsibilities in the world of commerce. That rule can no longer be relied upon as a means of rewarding fraud and deception, *Federal Trade Commission* v. *Standard Education Society,* 302 U.S. 112, 116, 58 S.Ct. 113, 82 L.Ed. 141 (1937), and has been replaced by a rule which gives to the consumer the right to rely upon representations of facts as the truth, *Goodman* v. *Federal Trade Commission,* 244 F.2d 584, 603 (9th Cir., 1957). In order best to implement the prophylactic purpose of the statute, it has been consistently held that advertising falls within its proscriptions not only when there is proof of actual deception, but also when the representations made have a capacity or tendency to deceive, i.e., when there is a likelihood or fair probability that the reader will be misled. . . . For the same reason, proof of intention to deceive is not requisite to a finding of violation of the statute, *Gimbel Bros., Inc.* v. *Federal Trade Commission,* 116 F.2d 578 (2d Cir., 1941); since the purpose of the statute is not to punish the wrongdoer but to protect the public, the cardinal factor is the probable effect which the advertiser's handiwork will have upon the eye and mind of the reader. It is therefore necessary in these cases to consider the advertisement in its entirety and not to engage in disputatious dissection. The entire mosaic should be viewed rather than each tile separately. "[T]he buying public does not ordinarily carefully study or weigh each word in an advertisement. The ultimate impression upon the mind of the reader arises from the sum total of not only what is said but also of all that is reasonably implied" [*Aronberg* v. *Federal Trade Commission,* 132 F.2d 165, 167 (7th Cir., 1942)].

Unlike that abiding faith which the law has in the "reasonable man," it has very little faith indeed in the intellectual acuity of the "ordinary purchaser" who is the object of the advertising campaign.

> The general public has been defined as "that vast multitude which includes the ignorant, and unthinking and the credulous, who, in making purchases, do not stop to analyze but too often are governed by appearances and general impressions." The average purchaser has been variously characterized as not "straight thinking," subject to "impressions," uneducated, and grossly misinformed; he is influenced by prejudice and superstition; and he wishfully believes in miracles, allegedly the result of progress in science. . . . The language of the ordinary purchaser is casual and unaffected. He is not an "expert in grammatical construction" or an "educated analytical reader" and, therefore, he does not normally subject every word in the advertisement to careful study.

[Callman, Unfair Competition and Trademarks § 19.2(a) (1), at 341–44 (1950), and the cases there cited.]

It is well established that advertising need not be literally false in order to fall within the proscription of the act. Gone for the most part, fortunately, are the days when the advertiser was so lacking in subtlety as to represent his nostrum as superlative for "arthritis, rheumatism, neuralgia, sciatica, lumbago, gout, coronary thrombosis, brittle bones, bad teeth, malfunctioning glands, infected tonsils, infected appendix, gallstones, neuritis, underweight, constipation, indigestion, lack of energy, lack of vitality, lack of ambition, and inability to sleep. . . ." See *Federal Trade Commission* v. *National Health Aids, Inc.,* 108 F.Supp. 340, 342 (D.Md. 1952). The courts are no longer content to insist simply upon the "most literal truthfulness," *Moretrench Corp.* v. *Federal Trade Commission,* 127 F.2d 792 at 795, for we have increasingly come to recognize that "advertisements as a whole may be completely misleading although every sentence separately considered is literally true. This may be because things are omitted that should be said, or because advertisements are composed or purposefully printed in such way as to mislead." . . . There are two obvious methods of employing a true statement so as to convey a false impression: one is the half truth, where the statement is removed from its context and the nondisclosure of its context renders the statement misleading, see *P. Lorillard Co.* v. *Federal Trade Commission,* 186 F.2d 52, 58 (4th Cir., 1950); a second is the ambiguity, where the statement in context has two or more commonly understood meanings, one of which is deceptive.

The Federal Trade Commission asserts here that the vice of the Bayer advertisement is of these types. It concedes that none of the statements made therein is literally false, but it contends that the half-truths and ambiguities of the advertisement give it "reason to believe" that our hypothetical sub-intelligent, less-than-careful reader will be misled thereby. Thus, we are told that the reference in large type to a "Government-Supported Medical Team" gives the misleading impression that the United States Government endorsed or approved the findings of the research team. Surely the fact that the word "supported" might have alternative dictionary definitions of "endorsed" or "approved" is not alone sufficient to show reason to believe that the ordinary reader will probably construe the word in this manner. Most words *do* have alternative dictionary definitions; if that in itself were a sufficient legal criterion, few advertisements would survive. Here, no impression is conveyed that the *product itself* has its source in or is being endorsed by the Government; for this reason, the cases cited by the Commission are inapt. If the reader of the advertisement believes that the Government in some way vouched for the soundness of the study's conclusions, then this impression would have also been conveyed had the advertisement "told the whole story," relating in full detail the extent of the Commission's participation: it selected the research team, supported the study with a grant, and authorized the publication of the report. The capsulized expression "Government-Supported" cannot, therefore, be characterized as misleading. The commission indicated to us upon argument that it would have been equally unhappy had the advertisement stated that the medical team was "Government-Financed" or "Government-Subsidized." But surely the concise statement of an established fact, immediately thereafter expanded—"This important new medical study supported by a grant from the federal government . . ."—cannot fairly be proscribed by the Commission; the alternatives are complete omission of the admittedly true statement or long-winded qualification and picayune circumlocution, neither of which we believe was in the contemplation of Congress.

The commission's attack upon the use of the phrase "Findings reported in the highly authoritative *Journal of the American Medical Association*," as misleadingly connoting endorsement and approval, is similarly unfounded, for much the same reasons already discussed. To assert that the ordinary reader would conclude from the use of the word "authoritative" that the study was endorsed by the *Journal* and the Association is to attribute to him not only a careless and imperceptive mind but also a propensity for unbounded flights of fancy. This we are not yet prepared to do. If the reader's natural reaction is to think that the study, because of publication in the *Journal,* is likely to be accurate, intelligent, and well-documented, then the reaction is wholly justified and one which the advertiser has every reason to expect and to seek to inculcate. We, as judges, know that an article on the law which has survived the rigorous selection and editing process of one of the major law publications is most probably more reliable and more thoroughly researched than the report of a recent trial or judicial decision carried in the *Podunk Daily Journal.* But we hardly think that there is "reason to believe" that either we or the lay observer would tend to construe the views expressed in the article as having secured the wholehearted endorsement and approval of the "authoritative" periodical in which it appears.

The commission's third objection deals with the probable vulnerability of the ordinary reader to Bayer's representations concerning stomach upset. We pass without comment the commission's claim that the Bayer advertisement represented that no other available analgesic product was more gentle to the stomach; clearly, any comparative statements made in the advertisement could only be understood to refer to the four other products tested. More seriously pressed upon us is the claim that the reader will be deceived by the statement that "Bayer Aspirin, taken as directed, is as gentle to the stomach as a plain sugar pill." "Sugar pill," we are told, is misleading terminology; the advertisement should have used the word "placebo." Again, we are confronted by a simple problem of communication. For how can we expect our hypothetically slow-witted reader to react when he reads that "Bayer Aspirin is as gentle to the stomach as a placebo"! Most likely, he will either read on, completely unaware of the significance of the statement or impatiently turn the page. Perhaps he will turn to his neighbor, and in response to a request for a definition of the troublesome word be greeted with the plausible query, "A *what*?" (This assumes that the reader will have been able to muster the correct pronunciation of the word.) But, all this aside, the pill used as a control in this case was indeed constituted of milk sugar, and the use of the term "sugar pill" was neither inaccurate nor misleading.

The commission next shifts its focus to the words "as gentle as," alleging that it has reason to believe that the reader will conclude that Bayer is not in the slightest bit harmful to the stomach; this can be rectified, we are told, by stating that Bayer is "no more upsetting" than the placebo, which did in fact cause a very minor degree of stomach upset. Unlike the standard of the average reader which the Commission avidly endorses throughout these proceedings, it here would have us believe that he is linguistically and syntactically sensitive to the difference between the phrases "as gentle as" and "no more upsetting than." We do not find that the Commission has reason to believe that this will be the case, and we therefore reject its contentions.

Finally, the commission attacks the manner in which the Bayer advertisement treated results of the study on speed and effectiveness of pain relief. As we understand the commission's argument, no objection is taken to the statement that, "The study shows that there is no significant difference among the products tested in rapidity of onset, strength, or duration of relief." Indeed, no objection can properly be taken, for the statement reproduces almost verbatim one of the conclusions enumerated in the article. It is thought, however, that the advertisement improperly represents greater short-run pain relief with Bayer Aspirin by stating that, "Nonetheless, it is interesting to note that within just fifteen minutes, Bayer Aspirin had a somewhat higher pain relief score than any of the other products." As we have seen, the statement is literally true, for Bayer's "score" after fifteen minutes was 0.94 while its closest competitor at the time interval was rated 0.90. The fact that the margin of accuracy of that scoring system was 0.124—meaning that the second-place drug might fare as well as or better than Bayer over the long run of statistical tests—does not detract from the fact that on this particular test, Bayer apparently fared better than any other product in relieving pain within fifteen minutes after its administration. It is true that a close examination of the statistical chart drawn up by the three investigators reveals that they thought the difference between all of the drugs at that time interval not to be "significantly different." But that is precisely what the Bayer advertisement stated in the sentence preceding its excursion into the specifics of the pain-relief scores. We cannot, therefore, conclude that Judge Dawson clearly erred in finding that the commission failed properly to carry its statutory burden of proof, however slim that burden might be. Not even the commission contends that in a proceeding under section 13(a) the judge is merely a rubber stamp, stripped of the power to exercise independent judgment on the issue of the commission's "reason to believe."

The commission relies heavily, especially as to the pain-relief aspects of its case, upon *P. Lorillard Co.* v. *Federal Trade Commission,* 186 F.2d 52 (4th Cir., 1950). There, *Reader's Digest* sponsored a scientific study of the major cigarettes, investigating the relative quantities of nicotine, tars, and resins. It accompanied its conclusions with a chart which revealed that, although Old Gold cigarettes ranked lowest in these deleterious substances, the quantitative differences between the brands were insignificant and would have no effect in reducing physiological harm to the smoker. The tenor of the study is revealed by its cheery words to the smoker "who need no longer worry as to which cigarette can most effectively nail down his coffin. For one nail is just about as good as another." Old Gold trumpeted its dubious success, claiming that it was found lowest in nicotine, tars, and resins, and predicting that the reader upon examining the results of the study would say "From now on, my cigarette is Old Gold." The Court quite properly upheld a cease-and-desist order issued by the Commission. An examination of that case shows that it is completely distinguishable in at least two obvious and significant respects. Although the statements made by Old Gold were at best literally true, they were used in the advertisement to convey an impression diametrically opposed to that intended by the writer of the article. As the Court noted, "The company proceeded to advertise this difference as though it had received a citation for public service instead of a castigation from the *Reader's Digest*" 186 F.2d at 57. Moreover, as to the specifics of brand-comparison, it was found that anyone reading the advertisement would gain "the very definite impression that Old Gold cigarettes were less irritating to the throat and less harmful than other leading brands of cigarettes. . . . The truth was exactly the opposite" 186 F.2d at 58. In the instant case, Sterling Drug can in no sense be said to have conveyed a misleading impression as to either the spirit or the specifics of the article published in the *Journal of the American Medical Association.*

Case Study
Manuel G. Velasquez

Toy Wars

Early in 1986, Tom Daner, president of the advertising company of Daner Associates, was contacted by the sales manager of Crako Industries, Mike Teal. Crako Industries is a family-owned company that manufactures children's toys and had long been a favorite and important client of Daner Associates. The sales manager of Crako Industries explained that the company had just developed a new toy helicopter. The toy was modeled on the military helicopters that had been used in Vietnam and that had appeared in the "Rambo" movies. Mike Teal explained that the toy was developed in response to the craze for military toys that had been sweeping the nation in the wake of the Rambo movies. The family-owned toy company had initially resisted moving into military toys since members of the family objected to the violence associated with such toys. But as segments of the toy market were increasingly taken over by military toys, the family came to feel that entry into the military toy market was crucial for their business. Consequently, they approved development of a line of military toys, hoping that they were not entering the market too late. Mike Teal now wanted Daner Associates to develop a television advertising campaign for the toy.

The toy helicopter Crako designers had developed was about one and one-half feet long, battery-operated, and made of plastic and steel. Mounted to the sides were detachable replicas of machine guns and a detachable stretcher modeled on the stretchers used to lift wounded soldiers from a battlefield.

Mike Teal of Crako explained that they were trying to develop a toy that had to be perceived as "more macho" than the top-selling "G.I. Joe" line of toys. If the company was to compete successfully in today's toy market, according to the sales manager, it would have to adopt an advertising approach that was even "meaner and tougher" than what other companies were doing. Consequently, he continued, the advertising clips developed by Daner Associates would have to be "mean and macho." Television advertisements for the toy, he suggested, might show the helicopter swooping over buildings and blowing them up. The more violence and mayhem the ads suggested, the better. Crako Industries was relying heavily on sales from the new toy and some Crako managers felt that the company's future might depend on the success of this toy.

Tom Daner was unwilling to have his company develop television advertisements that would increase what he already felt was too much violence in television aimed at children. In particular he recalled a television ad for a tricycle with a replica machine gun mounted on the handle-bars. The commercial showed the tricycle being pedaled through the woods by a small boy as he chased several other boys fleeing before him over a dirt path. At one point the camera closed in over the shoulder of the boy, focused through the gunsight, and showed the gunsight apparently trying to aim at the backs of the boys as they fled before the tricycle's machine gun. Ads of that sort had disturbed Tom Daner and had led him to think that advertisers should find other ways of promoting these toys. He suggested, therefore, that instead of promoting the Crako helicopter through violence, it should be presented in some other manner. When Teal asked what he had in mind, Tom was forced to reply that he didn't know. But at any rate, Tom pointed out, the three television networks would not accept a violent commercial aimed at children. All three networks adhered to an advertising code that prohibited violent, intense, or unrealistic advertisements aimed at children.

This seemed no real obstacle to Teal, however. Although the networks might turn down children's ads when they were too violent, local television stations were not as squeamish. Local television stations around the country regularly accepted ads aimed at children that the networks had rejected as too violent. The local stations inserted the ads as spots on their non-network programming, thereby circumventing the Advertising Codes of the three national networks. Daner Associates would simply have to place the ads they developed for the Crako helicopter through local television stations around the country. Mike Teal was firm: If Daner Associates would not develop a "mean and tough" ad campaign, the toy company would move their account to an advertiser who would. Reluctantly, Tom Daner agreed to develop the advertising campaign. Crako Industries accounted for $1 million of Daner's total revenues.

Like Crako Industries, Daner Associates was also a family-owned business. Started by his father almost fifty years ago, the advertising firm that Tom Daner now ran had grown dramatically under his leadership. In 1975 the business had grossed $3 million; ten years later it had revenues of $25 million and provided a full line of advertising services. The company was divided into three departments (creative, media, and account executive), each of which had about twelve employees. Tom Daner credited much of the company's success to the many new people he had hired, especially a group with M.B.A.s who had developed new marketing strategies based on more thorough market and consumer analyses. Most decisions, however, were made by a five-person executive committee consisting of Tom Daner, the senior accountant, and the three department heads. As owner-president, Tom's views tended to color most decisions, producing what one member of the committee called a "benevolent dictatorship." Tom himself was an enthusiastic, congenial, intelligent, and well-read person. During college he had considered becoming a missionary priest but had changed his mind and was now married and the father of three daughters. His personal heroes included Thomas Merton, Albert Schweitzer, and Tom Dooley.

When Tom Daner presented the Crako deal to his executive committee he found that they did not share his misgivings. The other committee members felt that Daner Associates should give Crako exactly the kind of ad Crako wanted: one with a heavy content of violence. Moreover, the writers and artists in the creative department were enthused with the prospect of letting their imaginations loose on the project, several feeling that they could easily produce an attention-grabbing ad by "out-violencing" current television programming. The creative department, in fact, quickly produced a copy-script that called for videos showing the helicopter "flying out of the sky with machine-guns blazing" at a jungle village below. This kind of ad, they felt, was exactly what they were being asked to produce by their client.

But after viewing the copy, Tom Daner refused to use it. They should produce an ad, he insisted, that would meet their client's needs but that would also meet the guidelines of the national networks. The ad should not glorify violence and war but should somehow support cooperation and family values. Disappointed and somewhat frustrated, the creative department went back to work. A few days later, they presented a second proposal: an ad that would show the toy helicopter flying through the family room of a home as a little boy plays with it; then the scene shifts to show the boy on a rock rising from the floor of the family room; the helicopter swoops down and picks up the boy as though rescuing him from the rock where he had been stranded. Although the creative department was mildly pleased with their attempt, they felt it was too "tame." Tom liked it, however, and a version of the ad was filmed.

A few weeks later Tom Daner met with Mike Teal and his team and showed them the film. The viewing was not a success. Teal turned down the ad. Referring to the network regulations which other toy advertisements were breaking as frequently as motorists broke the 55 mile per hour speed law, he said "That commercial is going only 55 miles an hour when I want one that goes 75." If the next version was not "tougher and meaner," Crako Industries would be forced to look elsewhere.

Disappointed, Tom Daner returned to the people in his creative department and told them to go ahead with designing the kind of ad they had originally wanted: "I don't have any idea what else to do." In a short time the creative department had an ad proposal on his desk that called for scenes showing the helicopter blowing up villages. Shortly afterwards a small set was constructed depicting a jungle village sitting next to a bridge stretching over a river. The ad was filmed using the jungle set as a background.

When Tom saw the result he was not happy. He decided to meet with his creative department and air his feelings. "The issue here," he said, "is basically the issue of violence. Do we really want to present toys as instruments for beating up people? This ad is going to promote aggression and violence. It will glorify dominance and do it with kids who are terrifically impressionable. Do we really want to do this?" The members of the creative department, however, responded that they were merely giving their client what the client wanted. That client, moreover, was an important account. The client wanted an aggressive "macho" ad, and that was what they were providing. The ad might violate the regulations of the television networks, but there were ways to get around the networks. Moreover, they said, every other advertising firm in the business was breaking the limits against violence set by the networks. Tom made one last try: why not market the toy as an adventure and fantasy toy? Film the ad again, he suggested, using the same jungle backdrop. But instead of showing the helicopter shooting at a burning village, show it flying in to rescue people from the burning village. Create an ad that shows excitement, adventure, and fantasy, but no aggression. "I was trying," he said later, "to figure out a new way of approaching this kind of advertising. We have to follow the market or we can go out of business trying to moralize to the market. But why not try a new approach? Why not promote toys as instruments that expand the child's imagination in a way that is positive and that promotes cooperative values instead of violence and aggression?"

A new film version of the ad was made, now showing the helicopter flying over the jungle set. Quick shots and heightened background music give the impression of excitement and danger. The helicopter flies dramatically through the jungle and over a river and bridge to rescue a boy from a flaming village. As lights flash and shoot haphazardly through the scene the helicopter rises and escapes into the sky. The final ad was clearly exciting and intense. And it promoted the saving of a life instead of violence against life.

It was clear when the final version was shot, however, that it would not clear the network censors. Network guidelines require that sets in children's ads must depict things that are within the reach of most children so that they do not create unrealistic expectations. Clearly the elaborate jungle set (which cost $25,000 to construct) was not within the reach of most children and consequently most children would not be able to recreate the scene of the ad by buying the toy. Moreover, network regulations stipulate that in children's ads scenes must be filmed with normal lighting that does not create undue intensity. Again clearly the helicopter ad which created excitement by using quick changes of light and fast cuts did not fall within these guidelines.

After reviewing the film Tom Daner reflected on some last-minute instructions Crako's sales manager had given him when he had been shown the first version of the ad: the television ad should show things being blown up by the guns of the little helicopter and perhaps even some blood on the fuselage of the toy; the ad had to be violent. Now Tom had to make a decision. Should he risk the account by submitting only the rescue mission ad? Or should he let Teal also see the ad that showed the helicopter shooting up the village, knowing that he would probably prefer that version if he saw it? And was the rescue mission ad really that much different from the ad that showed the shooting of the village? Did it matter that the rescue mission ad still violated some of the network regulations? What if he offered Teal only the rescue mission ad and Teal accepted the "rescue approach" but demanded he make it more violent; should he give in? And should Tom risk launching an ad campaign that was based on this new untested approach? What if the ad failed to sell the Crako toy? Was it right to experiment with a client's product, especially a product that was so important to the future of the client's business? Tom was unsure what he should do. He wanted to show Teal only the rescue mission commerical but he felt he first had to resolve these questions in his own mind.

For Discussion

1. From a moral point of view, what, in your judgment, should Tom Daner's final decision be? Justify your answer. What should Tom do if he is asked to make the final ad more violent than the rescue ad he had filmed?

2. Answer the questions Tom Daner asked himself: Was the rescue mission ad really that much different from the ad that showed the shooting of the village? Did it matter that the rescue mission ad still violated some of the network regulations? Was it right to experiment with a client's product, especially a product that was so important to the future of the client's business?

The Advertising Code of American Business

We hold that advertising has a responsibility to inform and serve the American public and to further the economic life of this nation. Believing this, the following principles are hereby affirmed.

1. **Truth**

   Advertising shall tell the truth, and shall reveal material facts, the concealment of which might mislead the public.

2. **Responsibility**

   Advertising agencies and advertisers shall be willing to provide substantiation of claims made.

3. **Taste and Decency**

   Advertising shall be free of statements, illustrations, or implications which are offensive to good taste or public decency.

4. **Disparagement**

   Advertising shall offer merchandise or service on its merits, and refrain from attacking competitors or disparaging their products, services or methods of doing business.

5. **Bait Advertising**

   Advertising shall be bona fide and the merchandise or service offered shall be readily available for purchase at the advertised price.

6. **Guarantees and Warranties**

   Advertising of guarantees and warranties shall be explicit. Advertising of any guarantee or warranty shall clearly and conspicuously disclose its nature and extent, the manner in which the guarantor or warrantor will perform and the identity of the guarantor or warrantor.

7. Price Claims

Advertising shall avoid price or savings claims which are unsupported by facts or which do not offer bona fide bargains or savings.

8. Unprovable Claims

Advertising shall avoid the use of exaggerated or unprovable claims.

9. Testimonials

Advertising containing testimonials shall be limited to those of competent witnesses who are reflecting a real and honest choice.

John Z. Miller

Ethics and Advertising

I don't intend to state anything original. Instead, I want to remind you of criticisms of advertising that indicate that all is not well in Adland. Of course, we all realize that our industry is enormously successful; we are a $100 billion a year industry, with over seven thousand competing firms. We are coming off a decade of unprecedented growth. But commercial success does not imply ethical behavior, and it is quite clear that the American public is concerned about advertising. There are deep reasons for this distrust.

Although we all know what the free market is, let's highlight a couple of its features in order to better see what is ethically problematic about advertising. First, economists all assume people have certain wants and are free to choose products based on those wants. The consumer is said to be king; producers merely satisfy preexisting wants. Ads provide information about products; consumers are then free to try products and see whether they satisfy their wants. Second, for the market to work well, both consumers and producers need reasonably complete transaction information. Advertising enters here, for it supposedly supplies the bulk of such information. To make a long story short, one moral defense of the free market is that it gives consumers what they want more efficiently than other economic systems. And advertising is central to this efficiency because it informs people about products that may satisfy their wants.

The claim that the consumer is king is seriously questioned by John Kenneth Galbraith. In *The Affluent Society* he showed that advertising does not simply satisfy antecedently specified consumer wants; instead, ads create wants. Everyone has seen the graph that shows cigarette consumption maps directly onto ad expenditures, and everyone knows that cigarette ads associating smoking with glamour and sex in some cases created the desire to smoke. To those of you who claim that it cannot be proven that ads even influenced people to smoke I say: get real. Many of today's kids want to avoid smoke altogether, in large part because of negative advertising. In the early 1970s Lee Iacocca was fond of saying "Safety doesn't sell," implying that consumers didn't want safe autos. That may well have been true at the time. Clearly, however, ads which for decades showed acceleration, speed, and power mixed with sex, and which omitted any reference to the dangers of speed, etc., were a big factor in determining what the public wanted. In some cases ads take rather indefinitely specified wants and give them a specific shape. Everyone needs a sense of self-esteem, a feeling of confidence and satisfaction with oneself. Advertising did not create that need or want. In the 1950s, however, Americans wanted large autos, and they wanted large autos because they were convinced that large autos were necessary for self-esteem and they were so convinced largely by advertising and by the auto producers who offered them only large autos. Fashion provides another example. Annually, designers and producers make clothes that are distinct from the previous year's clothes. Marketers then create a desire for the new line of clothes, which retailers then stock. Advertisers do not create a desire for clothing, but it is clear they create a desire for a line of clothes that is already produced and for which consumers had no desire before the ad campaign began.

Galbraith's point is that over a large domain of products the producer is king. He creates desires in consumers, which he then satisfies through production. And this is ethically troublesome on two accounts. First, we take it that autonomy is valuable and that anything that undercuts it is bad. The free-market model assumes wants are antecedent to ads and that consumers are autonomous agents. Yet, if producers via ads create and shape desires, then the consumer is not entirely autonomous. Second, the standard defense of the free market, namely, that it satisfies more wants better than other economic systems, is undercut if advertising creates the wants it satisfies. If we agree that the American market with its heavy advertising creates and satisfies wants, it doesn't follow that the consumer is better off having the wants the advertiser has created. If a drug pusher creates a desire for cocaine in you, he expands your range of wants but you are not better off for having that want. Consumers have an ethical concern here; after all, the producer will market anything that will legally make him a profit.

Advertising in America also influences wants negatively because of the materialism and sameness of the products it promotes and because of its pervasiveness. The wants ads influence are directed at beer, gasoline, diamonds, trucks, moisturizers, furs, fried chicken, foundation garments, watches, tissues, money, autos, tacos, cigarettes, chocolates, refrigerators, toys, nylons, electricity, shaving cream, batteries, and mouthwash. Although some of these products are unobjectionable, the idea that assaults us unrelentingly is that our problems are eliminable by an object. Success, happiness, joy—all are depicted as produced by an external consumable thing, and not the result of years of hard work, learning, and commitment. I am not claiming that advertising is the sole or even the primary cause of American materialism, but that it is a significant partial cause is obvious.

In part because they focus almost entirely on material consumables, ads are also deadeningly similar. Ads stereotype people, primarily as consumers, but also by addressing concocted psychological inadequacies and by portraying the American ideal as young, successful, white, and suburban. All of these negative effects are compounded by advertising's pervasiveness. Television, radio, newspapers, magazines, the roadways—all are saturated with ads hawking commercial products. On average, each of us sees 1,600 ads per day. Children watch television six hours a day and talk with their parents for fifteen minutes; they are in school six hours a day for twelve years, but are bombarded by ads throughout their lives.

Finally, although some ads are amusing, they generally deaden taste. Ads are repeated endlessly, are often intentionally irritating, and appeal to the lowest level of cognitive ability. It is often said that the fact that ads are unaesthetic does not mean they are unethical. In a deep sense, however, our moral capacity depends on our ability to reason, assess facts, exercise our imagination, and empathize with others. A practice, then, is ethical to the extent that it exercises and improves our cognitive, imaginative and affective capacities. In this sense, much of education is ethical while advertising fails the test.

It is sometimes claimed that ads control people; subliminal ads are often cited. Yet, even if subliminal ads do cause people to act in certain ways, it is difficult to see how this could be true of the typical ad. "Bud Light: Everything Else Is Just A Light." Cute, but it is hard to see how the ad could totally preclude choice, which is what "control" implies. Yet, even if such ads do not control a viewer as a brainwasher controls his victim, the viewer is in a subtle sense manipulated by the ads. A clean-cut, handsome young man is shown enjoying a beer, and then pictured in the presence of an attractive, scantily-clad young lady. Now the person who buys that brand of beer may well say he is buying it because he likes it or prefers its taste, but the ad works by linking the brand with his unconscious desire for sex, and the link is established between the brand and the fulfillment of that desire in the ad. So the real reason he buys the brand is the link set up between the brand and his unconscious desire, and he is not consciously aware of this link or the desire. In this way we are manipulated, if not controlled, by advertising.

As I see it, although no ad controls us, it is very difficult in America to avoid being heavily influenced or manipulated by the aim of advertisers, which is to get us to consume things, and by the pervasiveness and numbing sameness of the messages. The freedom to choose between this material object and that material object, between beer and pop, doesn't amount to much. We are perhaps truly free to the extent that we can step back, critically assess, and significantly change our entire way of living our lives. Advertising, however, mainly offers us beer or pop. This massive lifestyle conditioning is the threat advertising poses; it grinds down one's ability to entertain alternative lifestyles. Think of the bumperstickers you see. (1) "Born To Shop." Advertising's conditioning is so relentless that the consumer believes that shopping (for advertised products) is innate, natural, inevitable. (2) "A Woman's Place Is In The Mall." It is not the use of the advertised product that is significant or worthwhile, no, the *purchasing* of things gives women significance; their place is where things can be bought. (3) "When The Going Gets Tough, The Tough Go Shopping." Our deepest problems are solved by buying things advertised—typically on soap operas. (4) "Shop Till You Drop." Shopping is an all-consuming activity worth pursuing until you and your credit line are exhausted. While in some cases used as spoofs, it is sad that these slogans often reflect Americans' lives, and inescapably true that advertising must bear some responsibility for this sorry state of affairs.

Having shown that in many cases it is the producer via advertising who is king, and not the consumer, we can now examine the other primary prop of advertising, namely, that for the free market to work well both consumers and producers need reasonably complete market information and that ads supply the information. The indictment is that the "information" ads provide is often deceptive, misleading, or simply absent. Before we develop these charges we must examine the claim that ads are essentially lies.

Now, of course, very few advertisers sanction outright lying. The liar makes a claim that he believes is false with the intent to get his hearer to accept the claim as true. Both conditions must be met in order to label a claim a lie. This enables the advertiser to say with a straight face: "Everybody's talking about the new Starfire [automobile]." This isn't a lie because nobody believes that everybody is talking about the new Starfire. Hence, the second condition for lying is not met; since the advertiser knows nobody will accept the claim as true, he has not lied. He is engaged in mere "puffery." Although there isn't much outright lying in advertising, at least among large firms, the industry's standards are supposed to be much higher than the mere avoidance of lying. The advertising industry itself has a brief code of ethics that admonishes advertisers to tell the truth and not mislead consumers, and it says ads should avoid exaggerated or unprovable claims. Furthermore, the FTC is legally responsible for seeing that ads are not false. But it is false that everybody is talking about the new Starfire; the claim is certainly unprovable. In too many cases the industry and FTC are all too content to let a false claim slip by with the rationalization that at least it isn't a lie.

Although a liar asserts what he believes is false, ads can be deceptive without making false statements. An ad is deceptive if it causes consumers to have false beliefs about a product. Deceptive ads are unethical because the consumer who purchases based on false beliefs will not match products adequately with his interests. Since its founding in 1914, the FTC has sought to ban deceptive ads, but it must be admitted that deception is still rampant. Let's look at a few examples.

Volvo's ads have always stressed safety and chassis strength. In 1989 it ran an ad showing a six-ton truck being lowered onto a Volvo auto, which did not sag at all under the truck's weight. The ad was similar to Volvo ads from the early 1970s, which showed a Volvo holding up six other Volvos, again without sagging.

Now many viewers undoubtedly believed that the suspension and tires of the Volvo must be extraordinary to support such weight. In fact, however, in the 1989 ad jacks were hidden behind the tires and used to prop up the auto. Viewers saw the Volvo holding up the truck but did not see the jacks. After the ads were questioned, a Volvo spokesperson said the ads would not have looked the same without the jacks: "The tires would have exploded, and the springs would have compressed."

Volvo claimed the ads were not deceptive, because they were intended to exhibit the strength of Volvo's bodies and roofs, not the suspension or tires. However, the print version of Volvo's ad did not refer to body and roof strength; it simply said: "What you see here is exactly what you think you see here." Now, I'm not going to accuse Volvo or its advertisers of lying, but surely many readers believed that the Volvo has extraordinary suspension and tire strength. Certainly many readers believed the Volvo had suspension and tire strength sufficient to support a truck. But these are false beliefs produced by the ad. The TV ad that showed the truck being lowered onto the Volvo said "How well does your car stand up to heavy traffic?" Undoubtedly, many drivers of makes with suspension systems better than or equal to the Volvo's formed the belief that their make does not have a suspension system as good as Volvo's, and this false belief was produced by the ad. So these ads were deceptive.

In 1990 Volvo ran a TV ad that showed a pickup with huge tires being repeatedly driven over a line of autos, all of which were crushed except the Volvo. However, the Volvo's roof was reinforced with steel that viewers could not see and the other cars' roof support systems were cut through or weakened. No statements were made, so no false claims were made, yet clearly viewers would believe falsely that the Volvo's body strength was superior. Such ads are deceptive and unethical.

A 1990 ad showed an Oldsmobile dropped by parachute from a cargo plane. It hits the ground and drives away. But two Olds 98s are involved. The one dropped is an empty shell. The verbal part of the ad discusses Oldsmobile's customer satisfaction program. The company says the parachute represents the security provided by the program. Since the ad didn't mention anything about the car's performance and didn't claim that the car could be driven away after a parachute drop, Oldsmobile claimed the ad wasn't deceptive. But even though no performance claims are made, the visual focus of the ad is on the parachute drop. Many viewers falsely believe the Olds can be dropped and driven off, somewhat akin to the tanks we see dropped and then driven off in Airborne ads. Such an ad is deceptive even though it makes no false claims.

Since children are highly impressionable, advertisers have particular obligations to them, obligations that are often not met. A notorious case in point was Hudson Pharmaceutical Corporation's ads for "Spiderman" vitamins. Hudson's TV ads, aimed at preteens, featured Spiderman, an agile cartoon hero of immense strength. The ads depicted Spiderman gobbling a handful of Spiderman vitamins and then dispatching a bunch of bad guys, just like in the cartoons. However, children find it difficult to distinguish programming from advertisements, and the Spiderman of the cartoons looked like the Spiderman of the ads. So it was easy for viewers to falsely believe that eating a handful of vitamins will enable one to demonstrate incredible feats of strength. These ads were clearly deceptive. Furthermore, tests revealed that some of the Spiderman vitamins were very harmful when ingested in large amounts. The FTC ordered Hudson to stop the ads, but that the government had to intervene is an embarrassment to the advertising industry.

Of course, many advertisements do provide quite useful information. A picture may show you what a desk looks like, list its dimensions, and indicate its price, all of which will be informative. In such cases it will generally pay the advertiser to be truthful, for the consumer can verify whether the object has the features advertised. Still, there will be many cases in which ads convey only truthful information but are immoral. An ad may state all the beneficial features of a product but simply omit all negative features. It tells the truth, but only a half-truth. An advertisement will mention all the good features of a refrigerator, while overlooking all the defects and shortcomings that you can find if you read *Consumer Reports.* Now, clearly the producer and/or advertiser know their product's defects and shortcomings, but they present an ad which implies that the product has only good points. The consumer wants a product that satisfies his interests. If he believes that the product has only the advertised qualities but it actually has negative qualities that are unadvertised, then his interests will not be satisfied. Selling based on such advertised half-truths is unfair to the consumer.

I am not claiming that advertisers should be required to list *all* the positive and negative features of products. Ads would become prohibitively lengthy and confusing. But if not mentioning a feature clearly encourages consumers to buy a product for a use for which it was not intended and will not work, then it is ethical to mention it even though sales will be lost. And if not mentioning a negative feature will probably result in serious harm, then that feature should be mentioned. For example, it seems entirely appropriate to require advertisers of salt substitutes (which contain potassium) to state that the product is not appropriate for those on potassium-restricted diets, even though the salt substitute package itself lists potassium as an ingredient.

Many ballyhooed ads don't really provide any information. Coca-Cola ads are always right at the top of the "most memorable" ad list, but what information is conveyed by "Coke is the Real Thing" or "Coke Adds Life"? Such ads contain no factual information. To show Coca-Cola being used by a bunch of joyful, jumping juveniles associates the product with a stereotyped "good life," but no information is conveyed. Let's not pretend that such ads facilitate the free market by providing reasonably complete transaction information. The aim here is to sell pop by persuasion based on psychological association. The ads are repeated relentlessly as a form of psychological conditioning. Now there is nothing unethical about selling products, and nothing intrinsically wrong about persuasion. We can persuade by providing information or by other (mainly psychological) means. Again, there is nothing intrinsically wrong with the latter. But let's not pretend that ads which provide no information are somehow vital to satisfying a condition that free-market theorists regard as necessary to such a market, namely, that market transactions should rest on consumers' knowledge of the qualities of products they are purchasing.

For an efficient market, consumers as well as producers need reasonably complete market information. Ads, along with sources like *Consumer Reports,* can provide such information. In all too many cases, however, ads are deceptive, convey misleading half-truths, or simply don't present any information at all.

Advertisers have taken full advantage of the 1980s, the decade of the "me" generation and lax regulation. At some point the pendulum will swing toward tighter regulation because so much of advertising is ethically suspect. We need to help move advertising more toward the status of a profession, with a balanced commitment to the public as well as our clients. We need a more developed and better enforced code of ethics. We need a stronger commitment to provide consumers with more and better information, while also cleaning up the ad clutter that is so deadening today. We can and ought to discipline ourselves for the benefit of the common good.

Charles Collins

In Defense of Advertising

Advertising never has had much appeal to the cognoscenti. It doesn't have an abstract foundation that would enable it to find a niche within the theoretical tidiness of economics, and for those in the humanities who appeal to the "higher" values, advertising is too tied to mammon. Critics of advertising, ranging from philosophers, who contend that the market is "unfair," to economists, such as Galbraith, who decry the market's bad effects, used to have socialism on which to fall back. In the new age, philosopher-kings would determine production and distribution; advertising would be eliminated. And, in fact, as socialism was practiced advertisements were not needed; in socialist utopias such as the former USSR, Albania, Cuba, and North Korea it turned out that there were no goods to distribute. Socialism did satisfy the philosophers' demand for fairness; everyone shared equally in nothing. Since socialism, through its own internal contradictions, is reducing itself to absurdity, we are left with the market, messy as it may be. In fact, critics of advertising never had much of a case. Let's see why this is so.

Advertising's critics typically focus just on its negative aspects, of which admittedly there are some. However, if this sort of evidence is used to argue that advertising should be banned, the evidence is woefully insufficient for two reasons. First, advertising may well have benefits that outweigh its negative aspects. Second, to conclude that we should adopt some other method of conveying market information to consumers requires critics to propose and defend a method superior to advertising. This they have not done. Let us examine these two points.

Let's admit that in some cases advertising contributes to oligopoly, as in beer and cereals. Let's admit that in some cases it raises the cost of products to consumers, who pay for the cost of advertising. So what? In other cases advertising enables a company to gain market entry, which fosters competition. In many cases advertising increases sales, thereby lowering unit costs, which leads to lower prices. So the benefits of advertising must be discussed as well as its drawbacks, and no good empirical evidence exists to show that overall the negatives outweigh the positives as regards the issues of anticompetitiveness and prices.

Second, to show that advertising in some cases has some bad aspects does nothing to establish that there is some other method better at doing what advertising does. Of course, there is considerable controversy over what advertising does or should do. Yet if the suggestion is that we should ban advertising and replace it with, say, direct selling, this is just nonsense in a complex society such as ours. If the suggestion is that we replace advertising with a government controlled operation that would put out a product like *Consumer Reports,* then the burden is on those who make the proposal to show that such a system would be better than advertising. Of course, free-market defenders have no quarrel with *Consumer Reports* as it exists today; there is room in a free society both for *Consumer Reports* and commercial advertising.

Those who would ban advertising also need to recognize that businesses have a right to advertise, a right based on the right to free speech. The general benefits of free speech are well known. It promotes the independence and autonomy of speaker and hearer. It encourages criticism and reasoned deliberation, both important aspects of human development. Finally, free speech and the competition of ideas tend to help us establish the truth about issues. Since advertising is a form of speech, producers have a right to advertise. In some areas, such as political speech, the right to freedom of speech is almost unqualified; politicians can lie about their opponents and still avoid prosecution. Those of us who advocate a right to commercial speech recognize that the right is qualified. In the United States we require advertisers to tell the truth, and there is a good justification for prosecuting advertisers who make false claims. Advertising performs its function by providing information to the consumer; it cannot do so by making false claims. Nevertheless, within certain constraints companies do have a right to advertise.

Although there do not appear to be good reasons for banning advertising altogether, critics argue that regulation of advertising should be tightened considerably. One line of reasoning often voiced is inconsistent. Liberals often argue that freedom of speech in the political arena should not be restricted, on the assumption that the American public is sophisticated enough to filter the lies, falsehoods, misleading claims, and deceptive tactics that politicians employ. But they also argue that the American public is not sophisticated enough to filter out exaggeration and deception in advertising, even though advertisers cannot by law lie or make false claims. Although liberals often have blinders on when it comes to governmental paternalism, it should be clear that they cannot consistently maintain both positions.

Some critics object that advertisements often fail to provide informational content. So, it might be granted that advertising's function is to inform consumers, but then claimed that advertisements often do not inform. However, Phillip Nelson has recently developed arguments to the strong conclusion that all advertising is informative.[1] Clearly, some advertisements are informative, e.g., they state a product's function, size, cost, and so on. Generally, it will be in the producer's interest to state these features truthfully. The size and cost of a suit, for example, can be directly verified by a consumer prior to purchase. And it will generally pay to advertise a product's function truthfully; the producer who advertises an analgesic as a laxative will not get many repeat purchases. Accordingly, much advertising is informative. But what of advertisements such as "It's Miller Time" or "Coca-Cola Classic is the Real Thing"? Nelson argues that even if the message is not informative the fact that the product is advertised is informative. It pays to advertise those products that do satisfy consumers' wants; it does not pay to advertise products that fail to satisfy consumers' wants. Since repeat purchasing by consumers will typically increase the advertising budget, the amount of advertising provides consumers with information about what brands satisfy consumer wants. So advertising can provide valuable information to consumers even though it is as empty as "Coca-Cola Classic is the Real Thing."

Much of the critics' fire has been directed at "deceptive" advertising. Let's begin by differentiating lying from deception. A lie is a statement by a person who, knowing the statement is false, intends that his listeners will take the statement as true. To deceive a person is to cause him to have false beliefs. An advertisement, then, lies if it makes a false statement and the producer/advertiser intends that the consumer will take the statement to be true. An advertisement is deceptive if it causes a consumer to have false beliefs about the product advertised. Some refinement of the definition of "deception" will be required, but we can start here in order to see the difference between these concepts.

According to these definitions, an advertisement that lies involves a false claim, but a deceptive advertisement may not contain any false claims. It may tell the truth, yet still cause the consumer to have a false belief. So some deceptive advertisements are not lies. Furthermore, although all lies involve making a false claim, some false claims are not deceptive. If I lie in poker, you may not believe me, i.e., you are not deceived. So, some lies do not involve deception. One may say that a liar attempts to deceive his hearer; he does not always succeed. A person who is deceived by an advertisement does actually have a false belief as a result of the advertisement, irrespective of whether the deceiver makes a false claim.

Lying is not a major concern in advertising. For one thing, it is illegal. The 1937 Wheeler Amendment prohibits unfair or deceptive advertising, and explicitly says that a false advertisement is unfair or deceptive. Since a lie must contain a false statement, advertisements can neither make false claims nor lie. The advertising profession also explicitly bans lying because it prohibits false claims. It does so by insisting that advertisements contain true claims. The Advertising Code of the American Advertising Federation says: "Advertising shall tell the truth . . . be willing to provide substantiation of claims made . . . and avoid the use of unprovable claims." The profession monitors and polices advertisements, and believe me, if an advertisement makes a false claim, competitors let everyone in the professional body and at the FTC know about it. The FTC acts quickly to prohibit false advertisements. Accordingly, consumers need not worry that advertisements lie; they need not even worry that they contain false claims.

So far we have argued that all advertisements provide some information to consumers and that an overwhelming percentage of advertisements not only do not lie, they do not contain false claims. Are some advertisements, nonetheless, deceptive? According to our initial definition, many advertisements will be deceptive. We said that an advertisement is deceptive if it causes a consumer to have false beliefs about the product advertised. Judging from surveys which indicate that a rather high percentage of Americans believe that the Abominable Snowman exists, we could probably find some consumer whose false belief that the Jolly Green Giant exists and eats beans was caused by Pillsbury's advertisements. Such an advertisement would be deceptive on this definition of "deception."

From a legal standpoint, we know that the 1937 Wheeler Amendment broadened the FTC's powers to include the prohibition of deceptive advertising. So the issue is whether the FTC should adopt the above definition of deception. Ivan Preston has called the above definition the basis of the "ignorant man" standard, the idea being that the law should protect even the most ignorant person against "deceptive" advertising.[2] Preston points out that the FTC placed a strong emphasis on the ignorant man standard from roughly 1919 to 1963, but his tracing out of cases reveals a reduction to absurdity of the standard. The FTC, for example, outlawed Charles of the Ritz's use of "Rejuvenescence" as a facial cream name because it might cause consumers to falsely believe that it would literally restore youth and the appearance of youth. The FTC banned Clairol from saying that its dye would "color hair permanently" because one witness said she thought that someone might be caused to falsely believe that all the hair a person grows over a lifetime would be colored, even though the witness admitted that she would not be so fooled. The court itself said that it didn't see how anyone would be deceived, but had to admit that someone could be deceived, which seemed to preclude use of the advertisement by the ignorant man standard. The court sided with the FTC. The point is that any advertisement, no matter how truthful, will probably cause some ignoramus to have some false belief about a product. The FTC recognized the reduction to absurdity in 1963: "An advertiser cannot be charged with liability in respect of every conceivable misconception, however outlandish, to which his representations might be subject among the foolish or feeble-minded. . . . A representation does not become 'false and deceptive' merely because it will be unreasonably misunderstood by an insignificant and unrepresentative segment of the class of persons to whom the representation is addressed."[3]

If pressed to its logical conclusion, the ignorant man standard precludes or severely restricts advertising. Of course, many of advertising's critics desire that result. Again, however, no such proposal can be seriously entertained unless the legislation's costs are weighed against advertising's benefits. Furthermore, the burden is on the critics to show that the harm of advertising as presently practiced outweighs its benefits. Now we know that: (1) all advertising provides some information; (2) the law requires that advertisements not make false claims; (3) severely restricting advertising would increase consumers' search costs; (4) the cost of ignoramus-based litigation would be high; and (5) a basic assumption of democratic society is that individuals are able to detect and deflect the attempt to deceive. All this suggests that instead of banning or severely restricting advertising based on the ignorant man standard we should reject the concept of deception on which it rests.

Let us say, then, that an advertisement is deceptive if a reasonable person to whom the advertisement is directed would have false beliefs about the product advertised as a result of the advertisement. This was the standard employed in common law prior to establishment of the FTC in 1914, and it has been the standard followed in recent years by the FTC, roughly since 1963. This standard would permit Charles of the Ritz to use "Rejuvenescence" as the name of a facial cream and allow Clairol to claim that a dye "colors hair permanently." It would also allow "Coca-Cola Classic is the Real Thing"; this metaphor is outside the true/false domain. No reasonable person would be deceived by it. The reasonable man standard also permits the "half-truths" that critics find so disturbing about advertising. To tell the whole truth about whether a product is the best for a consumer to buy, the advertiser would have to list all of a product's features and compare those with all competing products—an impossible task in an advertisement. But every reasonable consumer knows that advertisers will present only those features favoring their products, so he is not deceived.

We should, in no uncertain terms, prohibit deceptive advertising, since advertising cannot fulfill its function of providing information to the consumer if the consumer is deceived about advertised products. And some advertisements are unquestionably deceptive. The recent Volvo advertisement, showing a pickup with monster tires being driven over the roofs of a row of automobiles with only the Volvo's roof holding up while the other automobiles' roofs caved in, was deceptive. Volvo had reinforced the roof of its automobile, but had cut the roof supports of the other automobiles. Clearly, the reasonable consumer could not know these facts, and probably would be deceived; it would be reasonable to form the false belief that the Volvo's roof support system is much better that its competitors'. However, you will note that this advertisement had a very short run; it was quickly fingered as deceptive and withdrawn. The upshot is that the advertising profession should work hard to prevent deceptive advertising and should take quick action to remove it when it occurs. But to inform the consumer adequately we need the reasonable man definition of "deception" rather than the ignorant man standard.

Let us now turn from the issues of truth and deception to advertising's effects. We consider two aspects of this issue: whether advertising creates desires and whether it controls consumers.

The traditional view of the market is that consumers have desires and producers make products to satisfy those desires. However, Galbraith argues that producers create certain desires through advertising, which they then satisfy through production.[4] So the producer is actually sovereign, not the consumer. Galbraith calls this the "dependence effect." Of course, certain desires, e.g., the desire for food, sex, and shelter are not created; they are basic or "original" to consumers in the sense that they are wired into people at birth. But other desires, e.g., for mouthwash, off-road vehicles, earrings, soda pop, and air conditioners, are nonbasic; they are, in Galbraith's term, "contrived," largely by advertising. Galbraith believes that as a capitalist society becomes more affluent desires are increasingly created by the very process by which they are satisfied, primarily by advertisers hired by those who produce the products.

According to Galbraith, the dependence effect has two bad consequences. To continuously increase production and make increasing profits, producers must create ever more desires, which puts consumers on a squirrel-wheel of materialistic consumption. Second, our preoccupation with our own consumption, constantly reinforced by advertising, leads to a neglect of public goods, such as schools, environmental quality, and mass transit. We have too much perfume and not enough parks.

Galbraith doesn't precisely detail which desires advertising creates, but he is mistaken in thinking that it creates any desires. Of course, people didn't desire the automobile before it was invented. However, they did desire mobility, and once the automobile was invented many thought it was a good means to mobility. People couldn't have desired a Fedders air conditioner prior to the invention of air conditioning, but they did desire comfort, and when the air conditioner was invented many thought the Fedders that they saw advertised was a good means to achieve comfort. So they tried it out. Men couldn't have desired Aramis before that scent was concocted, but they desired to attract women, and when Aramis became available many thought Aramis was a good means to attract women. Advertising may have persuaded them to give Aramis a try, but it certainly didn't create the desire. Critics castigate advertising for creating the desire to smoke, but overlook the popularity of marijuana, heroin, and cocaine, none of which is advertised. In general, then, advertising does not create desires; given a certain desire, the advertiser brings to the consumer's attention a product that may satisfy that desire. If the consumer chooses to try the product, it may or may not satisfy the desire. If it does, he may purchase the product again; if it doesn't, he probably won't buy it again.

Advertising simply doesn't have the power Galbraith attributes to it. Thousands of new products are introduced annually, many of which are heavily advertised. The vast majority fail to gain a market niche and are withdrawn. It is true that those products heavily advertised succeed more often than those not advertised. However, this is due to the fact that producers advertise those products they have good reason (via test marketing) to believe will satisfy consumers' desires, and not because they believe advertising can create desires.

Galbraith draws a loosely specified distinction between basic/original/real desires on the one hand and nonbasic/derived/contrived desires on the other.

The latter are said to be less worthy of satisfaction or less important than the former. But, as critics such as von Hayek have noted, all of the arts fall into the latter category.[5] We may be born with the desire for food, but the desire for Mozart is no less contrived than the desire for air conditioning— on the assumption that desires are contrived. A veritable army of educators is engaged in the task of contriving a desire for Mozart, Shakespeare, and Rembrandt. Are these desires, contrived by the producer (the educational system), unimportant or in some sense unworthy of satisfaction? Clearly, Galbraith would say no. So the overall dilemma for Galbraith is that either desires are not created, or, if some are, the mere fact that they are created does not mean they are unworthy of satisfaction.

It is precisely here that Galbraith's socialism becomes manifest. Among the set of contrived desires, some, contrived by Big Brother and intellectuals like Galbraith, are worthy of satisfaction, while others, contrived by advertising, are unimportant. Control advertising and you curb unimportant desires. Socialism, having failed totally to solve the problem of the production and distribution of goods, reemerges in new guise by telling us that most goods are unnecessary and that Big Brother and the professors will determine for us what goods are important or unimportant.

The remaining major criticism of advertising is that it in some sense "controls" consumers. Typically, it is assumed that some advertising, notably subliminal advertising, does control consumers. So, it is assumed that if "eat" is flashed on a theater screen in a way that is below the threshold of conscious recognition of the term, moviegoers will stream out to buy popcorn or candy. It is then argued that other forms of advertising analogously control consumers.

One problem is that there is simply no evidence that subliminal advertising works. For example, Moore argues that theoretical considerations are inconsistent with the claim that subliminal advertising can get a person to do anything,[6] and McDaniel, et al., point out that empirical research fails to support the claim that purchasing behavior is influenced by subliminal stimuli.[7] Ever since Wilson Key wrote Subliminal Seduction, he has made a nice living by going from campus to campus pointing out hidden sexual symbolism in just about any advertisement.[8] He intimates to kids who desperately want to be free that that devil, the advertiser, can manipulate them into buying just about anything via subliminal messages. But, as with an inkblot, there is no telling what a viewer will see in an advertisement. It is perhaps curious and amusing that Key sees sex in a Sunkist orange, but, even if some advertisements do contain subliminal messages, there is no theoretical or empirical basis for his assertion that such messages control or even influence consumers.

Once the claim that subliminal advertising works is undercut it is difficult to see how advertising could be said to "control" consumer behavior. In one sense I control your behavior if I can actually get you to do what I want you to do. The advertiser wants you to purchase the advertised product, but he certainly cannot ensure that you will do so. Again, advertising simply does not have the power critics attribute to it.

It is also claimed that some advertising controls consumers by linking a product with certain "unconscious" desires.[9] For example, after watching a beer commercial that portrays a young man drinking a Budweiser and then cozying up to an attractive young lady, I may subsequently purchase a Budweiser and, when asked, say I purchased it because I like that brand of beer. But, say the critics, the real reason I bought the Bud is that the commercial linked that brand with my unconscious sexual desire. The problem here is that the desire is not "unconscious." Of course I desire sex. I am also aware that I desire sex. I believe that sex is desirable, and am aware I have this belief. Furthermore, I think that Budweiser sometimes works as a means to sex (although I know from experience that Colt-45 does not "work every time"). In certain cases it doesn't; one has to experiment. Finally, I am aware I like Budweiser. So, all of this is within the orbit of my conscious awareness. I choose; I am not controlled.

It has been argued that the consumer only rarely understands the full range of the object's features, what it will do, and what the consequences of using it will be; hence, advertising can cause consumers to make irrational choices, i.e., choices they would not make if they knew all the relevant facts. As Arrington has recently argued, however, if we require every fact about a product to be known before we can be said to rationally desire the product, then, since this is impossible, no desire will be rational. On the other hand, if we require only knowledge of the relevant information to label the desire rational, then prior desires establish the relevance of information.[10] Now it is precisely advertising that enables us to fulfill those prior desires. It does so by providing information to the consumer and by laying out an array of means that may enable the consumer to satisfy such desires. A consideration of a variety of means to realize a given desire is certainly a prime instance of what we regard as rational behavior. So advertising cannot be convicted of causing irrational desires.

So the claim that advertising controls consumers' behavior is indefensible. Nobody really believes that an automobile advertisement linking, as most do, the twin desires of mobility and sex, could control a consumer. In fact, most automobile advertisers explicitly tell their clients that their advertisement will not sell the automobile; at best it persuades the consumer to go to a dealer's showroom to see and try the product. The advertisement cannot, and should not be expected to, list all the automobile's features or compare it to all competing automobiles. The consumer must drive this and other automobiles and read automotive magazines to get that information.

If we put aside the professors' theorizing, do we find *any* evidence that advertising in *any* sense "controls" consumers? No, we don't. No empirical studies show this. Information Resources, Inc., recently released the results of an exhaustive six-year study of 30,000 households' television viewing and reading patterns and their purchasing behavior.[11] The study was unique in that it focused on individuals rather than on aggregate behavior patterns. The firm knew, for example, what television commercials a subject viewed, what products he purchased with what coupons, even what he ate for lunch. The detailed study promised to indicate whether advertising works, and, if so, point to or explain how it works. What were the results? Well, the study concluded that there is no "simple correspondence" between more advertising and higher sales, that new brands need to be advertised more heavily when they are introduced, and that it is better to advertise during prime-time than other times. Ho hum. Interestingly, one of the advertisers' stock assumptions was shot down. Advertisers often test an advertisement on a sample of consumers to see whether they can recall it. But Information Resources' research reveals that the relation between high recall and increased sales is "tenuous at best." This study certainly explodes the myth that advertising controls behavior: for X to control Y there must be at least a correlation between X and Y, but even that seems questionable in the case of advertising and sales.

In conclusion, advertising is defensible. Since advertising is a form of speech, producers have a right to advertise unless they harm consumers or deny them certain rights. But advertising does not violate consumers' rights. It does not manipulate them by creating desires, and it cannot be said to control consumers' behavior. Instead, it simply presents choices to consumers; in total, advertising presents a wide variety of means to satisfy consumers' desires. Whether the consumer tries the product is his free choice. Whether the product satisfies the consumer's desire is up to the consumer to decide. If it does, he may repurchase the product; if not, he will try something else. Advertising should provide information to consumers, and all advertising does so. We have in place professional and governmental mechanisms to prevent or quickly withdraw advertisements that lie or make false claims. We do need to protect consumers against deceptive advertising, but to do so we should continue to employ the "reasonable" man standard rather than the "ignorant" man standard. Although this standard permits puffery and half-truths, such practices are permissible, since reasonable people are not deceived by them. Undoubtedly, advertising has some bad effects, but it certainly has not been shown that they outweigh its numerous good effects. To ban or severely restrict advertising, critics will have to provide consumers with product information. Such an alternative will have to be compatible with the free-market, for the socialist option has recently been consigned to the dustbin of history.

NOTES

1. Phillip Nelson, "Advertising and Ethics," in *Ethics, Free Enterprise, and Public Policy,* Richard T. De George and Joseph A. Pichler, eds., (New York: Oxford University Press, 1978), pp. 187–98.

2. Ivan Preston, *The Great American Blow-up: Puffery in Advertising and Selling* (Madison: University of Wisconsin Press, 1975).

3. Heinz W. Kirchner, 63 FTC 1282 (1963).

4. John Kenneth Galbraith, *The Affluent Society* (Boston: Houghton Mifflin Co., 1958).

5. F. A. von Hayek, "The Non Sequitur of the 'Dependence Effect,' " *Southern Economic Journal* 27 (1961): 346–48.

6. Timothy E. Moore, "Subliminal Advertising: What You See is What You Get," *Journal of Marketing* 46 (Spring 1982): 38–47.

7. Stephen McDaniel, Sandra Hart, and James McNeal, "Subliminal Stimulation as a Marketing Tool," *The Mid-Atlantic Journal of Business* 20 (1983): 41–48.

8. Wilson Key, *Subliminal Seduction* (New York: New American Library, 1973).

9. Roger Crisp, "Persuasive Advertising, Autonomy, and the Creation of Desire," *Journal of Business Ethics* 6 (1987): 413–18.

10. Robert L. Arrington, "Advertising and Behavior Control," *Journal of Business Ethics* 1 (1982): 3–12.

11. *Wall Street Journal,* November 4, 1991, B1, 6.

Corporate Policy Statement

BACKGROUND OBJECTIVES

We participate in competitive businesses in which the consumer or user has a choice of many products besides our own. It is the role of advertising to inform the public about our products and their benefits so that the consumer can make an intelligent, informed buying decision.

While our company image and reputation with the general public is based primarily on product performance, we recognize that it is also influenced by the quality and effectiveness of our product advertising.

Policy

1. Product advertising will inform the potential users about our products and their benefits so they can make an intelligent, informed buying decision.

2. Advertising will be truthful. It will not over-promise or create unrealistic expectations about the performance of our products. Performance and other claims, either actual or implied, will be substantiated by appropriate technical or consumer support.

3. All product advertising will be in good taste. It should not be inconsistent with our image, or cause consumers to react unfavorably, or portray people in a demeaning or embarrassing manner, or make unfair,

misleading, inaccurate, or disparaging statements about competitors or their products.

4. Product advertising is a reflection of our company, and it should not be placed in media which will offend generally accepted standards of propriety and decency or which present highly controversial subject matter in a biased or exploitive way. "Media," in this context, could be, for example, either a magazine or a particular issue of that magazine; a television program or a particular episode of that program.

5. Each company will be aware of, and responsive to, national concerns, for example, the representation of appropriate ethnic or other minorities in their product advertising.

Definition

Product advertising is whatever the company says or shows about our products to the public, especially through such media as television, newspapers, magazines, radio, billboards, brochures and the like, whether consumer or trade oriented. It also includes product advertising communicated through labels, packages, and sales promotion materials.

Practices

Each company will establish its own procedures for the approval of all forms of product advertising before such advertising is released. The approval will include review by R&D, legal and other functions, as appropriate.

The responsibility for maintaining the product advertising standards described in this policy is with the general manager of a subsidiary company, and the appropriate Operations head for U.S. Consumer Products and for U.S. Innochem operations.

Advertising Policy

During the early days of radio and TV, the company sponsored its own programs. This practice assured us that the program environment was not incompatible with our commercials. Today, like most other advertisers, the company no longer sponsors its own programs; our commericals appear on many different programs. The following policy guides our selection of these programs from among those offered by the networks and other suppliers of TV entertainment.

Policy

As a responsible television advertiser, Johnson Wax will actively seek out programs which not only satisfy our specific advertising needs, but also support and enhance our reputation as a socially responsible corporation. We recognize that most programs made available to us will not satisfy both of these objectives, since much of what is on television must appeal to a wide range of interests, tastes, and preferences. However, in selecting from available programs, we will specifically avoid those whose appeal is based on excessive violence or the manifest exploitation of controversial subjects; additionally, we will take care to insure that the content of programs on which we advertise is appropriate to the time period in which they are shown.

IMPLEMENTING GUIDELINES

In carrying out this policy, we and advertising agencies acting in our behalf will avoid placing our advertising on programs or program episodes which could be characterized as follows:

> Programs which include violence for its own sake and when it makes no significant contribution to the understanding of the story line.

> Programs which sensationalize acts of brutality or human suffering through overly realistic presentation.

> Programs which dramatize anti-social actions in a moment that might encourage or stimulate imitations.

> Programs which involve the discussion of subjects or depiction of behavior which is of a highly controversial nature in an exploitive manner, including exploitive depiction of human sexuality.

We believe this course is in our self-interest, as a company making quality consumer products and also in the interest of the public at large.

Practices

Selection of programs on which the company will place its advertising will be made by the Director of Advertising Services, who will adhere to the above implementing guidelines. In instances where a proposed program "buy" may appear to conflict with one or more of the guidelines, the Director of Advertising Services and the Director of Public Affairs will preview the program to determine whether it fits within this policy.

Johnson Wax

SELLING

Case Study
Clinton L. Oaks

Roger Hixon: Let the Buyer Beware

What obligation, if any, does a vendor have to point out to a prospective buyer the flaws or defects in his product? Roger Hixon, a former executive with a national firm and now a teacher of business policy at a western college, raised this question with respect to the remarks of a guest speaker in a previous class period. The speaker had talked about various levels of business ethics among the salesmen for companies with whom he dealt regularly. He had concluded that while some companies had a very strict policy calling for honesty and complete disclosure, many did not.

During the ensuing discussion, one student commented,"I hear all these platitudes being mouthed about how 'complete disclosure is always good business practice.' How many of you practice complete disclosure in your personal business dealings? I am sure I don't." At this point, just as the discussion was beginning to get a little heated, the instructor noted that the class period was nearly over. He invited several of those who were participating most actively in the discussion to write up a specific incident for discussion the next time the class met.

JOAN STULLARD

"My parents, who live in a small college town in the northern part of the state, decided a year ago last spring to try to sell their home and move into a condominium. Since my father is pretty close to retirement, they tried to sell the place themselves rather than going through a real estate agent. The real estate market up there, unlike that in many urban areas, was quite slow. By late August, they had only had one potential buyer who had shown enough interest to come back several times.

"One of the nicest features of our home was its large backyard. A huge cottonwood tree standing in one corner of the yard provided the entire house and yard with shade against the late afternoon sun. The tree was very large —its trunk had a circumference of nearly fifteen feet. The only problem with it was that it was dying. While it looked healthy and green from our house, our neighbors behind the tree could see many dead and potentially dangerous branches. A violent storm would often litter their yards and prompt them to call us and demand that we cut down the tree.

"The prospective buyer who had shown the greatest interest in the place was standing on the patio one afternoon with my father. 'That sure is a nice, big tree,' he said. I was standing at the door, and overheard his remark. His comment wasn't one that required an answer. I found myself wondering what, if anything, my father would say."

MARK BASCOM

"My brother is working as a used car salesman at Clark Motors. He tells me that the manager of the used car lot keeps a folder on every car in stock. Everything that is known about the car is recorded in the folder. This would include information about the previous owner, any major body or engine repairs, the mechanic's evaluation at the time the car came on the lot, etc.

"Before school started, my brother got permission to borrow a Buick Estate Wagon for several days to take a short vacation. He said he and his wife really enjoyed the car but they were appalled at the gas mileage—less than eight miles per gallon on the open road. When he returned the car, he made a note of this in the car's folder. He also talked to one of the mechanics about it. 'I'm not surprised,' the mechanic commented. 'As you know, we clean the carburetor, put in new plugs and points, adjust the timing and so forth whenever we get a car—but that particiular model always was a gas hog.'

"A few days later a young couple who were looking at cars on the lot expressed a great deal of interest in this car. They asked my brother a lot of questions and he, having had some personal experience with the car, was able to answer them in greater detail than was normally the case. He was also able to point out some of the features of the car that might have otherwise been overlooked. The longer they talked, the more enthusiastic the couple became. Almost the only question they didn't ask was about the car's mileage. They had to leave at 4:30 to pick up their child at the babysitter's but made an appointment to come back at 9:30 the next morning to work out the details of the sale.

"That night my brother came over to talk about a deal we were working on together. While he was there he told me about what had happened and said, 'As you know, things have been really tight for Jean and me since we took that trip, and the commission on this sale would really help us right now. I have always tried, as a matter of policy, to answer honestly any question that a prospective buyer raises. If I were to tell this couple about the gas mileage on that car, however, I'm pretty sure they would back out of the sale. I don't intend to try to deceive them, but do I have any obligation to tell them about it if they don't ask?' "

JEFF MOYER

"My wife and I live approximately thirty-five miles away from the university. She teaches school in a district that is also about thirty miles from where we live, but in the opposite direction. As you can imagine, transportation is a big item in our budget. Neither of us has been successful in finding a car pool. Fortunately, my wife's parents have graciously allowed us to continue to use the car my wife drove before we were married. We own an older car, and with the two cars we have been able to get by up to now.

"When my wife accepted the teaching position we knew the travel involved would be both time consuming and expensive. However, our projections on costs were painfully underestimated. Not only have gas and oil prices increased sharply, but we hadn't realized that both cars would need new tires. Because we drive as far as we do, we have had to have tune-ups on both cars more frequently than anticipated. In addition to all this, we have had to have work done on our own car's distributor, muffler, and lights—all of which has cost us well over two hundred dollars. Just recently we had more trouble requiring a mechanic's examination. His diagnosis was 'You need a valve job.'

"While I was trying to figure out where I could borrow the projected $240 for the valve job, the mechanic said, 'The engine block is pitted and needs to be ground down. If you are going to do that you might as well overhaul the whole engine.'

" 'How much will that be over the $240?' I asked, bracing for the shock.

" 'About $360,' the mechanic replied.

"Fighting the churning feeling in my stomach, I asked what would happen if he didn't grind down the block. I was told that the engine head and block might not seal when put back together after the work was done on the valves. 'Just try to get it to seal,' I told him, knowing our budget was already dripping with red ink.

"The mechanic put the engine back together and I crossed my fingers. Evidently it sealed because the car is running now. I suspect that with all the miles that it travels weekly it may need the overhaul before long. I can't begin to afford that. Both my father and father-in-law have given me the same advice. 'Get rid of the car while it is still running.'

"I checked on the Blue Book value of this model and it ranged from $1600 to $2300. I was pretty sure that if I were to tell the buyer about the engine block, I would have more difficulty in selling it and I would probably have to knock $400 to $800 off the going price.

"I try to think of myself as an honest person, and I don't think I could lie about it if someone asked me whether or not the car engine needed an overhaul. But suppose they didn't ask? Am I obligated to tell them anyway?

"Suppose I were to trade in the car on another car at an auto dealership. A dealer will almost always have a mechanic check out the car before he makes you an offer. Do I need to say anything in a situation like that? If I said anything I am sure it would lower the offer the dealer would make to me, but I am not at all sure, based upon my past experience, that the dealer would pass this information and a lower price on to another customer. In such a transaction isn't there almost a mutual understanding that everyone is governed by the old merchant's law of 'Let the buyer beware'?

"Having decided not to keep the car, I felt my choices were: (1) tell whoever buys the car about the engine; (2) tell whoever buys the car about the engine only if he or she asks if I know of any mechanical flaws; (3) tell about the engine only if I sell the car myself instead of trading it in; and (4) don't tell anyone about the engine even if asked. What should I have done?"

DON CASE

"Just after I turned sixteen, I spent a summer working with my best friend on his dad's used car lot. Our job was to 'clean-up' and 'recondition' cars before they were put on the sales lot. We were to make them presentable so they could be shown to prospective buyers.

"Some of the things we had to do were what you might expect. We washed and waxed the body, scrubbed the seats and door interiors and shampooed the rugs. We also tightened any loose screws and repositioned the carpet, tightening down the carpet edges.

"My friend's dad taught us how to do a lot of other things as well. We were to use a powerful grease cutting detergent to wash the engine and eliminate the dirt, oil, and grease that had accumulated on it. 'A buyer is always impressed with a clean engine,' he told us, 'and besides he won't be alarmed by any evidence that oil is leaking from the engine.' We were also shown how to use a spray shellac on all the rubber hoses so that they would look like they were new.

"If the car was burning any oil, we were to add a can of STP. If the blue smoke coming out of the back end was heavy we would add two cans and sometimes three.

"Rust had often eaten through the steel from the wheel well and would show around the fenders. With the help of a steel brush and a can of spray paint this was easily hidden and the rust would not show through the paint again for at least a month.

"Sometimes the carpets were too stained with grease and dirt to be cleaned. A coat of dark spray coloring hid the stains and would make the carpets look nice for at least a week or two after the car was purchased.

"I was young enough at the time and grateful enough to have a job that I don't ever remember even questioning the rightness or wrongness of the things we did. My friend's dad's conscience must have troubled him a little, however, because he was always telling us that there wasn't anything wrong or illegal about what we were doing. He told us that every used car lot did the same thing and he had to do it to remain competitive. 'We never turn back an odometer,' he said. 'That is illegal. The buyer expects that a used car lot will do everything possible to make a used car look good—and part of his job as a buyer is to check out anything that might be wrong.'

"Two or three years later, I had a used car of my own to sell. Without thinking much about it, I gave it some treatment we used to give cars on the lot, including the addition of two cans of STP. I put a "For Sale" sign in the window and parked it on our curb. The next night, a girl about my age who evidently didn't know much about cars, came by to ask me how much I was asking for it. After I told her, she asked, 'Is the car in good condition? Do you know of any problems that I am likely to have with it?' What should I have said?"

NED OSBORNE

"At the end of last spring semester, one of my roommates transferred to a school down in Texas. Before he left, he turned over to me two pairs of skis, both virtually new. He said, 'There isn't any market for these right now but they should be easy to sell in the fall. Why don't you keep them for me until then?'

"Knowing that he wasn't much of a skier, I asked him, 'Where did you get them?' He replied, 'One of the guys I run around with gave them to me. I don't know for sure but I wouldn't be surprised if he picked them up off an unlocked ski rack on a car parked in front of the motel where he used to work. At any event there aren't any identifying marks on them. I checked in the local ski shops around here and both pairs retail for around $300. Sell them for whatever you can get and you keep half of it.' Before I had any chance to protest, he took off.

"Those skis stood in my closet for nearly six months. Late in the fall, we got a little cramped for room and I decided I had better do something with them. I was half tempted to just turn them over to campus security and tell them they had been left in my apartment and I didn't know whose they were.

"One day when I was trying to rearrange some of the things in the closet, I had both pairs of skis out on my bed. A friend of another roommate saw them and said, 'You wouldn't like to sell a pair of skis, would you? I am really in the market and they look just like what I have been looking for.'

"Without stopping to think about it, I asked, 'What will you give me?' He said, 'I'll give you $150.00 for the pair on the right.'

"What should I have done? My textbooks that fall had cost me about twice what I had estimated and I was really strapped for cash. I hadn't stolen the skis—in fact I didn't know for sure they had been stolen. I could truthfully say that a roommate had left them with me to sell and let it go at that. Was I obligated to tell a prospective purchaser that they might have been stolen? I can imagine what effect that might have had on the reputation of those of us living in the apartment.

"If the skis were stolen, it was extremely unlikely that the rightful owners could ever be located. In view of this, what difference did it make whether or not they had been stolen? If I turned them over to campus security, they would probably just keep them for a while and then sell them at an auction. If the end result would be the same—that is, that the skis would end up with some third party who didn't know who the original owner was and who could care less—why shouldn't I pick up a few dollars to cover my 'costs of handling' "?

For Discussion

Joan Stullard

Should Joan's father disclose to prospective buyers the status of the cottonwood tree?

Mark Bascom

How should Mark respond to his brother?

Jeff Moyer

Which of Jeff's four strategies should he adopt?

Don Case

How should Don respond? Does the fact that an action is a customary industry practice make a moral difference?

Ned Oborne

Should Ned sell the skis?

David M. Holley

A Moral Evaluation of Sales Practices

A relatively neglected area in recent literature on business ethics is the ethics of sales practices. Discussions of the moral dimensions of marketing have tended to concentrate almost exclusively on obligations of advertisers or on the moral acceptability of the advertising system. By contrast, little attention has been given to the activities of individual salespersons.[1]

This neglect is surprising on several counts. First, efforts to sell a product occupy a good deal of the time of many people in business. Developing an advertising campaign may be a more glamorous kind of activity, but it is sales on the individual level that provides the revenue, and for most businesses the number of persons devoted to selling will far exceed the number devoted to advertising. Second, the activity of selling something is of intrinsic philosophical significance. It furnishes a paradigm case of persuasive communication, raising such issues as deception, individual autonomy, and the social value of a marketing-oriented system for distributing goods and services. While the practice of advertising raises these same issues, the potential for manipulation of vulnerable consumers comes into much sharper focus at the level of individual sales.

In this paper I will attempt to develop a framework for evaluating the morality of various sales practices. Although I recognize that much of the salesforce in companies is occupied exclusively or primarily with sales to other businesses, my discussion will focus on sales to the individual consumer. Most of what I say should apply to any type of sales activity, but the moral issues

Originally published in *Business and Professional Ethics* 5, no. 1 (Fall 1987). This edited version appeared in *Ethical Theory and Business,* 3d. ed., edited by Tom Beauchamp and Norman E. Bowie (Englewood Cliffs, N.J.: Prentice Hall, 1988), pp. 448–57.

arise most clearly in cases in which a consumer may or may not be very sophisticated in evaluating and responding to a sales presentation.

My approach will be to consider first the context of sales activities, a market system of production and distribution. Since such a system is generally justified on teleological grounds, I describe several conditions for its successful achievement of key goals. Immoral sales practices are analyzed as attempts to undermine these conditions.

I

The primary justification for a market system is that it provides an efficient procedure for meeting people's needs and desires for goods and services.[2] This appeal to economic benefits can be elaborated in great detail, but at root it involves the claim that people will efficiently serve each other's needs if they are allowed to engage in voluntary exchanges.

A crucial feature of this argument is the condition that the exchange be voluntary. Assuming that individuals know best how to benefit themselves and that they will act to achieve such benefits, voluntary exchange can be expected to serve both parties. On the other hand, if the exchanges are not made voluntarily, we have no basis for expecting mutually beneficial results. To the extent that mutual benefit does not occur, the system will lack efficiency as a means for the satisfaction of needs and desires. Hence, this justification presupposes that conditions necessary for the occurrence of voluntary exchange are ordinarily met.

What are these conditions? For simplicity's sake, let us deal only with the kind of exchange involving a payment of money for some product or service. We can call the person providing the product the *seller* and the person making the monetary payment the *buyer*. I suggest that voluntary exchange occurs only if the following conditions are met:

1. Both buyer and seller understand what they are giving up and what they are receiving in return.

2. Neither buyer nor seller is compelled to enter into the exchange as a result of coercion, severely restricted alternatives, or other constraints on the ability to choose.

3. Both buyer and seller are able at the time of the exchange to make rational judgments about its costs and benefits.

I will refer to these three conditions as the knowledge, noncompulsion, and rationality conditions, respectively.[3] If the parties are uninformed, it is possible that an exchange might accidentally turn out to benefit them. But given the lack of information, they would not be in a position to make a rational judgment about their benefit, and we cannot reasonably expect beneficial results as a matter of course in such circumstances. Similarly, if the exchange is made under compulsion, then the judgment of personal benefit is not the basis of the exchange. It is possible for someone to be forced or manipulated into an arrangement that is in fact beneficial. But there is little reason to think that typical or likely.[4]

It should be clear that all three conditions are subject to degrees of fulfillment. For example, the parties may understand certain things about the exchange but not others. Let us posit a theoretical situation in which both parties are fully informed, fully rational, and enter into the exchange entirely of their own volition. I will call this an *ideal exchange*. In actual practice there is virtually always some divergence from the ideal. Knowledge can be more or less adequate. Individuals can be subject to various irrational influences. There can be borderline cases of external constraints. Nevertheless, we can often judge when a particular exchange was adequately informed, rational, and free from compulsion. Even when conditions are not ideal, we may still have an *acceptable exchange.*

With these concepts in mind, let us consider the obligations of sales personnel. I suggest that the primary duty of salespeople to customers is to avoid undermining the conditions of acceptable exchange. It is possible by act or omission to create a situation in which the customer is not sufficiently knowledgeable about what the exchange involves. It is also possible to influence the customer in ways that short-circuit the rational decision-making process. To behave in such ways is to undermine the conditions that are presupposed in teleological justifications of the market system. But the moral acceptability of the system may become questionable if the conditions of acceptable exchange are widely abused. The individual who attempts to gain personally by undermining these conditions does that which, if commonly practiced, would produce a very different system from the one that supposedly provides moral legitimacy to that individual's activities.

II

If a mutually beneficial exchange is to be expected, the parties involved must be adequately informed about what they are giving up and what they are receiving. In most cases this should create no great problem for the seller[5], but what about the buyer? How is she to obtain the information needed? One answer is that the buyer is responsible for doing whatever investigation is necessary to acquire the information. The medieval principle of *caveat emptor* encouraged buyers to take responsibility for examining a purchase thoroughly to determine whether it had any hidden flaws. If the buyer failed to find defects, that meant that due caution had not been exercised.

If it were always relatively easy to discover defects by examination, then this principle might be an efficient method of guaranteeing mutual satisfaction. Sometimes, however, even lengthy investigation would not disclose what the buyer wants to know. With products of great complexity, the expertise needed for an adequate examination may be beyond what could reasonably be expected of most consumers. Even relatively simple products can have hidden flaws that most people would not discover until after the purchase, and to have the responsibility for closely examining every purchase would involve a considerable amount of a highly treasured modern commodity, the buyer's time. Furthermore, many exchange situations in our context involve products that cannot be examined in this way—goods that will be delivered at a later time or sent through the mail, for example. Finally, even if we assume that most buyers, by exercising enough caution, can protect their interests, the system of *caveat emptor* would take advantage of those least able to watch out for themselves. It would in effect justify mistreatment of a few for a rather questionable benefit.

In practice the buyer almost always relies on the seller for some information, and if mutually beneficial exchanges are to be expected, the information needs to meet certain standards of both quality and quantity. With regard to quality, the information provided should not be deceptive. This would include not only direct lies but also truths that are intended to mislead the buyer. Consider the following examples:

1. An aluminum siding salesperson tells customers that they will receive "bargain factory prices" for letting their homes be used as models in a new advertising campaign. Prospective customers will be brought to view the houses, and a commission of $100 will be paid for each sale that results. In fact, the price paid is well above market rates, the workmanship and materials are substandard, and no one is ever brought by to see the houses.[6]

2. A used car salesperson turns back the odometer reading on automobiles by an average of 25,000 to 30,000 miles per car. If customers ask whether the reading is correct, the salesperson replies that it is illegal to alter odometer readings.

3. A salesperson at a piano store tells an interested customer that the "special sale" will be good only through that evening. She neglects to mention that another "special sale" will begin the next day.

4. A telephone salesperson tells people who answer the phone that they have been selected to receive a free gift, a brand new freezer. All they have to do is buy a year's subscription to a food plan.

5. A salesperson for a diet system proclaims that under this revolutionary new plan the pounds will melt right off. The system is described as a scientific advance that makes dieting easy. In fact, the system is a low-calorie diet composed of foods and liquids that are packaged under the company name but are no different from standard grocery store items.

The possibilities are endless, and whether or not a lie is involved, each case illustrates a salesperson's attempt to get a customer to believe something that is false in order to make the sale. It might be pointed out that these kinds of practices would not deceive a sophisticated consumer. Perhaps so, but whether they are always successful deceptions is not the issue. They are attempts to mislead the customer, and given that the consumer must often rely on information furnished by the salesperson, they are attempts to subvert the conditions under which mutually beneficial exchange can be expected. The salesperson attempts to use misinformation as a basis for customer judgment rather than allowing that judgment to be based on accurate beliefs. Furthermore, if these kinds of practices were not successful fairly often, they would probably not be used.

In the aluminum siding case, the customer is led to believe that there will be a discount in exchange for a kind of service, allowing the house to be viewed by prospective customers. This leaves the impression both that the job done will be of high quality and that the price paid will be offset by commissions. The car salesperson alters the product in order to suggest false information about the extent of its use. With such information, the customer is not able to judge accurately the value of the car. The misleading reply to inquiries is not substantially different from a direct lie. The piano salesperson deceives the customer about how long the product will be obtainable at a discount price. In this case the deception occurs through an omission. The telephone solicitor tries to give the impression that there has been a contest of some sort and that the freezer is a prize. In this way, the nature of the exchange is obscured.

The new diet-system case raises questions about how to distinguish legitimate "puffery" from deception. Obviously, the matter will depend to some extent on how gullible we conceive the customer to be. As described, the case surely involves an attempt to get the customer to believe that dieting will be easier under this system and that what is being promoted is the result of some new scientific discovery. If there were no prospect that a customer would be likely to believe this, we would probably not think the technique deceptive. But in fact a number of individuals are deceived by claims of this type.

Some writers have defended the use of deceptive practices in business contexts on the grounds that there are specific rules applying to those contexts that differ from the standards appropriate in other contexts. It is argued, for example, that deception is standard practice, understood by all participants as something to be expected and, therefore, harmless, or that it is a means of self-defense justified by pressures of the competitive context.[7] To the extent that the claims about widespread practice are true, people who know what is going on may be able to minimize personal losses, but that is hardly a justification of the practice. If I know that many people have installed devices in their cars that can come out and puncture the tires of the car next to them, that may help keep me from falling victim, but it does not make the practice harmless. Even if no one is victimized, it becomes necessary to take extra precautions, introducing a significant disutility into driving conditions. Analogously, widespread deception in business debases the currency of language, making business communication less efficient and more cumbersome.

More importantly, however, people are victimized by deceptive practices, and the fact that some may be shrewd enough to see through clouds of misinformation does not alter the deceptive intent. Whatever may be said with regard to appropriate behavior among people who "know the rules," it is clear that many buyers are not aware of having entered into some special domain where deception is allowed. Even if this is naive, it does not provide a moral justification for subverting those individuals' capacity for making a reasoned choice.

Only a few people would defend the moral justifiability of deceptive sales practices. However, there may be room for much more disagreement with regard to how much information a salesperson is obligated to provide. In rejecting the principle of *caveat emptor*, I have suggested that there are pragmatic reasons for expecting the seller to communicate some information about the product. But how much? When is it morally culpable to withhold information? Consider the following cases:

1. An automobile dealer has bought a number of cars from another state. Although they appear to be new or slightly used, these cars have been involved in a major flood and were sold by the previous dealer at a discount. The salesperson knows the history of the cars and does not mention it to customers.

2. A salesperson for an encyclopedia company never mentions the total price of a set unless he has to. Instead he emphasizes the low monthly payment involved.

3. A real estate agent knows that one reason the couple selling a house with her company wants to move is that the neighbors often have loud parties and neighborhood children have committed minor acts of vandalism. The agent makes no mention of this to prospective customers.

4. An admissions officer for a private college speaks enthusiastically about the advantages of the school. He does not mention the fact that the school is not accredited.

5. A prospective retirement home resident is under the impression that a particular retirement home is affiliated with a certain church. He makes it known that this is one of the features he finds attractive about the home. Though the belief is false, the recruiters for the home make no attempt to correct the misunderstanding.

In all these cases the prospective buyer lacks some piece of knowledge that might be relevant to the decision to buy. The conditions for ideal exchange are not met. Perhaps, however, there can be an acceptable exchange. Whether or not this is the case depends on whether the buyer has adequate information to decide if the purchase would be beneficial. In the case of the flood-damaged autos, there is information relevant to evaluating the worth of the car that the customer could not be expected to know unless informed by the seller. If this information is not revealed, the buyer will not have adequate knowledge to make a reasonable judgment. Determining exactly how much information needs to be provided is not always clear-cut. We must in general rely on our assessments of what a reasonable person would want to know. As a practical guide, a salesperson might consider, "What would I want to know if I were considering buying this product?"

Surely a reasonable person would want to know the total price of a product. Hence the encyclopedia salesperson who omits this total is not providing adequate information. The salesperson may object that this information could be inferred from other information about the monthly payment, length of term, and interest rate. But if the intention is not to have the customer act without knowing the full price, then why shouldn't it be provided directly? The admissions officer's failure to mention that the school is unaccredited also seems unacceptable when we consider what a reasonable person would want to know. There are some people who would consider this a plus, since they are suspicious about accrediting agencies imposing some alien standards (e.g., standards that conflict with religious views). But regardless of how one evaluates the fact, most people would judge it to be important for making a decision.

The real estate case is more puzzling. Most real estate agents would not reveal the kind of information described, and would not feel they had violated any moral duties in failing to do so. Clearly, many prospective customers would want to be informed about such problems. However, in most cases failing to know these facts would not be of crucial importance. We have a case of borderline information. It would be known by all parties to an ideal exchange, but we can have an acceptable exchange even if the buyer is unaware of it. Failure to inform the customer of these facts is not like failing to inform the customer that the house is on the site of a hazardous waste dump or that a major freeway will soon be adjacent to the property.

It is possible to alter the case in such a way that the information should be revealed or at least the buyer should be directed another way. Suppose the buyer makes it clear that his primary goal is to live in a quiet neighborhood where he will be undisturbed. The "borderline" information now becomes more central to the customer's decision. Notice that thinking in these terms moves us away from the general standard of what a reasonable person would want to know to the more specific standard of what is relevant given the criteria of this individual. In most cases, however, I think that a salesperson would be justified in operating under general "reasonable person" standards until particular deviations become apparent.[8]

The case of the prospective retirement home resident is a good example of how the particular criteria of the customer might assume great importance. If the recruiters, knowing what they know about this man's religious preferences, allow him to make his decision on the basis of a false assumption, they will have failed to support the conditions of acceptable exchange. It doesn't really matter that the misunderstanding was not caused by the salespeople. Their allowing it to be part of the basis for a decision borders on deception. If the misunderstanding was not on a matter of central importance to the individual's evaluation, they might have had no obligation to correct it. But the case described is not of that sort.

Besides providing nondeceptive and relatively complete information, salespeople may be obligated to make sure that their communications are understandable. Sales presentations containing technical information that is likely to be misunderstood are morally questionable. However, it would be unrealistic to expect all presentations to be immune to misunderstanding. The salesperson is probably justified in developing presentations that would be intelligible to the average consumer of the product he or she is selling and making adjustments in cases where it is clear that misunderstanding has occurred.

III

The condition of uncompelled exchange distinguishes business dealings from other kinds of exchanges. In the standard business arrangement, neither party is forced to enter the negotiations. A threat of harm would transform the situation to something other than a purely business arrangement. Coercion is not the only kind of compulsion, however. Suppose I have access to only one producer of food. I arrange to buy food from this producer, but given my great need for food and the absence of alternatives, the seller is able to dictate the terms. In one sense I choose to make the deal, but the voluntariness of my choice is limited by the absence of alternatives.

Ordinarily, the individual salesperson will not have the power to take away the buyer's alternatives. However, a clever salesperson can sometimes make it seem as if options are very limited and can use the customer's ignorance to produce the same effect. For example, imagine an individual who begins to look for a particular item at a local store. The salesperson extolls the line carried by his store, warns of the deficiencies of alternative brands, and warns about the dishonesty of competitors, in contrast to his store's reliability. With a convincing presentation, a customer might easily perceive the options to be very limited. Whether or not the technique is questionable may depend on the accuracy of the perception. If the salesperson is attempting to take away a legitimate alternative, that is an attempt to undermine the customer's voluntary choice.

Another way the condition of uncompelled choice might be subverted is by involving a customer in a purchase without allowing her to notice what is happening. This would include opening techniques that disguise the purpose of the encounter so there can be no immediate refusal. The customer is led to believe that the interview is about a contest or a survey or an opportunity to make money. Not until the end does it become apparent that this is an attempt to sell something, and occasionally if the presentation is smooth enough, some buyers can be virtually unaware that they have bought anything. Obviously, there can be degrees of revelation, and not every approach that involves initial disguise of certain elements that might provoke an immediate rejection is morally questionable. But there are enough clear cases in which the intention is to get around, as much as possible, the voluntary choice of the customer. Consider the following examples:

1. A seller of children's books gains entrance to houses by claiming to be conducting an educational survey. He does indeed ask several "survey" questions, but he uses these to qualify potential customers for his product.

2. A salesperson alludes to recent accidents involving explosions of furnaces and, leaving the impression of having some official government status, offers to do a free inspection. She almost always discovers a "major problem" and offers to sell a replacement furnace.

3. A man receives a number of unsolicited books and magazines through the mail. Then he is sent a bill and later letters warning of damage to his credit rating if he does not pay.

These are examples of the many variations on attempts to involve customers in exchanges without letting them know what is happening. The first two cases involve deceptions about the purpose of the encounter. Though they resemble cases discussed earlier that involved deception about the nature or price of a product, here the salesperson uses misinformation as a means of limiting the customers' range of choice. The customer does not consciously choose to listen to a sales presentation but finds that this is what is happening. Some psychological research suggests that when people do something that appears to commit them to a course of action, even without consciously choosing to do so, they will tend to act as if such a choice had been made in order to minimize cognitive dissonance. Hence, if a salesperson successfully involves the customer in considering a purchase, the customer may feel committed to give serious thought to the matter. The third case is an attempt to get the customer to believe that an obligation has been incurred. In variations on this technique, merchandise is mailed to a deceased person to make relatives believe that some payment is owed. In each case, an effort is made to force the consumer to choose from an excessively limited range of options.

IV

How can a salesperson subvert the rationality condition? Perhaps the most common way is to appeal to emotional reactions that cloud an individual's perception of relevant considerations. Consider the following cases:

1. A man's wife has recently died in a tragic accident. The funeral director plays upon the husband's love for his wife and to some extent his guilt about her death to get him to purchase a very expensive funeral.

2. A socially insecure young woman has bought a series of dance lessons from a local studio. During the lessons, an attractive male instructor constantly compliments her on her poise and natural ability and tries to persuade her to sign up for more lessons.[9]

3. A life insurance salesperson emphasizes to a prospect the importance of providing for his family in the event of his death. The salesperson tells several stories about people who put off this kind of preparation.

4. A dress salesperson typically tells customers how fashionable they look in a certain dress. Her stock comments also include pointing out that a dress is slimming or sexy or "looks great on you."

5. A furniture salesperson regularly tells customers that a piece of furniture is the last one in stock and that another customer recently showed great interest in it. He sometimes adds that it may not be possible to get any more like it from the factory.

These cases remind us that emotions can be important motivators. It is not surprising that salespeople appeal to them in attempting to get the customer to make a purchase. In certain cases the appeal seems perfectly legitimate. When the life insurance salesperson tries to arouse the customer's fear and urges preparation, it may be a legitimate way to get the customer to consider something that is worth considering. Of course, the fact that the fear is aroused by one who sells life insurance may obscure to the customer the range of alternative possibilities in preparing financially for the future. But the fact that an emotion is aroused need not make the appeal morally objectionable.

If the appeal of the dress salesperson seems more questionable, this is probably because we are not as convinced of the objective importance of appearing fashionable, or perhaps because repeated observations of this kind are often insincere. But if we assume that the salesperson is giving an honest opinion about how the dress looks on a customer, it may provide some input for the individual who has a desire to achieve a particular effect. The fact that such remarks appeal to one's vanity or ambition does not in itself make the appeal unacceptable.

The furniture person's warnings are clearly calculated to create some anxiety about the prospect of losing the chance to buy a particular item unless immediate action is taken. If the warnings are factually based, they would not be irrelevant to the decision to buy. Clearly, one might act impulsively or hastily when under the spell of such thoughts, but the salesperson cannot be faulted for pointing out relevant considerations.

The case of the funeral director is somewhat different. Here there is a real question of what benefit is to be gained by choosing a more expensive funeral package. For most people, minimizing what is spent on the funeral would be a rational choice, but at a time of emotional vulnerability it can be made to look as if this means depriving the loved one or the family of some great benefit. Even if the funeral director makes nothing but true statements, they can be put into a form designed to arouse emotions that will lessen the possibility of a rational decision being reached.

The dance studio case is similar in that a weakness is being played upon. The woman's insecurity makes her vulnerable to flattery and attention, and this creates the kind of situations in which others can take advantage of her. Perhaps the dance lessons fulfill some need, but the appeal to her vanity easily becomes a tool to manipulate her into doing what the instructor wants.

The key to distinguishing between legitimate and illegitimate emotional appeals lies in whether the appeal clouds one's ability to make a decision based on genuine satisfaction of needs and desires. Our judgment about whether this happens in a particular case will depend in part on whether we think the purchase likely to benefit the customer. The more questionable the benefits, the more an emotional appeal looks like manipulation rather than persuasion. When questionable benefits are combined with some special vulnerability on the part of the consumer, the use of the emotional appeal appears even more suspect.

In considering benefits, we should not forget to consider costs as well. Whether a purchase is beneficial may depend on its effects on the family budget. Ordinarily it is not the responsibility of a salesperson to inquire into such matters, but if it becomes clear that financial resources are limited, the use of emotional appeals to get the customer to buy more than she can afford becomes morally questionable. Occasionally we hear about extreme cases in which a salesperson finds out the amount of life insurance received by a widow and talks her into an unnecessary purchase for that amount, or in which the salesperson persuades some poor family to make an unwise purchase on credit requiring them to cut back on necessities. The salesperson is not responsible for making a rational calculation for the customer, but when a salesperson knowingly urges an action that is not beneficial to the consumer, that is in effect trying to get the consumer to make an irrational judgment. Any techniques used to achieve this end would be attempts to subvert the conditions of mutually beneficial exchange.

For obvious reasons, salespeople want as many customers as possible to make purchases, and therefore they try to put the decision to purchase in the best possible light. It is not the job of a salesperson to present all the facts as objectively as possible. But if playing on a customer's emotions is calculated to obscure the customer's ability to make rational judgments about whether a purchase is in her best interest, then it is morally objectionable.

V

I have attempted to provide a framework for evaluating the morality of a number of different types of sales practices. The framework is based on conditions for mutually beneficial exchange and ultimately for an efficient satisfaction of economic needs and desires. An inevitable question is whether this kind of evaluation is of any practical importance.

If we set before ourselves the ideal of a knowledgeable, unforced, and rational decision on the part of a customer, it is not difficult to see how some types of practices would interfere with this process. We must, of course, be careful not to set the standards too high. A customer may be partially but adequately informed to judge a purchase's potential benefits. A decision may be affected by nonrational and even irrational factors and yet still be rational enough in terms of being plausibly related to the individual's desires and needs. There may be borderline cases in which it is not clear whether acting in a particular way would be morally required or simply overscrupulous, but that is not an objection to this approach, only a recognition of a feature of morality itself.

NOTES

1. In a survey of the major textbooks in the field of business ethics, I discovered only one with a chapter on sales practices: David Braybrooke's *Ethics in the World of Business,* chapter 4 (Totowa, N.J.: Rowman and Allanheld, 1983). That chapter contains only a brief discussion of the issue; most of the chapter is devoted to excerpts from court cases and the quotation of a code of ethics for a direct-mail marketing association.

2. The classic statement of the argument from economic benefits is found in Adam Smith, *The Wealth of Nations* (1776) (London: Methusen and Co. Ltd., 1930). Modern proponents of this argument include Ludwig von Mises, Friedrich von Hayek, and Milton Friedman.

3. One very clear analysis of voluntariness making use of these conditions may be found in John Hospers's *Human Conduct: Problems of Ethics,* 2d ed. (New York: Harcourt Brace Jovanovich, 1982), pp. 385–88.

4. I will refer to the three conditions indifferently as conditions for voluntary exchange or conditions for mutually beneficial exchange. By the latter designation I do not mean to suggest that they are either necessary or sufficient conditions for the occurrence of mutual benefit, but that they are conditions for the reasonable expectation of mutual benefit.

5. There are cases, however, in which the buyer knows more about a product than the seller. For example, suppose Cornell has found out that land Fredonia owns contains minerals that make it twice as valuable as Fredonia thinks. The symmetry of my conditions would lead me to conclude that Cornell should give Fredonia the relevant information unless perhaps Fredonia's failure to know was the result of some culpable negligence.

6. This case is described in Warren Magnuson and Jean Carper, *The Dark Side of the Marketplace* (Englewood Cliffs, N.J.: Prentice Hall, 1968), pp. 3–4.

7. Albert Carr, "Is Business Bluffing Ethical?" *Harvard Business Review* 46 (January–February 1968): 143–153. See also Thomas L. Carson, Richard E. Wokutch, and Kent F. Murrmann, "Bluffing in Labor Negotiations: Legal and Ethical Issues," *Journal of Business Ethics* 1 (1982): 13–22.

8. My reference to a reasonable person standard should not be confused with the issue facing the FTC of whether to evaluate advertising by the reasonable consumer or ignorant consumer standard as described in Ivan Preston, "Reasonable Consumer or Ignorant Consumer: How the FTC Decides," *Journal of Consumer Affairs* 8 (Winter 1974): 131–143. There the primary issue is with regard to whom the government should protect from claims that might be misunderstood. My concern here is with determining what amount of information is necessary for informed judgment. In general I suggest that a salesperson should begin with the assumption that informa-

tion a reasonable consumer would regard as important needs to be revealed and that when special interests and concerns of the consumer come to light they may make further revelations necessary. This approach parallels the one taken by Tom Beauchamp and James Childress regarding the information that a physician needs to provide to obtain informed consent. See their *Principles of Biomedical Ethics,* 2d ed. (New York: Oxford University Press, 1983), pp. 74–79.

9. This is adapted from a court case quoted in Braybrooke, pp. 68–70.

Corporate Policy Statement

CONDUCT INVOLVING CUSTOMERS

General

Restrictive agreements or understandings with distributors, dealers, OEMs, or others may be illegal, particularly where the customer is in the resale business. Hewlett-Packard (HP) may never deprive a customer of its right to determine its own resale prices; and HP may impose nonprice restrictions on a customer's resale business only in limited, well-defined circumstances.

Prospective Customers

Numerous retail and wholesale customers ask to become HP distributors, dealers, or OEMs. HP has established procedures for entering into agreements with these firms and all HP personnel are expected to comply with those procedures. Within the United States, HP generally may be selective in choosing its customers. If HP decides not to do business with a customer, the customer should be informed in writing that HP has made a business decision not to deal with it. HP need not offer any other explanation for such a decision and it is best not to do so.

Resale Price Maintenance

Once HP sells its products, it must leave the customer free to set any real prices. HP will not engage in any effort to influence resale prices, other than merely suggesting resale prices. Furthermore, HP will not enter into any understanding with a customer as to the terms upon which HP will deal with another customer. Communications from one customer about a second customer's resale prices must be handled so that it is clear that HP will not try to affect the conduct of the second customer.

Other Restrictions on Resale

Under limited circumstances, HP may establish territorial restrictions or other non-price-related rules for resale channels. Any proposal to impose such restrictions must be approved by the General Legal Department prior to implementation.

Boycotts

Having an agreement or understanding with an HP competitor or customer not to deal with a particular customer, supplier, or service organization may be illegal. This underscores the need for extreme care if HP discusses a customer's resale pricing or other competitive policies with another customer. A unilateral decision not to sell to a prospective customer is usually legal in the United States, but an unlawful agreement might be inferred where the decision follows a discussion with another customer.

Exclusive Dealing

HP may not require its customers to agree either to buy products or services exclusively from HP or to refrain from purchasing the goods of a competitor where the probable effect is to substantially lessen competition.

Tying Agreements

A tying agreement is a refusal to sell a unique or highly desirable product or service unless a second product or service is also purchased. Such agreements are generally illegal since they force customers to buy a product or service they do not want in order to get one they do want. A "package" price is not a tying agreement if the components are separately available on reasonable terms.

Reciprocal Deals

Reciprocal deals are understandings that one firm will buy another firm's products or services only if the favor is returned. Attempts to coerce a customer into reciprocal deals are usually illegal, and certainly unethical.

* * *

General Rule

It is HP's policy to emphasize the quality of its products and to abstain from making disparaging comments or casting doubt on competitors or their products. If statements (oral or written) are made concerning a competitor or its products, they must be fair, factual, and complete.

Advertising

All HP advertising must comply with HP's Advertising and Sales Promotion policies and guidelines. HP generally discourages comparative advertising in the United States, and in certain other countries comparative advertising may be unlawful. Any comparisons with competitive products must be substantiated before the comparsion is published.

Specific Practices

HP employees should comply with the following rules when communicating about a competitor or its products:

1. Do not make comments about a competitor's character or business practices. For example, do not tell a customer that a competitor's sales representative is immoral or untrustworthy.

2. Sell on the basis of HP's capabilities, know-how, and benefits to the customer and not on the basis of a competitor's deficiencies.

3. Avoid references to a competitor's troubles or weak points. For example, do not mention financial difficulties, pending lawsuits, or government investigations involving the competitor.

4. Do not make any statement about the specifications, quality, utility, or value of a competitor's product unless the statement is based on the competitor's current published information or other factual data. Even statements based on factual data must be complete. In some countries, such statements also must relate to the positive aspects of the competitive product.

5. Do not make unsubstantiated claims that HP originated a product or one of its features.

Hewlett-Packard

455

SELECT BIBLIOGRAPHY

Beauchamp, T., and N. Bowie. *Ethical Theory and Business.* 3d ed. Englewood Cliffs, N.J.: Prentice-Hall, 1988, pp. 194–226; 398–471.

Business and Professional Ethics Journal 3 (1984). An issue focusing solely on ethics and advertising.

Carson, T., et al. "An Ethical Analysis of Deception in Advertising." *Journal of Business Ethics* 4 (1985), 93–104.

Desjardins, J., and J. McCall. *Contemporary Issues in Business Ethics.* Belmont, Calif.: Wadsworth Publishng Co., 1985, pp. 48–197.

Fletcher, G. "Fairness and Utility in Tort Theory," *Harvard Law Review* 85 (January 1972): 537–73.

Goldman, A. "Ethical Issues in Advertising," in *Just Business.* T. Regan, ed. New York: Random House, 1984, pp. 235–70.

Gray, I. *Product Liability: A Management Response.* New York: Amacom, 1975, ch. 6.

Hyman, A., and M. Johnson, eds. *Advertising and Free Speech.* Lexington, Mass.: D. C. Heath, 1977.

Keeton, W., et al. *Products Liability and Safety.* Mineola, N.Y.: Foundation Press, 1980.

Laczniack, G., and P. Murphy, eds. *Marketing Ethics.* Lexington: Lexington Books, 1987.

Morgan, F. "Marketing and Product Liability: A Review and Update." *Journal of Marketing* 46 (Summer 1982): 69–78.

Moskin, J., ed. *The Case for Advertising.* New York: American Association of Advertising Agencies, 1973.

Packard, V. *The Hidden Persuaders.* New York: David McKay, 1957.

Posner, R. "Strict Liability: A Comment." *Journal of Legal Studies* 2 (January 1973): 205–221.

Preston, J. *The Great American Blow-up: Puffery in Advertising and Selling.* Madison: University of Wisconsin Press, 1975.

Velasquez, M. *Business Ethics.* 2d ed. Englewood Cliffs, N.J.: Prentice-Hall, 1988, pp. 269–306.

Weinstein, A., et al. *Products Liability and the Reasonably Safe Product.* New York: John Wiley and Sons, 1978.

Wright, J., and J. Mertes, eds. *Advertising's Role in Society.* St. Paul: West, 1974.

7

BUSINESS AND THE ENVIRONMENT

INTRODUCTION

Most of us favor economic growth. We also are interested in a clean environment. These interests often clash: nuclear power, oil and chemical spills, ozone depletion, automobile exhaust, pesticides, fertilizers, timber cutting, hydroelectricity, resource depletion, landfills, toxic waste, acid rain, strip mining, global warming, commercial fishing and netting, wetlands drainage—all illustrate contests between commercial interests and environmentalists. In this chapter we explore ethical approaches to these complex issues.

Wilfred Beckerman is convinced that extreme environmentalists have exaggerated the facts about the results of economic growth and the facts about pollution. He argues that pollution can and is being controlled, and claims there are no compelling reasons to believe that economic growth will exhaust our resources in a catastrophic or tragic way. Beckerman believes one should estimate the costs and benefits involved in production and pollution control, and that, while this approach would turn out to justify some controls, it would not support the demand of the "eco-doomsters" for a total stop to economic growth or for a pursuit of extreme measures to eradicate pollution.

William Blackstone approaches the environmental issue from a rights perspective, claiming that a livable environment is not only desirable but a human right. We have a human (or moral) right to a decent environment because such a state is necessary if people are to fulfill their human capacities. Because we have a human right to a livable environment, business and society have obligations not to interfere with that right; accordingly, Blackstone argues we should incorporate this right into our legal system, even though doing so will restrict businesses' economic and property rights. Blackstone's rights approach leaves several difficult questions unanswered. Is pollution to be banned completely? How far are property and commercial rights to be restricted to preserve environmental rights? What should we do when the cost of removing

457

a pollutant is very high and the benefit of doing so is minimal? Manuel Velasquez discusses these issues from a utilitarian/free market perspective, pointing out the advantages and disadvantages of employing utilitarianism to address pollution problems.

Two cases place the reader in a decision-maker's role. "High Tech Spills" asks what corporate executives should do when faced with a certain sort of environmental problem. The Macklin Mining case asks for your opinion on how a judge should decide a legal case.

Traditional ethical approaches to the environment all stress *human* values; for example, Blackstone's concern is with a human right to a clean environment, and utilitarians standardly focus on utility for humans. Many of today's environmentalists take sharp issue with the view that nature should be protected only if doing so promotes human interests or rights. Christopher Stone argues that the notion of a right should be extended to cover natural objects in the environment. Having rights would give these objects legal recourse when they are harmed by pollution. The position Stone points toward represents a radical break from previous ethical theories. According to Stone, natural objects have rights and interests quite independent of our relation to them, and it is important to protect their interests. Granting rights to natural objects implies that we cannot justifiably "exploit" them for our own (business) purposes because doing so rests on the (unjustified) assumption that our human interests and rights are all that count. In response to Stone, Hobbs argues that for natural objects to have rights they must have interests; arguing that they lack interests, he concludes that natural objects cannot have moral or legal rights. The Supreme Court case *Sierra* Club v. *Morton* discusses Disney's plan to build a recreational complex in a national forest.

ENVIRONMENTAL RESPONSIBILITY

Case Study
Manuel G. Velasquez

High Tech Spills

On November 17, 1981, officials of Fairchild Camera and Instrument Corporation came across evidence indicating that several thousand gallons of 1,1,1 trichloroethane (TCA) had leaked from one of their underground chemical waste storage tanks at the company's plant in San Jose, California. TCA, an industrial cleaning solvent, is commonly used in the electronics industry to clean and degrease computer chips. Further investigations confirmed the managers' suspicions and in early December the company notified the state and city officials of the leak. City tests of a water well located 2,000 feet from the tank on December 7 showed that the water contained TCA levels of 1,700 parts per billion, almost six times what state standards allowed. The well, which provided drinking water to Los Paseos, a nearby residential neighborhood, was closed down the same day by the Great Oaks Water Company, owner of the contaminated well.[1]

Residents of the neighborhood surrounding the well were understandably upset, since several had earlier noticed what appeared to be a high number of birth defects and miscarriages. One resident, Lorraine Ross, wrote a letter on January 27, 1982, to Betty Roeder, president of the water company that owned the well, asking her to look into the possibility that the defects and miscarriages were linked to the chemical spill and the contaminated well. Roe-

From Manuel G. Velasquez, *Business Ethics: Concepts & Cases,* 2e, copyright © 1984, pp. 265–67. Adapted by permission of Prentice Hall, Englewood Cliffs, New Jersey.

der replied that she had notified state and county health officials who would look into the matter.

The County Health Department director convened an advisory committee that met with state and health experts to plan an investigation of the residents' suspicions. The committee conducted a review of the scientific literature, but found no human epidemiologic studies that discussed the reproductive effects of TCA. Animal studies were also inconclusive, one study having concluded that TCA caused cancer in female mice but not in rats. However, the committee decided to investigate the possibility of health defects anyway. Public money was tight at the time and due to a state spending freeze, work in the investigation did not get underway until spring of 1983. At that time investigators conducted a questionnaire survey of all the households in the area, and then had extensive interviews with all women reporting defects or miscarriages. The interviews were followed by a careful analysis of hundreds of local hospital records, and the results were compared with an adjoining "control" community with similar demographic characteristics.

On January 16, 1985 the committee finally released the results of its investigation: From 1980 to 1981 birth defects in the neighborhood around the contaminated well by the Fairchild plant were 300 percent higher than normal, miscarriages were 200 percent above normal levels, and 200 percent more infants were born with major heart defects than would have been expected.[2] The study, however, did not attribute the cluster of excess defects and miscarriages to the Fairchild leak, noting that the birth defects occurred before Fairchild records indicated the leak would have begun, and noting that the birth defects extended beyond the area surrounding the Great Oaks Water Company's contaminated well. The study read:

> The time trends of spontaneous abortions and congenital malformation rates in the Los Paseos area do not correspond to the timing of the leak according to the Fairchild Co.'s material balance sheet. The Fairchild material balance sheet suggests that the leak increased in the second half of 1980 and peaked sharply at the end of 1981. However, this balance sheet was constructed in 1982 after the purported cluster of spontaneous abortions and congenital malformations had been identified. It was based on company estimates of input and outflow of materials and there is uncertainty about the validity of these data.[3]

Residents were not convinced that Fairchild was not the culprit. Several suggested that the company's records were not accurate or that earlier Fairchild leaks that had gone undetected might have been contaminating the water for a long period of time. Others pointed out that since Great Oaks Water Company mixed water from several wells before selling it to customers throughout the area, the contaminated water might have caused the defects that occurred outside the Los Paseos neighborhood.

A few months after the birth defect report was issued, an MBA student named Jack Johnson began working as a summer intern for Infotek, a major manufacturer of a wide variety of electronic components and integrated circuits whose offices and plants were located in Santa Clara, a few miles from the Fairchild plant.[4] He was to sit in on all the meetings of Infotek's corporate affairs officer, Robert Stone, an alumnus of the same MBA program, so that the two could "brainstorm" about possible solutions to problems that might arise. In their initial interview Stone had emphasized the confidentiality that would be required from Johnson. Already, in his first two weeks, Johnson had been astonished by the number of sensitive discussions he was invited to sit in on.

Johnson later recalled one particular series of conversations he had sat in on in Stone's office, recounting the events without revealing the true names of the company or people involved:

> Stone called me into his office, and pointing to some folders on his desk he said, "These environmental test results just came in this morning. As you know, we've dug test wells all around our property and sample the wells every week. You might remember that two city wells west of us were shut down two years ago because they found chemicals in them. Well, these new tests results aren't too good. One of our wells shows an increase of twenty times more Hydrochlorbenzine (HCB) than was there last week. Last week that well had only 2.25 parts per billion of HCB; now it's showing 45 parts."
>
> "How high a level is safe?" I asked.
>
> "No one knows," Stone replied. "The EPA hasn't issued standards for that chemical, and they might not do it for years. Of course, if the stuff stays put on our property, we're fine. But if it moves west underground toward the city's water wells, that's a problem." He paused, then continued. "Everyone loves living here in the middle of a high-tech boom. Low unemployment, clean jobs, and no dirty smoke-belching factory chimneys. But electronics manufacturing uses a lot of chemical solvents, and we didn't used to be too careful with them. Sometimes we would just pour the stuff down the drain at the end of the day! A couple of years ago, two city wells turned up contaminated, and there was no way of knowing which of the firms in the area was responsible. Chances are all of us were. We're a lot more careful now, but as you can see by these test results, we still run into problems."
>
> "How much would it cost to clean up the chemicals around our well?" I asked.
>
> "We don't know. Two months ago, one of our other wells showed a lower level of HCB—7.5 parts per billion—and I called a friend at Dow Chemical. He said that HCB probably causes cancer at high enough concentrations, but no one is sure just how high. He gave me the name of an environmental consulting firm that I hired to help us work out a program for all of our chemicals. I called them this morning and told them about the latest results. They couldn't give me any hard figures, but based on my description, one guy said cleaning up the well probably wouldn't take any longer than two weeks or cost more than $1 million. Really, my biggest problem is figuring out whether we should report this test result to the county or the state right away."

Stone asked me to spend the rest of the day tracking down and reading materials on the company's legal responsibilities under the new laws that had recently been passed. Later that day he called me into his office and I told him what I'd found: "Under the law, any spill or knowledge of a spill has to be reported immediately to the EPA and the State Department of Environmental Control. A 'spill' is defined as any unauthorized release of a regulated substance into the environment. HCB is a regulated substance, and since it doesn't occur naturally, finding it in the environment means that someone had to release it. From a liability side, the law holds property owners responsible for spills on their property, unless they can show they were not at fault, but even then, they may still be responsible for cleanup."

After we talked about it for a while, Stone placed a call to Infotek's senior vice president and chief legal counsel, George Boggs. Boggs was finally reached in London where he was vacationing, and Stone quickly briefed him on the problem.

"I suggest that you all slow down a little before doing anything," Boggs said. "I just saw that our stock closed down half a point yesterday, which is three points since May. Can you imagine what's going to happen to the stock price if this is handled the wrong way? Let's not go off half-cocked. The law says we report it immediately. But what's 'immediately'? We didn't report those test results we had with that other well two months ago and the situation improved. Before we report this we better have an explanation of why we didn't report that and we better have a plan of action."

"George," Stone said, "We better not do anything that will expose us to shareholder suits. If this has a material impact on our earnings and we keep silent, we may run into trouble."

"You're projecting maybe $1 million to clean this up," Boggs replied. "That's a lot less than five percent of projected earnings, so don't worry about it. It's not material. Just worry about keeping this situation under control. How many people know about this?"

Stone explained the people he'd talked to, and Boggs replied that he would think it all over and call him back later. Two days later Stone reminded me again about the need to maintain confidentiality and asked me to start work on another project under another manager. The HCB project was being turned over to a high level corporate task force. I wasn't asked to do any more work on the HCB issue and when the summer ended I went back to school.

For Discussion

1. From a moral point of view, what, in your judgment, should each of the parties (including Stone and Boggs) of Infotek have done? What should Jack Johnson have done? Justify your answer.

2. Who, in your judgment, should pay the costs for treating the many children born with birth defects and the miscarriages that were suffered by those living around the Fairchild plant? Should the parents be forced to pay these costs themselves? Should the government? Fairchild? To what extent do the uncertainties involved either eliminate or mitigate the responsibility of the various parties?

3. If a later study around the Infotek plant shows a cluster of birth defects and miscarriages similar to those around the Fairchild plant, what would be the responsibility, if any, of the various Infotek parties for these defects and miscarriages? What, if any, would be the moral responsibility of Jack Johnson?

NOTES

1. "How Researchers Hunted Down Birth-defect Cluster," *San Jose Mercury News*, 21 January 1985, p. 1.

2. "Spill Area Has High Birth Defect Rate," *San Jose Mercury News*, 17 January 1985, p. 1.

3. Quoted in "What the State's Leak Studies Said," *San Jose Mercury News*, 17 January 1985, p. 6a.

4. Although based on a real incident, the name and location of the company here referred to as "Infotek" are disguised, as are the names of all other parties involved in the Infotek incident. This portion of the case is based on a case prepared for discussion purposes by Jeff Zimman.

Macklin Mining Company

The 1972 Federal Water Pollution Act aims to eliminate discharges of pollutants into the nation's waters. Although the act leaves the primary prevention and enforcement responsibilities to the states, it establishes broad guidelines to which states must conform. It requires industries that discharge pollutants to use the "best available" technology to eliminate them. In establishing the best available technology, consideration is to be given to the cost of control, the age of the industrial facility, the control process used, and the overall environmental impact of the controls. The law also authorizes loans to help small businesses meet water-pollution control requirements. In addition, it sets water quality standards and requires states to set daily load limits for pollutants that will not impair propagation of fish and wildlife. With respect to enforcement, the law requires polluters to keep proper records, to install and use monitoring equipment, and to sample their discharges. States, upon approval of the Federal Environmental Protection Agency (EPA), are authorized to enter and inspect any polluting facility. Penalties for violating the law range from $2,500 to $25,000 per day and up to one year in prison for the first offense, and up to $50,000 a day and two years in prison for subsequent violations.

Macklin Mining Company is primarily a coal mining company that operates three mines in Tennessee. Macklin's is a marginal operation, with revenue/net income over the last three years of: 1989, $3.2 million/$22 thousand; 1988, $2.7 million/$6 thousand; 1987, $1.6 million/$26 thousand. The company operates the Macklin mine in Bone County, Tennessee, where it employs 42 people. The mine is situated in a low area near Talk Creek, which flows into the Bone River, four miles downstream.

Because of its setting, Macklin has always had a drainage problem with its Talk Creek mine. Prior to 1983, it dumped mine drainage directly into Talk Creek. In 1983 the Tennessee Pollution Control Administration (TPCA) ordered Macklin to cease dumping into Talk Creek. After two years of negotiation, the company proposed to build a settling pond for drainage adjacent to the mouth of the mine and Talk Creek. The pond was finished in 1986 at a cost of $17,000. By 1987 the river was relatively free of contaminants, and residents reported the return of fish to Talk Creek.

In late 1989, however, the TPCA received reports that Talk Creek was again being polluted, and on February 29, 1990, the TPCA filed a complaint against Macklin, claiming that discharge from the firm's settling pond was responsible for extensive pollution of Talk Creek. Macklin responded, claiming that it was not in violation of the Tennessee statute that prohibits discharge of contaminants into state waters.

The TPCA's complaint was filed with the Tennessee Environmental Council (TEC), which hears such cases and, if the charged party is in violation of law, fixes a penalty. The TEC has broad responsibilities and can assess any combination of the following penalties: (1) a maximum penalty of $25,000 for a violation of the State Pollution Control Act, (2) a maximum penalty of $1,500 for each day the violation continues, (3) institution of a program to bring the violator into compliance with the law, and/or (4) an injunction shutting down the firm until compliance is effected.

A hearing before the TEC was held on August 3, 1990. John Benn, regional manager for the TPCA, presented the state's case. He said that the TPCA initially investigated the complaint of nearby residents, who thought Talk Creek was again being polluted. The initial investigation was delayed by a heavy case load, but on November 29, 1989, Benn said, a TPCA inspector found that, although Talk Creek was of relatively clear appearance above the Macklin mine, it was a dark, reddish color below the firm's settling pond. Photographs showing this were submitted. Subsequent water analysis showed the water above the pond to have a slightly alkaline pH of 7.1, whereas below the pond the pH was a somewhat acidic 6.8. Analysis indicated that the dissolved mineral content (mainly iron) below the pond was 132% greater than above it. The suspended solids count was 267% higher below the pond than above it. Analysis also revealed that the water below the pond had a very low dissolved oxygen content, much lower than above the pond. There were also increased sulphate, chloride, bromide, and phosphate concentrations below the pond. Benn stated that the TPCA repeated these experiments on December 14, 1989, again on January 2, 1990, and a third time on January 8, 1990, with very similar results. Benn testified that on January 14, 1990 a Tennessee State biologist sampled Talk Creek and found that, although there was an abundance of organic life and numerous fish above the Macklin mine, there were no fish discovered in shocking experiments just below the settling pond or at four 1,000 yard intervals below the pond. His investigators and scientists concluded that the absence of dissolved oxygen caused the fish to die.

Benn stated that although inspectors could not directly observe a concentrated flow at any one point, an aerial photograph indicated general seepage along the 170 yards that the settling pond fronts Talk Creek. He concluded by saying that in his opinion the environmental damage was extensive, that it had effectively eradicated life in lower Talk Creek.

Speaking for twelve families who live along lower Talk Creek, Jim Clance said they all worried about their drinking water. He added that the Macklin's "only know money" and that the TEC should "shut 'em down or fine 'em to the gills."

Jim Kelly spoke on behalf of the local sportsmen's association. He said that although he was no expert on environmental matters, his association was very concerned with Macklin's pollution of a very fine fishing stream and he wanted to point out certain aspects of the 1972 Federal Water Pollution Act Amendments (FWPAA). According to these amendments "States must establish the total maximum daily load of pollutants . . . that will not impair propagation of fish and wildlife." Since all fish were killed in Talk Creek, Kelly pointed out that Macklin clearly violated the FWPAA, whatever standards the state set. He also pointed out the FWPAA's provision that "Any citizen or group of citizens whose interests may be adversely affected has the right to take court action against anyone violating an effluent standard or limitation or an order issued by EPA or a State, under the law." Kelly said his association had retained a lawyer and would take legal action against Macklin if the state failed to act. Finally, he noted the FWPAA provision that "A State's permit program is subject to revocation by EPA, after a public hearing, if the State fails to implement the law adequately." He indicated that his association would also pursue this course of action if the state failed to act.

Jim Robbis, manager of the Talk Creek mine, testified for Macklin. He said there was no health hazard: "The state itself indicated it is an iron problem; nobody ever died from rust in their water. And people don't obtain their oxygen by taking in water."

Robbis said that Macklin installed the settling pond in 1986, that it was built to comply with stringent TPCA specifications, that the TPCA approved it upon completion, and that the company had maintained the pond to state standards. He said that Macklin employed Environmental Monitors, an independent firm, to test the site, and that on September 16, 1989, that firm reported to Macklin and the TPCA that Macklin was in full compliance with the law. He noted that Environmental Monitors had tested the site triannually, as required by law, since 1986, and that it had always been in compliance, except for one period during 1987 when heavy rains caused a small spillover of the settling pond. Robbis added that although Environmental Monitors was scheduled at the site during the third week of January 1990, an equipment breakdown caused the testing firm to delay its check until mid-February. By that time the TPCA had filed its complaint.

Robbis said that he noticed some water discoloration in the creek in mid-October 1989, but he recalled that it extended above the mine and thought it was caused by heavy rains. He added that pockets of iron leech out above the mine periodically, and he didn't think anything of the light red tinge.

John Macklin, president of the firm, then spoke. He said he lived in Bone County all his life, and that he knows all the men at the mine—Bone County's third largest employer. He noted the unemployment rate of over 15 percent there, pointed out the firm's annual wages totaled over $600,000 in 1989, and said he was especially concerned about six employees who were close to pension eligibility.

He said that the TPCA had not conclusively proven its case. But he added that if his company had violated the letter of the law it was completely unintentional.

Mr. Macklin said that although coal has a bright future, the past three years had been difficult: profits were higher ten years ago than in 1989. Compliance with Occupational Safety and Health Administration and environmental legislation had made the Talk Creek operation marginal. A full fine of $25,000, he noted, would wipe out last year's profit. Fines of $1,500 per day could mean bankruptcy for the entire firm. He pointed out that the pricing situation in the coal industry was rapidly improving, and he believed profits would increase substantially in the next year. An injunction shutting down the mine until compliance could be effected would not only penalize employees, it would wipe out Macklin's chance for the profit necessary to keep the mine open. He could agree to a more extensive test procedure to see if the pond was really responsible for the discharge. If so, there was only one reasonable alternative. A new pond would be constructed south of the present one. The present mine and pond would continue as is until the drainage could be shifted to the new pond in a year or so. This was the only way that Macklin could cover the cost of the new pond. This would mean the discharge into Talk Creek would continue, but the creek had snapped back before and would do so again.

For Discussion

If you were the TEC judge, what judgment would you reach in this case? Why? If you believe Macklin is guilty, what penalty would you assess? Why? What factors must be weighed in making your decision?

Wilfred Beckerman

The Case for Economic Growth

For some years now it has been very unfashionable to be in favor of continued long-run economic growth. Unless one joins in the chorus of scorn for the pursuit of continued economic growth, one is in danger of being treated either as a coarse Philistine, who is prepared to sacrifice all the things that make life really worth living for vulgar materialist goods, or as a shortsighted, complacent, Micawber who is unable to appreciate that the world is living on the edge of a precipice. For it is widely believed that if growth is not now brought to a halt in a deliberate orderly manner, either there will be a catastrophic collapse of output when we suddenly run out of key raw materials, or we shall all be asphyxiated by increased pollution. In other words, growth is either undesirable or impossible, or both. Of course, I suppose this is better than being undesirable and inevitable, but the anti-growth cohorts do not seem to derive much comfort from the fact that, although growth would be unpleasant, we cannot—according to them—go on having it anyway. . . .

Hence it is not entirely surprising that the anti-growth movement has gathered so much support over the past few years even though it is 99 percent nonsense. Not 100 percent nonsense. There does happen to be a one per cent grain of truth in it.

This is that, in the absence of special government policies (policies that governments are unlikely to adopt if not pushed hard by communal action from citizens), pollution will be excessive. This is because—as economists have known for many decades—pollution constitutes what is known in the jargon

From "The Case for Economic Growth," *Public Utilities Fortnightly,* 94 (September 26, 1974):37–41. Reprinted by permission of Public Utilities Reports, Inc.

as an "externality." That is to say, the costs of pollution are not always borne fully—if at all—by the polluter. The owner of a steel mill that belches smoke over the neighborhood, for example, does not usually have to bear the costs of the extra laundry, or of the ill-health, that may result. Hence, although he is, in a sense, "using up" some of the environment (the clean air) to produce his steel he is getting this particular factor of production free of charge. Naturally, he has no incentive to economize in its use in the same way as he has for other factors of production that carry a cost, such a labor or capital. In all such cases of "externalities," or "spillover effects" as they are sometimes called, the normal price mechanism does not operate to achieve the socially desirable pattern of output or of exploitation of the environment. This defect of the price mechanism needs to be corrected by governmental action in order to eliminate excessive pollution.

But, it should be noted that the "externality" argument, summarized above, only implies that society should cut out "excessive" pollution; not all pollution. Pollution should only be cut to the point where the benefits from reducing it further no longer offset the costs to society (labor or capital costs) of doing so.

Mankind has always polluted his environment, in the same way that he has always used up some of the raw materials that he has found in it. When primitive man cooked his meals over open fires, or hunted animals, or fashioned weapons out of rocks and stones, he was exploiting the environment. But to listen to some of the extreme environmentalists, one would imagine that there was something immoral about this (even though God's first injunction to Adam was to subdue the earth and every living thing that exists in it). If all pollution has to be eliminated we would have to spend the whole of our national product in converting every river in the country into beautiful clear-blue swimming pools for fish. Since I live in a town with a 100,000 population but without even a decent swimming pool for the humans, I am not prepared to subscribe to this doctrine.

Anyway, most of the pollution that the environmentalists make such a fuss about, is not the pollution that affects the vast mass of the population. Most people in industrialized countries spend their lives in working conditions where the noise and stench cause them far more loss of welfare than the glamorous fashionable pollutants, such as PCB's or mercury, that the antigrowth lobby make such a fuss about. Furthermore, such progress as has been made over the decades to improve the working conditions of the mass of the population in industrialized countries has been won largely by the action of working-class trade unions, without any help from the middle classes that now parade so ostentatiously their exquisite sensibilities and concern with the "quality of life."

The extreme environmentalists have also got their facts about pollution wrong. In the Western world, the most important forms of pollution are being reduced, or are being increasingly subjected to legislative action that will shortly reduce them. In my recently published book (*In Defense of Economic Growth*)[1] I give the facts about the dramatic decline of air pollution in British cities over the past decade or more, as well as the improvement in the quality of the rivers. I also survey the widespread introduction of antipollution policies in most of the advanced countries of the world during the past few years, which will enable substantial cuts to be made in pollution. By comparison with the reductions already achieved in some cases, or envisaged in the near future, the maximum pollution reductions built into the computerized calculations of the Club of Rome[2] can be seen to be absurdly pessimistic.

The same applies to the Club of Rome's assumption that adequate pollution abatement would be so expensive that economic growth would have to come to a halt. For example, the dramatic cleaning up of the air in London cost a negligible amount per head of the population of that city. And, taking a much broader look at the estimates, I show in my book that reductions in pollution many times greater than those which the Club of Rome purports to be the upper limits over the next century can, and no doubt will, be achieved over the next decade in the advanced countries of the world at a cost of only about one percent to 2 percent of annual national product.

When confronted with the facts about the main pollutants, the anti-growth lobby tends to fall back on the "risk and uncertainty" argument. This takes the form, "Ah yes, but what about all these new pollutants, or what about undiscovered pollutants? Who knows, maybe we shall only learn in a 100 years' time, when it will be too late, that they are deadly." But life is full of risk and uncertainty. Every day I run the risk of being run over by an automobile or hit on the head by a golf ball. But rational conduct requires that I balance the probabilities of this happening against the costs of insuring against it. It would only be logical to avoid even the minutest chance of some catastrophe in the future if it were costless to do so. But the cost of stopping economic growth would be astronomic. This cost does not merely comprise the loss of any hope of improved standards of living for the vast mass of the world's population, it includes also the political and social costs that would need to be incurred. For only a totalitarian regime could persist on the basis of an antigrowth policy that denied people their normal and legitimate aspirations for a better standard of living.

But leaving aside this political issue, another technical issue which has been much in the public eye lately has been the argument that growth will be brought to a sudden, and hence catastrophic, halt soon on account of the impending exhaustion of raw material supplies. This is the "finite resources" argument; i.e., that since the resources of the world are finite, we could not go on using them up indefinitely.

Now resources are either finite or they are not. If they are, then even zero growth will not save us in the longer run. Perhaps keeping Gross National Product at the present level instead of allowing it to rise by, say, 4 percent per annum, would enable the world's resources to be spread out for 500 years instead of only 200 years. But the day would still come when we would run out of resources. (The Club of Rome's own computer almost gave the game away and it was obliged to cut off the printout at the point where it becomes clear that, even with zero growth, the world eventually begins to run out of resources!) So why aim only at zero growth? Why not cut output? If resources are, indeed, finite, then there must be some optimum rate at which they should be spread out over time which will be related to the relative importance society attaches to the consumption levels of different generations. The "eco-doomsters" fail to explain the criteria that determine the optimum rate and why they happen to churn out the answer that the optimum growth rate is zero.

And if resources are not, after all, finite, then the whole of the "finite resources" argument collapses anyway. And, in reality, resources are not finite in any meaningful sense. In the first place, what is now regarded as a resource may not have been so in past decades or centuries before the appropriate techniques for its exploitation or utilization had been developed. This applies, for example, to numerous materials now in use but never heard of a century ago, or to the minerals on the sea bed (e.g., "manganese nodules"), or even the sea water itself from which unlimited quantities of certain basic minerals can eventually be extracted.

In the second place, existing known reserves of many raw materials will never appear enough to last more than, say, twenty or fifty years at current rates of consumption, for the simple reason that it is rarely economically worthwhile to prospect for more supplies than seem to be saleable, at prospective prices, given the costs of exploitation and so on. This has always been the case in the past, yet despite dramatic increases in consumption, supplies have more or less kept pace with demand. The "finite resource" argument fails to allow for the numerous ways that the economy and society react to changes in relative prices of a product, resulting from changes in the balance between supply and demand.

For example, a major United States study in 1929 concluded that known tin resources were only adequate to last the world ten years. Forty years later, the Club of Rome is worried because there is only enough to last us another fifteen years. At this rate, we shall have to wait another century before we have enough to last us another thirty years. Meanwhile, I suppose we shall just have to go on using up that ten years' supply that we had back in 1929.

And it is no good replying that demand is growing faster now than ever before, or that the whole scale of consumption of raw materials is incomparably greater than before. First, this proposition has also been true at almost any time over the past few thousand years, and yet economic growth continued. Hence, the truth of such propositions tells us nothing about whether the balance between supply and demand is likely to change one way or the other. And it is this that matters. In other words, it may well be that demand is growing much faster than ever before, or that the whole scale of consumption is incomparably higher, but the same applies to supply. For example, copper consumption rose about forty-fold during the nineteenth century and demand for copper was accelerating, around the turn of the century, from an annual average growth rate of about 3.3 percent per annum (over the whole century) to about 6.4 percent per annum during the period 1890 to 1910. Annual copper consumption had been only about 16,000 tons at the beginning of the century, and was about 700,000 tons at the end of it; i.e., incomparably greater. But known reserves at the end of the century were greater than at the beginning.

And the same applies to the postwar period. In 1946 world copper reserves amounted to only about 100 million tons. Since then the annual rate of copper consumption has trebled and we have used up 93 million tons. So there should be hardly any left. In fact, we now have about 300 million tons!

Of course, it may well be that we shall run out of some individual materials; and petroleum looks like one of the most likely candidates for exhaustion of supplies around the end of this century—if the price did not rise (or stay up at its recent level). But there are two points to be noted about this. First, insofar as the price does stay up at its recent level (i.e., in the $10 per barrel region) substantial economies in oil use will be made over the next few years, and there will also be a considerable development of substitutes for conventional sources, such as shale oil, oil from tar sands, and new ways of using coal reserves which are, of course, very many times greater than oil reserves (in terms of common energy units).

Second, even if the world did gradually run out of some resources it would not be a catastrophe. The point of my apparently well-known story about "Beckermonium" (the product named after my grandfather who failed to discover it in the nineteenth century) is that we manage perfectly well without it. In fact, if one thinks about it, we manage without infinitely more products than we manage with! In other words, it is absurd to imagine that if, say, nickel or petroleum had never been discovered, modern civilization would never have existed, and that the eventual disappearance of these or other products must, therefore, plunge us back into the Dark Ages.

The so-called oil crisis, incidentally, also demonstrates the moral hypocrisy of the antigrowth lobby. For leaving aside their mistaken interpretation of the technical reasons for the recent sharp rise in the oil price (i.e., it was not because the world suddenly ran out of oil), it is striking that the antigrowth lobby has seized upon the rise in the price of oil as a fresh argument for abandoning economic growth and for rethinking our basic values and so on. After all, over the past two or three years the economies of many of the poorer countries of the world, such as India, have been hit badly by the sharp rise in the price of wheat. Of course, this only means a greater threat of starvation for a few more million people in backward countries a long way away. That does not, apparently, provoke the men of spiritual and moral sensibility to righteous indignation about the values of the growth-oriented society as much as does a rise in the price of gasoline for our automobiles!

The same muddled thinking is behind the view that mankind has some moral duty to preserve the world's environment or supplies of materials. For this view contrasts strangely with the antigrowth lobby's attack on materialism. After all, copper and oil, and so on are just material objects, and it is difficult to see what moral duty we have to preserve indefinitely the copper species from extinction.

Nor do I believe that we have any overriding moral duty to preserve any particular animal species from extinction. After all, thousands of animal species have become extinct over the ages, without any intervention by mankind. Nobody really loses any sleep over the fact that one cannot now see a live dinosaur.

How many of the people who make a fuss about the danger that the tiger species may disappear even bother to go to a zoo to look at one? . . . It is now time to recognize that the various antigrowth arguments are devoid of true moral sense, of logic, and of any real factual basis. It is time now to return to the analysis of the real problems facing society. These include problems of income distribution, food and population control, housing, education, crime, drugs, racial tolerance, international relations, old-age, and many other serious problems.

Whilst economic growth alone may never provide a simple means of solving any of these problems, and it may well be that, by its very nature, human society will always create insoluble problems of one kind or another, the absence of economic growth will only make our present problems a lot worse.

NOTES

1. Jonathan Cape, London. The U.S.A. edition, under the title *Two Cheers for the Affluent Society,* [was] published by the St. Martins Press in the fall of 1974.

2. The Club of Rome is an informal international organization of educators, scientists, economists, and others which investigates what it conceives to be the overriding problems of mankind. Its study, "The Limits of Growth," has become the bible of no-growth advocates (Potomac Associates, 1707 L Street, N.W., Washington, D.C., $2.75). The study assembled data on known reserves of resources and asked a computer what would happen if demand continued to grow exponentially. Of course, the computer replied everything would break down. The theory of "Beckermonium" lampoons this. Since the author's grandfather failed to discover "Beckermonium" by the mid-1800s, the world has had no supplies of it at all. Consequently, if the club's equations are followed, the world should have come to a halt many years ago. "Beckermonium's" foundation is that the things man has not yet discovered are far more numerous and of greater importance than what has been discovered. (Editor's Note.)

William T. Blackstone

Ethics and Ecology

THE RIGHT TO A LIVABLE ENVIRONMENT AS A HUMAN RIGHT

Let us first ask whether the right to a livable environment can properly be considered to be a human right. For the purposes of this paper, however, I want to avoid raising the more general question of whether there are any human rights at all. Some philosophers do deny that any human rights exist.[1] In two recent papers I have argued that human rights do exist (even though such rights may properly be overridden on occasion by other morally relevant reasons) and that they are universal and inalienable (although the actual exercise of such rights on a given occasion is alienable).[2] My argument for the existence of universal human rights rests, in the final analysis, on a theory of what it means to be human, which specifies the capacities for rationality and freedom as essential, and on the fact that there are no relevant grounds for excluding any human from the opportunity to develop and fulfill his capacities (rationality and freedom) as a human. This is not to deny that there are criteria which justify according human rights in quite different ways or with quite different modes of treatment for different persons, depending upon the nature and degree of such capacities and the existing historical and environmental circumstances.

If the right to a livable environment were seen as a basic and inalienable human right this could be a valuable tool (both inside and outside of

From *Philosophy and Environmental Crisis* by William T. Blackstone (Athens, Ga.: The University of Georgia Press, 1974), pp. 30–42. Reprinted in edited form with the permission of the publisher.

legalistic frameworks) for solving some of our environmental problems, both on a national and on an international basis. Are there any philosophical and conceptual difficulties in treating this right as an inalienable human right? Traditionally we have not looked upon the right to a decent environment as a human right or as an inalienable right. Rather, inalienable human or natural rights have been conceived in somewhat different terms: equality, liberty, happiness, life, and property. However, might it not be possible to view the right to a livable environment as being entailed by, or as constitutive of, these basic human or natural rights recognized in our political tradition? If human rights, in other words, are those rights which each human possesses in virtue of the fact that he is human and in virtue of the fact that those rights are essential in permitting him to live a human life (that is, in permitting him to fulfill his capacities as a rational and free being), then might not the right to a decent environment be properly categorized as such a human right? Might it not be conceived as a right which has emerged as a result of changing environmental conditions and the impact of those conditions on the very possibility of human life and on the possibility of the realization of other rights such as liberty and equality? Let us explore how this might be the case.

Given man's great and increasing ability to manipulate the environment, and the devastating effect this is having, it is plain that new social institutions and new regulative agencies and procedures must be initiated on both national and international levels to make sure that the manipulation is in the public interest. It will be necessary, in other words, to restrict or stop some practices and the freedom to engage in those practices. Some look upon such additional state planning, whether national or international, as unnecessary further intrusion on man's freedom. Freedom is, of course, one of our basic values, and few would deny that excessive state control of human action is to be avoided. But such restrictions on individual freedom now appear to be necessary in the interest of overall human welfare and the rights and freedoms of *all* men. Even John Locke with his stress on freedom as an inalienable right recognized that this right must be construed so that it is consistent with the equal right to freedom of others. The whole point of the state is to restrict unlicensed freedom and to provide the conditions for equality of rights for all. Thus it seems to be perfectly consistent with Locke's view and, in general, with the views of the founding fathers of this country to restrict certain rights or freedoms when it can be shown that such restriction is necessary to insure the equal rights of others. If this is so, it has very important implications for the rights to freedom and to property. These rights, perhaps properly seen as inalienable (though this is a controversial philosophical question), are not properly seen as unlimited or unrestricted. When values which we hold dear conflict (for example, individual or group freedom and the freedom of all, individual or group rights and the rights of all, and individual or group welfare and the welfare of the general public) something has to give; some priority must be established. In the case of the abuse and waste of environmental resources, less individual freedom and fewer individual rights for the sake of greater public welfare and equality of rights seem justified.

What in the past had been properly regarded as freedoms and rights (given what seemed to be unlimited natural resources and no serious pollution problems) can no longer be so construed, at least not without additional restrictions. We must recognize both the need for such restrictions and the fact that none of our rights can be realized without a livable environment. Both public welfare and equality of rights now require that natural resources not be used simply according to the whim and caprice of individuals or simply for personal profit. This is not to say that all property rights must be denied and that the state must own all productive property, as the Marxist argues. It is to insist that those rights be qualified or restricted in the light of new ecological data and in the interest of the freedom, rights, and welfare of all.

The answer then to the question, Is the right to a livable environment a human right? is yes. Each person has this right qua being human and because a livable environment is essential for one to fulfill his human capacities. And given the danger to our environment today and hence the danger to the very possibility of human existence, access to a livable environment must be conceived as a right which imposes upon everyone a correlative moral obligation to respect.

A good case can be made for the view that not all moral or human rights should be legal rights and that not all moral rules should be legal rules. It may be argued that any society which covers the whole spectrum of man's activities with legally enforceable rules minimizes his freedom and approaches totalitarianism. There is this danger. But just as we argued that certain traditional rights and freedoms are properly restricted in order to insure the equal rights and welfare of all, so also it can plausibly be argued that the human right to a livable environment should become a legal one in order to assure that it is properly respected. Given the magnitude of the present dangers to the environment and to the welfare of all humans, and the ingrained habits and rules, or lack of rules, which permit continued waste, pollution, and destruction of our environmental resources, the legalized status of the right to a livable environment seems both desirable and necessary.

Such a legal right would provide a tool for pressing environmental transgressions in the courts. At the present the right to a livable environment, even if recognized as a human right, is not generally recognized as a legal one. One cannot sue individuals or corporations for polluting the environment, if the pollution harms equally every member of a community. One can sue such individuals or corporations if they damage one's private property but not if they damage the public environment.

The history of government, in this country and elsewhere, has been that of the gradual demise of a laissez-faire philosophy of government. Few deny that there are areas of our lives where government should not and must not intrude. In fact, what we mean by a totalitarian government is one which exceeds its proper bounds and attempts to control nearly all human activities. But in some areas of human life, it has been seen that the "keep-government-out-of-it" attitude just will not work. The entire quality of life in a society is determined by the availability and distribution of goods and services in such vital areas as education, housing, medical treatment, legal treatment, and so on. In the field of education, for example, we have seen the need for compulsory education and, more recently, for unitary school systems in order to provide equality of educational opportunity.

In the same way, it is essential that government step in to prevent the potentially dire consequences of industrial pollution and the waste of environmental resources. Such government regulations need not mean the death of the free enterprise system. The right to private property can be made compatible with the right to a livable environment, for if uniform antipollution laws were applied to all industries, then both competition and private ownership could surely continue. But they would continue within a quite different set of rules and attitudes toward the environment. This extension of government would not be equivalent to totalitarianism. In fact it is necessary to insure equality of rights and freedom, which is essential to a democracy.

ECOLOGY AND ECONOMIC RIGHTS

We suggested above that it is necessary to qualify or restrict economic or property rights in the light of new ecological data and in the interest of the freedom, rights, and welfare of all. In part, this suggested restriction is predicated on the assumption that we cannot expect private business to provide solutions to the multiple pollution problems for which they themselves are responsible. Some companies have taken measures to limit the polluting effect of their operations, and this is an important move. But we are deluding ourselves if we think that private business can function as its own pollution police. This is so for several reasons: the primary objective of private business is economic profit. Stockholders do not ask of a company, "Have you polluted the environment and lowered the quality of the environment for the general public and for future generations?" Rather they ask, "How high is the annual dividend and how much higher is it than the year before?" One can hardly expect organizations whose basic norm is economic profit to be concerned in any great depth with the long-range effects of their operations upon society and future generations or concerned with the hidden cost of their operations in terms of environmental quality to society as a whole. Second, within a free enterprise system companies compete to produce what the public wants at the lowest possible cost. Such competition would preclude the spending of adequate funds to prevent environmental pollution, since this would add tremendously to the cost of the product—unless all other companies would also conform to such antipollution policies. But in a free enterprise economy such policies are not likely to be self-imposed by businessmen. Third, the basic response of the free enterprise system to our economic problems is that we must have greater economic growth or an increase in gross national product. But such growth many ecologists look upon with great alarm, for it can have devastating long-range effects upon our environment. Many of the products of uncontrolled growth are based on artificial needs and actually detract from, rather than contribute to, the quality of our lives. A stationary economy, some economists and ecologists suggest, may well be best for the quality of man's environment and of his life in the long run. Higher GNP does not automatically result in an increase in social well-being, and it should not be used as a measuring rod for assessing economic welfare. This becomes clear when one realizes that the GNP

> aggregates the dollar value of all goods and services produced—the cigarettes as well as the medical treatment of lung cancer, the petroleum from offshore wells as well as the detergents required to clean up after oil spills, the electrical energy produced and the medical and cleaning bills resulting from the air-pollution fuel used for generating the electricity. The GNP allows no deduction for negative production, such as lives lost from unsafe cars or environmental destruction perpetrated by telephone, electric and gas utilities, lumber companies, and speculative builders.[3]

To many persons, of course, this kind of talk is not only blasphemy but subversive. This is especially true when it is extended in the direction of additional controls over corporate capitalism. The fact of the matter is that the ecological attitude forces one to reconsider a host of values which have been held dear in the past, and it forces one to reconsider the appropriateness of the social and economic systems which embodied and implemented those values. Given the crisis of our environment, there must be certain fundamental changes in attitudes toward nature, man's use of nature, and man himself. Such changes in attitudes undoubtedly will have far-reaching implications for the institutions of private property and private enterprise and the values embodied in these institutions. Given that crisis we can no longer look upon water and air as free commodities to be exploited at will. Nor can the private ownership of land be seen as a lease to use that land in any way which conforms merely to the personal desires of the owner. In other words, the environmental crisis is forcing us to challenge what had in the past been taken to be certain basic rights of man or at least to restrict those rights. And it is forcing us to challenge institutions which embodied those rights.

Much has been said about the conflict between these kinds of rights, and the possible conflict between them is itself a topic for an extensive paper. Depending upon how property rights are formulated, the substantive content of those rights, it seems plain to me, can directly conflict with what we characterize as human rights. In fact our moral and legal history demonstrate exactly that kind of conflict. There was a time in the recent past when property rights embodied the right to hold human beings in slavery. This has now been rejected, almost universally. Under nearly any interpretation of the substantive content of human rights, slavery is incompatible with those rights.

The analogous question about rights which is now being raised by the data uncovered by the ecologist and by the gradual advancement of the ecological attitude is whether the notion of property rights should be even further restricted to preclude the destruction and pollution of our environmental resources upon which the welfare and the very lives of all of us and of future generations depend. Should our social and legal system embrace property rights or other rights which permit the kind of environmental exploitation which operates to the detriment of the majority of mankind? I do not think so. The fact that a certain right exists in a social or legal system does not mean that it ought to exist. I would not go so far as to suggest that all rights are merely rule-utilitarian devices to be adopted or discarded whenever it can be shown that the best consequences thereby follow.[4] But if a right or set of rights systematically violates the public welfare, this is prima facie evidence that it ought not to exist. And this certainly seems to be the case with the exercise of certain property rights today.

In response to this problem, there is today at least talk of "a new economy of resources," one in which new considerations and values play an important role along with property rights and the interplay of market forces. Economist Nathaniel Wollman argues that "the economic past of 'optimizing' resource use consists of bringing into an appropriate relationship the ordering of preferences for various experiences and the costs of acquiring those experiences. Preferences reflect physiological-psychological responses to experience or anticipated experience, individually or collectively revealed, and are accepted as data by the economist. A broad range of noneconomic investigations is called for to supply the necessary information."[5]

Note that Wollman says that noneconomic investigations are called for. In other words the price system does not adequately account for a number of value factors which should be included in an assessment. "It does not account for benefits or costs that are enjoyed or suffered by people who were not parties to the transaction."[6] In a system which emphasizes simply the interplay of market forces as a criterion, these factors (such as sights, smells, and other aesthetic factors, justice, and human rights—factors which are important to the well-being of humans) are not even considered. Since they have no direct monetary value, the market places no value whatsoever on them. Can we assume, then, that purely economic or market evaluations provide us with data which will permit us to maximize welfare, if the very process of evaluation and the normative criteria employed exclude a host of values and considerations on which human welfare depends? The answer to this question is plain. We cannot make this assumption. We cannot rely merely upon the interplay of market forces or upon the sovereignty of the consumer. The concept of human welfare and consequently the notion of maximizing that welfare requires a much broader perspective than the norms offered by the traditional economic perspective. A great many things have value and use which have no economic value and use. Consequently we must broaden our evaluational perspective to include the entire range of values which are essential not only to the welfare of man but also to the welfare of other living things and to the environment which sustains all of life. And this must include a reassessment of rights.

ETHICS AND TECHNOLOGY

I have been discussing the relationship of ecology to ethics and to a theory of rights. Up to this point I have not specifically discussed the relation of technology to ethics, although it is plain that technology and its development is responsible for most of our pollution problems. This topic deserves separate treatment, but I do want to briefly relate it to the thesis of this work.

We tend too readily to assume that new technological developments will always solve man's problems. But this is simply not the case. One technological innovation often seems to breed a half-dozen additional ones which themselves create more environmental problems. We certainly do not solve pollution problems, for example, by changing from power plants fueled by coal to power plants fueled by nuclear energy, if radioactive waste from the latter is worse than pollution from the former. Perhaps part of the answer to pollution problems is less technology. There is surely no real hope of returning to nature (whatever that means) or of stopping *all* technological and scientific development, as some advocate. Even if it could be done, this would be too extreme a move. The answer is not to stop technology, but to guide it toward proper ends, and to set up standards of antipollution to which all technological devices must conform. Technology has been and can be used to destroy and pollute an environment, but it can also be used to save and beautify it. What is called for is purposeful environmental engineering, and this engineering calls for a mass of information about our environment, about the needs of persons, and about basic norms and values which are acceptable to civilized men. It also calls for priorities on goals and for compromises where there are competing and conflicting values and objectives. Human rights and their fulfillment should constitute at least some of those basic norms, and technology can be used to implement those rights and the public welfare.

NOTES

1. See Kai Nielsen's "Skepticism and Human Rights," *Monist* 52, no. 4 (1968): 571–94.

2. See my "Equality and Human Rights," *Monist* 52, no. 4 (1968): 619–639 and my "Human Rights and Human Dignity" in Laszlo and Gotesky, eds., *Human Dignity.*

3. See Melville J. Ulmer, "More Than Marxist," *New Republic,* 26 December 1970, p. 14.

4. Some rights, I would argue, are inalienable, and are not based merely on a contract (implicit or explicit) or merely upon the norm of maximizing good consequences. (See David Braybrooke's *The Test for Democracy: Personal Rights, Human Welfare, Collective Preference* [New York: Random House, 1968], which holds such a rule-utilitarian theory of rights, and my "Human Rights and Human Dignity" for a rebuttal.)

5. Nathaniel Wollman, "The New Economics of Resources," *Daedalus* 96, no. 2, (Fall 1967): 1100.

6. Ibid.

Manuel G. Velasquez

Utilitarianism and the Environment

. . . A fundamentally utilitarian approach to environmental problems is to see them as market defects. If an industry pollutes the environment, the market prices of its commodities will no longer reflect the true cost of producing the commodities; the result is a misallocation of resources, a rise in waste, and an inefficient distribution of commodities. Consequently, society as a whole is harmed as its overall economic welfare declines.[1] Utilitarians therefore argue that individuals should avoid pollution because they should avoid harming society's welfare.[2] The following paragraphs explain this utilitarian argument in greater detail. . . .

PRIVATE COSTS AND SOCIAL COSTS

Economists often distinguish between what it costs a private manufacturer to make a product and what the manufacture of that product costs society as a whole. Suppose, for example, that an electric firm consumes a certain amount of fuel, labor, and equipment to produce one kilowatt of electricity. The cost of these resources are its *private* costs: the price it must pay out of its own pocket to manufacture one kilowatt of electricity. But producing the kilowatt of electricity may also involve other "external" costs for which the firm does not pay.[3] When the firm burns fuel, for example, it may generate smoke and soot that settles on surrounding neighbors, who have to bear the costs of cleaning

From Manuel G. Velasquez, *Business Ethics: Concepts & Cases,* 2e, copyright © 1988, pp. 240–51. Adapted by permission of Prentice Hall, Englewood Cliffs, New Jersey.

up the grime and of paying for any medical problems the smoke creates. From the viewpoint of society as a whole, then, the costs of producing the kilowatt of electricity include not only the "internal" costs of fuel, labor, and equipment for which the manufacturer pays, but also the "external" costs of cleanup and medical care that the neighbors pay. This *sum total* of costs (the private internal costs plus the neighbors' external costs) are the *social* costs of producing the kilowatt of electricity: the total price society must pay to manufacture one kilowatt of electricity. Of course, private costs and social costs do not always diverge as in this example: Sometimes the two coincide. If a producer pays for *all* the costs involved in manufacturing a product, for example, or if manufacturing a product imposes no external costs, then the producer's costs and the total social costs will be the same.

Thus, when a firm pollutes its environment in any way, the firm's private costs are always *less* than the total social costs involved. Whether the pollution is localized and immediate, as in the neighborhood effects described in the example above, or whether the pollution is global and long-range as in the "hot-house" effects predicted to follow from introducing too much carbon dioxide into the atmosphere, pollution always imposes "external" costs, that is, costs for which the person who produces the pollution does not have to pay. Pollution is fundamentally a problem of this divergence between private and social costs.

Why should this divergence be a problem? It is a problem because when the private costs of manufacturing a product diverge from the social costs involved in its manufacture, markets no longer price commodities accurately; consequently, they no longer allocate resources efficiently. As a result, society's welfare declines. . . . Three deficiencies, in particular, can be noted.

First, allocation of resources in markets that do not take all costs into account is not optimal, because from the point of view of society as a whole, more of the commodity is being produced than society would demand if society had available an accurate measure of what it is actually paying to produce the commodity. Since the commodity is being overproduced, more of society's resources are being consumed to produce the commodity than is optimal. The resources being consumed by overproduction of the commodity are resources that could be used to produce other commodities for which there would be greater demand if prices accurately reflected costs. Resources are thereby being misallocated.

Second, when external costs are not taken into account by producers, producers ignore these costs and make no attempt to minimize them. So long as the firm does not have to pay for external costs, it has no incentive to use technology that might decrease or eliminate them. Consequently, the resources being consumed by these external costs (such as clean air) are being unnecessarily wasted. There may be technologically feasible ways of producing the same commodities without imposing as many external costs, but the producer will make no attempt to find them.

Third, when the production of a commodity imposes external costs on third parties, goods are no longer efficiently distributed to consumers. External costs introduce effective price differentials into markets: Everyone does not pay equal price for the same commodities. . . .

Pollution, then, imposes "external costs" and this in turn means that the private costs of production are less than the social costs. As a consequence, markets do not impose an optimal discipline on producers, and the result is a drop in social utility. Pollution of the environment, then, is a violation of the utilitarian principles that underlie a market system.

REMEDIES: THE DUTIES OF THE FIRM

The remedy for external costs, according to the utilitarian argument sketched above, is to ensure that the costs of pollution are internalized, that is, that they are absorbed by the producer and taken into account when determining the price of his goods.[4] In this way goods will be accurately priced, market forces will provide the incentives that will encourage producers to minimize external costs, and some consumers will no longer end up paying more than others for the same commodities.

There are various ways of internalizing the external costs of pollution. One way is for the polluting agent to pay to all of those being harmed, voluntarily or by law, an amount equal to the costs the pollution imposes on them. When Union Oil's drilling in the Santa Barbara channel on the California coast led to an oil spill, the total costs that the spill imposed on local residents and on state and federal agencies were estimated at about $16,400,000 (including costs of cleanup, containment, administration, damage to tourism and fishing, recreational and property damages, and loss of marine life). Union Oil paid about $10,400,000 of these costs voluntarily by paying for all cleanup and containment of the oil, and it paid about $6,300,000 in damages to the affected parties as the result of litigation.[5] Thus, the costs of the oil spill were "internalized," in part through voluntary action and in part through legal action. When the polluting firm pays those on whom its manufacturing processes impose costs, as Union Oil did, it is led to figure these costs into its own subsequent price determinations. Market mechanisms then lead it to come up with ways of cutting down pollution in order to cut down its costs. Since the Santa Barbara oil spill, for example, Union Oil and other petroleum firms have invested considerable amounts of money in developing methods to minimize pollution damage from oil spills.

A problem with this way of internalizing the costs of pollution, however, is that when several polluters are involved, it is not always clear just who is being damaged by whom. How much of the environmental damage caused by several polluters should be counted as damages to my property and how much should be counted as damages to your property, when the damages are inflicted on things such as air or public bodies of water, and for how much of the damage should each polluter be held responsible? Moreover, the administrative and legal costs of assessing damages for each distinct polluter and of granting separate compensations to each distinct claimant can become substantial.

A second remedy is for the polluter to stop pollution at its source by installing pollution-control devices. In this way, the external costs of polluting the environment are translated into the internal costs the firm itself pays to install pollution controls. Once costs are internalized in this way, market mechanisms again provide cost-cutting incentives and ensure that prices reflect the true costs of producing the commodity. In addition, the installation of pollution-control devices serves to eliminate the long-range and potentially disastrous worldwide effects of pollution.

JUSTICE

This utilitarian way of dealing with pollution (that is, by internalizing costs) seems to be consistent with the requirements of distributive justice insofar as distributive justice favors equality. Observers have noted that pollution often has the effect of increasing inequality.[6] If a firm pollutes, its stockholders benefit because their firm does not have to absorb the external costs of pollution and this leaves them with greater profits, and those customers who purchase the firm's products also benefit because the firm does not charge them for all the costs involved in making the product. The *beneficiaries* of pollution, therefore, tend to be those who can afford to buy a firm's stock and its products. On the other hand, the external *costs* of pollution are borne largely by the poor.[7] Property values in polluted neighborhoods are generally lower, and consequently they are inhabited by the poor and abandoned by the wealthy. Pollution, therefore, may produce a net flow of benefits away from the poor and toward the well-off, thereby increasing inequality. To the extent that this occurs, pollution violates distributive justice. Internalizing the costs of pollution, as utilitarianism requires, would rectify matters by removing the burdens of external costs from the backs of the poor and placing them in the hands of the wealthy: the firm's stockholders and its customers. By and large, therefore, the utilitarian claim that the external costs of pollution should be internalized is consistent with the requirement of distributive justice.

We should note, however, that if a firm makes basic goods (food products, clothing, gasoline, automobiles) for which the poor must allocate a larger proportion of their budgets than the affluent, then internalizing costs may place a heavier burden on the poor than on the affluent, because the prices of these basic goods will rise. The poor may also suffer if the costs of pollution control rise so high that unemployment results (although current studies indicate that the unemployment effects of pollution-control programs are transitory and minimal). There is some rudimentary evidence that tends to show that current pollution-control measures place greater burdens on the poor than on the wealthy. This suggests the need to integrate distributional criteria into our pollution-control programs.

Internalizing external costs also seems to be consistent with the requirements of retributive and compensatory justice.[8] Retributive justice requires that those who are responsible for and who benefit from an injury should bear the burdens of rectifying the injury, while compensatory justice requires that those who have been injured should be compensated by those who injure them. Taken together, these requirements imply that (1) the costs of pollution control should be borne by those who cause pollution and who have benefited from pollution activities, while (2) the benefits of pollution control should flow to those who have had to bear the external costs of pollution. Internalizing external costs seems to meet these two requirements: (1) The costs of pollution control are borne by stockholders and by customers, both of whom benefit from the polluting activities of the firm, and (2) the benefits of pollution control flow to those neighbors who once had to put up with the firm's pollution.

COSTS AND BENEFITS

The technology for pollution control has developed effective but costly methods for abating pollution. Up to 60 percent of water pollutants can be removed through "primary" screening and sedimentation processes; up to 90 percent can be removed through more expensive "secondary" biological and chemical processes; and amounts over 95 percent can be removed through even more expensive "tertiary" chemical treatment.[9] Air pollution abatement techniques include: the use of fuels and combustion procedures that burn more cleanly; mechanical filters that screen or isolate dust particles in the air; "scrubbing" processes that pass polluted air through liquids that remove pollutants; and chemical treatment that transforms gases into more easily removed compounds.[10]

It is possible, however, for a firm to invest *too much* in pollution control devices. Suppose, for example, that the pollution from a certain firm causes $100 worth of environmental damage, and suppose that the only device that can eliminate this pollution would cost the firm at least $1,000. Then, obviously, the firm should not install the device, for if it does so, the economic utility of society will decline: the costs of eliminating the pollution will be greater than the benefits society will reap, thereby resulting in a shrinkage of total utility.

How much should a firm invest in pollution control, then? Consider that the costs of controlling pollution and the benefits derived from pollution control are inversely related. As one rises, the other falls. Why is this so? Think for a moment that if a body of water is highly polluted, it will probably be quite easy and consequently quite cheap to filter out a certain limited amount of pollutants. To filter out a few more pollutants, however, will require finer and therefore additional and more expensive filters. Costs will keep climbing for each additional level of purity desired, and getting out the last few molecules of impurities would require astronomically expensive additional equipment. However, getting out those last traces of impurities will probably not matter much to people and will therefore be unnecessary. At the other end of the scale, however, getting rid of the first gross amounts of pollutants will be highly beneficial to people: The costs of damages from these pollutants are substantial. Consequently, if we plot as curves on a graph the costs of removing pollution and the benefits of removing pollution (which are equivalent to the external costs removed) the result will be two intersecting curves. What is the optimal amount of pollution control? Obviously, the point at which the two lines cross. At this point, the costs of pollution control exactly equal its benefits. If the firm invests additional resources in removing pollution, society's net utility will decline. Beyond this point, the firm should resort to directly or indirectly (that is, through taxes or other forms of social investment) paying society for the costs of polluting the environment.

To enable the firm to make such cost-benefit analyses, researchers have devised an array of theoretical methods and techniques for calculating the costs and benefits of removing pollution. These make use of estimates of consumer surplus, rents, market prices and "shadow prices," adjustment for "transfers," discounted future values, and recognition of risk factors.[11] Thomas Klein summarizes the procedures for cost-benefit analysis as follows:

1. Identify costs and benefits of the proposed program and the person or sectors incurring or receiving them. Trace transfers.

2. Evaluate the costs and benefits in terms of their value to beneficiaries and donors. The standard of measure is the value of each marginal unit to demanders and suppliers ideally captured in competitive prices. Useful refinements involve:
   a. Incorporating time values through the use of a discount rate.
   b. Recognizing risk by factoring possible outcomes according to probabilities and, where dependent, probability trees.

3. Add up costs and benefits to determine the net social benefit of a project or program.[12]

In order to avoid "erratic" and "costly" use of these procedures, Klein recommends that firms introduce a system of "social accounting" that "routinely measures, records, and reports external effects to management and other parties."[13]

It is at this point, however, that a fundamental difficulty in the utilitarian approach to pollution emerges. The cost-benefit analyses just described assume that the costs and benefits of reducing pollution can be accurately measured.[14] In some cases (limited and local in character) cost-benefit measurements are available: The costs and benefits of cleaning up the oil spilled by Union Oil at Santa Barbara, for example, were more or less measurable. But the costs and benefits of pollution removal are difficult to measure when they involve damages to human health and loss of life: What is the price of life?[15]

Measurement is also difficult when the effects of pollution are uncertain and, consequently, difficult to predict: What will be the effects of increasing the carbon dioxide content of our atmosphere by burning more coal, as the United States is now starting to do? In fact, perhaps the major problem involved in obtaining the measurements needed to apply cost-benefit analysis to pollution problems is the problem of estimating and evaluating *risk* (that is, the probability of future costly consequences).[16] Many new technologies carry with them unknown degrees of risk to present and future generations.

The use of nuclear technology, for example, involves some probability of damages to health and loss of life for present and future generations: there are the risks of health damages from mining and the use and disposal of radioactive materials, plus the risks of sabotage and of a proliferation of the materials used in atomic weapons. But there are insurmountable obstacles in the way of measuring these risks accurately. We cannot use trial and error (a usual method for learning what the probabilities of an event are) to learn the risk, for example, of a nuclear accident, since the lesson would obviously be too costly and some of the health effects of radioactivity would not appear until decades after it is too late to correct them. Moreover, the mathematical models that we must rely on to measure risk in the absence of trial and error learning are not useful when all the possible things that can go wrong with a technology are not known. Human error, carelessness, and malice have been involved in most nuclear mishaps. The human factor is notoriously impossible to predict, and therefore impossible to incorporate into a measurement of the risks associated with using nuclear power. Moreover, even if the numerical risk associated with a new technology were known, it is unclear how much weight it should be given in a social cost-benefit analysis. Imagine, for example, that society currently accepts with some indifference a .01 risk of death associated with driving. Does it then follow that society also should be indifferent to accepting a .01 risk of death from the introduction of a certain new technology? Obviously not, because risk is cumulative: The new technology will *double* society's risk of death to .02, and while society may be indifferent to carrying a .01 risk of death, it may find a .02 risk unacceptable. Knowing the risk of a certain costly future event does not, then, necessarily tell us the value that society will place on that risk once it is added to the other risks a society already runs. And, to make matters worse, individuals differ substantially in their aversion to risk: Some individuals *like* to gamble while others find it extremely distasteful.

The almost insurmountable problems involved in getting accurate pollution measurements are illustrated by the few federal estimates of the *benefits* produced by pollution control activities.[17] The present financial *costs* of pollution control are fairly easy to obtain by examining reports on expenditures for pollution equipment. Total 1978 expenditures for pollution control, including government and private expenditures, were $46.7 billion. But the *benefits* associated with these expenditures have never been accurately measured. The federal government estimated that the annual benefits from air pollution control alone were approximately $21.4 billion in 1978, and earlier studies had estimated the annual benefits of water pollution control alone would be $12.3 billion by 1978. But these estimates are based on exceedingly unreliable methodologies and deliberately omit many of the effects of pollution, especially long-range global effects such as the effects of carbon dioxide build-up and ozone depletion, as well as the health benefits from the elimination of chemical contamination in drinking water.

The problems involved in getting accurate measurements of the benefits of pollution control are also illustrated by the difficulties businesses have encountered in trying to construct a "social audit" (a report of the social costs and social benefits of the firm's activities). Those who advocate that a corporation should measure and report the social impacts of its activities have been forced to recognize that the goal of measuring all impacts of all actions upon all conditions and all publics, using standard techniques and units, considerably exceeds current capabilities and that compromises and modifications are inevitable. Due to this inability to measure benefits, so-called "social audits" are usually nothing more than qualitative descriptions of what a firm is doing. But without definite quantitative measurements of the benefits deriving from its attempts to reduce pollution, a firm has no way of knowing whether its efforts are cost-effective from a social point of view.

These failures of measurement pose significant technical problems for utilitarian approaches to pollution. In addition, the use of utilitarian cost-benefit analysis is sometimes based on assumptions that are inconsistent with people's moral rights. Advocates of utilitarian cost-benefit analysis sometimes assume that if the benefits of a certain technology or manufacturing process "clearly" outweigh its costs, then it is morally permissible to impose the process on unwilling citizens. A recent government report, for example, makes the following recommendations:

> Because nuclear problems are such highly emotional issues and becoming even more so, as evidenced by the states that have indicated an unwillingness to permit nuclear waste disposal within their boundaries, it may be impossible to get the public and political support necessary for a given state to accept nuclear waste. Ultimately, if state approval for waste repository sites cannot be obtained within an established time, the federal government might have to mandate selections. While such action would not be easy it may be necessary if the waste problem is to be solved in a reasonable time.[18]

But recommendations of this type seem to violate the basic moral right that underlies democratic societies: Persons have a moral right to be treated only as they have consented to be treated beforehand. If people have not consented to take on the costs of a technology (and indicate this unwillingness, for example, through local legislation, hearings, or opinion surveys), then their moral right of consent is violated when these costs are imposed on them anyway. Using only cost-benefit analysis to determine whether a new technology or manufacturing process should be used, then, ignores the question of whether the costs involved are *voluntarily* accepted by those who must bear them, or whether they are unilaterally *imposed* on them by others.

It should be noted that although the right of consent seems to imply that decisions concerning pollution control always should be left in the hands of the ordinary citizen, this implication is not necessarily correct. For people can give their informed consent to a risky project only if they have an adequate understanding of the project and its attendant risks. But contemporary technology is often so complex that even experts disagree when estimating and assessing the risks it may involve (scientists disagree wildly, for example, over the safety of using nuclear power). So it may be impossible for ordinary citizens to understand and assess the risks that a certain polluting technology will impose on them, and, consequently, it may be impossible, in principle, for them to give their informed consent to it.

In view of all the problems raised by utilitarian approaches to pollution, it may be that alternative approaches are more adequate. In particular, it may be that the absolute bans on pollution which are still incorporated in many federal laws, and the rights theory on which these absolute bans rest, are, for the present at least, a more adequate approach to pollution issues than utilitarianism. Alternatively, some writers have suggested that when risks cannot be reliably estimated it is best to choose only those projects that carry no risk of irreversible damages. For example, if there is a probability that the pollution from a certain technology may bring about catastrophic consequences that will continue to plague us forever, then the technology should be rejected in favor of other technologies that will not close off our options in the same permanent way. Others suggest that when risks cannot be assessed, we should, in justice, identify those who are most vulnerable and who would have to bear the heaviest costs if things should go wrong, and then take steps to ensure that they are protected. Future generations and children, for example, should be protected against our polluting choices. Finally, others suggest that when risks cannot be measured, the only rational procedure is to first assume that the worst will happen and then choose the option that will leave us best off when the worst happens (this is the so-called maximum rule of probability theory). It is unclear which of these alternative approaches should be adopted when utilitarian cost-benefit analysis fails.

NOTES

1. There are a number of texts describing this approach. An elementary text is Tom Tietenberg, *Environmental and Natural Resource Economics* (Glenview, IL: Scott, Foresman & Company, 1984); a more compact treatment is Edwin S. Mills, *The Economics of Environmental Quality* (New York: W. W. Norton & Co., Inc., 1978), ch. 3; for several viewpoints consult Robert Dorfman and Nancy Dorman, eds., *Economics of the Environment* (New York: W. W. Norton & Co., Inc., 1977).

2. Mills, *Economics of Environmental Quality,* pp. 68–70.

3. For a compact review of the literature on external costs, see E. J. Mishan, "The Postwar Literature on Externalities: An Interpretative Essay," *Journal of Economic Literature* 9, no. 1 (March 1971): 1–28.

4. See E. J. Mishan, *Economics for Social Decisions* (New York: Praeger Publishers, Inc., 1973), pp. 85 ff.; also E. J. Mishan, *Benefit Analysis,* 3d ed. (London: Allen & Unwin: 1982).

5. S. Prakesh Sethi, *Up Against the Corporate Wall* (Englewood Cliffs, N.J.: Prentice Hall, 1977), p. 21.

6. See Mishan, "The Postwar Literature on Externalities," p. 24.

7. William J. Baumal and Wallace E. Oates, *Economics, Environmental Policy, and the Quality of Life* (Englewood Cliffs, N.J.: Prentice Hall, 1979), p. 177.

8. Mishan, "The Postwar Literature on Externalities," p. 24.

9. Mills, *Economics of Environmental Quality*, pp. 111–12.

10. Frederick D. Sturdivant, *Business and Society* (Homewood, IL: Richard D. Irwin, Inc., 1977), p. 307.

11. For a number of cases that apply these techniques, see Yusuf J. Ahmad, Partha Dasgupta, and Karl-Goran Maler, eds., *Environmental Decision-Making* (London: Hodder and Stoughton, 1984).

12. Thomas A. Klein, *Social Costs and Benefits of Business* (Englewood Cliffs, N.J.: Prentice Hall, 1977), p. 118.

13. Ibid., p. 119; the literature on social accounting for business firms is vast; see U.S. Department of Commerce, *Corporate Social Reporting in the United States and Western Europe* (Washington, D.C.: U.S. Government Printing Office, 1979); Committee on Social Measurement, *The Measurement of Corporate Social Performance* (New York: American Institute of Certified Public Accountants, Inc., 1977).

14. See Boyd Collier, *Measurement of Environmental Deterioration* (Austin, TX: Bureau of Business Research, The University of Texas at Austin, 1971).

15. See Michael D. Bayles, "The Price of Life," *Ethics* 89, no. 1 (October 1978): 20–34; for other problems with using cost-benefit analysis in environmental areas, see Mark Sagoff, "Ethics and Economics in Environmental Law," in Regan, ed., *Earthbound*, pp. 147–78, and Rosemarie Tong, *Ethics in Policy Analysis* (Englewood Cliffs, N.J.: Prentice Hall, 1986), pp. 14–29.

16. Much of the material in this and the following paragraphs is based on the superb analysis in Robert E. Goodwin, "No Moral Nukes," *Ethics* 90, no. 3 (April 1980): 417–49.

17. Council on Environmental Quality, *Environmental Quality*, eighth annual report (Washington, D.C.: U.S. Government Printing Office, 1979), pp. 323–25.

18. U.S. General Accounting Office, *The Nation's Nuclear Waste* (Washington, D.C.: U.S. Government Printing Office, 1979), p. 12. For a criticism of this kind of policy analysis see Tong, *Ethics in Policy Analysis*, pp. 39–54.

Nonhuman Rights

Sierra Club v. *Morton*

In 1965 the U.S. Forest Service invited proposals for development of a year-round recreational project in the Sequoia National Forest's Mineral King Valley. Walt Disney's proposal was judged the best; a $35 million complex on eighty acres, it included ski trails, twenty ski lifts, ten restaurants, a railway, roads, and structures to accommodate 14,000 visitors daily. In announcing the Disney contract, the Forest Service said its plan would enable more people to enjoy Mineral King, while also preserving the environment.

Shortly thereafter the Sierra Club sued, claiming the government acted illegally and sanctioned "permanent destruction of natural values" and "irreparable harm to the public interest" (433 Fed. 2d. 27-8). The Supreme Court held against the Sierra Club four to three, with two justices abstaining. The Court said the Sierra Club lacked "standing." A person or organization has legal standing to seek judicial review only if he or it can show that he (or it) has suffered or will suffer injury. Since the Sierra Club did not show that it would be injured, it lacked standing to seek legal redress and its suit was dismissed.

[*What follows are portions of the majority opinion by Justice Stewart, and the dissenting opinion by Justice Douglas. Footnotes have been dropped—* Eds.]

Justice Stewart delivered the opinion of the Court.

405 U.S. 727 (1972).

491

The first question presented is whether the Sierra Club has alleged facts that entitle it to obtain judicial review of the challenged action. Whether a party has a sufficient stake in an otherwise justiciable controversy to obtain judicial resolution of that controversy is what has traditionally been referred to as the question of standing to sue. Where the party does not rely on any specific statute authorizing invocation of the judicial process, the question of standing depends upon whether the party has alleged such a "personal stake in the outcome of the controversy," *Baker* v. *Carr,* 369 U.S. 186, 204, as to ensure that "the dispute sought to be adjudicated will be presented in an adversary context and in a form historically viewed as capable of judicial resolution." *Flast* v. *Cohen,* 392 U.S. 83, 101. . . .

The injury alleged by the Sierra Club will be incurred entirely by reason of the change in the uses to which Mineral King will be put, and the attendant change in the aesthetics and ecology of the area. Thus, in referring to the road to be built through Sequoia National Park, the complaint alleged that the development "would destroy or otherwise adversely affect the scenery, natural and historic objects and wildlife of the park and would impair the enjoyment of the park for future generations." We do not question that this type of harm may amount to an "injury in fact" sufficient to lay the basis for standing. Aesthetic and environmental well-being, like economic well-being, are important ingredients of the quality of life in our society, and the fact that particular environmental interests are shared by the many rather than the few does not make them less deserving of legal protection through the judicial process. But the "injury in fact" test requires more than an injury to a cognizable interest. It requires that the party seeking review be himself among the injured.

The impact of the proposed changes in the environment of Mineral King will not fall indiscriminately upon every citizen. The alleged injury will be felt directly only by those who use Mineral King and Sequoia National Park, and for whom the aesthetic and recreational values of the area will be lessened by the highway and ski resort. The Sierra Club failed to allege that it or its members would be affected in any of their activities or pastimes by the Disney development. Nowhere in the pleadings or affidavits did the club state that its members use Mineral King for any purpose, much less that they use it in any way that would be significantly affected by the proposed actions of the respondents.

The club apparently regarded any allegations of individualized injury as superfluous, on the theory that this was a "public" action involving questions as to the use of natural resources, and that the club's longstanding concern with and expertise in such matters were sufficient to give it standing as a "representative of the public." This theory reflects a misunderstanding of our cases involving so-called "public actions" in the area of administrative law. . . .

Some courts have indicated a willingness to confer standing upon organizations that have demonstrated "an organizational interest in the problem" of environmental or consumer protection. *Environmental Defense Fund* v. *Hardin,* 138 U.S. App. D. C. 391, 395, 428 F. 2d 1093, 1097. It is clear that an organization whose members are injured may represent those members in a proceeding for judicial review. See, *e.g., NAACP* v. *Button,* 371 U.S. 415, 428. But a mere "interest in a problem," no matter how longstanding the interest and no matter how qualified the organization is in evaluating the problem, is not sufficient by itself to render the organization "adversely affected" or "aggrieved" within the meaning of the APA. The Sierra Club is a large and long-established organization, with a historic commitment to the cause of protecting our Nation's natural heritage from man's depredations. But if a "special interest" in this subject were enough to entitle the Sierra Club to commence this litigation, there would appear to be no objective basis upon which to disallow a suit by any other bona fide "special interest" organization, however small or short-lived. And if any group with a bona fide "special interest" could initiate such litigation, it is difficult to perceive why any individual citizen with the same bona fide special interest would not also be entitled to do so. . . .

Mr. Justice Douglas, dissenting.

The critical question of "standing" would be simplified and also put neatly in focus if we fashioned a federal rule that allowed environmental issues to be litigated before federal agencies or federal courts in the name of the inanimate object about to be despoiled, defaced, or invaded by roads and bulldozers and where injury is the subject of public outrage. Contemporary public concern for protecting nature's ecological equilibrium should lead to the conferral of standing upon environmental objects to sue for their own preservation. See Stone, Should Trees Have Standing?—Toward Legal Rights for Natural Objects, 45 S. Cal. L. Rev. 450 (1972). This suit would therefore be more properly labeled as *Mineral King* v. *Morton.*

Inanimate objects are sometimes parties in litigation. A ship has a legal personality, a fiction found useful for maritime purposes. The corporation sole —a creature of ecclesiastical law—is an acceptable adversary and large fortunes ride on its cases. The ordinary corporation is a "person" for purposes of the adjudicatory processes, whether it represents proprietary, spiritual, aesthetic, or charitable causes.

So it should be as respects valleys, alpine meadows, rivers, lakes, estuaries, beaches, ridges, groves of trees, swampland, or even air that feels the destructive pressures of modern technology and modern life. The river, for example, is the living symbol of all the life it sustains or nourishes—fish, aquatic insects, water ouzels, otter, fisher, deer, elk, bear, and all other animals, including man, who are dependent on it or who enjoy it for its sight, its sound, or its life. The river as plaintiff speaks for the ecological unit of life that is part of it. Those people who have a meaningful relation to that body of water— whether it be a fisherman, a canoeist, a zoologist, or a logger—must be able to speak for the values which the river represents and which are threatened with destruction. . . .

Mineral King is doubtless like other wonders of the Sierra Nevada such as Tuolomne Meadows and the John Muir Trail. Those who hike it, fish it, hunt it, camp in it, frequent it, or visit it merely to sit in solitude and wonderment are legitimate spokesmen for it, whether they may be few or many. Those who have that intimate relation with the inanimate object about to be injured, polluted, or otherwise despoiled are its legitimate spokesmen. . . . [T]he problem is to make certain that the inanimate objects, which are the very core of America's beauty, have spokesmen before they are destroyed. It is, of course, true that most of them are under the control of a federal or state agency. The standards given those agencies are usually expressed in terms of the "public interest." Yet "public interest" has so many differing shades of meaning as to be quite meaningless on the environmental front. . . .

The pressures on agencies for favorable action one way or the other are enormous. The suggestion that Congress can stop action which is undesirable is true in theory; yet even Congress is too remote to give meaningful direction and its machinery is too ponderous to use very often. The federal agencies of which I speak are not venal or corrupt. But they are notoriously under the control of powerful interests who manipulate them through advisory committees, or friendly working relations, or who have that natural affinity with the agency which in time develops between the regulator and the regulated. . . .

The Forest Service—one of the federal agencies behind the scheme to despoil Mineral King—has been notorious for its alignment with lumber companies, although its mandate from Congress directs it to consider the various aspects of multiple use in its supervision of the natural forests.

The voice of the inanimate object, therefore, should not be stilled. That does not mean that the judiciary takes over the managerial functions from the federal agency. It merely means that before these priceless bits of Americana (such as a valley, an alpine meadow, a river, or a lake) are forever lost or are so transformed as to be reduced to the eventual rubble of our urban environment, the voice of the existing beneficiaries of these environmental wonders should be heard.

Perhaps they will not win. Perhaps the bulldozers of "progress" will plow under all the aesthetic wonders of this beautiful land. That is not the present question. The sole question is, who has standing to be heard?

Those who hike the Appalachian Trail into Sunfish Pond, New Jersey, and camp or sleep there, or run the Allagash in Maine, or climb the Guadalupes in West Texas, or who canoe and portage the Quetico Superior in Minnesota, certainly should have standing to defend those natural wonders before courts or agencies, though they live 3,000 miles away. Those who merely are caught up in environmental news or propaganda and flock to defend these waters or areas may be treated differently. That is why these environmental issues should be tendered by the inanimate object itself. Then there will be assurances that all of the forms of life which it represents will stand before the court—the pileated woodpecker as well as the coyote and bear, the lemmings as well as the trout in the streams. Those inarticulate members of the ecological group cannot speak. But those people who have so frequented the place as to know its values and wonders will be able to speak for the entire ecological community.

Ecology reflects the land ethic; and Aldo Leopold wrote in *A Sand County Almanac* 204 (1949), "The land ethic simply enlarges the boundaries of the community to include soils, waters, plants, and animals, or collectively: the land."

That, as I see it, is the issue of "standing" in the present case and controversy.

Christopher D. Stone

Should Trees Have Standing?—
Toward Legal Rights for Natural Objects

Throughout legal history, each successive extension of rights to some new entity has been, theretofore, a bit unthinkable. We are inclined to suppose the rightlessness of rightless "things" to be a decree of Nature, not a legal convention acting in support of some status quo. It is thus that we defer considering the choices involved in all their moral, social, and economic dimensions. And so the United States Supreme Court could straight-facedly tell us in *Dred Scott* that blacks had been denied the rights of citizenship "as a subordinate and inferior class of beings, who had been subjugated by the dominant race. . . ."[1] In the nineteenth century the highest court in California explained that Chinese had not the right to testify against white men in criminal matters because they were "a race of people whom nature has marked as inferior, and who are incapable of progress or intellectual development beyond a certain point . . . between whom and ourselves nature has placed an impassable difference."[2] The popular conception of the Jew in the 13th century contributed to a law which treated them as "men *ferae naturae,* protected by a quasi-forest law. Like the roe and the deer, they form an order apart."[3] Recall, too, that it was not so long ago that the foetus was "like the roe and the deer." In an early suit attempting to establish a wrongful death action on behalf of a negligently killed foetus (now widely accepted practice), Holmes, then on the Massachusetts Supreme Court, seems to have thought it simply inconceivable

From *Southern California Law Review* 45 (1972):450, 453–60, 463–64, 480–81, 486–87. Reprinted by permission.

"that a man might owe a civil duty and incur a conditional prospective liability in tort to one not yet in being."[4] The first woman in Wisconsin who thought she might have a right to practice law was told that she did not, in the following terms:

> The law of nature destines and qualifies the female sex for the bearing and nurture of the children of our race and for the custody of the homes of the world. . . . [A]ll life-long callings of women, inconsistent with these radical and sacred duties of their sex, as is the profession of the law, are departures from the order of nature; and when voluntary, treason against it. . . . The peculiar qualities of womanhood, its gentle graces, its quick sensibility, its tender susceptibility, its purity, its delicacy, its emotional impulses, its subordination of hard reason to sympathetic feeling, are surely not qualifications for forensic strife. Nature has tempered woman as little for the juridical conflicts of the court room, as for the physical conflicts of the battle field. . . .[5]

The fact is, that each time there is a movement to confer rights onto some new "entity," the proposal is bound to sound odd or frightening or laughable. This is partly because until the rightless thing receives its rights, we cannot see it as anything but a *thing* for the use of "us"—those who are holding rights at the time. In this vein, what is striking about the Wisconsin case above is that the court, for all its talk about women, so clearly was never able to see women as they are (and might become). All it could see was the popular "idealized" version of *an object it needed*. Such is the way the slave South looked upon the black. There is something of a seamless web involved: there will be resistance to giving the thing "rights" until it can be seen and valued for itself, yet it is hard to see it and value it for itself until we can bring ourselves to give it "rights"—which is almost inevitably going to sound inconceivable to a large group of people.

The reason for this little discourse on the unthinkable, the reader must know by now, if only from the title of the paper. I am quite seriously proposing that we give legal rights to forests, oceans, rivers and other so-called "natural objects" in the environment—indeed, to the natural environment as a whole.

As strange as such a notion may sound, it is neither fanciful nor devoid of operational content. In fact, I do not think it would be a misdescription of recent developments in the law to say that we are already on the verge of assigning some such rights, although we have not faced up to what we are doing in those particular terms. We should do so now, and begin to explore the implications such a notion would hold.

TOWARD RIGHTS FOR THE ENVIRONMENT

Now, to say that the natural environment should have rights is not to say anything as silly as that no one should be allowed to cut down a tree. We say human beings have rights, but—at least as of the time of this writing—they can be executed. Corporations have rights, but they cannot plead the fifth amendment; *In re Gault* gave fifteen-year-olds certain rights in juvenile proceedings, but it did not give them the right to vote. Thus, to say that the environment should have rights is not to say that it should have every right we can imagine, or even the same body of rights as human beings have. Nor is it to say that everything in the environment should have the same rights as every other thing in the environment.

But for a thing to be *a holder of legal rights*, something more is needed than that some authoritative body will review the actions and processes of those who threaten it. As I shall use the term, "holder of legal rights," each of three additional criteria must be satisfied. All three, one will observe, go toward making a thing *count* jurally—to have a legally recognized worth and dignity in its own right, and not merely to serve as a means to benefit "us" (whoever the contemporary group of rights-holders may be). They are, first, that the thing can institute legal actions *at its behest;* second, that in determining the granting of legal relief, the court must take *injury to it* into account; and, third, that relief must run to the *benefit of it.*

The Rightlessness of Natural Objects at Common Law

Consider, for example, the common law's posture toward the pollution of a stream. True, courts have always been able in some circumstances, to issue orders that will stop the pollution. . . . But the stream itself is fundamentally rightless, with implications that deserve careful reconsideration.

The first sense in which the stream is not a rights-holder has to do with standing. The stream itself has none. So far as the common law is concerned, there is in general no way to challenge the polluter's actions save at the behest of a lower riparian—another human being—able to show an invasion of *his* rights. This conception of the riparian as the holder of the right to bring suit has more than theoretical interest. The lower riparians may simply not care about the pollution. They themselves may be polluting, and not wish to stir up legal waters. They may be economically dependent on their polluting neighbor. And, of course, when they discount the value of winning by the costs of bringing suit and the chances of success, the action may not seem worth undertaking. . . .

The second sense in which the common law denies "rights" to natural objects has to do with the way in which the merits are decided in those cases in which someone is competent and willing to establish standing. At its more primitive levels, the system protected the "rights" of the property owning human with minimal weighing of any values: "*Cujus est solum, ejus est usque ad coelum et ad infernos.*" Today we have come more and more to make balances—but only such as will adjust the economic best interests of identifiable humans.

. . . None of the natural objects, whether held in common or situated on private land, has any of the three criteria of a rights-holder. They have no standing in their own right; their unique damages do not count in determining outcome; and they are not the beneficiaries of awards. In such fashion, these objects have traditionally been regarded by the common law, and even by all but the most recent legislation, as objects for man to conquer and master and use—in such a way as the law once looked upon "man's" relationships to African Negroes. Even where special measures have been taken to conserve them, as by seasons on game and limits on timber cutting, the dominant motive has been to conserve them *for us*—for the greatest good of the greatest number of human beings. Conservationists, so far as I am aware, are generally reluctant to maintain otherwise. As the name implies, they want to conserve and guarantee our consumption and our enjoyment of these other living things. In their own right, natural objects have counted for little, in law as in popular movements. . . .

As I mentioned at the outset, however, the rightlessness of the natural environment can and should change; it already shows some signs of doing so.

Toward Having Standing in Its Own Right

It is not inevitable, nor is it wise, that natural objects should have no rights to seek redress in their own behalf. It is no answer to say that streams and forests cannot have standing because streams and forests cannot speak. Corporations cannot speak either; nor can states, estates, infants, incompetents, municipalities or universities. Lawyers speak for them, as they customarily do for the ordinary citizen with legal problems. One ought, I think, to handle the legal problems of natural objects as one does the problems of legal incompetents—human beings who have become vegetable. If a human being shows signs of becoming senile and has affairs that he is *de jure* incompetent to manage, those concerned with his well being make such a showing to the court, and someone is designated by the court with the authority to manage the incompetent's affairs. The guardian (or "conservator" or "committee"— the terminology varies) then represents the incompetent in his legal affairs. Courts make similar appointments when a corporation has become "incompetent"—they appoint a trustee in bankruptcy or reorganization to oversee its affairs and speak for it in court when that becomes necessary.

On a parity of reasoning, we should have a system in which, when a friend of a natural object perceives it to be endangered, he can apply to a court for the creation of a guardianship. . . .

. . . One reason for making the environment itself the beneficiary of a judgment is to prevent it from being "sold out" in a negotiation among private litigants who agree not to enforce rights that have been established among themselves. Protection from this will be advanced by making the natural object a party to an injunctive settlement. Even more importantly, we should make it a beneficiary of money awards. . . .

The idea of assessing damages as best we can and placing them in a trust fund is far more realistic than a hope that a total "freeze" can be put on the environmental status quo. Nature is a continuous theater in which things and species (eventually man) are destined to enter and exit. In the meantime, coexistence of man and his environment means that *each* is going to have to compromise for the better of both. Some pollution of streams, for example, will probably be inevitable for some time. Instead of setting an unrealizable goal of enjoining absolutely the discharge of all such pollutants, the trust fund concept would (a) help assure that pollution would occur only in those instances where the social need for the pollutant's product (via his present method of production) was so high as to enable the polluter to cover *all* homocentric costs, plus some estimated costs to the environment *per se,* and (b) would be a corpus for preserving monies, if necessary, while the technology developed to a point where repairing the damaged portion of the environment was feasible. Such a fund might even finance the requisite research and development.

I do not doubt that other senses in which the environment might have rights will come to mind, and, as I explain more fully below, would be more apt to come to mind if only we should speak in terms of their having rights, albeit vaguely at first. "Rights" might well lie in unanticipated areas. It would seem, for example, that Chief Justice Warren was only stating the obvious when he observed in *Reynolds v. Sims* that "legislators represent people, not trees or acres." Yet, could not a case be made for a system of apportionment which did take into account the wildlife of an area? It strikes me as a poor idea that Alaska should have no more congressmen than Rhode Island primarily *because there are in Alaska all those trees and acres, those waterfalls and forests.* I am not saying anything as silly as that we ought to overrule *Baker v. Carr* and retreat from one man-one vote to a system of one man-or-tree one vote. Nor am I even taking the position that we ought to count each acre, as we once counted each slave, as three-fifths of a man. But I am suggesting that there is nothing unthinkable about, and there might on balance even be a prevailing case to he made for, an electoral apportionment that made some systematic effort to allow for the representative "rights" of non-human life. And if a case can be made for that, which I offer here mainly for purpose of illustration, I suspect that a society that grew concerned enough about the environment to make it a holder of rights would be able to find and quite a number of "rights" to have waiting for it when it got to court.

NOTES

1. *Dred Scott v. Sandford,* 60 U.S. (19 How.) 396, 404–405 (1856).
2. *People v. Hall,* 4 Cal. 399, 405 (1854).
3. Schechter, "The Rightlessness of Mediaeval English Jewry," 45 *Jewish Quarterly Review,* 121, 135 (1954) quoting from M. Bateson, *Medieval England,* 139 (1904).
4. *Dietrich v. Inhabitants of Northampton,* 138 Mass. 14, 16 (1884).
5. *In re* Goddell, 39 Wisc. 232, 245 (1875).

Clayton Hobbs

Only Humans Have Rights

Although humans have numerous legal rights, animals today do not unless they are members of an endangered species. Recently, however, activists have clamored for nonhuman rights; Christopher Stone, for example, argues that animals, trees, rivers, indeed, the "natural environment as a whole" should have legal rights.[1] Businessmen and farmers are justifiably concerned about the emerging "rights" movement; we already face too many lawsuits, many of which are entirely frivolous yet costly. Imagine being sued because your grading for a new factory foundation violates the rights of dirt, or imagine a farmer being sued because he allegedly violated the rights of barley or chickens. All of the arguments that conclude we should confer legal rights on nonhumans are based on the notion that such entities have "moral" rights. I shall argue that we should not confer legal rights on natural nonhuman entities. To make my argument manageable, I make three assumptions: (1) some objects, e.g., manmade utilitarian objects, such as knives and staplers, have no moral rights; (2) if animals have no moral rights, then other "lower" natural nonhumans, e.g., barley and rocks, have no moral rights; and, (3) entities which have no moral rights should not have legal rights conferred on them. I will only argue for (4): animals have no moral rights. Given 1, 2, and 3, proof of 4 will establish my thesis: we should not confer legal rights on nonhuman entities.

Animal rights activists often argue that: (R_1) having interests is both necessary and sufficient for an entity's having moral rights, and (R_2) animals have interests; hence, animals have moral rights.[2] Let us examine this argument.[3]

Following Tom Regan, we can distinguish two senses of "interest": (S_1)

the sense in which we say "X is in Sam's interest," and (S₂) the sense in which we say "Sam is interested in X."[4] These are distinct since S₁ may be true but S₂ false and vice versa (X = cigarettes).

Animals possess interests in sense S₁; accordingly, R₂ is true using S₁. In this sense (X is in Sam's interest), an interest is tied to a state of "goodness" to which X contributes, e.g., "Drinking milk is in Sam's interest" means that milk is *good for* Sam. Certainly there are things such as water that are in my cat Tabby's interest in the sense that they are good for him and things such as being kicked that are not in Tabby's interest, i.e., are not good for him. However, if S₁ establishes R₂ in the case of animals, it undercuts R₁; for manmade utilitarian objects have interests in sense S₁ but, per our assumption, have no moral rights. For example, it is in a meat-cutting knife's interest (S₁) to be sharp, since this means it is good for the knife to be sharp. Just as drinking milk is in Sam's interest (i.e., is good for Sam) in that it enables him to function well, so being sharp is in the knife's interest (i.e., is good for the knife) in that it enables it to cut meat well. The upshot is that R₁ is false if "interest" is used in sense S₁.

In sense S₂, the sense in which we say "Sam is interested in X," can animals have interests? In this sense to be interested in X is to want X or (minimally) to desire X. Can animals desire? Although I will not here be concerned with behaviorist accounts of desire, it should be noted that if any one of them is correct, then animals do not have desires. Our concern is with the ordinary and typical use of "desire." If I desire something in this sense (say the new John Deere tractor due at dealers in two months), I standardly do not have it. So, however complex my desire is, it (minimally) contains a *belief,* namely, that I do not have the new Deere. In other cases I have the desired object in hand, e.g., I desire that pizza on the plate in front of me. Still, I have beliefs, e.g., the object really is a pizza, it is edible, would taste good, etc. In general, then, when I desire X I have a belief about X, more specifically, a belief of the form "I believe that p," where p is a proposition expressible in a sentence.

So the situation boils down to this: to have an interest in X in sense S₂ an entity must have a desire for X, and to have a desire for X the entity must have a belief about X, namely, of the form: I believe that p, where p is a proposition expressible in a sentence. Accordingly, the ability to use language is necessary for having beliefs of the sort necessary for having interest S₂. If this is correct, then animals do not possess interests in sense S₂, because they lack the ability to use language.

I recognize that considerable controversy attends specifying necessary and sufficient conditions for the correct attribution of "language," but nobody seriously believes that cats have language capacity. Some researchers contend that chimpanzees possess language, but two points are worthy of note. First, this claim is arguable; it certainly has not been established that chimpanzees have language capacity, and there are arguments for thinking they do not. The burden of proof is on those who claim chimpanzees have a language, and they have not met the burden. Second, even if it were eventually established that chimpanzees do have language, that would only establish that a very limited class of animals is capable of language and hence a candidate for moral rights. So this argument could not establish broad claims of nonhuman rights.

So the dilemma for animal rights defenders is this: to establish that animals have moral rights they argue that (R_1) having interests is both necessary and sufficient for having moral rights, and (R_2) animals have interests. But "interests" used in sense S_1 makes R_1 false and "interests" used in sense S_2 makes R_2 false. So the defenders of animal rights have not established that animals have moral rights.

Animal rights advocates have a quick counter to the argument just developed. Stone, for example, says:

> It is not inevitable, nor is it wise, that natural objects have no rights to seek redress in their own behalf. It is no answer to say that streams and forests cannot have standing because streams and forests cannot speak. Corporations cannot speak either; nor can states, estates, infants, incompetents, municipalities or universities. Lawyers speak for them, as they customarily do for the ordinary citizen with legal problems. One ought, I think, to handle the legal problems of natural objects as one does the problems of legal incompetents—human beings who have become vegetable. If a human being shows signs of becoming senile and has affairs that he is *de jure* incompetent to manage, those concerned with his well-being make such a showing to the court, and someone is designated by the court with the authority to manage the incompetent's affairs. The guardian . . . then represents the incompetent in his legal affairs. . . . On a parity of reasoning, we should have a system in which, when a friend of a natural object perceives it to be endangered [injured], he can apply to a court for the creation of a guardianship. . . .

This line of reasoning can be employed against our argument. The claim that having beliefs expressible in language is necessary for having interests (and hence moral rights) is undercut by the case of the brain-dead (or babies), neither of whom have language but who do have moral rights.

Stone's own words, however, negate this criticism. He speaks of "human beings who have become vegetable." In the normal state humans do have language capability. Although some "become vegetable," they are still members of a general class, the normal or typical members of which do have language capability. But cats are not members of a class, the normal or typical members of which do have language capability. Similarly, the newborn baby has potential language capability; in the normal state of affairs he will mature into a being that uses language. But that certainly isn't true of Tabby; no cat develops into a language user. So the argument of Stone and others, essentially:

1. Animals are like babies and the brain-dead in that neither uses language (the criterion animal rights critics' use to differentiate humans from animals).

2. Babies and the brain-dead have rights.

Therefore, animals should have rights.

is not acceptable. We certainly accept (2) but (1) is false; the language-use criterion we used to exclude animals from the status of rights-holders does note exclude babies and the brain-dead.

Having shown that animals (and by extension all "lower" nonhuman entities, e.g., barley and rocks) are not bearers of moral rights, it follows that they should not be extended legal rights. Nonhuman entities should not have legal standing to the extent that is based on moral rights; there is no moral right basis for their having a legal right to have redress sought in their own behalf.

Those of us who argue there is no rational basis for extending rights (moral or legal) to nonhuman entities will seem insensitive or immoral to many animal lovers, who will claim our position permits humans to do anything whatsoever to animals. This does not follow. Even though cats do not have interests (S_2) and hence lack moral rights, they do have needs; cats need water to survive, and it would be wrong to deny a healthy cat water. Furthermore, I believe some animals experience pain and that it is wrong to inflict pain on animals for no reason whatsoever, even though I agree with Frey that being able to experience pain is neither necessary nor sufficient for having interests and hence moral rights.[5] Accordingly, I reject the claim that if we deny moral rights to nonhuman entities, we morally sanction humans to do anything they want to nonhumans.

NOTES

1. Christopher Stone, "Should Trees Have Standing?" *Southern California Law Review* 45 (1972): 453 ff.

2. Leonard Nelson, *A System of Ethics* (New Haven, Conn.: Yale University Press, 1956), 136–44.

3. The argument I develop is based largely on: R. G. Frey, *Interests and Rights* (Oxford: Oxford University Press, 1980).

4. Tom Regan, "McCloskey on Why Animals Cannot Have Rights," *Philosophical Quarterly* 26 (1976): 251–57.

5. Frey, 140–67.

SELECT BIBLIOGRAPHY

Attfield, R. *The Ethics of Environmental Concern*. New York: Columbia University Press, 1983.

Barbour, I. *Technology, Environment, and Human Values*. New York: Draeger, 1980.

Baxter, W. *People or Penguins? The Case for Optimal Pollution*. New York: Columbia University Press, 1974.

Blackstone, W., ed. *Philosophy and Environmental Crisis*. Athens: University of Georgia Press, 1974.

Brunner, D., et al., eds. *Corporations and the Environment: How Should Decisions Be Made?* Stanford, Calif.: Committee on Corporate Responsibility, 1981.

Callicott, J., ed. *In Defense of the Land Ethic*. Albany, N.Y.: State University of New York Press, 1989.

Davidson, D.. *The Environmental Factor: An Approach for Managers*. New York: John Wiley and Sons, 1978.

Gibson, M. *To Breathe Freely: Risk, Consent, and Air*. Totowa, N.J.: Rowman and Allanheld, 1985.

Goodpaster, K., and K. Sayre, eds. *Ethics and Problems of the 21st Century*. Notre Dame, Ind.: University of Notre Dame Press, 1979.

Hardin, G., and J. Baden. *Managing the Commons*. San Francisco: W. H. Freeman, 1977.

Leonard, H. J., et al., eds. *Business and Environment: Toward Common Ground*. Washington, D.C.: The Conservation Foundation, 1977.

Regan, T., ed. *Earthbound: New Introductory Essays in Environmental Ethics*. New York: Random House, 1984.

Rohrlich, G. *Environmental Management*. Cambridge, Mass.: Ballinger, 1976.

Rolston, H. *Environmental Ethics*. Philadelphia: Temple University Press, 1988.

Scherer, D., and T. Attig, eds. *Ethics and the Environment*. Englewood Cliffs, N.J.: Prentice-Hall, 1983.

Schrader-Frechette, K. *Environmental Ethics*. Pacific Grove, Calif.: Boxwood Press, 1982.

Taylor, P. *Respect for Nature*. Princeton, N.J.: Princeton University Press, 1986.

Tietenberg, T. *Environmental and Natural Resource Economics*. Glenview, Ill.: Scott, Foresman & Co., 1984.

8

MULTINATIONAL CORPORATIONS

INTRODUCTION

Multinational corporations, those that produce and/or market goods in more than one country, pose a host of ethical problems. Should a multinational have one conflict of interest policy and one employee rights policy applicable transnationally, or should these be tailored to the business climate in different countries? How much profit should be repatriated to the country where the firm is headquartered, and how much should be reinvested in the host country? Should products sold be uniform across national boundaries, e.g., should drugs be marketed abroad that do not meet Food and Drug Administration (FDA) safety standards in the U.S.? Should American firms be allowed to operate in countries that are ruled by repressive governments?

Discussion of these issues is complicated by the fact that there is no effective organization for policing multinational operations. In any specific country, laws can be passed to curb practices judged to be immoral and detrimental to society, but critics charge that the absence of a transnational legal body and enforcement mechanism invites multinationals to sidestep moral issues and operate in a purely egoistic fashion.

James Kiersky's article discusses the numerous ethical complexities facing multinational managers, complexities illustrated in the Bhopal case study. Thomas Donaldson develops an algorithm or system that multinational managers can employ to resolve international ethical conflicts.

Although bribes and kickbacks are illegal and considered immoral in the U.S., similar practices are commonplace in some foreign countries, particularly in those lacking a vigorous free market. The case study on Lockheed's selling of the TriStar aircraft in Japan provides insight into the reasons used by the executives of one corporation to justify making payoffs to foreign government officials in order to make a sale, and raises the question of what ethical principles or values American firms should adopt in such contexts. Mark Pastin and

Michael Hooker argue that the 1977 Foreign Corrupt Practices Act, which bans corporate payoffs to foreign government officials for the purpose of securing or retaining business, has no moral basis and hence should be repealed. In contrast, James Humber criticizes the arguments of Pastin and Hooker, and argues that the Foreign Corrupt Practices Act rests on a solid ethical foundation.

Multinational Decision Making

Union Carbide and Bhopal

Between midnight and the pre-dawn hours of December 3, 1984, in Bhopal, India, the worst industrial accident in terms of immediate loss of human life occurred at a Union Carbide plant that manufactured agricultural pesticides. When somewhere between twenty-one and forty tons of methyl isocyanate (MIC) escaped from a holding tank into the foggy night air, the resulting yellowish white cloud descended onto the city of 800,000 sleeping residents. Because this gas is heavier than air, the cloud hovered close to the ground. For this reason, only those denizens of the upper floors of well-sealed buildings would not have to flee the city. The remaining hundreds of thousands overflowed into the streets to join what has been called the "largest unplanned human exodus of the industrial age." Many did not make it to safety; 3,800 people died and 300,000 were injured, at least 20,000 of whom were injured seriously.

In 1984 Union Carbide was America's third largest chemical company and thirty-fifth largest industrial corporation. With sales of approximately $10 billion, Union Carbide employed almost 100,000 people in forty countries. The company had operated in India since the 1920s and incorporated there in 1934 as Union Carbide India Ltd (UCIL). Union Carbide owned 50.8 percent of UCIL, the Indian government owned 22 percent, and some 23,000 Indian citizens owned the remaining 27.2 percent.

In 1969, in part at the request of the Indian government, UCIL and the parent company, Union Carbide, decided to construct a pesticide manufacturing plant in Bhopal. The Indian government wanted to increase pesticide use, since doing so would increase crop yield and enable the country to feed an additional 100 million people. The Indian government also wanted to improve its balance of trade by lowering imports, and also wanted to increase the number of jobs available to Indians. One advantage of locating in India to Union Carbide was that the government leased eighty acres of governmental land to the company at $40 per acre per year. The relatively low fixed investment, coupled with low labor costs and a large market, led Union Carbide to think it could achieve a good return on its Bhopal investment.

Union Carbide initially shipped basic chemicals, including MIC, to Bhopal, and reacted them there to make the final product, a pesticide called Sevin. By 1975, however, the Indian government wanted Union Carbide to reduce further its imports, and, in order to keep its Indian operating license, the company was forced to construct a second plant in Bhopal. This complex included a facility to make MIC, which was then reacted with other chemicals to produce Sevin. The new facility was designed and constructed between 1975 and 1980. When the plant was authorized and construction began the site was located outside of Bhopal proper and there were alleged to be no residential dwellings within one and one half miles of the facility's fence. However, since India had virtually no land use control laws, by the time the plant reached operational status in 1980, "shantytowns" of Indian citizens, many of them laborers at the construction site, had sprung up, filling in most of the previously uninhabited land between the site and the city.

As noted, Union Carbide owned a majority interest in UCIL, with minority stakes held by the Indian government and Indian citizens. As majority owner, Union Carbide had primary legal responsibility for UCIL's fourteen facilities in India, including the one in Bhopal. However, except for five Union Carbide representatives on UCIL's board of directors, all UCIL employees were Indian nationals, in accordance with the Indian government's desire to train and employ Indians. The Indian government had primary responsibility for governmental safety inspections, and problems existed at the Bhopal plant; as John F. Steiner reported:

> In 1980, the project was finished, and the MIC Unit began operation . . . the plant had become far more dangerous, for it now manufactured the basic chemical ingredients of pesticides rather than simply making them from shipped-in ingredients. One step in the manufacture of MIC, for example, involves the production of phosgene, the lethal "mustard gas" used in World War I.
>
> In 1981, a phosgene gas leak at the Bhopal plant killed one worker, and a crusading Indian journalist wrote a series of articles about the plant and its potential dangers to the population. No one heeded these articles. In 1982, a second phosgene leak forced the temporary evacuation of some surrounding slum areas. Also in 1982, a safety survey of the plant by three Carbide engineers from the United States cited approximately fifty safety defects, most of them minor, and noted "no situation involving imminent danger or requiring immediate correction." Subsequently, all suggested changes in safety systems and procedures were made (except the replacement of one troublesome valve outside the accident area). Worker safety and environmental inspections of the plant were carried out by the Department of Labor in Madhya Pradesh. The agency had only fifteen factory inspectors to cover 8,000 plants and had

a record of lax enforcement. This was in keeping with the generally low commitment to pollution control in India by regulators at all levels.

Exactly what happened on December 3, 1984, will probably never be known, since the Bhopal case did not come to trial. We do know that on the evening of December 2, 1984, a pressurized storage tank was partially filled with about 12,000 gallons of MIC. The two adjacent storage tanks were nearly full of MIC, a practice inconsistent with operational policy, since one tank was supposed to remain empty for safety considerations. Somehow 120 to 240 gallons of water entered the MIC tank, setting off a heat-generating reaction. Operators of the Bhopal facility were initially unaware of the heat-building, which went on unconstrained because the plant's refrigeration unit had been shut off for several months to reduce costs. As pressure and heat increased in the tank, a leak developed, releasing some MIC. Although the leak was reported, the plant's managers decided to repair it after a break for tea. Shortly thereafter, the pressure blew out a valve, releasing MIC. Two standard safety mechanisms, one designed to neutralize MIC and the other designed to burn MIC vapor, were shut down for maintenance and could not be employed. Attempts to spray the MIC vapor with water were ineffective. Almost all of the plant's employees fled in panic. Over a span of approximately two hours about 85 percent of the MIC in the storage tank escaped and spread over the city of Bhopal.

The cause of the Bhopal disaster was not established. A team of Indian scientists claimed that a worker who had been ordered to clean out filters by washing them with water had done so without installing a device that was used standardly to prevent water from running into the MIC tank. Union Carbide disputed this theory, claiming that water could not have reached the MIC tank via this route because valves placed between the cleaned filters and the MIC tank were closed prior to the disaster. Union Carbide claimed to have evidence that an employee upset at not being promoted intentionally sabotaged the plant by running water into the MIC tank. Since the case never came to trial, we will probably never know what caused the Bhopal disaster.

Union Carbide and the Indian authorities also disagreed on the plant's management. The company maintained that initially, while it had control of the plant, operations were essentially identical to those in effect at the Union Carbide pesticide plant in West Virginia. But, because the Indian government wanted more and more control of the plant, not only in terms of ownership but also in terms of day-to-day operations, the parent company had gradually been phased out to the point where at the time of the accident all personnel in any way connected with the plant were of Indian origin and descent with no outside aid or assistance, with the exception of periodic and announced safety inspections by Union Carbide personnel who were of U.S. origin. According to this interpretation, what happened was that an increasing number of safety violations were allowed to occur because (a) despite Union Carbide's continued training of UCIL's personnel, there was little understanding by the latter of the potential danger the plant posed, and (b) those in charge of running the Bhopal facility as well as its employees all took a much more Eastern and passive, fatalistic approach to daily operations than their Western predecessors.

Indian authorities challenged the veracity of Union Carbide's claim that its domestic operations were conducted in precisely the same manner as its operations in developing countries. They pointed, for example, to the fact that the West Virginia plant was computerized, whereas the Bhopal plant was not. The company's rejoinder was that the Bhopal plant and personnel did not have the kind of expertise necessary to utilize sophisticated computer technology and that the West Virginia facility essentially relied on the same mechanical controls as the one in Bhopal. It was also alleged that the profit motive led Union Carbide to cut many safety corners, that management had permitted both the plant and its equipment to deteriorate, and that the company permitted attrition among qualified employees and lowered entrance standards. Such managerial weaknesses were alleged to be due to higher management's decision to sell the plant to Indian nationals. From the perspective of Indian authorities, the Bhopal plant was still alleged to be profitable, accounting for as much as 3 percent of Union Carbide's worldwide profit. Union Carbide maintained that the plant was never profitable and that it was on account of annual net losses of millions of dollars in addition to repeated pressure from Indian interests that the sale of the plant was contemplated. The losses were said to be due to unexpected competition which never allowed Bhopal production to reach a fraction of its capacity.

U.S. safety authorities agreed that until the time of the accident Union Carbide's safety record worldwide was exemplary. The company had continually expressed concerns about the Bhopal facility and wanted the Indian government to make periodic and *unannounced* inspections of the plant.

Environmentalists who studied the Bhopal disaster reached a quite different conclusion as to its "cause." They tended to focus on the use of "toxic" chemical pesticides in agriculture and argued we should eliminate their use. Although we are now led to believe that such chemicals are a necessary part of our food production cycle if we are not to starve hundreds of millions of people, ecologists are not convinced that this argument is a sound one. Many of them believe we can feed an entire planet a healthy diet without poisoning ourselves or our habitat and even make use of a large global force of poor and unemployed workers in the bargain.

Environmentalists also pointed out some questionable connections between governments and pesticide manufacturers. A number of chemical pesticides are composed of chemical compounds that were formerly used in weapons. MIC, for example, has phosgene, a World War I nerve gas, as one of its components. So it turns out to be convenient and mutually beneficial for governments to dispose of their environmentally hazardous materials and receive some recompense at the same time that multinational corporations can pick up their raw materials at bargain-basement prices. In this way war materials now find a "useful" outlet as ingredients in the new warfare against bugs.

Immediately after the disaster, Union Carbide dispatched physicians and medical supplies to Bhopal; it also sent technicians to determine what happened. Within forty-eight hours of the incident Chairman Warren Anderson and other Union Carbide managers flew to Bhopal. Anderson said the company accepted "moral responsibility" for the situation. On arrival, Anderson was arrested, charged with criminal negligence, and then asked to leave India.

About the time that the Bhopal gas cloud was dissipating, lawyers from the United States flocked into the shantytowns of Bhopal in search of potential litigants for compensatory and punitive damage claims against Union Carbide. The lists that they compiled were sold for profit, which led a *Wall Street Journal* editorial writer to call this Bhopal's "second tragedy." In defense of their actions, these attorneys offered several lines of justification, three of which certainly bear on ethical and moral concerns. First, they claimed that recent verdicts by sympathetic juries against firms such as A. H. Robins Company and Manville Corporation go a long way in fighting if not curtailing corporate irresponsibility. Second, by effectively moving the *venue* of the trials to the United States, a huge step would be taken toward holding multinational corporations accountable to a single, worldwide safety standard. And third, by keeping the tragedy and its victims at the center of worldwide attention, there was more chance of the victims' families receiving a "just" compensation and less chance that the horrible nightmare would soon be forgotten.

Four days after the MIC leakage the first lawsuits were filed against Union Carbide in U.S. federal district court in West Virginia. American attorneys, hoping to have the cases heard in American courts where they were licensed to practice, sought fifty billion dollars in damages against Union Carbide. Before the courts made any decision concerning the cases (which increased to more than 140 and represented more than 200,000 Indian plaintiffs), the Indian parliament itself passed the Bhopal Gas Leak Disaster Act, which granted Indians the exclusive right to represent Indian plaintiffs in India or any other country. The Indian government then brought charges against Union Carbide in United States' courts, since American juries routinely returned verdicts that valued a human life much more highly in monetary terms than Indian juries. Furthermore, cases reach the trial stage much more rapidly in the United States than in India.

In May of 1986 District Court Judge John Keenan ruled that the cases would have to be heard in India, partly on the grounds of a legal principle of *forum non conveniens,* which allows a court to refuse jurisdiction in a case where there is a more reasonable and convenient trial venue or location. Since the plaintiffs, evidence, and witnesses were all in India, it was the reasonable place to try the case. The decision was timely for several reasons. Union Carbide had just offered to settle the almost half million claims for 350 million dollars and the U.S. lawyers, who were afraid that Judge Keenan might do what he in fact did, pressed for immediate acceptance of the settlement. The government of India held out in hopes of a larger verdict. Judge Keenan expressed contempt in his ruling for what American attorneys had done to tarnish the worldwide image of the United States, but also expressed hope that India could reach a just verdict.

Suits against Union Carbide amounting to $3.3 billion were filed in India in September, 1986. After considerable preliminary legal maneuvering, a settlement was tentatively reached in early 1989. Union Carbide agreed to pay $470 million to settle all claims and the Indian government agreed to initiate no new lawsuits on behalf of Indians. The settlement means an award of about $1,500 per person injured or killed at Bhopal. In October, 1991, the Supreme Court of India upheld the $470 million settlement already paid by Union Carbide. However, it revoked the immunity from criminal prosecution of Union Carbide's top executives, including then CEO Warren Anderson. The likelihood of any further actions being taken against Anderson or any other Union Carbide executive is probably miniscule, but the precedent is there in case any future industrial accidents occur.

The Union Carbide that survived this disaster is a vastly different organization. In order to meet the exigencies of the Bhopal situation, to pay off the legal claims, and at the same time survive a hostile takeover attempt by GAF Corporation, the company had to sell off many of its prime assets including Eveready Batteries, Glad Bags, and Prestone Antifreeze; it also restructured and cut its nu;mber of employees from 98,000 to 43,000.

For Discussion

List those parties who could be considered responsible for the Bhopal disaster. Who is responsible? Is one person or organization primarily responsible or should blame be apportioned on a *pro rata* basis among the various parties involved? Why? In cases such as Bhopal that involve multinational corporations, should there be a global legal standard by which any multinational should be judged? If so, why? If not, which country should have legal jurisdiction? What sort of safety standards should a multinational corporation adopt?

SOURCES

David Weir, *The Bhopal Syndrome* (San Francisco; Sierra Club Books, 1987); Jack Behrman, *Essays on Ethics in Business and the Professions* (Englewood Cliffs, N.J.: Prentice-Hall, 1988), pp. 277–80; Manuel Velasquez, *Business Ethics,* 2d ed. (Englewood Cliffs, N.J.: Prentice-Hall, 1988), pp. 2–7; Clayton Trotter, et al., "Bhopal, India, and Union Carbide: The Second Tragedy," *Journal of Business Ethics* 8 (1989), pp. 439–54; John Steiner, *Industry, Society and Change* (New York: McGraw-Hill, 1991), pp. 295–319.

James Kiersky

Ethical Complexities Involving Multinational Corporations

By no means a new phenomenon on the business scene, multinational corporations (MNCs) present a number of distinctive ethical problems peculiar to their organizational format. These problems are not simply a function of MNCs' size, for many localized national corporations (LNCs) are larger in terms of financial net worth, number of shareholders, gross sales, or number of employees.

The first and most obvious set of conditions that gives rise to ethical problems grows out of the fact that MNCs function in three domains: (A) a home base of operation where the MNC is headquartered and chartered, (B) a foreign base of operation in a host country, and (C) additional foreign markets beyond both (A) and (B). Each of these domains has a unique web of ethical beliefs and principles which often conflicts with those of the other domains. A major problem, peculiar to MNCs, concerns one of *venue:* when a situation arises involving conflicting claims among the different domains of (A), (B) and/or (C), where is the appropriate place to adjudicate the conflict legally or ethically— the parent company's national court system, the host country's courts, the place where the problems occurred, a neutral site, a place most likely to render a "just" verdict, or a mutually agreed upon location?

What seems to create this particular niche of ethical complexities for the international business community are the permutations and combinations of factors already present in most business operations of any size. In other words, for most businesses the following identifiable "players" are involved:

(1) Managers—who make the decisions

(2) Employees—who carry out those decisions

(3) Shareholders—who finance those decisions and expect to profit from them

(4) Consumers—who utilize the fruits of those decisions

(5) Environmental community—which is affected by those decisions

(6) Governments—who regulate those decisions

(7) Competitors—who must contend with those decisions

Of course, there are other "players," for example, lending institutions, who do not fit neatly into any one of these main categories. The list is not meant to be complete; it merely identifies the range of concerns at play. While there are invariably conflicting interests and different values motivating each of these "players," the MNC not only involves all seven of them, but creates interesting sub-alliances by virtue of the fact that each domain of the MNC—(A), (B), and (C) above—has its own set of the seven players. With each issue that emerges, the sub-alliances seem to change team members.

In order to illustrate more concretely the general complexities being characterized, consider a few scenarios. For example, in the hopes of being able to meet foreign competition the chief executive officer of a manufacturing MNC wishes to move production plants to a host country (B) where the labor market is significantly cheaper than in the home country (A). While many stockholders of that MNC (which would include A-3, B-3, and C-3 above) may applaud such a move, along with labor unions, prospective employees, and the government in the host country (B-2 and B-6), there is likely to be an outcry of betrayal from the home labor market (A-2), the home government (A-6), the general populace of the home country (A-4 and A-5), as well as from foreign competitors (C-7), and possibly competitors in the host nation (B-7).

A second, rather different sort of scenario involves an MNC home-based in a nation (A) which is committed to human rights, egalitarianism, and/or affirmative action programs but which has overseas affiliates operating in a host nation (B) committed to programs which are dictatorial and openly racist. The conflict of values which may take shape in this case will depend upon what actions are taken or contemplated. For instance, hiring and termination practices in affiliates in the host country will have different repercussions not only in the different domains of (A), (B), and (C), but within one and the same domain. A minority of citizens and consumers in (B) may vehemently oppose the same practices strongly endorsed by a majority of citizens and consumers in (B), or in (A) or (C) for that matter. The consequences of business activities proposed as well as undertaken are likely to have further effects in all three domains which may not have been foreseen.

A third type of situation is likely to find its way into newsprint in the 1990s. An MNC home-based in (A) has been operating in country (B) for many years. Country (B) has recently upgraded its environmental legislation and now decides to press civil claims against that MNC for long-term damage to its waterways, soil, air, and its citizenry. The entire host affiliate of that MNC in country (B) is not even financially equivalent to the amount of the claims, so that the MNC in country (A) decides to sue its own insurance company, itself an MNC, headquartered in country (C). Who is to be held responsible, both ethically and legally and, furthermore, which set of ethical and legal standards is the appropriate one to decide such an issue? The same questions are similarly applicable to product liability issues, or industrial "accidents."

In many of the cases of the types mentioned a need seems to be indicated to at least examine the feasibility of establishing an "international marketplace" with "internationally acceptable rules of the game" and "international court and enforcement mechanisms." Just how these could be established and financed, what would be the chief obstacles and sources of opposition as well as support are questions that should be explored.

Thomas Donaldson

Multinational Decision Making: Reconciling International Norms

Jurisprudence theorists are often puzzled when, having thoroughly analyzed an issue within boundaries of a legal system, they must confront it again outside those boundaries. For international issues, trusted axioms often fail as the secure grounds of legal tradition and national consensus erode. Much the same happens when one moves from viewing a problem of corporate ethics against a backdrop of national moral consensus to the morally inconsistent backdrop of international opinion. Is the worker who appeals to extra-national opinion while complaining about a corporate practice accepted within his or her country, the same as an ordinary whistleblower? Is a factory worker in Mexico justified in complaining about being paid three dollars an hour for the same work a U.S. factory worker, employed by the same company, is paid eight dollars?[1] Is he justified when in Mexico the practice of paying workers three dollars an hour—and even much less—is widely accepted? Is an asbestos worker in India justified in drawing world attention to the lower standards of in-plant asbestos pollution maintained by an English multinational relative to standards in England, when the standards in question fall within Indian government guidelines and, indeed, are stricter than the standards maintained by other Indian asbestos manufacturers?

What distinguishes these issues from standard ones about corporate practices is that they involve reference to a conflict of norms, either moral or legal, between home and host country. This paper examines the subclass of conflicts

---

From the *Journal of Business Ethics* 4 (1985): 357-66. Copyright ⊕ 1985 by Thomas Donaldson, Georgetown University.

in which host country norms appear substandard from the perspective of home country, and evaluates the claim often made by multinational executives that the prevalence of seemingly lower standards in a host country warrants the adoption by multinationals of the lower standards. It is concerned with cases of the following form: A multinational company (C) adopts a corporate practice (P) which is morally and/or legally permitted in C's home country (A). The paper argues that the presence of lower standards in B justifies C's adopting the lower standards only in certain, well-defined contexts. It proposes a conceptual test, or ethical algorithm, for multinationals to use in distinguishing justified from unjustified applications of standards. This algorithm ensures that multinational practice will remain faithful at least to the enlightened standards of home country morality.

If C is a non-national, that is to say a multinational, corporation, then one may wonder why home country opinion should be a factor in C's decision-making. One reason is that although global companies are multinational in doing business in more than one country, they are uninational in composition and character. They are chartered in a single country, typically have over ninety-five percent of their stock owned by citizens of their home country, and have managements dominated by citizens of their home country. Thus, in an important sense the term 'multinational' is a misnomer. For our purposes it is crucial to acknowledge that the moral foundation of a multinational, i.e., the underlying assumptions of its managers infusing corporate policies with a basic sense of right and wrong, is inextricably linked to the laws and mores of the home country.

Modern textbooks dealing with international business consider cultural relativity to be a powerful factor in executive decision-making. Indeed they often use it to justify practices abroad which, although enhancing corporate profits, would be questionable in the multinational's home country. One prominent text, for example, remarks that "In situations where patterns of dominance-subordination are socially determined, and not a function of demonstrated ability, management should be cautioned about promoting those of inferior social status to positions in which they are expected to supervise those of higher social status."[2] Later, referring to multiracial societies such as South Africa, the same text offers managers some practical advice: ". . . the problem of the multiracial society manifests itself particularly in reference to promotion and pay. An equal pay for equal work policy may not be acceptable to the politically dominant but racial minority group . . ."[3]

Consider two actual instances of the problem at issue:

Charles Pettis. In 1966 Charles Pettis, employee of Brown and Root Overseas, Inc., an American multinational, became resident engineer for one of his company's projects in Peru: a 146 mile, $46 million project to build a highway across the Andes. Pettis soon discovered that Peruvian safety standards were far below those in the United States. The highway design called for cutting channels through mountains in areas where rock formations were unstable. Unless special precautions were taken, slides could occur. Pettis blew the whistle, complaining first to Peruvian government officials and later to U.S. officials. No special precautions were taken, with the result that thirty-one men were killed by slides during the construction of the road. Pettis was fired for his trouble by Brown and Root and had difficulty finding a job with another company.[4]

American bank in Italy. A new American bank in Italy was advised by its Italian attorneys to file a tax return that misstated income and expenses and consequently grossly underestimated actual taxes due. The bank learned, however, that most other Italian companies regarded the practice as standard operating procedure and merely the first move in a complex negotiating process with the Italian Internal Revenue Service. The bank initially refused to file a fallacious return on moral grounds and submitted an 'American style' return instead. But because the resulting tax bill was many times higher than what comparable Italian companies were asked to pay, the bank changed policy in later years to agree with 'Italian style.'[5]

A. THE MORAL POINT OF VIEW

One may well decide that home country standards were mandatory in one of the above cases, but not in the other. One may decide that despite conforming to Peruvian standards, Peruvian safety precautions were unacceptable, while at the same time acknowledging that however inequitable and inefficient Italian tax mores may be, a decision to file 'Italian style' is permissible.

Despite claims to the contrary, one must reject the simple dictum that whenever P violates a moral standard of country A, it is impermissible for C. Arnold Berleant has argued that the principle of equal treatment endorsed by most U.S. citizens requires that U.S. corporations pay workers in less developed countries exactly the same wages paid to U.S. workers in comparable jobs (after appropriate adjustments are made for cost of living levels in the relevant areas).[6] But most observers, including those from the less developed countries, believe this stretches the doctrine of equality too far in a way detrimental to host countries. By arbitrarily establishing U.S. wage levels as the benchmark for fairness one eliminates the role of the international market in establishing salary levels, and this in turn eliminates the incentive U.S. corporations have to hire foreign workers. If U.S. companies felt morally bound to pay Korean workers exactly the wages U.S. workers receive for comparable work, they would not locate in Korea. Perhaps U.S. firms should exceed market rates for foreign labor as a matter of moral principle, but to pay strictly equal rates would freeze less developed countries out of the international labor market.[7] Lacking, then, a simple formula of the sort, 'P is wrong when P violates A's norms,' one seems driven to undertake a more complex analysis of the types and degrees of responsibilities multinationals possess.

The first task is to distinguish between responsibilities that hold as minimum conditions, and ones that exceed the minimum. We are reminded of the distinction, eloquently articulated by Kant, between perfect and imperfect duties. Perfect duties are owed to a specific class of persons under specified conditions, such as the duty to honor promises. They differ from imperfect duties, such as the duty of charity, which, although mandatory, allow considerable discretion as to when, how, and to whom they are fulfilled. The perfect-imperfect distinction, however, is not appropriate for corporations since it is doubtful whether economic entities such as corporations must assume the same imperfect burdens, e.g., of charity, as individual persons.

For purpose of discussing multinationals, then, it is best to recast the distinction into one between 'minimal' and 'enlightened' duties, where a minimal duty is one the persistent failure of which to observe would deprive the corporation of its moral right to exist, i.e., a strictly mandatory duty, and an enlightened duty is one whose fulfillment would be praiseworthy but not mandatory in any sense. In the present context, it is the determination of minimal duties that has priority since in attempting to answer whether P is permissible for C in B, the notion of permissibility must eventually be cashed in terms of minimal standards. Thus, P is not impermissible for C simply because C fails to achieve an ideal vision of corporate conduct; and C's failure to contribute generously to the United Nations is a permissible, if regrettable, act.

Because minimal duties are our target, it is appropriate next to invoke the language of rights, for rights are entitlements that impose minimum demands on the behavior of others.

B. THE APPEAL TO RIGHTS

Theorists commonly analyze the obligations of developed to less developed countries in terms of rights. James Sterba argues that "distant peoples" (e.g., persons in Third World countries) enjoy welfare rights that members of the developed countries are obliged to respect.[8] Welfare rights are defined as rights to whatever is necessary to satisfy "basic needs," and "basic needs," in turn, as needs "which must be satisfied in order not to seriously endanger a person's health and sanity."[9] It follows that multinationals are obliged to avoid workplace hazards that seriously endanger workers' health.

A similar notion is advanced by Henry Shue in his book, *Basic Rights*. The substance of a basic right for Shue is "something the deprivation of which is one standard threat to rights generally."[10] He considers it a "minimal demand" that "no individuals or institutions, including corporations, may ignore the universal duty to avoid depriving persons of their basic rights."[11] Since one's physical security, including safety from exposure to harmful chemicals or pollution, is a condition for one's enjoyment of rights generally, it follows that the right to physical security is a basic right that imposes specific obligations on corporations.

Equally important for our purposes is Shue's application elsewhere of the "no harm" principle to the actions of U.S. multinationals abroad.[12] Associated with Mill and traditional liberalism, the "no harm" principle reflects a rights based approach emphasizing the individuals' right to liberty, allowing maximal liberty to each so long as each inflicts no avoidable harm on others. Shue criticizes as a violation of the no-harm principle a plan by a Colorado based company to export millions of tons of hazardous chemical waste from the U.S. for processing and disposal in the West African nation of Sierra Leone.[13] Using the same principle, he is able to criticize any U.S. asbestos manufacturing corporation which, in order to escape expensive regulations at home, moves its plant to a foreign country with lower standards.[14]

Thus the Shue-Sterba rights based approach recommends itself as a candidate for evaluating multinational conduct. It is irrelevant whether the standards of B comply or fail to comply with home country standards; what is relevant is whether they meet a universal, objective minimum. In the present context, the principal advantage of a rights based approach is to establish a firm limit to appeals made in the name of host country laws and morals— at least when the issue is a clear threat to workers' safety. Clear threats such as in-plant asbestos pollution exceeding levels recommended by independent scientific bodies, are incompatible with employees' rights, especially their right not to be harmed. It is no excuse to cite lenient host country regulations or ill-informed host country public opinion.

But even as a rights oriented approach clarifies a moral bottom line for extreme threats to workers' safety, it leaves obscure not only the issue of less extreme threats, but of harms other than physical injury. The language of rights and harm is sufficiently vague so as to leave shrouded in uncertainty a formidable list of issues crucial to multinationals.

When refined by the traditions of a national legal system, the language of rights achieves great precision. But left to wander among the concepts of general moral theory, the language proves less exact. Granted, the celebrated dangers of asbestos call for recognizing the right to workers' safety no matter how broadly the language of rights is framed. But what are we to say of a less toxic pollutant? Is the level of sulfer-dioxide air pollution we should demand in a struggling nation, say, one with only a few fertilizer plants working overtime to help feed its malnourished population, the same we should demand in Portland, Oregon? Or taking a more obvious case, should the maximal level of thermal pollution generated by a poor nation's electric power plants be the same as West Germany's? Since thermal pollution raises the temperature of a given body of water, it lowers the capacity of the water to hold oxygen and in turn the number of "higher" fish species, e.g., salmon and trout. But whereas the tradeoff between more trout and higher output is rationally made by the West German in favor of the trout, the situation is reverse for the citizen of Chad, Africa. This should not surprise us. It has long been recognized that many rights, e.g., the right to medical care, are dependent for their specification on the level of economic development of the country in question.[15]

Nor is it clear how a general appeal to rights will resolve issues that turn on the interpretation of broad social practices. For example, in the Italian tax case mentioned earlier, the propriety of submitting an "Italian" versus "American" style tax return hinges more on the appraisal of the value of honesty in a complex economic and social system, than on an appeal to inalienable rights.

C. AN ETHICAL ALGORITHM

What is needed, then, is a test for evaluating P that is more comprehensive than a simple appeal to rights. In the end nothing short of a general moral theory working in tandem with an analysis of the foundations of corporate existence is needed. That is, ultimately there is no escape for the multinational executive from merging the ordinary canons of economic decision-making, of profit maximization and market share, with the principles of basic moral theory.[16] But this formidable task, essential as it is, does not preclude the possibility of discovering lower-order moral concepts to clarify the moral intuitions already in use by multinational decision-makers. Apart from the need for general theories of multinational conduct there is need for pragmatic aids to multinational decision-making that bring into relief the ethical implications of views already held. This suggests, then, the possibility of generating an interpretive mechanism, or algorithm, that managers of multinationals could use in determining the implications of their own moral views about cases of the form, "Is P permissible for C when P is acceptable in B but not in A?"

The first step in generating such an ethical algorithm is to isolate distinct senses in which B's norms may conflict with the norms of A. Now, if P is morally and/or legally permitted in B, but not in A then either:

(1) The moral reasons underlying B's view that P is permissible refer to B's relative level of economic development; or

(2) The moral reasons underlying B's view that P is permissible are independent of B's relative level of economic development.

Let us call the conflict of norms described in (1) a 'type #1' conflict. In such a conflict, an African country that permits slightly higher levels of thermal pollution from electric power generating plants, or a lower minimum wage, than those prescribed in European countries would do so not because higher standards would be undesirable *per se,* but because its level of economic development requires an ordering of priorities. In the future when it succeeds in matching European economic achievements, it may well implement the higher standards.

Let us call the conflict of norms described in (2) a 'type #2' conflict. In such cases levels of economic development play no role. For example, low level institutional nepotism, common in many underdeveloped countries, is justified not on economic grounds, but on the basis of clan and family loyalty. Presumably the same loyalties should be operative even after the country has risen to economic success—as the nepotism prevalent in Saudi Arabia would indicate. The Italian tax case also reflects an Italian cultural style with a penchant for personal negotiation and an unwillingness to formalize transactions, more than a strategy based on level of economical development.

When the conflicts of norms occur for reasons other than relative economic development (type #2), then the possibility is increased that there exists what Richard Brandt has called an "ultimate ethical disagreement." An ultimate disagreement occurs when two cultures are able to consider the same set of facts surrounding a moral issue while disagreeing on the moral issue itself. An ultimate disagreement is less likely in a type #1 cases since after suitable reflection about priorities imposed by differing economic circumstance, the members of *A* may come to agree that *given* that facts of *B*'s level of economic development, *P* is permissible. On the other hand, a type #2 dispute about what Westerners call "nepotism" will continue even after economic variables are discounted.[17]

The status of the conflict of norms between *A* and *B*, i.e., whether it is of type #1 or #2, does not fix the truth value of *B*'s claim that *P* is permissible. *P* may or may not be permissible whether the conflict is of type #1 or #2. This, however, is not to say that the truth value of *B*'s claim is independent of the conflict's type status, for a different test will be required to determine whether *P* is permissible when the conflict is of type #1 rather than type #2. In a type #1 dispute, the following formula is appropriate:

> *P* is permissible if and only if the members of *A* would, under conditions of economic development relevantly similar to those of *B*, regard *P* as permissible.

Under this test, excessive levels of asbestos pollution would almost certainly not be tolerated by the members of *A* under relevantly similar economic conditions, whereas higher levels of thermal pollution would be. The test, happily, explains and confirms our initial moral intuitions.

Yet, when as in type #2 conflicts the dispute between *A* and *B* depends upon a fundamental difference of perspective, the step to equalize hypothetically the levels of economic development is useless. A different test is needed. In type #2 conflicts the opposing evils of ethnocentricism and ethical relativism must be avoided. A multinational must forego the temptation to remake all societies in the image of its home society, while at the same time rejecting a relativism that conveniently forgets ethics when the payoff is sufficient. Thus, the task is to tolerate cultural diversity while drawing the line at moral recklessness.

Since in type #2 cases *P* is in conflict with an embedded norm of *A*, one should first ask whether *P* is necessary to business in *B*, for if not, the solution clearly is to adopt some other practice that is permissible from the standpoint of *A*. If petty bribery of public officials is unnecessary for the business of the Cummins Engine Company in India, then the company is obliged to abandon such bribery. If, on the other hand, *P* proves necessary for business, one must next ask whether *P* consitutes a direct violation of a basic human right. Here the notion of a right, specifying a minimum below which corporate conduct should not fall, has special application. If Polaroid, an American company, confronts South African laws that mandate systematic discrimination against nonwhites, then Polaroid must refuse to comply with the laws. Thus, in type #2 cases, *P* would be permissible if and only if the answer to both of the following questions is no.

(a) Is it possible to conduct business successfully in *B* without undertaking *P*?

(b) Is *P* a clear violation of a basic human right?

What sorts of practice might pass both conditions a and b? Consider the practice of low-level bribery of public officials in some under-developed nations. In some South American countries, for example, it is impossible for any company, foreign or national, to move goods through customs without paying low-level officials a few dollars. Indeed, the salaries of such officials are sufficiently low that one suspects they are set with the prevalence of the practice in mind. The payments are relatively small, uniformly assessed, and accepted as standard practice by the surrounding culture. Here, the practice of petty bribery would pass the type #2 test and, barring other moral factors, would be permissible.

A further condition, however, should be placed on multinationals undertaking *P* in type #2 contexts. The companies should be willing to speak out against, and be willing to work for, change of *P*. Even if petty bribery or low-level nepotism passes the preceding tests, it may conflict with an embedded norm of country *A*, and as a representative of *A*'s culture, the company is obliged to take a stand. This would be true even for issues related exclusively to financial practice, such as the Italian tax case. If the practice of underestimating taxes due is (1) accepted in *B*, (2) necessary for successful business, and (3) does not violate any basic human rights, then it satisfies the necessary conditions of permissibility. Yet insofar as it violates a norm accepted by *A*, *C* should make its disapproval of the practice known.

To sum up, then, two complementary tests have been proposed for determining the ultimate permissibility of *P*. If *P* occurs in a type #1 context, then *P* is not permissible if:

> The members of *A* would not, under conditions of economic development relevantly similar to those of *B*, regard *P* as permissible.

If *P* occurs in a type #2 context, then *P* is not permissible if either:

(1) It is possible to conduct business successfully in *B* without undertaking *P*, or

(2) *P* is a direct violation of a basic human right.

Notice that the type #1 criterion is not reducible to the type #2 criterion. In order for the two criteria to have equivalent outcomes, four propositions would need to be true: (1) If *P* passes #1, it passes #2; (2) if *P* fails #1, it fails #2; (3) if *P* passes #2, it passes #1; and (4) if *P* fails #2, it fails #1. But none of these propositions is true. The possibility matrix below lists in rows *A* and *B* the only combinations of outcomes that are possible on the assumption that the two criteria are equivalent. But they are not equivalent because the combinations of outcomes in *C* and *D* are also possible. To illustrate, *P* may pass #2 and fail #1; for example, the practice of petty bribery may be necessary for business, may not violate basic human rights, but may nonetheless be unacceptable in A under hypothetically lowered levels of economic development; similarly, the practice of allowing a significant amount of water pollution may be necessary for business, may not violate basic rights, yet may be hypothetically unacceptable in A. Or, P may fail #2 and pass #1; for example, the practice of serving alcohol at executive dinners in a strongly Moslem country may not be necessary for business in B (and thus impermissible by criteria #2) while being thoroughly acceptable to the members of A under hypothetically lowered economic conditions. It follows, then, that the two tests are not mutually reducible. This underscores the importance of the preliminary step of classifying a given case under either type #1 or type #2. The prior act of classification explains, moreover, why not all cases in row C or in row D will have the same moral outcome. Consider, for example, the two Fail-Pass cases from row C mentioned above, i.e., the cases of water pollution and petty bribery. If classified as a type #1 case, the water pollution would *not* be permissible, while petty bribery, if classified as a type #2 case, *would* be.

	Criterion #1	Criterion #2	
A	Fail	Fail	
			equivalent outcomes
B	Pass	Pass	

	Criterion #1	Criterion #2	
C	Fail	Pass	
			non-equivalent outcomes
D	Pass	Fail	

D. SOME PRACTICAL CONSIDERATIONS AND OBJECTIONS

The algorithm does not obviate the need for multinational managers to appeal to moral concepts both more general and specific than the algorithm itself. It is not intended as a substitute for a general theory of morality or even an interpretation of the basic responsibilities of multinationals. Its power lies in its ability to tease out implications of the moral presuppositions of a manager's acceptance of 'home' morality and in this sense to serve as a clarificatory device for multinational decision-making. But insofar as the context of a given conflict of norms categorizes it as a type #1 rather than type #2 conflict, the algorithm makes no appeal to a universal concept of morality (as the appeal to basic human rights does in type #2 cases) save for the purported universality of the ethics endorsed by culture *A*. This means that the force of the algorithm is relativized slightly in the direction of a single society. When *A*'s morality is wrong or confused, the algorithm can reflect this ethnocentricity, leading either to a mild paternalism or to the imposition of parochial standards. For example, *A*'s oversensitivity to aesthetic features of the environment may lead it to reject a given level of thermal pollution even under hypothetically lowered economic circumstances, thus yielding a paternalistic refusal to allow such levels in *B*, despite *B*'s acceptance of the higher levels and *B*'s belief that tolerating such levels is necessary for stimulating economic development. Or, *A*'s mistaken belief that the practice of hiring twelve-year-olds for full-time, permanent work, although happily unnecessary at its relatively high level of economic development, would be acceptable and economically necessary at a level of economic development relevantly similar to *B*'s, might lead it both to tolerate and undertake the practice in *B*.

Nor is the algorithm a substitute for more specific guides to conduct such as the numerous codes of ethics now appearing on the international scene. A need exists for topic-specific and industry-specific codes that embody detailed safeguards against self-serving interpretations. Consider the Sullivan Standards, designed by the black American minister, Leon Sullivan, drafted for the purpose of ensuring non-racist practices by U.S. multinationals operating in South Africa. As a result of a lengthy lobbying campaign by U.S. activists, the Sullivan principles are now endorsed and followed by almost one third of all American multinationals with South African subsidiaries. Among other things, companies complying with the Sullivan principles must:

Remove all race designation signs.

Support the elimination of discrimination against the rights of blacks to form or belong to government registered unions.

Determine whether upgrading of personnel and/or jobs in the lower echelons is needed (and take appropriate steps).[18]

A variety of similar codes are either operative or in the process of development, e.g., the European Economic Community's Vredeling Proposal on labor-management consultations; the United Nations' Code of Conduct for Transnational Corporations and its International Standards of Accounting and Reporting; the World Health Organizations's Code on Pharmaceuticals and Tobacco; the World Intellectual Property Organization's Revision of the Paris Convention for the Protection of Industrial Patents and Trademarks; the International Chamber of Commerce's Rules of Conduct to Combat Extortion and Bribery; and the World Health Organization's Infant Formula Code against advertising of breast-milk substitutes.[19]

Despite these limitations, the algorithm has important applications in countering the well documented tendency of multinationals to mask immoral practices in the rhetoric of 'tolerance' and 'cultural relativity.' Utilizing it, no multinational manager can naively suggest that asbestos standards in Chile are permissible because they are accepted there. Nor can he infer that the standards are acceptable on the grounds that the Chilean economy is, relative to his home country, underdeveloped. A surprising amount of moral blindness occurs not because people's fundamental moral views are confused, but because their cognitive application of those views to novel situations is misguided.

What guarantees that either multinationals or prospective whistleblowers possess the knowledge or objectivity to apply the algorithm fairly? As Richard Barnet quips, "On the 56th floor of a Manhatten skyscraper, the level of self-protective ignorance about what the company may be doing in Colombia or Mexico is high."[20] Can Exxon or Johns Manville be trusted to have a sufficiently sophisticated sense of 'human rights,' or to weigh dispassionately the hypothetical attitudes of their fellow countrymen under conditions of 'relevantly similar economic development'? My answer to this is 'probably not,' at least given the present character of the decision-making procedures in most global corporations. I would add, however, that this problem is a contingent and practical one. It is no more a theoretical flaw of the proposed algorithm that it may be conveniently misunderstood by a given multinational, than it is of Rawl's theory that it may be conveniently misunderstood by a trickle-down capitalist.

What would need to change in order for multinationals to make use of the algorithm? At a minimum they would need to enhance the sophistication of their decision-making mechanisms. They would need to alter established patterns of information flow and collection in order to accommodate moral information. The already complex parameters of corporate decision-making would become more so. They would need to introduce alongside analyses of the bottom line analyses of historical tendencies, nutrition, rights, and demography. And they would need to introduce a new class of employee to provide expertise in these areas. However unlikely such changes are, I believe they are within the realm of possibility. Multinationals, the organizations capable of colonizing our international future, are also capable of looking beyond their national borders and applying—at a minimum—the same moral principles they accept at home.

NOTES

1. An example of disparity in wages between Mexican and U.S. workers is documented in the case study, "Twin-Plants and Corporate Responsibilites," by John H. Haddox, in *Profits and Responsibility,* Patricia Werhane and Kendall D'Andrade, eds. (New York: Random House, 1985).

2. Richard D. Robinson, *International Business Management: A Guide to Decision Making,* 2d ed. (Hinsdale, Ill.: The Dryden Press, 1978), p. 241.

3. Robinson, p. 241.

4. Charles Peters and Taylor Branch, *Blowing the Whistle: Dissent in the Public Interest* (New York: Praeger Publishers, 1972), pp. 182–85.

5. Arthur Kelly, 'Italian Bank Mores,' in *Case-Studies in Business Ethics,* ed. T. Donaldson (Englewood Cliffs, N.J.: Prentice-Hall, Inc., 1984).

6. Arnold Berleant, "Multinationals and the Problem of Ethical Consistency," *Journal of Business Ethics* 3 (August 1982): 185–95.

7. One can construct an argument attempting to show that insulating the economies of the less developed countries would be advantageous to the less developed countries in the long run. But whether correct or not, such an argument is independent of the present issue, for it is independent of the claim that if *P* violates the norms of *A*, then *P* is impermissible.

8. James Sterba, "The Welfare Rights of Distant Peoples and Future Generations: Moral Side Constraints on Social Policy," in *Social Theory and Practice* 7 (Spring 1981), p. 110.

9. Sterba, "Hazards," p. 111.

10. Henry Shue, *Basic Rights, Subsistence, Affluence, and U.S. Foreign Policy* (Princeton, N.J.: Princeton University Press, 1981), p. 34.

11. Shue, *Basic Rights,* p. 170.

12. Henry Shue, "Exporting Hazards," *Ethics* 91 (July 1981): 579–606.

13. Shue, "Hazards," pp. 579–80.

14. Considering a possible escape from the principle, Shue considers whether inflicting harm is acceptable in the event overall benefits outweigh the costs. Hence, increased safety risks under reduced asbestos standards might be acceptable insofar as the economic benefits to the country outweighed the costs. The problem, as Shue correctly notes, is that this approach fails to distinguish between the no-harm principle and a naive greatest happiness principle. Even classical defenders of the no-harm principle were unwilling to accept a simple-minded utilitarianism that sacrificed individual justice on the altar of maximal happiness. Even classical utilitarians did not construe their greatest happiness principle to be a "hunting license." (Shue, "Hazards," pp. 592–93.

Still another escape might be by way of appealing to the rigors of international economic competition. That is, is it not unreasonable to expect firms to place themselves at a competitive disadvantage by installing expensive safety equipment in a market where other firms are brutally cost conscious? Such policies, argue critics, could trigger economic suicide. The obligation not to harm, in turn, properly belongs to the government of the host country. Here, too, Shue's rejoinder is on-target. He notes first that the existence of an obligation by one party does not cancel its burden on another party; hence, even if the host country's government does have an obligation to protect its citizens from dangerous workplace conditions, its duty does not cancel that of the corporation. (Shue, "Hazards," p. 600.) Second, governments of poor countries are themselves forced to compete for scarce foreign capital by weakening their laws and regulations, with the result that any "competitive disadvantage" excuse offered on behalf of the corporation would also apply to the government. (Shue, "Hazards," p. 601.)

15. Sterba himself reflects this consensus when he remarks that for rights ". . . an acceptable minimum should vary over time and between societies at least to some degree." (Sterba, "Distant Peoples," p. 112.)

16. For the purpose of analyzing the moral foundations of corporate behavior, I prefer a social contract theory, one that interprets a hypothetical contract between society and productive organizations, and which I have argued for in my book, *Corporations and Morality,* Thomas Donaldson, *Corporations and Morality* (Englewood Cliffs, N.J.: Prentice-Hall, 1982); see especially Chapter 3. There I argue that corporations are artifacts; that they are in part the products of our moral and legal imagination. As such, they are to be molded in the image of our collective rights and societal ambitions. Corporations, as all productive organizations, require from society both recognition as single agents, and the authority to own or use land and natural

resources, and to hire employees. In return for this, society may expect that productive organizations will, all other things being equal, enhance the general interests of consumers and employees. Society may reasonably expect that in doing so corporations honor existing rights and limit their activities to accord with the bounds of justice. This is as true for multinationals as it is for national corporations.

17. Richard Brandt, "Cultural Relativism," in *Ethical Issues in Business,* 2d ed. T. Donaldson and P. Werhane, eds. (Englewood Cliffs, N.J.: Prentice-Hall, Inc., 1983).

18. See "Dresser Industries and South Africa," by Patricia Mintz and Kirk O. Hanson, in *Case Studies in Business Ethics,* Thomas Donaldson, ed. (Englewood Cliffs, N.J.: Prentice-Hall, 1984).

19. For a concise and comprehensive account of the various codes of conduct for international business now under consideration, see "Codes of Conduct: Worry over New Restraints on Multinationals," *Chemical Week* (July 15, 1981): 48–52.

20. Richard J. Barnet and Ronald Muller, *Global Reach: The Power of Multinational Corporations* (New York: Simon and Schuster, 1974), p. 185.

INTERNATIONAL MARKETING

Case Study

Selling the Lockheed TriStar

In 1966, Lockheed Corporation earned $5.29 per share, had a net worth of $320 million, and had $140 million in debt. Its stock sold at a high of $74 per share. Earnings then declined for four years, and in 1970 the firm lost $7.60 per share, saw its net worth reduced to $266 million, its debt increase to $761 million, and its stock reach a low of $7 per share. By mid-1971, Lockheed was near bankruptcy. The crisis was primarily caused by cost overruns on major defense projects, which cost the firm $480 million. In addition, in early 1969 a test model of Lockheed's armed helicopter, the Cheyenne, crashed during a test flight, and shortly thereafter the government cancelled the Cheyenne contract, charging default. Lockheed had to write off $132 million in development costs. In late 1969, Congress and the press began objecting to Lockheed's development costs for the C5A Galaxy transport, and the Air Force reduced its order from 115 units to 81.

Lockheed was also having difficulties on the nongovernmental side of its business. The company began developing the L-1011, or "TriStar," in 1967 to compete with Boeing's 747 and McDonnell-Douglas's DC-10. Since the DC-10 was based on earlier models, and the TriStar was a new plane, McDonnell-Douglas completed its development work earlier, and thereby gained the initial advantage in securing orders. Lockheed did secure early 1968 orders from TWA, Delta, and Eastern Airlines, but was hindered by the financial difficulties of its engine maker, Rolls-Royce, which itself was on the verge of bankruptcy throughout 1969-70. Early in 1971, Rolls-Royce went into receivership and announced that it would be unable to produce engines for the TriStar. After two months of negotiations the British government decided to continue production of Rolls-Royce engines for the TriStar, but at a sharply escalated price. It also demanded that the U.S. government provide some guarantee of Lockheed's financial viability. President Nixon then proposed a U.S. government loan guarantee of $250 million for Lockheed. The bill passed the U.S. House by three votes and the Senate by one vote in mid-1971.

By mid-1972, McDonnell-Douglas had 168 firm orders for the DC-10 and had delivered 43 planes. Lockheed had delivered 7 planes and had 100 firm orders. Lockheed claimed it could recoup development costs by selling 275 planes, but knowledgeable industry sources put the figure at 370. The variation was due to the fact that Lockheed did not break out development costs. Outside analysts concurred that Lockheed's inventory account included over $400 million in capitalized development costs for the TriStar, i.e., not really assets, but $400 million in deferred costs. If these figures were correct, and Lockheed had to write off its deferred development costs, the firm would have had negative net worth. In that case, the betting was that Lockheed would be forced into receivership in spite of its U.S. government loan guarantee. Lockheed's problems were compounded by the fact that by mid-1972 most of the U.S. market had been sold on either the TriStar or the DC-10, and furthermore, the DC-10 had already captured most of the European market. These facts dictated an all-out drive to secure sales in the largest market then untapped—Japan.

Lockheed recognized the importance of the Japanese market early on; in fact, in 1970, Lockheed's president, A. Carl Kotchian, said, "There is no way left but to win in the biggest market, Japan." Kotchian himself had experience in serving Lockheed in Japan. He had been there in 1961, shortly after Lockheed sold its F-104 fighter to the Japanese government. Kotchian returned in 1968 to scout prospects for selling the TriStar. Between 1968 and 1972 he returned ten times to work for sales of the TriStar. In Japan, Lockheed was officially represented by Marubeni Corporation, which handled most of the contacts with Japan's airline officials and Japanese politicians. Lockheed also had a secret agent, Yoshio Kodama, who had worked for the company since the late 1950s, and who had been helpful in obtaining the F-104 contract for Lockheed in 1960. Kodama was an ultranationalist who had been sentenced to jail both before World War II and during the American occupation, but who amassed a fortune during the war. Upon his release from prison in 1948, he was probably the wealthiest man in Japan. Kodama helped finance the birth of Japan's dominant Liberal party, and was a close, active supporter of most of Japan's postwar prime ministers.

On August 19, 1972, Kotchian flew to Tokyo to "devote all my energy and time to the sales campaign in Japan." On August 22, Toshiharu Okubu, a Marubeni representative, informed Kotchian that, at the latter's request, Marubeni officials would be meeting with Japanese Prime Minister Kakuei Tanaka on the next day. Okubu suggested that Kotchian make a pledge to pay $1.7 million for the favor. Kotchian said later that although the request did not "appall and outrage" him, it did "astonish" him that the political connection was so explicit. For, in response to the question of how the money was to be delivered by Marubeni, Okubu said a Marubeni representative was "very close to Mr. Enomoto, the prime minister's secretary." Kotchian said the exchange left him with "no doubt that the money was going to the office of Japan's prime minister." Later, on the same day, Kotchian consulted with Kodama about enlisting the aid of another important intimate of Tanaka, and Kodama said, "In order to include Mr. Osano, we need an extra $1.7 million." This amount was in addition to the $1.7 million that allegedly went to Tanaka, and the $1.8 that had already been pledged to Kodama.

On August 23, Hiro Hiyama, president of Marubeni, and Okubu met with Tanaka. Hiyama is alleged to have said that if Tanaka would help Lockheed he would be given $1.6 million. Tanaka replied, "O.K., O.K." On August 29 Tanaka called the president of All Nippon Airways (ANA) and asked him if he had decided to buy the TriStar. To the somewhat vague response, Tanaka said, "It will be convenient if you decide."

On August 31, Tanaka met with President Nixon in Hawaii. Tanaka had only been in office for two months, so the meeting was exploratory. But the subject of aircraft was discussed. At Nixon's request Tanaka agreed to purchase $720 million of products to reduce America's trade imbalance with Japan, and that was to include $320 million worth of commercial aircraft. Whether Lockheed was explicitly discussed is unknown, but Tanaka, on his return to Japan, claimed that Nixon spoke in favor of Lockheed. And Kotchian allowed that he encouraged the "idea of the Lockheed company being closely supported by the Nixon administration." In mid-September British Prime Minister Edward Heath met with Tanaka, and the subject included support for Rolls-Royce on the basis of Britain's trade imbalance with Japan.

During September and October, Kotchian, Kodama, and Marubeni's officials held a series of meetings with Japanese government officials and top managers of Japanese airlines to solidify Lockheed's case. On October 29, Kotchian received a call from Okubu, the Marubeni representative, suggesting that if Lockheed, through Marubeni, paid $300 thousand to the president of All Nippon Airways and a total of $100 thousand to six politicians, the airline would purchase the TriStar. Later, Kotchian said:

> If some third party had heard this conversation, he could ask why I responded to this request for secret payments. However, I must admit that it was extremely persuasive and attractive at that time to have someone come up to me and confidently tell me, "If you do this, you will surely get ANA's order in twenty-four hours." What businessman who is dealing with commercial and trade matters could decline a request for certain amounts of money when that money would enable him to get the contract? For someone like myself who had been struggling against plots and severe competition for over two months, it was almost impossible to dismiss this opportunity.

On October 30, the payments were made and that same afternoon it was announced that All Nippon Airways would purchase six TriStars and take an option on more.

When the Watergate scandal engulfed the Nixon administration, many corporations were discovered to have made illegal contributions to Nixon's campaign. Although Lockheed did not make such contributions, its foreign payoffs were revealed in the subsequent investigation. In April, 1976, Lockheed consented, without acknowledging or denying, to a Securities and Exchange Commission (SEC) complaint that it made at least $25 million in secret payments to foreign government officials since 1968. It also admitted to payments in excess of $200 million since 1970 to "various consultants, commission agents and others." The SEC also charged that Lockheed kept secret funds not recorded on the books and records of Lockheed, and that the monies were disbursed "without adequate records and controls . . . and a portion of these funds were used for payments to certain foreign government officials." It was revealed that Lockheed's payments in Japan totaled $12.6 million. Kotchian estimated that $2.8 million went to high-ranking Japanese government officials. Kodama was reported to have received $7 million for his own use and disbursement to government officials. In defense of the payments, Kotchian offered several arguments:

> The *first* is that the Lockheed payments in Japan, totaling about $12 million, were worthwhile from Lockheed's standpoint, since they amounted to less than 3 percent of the expected sum of about $430 million that we would receive from ANA for 21 TriStars. Further, as I've noted, such disbursements *did not violate American laws.* I should also like to stress that my decision to make such payments stemmed from my judgment that the TriStar payments to ANA would provide Lockheed workers with jobs and thus redound to the benefit of their communities, and stockholders of the corporation.

> *Secondly,* I should like to emphasize that the payments to the so-called "high Japanese government officials" were all requested by Okubu and *were not brought up from my side.* When he told me "five hundred million yen is necessary for such sales," from a purely ethical and moral standpoint I would have declined such a request. However, in that case, I would most certainly have sacrificed commercial success.

> *Finally,* I want to make it clear that I never discussed money matters with Japanese politicians, government officials, or airline officials.

> . . . Much has been made in press accounts in both Japan and the United States of secret agents and secret channels for sales efforts. Of course these consultations with advisers were secret: competitors do not tell each other their strategy or even their sales targets.

> And if Lockheed had not remained competitive by the rules of the game as then played, we would not have sold the TriStar and would not have provided work for tens of thousands of our employees or contributed to the future of the corporation. Nor would ANA have had the services of this excellent airplane.

> From my experience in international sales, I knew that if we wanted our product to have a chance to win on its own merits, we had to follow the functioning system. If we wanted our product to have a chance, we

understood that we would have to pay, or pledge to pay, substantial sums of money in addition to the contractual sales commissions. We never *sought* to make these extra payments. We would have preferred not to have the additional expenses for the sale. But, always, they were recommended by those whose experience and judgment we trusted and whose recommendations we therefore followed.

In Senate hearings Lockheed was not apologetic. It claimed the payments "were made with the knowledge of management and management believes they were necessary . . . and consistent with practices engaged in by numerous other companies abroad, including many of its competitors." The company also argued that its practices were consistent with business customs in many countries. When questioned as to whether such payments really were necessary, Lockheed's Chairman, Daniel Haughton, said, "If payments are made and you get the contract, it is good evidence that you needed to make the payments." Other American aerospace experts disagreed; one said, "They overpaid. . . . They could have gotten by for maybe $100 thousand. There was no need to pay a million bucks to anyone. It reflects their lack of expertise."

Haughton also refused to classify the payments as bribes, preferring instead to call them "kickbacks," presumably because bribes to government officials are illegal in most countries, whereas the legal status of kickbacks is less clear. At the time of the Japanese payments, however, the bribery of a foreign government official by a U.S. business was not illegal in the U.S. When it was revealed that Lockheed paid $1 million to a "high Dutch official" (later identified as Prince Bernhard, husband of Queen Juliana), Kotchian allowed that he knew "absolutely" that Bernhard received the money, but said it was a gift, not a bribe. Kotchian said the gift was made to assist in the sale of aircraft, but was paid after an initial idea of presenting Bernhard with the gift of a private aircraft was dropped because of difficulties in transferring title. When pressed by Senator Church as to whether the payoff really was a bribe, Kotchian said, "It brought a climate of goodwill. I consider it more as a gift, but I don't want to quibble."

Some support for Lockheed's position is based on a 1976 Italian court case in which government officials were charged with extorting money from Lockheed. The charges alleged that the Italian Air Force Chief of Staff "abused his position . . . and with others induced the Lockheed company to pay sums of money not less than one billion lire." Several observers saw this as placing Lockheed in the position of a victim rather than a willing participant in corruption.

Reaction to the Lockheed disclosures was mixed. Edwin Reischauer, former U.S. ambassador to Japan (1961–66), said: "We should devise legislation to prevent bribery of government officials abroad. In the Lockheed case the stupidities committed have been almost beyond belief. In a country not given to official bribery, in competition with American, not foreign, companies, Lockheed officials allegedly paid exorbitant bribes through Yoshio Kodama, a somewhat disreputable right-wing extremist, whose involvement in any cause is likely to do more harm than good." John Bierwirth, Grumman's chairman, argued that the prosecution of bribery abroad should be left to the country where the bribe occurred: "Most foreign governments don't want the U.S. to enact laws that define what is a crime in their countries. The thing that makes a bribe so bad is that it's a payment to get someone to take a less desirable product, and the people who are penalized are the people who use the less desirable product." A poll by the prestigious Conference Board showed that half of seventy-three business leaders surveyed said that they owed it to their companies to make payoffs in countries where such practices were accepted. Kenneth Keys, consultant to multinational firms, said: "Competition doesn't wholly explain the situation. In many areas of the world a market system doesn't exist; commerce is conducted by social connections that are lubricated by tribute. Even in Japan there are a variety of arrangements, such as, *On,* which requires that all favors be repaid, often in cash. Such payments are part of social convention, and failure to make them means loss of face." Senator Church said, "Lockheed's assertion that what it did is the industry norm and that there is nothing wrong with its actions underscores the need for congressional action to end these practices by American multinationals, especially those in the arms industry." Melvin Ness, corporate consultant, said: "You can pass a law banning bribes. But you have to deal with agents in many countries to do any business. The agent's fee is a legitimate tax-deductible business expense. How are you going to know whether part of that fee is passed on as a bribe? You can put a cap on an agent's fee, but the British, French, and Japanese won't do it, so U.S. firms won't be doing much business abroad."

The ramifications of the Lockheed case were widespread. In early 1976, Kotchian and Haughton were forced to resign. Tanaka was forced to resign and was arrested, along with several other Japanese officials, in 1974. In 1977, the U.S. passed the Foreign Corrupt Practices Act, which makes it a crime for U.S. corporations to offer or provide payments to foreign government officials for the purpose of securing or retaining business. Finally, in 1979, Lockheed pleaded guilty to hiding the Japanese payments from the U.S. government by falsely charging them off as marketing costs. The case was based on section 162C of the IRS Code stating that a deduction is impermissible for "any payment made, directly or indirectly, to any official or employee of any government if the payment constitutes an illegal bribe or kickback." Lockheed was found guilty of four counts of fraud and four counts of making misleading statements to the U.S. government. Kotchian, Haughton, and other Lockheed officials, were not indicted.

For Discussion

Carefully explain the differences between: bribery, kickbacks, and extortion, commissions, gifts, and agents' fees. How should Lockheed's payments be classified? Why? Do you believe Lockheed's payments in selling the TriStar were morally justified? Why or why not?

SOURCES

"Lockheed Digs Itself Out of a Hole," *Business Week,* January 29, 1972, pp. 72–74; "Lockheed Wins an L-1011 Lift," *Business Week,* November 4, 1972, pp. 24–25; "Who Will Save Lockheed?" *Forbes,* July 1, 1973, pp. 15–16; "Lockheed's Defiance: A Right to Bribe?" *Time,* August 18, 1975, pp. 66–67; "Show-and-Tell Time," *Newsweek,* August 18, 1975, p. 63; "I Prefer Not to Answer," *Newsweek,* September 8, 1975, p. 54; "Rules for Lockheed," *Time,* September 8, 1975, p. 60; "The Big Payoff," *Time,* February 23, 1976, pp. 28–36; "Payoffs: The Growing Scandal," *Newsweek,* February 23, 1976, pp. 26–33; "Extortion Alleged in Italy Lockheed Case," *Aviation Week and Space Technology,* March 29, 1976, pp. 14–15; "The Unfolding of a Tortuous Affair," *Fortune,* March, 1976, pp. 27–28; "Secret Payment Complaint Consented to by Lockheed," *Aviation Week and Space Technology,* April 19, 1976, p. 21; Edwin Reischauer, "The Lessons of the Lockheed Scandal," *Newsweek,* May 10, 1976, pp. 20–21; A. Carl Kotchian, "The Payoff," *Saturday Review* 4, no. 20 (July 9, 1977): 7–12; Robert Shaplen, "Annals of Crime: The Lockheed Incident," *New Yorker* 53 (January 23, 1978): 48–80 (January 30, 1978): 74–91; "Lockheed Pleads Guilty to Making Secret Payoffs," *San Francisco Chronicle,* June 2, 1979.

Mark Pastin
Michael Hooker

Ethics and the Foreign Corrupt Practices Act

Not long ago it was feared that as a fallout of Watergate, government officials would be hamstrung by artificially inflated moral standards. Recent events, however, suggest that the scapegoat of post-Watergate morality may have become American business rather than government officials.

One aspect of the recent attention paid to corporate morality is the controversy surrounding payments made by American corporations to foreign officials for the purpose of securing business abroad. Like any law or system of laws, the Foreign Corrupt Practices Act (FCPA), designed to control or eliminate such payments, should be grounded in morality, and should therefore be judged from an ethical perspective. Unfortunately, neither the law nor the question of its repeal has been adequately addressed from that perspective.

HISTORY OF THE FCPA

On December 20, 1977, President Carter signed into law S.305, the Foreign Corrupt Practices Act (FCPA), which makes it a crime for American corporations to offer or provide payments to officials of foreign governments for the purpose of obtaining or retaining business. The FCPA also establishes record keeping requirements for publicly held corporations to make it diffi-

From *Business Horizons* vol. 23, no. 6 (December 1980): 43–47. Copyright, 1980, by the Foundation for the School of Business at Indiana University. Reprinted by permission.

cult to conceal political payments proscribed by the Act. Violators of the FCPA, both corporations and managers, face severe penalties. A company may be fined up to $1 million, while its officers who directly participated in violations of the Act or had reason to know of such violations, face up to five years in prison and/or $10,000 in fines. The Act also prohibits corporations from indemnifying fines imposed on their directors, officers, employees, or agents. The Act does not prohibit "grease" payments to foreign government employees whose duties are primarily ministerial or clerical, since such payments are sometimes required to persuade the recipients to perform their normal duties.

At the time of this writing, the precise consequences of the FCPA for American business are unclear, mainly because of confusion surrounding the government's enforcement intentions. Vigorous objections have been raised against the Act by corporate attorneys and recently by a few government officials. Among the latter is Frank A. Weil, former Assistant Secretary of Commerce, who has stated, "The questionable payments problem may turn out to be one of the most serious impediments to doing business in the rest of the world."[1]

The potentially severe economic impact of the FCPA was highlighted by the fall 1978 report of the Export Disincentives Task Force, which was created by the White House to recommend ways of improving our balance of trade. The Task Force identified the FCPA as contributing significantly to economic and political losses in the United States. Economic losses come from constricting the ability of American corporations to do business abroad, and political losses come from the creation of a holier-than-thou image.

The Task Force made three recommendations in regard to the FCPA:

- The Justice Department should issue guidelines on its enforcement policies and establish procedures by which corporations could get advance government reaction to anticipated payments to foreign officials.

- The FCPA should be amended to remove enforcement from the SEC, which now shares enforcement responsibility with the Department of Justice.

- The administration should periodically report to Congress and the public on export losses caused by the FCPA.

In response to the Task Force's report, the Justice Department, over SEC objections, drew up guidelines to enable corporations to check any proposed action possibly in violation of the FCPA. In response to such an inquiry, the Justice Department would inform the corporation of its enforcement intentions. The purpose of such an arrangement is in part to circumvent the intent of the law. As of this writing, the SEC appears to have been successful in blocking publication of the guidelines, although Justice recently reaffirmed its intention to publish guidelines. Being more responsive to political winds, Justice may be less inclined than the SEC to rigidly enforce the Act.

Particular concern has been expressed about the way in which bookkeeping requirements of the Act will be enforced by the SEC. The Act requires that company records will "accurately and fairly reflect the transactions and dispositions of the assets of the issuer." What is at question is the interpretation the SEC will give to the requirement and the degree of accuracy and detail it will demand. The SEC's post-Watergate behavior suggests that it will be rigid in requiring the disclosure of all information that bears on financial relationships between the company and any foreign or domestic public official. This level of accountability in record keeping, to which auditors and corporate attorneys have strongly objected, goes far beyond previous SEC requirements that records display only facts material to the financial position of the company.

Since the potential consequences of the FCPA for American businesses and business managers are very serious, it is important that the Act have a rationale capable of bearing close scrutiny. In looking at the foundation of the FCPA, it should be noted that its passage followed in the wake of intense newspaper coverage of the financial dealings of corporations. Such media attention was engendered by the dramatic disclosure of corporate slush funds during the Watergate hearings and by a voluntary disclosure program established shortly thereafter by the SEC. As a result of the SEC program, more than 400 corporations, including 117 of the Fortune 500, admitted to making more than $300 million in foreign political payments in less than ten years.

Throughout the period of media coverage leading up to passage of the FCPA, and especially during the hearings on the Act, there was in all public discussions of the issue a tone of righteous moral indignation at the idea of American companies making foreign political payments. Such payments were ubiquitously termed "bribes," although many of these could more accurately be called extortions, while others were more akin to brokers' fees or sales commissions.

American business can be faulted for its reluctance during this period to bring to public attention the fact that in a very large number of countries, payments to foreign officials are virtually required for doing business. Part of that reluctance, no doubt, comes from the awkwardly difficult position of attempting to excuse bribery or something closely resembling it. There is a popular abhorrence in this country of bribery directed at domestic government officials, and that abhorrence transfers itself to payments directed toward foreign officials as well.

Since its passage, the FCPA has been subjected to considerable critical analysis, and many practical arguments have been advanced in favor of its repeal.[2] However, there is always lurking in back of such analyses the uneasy feeling that no matter how strongly considerations of practicality and economics may count against this law, the fact remains that the law protects morality in forbidding bribery. For example, Gerald McLaughlin, professor of law at Fordham, has shown persuasively that where the legal system of a foreign country affords inadequate protection against the arbitrary exercise of power to the disadvantage of American corporations, payments to foreign officials may be required to provide a compensating mechanism against the use of such arbitrary power. McLaughlin observes, however, that "this does not mean that taking advantage of the compensating mechanism would necessarily make the payment moral."[3]

The FCPA, and questions regarding its enforcement or repeal, will not be addressed adequately until an effort has been made to come to terms with the Act's foundation in morality. While it may be very difficult, or even impossible, to legislate morality (that is, to change the moral character and sentiments of people by passing laws that regulate their behavior), the existing laws undoubtedly still reflect the moral beliefs we hold. Passage of the FCPA in Congress was eased by the simple connection most Congressmen made between bribery, seen as morally repugnant, and the Act, which is designed to prevent bribery.

Given the importance of the FCPA to American business and labor, it is imperative that attention be given to the question of whether there is adequate moral justification for the law.

ETHICAL ANALYSIS OF THE FCPA

The question we will address is not whether each payment prohibited by the FCPA is moral or immoral, but rather whether the FCPA, given all its consequences and ramifications, is itself moral. It is well known that morally sound laws and institutions may tolerate such immoral acts. The First Amendment's guarantee of freedom of speech allows individuals to utter racial slurs. And immoral laws and institutions may have some beneficial consequences, for example, segregationist legislation bringing deep-seated racism into the national limelight. But our concern is with the overall morality of the FCPA.

The ethical tradition has two distinct ways of assessing social institutions, including laws: *End-Point Assessment and Rule Assessment.* Since there is no consensus as to which approach is correct, we will apply both types of assessment to the FCPA.

The End-Point approach assesses a law in terms of its contribution to general social well-being. The ethical theory underlying End-Point Assessment is utilitarianism. According to utilitarianism, a law is morally sound if and only if the law promotes the well-being of those affected by the law to the greatest extent practically achievable. To satisfy the utilitarian principle, a law must promote the well-being of those affected by it at least as well as any alternative law that we might propose, and better than no law at all. A conclusive End-Point Assessment of a law requires specification of what constitutes the welfare of those affected by the law, which the liberal tradition generally sidesteps by identifying an individual's welfare with what he takes to be in his interests.

Considerations raised earlier in the paper suggest that the FCPA does not pass the End-Point test. The argument is not the too facile one that we could propose a better law. (Amendments to the FCPA are now being considered.[4]) The argument is that it may be better to have *no* such law than to have the FCPA. The main domestic consequences of the FCPA seem to include an adverse effect on the balance of payments, a loss of business and jobs, and another opportunity for the SEC and the Justice Department to compete. These negative effects must be weighed against possible gains in the conduct of American business within the United States. From the perspective of foreign countries in which American firms do business, the main consequence of the FCPA seems to be that certain officials now accept bribes and influence from non-American businesses. It is hard to see that who pays the bribes makes much difference to these nations.

Rule Assessment of the morality of laws is often favored by those who find that End-Point Assessment is too lax in supporting their moral codes. According to the Rule Assessment approach: A law is morally sound if and only if the law accords with a code embodying correct ethical rules. This approach has no content until the rules are stated, and different rules will lead to different ethical assessments. Fortunately, what we have to say about Rule Assessment of the FCPA does not depend on the details of a particular ethical code.

Those who regard the FCPA as a worthwhile expression of morality, despite the adverse effects on American business and labor, clearly subscribe to a rule stating that it is unethical to bribe. Even if it is conceded that the payments proscribed by the FCPA warrant classification as bribes, citing a rule prohibiting bribery does not suffice to justify the FCPA.

Most of the rules in an ethical code are not *categorical* rules; they are *prima facie* rules. A categorical rule does not allow exceptions, whereas a prima facie rule does. The ethical rule that a person ought to keep promises is an example of a prima facie rule. If I promise to loan you a book on nuclear energy and later find out that you are a terrorist building a private atomic bomb, I am ethically obligated not to keep my promise. The rule that one ought to keep promises is "overridden" by the rule that one ought to prevent harm to others.

A rule prohibiting bribery is a prima facie rule. There are cases in which morality requires that a bribe be paid. If the only way to get essential medical care for a dying child is to bribe a doctor, morality requires one to bribe the doctor. So adopting an ethical code which includes a rule prohibiting the payment of bribes does not guarantee that a Rule Assessment of the FCPA will be favorable to it.

The fact that the FCPA imposes a cost on American business and labor weighs against the prima facie obligation not to bribe. If we suppose that American corporations have obligations, tantamount to promises, to promote the job security of their employees and the investments of shareholders, these obligations will also weigh against the obligation not to bribe. Again, if government legislative and enforcement bodies have an obligation to secure the welfare of American business and workers, the FCPA may force them to violate their public obligations.

The FCPA's moral status appears even more dubious if we note that many of the payments prohibited by the Act are neither bribes nor share features that make bribes morally reprehensible. Bribes are generally held to be malefic if they persuade one to act against his good judgment, and consequently purchase an inferior product. But the payments at issue in the FCPA are usually extorted *from the seller*. Further it is arguable that not paying the bribe is more likely to lead to purchase of an inferior product than paying the bribe. Finally, bribes paid to foreign officials may not involve deception when they accord with recognized local practices.

In conclusion, neither End-Point nor Rule Assessment uncovers a sound moral basis for the FCPA. It is shocking to find that a law prohibiting bribery has no clear moral basis, and may even be an immoral law. However, this is precisely what examination of the FCPA from a moral perspective reveals. This is symptomatic of the fact that moral conceptions which were appropriate to a simpler world are not adequate to the complex world in which contemporary business functions. Failure to appreciate this point often leads to righteous condemnation of business, when it should lead to careful reflection on one's own moral preconceptions.

NOTES

1. *National Journal,* June 3, 1978: 880.

2. David C. Gustman, "The Foreign Corrupt Practices Act of 1977," *The Journal of International Law and Economics* 13 (1979): 367–401, and Walter S. Surrey, "The Foreign Corrupt Practices Act: Let the Punishment Fit the Crime," *Harvard International Law Journal* (Spring 1979): 203–303.

3. Gerald T. McLaughlin, "The Criminalization of Questionable Foreign Payments by Corporations," *Fordham Law Review* 46: 1095.

4. "Foreign Bribery Law Amendments Drafted," *American Bar Association Journal* (February 1980): 135.

James M. Humber

Justifying the Foreign Corrupt Practices Act

Most people probably believe that it is morally proper to use the law to prohibit American businesspersons from bribing foreign government officials. However, if this is the common view, it clearly is not the opinion of Mark Pastin and Michael Hooker for, although these individuals allow that the Foreign Corrupt Practices Act (FCPA) is "a law prohibiting bribery," in "Ethics and the Foreign Corrupt Practices Act," they nevertheless argue that the law ought to be repealed because it "has no clear moral basis, and may even be . . . immoral. . . ." In what follows, I intend to show that Pastin and Hooker are wrong to advocate repeal of the FCPA. In support of my position, I shall: (1) examine the arguments Pastin and Hooker offer in support of their view, (2) show that those arguments are unsound, and then (3) demonstrate that the FCPA rests upon a solid moral foundation.

One reason Pastin and Hooker repeatedly give for advocating repeal of the FCPA is that many of the payments prohibited by the act are not truly bribes. Now, Pastin and Hooker never really offer a detailed explanation as to why they think this fact—if indeed it is a fact—counts against the FCPA. However, in the final analysis their reasoning appears to be something like the following: Bribes ordinarily are thought to be morally wrong. Thus, if the FCPA prohibited *only* bribes, there would be some reason to believe that the act was well grounded in morality. However, many of the payments prohibited by the FCPA are not bribes but, rather, brokers' fees, sales commissions, or payments extorted from American businesspersons by corrupt foreign officials. It is not obvious that we ought to have a law prohibiting Americans from submitting to extortion demands made by agents of foreign governments, and it seems wrong to forbid innocuous payments such as brokers' fees and sales commissions. Thus, the FCPA has no clear moral basis, and may even be immoral. A law such as this has no *raison d'etre,* and should be repealed.

If the above correctly represents the argument Pastin and Hooker mean to advance, it may be criticized in at least two ways. First, in order to provide adequate support for their conclusion, Pastin and Hooker must give us some reason to believe that many of the payments prohibited by the FCPA are not bribes. In point of fact, however, they provide no evidence whatsoever for this view; instead, they simply assert that many of the payments that the FCPA was designed to prohibit should not be classified as bribes; rather, these payments are extortions, brokers' fees, or sales commissions. Now, not only does this assertion lack support, there is good reason to believe that it is false. Without doubt, some of the money corporate executives pay to foreign officials should be called brokers' fees and sales commissions. But if a payment to a foreign official is properly called a brokers' fee or sales commission, it must be relatively small in size, proffered because local business customs require such payments, and given to a clerk, customs official, or some other low-level employee in order to ensure that the person's normal duties are performed. Payments of this sort are *permitted* by the FCPA. Thus, contrary to what Pastin and Hooker assert, the FCPA does not appear to be designed to prohibit brokers' fees and sales commissions. On the other hand, the act does seem to forbid payments which Pastin and Hooker would call extortions. However, "extortion" and "bribe" are not mutually exclusive categories, and just because a payment is extorted from a seller does not mean that it is not a bribe. For example, let us say that I represent a construction firm that wants to build a highway for state S. If I offer the governor of that state $50,000 in return for his recommendation that my company build the highway, it seems clear that I am trying to bribe this public official. But now change the example slightly. Let us say that I offer the governor nothing. Instead, the governor tells me that if I give him $50,000 he will recommend to the purchasing department that my firm be given the highway contract, and that if I do not give him the money he will recommend another firm. In this case Pastin and Hooker would say that the governor is engaging in extortion. However, if this is true, it seems clear that what the governor is trying to extort from me is a $50,000 *bribe.* Furthermore, it is precisely this sort of "extortion" that the FCPA attempts to prohibit. Thus, we can admit that the FCPA forbids extortion, and yet insist that Pastin and Hooker are wrong to believe that this shows that the FCPA prohibits payments which are not bribes.

Before introducing the second criticism of Pastin's and Hooker's attack upon the FCPA, it will be useful briefly to review the discussion as it has proceeded thus far. First, Pastin and Hooker argued that (a) the FCPA should be repealed because (b) the law is immoral, or at least, without any clear moral foundation. To support (b), Pastin and Hooker argued that (c) the FCPA prohibits many payments that are not bribes, and hence are not immoral. To prove (c), Pastin and Hooker simply asserted (without any supporting evidence) that (d) the FCPA does not allow American businesspersons to submit to extortion, or to pay brokers' fees and sales commissions to foreign officials. When we examined (d), we found that: (i) there is good reason to believe that the FCPA does not outlaw brokers' fees and sales commissions, and (ii) although the FCPA does prohibit extortion payments, this prohibition is really a prohibition on paying bribes, for the kind of extortion the FCPA forbids is the extortion of bribes. Now, if (i) and (ii) are true, we have no reason to accept (c); indeed, we have no reason to believe the FCPA prohibits anything but bribery. However, bribery ordinarily is thought to be morally wrong. Thus, if the FCPA prohibits nothing but bribery, the law seems to be in accord with morality and not "without any clear moral basis." And of course, if this is true, we have no reason to believe that the FCPA should be repealed.

If the argument of Pastin and Hooker is as we have outlined, we do not have to question the truth of premises (c) and (d) in order to show that the argument is unsound. Let us assume, for instance, that Pastin and Hooker are correct in asserting both (c) and (d). In this case we might well admit that *part* of the FCPA lacks a sound moral foundation, for it is not patently obvious that it is morally proper to prohibit payment of brokers' fees and sales commissions. However, even if many of the payments that the FCPA prohibits are of these rather innocuous sorts, other payments prohibited by the act *are* bribes. Moreover, insofar as the FCPA prohibits bribery, the law would seem to be morally proper. Thus, if we assume that (c) and (d) are true, we will not conclude that the entire FCPA lacks a solid moral foundation; rather, we will hold that part of the act is without firm moral support (viz., the part prohibiting payments of sums that are not bribes), and that another part is well-grounded (viz., the part prohibiting bribery). Now, given this state of affairs, we do not have an argument for *repealing* the FCPA, but rather for *revising* the act so as to ensure that it totally accords with morality. Or to put the matter another way, even if everything Pastin and Hooker say is true, they cannot prove that the FCPA should be repealed because their argument does not apply to the FCPA as a whole.

We have argued that Pastin and Hooker are wrong to believe that the FCPA should be repealed, primarily because they are wrong to believe that no part of the act rests upon a sound moral basis. On the other hand, when we developed our argument we unquestioningly accepted two beliefs. Specifically, we simply assumed that: (1) all bribery is morally wrong, and (2) if bribery is wrong, any law prohibiting such action is morally proper. Now, Pastin and Hooker refuse to accept these assumptions; indeed, they present an argument in which they reject both (1) and (2). Furthermore, if this argument is sound, it may well be that the FCPA is immoral and properly to be repealed. Thus, we must evaluate the argument, and it is to this task that we now turn.

When Pastin and Hooker present their second attack upon the FCPA they do not try to show that the law errs because it proscribes transfers of funds that are not properly classified as bribes. Rather, they try to show that even if the prohibited payments are bribes, the law should be repealed because it lacks a clear moral basis. In the broadest terms, the arguments Pastin and

Hooker use to support their position are as follows: First, if we are to assess the morality of any law, we must do so by appealing to some moral theory. When we examine moral theories we find that they are of two different sorts; specifically, some theories are consequentialist in nature, and others are nonconsequentialist. Now utilitarianism is the most defensible consequentialist moral theory, and when we use this theory to judge the activity of paying bribes to foreign officials we find that the activity can be morally justified. Furthermore, when we use nonconsequentialist theories to assess the morality of the FCPA, we find that although theories of this sort allow that we have a general moral obligation not to bribe, they offer no support for the view that it is morally proper to use the law to prohibit American businesspersons from bribing foreign officials. In the end, then, neither consequentialist nor nonconsequentialist theories provide the FCPA with firm moral support, and the law should be repealed.

If the above argument were sound, it would demonstrate that the FCPA lacked a clear moral basis. However, it is not at all clear that the argument is sound. To see why this is so, we must examine the argument in greater detail.

Let us begin our evaluation by assuming that utilitarianism is true. In this case a morally right act will be one that would promote the well-being of those affected by the act to the greatest extent practically achievable. Pastin and Hooker argue that if we accept this definition we should conclude that is it morally right for corporate executives to bribe foreign officials whenever such bribes are required as a condition for doing business. This is so because not permitting such payments will produce numerous negative consequences and virtually no benefits. More specifically, if we use the FCPA to forbid foreign bribes, Pastin and Hooker claim that the main domestic consequences will be: (1) an adverse effect on the balance of payments, (2) a loss of business and jobs for U.S. corporations, and (3) confusion in interpreting and enforcing the law because of competition between the SEC and the Justice Department. At the same time, foreign officials will continue to take bribes (albeit from non-Americans), and then purchase non-American (inferior) products. In short, if foreign bribes are not paid, everyone will suffer; if the bribes are paid, the well-being of those affected by the act will be maximized to the greatest extent practically achievable. Hence, paying the bribes is morally proper.

There are at least two problems with the utilitarian argument advanced by Pastin and Hooker. For one thing, none of the consequences they enumerate seem to have been produced by the FCPA, even though that law has been in force for over ten years. Furthermore, it is not at all likely that any of the consequences predicted by Pastin and Hooker will occur in the future. It is easy to see why. First, contrary to what Pastin and Hooker appear to believe, bribery is *not* approved of in most foreign countries.[1] Indeed, in the past, when bribery demands of foreign officials were made public, those officials were punished.[2] Now, if the FCPA prohibits employees of American businesses from paying bribes to foreign officials, this gives American employees an incentive to "blow the whistle" on any person they suspect is guilty of demanding or accepting a bribe. Officials of foreign governments know this; they also know that if they are caught accepting a bribe, they are likely to be punished. Hence, the probable long-term effect of the FCPA will be to deter bribery and increase fair competition among those businesses operating in foreign markets. Furthermore, if competition in foreign markets is fair, and if U.S. corporations continue to produce quality products at reasonable prices, then there is no reason to believe that the FCPA will adversely affect our balance of payments, or to think that it will produce a loss of business and jobs for U.S. companies.

The second problem with the utilitarian argument, as advanced by Pastin and Hooker, is that it neglects to consider the principal negative consequence of bribery, and, in so doing, takes too narrow a view of the number of people who are affected by the act. The great strength of a properly functioning free market economy is that the system forces products to compete for consumers' funds on the basis of quality and pricing. This sort of competition creates pressure on manufacturers to innovate, improve existing products, and keep prices low. Thus, fair competition tends generally to provide consumers with the greatest value for their dollar. On the other hand, these benefits are lost in any system wherein the sale and consumption of goods is determined by bribery rather than by fair and open competition. In a system where bribery operates unchecked, manufacturers do not have an incentive to improve their products, or to keep prices low, but only to "out-bribe" their competitors. As a result, consumers tend to receive inferior products at high prices; that is to say, bribery strikes at the heart of a free market economy, and, in so doing, produces deleterious consequences for virtually *all* consumers. Moreover, the companies which engage in bribery also tend to suffer. Companies of this sort have no incentive to innovate or improve their products; thus they are ill equipped to compete in markets that refuse to tolerate bribery. Also, if knowledge of a corporation's bribing activity becomes public, that corporation's reputation may be irreparably harmed. In short, bribery produces harmful consequences for virtually everyone who is touched by the practice.

If our analysis thus far is correct, utilitarians have every reason to believe that bribery is harmful, and no reason to believe that the FCPA will produce any of the negative consequences enumerated by Pastin and Hooker. Hence, if we accept utilitarianism, we seem driven to the conclusion that bribery is immoral and properly prohibited by the FCPA. Still, utilitarianism is not the only moral theory available for judging actions. Indeed, nonconsequentialists claim that utilitarians are wrong to assess the morality of actions by appealing to those acts' consequences, and instead insist that we should judge actions by appealing to moral rules. Thus, for example, a nonconsequentialist will claim that an action is right if it conforms to requirements laid down in some set of moral laws (e.g., the Ten Commandments), and wrong if it violates those requirements. Now virtually all ethicists agree that it is possible for utilitarianism to be false and nonconsequentialism true. Thus, if we want to demonstrate that the FCPA rests upon a firm moral foundation, we must show that utilitarianism is not alone in supporting this conclusion, and that on this issue at least, utilitarianism and nonconsequentialism speak as one. Pastin and Hooker do not think that this can be done, for they believe that accepting nonconsequentialism forces one to conclude that the moral status of the FCPA is "dubious." When arguing in support of this view, Pastin and Hooker do not deny that nonconsequentialists accept a moral rule stating that it is wrong to bribe. Instead, they distinguish between different types of moral rules, and then try to use this distinction to make their point. Their argument is as represented below.

First, moral rules express moral duties or obligations, and are of two different sorts: categorical and *prima facie*. Categorical moral rules hold without exception; as a result, a morally wrong act is performed *whenever* a person violates a categorical rule. On the other hand, if a *prima facie* rule is violated, the person may not be acting immorally, for *prima facie* rules can be "overridden" or negated whenever they come into conflict with a more important moral duty. For example, most people accept a moral rule stating that it is right to keep one's promises. Thus, if I promise to meet you for lunch at noon, I have a moral duty to meet you at that time. However, if I must break my promise to you in order to save a human life, it is morally permissible for me to do so because my duty to keep promises is only *prima facie,* and properly "overridden" by the more important duty to save a life. Now, Pastin and Hooker claim that nonconsequentialists allow that our duty not to bribe, like our duty to keep promises, is merely *prima facie*. They then proceed to reason as follows:

1. Nonconsequentialists recognize that all individuals have a *prima facie* moral duty to keep their promises, and a *prima facie* moral duty not to bribe.

2. Corporate executives have tacitly promised to make money for shareholders and protect employees' jobs.

3. Therefore, corporate executives have a *prima facie* moral duty not to bribe, and *prima facie* duties to make money and protect jobs.

4. When bribery is required to do business in a foreign country, American businesspersons are forced to choose between: (a) keeping their promises to their employees and stockholders by violating their duty not to bribe, or (b) fulfilling their obligation not to bribe by breaking their promises to their employees and shareholders.

5. When corporate executives are forced to choose between (a) and (b), it is not certain which choice is morally proper, because it is not clear whether the duties to make money and protect jobs outweigh the duty not to bribe, or *vice-versa*.

6. When a person is in a situation where he or she must choose between alternatives, and it is not certain which alternative is morally proper,

it is "dubious" whether it is morally right to compel that person to select one alternative and reject the other(s).

7. When corporate executives must choose between (a) and (b), the FCPA compels them to choose (b) and reject (a).

8. Therefore, the FCPA possesses "dubious" moral status.

9. If a law's moral status is dubious, the law should be repealed.

10. Therefore, the FCPA should be repealed.

Pastin and Hooker's nonconsequentialist assault upon the FCPA is really no better than their utilitarian attack. For one thing, they misrepresent mainstream nonconsequentialism when they assert that most nonconsequentialist rules are *prima facie* rather than categorical in nature. To be sure, some nonconsequentialists hold this view; however, this cannot be said to be the view held by most nonconsequentialists. At least, it is not the position accepted by those who ally themselves with either of the most defensible nonconsequentialist moral theories, viz., Kantianism and Theologism. Now, if it is true, as most nonconsequentialists assert, that moral rules are categorical, and if it is true, as Pastin and Hooker allow, that most nonconsequentialists accept a moral rule proscribing bribery, then it follows that bribery is always wrong, and nonconsequentialism provides no support whatsoever for the position Pastin and Hooker wish to defend.

Apart from the above, there is a second problem with Pastin and Hooker's nonconsequentialist attack on the FCPA. That is, even if we accept the view that nonconsequentialist moral rules are *prima facie* rather than categorical in nature, Pastin and Hooker cannot show that the FCPA possesses a dubious moral status, because the argument they use to establish this conclusion rests upon three questionable assumptions. First, they assume that there are countries where American businesspersons must engage in bribery if they want to do business successfully. Now there may well be places in the world where corporate representatives must provide "grease" payments to low-level government officials in order to ensure that these persons do their jobs properly. But these payments are allowed by the FCPA and, as Pastin and Hooker themselves observe, payments of this sort are more properly called brokers' fees or sales commissions than bribes. Furthermore, Pastin and Hooker give us no reason to think that citizens of *any* country believe that it is morally right for corporations to bribe high-level officials by giving them huge sums of money. If this is so, though, we have no reason to believe that there are times when representatives of American corporations *must* choose between (a) and (b) when attempting to do business in foreign countries; for those representatives always have the option of blowing the whistle on corrupt foreign officials, and by focusing public attention on those individuals, ensuring that they perform their duties in a fair and equitable manner. This course of action would violate no nonconsequentialist moral rules, and it would accord totally with the directives of the FCPA. Thus, once we allow that (a) and (b) are not the only options available to American businesspersons operating abroad, we need not conclude that the FCPA rests upon a "dubious" moral foundation.

Second, the argument which Pastin and Hooker use to attack the FCPA not only assumes that there are times when corporate executives must choose between (a) and (b), it also assumes that executives who are faced with this choice have no way of determining which course of action is morally proper. This also is questionable. For example, let us assume that R represents American corporation C in foreign country F, and that R is attempting to get F to buy products manufactured by C. In the course of his discussion with officials of F, R is told by a cabinet minister M that if he provides M with a large sum of money, M will ensure that F buys goods from C rather than from one of C's competitors. In addition, let us assume that F is a country where R cannot "blow the whistle" on M, and that R is a nonconsequentialist who acknowledges that he has a *prima facie* duty not to bribe, as well as *prima facie* obligations to ensure job security and promote stockholders' investments. Now, if all of the above assumptions are true, how should R reason when reviewing his alternatives for action? Well, R *knows* that if he gives M money he will break his *prima facie* duty not to bribe. On the other hand, it is not at all obvious that by giving M money R will fulfill his obligations to C's employees and shareholders. First, since M is requesting a bribe, he cannot be described as morally upright and trustworthy. Thus, he may take R's money and do nothing. Second, even if M is trustworthy, he may not have the power to ensure that F buy C's products. Finally, R must remember that bribery is disapproved of in the United States. Thus, if knowledge of R's bribing M should become public, C's reputation could be severely damaged. In this case, then, C's employees could lose their jobs, and C's stockholders could lose money. Hence, if R bribes M there is good reason to doubt that he will fulfill *any* moral duty; on the other hand, if R refuses to give M money, it is *absolutely* certain that he will act in accordance with his duty not to bribe. Clearly, if R is a rational nonconsequentialist he should "play the odds" and refuse to bribe M. But this is precisely the course of action prescribed by the FCPA. Thus, we once again seem driven to the conclusion that nonconsequentialists will not hold that the FCPA's moral status is dubious, but rather that its injunctions accord with the dictates of morality.

Finally, to show that there are nonconsequentialist grounds for questioning the moral status of the FCPA, Pastin and Hooker assume that there are circumstances in which a corporate executive's duty not to bribe will conflict with tacit promises to promote job security and increase profits. However, if there is to be a conflict between these duties, the latter obligations must be interpreted in a totally unconditional or unrestricted manner and it is not clear that it is proper to interpret tacit promises in this fashion. To see why this is so, let us assume that corporate executives do make tacit promises to their employees and shareholders, and that all persons have at least a *prima facie* moral duty to keep their promises. The question, then, is this: What is the character of the promises made by executives to their employees and shareholders? If we interpret these promises in a totally unqualified or unrestricted manner, we shall take an executive's promise to shareholders to be something like the following: "I promise to increase profits." Now, if this is the character of the executive's promise to shareholders, we must admit that it is possible for the promise to increase profits to conflict with the duty not to bribe, for we can imagine circumstances in which bribing someone will maximize profits. However, we also can imagine cases where a corporate executive could increase profits by murdering someone. Does this mean that because the executive has tacitly promised to increase profits, a *prima facie* duty to murder exists? This sounds absurd. Rather, what we want to say is that the executive's promise to maximize profits imposes no duty at all on the executive to murder, because the promise was understood from the first to exclude murder as a legitimate means for maximizing income. If this is so, though, the executive's tacit promise to increase profits cannot be taken to be unconditional, but rather must be viewed as qualified in some manner. At the very least, the promise must assert something like the following. "I promise to increase profits by any means short of murder."

If corporate executives make tacit promises to their employees and stockholders, we now see that we have good reason to believe that those promises are not unconditional, but restricted in their forms. However, if the tacit promises of executives are restricted, what sorts of conditions should we see as being placed on those promises? A complete answer to this question may be impossible. However, if we adopt the reasonable assumption that it is in the interests of corporations to keep moral conflict to a minimum, we then shall conclude that executives' tacit promises must be understood as being limited by the demands of morality. Accepting this conclusion, we shall then interpret the tacit promise to increase profits and secure jobs as follows: "I promise to use all and only morally proper means to increase profits and secure jobs." Pastin and Hooker admit that nonconsequentialists accept a moral rule stating that bribery is immoral. If this is so, though, there is no conflict at all between a businessperson's duty not to bribe and that person's restricted promise to use morally proper means to increase shareholders' profits and secure employees' jobs. To put the matter another way, if we assume that: (1) D is a nonconsequentialist corporate executive who has tacitly promised to use only moral means to increase profits and secure jobs, and (2) D accepts a moral rule stating that bribery is *prima facie* wrong, then (3) when D finds himself in a situation where he can increase profits and secure jobs by bribing someone, he can be absolutely certain that the right thing to do is not to bribe; for by refusing to bribe, D not only avoids the immorality of bribery, he also keeps his restricted promise to obey all moral rules when attempting to maximize profits and secure jobs. Of course, if D were to adopt this course of action, he would act as the FCPA directs. Thus, if we judge the FCPA by nonconsequentialist moral standards, we once again conclude that the law rests upon a firm moral foundation.

CONCLUSION

We have examined the arguments Pastin and Hooker offer in support of the claim that the FCPA should be repealed because its moral status is dubious. Our analysis indicates that Pastin and Hooker's arguments are unsound, and that the FCPA supports the dictates of morality. In short, if our analysis is correct, we have no reason to believe that the FCPA should be repealed, and every reason to believe that it should be kept in force.

NOTES

1. See Patricia Werhane, "Ethical Relativism and Multinational Corporations," *Proceedings of the Second National Conference on Business Ethics* (UPA, 1979), pp. 28–32.

2. See "Selling the Lockheed TriStar" (this volume, p. 531).

Corporate Policy Statements

It is the policy of Occidental and its subsidiaries NOT to make any of the following types of payments. . . . Payments to Employees of Foreign Governments—Any payment to or for the benefit of any official or employee of a foreign government or of a corporation wholly or partly owned by a foreign government, as compensation for services specially rendered to Occidental; except that, Occidental may employ an official or employee of a foreign government provided that such employment is lawful under the laws of the country concerned, that either the Board of Directors or its Executive Committee and the employee have determined that the services rendered to Occidental do not conflict in any manner with the governmental duties of such persons, and that the employment does not violate the Foreign Corrupt Practices Act of 1977. Notice is taken of the fact that in many countries it is both customary and necessary to make facilitating payments or gratuities in various forms in the ordinary course of business to persons, some of whom may hold lower-echelon government employment, to expedite or advance the routine performance of their duties. Such customary gratuities for the purpose of facilitating the conduct of the company's business are not prohibited, provided that they are not in significant amounts, do not constitute a material factor in the company's business, and are accurately disclosed and properly recorded on the books of Occidental. Any officer or employee of Occidental found to have willfully violated these policies shall be subject to dismissal.

Occidental Petroleum Corp.

Facilitating payments or tips in nominal amounts to low level foreign government employees may be made to obtain or expedite the performance of ministerial or legitimate customary duties such as mail delivery, security, customs clearance and the like, where the practice is usual or customary in the foreign country. Before such payments are made, a corporate officer shall have determined that: (1) the governmental action or assistance sought is proper for the company to receive, (2) the payments are customary in the foreign country in which they are to be made, and (3) there is no reasonable alternative to making such payments. All such payments shall be reported to the Corporate Controller's office, quarterly.

Allied Chemical Corp.

In overseas jurisdictions where corporate political contributions may be legal, no majority owned or controlled unit of Wells Fargo shall make any contribution or expenditure whatever for political purposes without the approval of the Executive Office. . . .

Employees in foreign countries are not to accept or to offer any gift, rebate, hidden commission or other form of illegal payment or commercial bribery in connection with any business transaction, whether or not such a payment is customary in the particular locality. Any payment made in the form of a gratuity to expedite consideration of matters affecting the company will be fully disclosed on our company records. Similarly, payments made relative to the security of employees will be fully disclosed.

Wells Fargo Bank

556

SELECT BIBLIOGRAPHY

Basche, J. *Unusual Foreign Payments*. New York: The Conference Board, 1976.

Dixon, C., D. Drakakis-Smith, and H. Watts, eds. *Multinational Corporations and the Third World*. London: Croom Helm, 1986.

Donaldson, T. *The Ethics of International Business*. New York: Oxford University Press, 1989.

Fisher, B., and J. Turner, eds. *Regulating the Multinational Enterprise*. Westport, Conn.: Quorum, 1985.

Ghosh, P., ed. *Multinational Corporations and Third World Development*. Westport, Conn.: Greenwood Press, 1984.

Hoffman, W. et al., eds. *Ethics and the Multinational Enterprise*. Lanham, Md.: University Press of America, 1986.

Ives, J., ed. *The Export of Hazard: Transnational Corporations and Environmental Control Issues*. Boston: Routledge & Kegan Paul, 1985.

Jacoby, N., P. Nehemkis, and R. Eells. *Bribery and Extortion in World Business*. New York: Macmillan, 1977.

Kline, J. *International Codes and Multinational Business*. Westport, Conn.: Quorum, 1985.

La Palombara, J. *Multinational Corporations and Developing Countries*. New York: Conference Board, 1979.

Madden, C. ed. *The Case for the Multinational Corporation*. New York: Praeger, 1977.

Mattelart, A. *Multinational Corporations and the Control of Culture*. Atlantic Highlands, N.J.: Humanities Press, 1979.

Michaud, L., ed. *Multinational Corporations and Regional Development*. Rome: Herder, 1983.

Pearson, C. *Multinational Corporations, the Environment and Development*. Washington, D.C.: World Resources Institute, 1985.

Rubin, S., and G. Hufbauer, eds. *Emerging Standards of International Trade and Investment: Multinational Codes and Corporate Conduct*. Totowa, N.J.: Rowman & Allanheld, 1984.

Rubner, A. *The Might of the Multinationals*. Westport, Conn.: Praeger, 1990.

Schwamm, H., and D. Germidis, *Codes of Conduct for Multinational Companies*. Brussels: European Centre for Study and Information on Multinational Corporations, 1977.

Takamiya, S., and K. Turley, eds. *Japan's Emerging Multinationals*. Tokyo: University of Tokyo Press, 1985.